Levels 1 & 2

Paradigm PUBLISHING

Microsoft®

excel 2007

BENCHMARK SERIES

Nita Rutkosky

Pierce College at Puyallup
Puyallup, Washington

Denise Seguin

Fanshawe College
London, Ontario

Audrey Rutkosky Roggenkamp

Pierce College at Puyallup
Puyallup, Washington

Managing Editor	Sonja Brown
Production Editor	Donna Mears
Cover and Text Designer	Leslie Anderson
Copy Editor	Susan Capecchi
Desktop Production	John Valo, Desktop Solutions
Proofreader	Laura Nelson
Indexer	Nancy Fulton

Acknowledgments: The authors and editors wish to thank Pamela J. Silvers, Chairperson, Business Computer Technologies, Asheville-Buncombe Technical Community College, Asheville, North Carolina, for testing the instruction and exercises for accuracy.

Care has been taken to verify the accuracy of information presented in this book. However, the authors, editors, and publisher cannot accept responsibility for Web, e-mail, newsgroup, or chat room subject matter or content, or for consequences from application of the information in this book, and make no warranty, expressed or implied, with respect to its content.

Photo Credits: Introduction page 1 (clockwise from top), Lexmark International, Inc., courtesy of Dell Inc., all rights Hewlett-Packard Company, Logitech, Micron Technology, Inc.; Excel Level 1 pages 1, 3, 4 © Corbis; Excel Level 2 pages 1, 2, 4 © Corbis; photos in Student Resources CD, courtesy of Kelly Rutkosky and Michael Rutkosky.

Trademarks: Microsoft is a trademark or registered trademark of Microsoft Corporation in the United States and/or other countries. Some of the product names and company names included in this book have been used for identification purposes only and may be trademarks or registered trade names of their respective manufacturers and sellers. The authors, editors, and publisher disclaim any affiliation, association, or connection with, or sponsorship or endorsement by, such owners.

We have made every effort to trace the ownership of all copyrighted material and to secure permission from copyright holders. In the event of any question arising as to the use of any material, we will be pleased to make the necessary corrections in future printings. Thanks are due to the aforementioned authors, publishers, and agents for permission to use the materials indicated.

Paradigm Publishing is independent from Microsoft Corporation, and not affiliated with Microsoft in any manner. While this publication may be used in assisting individuals to prepare for a Microsoft Business Certification exam, Microsoft, its designated program administrator, and Paradigm Publishing do not warrant that use of this publication will ensure passing a Microsoft Business Certification exam.

ISBN 978-0-76383-363-3 (Hardcover Text)
ISBN 978-0-76383-208-7 (Hardcover Text + CD)
ISBN 978-0-76382-992-6 (Softcover Text)
ISBN 978-0-76383-007-6 (Softcover Text + CD)

© 2008 by Paradigm Publishing, Inc.
875 Montreal Way
St. Paul, MN 55102
E-mail: educate@emcp.com
Web site: www.emcp.com

Printed in the United States of America

16 15 14 13 12 11 10 09 08   3 4 5 6 7 8 9 10

CONTENTS

excel Levels 1 & 2

Benchmark Microsoft Excel 2007 is designed for students who want to learn how to use this powerful spreadsheet program to manipulate numerical data in resolving issues related to finances or other numbers-based information. No prior knowledge of spreadsheets is required. After successfully completing a course using this textbook, students will be able to

- Create and edit spreadsheets of varying complexity
- Format cells, columns, and rows as well as entire workbooks in a uniform, attractive style
- Analyze numerical data and project outcomes to make informed decisions
- Plan, research, create, revise, and publish worksheets and workbooks to meet specific communication needs
- Given a workplace scenario requiring a numbers-based solution, assess the information requirements and then prepare the materials that achieve the goal efficiently and effectively

In addition to mastering Excel skills, students will learn the essential features and functions of computer hardware, the Windows XP operating system, and Internet Explorer 7.0. Upon completing the text, they can expect to be proficient in using Excel to organize, analyze, and present information.

Achieving Proficiency in Excel 2007

Since its inception several Office versions ago, the Benchmark Series has served as a standard of excellence in software instruction. Elements of the book function individually and collectively to create an inviting, comprehensive learning environment that produces successful computer users. On this and following pages, take a visual tour of the structure and features that comprise the highly popular Benchmark model.

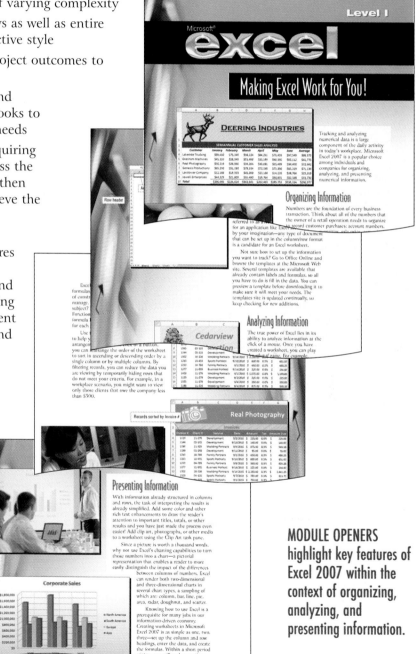

MODULE OPENERS highlight key features of Excel 2007 within the context of organizing, analyzing, and presenting information.

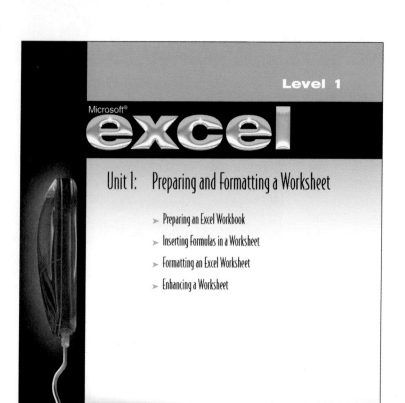

Level 1

Microsoft®
excel

Unit 1: Preparing and Formatting a Worksheet

➤ Preparing an Excel Workbook

➤ Inserting Formulas in a Worksheet

➤ Formatting an Excel Worksheet

➤ Enhancing a Worksheet

UNIT OPENERS display the unit's four chapter titles. Each level has two units, which conclude with a comprehensive unit performance assessment.

CHAPTER

Inserting Formulas in a
Worksheet

2

CHAPTER OPENERS present the Performance Objectives and highlight the practical relevance of the skills students will learn.

PERFORMANCE OBJECTIVES

Upon successful completion of Chapter 2, you will be able to:

• Write formulas with mathematical operators
• Type a formula in the Formula bar
• Copy a formula
• Use the Insert Function feature to insert a formula in a cell
• Write formulas with the AVERAGE, MAX, MIN, COUNT, PMT, FV, DATE, NOW, and IF functions
• Create an absolute and mixed cell reference

Tutorial 2.1
Inserting and Editing Formulas
Tutorial 2.2
Working with Cell References

CD icon identifies a folder of data files to be copied to student's storage medium.

The SNAP icon alerts students to corresponding SNAP tutorial titles.

Excel is a powerful decision-making tool containing data that can be manipulated to answer "what if" situations. Insert a formula in a worksheet and then manipulate the data to make projections, answer specific questions, and use as a planning tool. For example, the owner of a company might prepare a worksheet on production costs and then determine the impact on company revenues if production is increased or decreased.

Insert a formula in a worksheet to perform calculations on values. A formula contains a mathematical operator, value, cell reference, cell range, and a function. Formulas can be written that add, subtract, multiply, and/or divide values. Formulas can also be written that calculate averages, percentages, minimum and maximum values, and much more. As you learned in Chapter 1, Excel includes a Sum button in the Editing group in the Home tab that inserts a formula to calculate the total of a range of cells and also includes some commonly used formulas. Along with the Sum button, Excel includes a Formulas tab that offers a variety of functions to create formulas.

Note: Before beginning computer projects, copy to your storage medium the Excel2007L1C2 subfolder from the Excel2007L1 folder on the CD that accompanies this textbook and make Excel2007L1C2 the active folder.

A prominent note reminds students to copy the appropriate chapter data folder and make it active.

excel Level 1
Inserting Formulas in a Worksheet **37**

New! PROJECT APPROACH: Builds Skill Mastery within Realistic Context

Instruction and practice are organized into multipart projects that focus on related program features. A project overview identifies the tasks to accomplish and the key features to use in completing the work.

Project 1 Insert Formulas in a Worksheet

You will open a worksheet containing data and then insert formulas to calculate differences, salaries, and percentages of budgets.

Writing Formulas with Mathematical Operators

As you learned in Chapter 1, the Sum button in the Editing group in the Home tab creates the formula for you. You can also write your own formulas using mathematical operators. Commonly used mathematical operators and their functions are displayed in Table 2.1. When writing your own formula, begin the formula with the equals (=) sign. For example, to create a formula that divides the contents of cell B2 by the contents of cell C2 and inserts the result in cell D2, you would make D2 the active cell and then type =B2/C2.

Table 2.1 Mathematical Operators

Operator	Function
+	Addition
-	Subtraction
*	Multiplication
/	Division
%	Percent
^	Exponentiation

If a formula contains two or more operators, Excel uses the same order of operations used in algebra. From left to right in a formula, this order, called the *order of operations*, is: negations (negative number—a number preceded by -) first, then percents (%), then exponentiations (^), followed by multiplications (*), divisions (/), additions (+), and finally subtractions (-). If you want to change the order of operations, use parentheses around the part of the formula you want calculated first.

Copying a Formula with Relative Cell References

In many worksheets, the same basic formula is used repetitively. In a situation where a formula is copied to other locations in a worksheet, use a *relative cell reference*. Copy a formula containing relative cell references and the cell references change. For example, if you enter the formula =SUM(A2:C2) in cell [...] copy it relatively to cell D3, the formula in cell D3 displays as =SU[...] (Additional information on cell references is discussed later in this ch[...] "Using an Absolute Cell Reference in a Formula" section.)

Typically, a file remains open throughout a project. Students save their work incrementally.

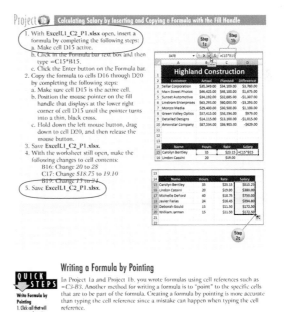

Project 1b Calculating Salary by Inserting and Copying a Formula with the Fill Handle

1. With **ExcelL1_C2_P1.xlsx** open, insert a formula by completing the following steps:
   a. Make cell D15 active.
   b. Click in the Formula bar text box and then type =C15*B15.
   c. Click the Enter button on the Formula bar.
2. Copy the formula to cells D16 through D20 by completing the following steps:
   a. Make sure cell D15 is the active cell.
   b. Position the mouse pointer on the fill handle that displays at the lower right corner of cell D15 until the pointer turns into a thin, black cross.
   c. Hold down the left mouse button, drag down to cell D20, and then release the mouse button.
3. Save **ExcelL1_C2_P1.xlsx**.
4. With the worksheet still open, make the following changes to cell contents:
   B16: Change 20 to 28
   C17: Change $18.75 to 19.10
   B19: Change 15 to 24
5. Save **ExcelL1_C2_P1.xlsx**.

Writing a Formula by Pointing

In Project 1a and Project 1b, you wrote formulas using cell references such as =C3-B3. Another method for writing a formula is to "point" to the specific cells that are to be part of the formula. Creating a formula by pointing is more accurate than typing the cell reference since a mistake can happen when typing the cell reference.

To write a formula by pointing, click the cell that will contain the formula, type the equals sign to begin the formula, and then click the cell you want to reference in the formula. This inserts a moving border around the cell and also changes the mode from Enter to Point. (The word *Point* displays at the left side of the Status bar.) Type the desired mathematical operator and then click the next cell reference. Continue in this manner until all cell references are specified and then press the Enter key. This ends the formula and inserts the result of the calculation of the formula in the active cell. When writing a formula by pointing, you can also select a range of cells you want included in a formula.

QUICK STEPS provide feature summaries for reference and review.

Following each project part, the text presents instruction on the features and skills necessary to accomplish the next task.

excel Levels 1 & 2

Each project exercise guides students step by step to the desired outcome. Screen captures illustrate what the screen should look like at key points.

Text in magenta identifies material to type.

Project 1a   **Writing a Formula by Pointing That Calculates Percentage of Down Time**

1. With **ExcelL1_C2_P1.xlsx** open, enter a formula by pointing that computes the percentage of equipment down time by completing the following steps:
   a. Make cell B45 active.
   b. Type the equals sign followed by the left parenthesis (=().
   c. Click cell B37. (This inserts a moving border around the cell and the mode changes from Enter to Point.)
   d. Type the minus symbol (-).
   e. Click cell B43.
   f. Type the right parenthesis followed by the forward slash ()/).
   g. Click cell B37.
   h. Make sure the formula looks like this =(B37-B43)/B37 and then press Enter.
2. Make cell B45 active, position the mouse pointer on the fill handle, drag across to cell G45, and then release the mouse button.
3. Enter a formula by dragging through a range of cells by completing the following steps:
   a. Click in cell B46 and then click the Sum button in the Editing group in the Home tab.
   b. Select cells B37 through D37.
   c. Click the Enter button on the Formula bar. (This inserts 7,260 in cell B46.)
4. Click in cell B47 and then complete steps similar to those in Step 3 to create a formula that totals hours available from April through June (cells E37 through G37). (This inserts 7,080 in cell B47.)
5. Click in cell B46 and notice the Trace Error button that displays. Complete the following steps to read about the error and then tell Excel to ignore the error:
   a. Click the Trace Error button.
   b. At the drop-down list that displays, click the *Help on this error* option.
   c. Read the information that displays in the Microsoft Excel Help window and then close the window.

   d. Click the Trace Error button again and then click *Ignore Error* at the drop-down list.
6. Remove the dark green triangle from cell B47 by completing the following steps:
   a. Click in cell B47.
   b. Click the Trace Error button and then click *Ignore Error* at the drop-down list.
7. Save, print, and then close **ExcelL1_C2_P1.xlsx**.

Project 2   **Insert Formulas with Statistical Functions**

You will use the AVERAGE function to determine average test scores, use the MINIMUM and MAXIMUM functions to determine lowest and highest averages, use the COUNT function to count number of students taking a test, and display formulas in a cell rather than the result of the formula.

Inserting Formulas with Functions

In Project 2a in Chapter 1, you used the Sum button to insert the formula =SUM(B2:B5) in a cell. The beginning section of the formula, =SUM, is called a *function*, which is a built-in formula. Using a function takes fewer keystrokes when creating a formula. For example, the =SUM function saved you from having to type each cell to be included in the formula with the plus (+) symbol between cell entries.

Excel provides other functions for writing formulas. A function operates on what is referred to as an *argument*. An argument may consist of a constant, a cell reference, or another function (referred to as a nested function). In the formula =SUM(B2:B5), the cell range *(B2:B5)* is an example of a cell reference argument. An argument may also contain a *constant*. A constant is a value entered directly into the formula. For example, if you enter the formula =SUM(B3:B9,100), the cell range B3:B9 is a cell reference argument and *100* is a constant. In this formula, 100 is always added to the sum of the cells. If a function is included in an argument within a function, it is called a *nested function*. (You will learn about nested functions later in this chapter.)

When a value calculated by the formula is inserted in a cell, this process is referred to as *returning the result*. The term *returning* refers to the process of calculating the formula and the term *result* refers to inserting the value in the cell.

You can type a function in a cell in a worksheet or you can use the Insert Function button on the Formula bar or in the Formulas tab to help you write the formula. Figure 2.1 displays the Formulas tab. The Formulas tab provides the Insert Function button as well as other buttons for inserting functions in a worksheet. The Function Library group in the Formulas tab contains a number of buttons for inserting functions from a variety of categories such as Financial, Logical, Text, and Date & Time.

Insert Function

At the end of the project, students save, print, and close the file. Locked, watermarked model answers in PDF format on the Student Resources CD allow students to check their work. This option rewards careful effort and builds software mastery.

CHAPTER REVIEW ACTIVITIES: A Hierarchy of Learning Assessments

CHAPTER SUMMARY captures the purpose and execution of key features.

COMMANDS REVIEW summarizes visually the major features and alternative methods of access.

CONCEPTS CHECK questions assess knowledge recall.

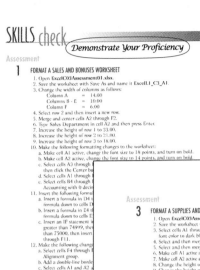

SKILLS check

Demonstrate Your Proficiency

Assessment

1 FORMAT A SALES AND BONUSES WORKSHEET

1. Open **ExcelC03Assessment01.xlsx**.
2. Save the worksheet with Save As and name it **ExcelL1_C3_A1**.
3. Change the width of columns as follows:
   - Column A = 14.00
   - Columns B - E = 10.00
   - Column F = 6.00
4. Select row 2 and then insert a new row.
5. Merge and center cells A2 through F2.
6. Type Sales Department in cell A2 and then press Enter.
7. Increase the height of row 1 to 53.00.
8. Increase the height of row 2 to 21.00.
9. Increase the height of row 3 to 18.00.
10. Make the following formatting changes to the worksheet:
    a. Make cell A1 active, change the font size to 18 points, and turn on bold.
    b. Make cell A2 active, change the font size to 14 points, and turn on bold.
    c. Select cells A3 through [...] then click the Center bu[...]
    d. Select cells A1 through [...]
    e. Select cells B4 through [...] Accounting with 0 decim[...]
11. Insert the following formu[...]
    a. Insert a formula in D4 t[...] formula down to cells D[...]
    b. Insert a formula in E4 t[...] formula down to cells E[...]
    c. Insert an IF statement in [...] greater than 74999, the[...] than 75000, then insert[...] through F11.
12. Make the following chang[...]
    a. Select cells F4 through [...] Alignment group.
    b. Add a double-line borde[...]
    c. Select cells A1 and A2 a[...]
    d. Select cells A3 through [...]
13. Save and then print the wo[...]
14. Apply the Verve theme to [...]
15. Save, print, and then close[...]

SKILLS CHECK exercises ask students to develop both standard and customized kinds of spreadsheet documents without how-to directions.

Assessment

3 FORMAT A SUPPLIES AND EQUIPMENT WORKSHEET

1. Open **ExcelC03Assessment03.xlsx**.
2. Save the worksheet with Save As and name it **ExcelL1_C3_A3**.
3. Select cells A1 through D19 and then change the font to Garamond and the font color to dark blue.
4. Select and then merge and center cells A1 through D1.
5. Select and then merge and center cells A2 through D2.
6. Make cell A1 active and then change the font size to 22 points and turn on bold.
7. Make cell A2 active and then change the font size to 12 points and turn on bold.
8. Change the height of row 1 to 36.00.
9. Change the height of row 2 to 21.00.
10. Change the width of column A to 15.00.
11. Select cells A3 through A17, turn on bold, and then click the Wrap Text button in the Alignment group.
12. Select cells A1 and A2 and then click the Middle Align button in the Alignment group.
13. Make cell B3 active and then change the number formatting to Currency with no decimal places.
14. Select cells C6 through C19 and then change the number formatting to Percentage with one decimal place.
15. Automatically adjust the width of column C.
16. Make cell D6 active and th[...] reference $B$5 with the pe[...] D7 through D19[...]
17. With cells D6 through D19[...] with no decimal places.
18. Make cell D8 active and th[...] command, F4, to clear the[...]
19. Add light green fill color to[...] A11–D11, A14–D14, and A[...]
20. Add borders and/or shading[...] the worksheet.
21. Save, print, and then close[...]

The chapter CASE STUDY requires planning and executing multi-part workplace projects.

5. Select cells B3 through D9, display the Format Cells dialog box with the Alignment tab selected, change the horizontal alignment to Right (Indent) and the indent to 2, and then close the dialog box.
6. Select cells A1 through D9 and then change the font size to 14.
7. Select cells B2 through D2 and then change the orientation to 45 degrees.
8. With cells B2 through D2 still selected, shrink the font size to show all data in the cells.
9. Save, print, and close **ExcelL1_C3_A4.xlsx**.

Assessment

4 FORMAT A FINANCIAL ANALYSIS [...]

1. Use the Help feature to lea[...] data in a cell (with an opti[...] tab selected).
2. Open **ExcelC03Assessment[...]**
3. Save the worksheet with Sa[...]
4. Make cell B9 active and th[...] in cells B3 through B8. C[...]

To complete certain exercises, students must first work with the program's Help feature, learning independently how to use a specific option.

CASE study

Apply Your Skills

Part
1

You are the office manager for HealthWise Fitness Center and you decide to prepare an Excel worksheet that displays the various plans offered by the health club. In this worksheet, you want to include yearly dues for each plan as well as quarterly and monthly payments. Open the **HealthWise.xlsx** workbook and then save it and name it **ExcelL1_C3_CS_P1A**. Make the following changes to the worksheet:

- Select cells B3 through D8 and then change the number formatting to Accounting with two decimal places and a dollar sign.
- Make cell B3 active and then insert 500.00.
- Make cell B4 active and then insert a formula that adds the amount in B3 with the product (multiplication) of B3 multiplied by 10%. (The formula should look like this: =B3+(B3*10%). The Economy plan is the base plan and each additional plan costs 10% more than the previous plan.)
- Copy the formula in cell B4 down to cells B5 through B8.
- Insert a formula in cell C3 that divides the amount in B3 by 4 and then copy the formula down to cells C4 through C8.
- Insert a formula in cell D3 that divides the amount in cell B3 by 12 and then copy the formula down to cells D4 through D8.
- Apply formatting to enhance the visual display of the worksheet.

Save and print the completed worksheet.

With **ExcelL1_C3_CS_P1A.xlsx** open, save the workbook with Save As and name it **ExcelL1_C3_CS_P1B**, and then make the following changes:

- You have been informed that the base rate for yearly dues has increased from $500.00 to $600.00. Change this amount in cell B3 of the worksheet.
- If clients are late with their quarterly or monthly dues payments, a late fee is charged. You decide to add the late fee information to the worksheet. Insert a new column to the right of Column C. Type Late Fees in cell D2 and also in cell F2.
- Insert a formula in cell D3 that multiplies the amount in C3 by 5%. Copy this formula down to cells D4 through D8.
- Insert a formula in cell F3 that multiplies the amount in E3 by 7%. Copy this formula down to cells F4 through F8. If necessary, change the number formatting for cells F3 through F8 to Accounting with two decimal places and a dollar sign.
- Apply any additional formatting to enhance the visual display of the worksheet.

Save, print, and then close **ExcelL1_C3_CS_P1B.xlsx**.

the fitness center and include the

[...]ss Center

[...]roll

[...]urs   Weekly Salary   Benefits

that multiplies the hourly wage by
[...] in the *Benefits* column that states that
[...]than 19, then insert "Yes" and if the
[...]pply formatting to enhance the visual
[...] and name it **ExcelL1_C3_CS_P2**.
[...]` to turn on the display of formulas
[...]Ctrl + ` to turn off the display of

Make the following changes to the worksheet:

- Change the hourly wage for Amanda Turney to $22.00.
- Increase the hours for Emily Dugan to 20.
- Remove the row for Grant Baker.
- Insert a row between Jean Overmeyer and Bonnie Haddon and then type the following information in the cells in the new row: Employee: Tonya McGuire; Hourly Wage: $17.50; Hours: 15.

Save and then print **ExcelL1_C3_CS_P2.xlsx**. Press Ctrl + ` to turn on the display of formulas and then print the worksheet. Press Ctrl + ` to turn off the display of formulas and then save and close **ExcelL1_C3_CS_P2.xlsx**.

Part
3

Your boss is interested in ordering new equipment for the health club. She is interested in ordering three elliptical machines, three recumbent bikes, and three upright bikes. She has asked you to use the Internet to research models and prices for this new equipment. She then wants you to prepare a worksheet with the information. Using the Internet, search for the following equipment:

- Search for elliptical machines for sale. Locate two different models and, if possible, find at least two companies that sell each model. Make a note of the company names, model numbers, and prices.

To complete one or more parts of the Case Study, students search the Web and/or use the Help feature to locate information.

UNIT PERFORMANCE ASSESSMENT: Cross-Disciplinary, Comprehensive Evaluation

Maintaining and Enhancing Workbooks — Unit 2

ASSESSING proficiency

In this unit, you have learned how to work with multiple windows; move, copy, link, and paste data between workbooks and applications; create and customize charts with data in a worksheet; save a workbook as a Web page; insert hyperlinks; and insert and customize pictures, clip art images, shapes, SmartArt diagrams, and WordArt.

*Note: Before beginning computer assessments, d_
*from your storage medium. Next, copy to your st_
*subfolder from the Excel2007L1 folder on the C_
*and then make Excel2007L1U2 the active folde_

**Assessment 1 Copy and Paste Data and Ins_
Scores Workbook**

1. Open ExcelU02Assessment01.xlsx an_
name it ExcelL1_U2_A1.
2. Delete row 15 (the row for *Kwieciak, Ke_
3. Insert a formula in cell D4 that averages_
4. Copy the formula in cell D4 down to c_
5. Make cell A22 active, turn on bold, an_
6. Display the Clipboard task pane and m_
7. Select and then copy each of the follow_
14, 16, and 18.
8. Make cell A23 active and then paste ro_
9. Make cell A24 active and then paste ro_
10. Make cell A25 active and then paste ro_
Theresa).
11. Make cell A26 active and then paste ro_
12. Make cell A27 active and then paste ro_
13. Click the Clear All button in the Clipb_
task pane.
14. Insert in cell A1 the text *Raseland* as We_
to add visual appeal to the worksheet.
15. Save, print, and then close ExcelL1_U2_

ASSESSING PROFICIENCY checks mastery of features.

WRITING activities

The following activities give you the opportunity to practice your writing skills along with demonstrating an understanding of some of the important Excel features you have mastered in this unit. Use correct grammar, appropriate word choices, and clear sentence constructions.

Activity 1 Prepare a Projected Budget

You are the accounting assistant in the financial department of McCormack Funds and you have been asked to prepare a yearly proposed department budget. The total amount for the department is $1,450,000. You are given the percentages for the proposed budget items, which are: Salaries, 45%; Benefits, 12%; Training, 14%; Administrative Costs, 10%; Equipment, 11%; and Supplies, 8%. Create a worksheet with this information that shows the projected yearly budget, the budget items in the department, the percentage of the budget, and the amount for each item. After the worksheet is completed, save the workbook and name it ExcelL1_U2_Act01. Print and then close the workbook.

Optional: Using Word 2007, write a memo to the McCormack Funds Finance Department explaining that the proposed annual department budget is attached for their review. Comments and suggestions are to be sent to you within one week. Save the file and name it ExcelL1_U2_Act01_Memo. Print and then close the file.

Activity 2 Create a Travel Tours Bar Chart

Prepare a worksheet in Excel for Carefree Travels that includes the following information:

Scandinavian Tours
Country	Tours Booked
Norway	52
Sweden	62
Finland	29
Denmark	38

Use the information in the worksh_
separate sheet. Save the workbook_
the sheet containing the chart and_

Activity 3 Prepare a Ski Vacation_

Prepare a worksheet for Carefree Tr_
the following information in the an_

• At the beginning of the work_
company name *Carefree Trav_
• Include the heading *Whistler_
• Include the following below_
  ○ Round-trip air transport_
  ○ Seven nights' hotel accom_
  ○ Four all-day ski passes: S_

WRITING ACTIVITIES involve applying program skills in a communication context.

○ Compact rental car with unlimited mileage: $250
○ Total price of the ski package: (calculate the total price)
• Include the following information somewhere in the worksheet:
  ○ Book your vacation today at special discount prices.
  ○ Two-for-one discount at many of the local ski resorts.

Save the workbook and name it ExcelL1_U2_Act03. Print and then close ExcelL1_U2_Act03.xlsx.

INTERNET research

Find Information on Excel Books and Present the Data in a Worksheet

Locate two companies on the Internet that sell new books. At the first new book company site, locate three books on Microsoft Excel. Record the title, author, and price for each book. At the second new book company site, locate the same three books and record the prices. Create an Excel worksheet that includes the following information:

• Name of each new book company
• Title and author of the three books
• Prices for each book from the two book company sites

Create a hyperlink for each book company to the URL on the Internet. Then save the completed workbook and name it ExcelL1_U2_InternetResearch. Print and then close the workbook.

INTERNET RESEARCH project reinforces research and spreadsheet analysis skills.

JOB study

Create a Customized Time Card for a Landscaping Company

You are the manager of a landscaping company and are responsible for employee time cards. Locate the time card template that is available with *Installed Templates* selected in the New Workbook dialog box. Use the template to create a customized time card for your company. With the template open, delete the Company Name that displays in the middle header pane. Insert additional blank rows to increase the spacing above the Employee row. Insert a clip art image related to landscaping or gardening and position and size it attractively in the form. Include a text box with the text Lawn and Landscaping Specialists inside the box. Format, size, and position the text attractively in the form. Fill in the form for the current week with the following employee information:

Employee = Jonathan Holder
Address = 12332 South 152nd Street, Baton Rouge, LA 70804
Manager = (Your name)
Employee phone = (225) 555-3092
Employee e-mail = None

JOB STUDY at the end of Unit 2 presents a capstone assessment requiring critical thinking and problem solving.

Student Courseware

Student Resources CD Each Benchmark Series textbook is packaged with a Student Resources CD containing the data files required for completing the projects and assessments. A CD icon and folder name displayed on the opening page of chapters reminds students to copy a folder of files from the CD to the desired storage medium before beginning the project exercises. Directions for copying folders are printed on the inside back cover. The Student Resources CD also contains the model answers in PDF format for the project exercises within chapters. Files are locked and watermarked, but students can compare their completed documents with the PDF files, either on screen or in hard copy (printed) format.

Internet Resource Center Additional learning tools and reference materials are available at the book-specific Web site at www.emcp.net/BenchmarkExcel07XP. Students can access the same resources that are on the Student Resources CD along with study aids, Web links, and tips for using computers effectively in academic and workplace settings.

SNAP Training and Assessment SNAP is a Web-based program that provides hands-on instruction, practice, and testing for learning Microsoft Office 2007 and Windows. SNAP course work simulates operations of Office 2007. The program is comprised of a Web-based learning management system, multimedia tutorials, performance skill items, a concept test bank, and online grade book and course planning tools. A CD-based set of tutorials teaching the basics of Office and Windows is also available for additional practice not requiring Internet access.

Class Connections Available for both WebCT and Blackboard e-learning platforms, Paradigm's Class Connection provides self-quizzes and study aids and facilitates communication among students and instructors via e-mail and e-discussion.

Instructor Resources

Curriculum Planner and Resources Instructor support for the Benchmark Series has been expanded to include a *Curriculum Planner and Resources* binder with CD. This all-in-one print resource includes planning resources such as Lesson Blueprints and sample course syllabi; presentation resources such as teaching hints and handouts; and assessment resources including an overview of assessment venues, model answers for intrachapter projects, and annotated model answers for end-of-chapter and end-of-unit assessments. Contents of the *Curriculum Planner and Resources* binder are also available on the Instructor's CD and on the password-protected Instructor's section of the Internet Resource Center for this title at www.emcp.com.

Computerized Test Generator Instructors can use ExamView test generating software and the provided bank of multiple-choice items to create customized Web-based or print tests.

What is the Microsoft Business Certification Program?

The Microsoft Business Certification program enables candidates to show that they have something exceptional to offer—proven expertise in Microsoft Office programs. The two certification tracks allow candidates to choose how they want to exhibit their skills, either through validating skills within a specific Microsoft product or taking their knowledge to the next level and combining Microsoft programs to show that they can apply multiple skill sets to complete more complex office tasks. Recognized by businesses and schools around the world, over 3 million certifications have been obtained in over 100 different countries. The Microsoft Business Certification Program is the only Microsoft-approved certification program of its kind.

What is the Microsoft Certified Application Specialist Certification?

Microsoft
CERTIFIED

*Application
Specialist*

The Microsoft Certified Application Specialist Certification exams focus on validating specific skill sets within each of the Microsoft® Office system programs. Candidates can choose which exam(s) they want to take according to which skills they want to validate. The available Application Specialist exams include:

- Using Microsoft® Windows Vista™
- Using Microsoft® Office Word 2007
- Using Microsoft® Office Excel® 2007
- Using Microsoft® Office PowerPoint® 2007
- Using Microsoft® Office Access 2007
- Using Microsoft® Office Outlook 2007

What is the Microsoft Certified Application Professional Certification?

Microsoft
CERTIFIED

*Application
Professional*

The Microsoft Certified Application Professional Certification exams focus on a candidate's ability to use the 2007 Microsoft® Office system to accomplish industry-agnostic functions, for example, Budget Analysis and Forecasting, or Content Management and Collaboration. The available Application Professional exams currently include:

- Organizational Support
- Creating and Managing Presentations
- Content Management and Collaboration
- Budget Analysis and Forecasting

What do the Microsoft Business Certification Vendor of Approved Courseware logos represent?

Microsoft
CERTIFIED

*Application
Specialist*

| **Approved Courseware**

Microsoft
CERTIFIED

*Application
Professional*

| **Approved Courseware**

The logos validate that the courseware has been approved by the Microsoft® Business Certification Vendor program and that these courses cover objectives that will be included in the relevant exam. It also means that after utilizing this courseware, you may be prepared to pass the exams required to become a Microsoft Certified Application Specialist or Microsoft Certified Application Professional.

For more information:

To learn more about Microsoft Certified Application Specialist or Professional exams, visit www.microsoft.com/learning/msbc.

To learn about other Microsoft Certified Application Specialist or Professional approved courseware from Paradigm Publishing, visit www.emcp.com/microsoft-certified-courseware.

The availability of Microsoft Certified Application exams varies by Microsoft Office program, program version, and language. Visit www.microsoft.com/learning for exam availability.

Microsoft, the Office Logo, Outlook, and PowerPoint are either registered trademarks or trademarks of Microsoft Corporation in the United States and/or other countries. The Microsoft Certified Application Specialist and Microsoft Certified Application Professional Logos are used under license from Microsoft Corporation.

System Requirements

This text is designed for the student to complete projects and assessments on a computer running a standard installation of Microsoft Office 2007, Professional Edition, and the Microsoft Windows XP operating system with Service Pack 2 or later. To effectively run this suite and operating system, your computer should be outfitted with the following:

- 500 MHz processor or higher; 256 MB RAM or higher
- DVD drive
- 2 GB of available hard-disk space
- CD-ROM drive
- 800 by 600 minimum monitor resolution; 1024 by 768 recommended
  Note: Screen captures in this book were created using 1024 by 768 resolution; screens with higher resolution may look different.
- Computer mouse or compatible pointing device

About the Authors

Nita Rutkosky began teaching business education courses at Pierce College in Puyallup, Washington, in 1978. Since then she has taught a variety of software applications to students in postsecondary Information Technology certificate and degree programs. In addition to co-authoring texts in the *Benchmark Office 2007 Series*, she has co-authored *Signature Word 2007*, *Marquee Office 2007*, and *Using Computers in the Medical Office: Microsoft Word, Excel, and PowerPoint 2003*. Other textbooks she has written for Paradigm Publishing include books on previous versions of Microsoft Office along with WordPerfect, desktop publishing, keyboarding, and voice recognition.

Denise Seguin has been teaching at Fanshawe College in London, Ontario, since 1986. She has taught a variety of software applications to learners in postsecondary Information Technology diploma programs and in Continuing Education courses. In addition to co-authoring texts in the *Benchmark Office 2007 Series*, she has co-authored *Marquee Office 2007* and *Using Computers in the Medical Office*. Other textbooks she has written for Paradigm Publishing include previous editions of the *Marquee Series*, *Macromedia Flash MX: Design and Application*, and books on Microsoft Outlook 2007, 2003, 2002, and 2000.

Audrey Rutkosky Roggenkamp has been teaching courses in the Business Information Technology department at Pierce College in Puyallup including keyboarding, skill building, and Microsoft Office programs. In addition to titles in the *Benchmark Office 2007 Series*, she has co-authored *Using Computers in the Medical Office*, *Marquee Office 2007*, and *Signature Word 2007*.

Getting Started in Office 2007

In this textbook, you will learn to operate several computer application programs that combine to make an application "suite." This suite of programs is called Microsoft Office 2007. The programs you will learn to operate are the software, which includes instructions telling the computer what to do. Some of the application programs in the suite include a word processing program named Word, a spreadsheet program named Excel, a database program named Access, and a presentation program named PowerPoint.

Identifying Computer Hardware

The computer equipment you will use to operate the suite of programs is referred to as hardware. You will need access to a microcomputer system that should consist of the CPU, monitor, keyboard, printer, drives, and mouse. If you are not sure what equipment you will be operating, check with your instructor. The computer system shown in Figure G.1 consists of six components. Each component is discussed separately in the material that follows.

Figure G.1 Microcomputer System

CPU

CPU stands for Central Processing Unit and it is the intelligence of the computer. All the processing occurs in the CPU. Silicon chips, which contain miniaturized circuitry, are placed on boards that are plugged into slots within the CPU. Whenever an instruction is given to the computer, that instruction is processed through circuitry in the CPU.

Monitor

The monitor is a piece of equipment that looks like a television screen. It displays the information of a program and the text being input at the keyboard. The quality of display for monitors varies depending on the type of monitor and the level of resolution. Monitors can also vary in size—generally from 14-inch size up to 21-inch size or larger.

Keyboard

The keyboard is used to input information into the computer. Keyboards for microcomputers vary in the number and location of the keys. Microcomputers have the alphabetic and numeric keys in the same location as the keys on a typewriter. The symbol keys, however, may be placed in a variety of locations, depending on the manufacturer. In addition to letters, numbers, and symbols, most microcomputer keyboards contain function keys, arrow keys, and a numeric keypad. Figure G.2 shows an enhanced keyboard.

Figure G.2 Keyboard

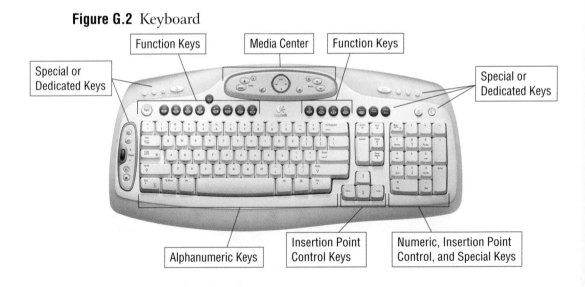

The 12 keys at the top of the keyboard, labeled with the letter F followed by a number, are called *function keys*. Use these keys to perform functions within each of the suite programs. To the right of the regular keys is a group of *special* or *dedicated keys*. These keys are labeled with specific functions that will be performed when you press the key. Below the special keys are arrow keys. Use these keys to move the insertion point in the document screen.

A keyboard generally includes three mode indicator lights. When you select certain modes, a light appears on the keyboard. For example, if you press the Caps Lock key, which disables the lowercase alphabet, a light appears next to Caps Lock. Similarly, pressing the Num Lock key will disable the special functions on the numeric keypad, which is located at the right side of the keyboard.

Disk Drives

Depending on the computer system you are using, Microsoft Office 2007 is installed on a hard drive or as part of a network system. Whether you are using Office on a hard drive or network system, you will need to have available a DVD or CD drive and a USB drive or other storage medium. You will insert the CD (compact disc) that accompanies this textbook in the DVD or CD drive and then copy folders from the CD to your storage medium. You will also save documents you complete at the computer to folders on your storage medium.

Printer

A document you create in Word is considered soft copy. If you want a hard copy of a document, you need to print it. To print documents you will need to access a printer, which will probably be either a laser printer or an ink-jet printer. A laser printer uses a laser beam combined with heat and pressure to print documents, while an ink-jet printer prints a document by spraying a fine mist of ink on the page.

Mouse

Many functions in the suite of programs are designed to operate more efficiently with a mouse. A mouse is an input device that sits on a flat surface next to the computer. You can operate a mouse with the left or the right hand. Moving the mouse on the flat surface causes a corresponding mouse pointer to move on the screen. Figure G.1 shows an illustration of a mouse.

Using the Mouse

The programs in the Microsoft Office suite can be operated using a keyboard or they can be operated with the keyboard and a mouse. The mouse may have two or three buttons on top, which are tapped to execute specific functions and commands. To use the mouse, rest it on a flat surface or a mouse pad. Put your hand over it with your palm resting on top of the mouse and your wrist resting on the table surface. As you move the mouse on the flat surface, a corresponding pointer moves on the screen.

When using the mouse, you should understand four terms—point, click, double-click, and drag. When operating the mouse, you may need to point to a specific command, button, or icon. Point means to position the mouse pointer on the desired item. With the mouse pointer positioned on the desired item, you may need to click a button on the mouse. Click means quickly tapping a button on the mouse once. To complete two steps at one time, such as choosing and then executing a function, double-click a mouse button. Double-click means to tap the left mouse button twice in quick succession. The term drag means to press and hold the left mouse button, move the mouse pointer to a specific location, and then release the button.

Using the Mouse Pointer

The mouse pointer will change appearance depending on the function being performed or where the pointer is positioned. The mouse pointer may appear as one of the following images:

- The mouse pointer appears as an I-beam (called the I-beam pointer) in the document screen and can be used to move the insertion point or select text.

- The mouse pointer appears as an arrow pointing up and to the left (called the arrow pointer) when it is moved to the Title bar, Quick Access toolbar, ribbon, or an option in a dialog box. For example, to open a new document with the mouse, position the I-beam pointer on the Office button located in the upper left corner of the screen until the pointer turns into an arrow pointer and then click the left mouse button. At the drop-down list that displays, make a selection by positioning the arrow pointer on the desired option and then clicking the left mouse button.

- The mouse pointer becomes a double-headed arrow (either pointing left and right, pointing up and down, or pointing diagonally) when performing certain functions such as changing the size of an object.

- In certain situations, such as moving an object or image, the mouse pointer becomes a four-headed arrow. The four-headed arrow means that you can move the object left, right, up, or down.

- When a request is being processed or when a program is being loaded, the mouse pointer may appear with an hourglass beside it. The hourglass image means "please wait." When the process is completed, the hourglass image is removed.

- The mouse pointer displays as a hand with a pointing index finger in certain functions such as Help and indicates that more information is available about the item.

Choosing Commands

Once a program is open, you can use several methods in the program to choose commands. A command is an instruction that tells the program to do something. You can choose a command using the mouse or the keyboard. When a program such as Word or PowerPoint is open, the ribbon contains buttons for completing tasks and contains tabs you click to display additional buttons. To choose a button on the Quick Access toolbar or in the ribbon, position the tip of the mouse arrow pointer on a button and then click the left mouse button.

The Office suite provides access keys you can press to use a command in a program. Press the Alt key on the keyboard to display KeyTips that identify the access key you need to press to execute a command. For example, press the Alt key in a Word document and KeyTips display as shown in Figure G.3. Continue pressing access keys until you execute the desired command. For example, if you want to begin spell checking a document, you would press the Alt key, press the R key on the keyboard to display the Review tab, and then press the letter S on the keyboard.

Figure G.3 Word KeyTips

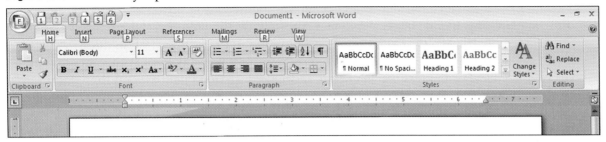

Choosing Commands from Drop-Down Lists

To choose a command from a drop-down list with the mouse, position the mouse pointer on the desired option and then click the left mouse button. To make a selection from a drop-down list with the keyboard, type the underlined letter in the desired option.

Some options at a drop-down list may be gray-shaded (dimmed), indicating that the option is currently unavailable. If an option at a drop-down list displays preceded by a check mark, that indicates that the option is currently active. If an option at a drop-down list displays followed by an ellipsis (…), a dialog box will display when that option is chosen.

Choosing Options from a Dialog Box

A dialog box contains options for applying formatting to a file or data within a file. Some dialog boxes display with tabs along the top providing additional options. For example, the Font dialog box shown in Figure G.4 contains two tabs—the Font tab and the Character Spacing tab. The tab that displays in the front is the

Figure G.4 Word Font Dialog Box

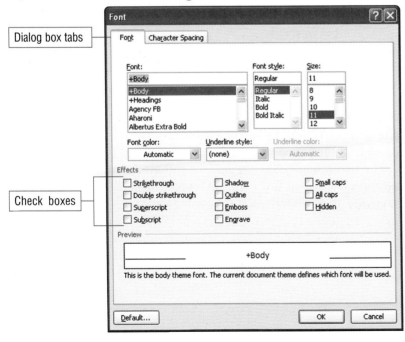

active tab. To make a tab active using the mouse, position the arrow pointer on the desired tab and then click the left mouse button. If you are using the keyboard, press Ctrl + Tab or press Alt + the underlined letter on the desired tab.

To choose options from a dialog box with the mouse, position the arrow pointer on the desired option and then click the left mouse button. If you are using the keyboard, press the Tab key to move the insertion point forward from option to option. Press Shift + Tab to move the insertion point backward from option to option. You can also hold down the Alt key and then press the underlined letter of the desired option. When an option is selected, it displays with a blue background or surrounded by a dashed box called a marquee. A dialog box contains one or more of the following elements: text boxes, list boxes, check boxes, option buttons, spin boxes, and command buttons.

Text Boxes

Some options in a dialog box require you to enter text. For example, the boxes below the *Find what* and *Replace with* options at the Excel Find and Replace dialog box shown in Figure G.5 are text boxes. In a text box, you type text or edit existing text. Edit text in a text box in the same manner as normal text. Use the Left and Right Arrow keys on the keyboard to move the insertion point without deleting text and use the Delete key or Backspace key to delete text.

Figure G.5 Excel Find and Replace Dialog Box

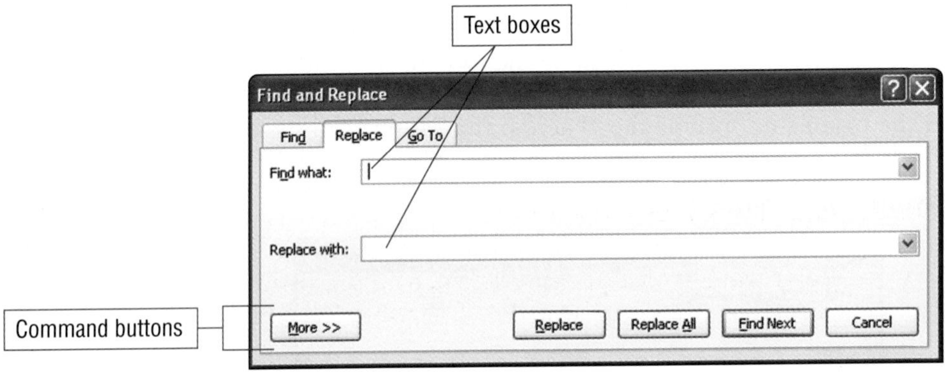

List Boxes

Some dialog boxes such as the Word Open dialog box shown in Figure G.6 may contain a list box. The list of files below the *Look in* option is contained in a list box. To make a selection from a list box with the mouse, move the arrow pointer to the desired option and then click the left mouse button.

Figure G.6 Word Open Dialog Box

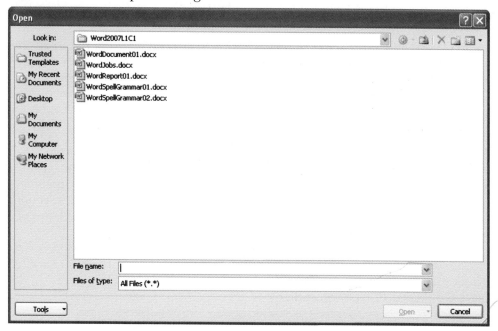

Some list boxes may contain a scroll bar. This scroll bar will display at the right side of the list box (a vertical scroll bar) or at the bottom of the list box (a horizontal scroll bar). You can use a vertical scroll bar or a horizontal scroll bar to move through the list if the list is longer than the box. To move down through a list on a vertical scroll bar, position the arrow pointer on the down-pointing arrow and hold down the left mouse button. To scroll up through the list in a vertical scroll bar, position the arrow pointer on the up-pointing arrow and hold down the left mouse button. You can also move the arrow pointer above the scroll box and click the left mouse button to scroll up the list or move the arrow pointer below the scroll box and click the left mouse button to move down the list. To move through a list with a horizontal scroll bar, click the left-pointing arrow to scroll to the left of the list or click the right-pointing arrow to scroll to the right of the list.

To make a selection from a list using the keyboard, move the insertion point into the box by holding down the Alt key and pressing the underlined letter of the desired option. Press the Up and/or Down Arrow keys on the keyboard to move through the list.

In some dialog boxes where enough room is not available for a list box, lists of options are inserted in a drop-down list box. Options that contain a drop-down list box display with a down-pointing arrow. For example, the *Underline style* option at the Word Font dialog box shown in Figure G.4 contains a drop-down list. To display the list, click the down-pointing arrow to the right of the *Underline style* option box. If you are using the keyboard, press Alt + U.

Check Boxes

Some dialog boxes contain options preceded by a box. A check mark may or may not appear in the box. The Word Font dialog box shown in Figure G.4 displays a variety of check boxes within the *Effects* section. If a check mark appears in the box, the option is active (turned on). If the check box does not contain a check mark, the option is inactive (turned off). Any number of check boxes can be active. For example, in the Word Font dialog box, you can insert a check mark in any or all of the boxes in the *Effects* section and these options will be active.

To make a check box active or inactive with the mouse, position the tip of the arrow pointer in the check box and then click the left mouse button. If you are using the keyboard, press Alt + the underlined letter of the desired option.

Option Buttons

The Word Print dialog box shown in Figure G.7 contains options in the *Print range* section preceded by option buttons. Only one option button can be selected at any time. When an option button is selected, a green circle displays in the button. To select an option button with the mouse, position the tip of the arrow pointer inside the option button and then click the left mouse button. To make a selection with the keyboard, hold down the Alt key and then press the underlined letter of the desired option.

Figure G.7 Word Print Dialog Box

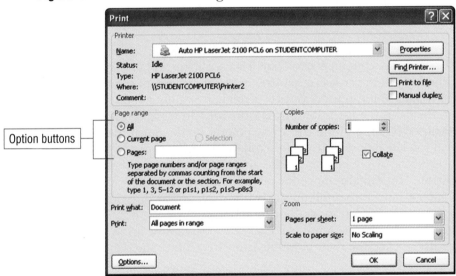

Spin Boxes

Some options in a dialog box contain measurements or numbers you can increase or decrease. These options are generally located in a spin box. For example, the Word Paragraph dialog box shown in Figure G.8 contains spin boxes located after the *Left, Right, Before,* and *After* options. To increase a number in a spin box, position the tip of the arrow pointer on the up-pointing arrow to the right of the desired option and then click the left mouse button. To decrease the number, click the down-pointing arrow. If you are using the keyboard, press Alt + the underlined letter of the desired option and then press the Up Arrow key to increase the number or the Down Arrow key to decrease the number.

Figure G.8 Word Paragraph Dialog Box

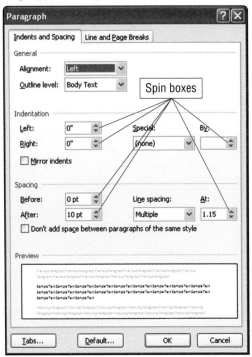

Command Buttons

In the Excel Find and Replace dialog box shown in Figure G.5, the boxes along the bottom of the dialog box are called command buttons. Use a command button to execute or cancel a command. Some command buttons display with an ellipsis (...). A command button that displays with an ellipsis will open another dialog box. To choose a command button with the mouse, position the arrow pointer on the desired button and then click the left mouse button. To choose a command button with the keyboard, press the Tab key until the desired command button contains the marquee and then press the Enter key.

Choosing Commands with Keyboard Shortcuts

Applications in the Office suite offer a variety of keyboard shortcuts you can use to executive specific commands. Keyboard shortcuts generally require two or more keys. For example, the keyboard shortcut to display the Open dialog box in an application is Ctrl + O. To use this keyboard shortcut, hold down the Ctrl key, type the letter O on the keyboard, and then release the Ctrl key. For a list of keyboard shortcuts, refer to the Help files.

Choosing Commands with Shortcut Menus

The software programs in the suite include menus that contain commands related to the item with which you are working. A shortcut menu appears in the file in the location where you are working. To display a shortcut menu, click the right mouse button or press Shift + F10. For example, if the insertion point is positioned in a paragraph of text in a Word document, clicking the right mouse button or pressing Shift + F10 will cause the shortcut menu shown in Figure G.9 to display in the document screen.

Figure G.9 Word Shortcut Menu

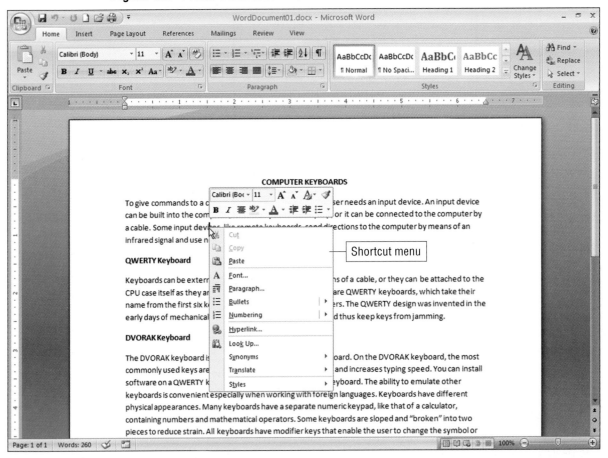

To select an option from a shortcut menu with the mouse, click the desired option. If you are using the keyboard, press the Up or Down Arrow key until the desired option is selected and then press the Enter key. To close a shortcut menu without choosing an option, click anywhere outside the shortcut menu or press the Esc key.

Working with Multiple Programs

As you learn the various programs in the Microsoft Office suite, you will notice how executing commands in each is very similar. For example, the steps to save, close, and print are virtually the same whether you are working in Word, Excel, or PowerPoint. This consistency between programs greatly enhances a user's ability to transfer knowledge learned in one program to another within the suite. Another appeal of Microsoft Office is the ability to have more than one program open at the same time. For example, you can open Word, create a document, and then open Excel, create a spreadsheet, and copy the spreadsheet into Word.

When you open a program, the name of the program displays in the Taskbar. If you open a file within the program, the file name follows the program name on the button on the Taskbar. If you open another program, the program name displays on a button positioned to the right of the first program button. Figure G.10 shows the Taskbar with Word, Excel, and PowerPoint open. To move from one program to another, click the button on the Taskbar representing the desired program file.

Figure G.10 Taskbar with Word, Excel, and PowerPoint Open

Completing Computer Projects

Some computer projects in this textbook require that you open an existing file. Project files are saved on the Student CD that accompanies this textbook. The files you need for each chapter are saved in individual folders. Before beginning a chapter, copy the necessary folder from the CD to your storage medium. After completing projects in a chapter, delete the chapter folder before copying the next chapter folder. (Check with your instructor before deleting a folder.)

The Student CD also contains model answers in PDF format for the project exercises within (but not at the end of) each chapter so you can check your work. To access the PDF files, you will need to have Adobe Acrobat Reader installed on your computer's hard drive. A free download of Adobe Reader is available at Adobe Systems' Web site at www.adobe.com.

Copying a Folder

As you begin working in a chapter, copy the chapter folder from the CD to your storage medium using the My Computer window by completing the following steps:

1. Insert the CD that accompanies this textbook in the CD drive.
2. Insert your storage medium in the appropriate drive.
3. At the Windows XP desktop, open the My Computer window by clicking the Start button and then clicking *My Computer* at the Start menu.
4. Double-click the CD drive in the contents pane (probably displays as *Office2007_Bench* or *Word2007, Excel 2007*, etc. followed by the drive letter).
5. Double-click the *StudentDataFiles* folder in the contents pane.
6. Double-click the desired folder name in the contents pane. (For example, if you are copying a folder for a Word Level 1 chapter, double-click the *Word2007L1* folder.)
7. Click once on the desired chapter subfolder name to select it.
8. Click the Copy this folder hyperlink in the *File and Folder Tasks* section of the task pane.
9. At the Copy Items dialog box, click the drive where your storage medium is located and then click the Copy button.
10. After the folder is copied to your storage medium, close the My Computer window by clicking the Close button (white X on red background) that displays in the upper right corner of the window.

Deleting a Folder

Before copying a chapter folder onto your storage medium, you may need to delete any previous chapter folders. Do this in the My Computer window by completing the following steps:

1. Insert your storage medium in the appropriate drive.
2. At the Windows XP desktop, open the My Computer window by clicking the Start button and then clicking *My Computer* at the Start menu.
3. Double-click the drive where you storage medium is located in the contents pane.
4. Click the chapter folder in the list box.
5. Click the <u>Delete this folder</u> hyperlink in the *File and Folder Tasks* section of the task pane.
6. At the message asking if you want to remove the folder and all its contents, click the Yes button.
7. If a message displays asking if you want to delete a read-only file, click the Yes to All button.
8. Close the My Computer window by clicking the Close button (white X on red background) that displays in the upper right corner of the window.

Viewing or Printing the Project Model Answers

If you want to access the PDF model answer files, first make sure that Adobe Acrobat Reader is installed on your hard drive. Double-click the folder, double-click the desired chapter subfolder name, and double-click the appropriate file name to open the file. You can view and/or print the file to compare it with your own completed exercise file.

Customizing the Quick Access Toolbar

The four applications in the Office 2007 suite—Word, Excel, PowerPoint, and Access—each contain a Quick Access toolbar that displays at the top of the screen. By default, this toolbar contains three buttons: Save, Undo, and Redo. Before beginning chapters in this textbook, customize the Quick Access toolbar by adding three additional buttons: New, Open, and Quick Print. To add these three buttons to the Word Quick Access toolbar, complete the following steps:

1. Open Word.
2. Click the Customize Quick Access Toolbar button that displays at the right side of the toolbar.
3. At the drop-down list, click *New*. (This adds the New button to the toolbar.)
4. Click the Customize Quick Access Toolbar button and then click *Open* at the drop-down list. (This adds the Open button to the toolbar.)
5. Click the Customize Quick Access Toolbar button and then click *Quick Print* at the drop-down list. (This adds the Quick Print button to the toolbar.)

Complete the same steps for Excel, Access, and PowerPoint. You will only need to add the buttons once to the Quick Access toolbar. These buttons will remain on the toolbar even when you exit and then reopen the application.

Using Windows XP

A computer requires an operating system to provide necessary instructions on a multitude of processes including loading programs, managing data, directing the flow of information to peripheral equipment, and displaying information. Windows XP Professional is an operating system that provides functions of this type (along with much more) in a graphical environment. Windows is referred to as a ***graphical user interface*** (GUI— pronounced *gooey*) that provides a visual display of information with features such as icons (pictures) and buttons. In this introduction, you will learn the basic features of Windows XP:

Tutorial WXP1
Exploring Windows XP
Tutorial WXP2
Working with Files and Folders
Tutorial WXP3
Customizing Windows
Tutorial WXP4
Using Applications

- Use desktop icons and the Taskbar to launch programs and open files or folders
- Organize and manage data, including copying, moving, creating, and deleting files and folders
- Customize the desktop by changing the theme, background, colors, and settings, and adding a screen saver
- Use the Help and Support Center features
- Customize monitor settings

Historically, Microsoft has produced two editions of Windows—one edition for individual users (on desktop and laptop computers) and another edition for servers (on computers that provide service over networks). Windows XP is an upgrade and a merging of these two Windows editions and is available in two versions. The Windows XP Home Edition is designed for home use and Windows XP Professional is designed for small office and workstation use. Whether you are using Windows XP Home Edition or Windows XP Professional, you will be able to complete the steps in the projects in this introduction.

Before using one of the software programs in the Microsoft Office suite, you will need to start the Windows XP operating system. To do this, turn on the computer. Depending on your computer equipment configuration, you may also need to turn on the monitor and printer. If you are using a computer that is part of a network system or if your computer is set up for multiple users, a screen will display showing the user accounts defined for your computer system. At this screen, click your user account name and, if necessary, type your password and then press the Enter key. The Windows XP operating system will start and, after a few moments, the desktop will display as shown in Figure W.1. (Your desktop may vary from what you see in Figure W.1.)

Figure W.1 Windows XP Desktop

icon

Taskbar

Exploring the Desktop

When Windows XP is loaded, the main portion of the screen is called the *desktop*. Think of the desktop in Windows as the top of a desk in an office. A business person places necessary tools—such as pencils, pens, paper, files, calculator—on the desktop to perform functions. Like the tools that are located on a desk, the desktop contains tools for operating the computer. These tools are logically grouped and placed in dialog boxes or panels that you can display using icons on the desktop. The desktop contains a variety of features for using your computer and software programs installed on the computer. The features available on the desktop are represented by icons and buttons.

Using Icons

Icons are visual symbols that represent programs, files, or folders. Figure W.1 identifies the *Recycle Bin* icon located on the Windows XP desktop. The Windows XP desktop on your computer may contain additional icons. Programs that have been installed on your computer may be represented by an icon on the desktop. Also, icons may display on your desktop representing files or folders. Double-click an icon and the program, file, or folder it represents opens on the desktop.

Using the Taskbar

The bar that displays at the bottom of the desktop (see Figure W.1) is called the Taskbar. The Taskbar, shown in Figure W.2, contains the Start button, a section that displays task buttons representing open programs, and the notification area.

Figure W.2 Windows XP Taskbar

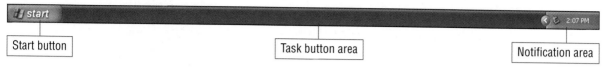

Start button   Task button area   Notification area

Click the Start button, located at the left side of the Taskbar, and the Start menu displays as shown in Figure W.3 (your Start menu may vary). You can also display the Start menu by pressing the Windows key on your keyboard or by pressing Ctrl + Esc. The left column of the Start menu contains *pinned programs*, which are programs that always appear in that particular location on the Start menu, and links to the most recently and frequently used programs. The right column contains links to folders, the Control Panel, online help, and the search feature.

Figure W.3 Start Menu

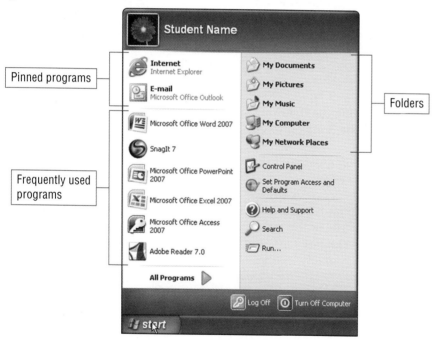

Pinned programs

Folders

Frequently used programs

To choose an option from the Start menu, drag the arrow pointer to the desired option (referred to as *pointing*) and then click the left mouse button. Pointing to options at the Start menu that are followed by a right-pointing arrow will cause a side menu to display with additional options. When a program is open, a task button representing the program appears on the Taskbar. If multiple programs are open, each program will appear as a task button on the Taskbar (a few specialized tools may not).

Project ① Opening Programs and Switching between Programs

1. Open Windows XP. (To do this, turn on the computer and, if necessary, turn on the monitor and/or printer. If you are using a computer that is part of a network system or if your computer is set up for multiple users, you may need to click your user account name and, if necessary, type your password and then press the Enter key. Check with your instructor to determine if you need to complete any additional steps.)
2. When the Windows XP desktop displays, open Microsoft Word by completing the following steps:
   a. Position the arrow pointer on the Start button on the Taskbar and then click the left mouse button.
   b. At the Start menu, point to *All Programs* (a side menu displays) and then point to *Microsoft Office* (another side menu displays).
   c. Drag the arrow pointer to *Microsoft Office Word 2007* in the side menu and then click the left mouse button.
   d. When the Microsoft Word program is open, notice that a task button representing Word displays on the Taskbar.

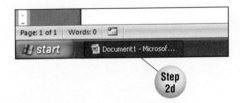

Step 2d

3. Open Microsoft Excel by completing the following steps:
   a. Position the arrow pointer on the Start button on the Taskbar and then click the left mouse button.
   b. At the Start menu, point to *All Programs* and then point to *Microsoft Office*.
   c. Drag the arrow pointer to *Microsoft Office Excel 2007* in the side menu and then click the left mouse button.
   d. When the Microsoft Excel program is open, notice that a task button representing Excel displays on the Taskbar to the right of the task button representing Word.
4. Switch to the Word program by clicking the task button on the Taskbar representing Word.

Step 4

Step 6

5. Switch to the Excel program by clicking the task button on the Taskbar representing Excel.
6. Exit Excel by clicking the Close button that displays in the upper right corner of the Excel window.
7. Exit Word by clicking the Close button that displays in the upper right corner of the Word window.

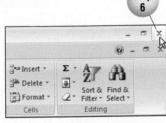

Exploring the Notification Area

The notification area is located at the right side of the Taskbar and contains the system clock along with small icons representing specialized programs that run in the background. Position the arrow pointer over the current time in the notification area of the Taskbar and today's date displays in a small yellow box above the time. Double-click the current time displayed on the Taskbar and the Date and Time Properties dialog box displays as shown in Figure W.4.

Figure W.4 Date and Time Properties Box

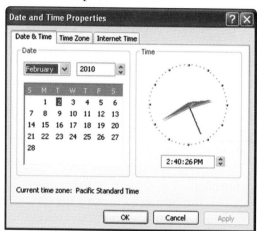

Change the date with options in the *Date* section of the dialog box. For example, to change the month, click the down-pointing arrow at the right side of the option box containing the current month and then click the desired month at the drop-down list. Change the year by clicking the up- or down-pointing arrow at the right side of the option box containing the current year until the desired year displays. To change the day, click the desired day in the monthly calendar that displays in the dialog box. To change the time, double-click either the hour, minute, or seconds and then type the appropriate time or use the up- and down-pointing arrows to adjust the time.

Some programs, when installed, will add an icon to the notification area of the Taskbar. Display the name of the icon by positioning the mouse pointer on the icon and, after approximately one second, the icon label displays in a small yellow box. Some icons may display information in the yellow box rather than the icon label. If more icons have been inserted in the notification area than can be viewed at one time, a left-pointing arrow button displays at the left side of the notification area. Click this left-pointing arrow button and the remaining icons display.

Setting Taskbar Properties

By default, the Taskbar is locked in its current position and size. You can change this default setting, along with other default settings, with options at the Taskbar and Start Menu Properties dialog box, shown in Figure W.5. To display this dialog box, position the arrow pointer on any empty spot on the Taskbar and then click the right mouse button. At the shortcut menu that displays, click *Properties*.

Figure W.5 Taskbar and Start Menu Properties Box

Each property is controlled by a check box. Property options containing a check mark are active. Click the option to remove the check mark and make the option inactive. If an option is inactive, clicking the option will insert a check mark in the check box and turn on the option (make it active).

Project ② Changing Taskbar Properties

1. Make sure Windows XP is open and the desktop displays.
2. Hide the Taskbar and remove the display of the clock by completing the following steps:
   a. Position the arrow pointer on any empty area on the Taskbar and then click the right mouse button.
   b. At the shortcut menu that displays, click *Properties*.
   c. At the Taskbar and Start Menu Properties dialog box, click *Auto-hide the taskbar*. (This inserts a check mark in the check box.)
   d. Click *Show the clock*. (This removes the check mark from the check box.)
   e. Click the Apply button.
   f. Click OK to close the dialog box.

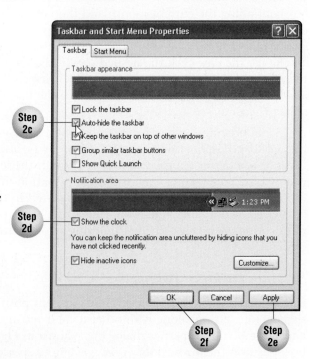

Step 2c

Step 2d

Step 2f

Step 2e

3. Display the Taskbar by positioning the mouse pointer at the bottom of the screen. When the Taskbar displays, notice that the time no longer displays at the right side of the Taskbar.
4. Return to the default settings for the Taskbar by completing the following steps:
   a. With the Taskbar displayed (if it does not display, position the mouse pointer at the bottom of the desktop), position the arrow pointer on any empty area on the Taskbar and then click the right mouse button.
   b. At the shortcut menu that displays, click *Properties*.
   c. At the Taskbar and Start Menu Properties dialog box, click *Auto-hide the taskbar*. (This removes the check mark from the check box.)
   d. Click *Show the clock*. (This inserts a check mark in the check box.)
   e. Click the Apply button.
   f. Click OK to close the dialog box.

Turning Off the Computer

When you are finished working with your computer, you can choose to shut down the computer completely, shut down and then restart the computer, put the computer on standby, or tell the computer to hibernate. Do not turn off your computer until your screen goes blank. Important data is stored in memory while Windows XP is running and this data needs to be written to the hard drive before turning off the computer.

To shut down your computer, click the Start button on the Taskbar and then click *Turn Off Computer* at the Start menu. At the Turn off computer window, shown in Figure W.6, click the *Stand By* option and the computer switches to a low power state causing some devices such as the monitor and hard drives to turn off. With these devices off, the computer uses less power. Stand By is particularly useful for saving battery power for portable computers. Tell the computer to "hibernate" by holding down the Shift key while clicking the *Stand By* option. In hibernate mode, the computer saves everything in memory, turns off the monitor and hard drive, and then turns off the computer. Click the *Turn Off* option if you want to shut down Windows XP and turn off all power to the computer. Click the *Restart* option if you want to restart the computer and restore the desktop exactly as you left it. You can generally restore your desktop from either standby or hibernate by pressing once on the computer's power button. Usually, bringing a computer out of hibernation takes a little longer than bringing a computer out of standby.

Figure W.6 Turn Off Computer Window

Managing Files and Folders

As you begin working with programs in Windows XP, you will create files in which data (information) is saved. A file might contain a Word document, an Excel workbook, or a PowerPoint presentation. As you begin creating files, consider creating folders into which those files will be stored. You can complete file management tasks such as creating a folder and copying and moving files and folders at the My Computer window. To display the My Computer window shown in Figure W.7, click the Start button on the Taskbar and then click My Computer. The various components of the My Computer window are identified in Figure W.7.

Figure W.7 My Computer Window

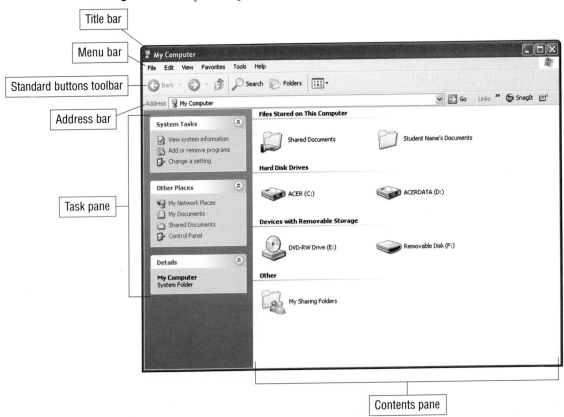

Copying, Moving, and Deleting Files/Folders

File and folder management activities might include copying and moving files or folders from one folder or drive to another, or deleting files or folders. The My Computer window offers a variety of methods for copying, moving, and deleting files/folders. You can use options in the task pane, drop-down menu options, or shortcut menu options. This section will provide you with the steps for copying, moving, and deleting files/folders using options in the task pane.

To copy a file/folder to another folder or drive, first display the file in the contents pane by identifying the location of the file. If the file is located in the My Documents folder, click the <u>My Documents</u> hyperlink in the *Other Places* section of the task pane. If the file is located on the hard drive, double-click the desired drive in the contents pane; if the file is located on a USB drive, DVD, or CD, double-click the desired drive letter. Next, click the folder or file name in the contents pane that you want to copy. This changes the options in the task pane to include management options such as renaming, moving, copying, and deleting folders or files. Click the Copy this folder (or Copy this file) hyperlink in the task pane and the Copy Items dialog box displays as shown in Figure W.8. At the Copy Items dialog box, click the desired folder or drive and then click the Copy button.

Figure W.8 Copy Items Dialog Box

To move adjacent files/folders, click the first file or folder, hold down the Shift key, and then click the last file or folder. This selects and highlights all files/folders from the first file/folder you clicked to the last file/folder you clicked. With the adjacent files/folders selected, click the Move the selected items hyperlink in the File and Folder Tasks section of the task pane and then specify the desired location at the Move Items dialog box. To select nonadjacent files/folders, click the first file/folder to select it, hold down the Ctrl key, and then click any other files/folders you want to move or copy.

You can easily remove (delete) a file or folder from the My Computer window. To delete a file or folder, click the file or folder in the contents pane, and then click the Delete this folder (or Delete this file) hyperlink in the task pane. At the dialog box asking you to confirm the deletion, click Yes. A deleted file or folder is sent to the Recycle Bin. You will learn more about the Recycle Bin in the next section.

In Project 3, you will insert the CD that accompanies this book into the DVD or CD drive. When the CD is inserted, the drive may automatically activate and a dialog box may display on the screen telling you that the disk or device contains more than one type of content and asking what you want Windows to do. If this dialog box displays, click Cancel to remove the dialog box.

Project ③ Copying a File and Folder and Deleting a File

1. At the Windows XP desktop, insert the CD that accompanies this textbook into the appropriate drive. If a dialog box displays telling you that the disk or device contains more than one type of content and asking what you want Windows to do, click Cancel.
2. At the Windows XP desktop, open the My Computer window by clicking the Start button on the Taskbar and then clicking *My Computer* at the Start menu.
3. Copy a file from the CD that accompanies this textbook to the drive containing your storage medium by completing the following steps:
   a. Insert your storage medium in the appropriate drive.
   b. In the contents pane, double-click the drive containing the CD (probably displays as *Office2007_Bench* followed by a drive letter). (Make sure you double-click the mouse button because you want the contents of the CD to display in the contents pane.)
   c. Double-click the *StudentDataFiles* folder.
   d. Double-click the *WindowsXP* folder in the contents pane.
   e. Click **WordDocument01.docx** in the contents pane to select it.
   f. Click the Copy this file hyperlink located in the *File and Folder Tasks* section of the task pane.

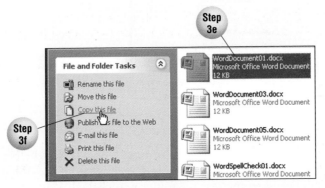

   g. At the Copy Items dialog box, click in the list box the drive containing your storage medium.
   h. Click the Copy button.

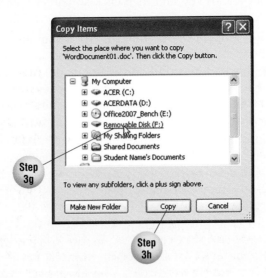

4. Delete **WordDocument01.docx** from your storage medium by completing the following steps:
   a. Click the <u>My Computer</u> hyperlink located in the *Other Places* section of the task pane.
   b. Double-click in the contents pane the drive containing your storage medium.
   c. Click ***WordDocument01.docx***.
   d. Click the <u>Delete this file</u> hyperlink in the *File and Folder Tasks* section of the task pane.

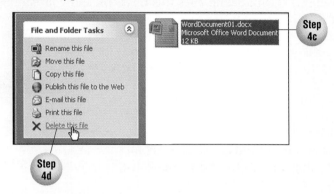

   e. At the message asking you to confirm the deletion, click Yes.
5. Copy the WindowsXP folder from the CD drive to the drive containing your storage medium by completing the following steps:
   a. Click the My Computer hyperlink in the *Other Places* section of the task pane.
   b. In the contents pane, double-click the drive containing the CD (probably displays as *Office2007_Bench* followed by a drive letter).
   c. Double-click the *StudentDataFiles* folder.
   d. Click the *WindowsXP* folder in the contents pane to select it.
   e. Click the <u>Copy this folder</u> hyperlink in the *File and Folder Tasks* section of the task pane.
   f. At the Copy Items dialog box, click the drive containing your storage medium.
   g. Click the Copy button.
6. Close the window by clicking the Close button (contains a white *X* on a red background) located in the upper right corner of the window. (You can also close the window by clicking File on the Menu bar and then clicking *Close* at the drop-down list.)

Selecting Files/Folders

You can move, copy, or delete more than one file or folder at the same time. Before moving, copying, or deleting files/folders, select the desired files or folders. Selecting files/folders is easier when you change the display in the contents pane to List or Details. To change the display, open the My Computer window and then click the Views button on the Standard Buttons toolbar. At the drop-down list that displays, click the *List* option or the *Details* option.

To move adjacent files/folders, click the first file or folder, hold down the Shift key, and click the last file or folder. This selects and highlights all files/folders from the first file/folder you clicked to the last file/folder you clicked. With the adjacent files/folders selected, click the <u>Move the selected items</u> hyperlink in the *File and Folder Tasks* section of the task pane and then specify the desired location at the Move Items dialog box. To select nonadjacent files/folders, click the first file/folder to select it, hold down the Ctrl key, and then click any other files/folders you want to move or copy.

Project ④ Copying and Deleting Files

1. At the Windows XP desktop, open the My Computer window by clicking the Start button and then clicking *My Computer* at the Start menu.
2. Copy files from the CD that accompanies this textbook to the drive containing your storage medium by completing the following steps:
   a. Make sure the CD that accompanies this textbook and your storage medium are inserted in the appropriate drives.
   b. Double-click the CD drive in the contents pane (probably displays as *Office2007_Bench* followed by the drive letter).
   c. Double-click the *StudentDataFiles* folder in the contents pane.
   d. Double-click the *WindowsXP* folder in the contents pane.
   e. Change the display to Details by clicking the Views button on the Standard Buttons toolbar and then clicking *Details* at the drop-down list.
   f. Position the arrow pointer on **WordDocument01.docx** in the contents pane and then click the left mouse button.
   g. Hold down the Shift key, click ***WordDocument05.docx***, and then release the Shift key. (This selects **WordDocument01.docx, WordDocument02.docx, WordDocument03.docx, WordDocument04.docx,** and **WordDocument05.docx.**)

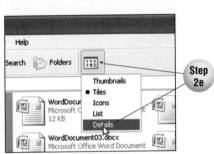

   h. Click the <u>Copy the selected items</u> hyperlink in the *File and Folder Tasks* section of the task pane.
   i. At the Copy Items dialog box, click the drive containing your storage medium and then click the Copy button.

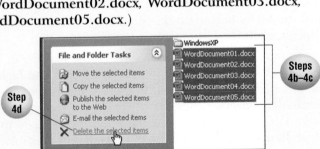

3. Display the files and folder saved on your storage medium by completing the following steps:
   a. Click the <u>My Computer</u> hyperlink in the *Other Places* section of the task pane.
   b. Double-click the drive containing your storage medium.
4. Delete the files from your storage medium that you just copied by completing the following steps:
   a. Change the view by clicking the Views button on the Standard Buttons toolbar and then clicking *List* at the drop-down list.
   b. Click ***WordDocument01.docx*** in the contents pane.
   c. Hold down the Shift key, click ***WordDocument05.docx***, and then release the Shift key. (This selects **WordDocument01.docx, WordDocument02.docx, WordDocument03.docx, WordDocument04.docx,** and **WordDocument05.docx.**)
   d. Click the <u>Delete the selected items</u> hyperlink in the *File and Folder Tasks* section of the task pane.
   e. At the message asking you to confirm the deletion, click Yes.
5. Close the window by clicking the Close button (white *X* on red background) that displays in the upper right corner of the window.

Manipulating and Creating Folders

As you begin working with and creating a number of files, consider creating folders in which you can logically group the files. To create a folder, display the My Computer window and then display in the contents pane the drive where you want to create the folder. Click File on the Menu bar, point to *New*, and then click *Folder* at the side menu. This inserts a folder icon in the contents pane and names the folder *New Folder*. Type the desired name for the new folder and then press Enter.

Project ⑤   Creating a New Folder

1. At the Windows XP desktop, open the My Computer window.
2. Create a new folder by completing the following steps:
   a. Double-click in the contents pane the drive that contains your storage medium.
   b. Double-click the *WindowsXP* folder in the contents pane. (This opens the folder.)
   c. Click File on the Menu bar, point to *New*, and then click *Folder*.
   d. Type **SpellCheckFiles** and then press Enter. (This changes the name from *New Folder* to *SpellCheckFiles*.)

Step 2c

3. Copy **WordSpellCheck01.docx**, **WordSpellCheck02.docx**, and **WordSpellCheck03.docx** into the SpellCheckFiles folder you just created by completing the following steps:

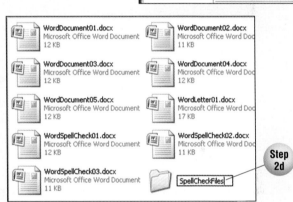

Step 2d

   a. Click the Views button on the Standard Buttons toolbar and then click *List* at the drop-down list.
   b. Click once on the file named **WordSpellCheck01.docx** located in the contents pane.
   c. Hold down the Shift key, click once on the file named **WordSpellCheck03.docx**, and then release the Shift key. (This selects **WordSpellCheck01.docx**, **WordSpellCheck02.docx**, and **WordSpellCheck03.docx**.)
   d. Click the Copy the selected items hyperlink in the *File and Folder Tasks* section of the task pane.
   e. At the Copy Items dialog box, click in the list box the drive containing your storage medium.
   f. Click *WindowsXP* in the list box.
   g. Click *SpellCheckFiles* in the list box.
   h. Click the Copy button.
4. Display the files you just copied by double-clicking the *SpellCheckFiles* folder in the contents pane.

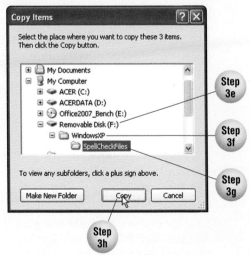

Step 3e

Step 3f

Step 3g

Step 3h

5. Delete the SpellCheckFiles folder and its contents by completing the following steps:
   a. Click the Up button on the Standard Buttons toolbar. (This displays the contents of the WindowsXP folder which is up one folder from the SpellCheckFiles folders.)
   b. Click the *SpellCheckFiles* folder in the contents pane to select it.
   c. Click the <u>Delete this folder</u> hyperlink in the *File and Folder Tasks* section of the task pane.
   d. At the message asking you to confirm the deletion, click Yes.
6. Close the window by clicking the Close button located in the upper right corner of the window.

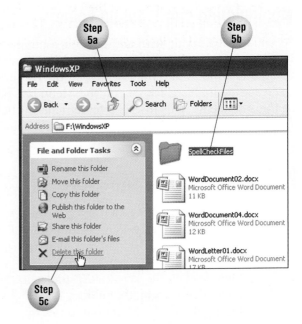

Using the Recycle Bin

Deleting the wrong file can be a disaster but Windows XP helps protect your work with the Recycle Bin. The Recycle Bin acts just like an office wastepaper basket; you can "throw away" (delete) unwanted files, but you can "reach in" to the Recycle Bin and take out (restore) a file if you threw it away by accident.

Deleting Files to the Recycle Bin

A file/folder or selected files/folders deleted from the hard drive are sent automatically to the Recycle Bin. Files/folders deleted from a disk are deleted permanently. (Recovery programs are available, however, that will help you recover deleted text. If you accidentally delete a file/folder from a disk, do not do anything more with the disk until you can run a recovery program.)

One method for deleting files is to display the My Computer window and then display in the contents pane the file(s) and/or folder(s) you want deleted. Click the file or folder or select multiple files or folders and then click the appropriate delete option in the task pane. At the message asking you to confirm the deletion, click Yes. Another method for deleting a file is to drag the file to the *Recycle Bin* icon on the desktop. Drag a file icon to the Recycle Bin until the *Recycle Bin* icon is selected (displays with a blue background) and then release the mouse button. This drops the file you are dragging into the Recycle Bin.

Recovering Files from the Recycle Bin

You can easily restore a deleted file from the Recycle Bin. To restore a file, double-click the *Recycle Bin* icon on the desktop. This opens the Recycle Bin window shown in Figure W.9. (The contents of the Recycle Bin will vary.) To restore a file, click the file you want restored, and then click the <u>Restore this item</u> hyperlink in the *Recycle Bin Tasks* section of the task pane. This removes the file from the Recycle Bin and returns it to its original location. You can also restore a file by positioning the arrow pointer on the file, clicking the right mouse button, and then clicking *Restore* at the shortcut menu.

Figure W.9 Recycle Bin Window

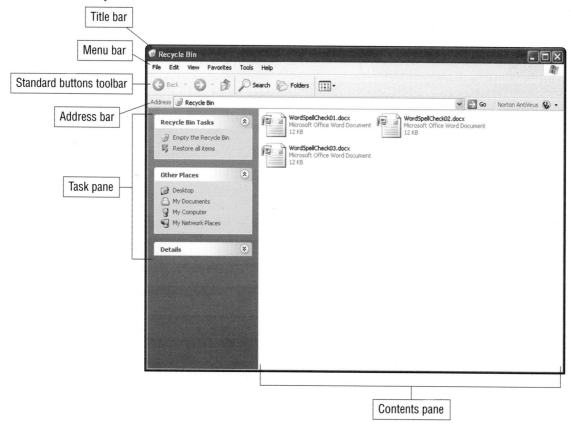

Project ⑥ Deleting Files to and Recovering Files from the Recycle Bin

Before beginning this project, check with your instructor to determine if you can copy files to the hard drive.

1. At the Windows XP desktop, open the My Computer window.
2. Copy files from your storage medium to the My Documents folder on your hard drive by completing the following steps:
    a. Double-click in the contents pane the drive containing your storage medium.
    b. Double-click the *WindowsXP* folder in the contents pane.
    c. Click the Views button on the Standard Buttons toolbar and then click *List* at the drop-down list.
    d. Position the arrow pointer on **WordSpellCheck01.docx** and then click the left mouse button.
    e. Hold down the Shift key, click *WordSpellCheck03.docx*, and then release the Shift key.

f. Click the Copy the selected items hyperlink in the *File and Folder Tasks* section of the task pane.

g. At the Copy Items dialog box, click *My Documents* in the list box.

h. Click the Copy button.

Step 2g

3. Click the <u>My Documents</u> hyperlink in the *Other Places* section of the task pane. (The files you copied, **WordSpellCheck01.docx** through **WordSpellCheck03.docx**, will display in the contents pane in alphabetical order.)

4. Delete **WordSpellCheck01.docx** through **WordSpellCheck03.docx** from the My Documents folder and send them to the Recycle Bin by completing the following steps:

   a. Select **WordSpellCheck01.docx** through **WordSpellCheck03.docx** in the contents pane. (If these files are not visible, you will need to scroll down the list of files.)

   b. Click the <u>Delete the selected items</u> hyperlink in the *File and Folder Tasks* section of the task pane.

   c. At the message asking you to confirm the deletion to the Recycle Bin, click Yes.

5. Click the Close button to close the window.

6. At the desktop, display the contents of the Recycle Bin by double-clicking the *Recycle Bin* icon.

7. At the Recycle Bin window, restore **WordSpellCheck01.docx** through **WordSpellCheck03.docx** to the My Documents folder by completing the following steps:

   a. Select **WordSpellCheck01.docx** through **WordSpellCheck03.docx** in the contents pane of the Recycle Bin window. (If these files are not visible, you will need to scroll down the list of files.)

   b. With the files selected, click the <u>Restore the selected items</u> hyperlink in the *Recycle Bin Tasks* section of the task pane.

Step 7a

Step 7b

8. Close the Recycle Bin window by clicking the Close button located in the upper right corner of the window.

9. Display the My Computer window.

10. Click the <u>My Documents</u> hyperlink in the *Other Places* section of the task pane.

11. Delete the files you restored by completing the following steps:

    a. Select **WordSpellCheck01.docx** through **WordSpellCheck03.docx** in the contents pane. (If these files are not visible, you will need to scroll down the list of files. These are the files you recovered from the Recycle Bin.)

    b. Click the <u>Delete the selected items</u> hyperlink in the *File and Folder Tasks* section of the task pane.

    c. At the message asking you to confirm the deletion, click Yes.

12. Close the window.

Emptying the Recycle Bin

Just like a wastepaper basket, the Recycle Bin can get full. To empty the Recycle Bin, position the arrow pointer on the *Recycle Bin* icon on the desktop and then click the right mouse button. At the shortcut menu that displays, click *Empty Recycle Bin*. At the message asking you to confirm the deletion, click Yes. You can also empty the Recycle Bin by double-clicking the *Recycle Bin* icon. At the Recycle Bin window, click the <u>Empty the Recycle Bin</u> hyperlink in the *Recycle Bin Tasks* section of the task pane. At the message asking you to confirm the deletion, click Yes. (You can also empty the Recycle Bin by clicking File on the Menu bar and then clicking *Empty Recycle Bin* at the drop-down menu.)

Emptying the Recycle Bin deletes all files/folders. You can delete a specific file/folder from the Recycle Bin (rather than all files/folders). To do this, double-click the *Recycle Bin* icon on the desktop. At the Recycle Bin window, select the file/folder or files/folders you want to delete. Click File on the Menu bar and then click *Delete* at the drop-down menu. (You can also right-click a selected file/folder and then click *Delete* at the shortcut menu.) At the message asking you to confirm the deletion, click Yes.

Project ⑦   Emptying the Recycle Bin

Before beginning this project, check with your instructor to determine if you can delete files/folders from the Recycle Bin.

1. At the Windows XP desktop, double-click the *Recycle Bin* icon.
2. At the Recycle Bin window, empty the contents of the Recycle Bin by completing the following steps:
   a. Click the <u>Empty the Recycle Bin</u> hyperlink in the *Recycle Bin Tasks* section of the task pane.

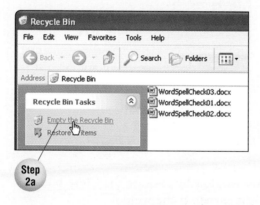

Step 2a

   b. At the message asking you to confirm the deletion, click Yes.
3. Close the Recycle Bin window by clicking the Close button located in the upper right corner of the window.

When you empty the Recycle Bin, the files cannot be recovered by the Recycle Bin or by Windows XP. If you have to recover a file, you will need to use a file recovery program such as Norton Utilities. These utilities are separate programs, but might be worth their cost if you ever need them.

Creating a Shortcut

If you use a file or program on a consistent basis, consider creating a shortcut to the file or program. A shortcut is a specialized icon that represents very small files that point the operating system to the actual item, whether it is a file, a folder, or an application. If you create a shortcut to a Word document, the shortcut icon is not the actual document but a path to the document. Double-click the shortcut icon and Windows XP opens the document in Word.

One method for creating a shortcut is to display the My Computer window and then display the drive or folder where the file is located. Right-click the desired file, point to *Send To*, and then click *Desktop (create shortcut)*. You can easily delete a shortcut icon from the desktop by dragging the shortcut icon to the Recycle Bin icon. This deletes the shortcut icon but does not delete the file to which the shortcut pointed.

Project 8 Creating a Shortcut

1. At the Windows XP desktop, display the My Computer window.
2. Double-click the drive containing your storage medium.
3. Double-click the *WindowsXP* folder in the contents pane.
4. Change the display of files to a list by clicking the Views button on the Standard Buttons toolbar and then clicking *List* at the drop-down list.
5. Create a shortcut to the file named **WordLetter01.docx** by right-clicking on **WordLetter01.docx**, pointing to *Send To*, and then clicking *Desktop (create shortcut)*.

Step
5

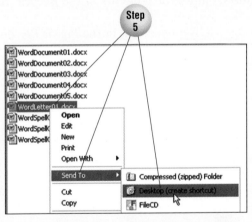

6. Close the My Computer window by clicking the Close button located in the upper right corner of the window.
7. Open Word and the file named **WordLetter01.docx** by double-clicking the *WordLetter01.docx* shortcut icon on the desktop.
8. After viewing the file in Word, exit Word by clicking the Close button that displays in the upper right corner of the window.
9. Delete the *WordLetter01.docx* shortcut icon by completing the following steps:
   a. At the desktop, position the mouse pointer on the *WordLetter01.docx* shortcut icon.
   b. Hold down the left mouse button, drag the icon on top of the *Recycle Bin* icon, and then release the mouse button.

Step
7

Customizing the Desktop

You can customize the Windows XP desktop to fit your particular needs and preferences. For example, you can choose a different theme, change the desktop background, add a screen saver, and apply a different appearance to windows, dialog boxes, and menus. To customize the desktop, position the arrow pointer on any empty location on the desktop and then click the right mouse button. At the shortcut menu that displays, click *Properties*. This displays the Display Properties dialog box with the Themes tab selected as shown in Figure W.10.

Figure W.10 Display Properties Dialog Box

Changing the Theme

A Windows XP theme specifies a variety of formatting such as fonts, sounds, icons, colors, mouse pointers, background, and screen saver. Windows XP contains two themes—Windows XP (the default) and Windows Classic (which appears like earlier versions of Windows). Other themes are available as downloads from the Microsoft Web site. Change the theme with the *Theme* option at the Display Properties dialog box with the Themes tab selected.

Changing the Desktop

With options at the Display Properties dialog box with the Desktop tab selected, as shown in Figure W.11, you can choose a different desktop background and customize the desktop. Click any option in the *Background* list box and preview the results in the preview screen. With the *Position* option, you can specify that the background image is centered, tiled, or stretched on the desktop. Use the *Color* option to change the background color and click the Browse button to choose a background image from another location or Web site.

Figure W.11 Display Properties Dialog Box with Desktop Tab Selected

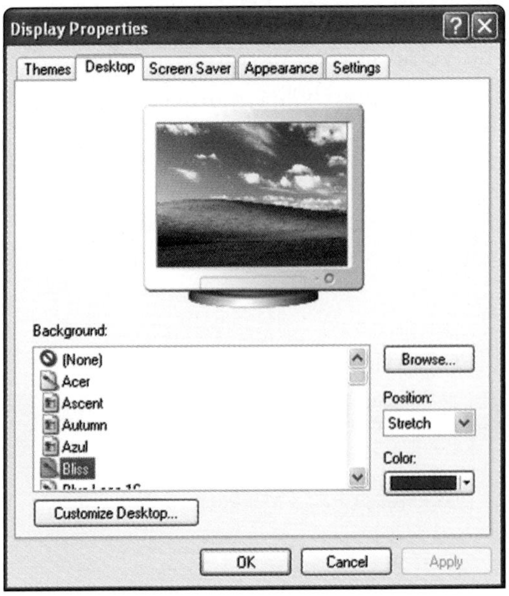

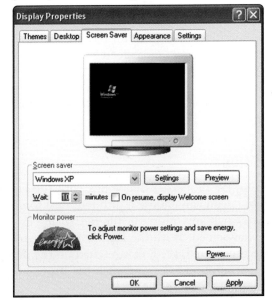

Adding a Screen Saver

If your computer sits idle for periods of time, consider adding a screen saver. A screen saver is a pattern that changes constantly, thus eliminating the problem of an image staying on the screen too long. To add a screen saver, display the Display Properties dialog box and then click the Screen Saver tab. This displays the dialog box as shown in Figure W.12.

Figure W.12 Display Properties Dialog Box with Screen Saver Tab Selected

Click the down-pointing arrow at the right side of the *Screen saver* option box to display a list of installed screen savers. Click a screen saver and a preview displays in the monitor located toward the top of the dialog box. Click the Preview button and the dialog box is hidden and the screen saver displays on your monitor. Move the mouse or click a button on the mouse and the dialog box will reappear. Click the Power button in the *Monitor power* section and a dialog box displays with options for choosing a power scheme appropriate to the way you use your computer. The dialog box also includes options for specifying how long the computer can be left unused before the monitor and hard disk are turned off and the system goes to standby or hibernate mode.

Changing Colors

Click the Appearance tab at the Display Properties dialog box and the dialog box displays as shown in Figure W.13. At this dialog box, you can change the desktop scheme. Schemes are predefined collections of colors used in windows, menus, title bars, and system fonts. Windows XP loads with the Windows XP style color scheme. Choose a different scheme with the Windows and buttons option and choose a specific color with the Color scheme option.

Figure W.13 Display Properties Dialog Box with Appearance Tab Selected

Changing Settings

Click the Settings tab at the Display Properties dialog box and the dialog box displays as shown in Figure W.14. At this dialog box, you can set color and screen resolution. The *Color quality* option determines how many colors your monitor displays. The more colors that are shown, the more realistic the images will appear. However, a lot of computer memory is required to show thousands of colors. Your exact choice is determined by the specific hardware you are using. The *Screen resolution* slide bar sets the screen's resolution. The higher the number, the more you can fit onto your screen. Again, your actual values depend on your particular hardware.

Figure W.14 Display Properties Dialog Box with Settings Tab Selected

Project ⑨   Customizing the Desktop

Before beginning this project, check with your instructor to determine if you can customize the desktop.

1. At the Windows XP desktop, display the Display Properties dialog box by positioning the arrow pointer on an empty location on the desktop, clicking the right mouse button, and then clicking *Properties* at the shortcut menu.
2. At the Display Properties dialog box, change the desktop background by completing the following steps:
   a. Click the Desktop tab.
   b. If a background is selected in the *Background* list box (other than the *(None)* option), make a note of this background name.
   c. Click *Blue Lace 16* in the *Background* list box. (If this option is not available, choose another background.)
   d. Make sure *Tile* is selected in the *Position* list box.
   e. Click OK to close the dialog box.

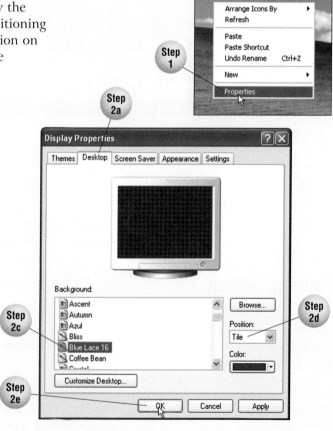

3. After viewing the desktop with the Blue Lace 16 background, remove the background image and change the background color by completing the following steps:
   a. Display the Display Properties dialog box.
   b. At the Display Properties dialog box, click the Desktop tab.
   c. Click *(None)* in the *Background* list box.
   d. Click the down-pointing arrow at the right side of the *Color* option and then click the dark red option at the color palette.
   e. Click OK to close the Display Properties dialog box.

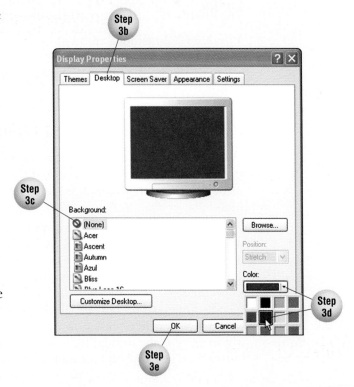

Step 3b

Step 3c

Step 3d

Step 3e

4. After viewing the desktop with the dark red background color, add a screen saver and change the wait time by completing the following steps:
   a. Display the Display Properties dialog box.
   b. At the Display Properties dialog box, click the Screen Saver tab. (If a screen saver is already selected in the *Screen saver* option box, make a note of this screen saver name.)
   c. Click the down-pointing arrow at the right side of the *Screen saver* option box.
   d. At the drop-down list that displays, click a screen saver that interests you. (A preview of the screen saver displays in the screen located toward the top of the dialog box.)
   e. Click a few other screen savers to see how they will display on the monitor.
   f. Click OK to close the Display Properties dialog box.
5. Return all settings back to the default by completing the following steps:
   a. Display the Display Properties dialog box.
   b. Click the Desktop tab.
   c. If a background and color were selected when you began this project, click that background name in the *Background* list box and change the color back to the original color.
   d. Click the Screen Saver tab.
   e. At the Display Properties dialog box with the Screen Saver tab selected, click the down-pointing arrow at the right side of the *Screen saver* option box, and then click *(None)*. (If a screen saver was selected before completing this project, return to that screen saver.)
   f. Click OK to close the Display Properties dialog box.

Exploring Windows XP Help and Support

Windows XP includes an on-screen reference guide providing information, explanations, and interactive help on learning Windows features. The on-screen reference guide contains complex files with hypertext used to access additional information by clicking a word or phrase.

Using the Help and Support Center Window

Display the Help and Support Center window shown in Figure W.15 by clicking the Start button on the Taskbar and then clicking *Help and Support* at the Start menu. The appearance of your Help and Support Center window may vary slightly from what you see in Figure W.15.

If you want to learn about a topic listed in the *Pick a Help topic* section of the window, click the desired topic and information about the topic displays in the window. Use the other options in the Help and Support Center window to get assistance or support from a remote computer or Windows XP newsgroups, pick a specific task, or learn about the additional help features. If you want help on a specific topic and do not see that topic listed in the *Pick a Help topic* section of the window, click inside the *Search* text box (generally located toward the top of the window), type the desired topic, and then press Enter or click the Start searching button (white arrow on a green background).

Figure W.15 Help and Support Center Window

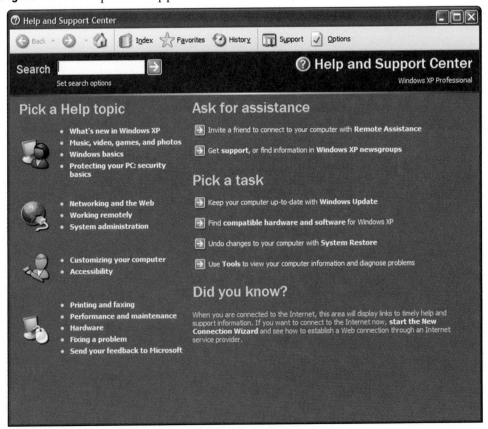

1. At the Windows XP desktop, use the Help and Support feature to learn about new Windows XP features by completing the following steps:

   a. Click the Start button on the Taskbar and then click *Help and Support* at the Start menu.

   b. At the Help and Support Center window, click the <u>What's new in Windows XP</u> hyperlink located in the *Pick a Help topic* section of the window.

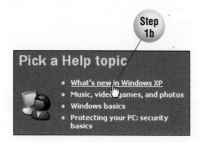

Step
1b

   c. Click the <u>What's new</u> hyperlink located in the *What's new in Windows XP* section of the window. (This displays a list of Help options at the right side of the window.)

   d. Click the <u>What's new in Windows XP</u> hyperlink located at the right side of the window below the subheading *Overviews, Articles, and Tutorials*.

   e. Read the information about Windows XP that displays at the right side of the window.

   f. Print the information by completing the following steps:

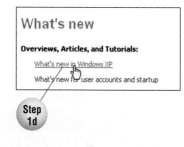

Step
1d

   1) Click the Print button located on the toolbar that displays above the information titled *What's new in Windows XP Professional*.

Step
1f1

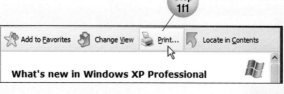

   2) At the Print dialog box, make sure the correct printer is selected and then click the Print button.

2. Return to the opening Help and Support Center window by clicking the Home button located on the Help and Support Center toolbar.

3. Use the *Search* text box to search for information on deleting files by completing the following steps:

   a. Click in the *Search* text box located toward the top of the Help and Support Center window.

   b. Type **deleting files** and then press Enter.

   c. Click the <u>Delete a file or folder</u> hyperlink that displays in the *Search Results* section of the window (below the *Pick a task* subheading).

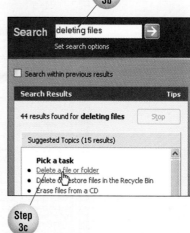

Step
3b

Step
3c

d. Read the information about deleting a file or folder that displays at the right side of the window and then print the information by clicking the Print button on the toolbar and then clicking the Print button at the Print dialog box.

e. Click the <u>Delete or restore files in the Recycle Bin</u> hyperlink that displays in the *Search Results* section of the window.

f. Read the information that displays at the right side of the window about deleting and restoring files in the Recycle Bin and then print the information.

4. Close the Help and Support Center window by clicking the Close button located in the upper right corner of the window.

Displaying an Index of Help and Support Topics

Display a list of help topics available by clicking the Index button on the Help and Support Center window toolbar. This displays an index of help topics at the left side of the window as shown in Figure W.16. Scroll through this list until the desired topic displays and then double-click the topic. Information about the selected topic displays at the right side of the window. If you are looking for a specific topic or keyword, click in the *Type in the keyword to find* text box, type the desired topic or keyword, and then press Enter.

Figure W.16 Help and Support Center Window with Index Displayed

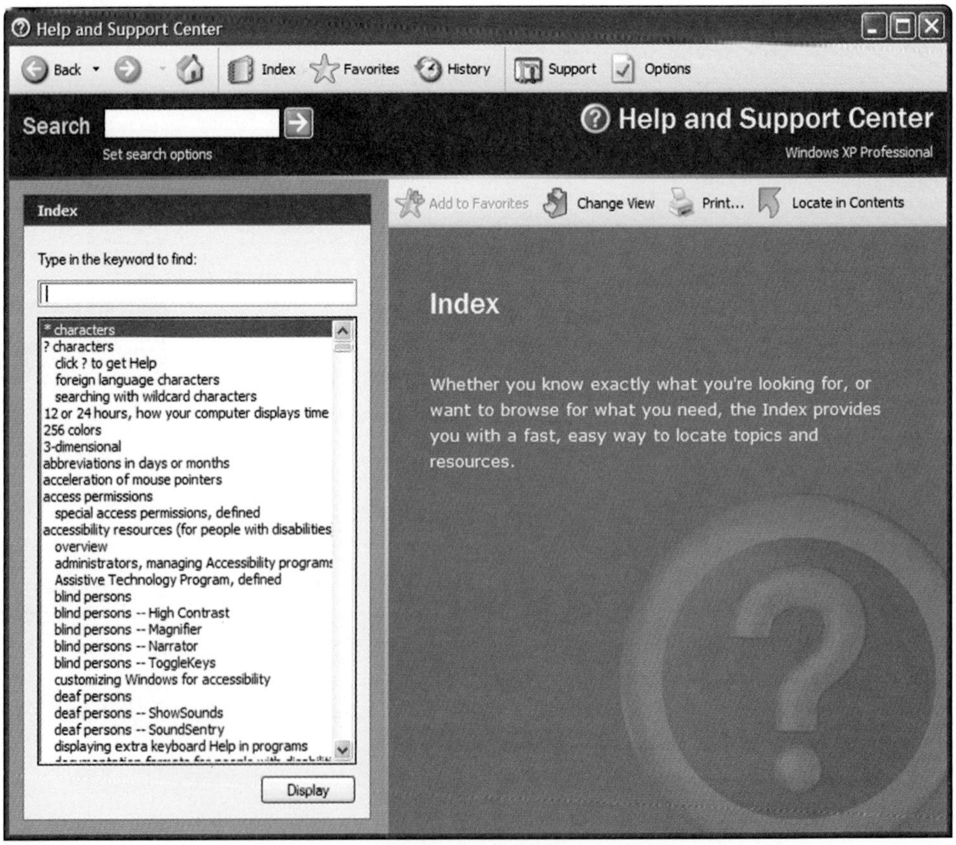

Project ⑪ Using the Index to Search for Information

1. At the Windows XP desktop, use the Index to display information on accessing programs by completing the following steps:
   a. Click the Start button on the Taskbar and then click *Help and Support* at the Start menu.
   b. Click the Index button on the Help and Support Center window toolbar.
   c. Scroll down the list of Index topics until *accessing programs* is visible and then double-click the subheading *overview* that displays below *accessing programs*.

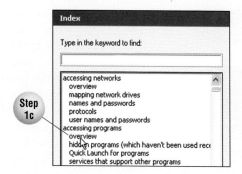

Step 1c

d. Read the information that displays at the right side of the window and then print the information.
2. Find information on adding a shortcut to the desktop by completing the following steps:
   a. Select and delete the text *overview* that displays in the *Type in the keyword to find* text box and then type **shortcuts**.
   b. Double-click the subheading *for specific programs* that displays below the *shortcuts* heading.

Step 2a

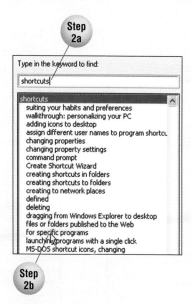

Step 2b

c. Read the information that displays at the right side of the window and then print the information.
3. Close the Help and Support Center window by clicking the Close button located in the upper right corner of the window.

Customizing Settings

Before beginning computer projects in this textbook, you may need to customize the monitor settings and turn on the display of file extensions. Projects in the chapters in this textbook assume that the monitor display is set to 1024 by 768 pixels and that the display of file extensions is turned on. To change the monitor display to 1024 by 768, complete the following steps:

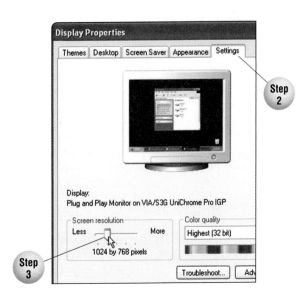

1. At the Windows XP desktop, right-click on any empty location on the desktop and then click *Properties* at the shortcut menu.
2. At the Display Properties dialog box, click the Settings tab.
3. Using the mouse, drag the slide bar button in the *Screen resolution* section to the left or right until *1024 by 768* displays below the slider bar.
4. Click the Apply button.
5. Click the OK button.

To turn on the display of file extensions, complete the following steps:

1. At the Windows XP desktop, click the Start button and then click *My Computer*.
2. At the My Computer window, click Tools on the Menu bar and then click *Folder Options* at the drop-down list.

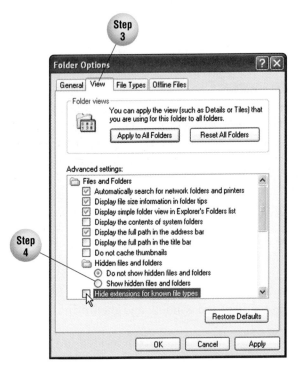

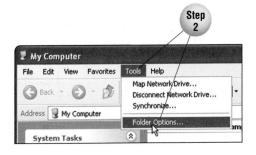

3. At the Folder Options dialog box, click the View tab.
4. Click the *Hide extentions for known file types* check box to remove the check mark.
5. Click the Apply button.
6. Click the OK button.

Browsing the Internet
Using Internet Explorer 7.0

Microsoft Internet Explorer 7.0 is a Web browser program with options and features for displaying sites as well as navigating and searching for information on the Internet. The *Internet* is a network of computers connected around the world. Users access the Internet for several purposes: to communicate using instant messaging and/or e-mail, to subscribe to newsgroups, to transfer files, to socialize with other users around the globe in "chat" rooms, and also to access virtually any kind of information imaginable.

Tutorial IE1
Browsing the Internet with Internet Explorer 7.0
Tutorial IE2
Gathering and Downloading Information and Files

Using the Internet, people can find a phenomenal amount of information for private or public use. To use the Internet, three things are generally required: an Internet Service Provider (ISP), a program to browse the Web (called a *Web browser*), and a *search engine*. In this section, you will learn how to:

- Navigate the Internet using URLs and hyperlinks
- Use search engines to locate information
- Download Web pages and images

Browsing the Internet

You will use the Microsoft Internet Explorer Web browser to locate information on the Internet. Uniform Resource Locators, referred to as URLs, are the method used to identify locations on the Internet. The steps for browsing the Internet vary but generally include: opening Internet Explorer, typing the URL for the desired site, navigating the various pages of the site, navigating to other sites using links, and then closing Internet Explorer.

To launch Internet Explorer 7.0, double-click the *Internet Explorer* icon on the Windows desktop. Figure IE.1 identifies the elements of the Internet Explorer, version 7.0, window. The Web page that displays in your Internet Explorer window may vary from what you see in Figure IE.1.

Figure IE.1 Internet Explorer Window

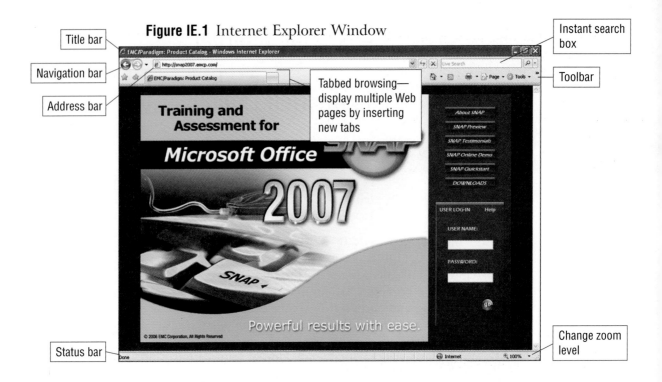

Title bar

Navigation bar

Address bar

Status bar

Instant search box

Toolbar

Tabbed browsing—display multiple Web pages by inserting new tabs

Change zoom level

If you know the URL for the desired Web site, click in the Address bar, type the URL, and then press Enter. The Web site's home page displays in a tab within the Internet Explorer window. URLs (Uniform Resource Locators) are the method used to identify locations on the Internet. The format of a URL is *http://server-name.path*. The first part of the URL, *http*, stands for HyperText Transfer Protocol, which is the protocol or language used to transfer data within the World Wide Web. The colon and slashes separate the protocol from the server name. The server name is the second component of the URL. For example, in the URL http://www.microsoft.com, the server name is *microsoft*. The last part of the URL specifies the domain to which the server belongs. For example, *.com* refers to "commercial" and establishes that the URL is a commercial company. Other examples of domains include *.edu* for "educational," *.gov* for "government," and *.mil* for "military."

Project ① Browsing the Internet Using URLs

1. Make sure you are connected to the Internet through an Internet Service Provider and that the Windows desktop displays. (Check with your instructor to determine if you need to complete steps for accessing the Internet such as typing a user name and password to log on.)
2. Launch Microsoft Internet Explorer by double-clicking the *Internet Explorer* icon located on the Windows desktop.
3. At the Internet Explorer window, explore the Web site for Yosemite National Park by completing the following steps:
   a. Click in the Address bar, type **www.nps.gov/yose**, and then press Enter.

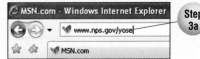

Step 3a

b. Scroll down the home page for Yosemite National Park by clicking the down-pointing arrow on the vertical scroll bar located at the right side of the Internet Explorer window.

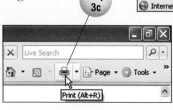

c. Print the home page by clicking the Print button located on the Internet Explorer toolbar.

4. Explore the Web site for Glacier National Park by completing the following steps:

a. Click in the Address bar, type **www.nps.gov/glac**, and then press Enter.

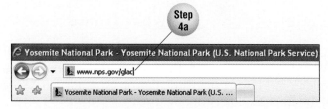

b. Print the home page by clicking the Print button located on the Internet Explorer toolbar.

5. Close Internet Explorer by clicking the Close button (contains an X) located in the upper right corner of the Internet Explorer window.

Navigating Using Hyperlinks

Most Web pages contain "hyperlinks" that you click to connect to another page within the Web site or to another site on the Internet. Hyperlinks may display in a Web page as underlined text in a specific color or as images or icons. To use a hyperlink, position the mouse pointer on the desired hyperlink until the mouse pointer turns into a hand, and then click the left mouse button. Use hyperlinks to navigate within and between sites on the Internet. The navigation bar in the Internet Explorer window contains a Back button that, when clicked, takes you to the previous Web page viewed. If you click the Back button and then want to return to the previous page, click the Forward button. You can continue clicking the Back button to back your way out of several linked pages in reverse order since Internet Explorer maintains a history of the Web sites you visit.

Project ② Navigating Using Hyperlinks

1. Make sure you are connected to the Internet and then double-click the *Internet Explorer* icon on the Windows desktop.

2. At the Internet Explorer window, display the White House Web page and navigate in the page by completing the following steps:

a. Click in the Address bar, type **whitehouse.gov**, and then press Enter.

b. At the White House home page, position the mouse pointer on a hyperlink that interests you until the pointer turns into a hand, and then click the left mouse button.

c. At the linked Web page, click the Back button. (This returns you to the White House home page.)

d. At the White House home page, click the Forward button to return to the previous Web page viewed.

e. Print the Web page by clicking the Print button on the Internet Explorer toolbar.

3. Display the Web site for Amazon.com and navigate in the site by completing the following steps:

a. Click in the Address bar, type **www.amazon.com**, and then press Enter.

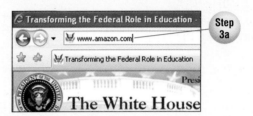

b. At the Amazon.com home page, click a hyperlink related to books.

c. When a book Web page displays, click the Print button on the Internet Explorer toolbar.

4. Close Internet Explorer by clicking the Close button (contains an X) located in the upper right corner of the Internet Explorer window.

Searching for Specific Sites

If you do not know the URL for a specific site or you want to find information on the Internet but do not know what site to visit, complete a search with a search engine. A search engine is a software program created to search quickly and easily for desired information. A variety of search engines are available on the Internet, each offering the opportunity to search for specific information. One method for searching for information is to click in the *Instant Search* box (displays the text *Live Search*) located at the right end of the navigation bar, type a keyword or phrase related to your search, and then click the Search button or press Enter. Another method for completing a search is to visit the Web site for a search engine and use options at the site.

Project ③ Searching for Information by Topic

1. Start Internet Explorer.

2. At the Internet Explorer window, search for sites on bluegrass music by completing the following steps:

a. Click in the *Instant Search* box (may display with *Live Search*) located at the right end of the of the navigation bar.

b. Type **bluegrass music** and then press Enter.

c. When a list of sites displays in the Live Search tab, click a site that interests you.

d. When the page displays, click the Print button.

3. Use the Yahoo! search engine to find sites on bluegrass music by completing the following steps:
   a. Click in the Address bar, type **www.yahoo.com**, and then press Enter.
   b. At the Yahoo! Web site, with the insertion point positioned in the *Search* text box, type **bluegrass music** and then press Enter. (Notice that the sites displayed vary from sites displayed in the earlier search.)

   c. Click hyperlinks until a Web site displays that interests you.
   d. Print the page.
4. Use the Google search engine to find sites on jazz music by completing the following steps:
   a. Click in the Address bar, type **www.google.com**, and then press Enter.
   b. At the Google Web site, with the insertion point positioned in the search text box, type **jazz music** and then press Enter.

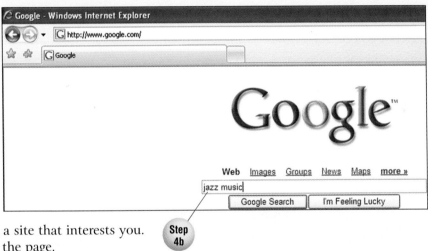

   c. Click a site that interests you.
   d. Print the page.
5. Close Internet Explorer.

Completing Advanced Searches for Specific Sites

The Internet contains an enormous amount of information. Depending on what you are searching for on the Internet and the search engine you use, some searches can result in several thousand "hits" (sites). Wading through a large number of sites can be very time-consuming and counterproductive. Narrowing a search to very specific criteria can greatly reduce the number of hits for a search. To narrow a search, use the advanced search options offered by the search engine.

Web Search

Project 4 Narrowing a Search

1. Start Internet Explorer.
2. Search for sites on skydiving in Oregon by completing the following steps:
   a. Click in the Address bar and then type www.yahoo.com.
   b. At the Yahoo! Web site, click the Web Search button next to the Search text box and then click the Advanced Search hyperlink.

Step 2b

   c. At the Advanced Web Search page, click in the search text box next to *all of these words*.
   d. Type **skydiving Oregon tandem static line**. (This limits the search to Web pages containing all of the words typed in the search text box.)

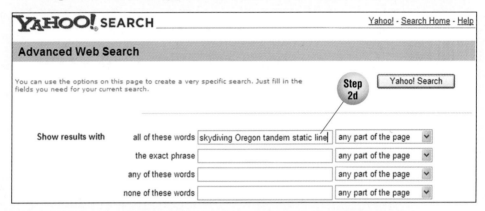

Step 2d

   e. Choose any other options at the Advanced Web Search page that will narrow your search.
   f. Click the Yahoo! Search button.
   g. When the list of Web sites displays, click a hyperlink that interests you.
   h. Print the page.
3. Close Internet Explorer.

Downloading Images, Text, and Web Pages from the Internet

The image(s) and/or text that display when you open a Web page as well as the Web page itself can be saved as a separate file. This separate file can be viewed, printed, or inserted in another file. The information you want to save in a separate file is downloaded from the Internet by Internet Explorer and saved in a folder of your choosing with the name you specify. Copyright laws protect much of the information on the Internet. Before using information downloaded from the Internet, check the site for restrictions. If you do use information, make sure you properly cite the source.

Project ⑤ **Downloading Images and Web Pages**

1. Start Internet Explorer.
2. Download a Web page and image from Banff National Park by completing the following steps:
   a. Search for sites on the Internet for Banff National Park.
   b. From the list of sites that displays, choose a site that contains information about Banff National Park and at least one image of the park.
   c. Save the Web page as a separate file by clicking the Page button on the Internet Explorer toolbar, and then clicking *Save As* at the drop-down list.
   d. At the Save Webpage dialog box, click the down-pointing arrow at the right side of the *Save in* option and then click the drive you are using as your storage medium at the drop-down list.
   e. Select the text in the *File name* text box, type **BanffWebPage**, and then press Enter.

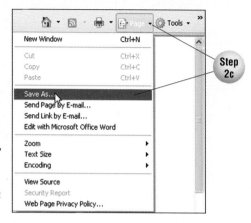

Step 2c

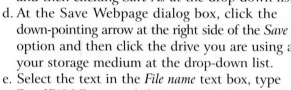

Step 2d

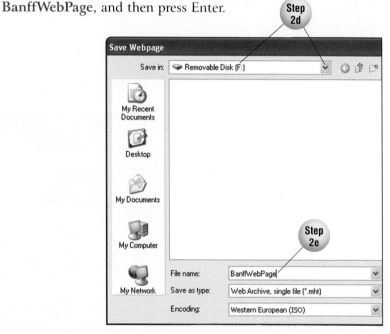

Step 2e

3. Save an image file by completing the following steps:
   a. Right-click an image that displays on the Web site. (The image that displays may vary from what you see below.)
   b. At the shortcut menu that displays, click *Save Picture As*.

Step 3b

c. At the Save Picture dialog box, change the *Save in* option to your storage medium.
d. Select the text in the *File name* text box, type **BanffImage**, and then press Enter.

4. Close Internet Explorer.

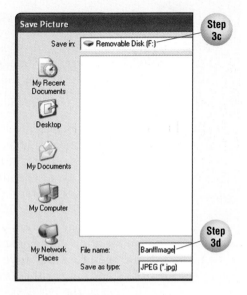

Step 3c

Step 3d

OPTIONAL

Project   Opening the Saved Web Page and Image in a Word Document

1. Open Microsoft Word by clicking the Start button on the Taskbar, pointing to *All Programs*, pointing to *Microsoft Office*, and then clicking *Microsoft Office Word 2007*.

2. With Microsoft Word open, insert the image in a document by completing the following steps:
   a. Click the Insert tab and then click the Picture button in the Illustrations group.
   b. At the Insert Picture dialog box, change the *Look in* option to the location where you saved the Banff image and then double-click ***BanffImage.jpg***.
   c. When the image displays in the Word document, print the document by clicking the Print button on the Quick Access toolbar.
   d. Close the document by clicking the Office button and then clicking *Close* at the drop-down menu. At the message asking if you want to save the changes, click No.

3. Open the **BanffWebPage.mht** file by completing the following steps:
   a. Click the Office button and then click *Open* at the drop-down menu.
   b. At the Open dialog box, change the *Look in* option to the location where you saved the Banff Web page and then double-click ***BanffWebPage.mht***.
   c. Print the Web page by clicking the Print button on the Quick Access toolbar.
   d. Close the **BanffWebPage.mht** file by clicking the Office button and then *Close*.

4. Close Word by clicking the Close button (contains an X) that displays in the upper right corner of the screen.

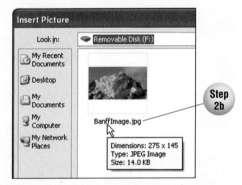

Step 2b

Step 3b

Microsoft®

excel

Making Excel Work for You!

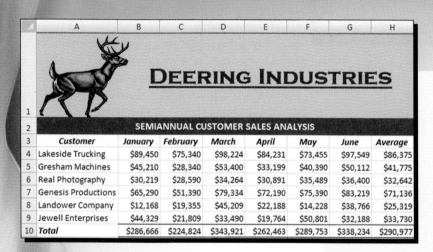

	A	B	C	D	E	F	G	H
	DEERING INDUSTRIES							
2	SEMIANNUAL CUSTOMER SALES ANALYSIS							
3	*Customer*	*January*	*February*	*March*	*April*	*May*	*June*	*Average*
4	Lakeside Trucking	$89,450	$75,340	$98,224	$84,231	$73,455	$97,549	$86,375
5	Gresham Machines	$45,210	$28,340	$53,400	$33,199	$40,390	$50,112	$41,775
6	Real Photography	$30,219	$28,590	$34,264	$30,891	$35,489	$36,400	$32,642
7	Genesis Productions	$65,290	$51,390	$79,334	$72,190	$75,390	$83,219	$71,136
8	Landower Company	$12,168	$19,355	$45,209	$22,188	$14,228	$38,766	$25,319
9	Jewell Enterprises	$44,329	$21,809	$33,490	$19,764	$50,801	$32,188	$33,730
10	*Total*	$286,666	$224,824	$343,921	$262,463	$289,753	$338,234	$290,977

Tracking and analyzing numerical data is a large component of the daily activity in today's workplace. Microsoft Excel 2007 is a popular choice among individuals and companies for organizing, analyzing, and presenting numerical information.

Organizing Information

Numbers are the foundation of every business transaction. Think about all of the numbers that the owner of a retail operation needs to organize to record customer purchases: account numbers, stock numbers, quantities, sale price, cost price, taxes, total due, amount received—just to name a few. Now consider a different scenario in which the manager of an apple orchard wants to track the volume of apples produced by each of 10 hybrids, along with the associated costs, in order to identify which hybrid apple trees are the most cost-effective. Factors to consider might include the number of apples produced weekly plus the costs of seed, fertilizer, general maintenance, and so on. These are just two examples of the type of information management for which you could use Excel.

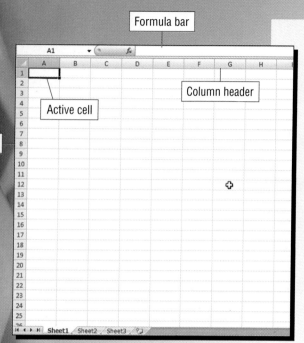

Formula bar

A1

Active cell

Column header

Row header

Sheet1 / Sheet2 / Sheet3

Spreadsheet software organizes data in columns and rows—an electronic version of an accountant's ledger—only with a lot more power and versatility. In Microsoft Excel, information is organized by creating column and row *headers*, also called headings or labels. Numbers, called *values*, are entered below and beside the headers and then formulas are created to perform calculations. The completed document is referred to as a *worksheet*. The potential uses for an application like Excel are only limited by your imagination—any type of document that can be set up in the column/row format is a candidate for an Excel worksheet.

Not sure how to set up the information you want to track? Go to Office Online and browse the templates at the Microsoft Web site. Several templates are available that already contain labels and formulas, so all you have to do is fill in the data. You can preview a template before downloading it to make sure it will meet your needs. The templates site is updated continually, so keep checking for new additions.

Analyzing Information

The true power of Excel lies in its ability to analyze information at the click of a mouse. Once you have created a worksheet, you can play the *what-if* game. For example, suppose you work in the sales department of a construction company and have used Excel to set up a worksheet that tracks sales quotas. You can use Excel's calculating and protecting features to answer questions: What kind of sales increase could we achieve if we added four more salespeople who each sold an average of the total current sales? What if we increase the existing sales quotas by 20 percent? Whenever you change a value in a worksheet, Excel automatically recalculates other values that are dependent on the number you changed. In an instant, you have your answer.

	A	B	C
1			*Cedarview Construction*
2			*Corporate Sales Quotas*
3	*Salesperson*	*Current Quota*	*Projected Quota*
4	Allejandro	$ 95,500	$114,600
5	Crispin	$ 137,000	$164,400
6	Frankel	$ 124,000	$148,800
7	Hiesmann	$ 85,500	$102,600
8	Jarvis	$ 159,000	$190,800
9	Littleman	$ 110,500	$132,600
10	Massey	$ 90,000	$108,000
11	Silverstein	$ 140,500	$168,600
12	Ting	$ 100,000	$120,000
13	Zimmerman	$ 115,500	$138,600
14			
15	20% Increase	1.2	

What would be the projected sales quotas with a 20% increase?

Answer appears as soon as you change the percentage.

Excel includes several predefined formulas, called *functions*, that make the task of constructing complex worksheets easier to manage. So math is not your favorite subject? Not a problem with Excel's Insert Function dialog box, which helps you build a formula by prompting you with explanations for each parameter.

Use the sorting and filtering in Excel to help you analyze the data in various arrangements. With the click of a button, you can rearrange the order of the worksheet to sort in ascending or descending order by a single column or by multiple columns. By filtering records, you can reduce the data you are viewing by temporarily hiding rows that do not meet your criteria. For example, in a workplace scenario, you might want to view only those clients that owe the company less than $500.

Original worksheet

Real Photography

Invoices

Invoice #	Client #	Service	Date	Amount	Tax	Amount Due
1199	03-288	Development	9/11/2010	$ 95.00	0.0%	$ 95.00
1326	04-325	Sports Portraits	9/3/2010	$ 750.00	8.5%	$ 813.75
1320	04-325	Sports Portraits	9/7/2010	$ 750.00	8.5%	$ 813.75
1270	04-789	Family Portraits	9/8/2010	$ 560.00	8.8%	$ 609.28
1345	05-335	Development	9/8/2010	$ 400.00	0.0%	$ 400.00
1144	05-335	Development	9/15/2010	$ 140.00	0.0%	$ 140.00
1302	10-226	Wedding Portraits	9/14/2010	$ 2,250.00	8.5%	$ 2,441.25
1233	10-455	Sports Portraits	9/10/2010	$ 600.00	8.5%	$ 651.00
1230	10-788	Family Portraits	9/1/2010	$ 450.00	8.5%	$ 488.25
1277	11-005	Business Portrait	9/14/2010	$ 225.00	8.8%	$ 244.80
1438	11-279	Wedding Portraits	9/1/2010	$ 1,075.00	8.8%	$ 1,169.60
1129	11-279	Development	9/2/2010	$ 225.00	0.0%	$ 225.00
1355	11-279	Development	9/4/2010	$ 350.00	0.0%	$ 350.00
1198	11-325	Wedding Portraits	9/4/2010	$ 875.00	8.5%	$ 949.38

Records sorted by Invoice #

Real Photography

Invoices

Invoice #	Client #	Service	Date	Amount	Tax	Amount Due
1129	11-279	Development	9/2/2010	$ 225.00	0.0%	$ 225.00
1144	05-335	Development	9/15/2010	$ 140.00	0.0%	$ 140.00
1198	11-325	Wedding Portraits	9/4/2010	$ 875.00	8.5%	$ 949.38
1199	03-288	Development	9/11/2010	$ 95.00	0.0%	$ 95.00
1230	10-788	Family Portraits	9/1/2010	$ 450.00	8.5%	$ 488.25
1233	10-455	Sports Portraits	9/10/2010	$ 600.00	8.5%	$ 651.00
1270	04-789	Family Portraits	9/8/2010	$ 560.00	8.8%	$ 609.28
1277	11-005	Business Portrait	9/14/2010	$ 225.00	8.8%	$ 244.80
1302	10-226	Wedding Portraits	9/14/2010	$ 2,250.00	8.5%	$ 2,441.25
1320	04-325	Sports Portraits	9/7/2010	$ 750.00	8.5%	$ 813.75
1326	04-325	Sports Portraits	9/3/2010	$ 750.00	8.5%	$ 813.75
1345	05-335	Development	9/8/2010	$ 400.00	0.0%	$ 400.00
1355	11-279	Development	9/4/2010	$ 350.00	0.0%	$ 350.00
1438	11-279	Wedding Portraits	9/1/2010	$ 1,075.00	8.8%	$ 1,169.60

Real Photog

Records filtered to display amounts less than $500.00

Invoices

Invoice	Client #	Service	Date	Amount	Tax	Amount Due
1199	03-288	Development	9/11/2010	$ 95.00	0.0%	$ 95.00
1345	05-335	Development	9/8/2010	$ 400.00	0.0%	$ 400.00
1144	05-335	Development	9/15/2010	$ 140.00	0.0%	$ 140.00
1230	10-788	Family Portraits	9/1/2010	$ 450.00	8.5%	$ 488.25
1277	11-005	Business Portrait	9/14/2010	$ 225.00	8.8%	$ 244.80
1129	11-279	Development	9/2/2010	$ 225.00	0.0%	$ 225.00
1355	11-279	Development	9/4/2010	$ 350.00	0.0%	$ 350.00

Presenting Information

With information already structured in columns and rows, the task of interpreting the results is already simplified. Add some color and other rich text enhancements to draw the reader's attention to important titles, totals, or other results and you have just made the process even easier! Add clip art, photographs, or other media to a worksheet using the Clip Art task pane.

Since a picture is worth a thousand words, why not use Excel's charting capabilities to turn those numbers into a chart—a pictorial representation that enables a reader to more easily distinguish the impact of the differences between columns of numbers. Excel can render both two-dimensional and three-dimensional charts in several chart types, a sampling of which are: column, bar, line, pie, area, radar, doughnut, and scatter.

Knowing how to use Excel is a prerequisite for many jobs in our information-driven economy. Creating worksheets in Microsoft Excel 2007 is as simple as one, two, three—set up the column and row headings, enter the data, and create the formulas. Within a short period of time, you will *excel* at creating, editing, and formatting worksheets!

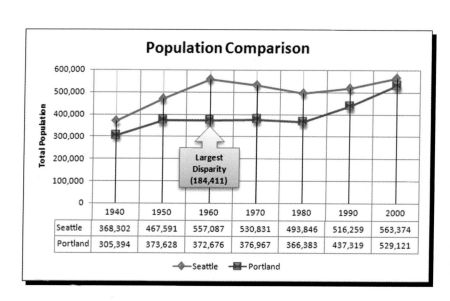

Microsoft®

excel

Unit 1:   Preparing and Formatting a Worksheet

- ➤ Preparing an Excel Workbook
- ➤ Inserting Formulas in a Worksheet
- ➤ Formatting an Excel Worksheet
- ➤ Enhancing a Worksheet

Benchmark Microsoft® Excel 2007 Level 1

Microsoft Certified Application Specialist Skills—Unit 1

Reference No.	Skill	Pages
1	**Creating and Manipulating Data**	
1.1	Insert data using AutoFill	
1.1.1	Fill a series	16-19
1.1.2	Copy a series	21
1.4	Change worksheet views	
1.4.1	Change views within a single window	79-80, 115-116
2	**Formatting Data and Content**	
2.1	Format worksheets	
2.1.1	Use themes to format worksheets	81-82
2.1.4	Format worksheet backgrounds	118
2.2	Insert and modify rows and columns	
2.2.1	Insert and delete cells, rows, and columns	71-74
2.2.2	Format rows and columns	75-78
2.2.3	Hide and unhide rows and columns	96-98
2.2.4	Modify row height and column width	68-71
2.3	Format cells and cell content	
2.3.1	Apply number formats	51-52, 82-84
2.3.3	Apply and modify cell styles	25-26
2.3.4	Format text in cells	75-78, 85-87
2.3.6	Merge and split cells	76-78
2.3.7	Add and remove cell borders	91-93
3	**Creating and Modifying Formulas**	
3.1	Reference data in formulas	
3.1.1	Create formulas that use absolute and relative cell references	56-59
3.2	Summarize data using a formula	
3.2.1	Use SUM, COUNT, COUNTA, AVERAGE, MIN, and MAX	43-49
3.8	Display and print formulas	49
5	**Collaborating and Securing Data**	
5.5	Set print options for printing data, worksheets, and workbooks	
5.5.1	Define the area of a worksheet to be printed	120-121
5.5.2	Insert and move a page break	114-116
5.5.3	Set margins	110-112
5.5.4	Add and modify headers and footers	121-123
5.5.5	Change the orientation of a worksheet	112-113
5.5.6	Scale worksheet content to fit a printed page	117-118

Note: The Level 1 and Level 2 texts each address approximately half of the Microsoft Certified Application Specialist skills. Complete coverage of the skills is offered in the combined Level 1 and Level 2 text titled *Benchmark Series Microsoft® Excel 2007: Levels 1 and 2,* which has been approved as certified courseware and which displays the Microsoft Certified Application Specialist logo on the cover.

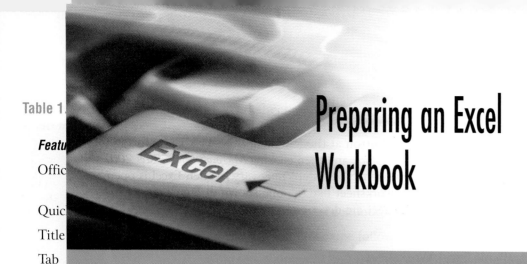

Preparing an Excel Workbook

PERFORMANCE OBJECTIVES

Upon successful completion of Chapter 1, you will be able to:

- Identify the various elements of an Excel workbook
- Create, save, and print a workbook
- Enter data in a workbook
- Edit data in a workbook
- Insert a formula using the Sum button
- Apply predesigned formatting to cells in a workbook
- Use the Help feature

excel Chapter 1

Tutorial 1.1
Creating an Excel Workbook

Many companies use a spreadsheet for numerical and financial data and to analyze and evaluate information. An Excel spreadsheet can be used for such activities as creating financial statements, preparing budgets, managing inventory, and analyzing cash flow. In addition, numbers and values can be easily manipulated to create "what if" situations. For example, using a spreadsheet, a person in a company can ask questions such as "What if the value in this category is decreased? How would that change affect the department budget?" Questions like these can be easily answered in an Excel spreadsheet. Change the value in a category and Excel will recalculate formulas for the other values. In this way, a spreadsheet can be used not only for creating financial statements or budgets, but also as a planning tool.

Note: Before beginning computer projects, copy to your storage medium the Excel2007L1C1 subfolder from the Excel2007L1 folder on the CD that accompanies this textbook. Steps on how to copy a folder are presented on the inside of the back cover of this textbook. Do this every time you start a chapter's projects.

Project ① Prepare a Worksheet with Employee Information

You will create a worksheet containing employee information, edit the contents, and then save and close the workbook.

The horizontal and vertical lines that define the cells in the worksheet area are called *gridlines*. When a cell is active (displays with a black border), the *cell address*, also called the *cell reference*, displays in the *Name box*. The cell reference includes the column letter and row number. For example, if the first cell of the worksheet is active, the cell reference *A1* displays in the Name box. A thick black border surrounds the active cell.

Entering Data in a Cell

Enter data such as a heading, number, or value in a cell. To enter data in a cell, make the desired cell active and then type the data. To make the next cell active, press the Tab key. Table 1.2 displays additional commands for making a specific cell active.

Table 1.2 Commands for Making a Specific Cell Active

To make this cell active	Press
Cell below current cell	Enter
Cell above current cell	Shift + Enter
Next cell	Tab
Previous cell	Shift + Tab
Cell at beginning of row	Home
Next cell in the direction of the arrow	Up, Down, Left, or Right Arrow keys
Last cell in worksheet	Ctrl + End
First cell in worksheet	Ctrl + Home
Cell in next window	Page Down
Cell in previous window	Page Up
Cell in window to right	Alt + Page Down
Cell in window to left	Alt + Page Up

Another method for making a specific cell active is to use the Go To feature. To use this feature, click the Find & Select button in the Editing group in the Home tab and then click Go To. At the Go To dialog box, type the cell reference in the *Reference* text box, and then click OK.

When you are ready to type data into the active cell, check the Status bar. The word *Ready* should display at the left side. As you type data, the word *Ready* changes to *Enter*. Data you type in a cell displays in the cell as well as in the Formula bar. If the data you type is longer than the cell can accommodate, the data overlaps the next cell to the right (it does not become a part of the next cell—it simply overlaps it). You will learn how to change column widths to accommodate data later in this chapter.

If the data you enter in a cell consists of text and the text does not fit into the cell, it overlaps the next cell. If, however, you enter a number in a cell, specify it as a number (rather than text) and the number is too long to fit in the cell, Excel changes the display of the number to number symbols (*###*). This is because Excel does not want you to be misled by a number when you see only a portion of it in the cell.

Along with the keyboard, you can use the mouse to make a specific cell active. To make a specific cell active with the mouse, position the mouse pointer, which displays as a white plus sign (called the *cell pointer*), on the desired cell, and then click the left mouse button. The cell pointer displays as a white plus sign when positioned in a cell in the worksheet and displays as an arrow pointer when positioned on other elements of the Excel window such as options in tabs or scroll bars.

Scroll through a worksheet using the horizontal and/or vertical scroll bars. Scrolling shifts the display of cells in the worksheet area, but does not change the active cell. Scroll through a worksheet until the desired cell is visible and then click the desired cell.

Saving a Workbook

Save an Excel workbook, which may consist of a worksheet or several worksheets, by clicking the Save button on the Quick Access toolbar or by clicking the Office button and then clicking *Save* at the drop-down list. At the Save As dialog box, type a name for the workbook in the *File name* text box and then press Enter or click the Save button. A workbook file name can contain up to 255 characters, including drive letter and any folder names, and can include spaces. Note that you cannot give a workbook the same name in first uppercase and then lowercase letters. Also, some symbols cannot be used in a file name such as:

forward slash (/)	question mark (?)
backslash (\)	quotation mark (")
greater than sign (>)	colon (:)
less than sign (<)	semicolon (;)
asterisk (*)	pipe symbol (|)

To save an Excel workbook in the Excel2007L1C1 folder on your storage medium, display the Save As dialog box and then click the down-pointing arrow at the right side of the *Save in* option box. At the drop-down list that displays, click the drive representing your storage medium and then double-click Excel2007L1C1 in the list box.

Save a Workbook
1. Click Save button.
2. Type workbook name.
3. Press Enter.

HINT
Ctrl + S is the keyboard command to save a document.

Save

Office button

1. Open Excel by clicking the Start button on the Taskbar, pointing to *All Programs*, pointing to *Microsoft Office*, and then clicking *Microsoft Office Excel 2007*. (Depending on your operating system, these steps may vary.)
2. At the Excel worksheet that displays, create the worksheet shown in Figure 1.3 by completing the following steps:
   a. Press the Enter key once to make cell A2 the active cell.
   b. With cell A2 active (displays with a thick black border), type **Employee**.
   c. Press the Tab key. (This makes cell B2 active.)
   d. Type **Location** and then press the Tab key. (This makes cell C2 active.)
   e. Type **Benefits** and then press the Enter key to move the insertion point to cell A3.
   f. With cell A3 active, type the name **Avery**.
   g. Continue typing the data shown in Figure 1.3. (For commands for making specific cells active, refer to Table 1.2.)
3. After typing the data shown in the cells in Figure 1.3, save the workbook by completing the following steps:
   a. Click the Save button on the Quick Access toolbar.
   b. At the Save As dialog box, click the down-pointing arrow to the right of the *Save in* option.
   c. From the drop-down list that displays, click the letter representing your storage medium.
   d. Double-click the Excel2007L1C1 folder that displays in the list box.
   e. Select the text in the *File name* text box and then type **ExcelL1_C1_P1**(for Excel Level 1, Chapter 1, Project 1).
   f. Press the Enter key or click the Save button.

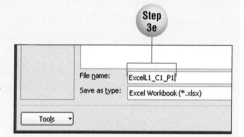

Figure 1.3 **Project 1a**

	A	B	C	D
1				
2	Employee	Location	Benefits	
3	Avery			
4	Connors			
5	Estrada			
6	Juergens			
7	Mikulich			
8	Talbot			
9				

Editing Data in a Cell

Edit data being typed in a cell by pressing the Backspace key to delete the character to the left of the insertion point or pressing the Delete key to delete the character to the right of the insertion point. To change the data in a cell, click the cell once to make it active and then type the new data. When a cell containing data is active, anything typed will take the place of the existing data.

If you want to edit only a portion of the data in a cell, double-click the cell. This makes the cell active, moves the insertion point inside the cell, and displays the word *Edit* at the left side of the Status bar. Move the insertion point using the arrow keys or the mouse and then make the needed corrections. If you are using the keyboard, you can press the Home key to move the insertion point to the first character in the cell or Formula bar, or press the End key to move the insertion point to the last character.

When you are finished editing the data in the cell, be sure to change out of the Edit mode. To do this, make another cell active. You can do this by pressing Enter, Tab, or Shift + Tab. You can also change out of the Edit mode and return to the Ready mode by clicking another cell or clicking the Enter button on the Formula bar.

Cancel

If the active cell does not contain data, the Formula bar displays only the cell reference (by column letter and row number). As you type data, the two buttons shown in Figure 1.4 display on the Formula bar to the right of the Name box. Click the Cancel button to delete the current cell entry. You can also delete the cell entry by pressing the Delete key. Click the Enter button to indicate that you are finished typing or editing the cell entry. When you click the Enter button on the Formula bar, the word *Enter* (or *Edit*) located at the left side of the Status bar changes to *Ready*.

Enter

Figure 1.4 Buttons on the Formula Bar

Cancel   Enter

Project **Editing Data in a Cell**

1. With **ExcelL1_C1_P1.xlsx** open, double-click cell A7 (contains *Mikulich*).
2. Move the insertion point immediately left of the *k* and then type a c. (This changes the spelling to *Mickulich*.)
3. Click once in cell A4 (contains *Connors*), type **Bryant**, and then press the Tab key. (Clicking only once allows you to type over the existing data.)
4. Edit cell C2 by completing the following steps:
   a. Click the Find & Select button in the Editing group in the Home tab and then click *Go To* at the drop-down list.
   b. At the Go To dialog box, type **C2** in the *Reference* text box, and then click OK.
   c. Type **Classification** (over *Benefits*).
5. Click once in any other cell.
6. Click the Save button on the Quick Access toolbar to save the workbook again.

Step 4b

HINT

Quick Print

Printing a Workbook

Click the Quick Print button on the Quick Access toolbar to print the active worksheet. If the Quick Print button does not display on the Quick Access toolbar, click the Customize Quick Access Toolbar button that displays at the right side of the toolbar and then click *Quick Print* at the drop-down list. You can also print a worksheet by clicking the Office button, pointing to the *Print* option, and then clicking *Quick Print* at the side menu.

Closing a Workbook

Close Window

To close an Excel workbook, click the Office button and then click *Close* at the drop-down list. You can also close a workbook by clicking the Close Window button located toward the upper right corner of the screen. Position the mouse pointer on the button and a ScreenTip displays with the name *Close Window*.

Exiting Excel

X Exit Excel

X

Close

To exit Excel, click the Close button that displays in the upper right corner of the screen. The Close button contains an X and if you position the mouse pointer on the button a ScreenTip displays with the name *Close*. You can also exit Excel by clicking the Office button and then clicking the Exit Excel button located at the bottom of the drop-down list.

Using Automatic Entering Features

Excel contains several features that help you enter data into cells quickly and efficiently. These features include **AutoComplete**, which automatically inserts data in a cell that begins the same as a previous entry; **AutoCorrect**, which automatically corrects many common typographical errors; and **AutoFill**, which will automatically insert words, numbers, or formulas in a series.

Print a Workbook
Click Quick Print button.
OR
1. Click Office button, *Print*.
2. Click OK.

Close a Workbook
Click Office button, *Close*.
OR
Click Close Window button.

Exit Excel
Click Close button.
OR
Click Office button, Exit Excel.

Using AutoComplete and AutoCorrect

The AutoComplete feature will automatically insert data in a cell that begins the same as a previous entry. If the data inserted by AutoComplete is the data you want in the cell, press Enter. If it is not the desired data, simply continue typing the correct data. This feature can be very useful in a worksheet that contains repetitive data entries. For example, consider a worksheet that repeats the word *Payroll*. The second and subsequent times this word is to be inserted in a cell, simply typing the letter *P* will cause AutoComplete to insert the entire word.

The AutoCorrect feature automatically corrects many common typing errors. To see what symbols and words are in the AutoCorrect feature, click the Office button and then click Excel Options located in the lower right corner of the drop-down list. At the Excel Options dialog box, click *Proofing* in the left panel and then click the AutoCorrect Options button located in the right panel. This displays the AutoCorrect dialog box with the AutoCorrect tab selected as shown in Figure 1.5 with a list box containing the replacement data.

Figure 1.5 AutoCorrect Dialog Box with AutoCorrect Tab Selected

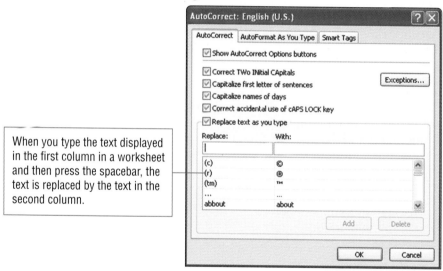

When you type the text displayed in the first column in a worksheet and then press the spacebar, the text is replaced by the text in the second column.

At the AutoCorrect dialog box, type the text shown in the first column in the list box and the text in the second column is inserted in the cell. Along with symbols, the AutoCorrect dialog box contains commonly misspelled words and common typographical errors.

1. With **ExcelL1_C1_P1.xlsx** open make cell A1 active.
2. Type the text in cell A1 as shown in Figure 1.6. Insert the ® symbol by typing (r). (AutoCorrect will change (r) to ®.)
3. Type the remaining text in the cells. When you type the W in *West* in cell B5, the AutoComplete feature will insert *West*. Accept this by pressing the Enter key. (Pressing the Enter key accepts *West* and also makes the cell below active.) Use the AutoComplete feature to enter *West* in B6 and B8 and *North* in cell B7. Use AutoComplete to enter the second and subsequent occurrences of *Salaried* and *Hourly*.
4. Click the Save button on the Quick Access toolbar.
5. Print **ExcelL1_C1_P1.xlsx** by clicking the Quick Print button on the Quick Access toolbar. (The gridlines will not print.) If the Quick Print button does not display on the Quick Access toolbar, click the Customize Quick Access Toolbar button that displays at the right side of the toolbar and then click *Quick Print* at the drop-down list.
6. Close the workbook by clicking the Close Window button (contains an X) that displays in the upper right corner of screen. (Make sure you click the Close Window button and not the Close button.)

Step 5

Step 6

Figure 1.6 **Project 1c**

	A	B	C	D
1	Team Net®			
2	Employee	Location	Classification	
3	Avery	West	Hourly	
4	Bryant	North	Salaried	
5	Estrada	West	Salaried	
6	Juergens	West	Salaried	
7	Mickulich	North	Hourly	
8	Talbot	West	Hourly	
9				

Project ② **Open and Format a Workbook and Insert Formulas**

You will open an existing workbook, insert formulas to find the sum and averages of numbers and apply predesigned formatting with table and cell styles.

Using AutoFill

When a cell is active, a thick black border surrounds it and a small black square displays in the bottom right corner of the border. This black square is called the AutoFill *fill handle* (see Figure 1.2). With the fill handle, you can quickly fill a range of cells with the same data or with consecutive data. For example, suppose you need to insert the year 2010 in a row or column of cells. To do this quickly, type 2010 in the first cell, position the mouse pointer on the fill handle, hold down the left mouse button, drag across the cells in which you want the year inserted, and then release the mouse button.

You can also use the fill handle to insert a series in a row or column of cells. For example, suppose you are creating a worksheet with data for all of the months in the year. Type **January** in the first cell, position the mouse pointer on the fill handle, hold down the left mouse button, drag down or across to 11 more cells, and then release the mouse button. Excel automatically inserts the other 11 months in the year in the proper order. When using the fill handle, the cells must be adjacent. Table 1.3 identifies the sequence inserted in cells by Excel when specific data is entered.

Table 1.3 AutoFill Fill Handle Series

Enter this data (Commas represent data in separate cells.)	And the fill handle will insert this sequence in adjacent cells
January	February, March, April, and so on . . .
Jan	Feb, Mar, Apr, and so on . . .
Jan 08, Jan 09	Jan-10, Jan-11, Jan-12, and so on . . .
Monday	Tuesday, Wednesday, Thursday, and so on . . .
Product 1	Product 2, Product 3, Product 4, and so on . . .
Qtr 1	Qtr 2, Qtr 3, Qtr 4
2, 4	6, 8, 10, and so on . . .

Certain sequences, such as *2, 4* and *Jan 08, Jan 09,* require that both cells be selected before using the fill handle. If only the cell containing *2* is active, the fill handle will insert *2*s in the selected cells. The list in Table 1.3 is only a sampling of what the fill handle can do. You may find a variety of other sequences that can be inserted in a worksheet using the fill handle.

An Auto Fill Options button displays when you fill cells with the fill handle. Click this button and a list of options displays for filling the cells. By default, data and formatting are filled in each cell. You can choose to fill only the formatting in the cells or fill only the data without the formatting.

HINT
If you do not want a series to increment, hold down the Ctrl key while dragging the fill handle.

Auto Fill Options

QUICK STEPS

Open a Workbook
1. Click Open button.
2. Display desired folder.
3. Double-click workbook name.

Open

Opening a Workbook

Open an Excel workbook by displaying the Open dialog box and then double-clicking the desired workbook name. Display the Open dialog box by clicking the Open button on the Quick Access toolbar or clicking the Office button and then clicking *Open* at the drop-down list. If the Open button does not display on the Quick Access toolbar, click the Customize Quick Access Toolbar button that displays at the right side of the toolbar and then click *Open* at the drop-down list. You can also use the keyboard shortcut Ctrl + O to display the Open dialog box.

Project 2a   Inserting Data in Cells with the Fill Handle

1. Open **ExcelC01Project02.xlsx**. (This workbook is located in the Excel2007L1C1 folder on your storage medium.)
2. Save the workbook with Save As and name it **ExcelL1_C1_P2**.
3. Add data to cells as shown in Figure 1.7. Begin by making cell B1 active and then typing **January**.
4. Position the mouse pointer on the fill handle for cell B1, hold down the left mouse button, drag across to cell G1, and then release the mouse button.

	A	B	C	D	E	F	G
1		January	February	March	April	May	June
2		100					125
3		150	150	150	150	175	175

Step 4

5. Type a sequence and then use the fill handle to fill the remaining cells by completing the following steps:
   a. Make cell A2 active and then type **Year 1**.
   b. Make cell A3 active and then type **Year 3**.
   c. Select cells A2 and A3 by positioning the mouse pointer in cell A2, holding down the left mouse button, dragging down to cell A3, and then releasing the mouse button.
   d. Drag the fill handle for cell A3 to cell A5. (This inserts *Year 5* in cell A4 and *Year 7* in cell A5.)
6. Use the fill handle to fill adjacent cells with a number but not the formatting by completing the following steps:
   a. Make cell B2 active. (This cell contains *100* with bold formatting.)
   b. Drag the fill handle for cell B2 to cell E2. (This inserts *100* in cells C2, D2, and E2.)
   c. Click the Auto Fill Options button that displays at the bottom right of the selected cells.
   d. Click the *Fill Without Formatting* option at the drop-down list.

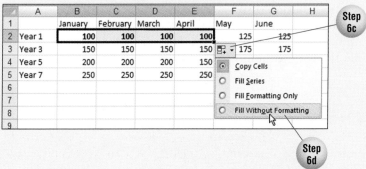

Step 6c

Step 6d

7. Use the fill handle to apply formatting only by
   completing the following steps:
   a. Make cell B2 active.
   b. Drag the fill handle to cell B5.
   c. Click the Auto Fill Options button and then
      click *Fill Formatting Only* at the drop-down list.
8. Make cell A10 active and then type **Qtr 1**.
9. Drag the fill handle for cell A10 to cell A13.
10. Save **ExcelL1_C1_P2.xlsx**.

▲	A	B	C	D	E
1		January	February	March	April
2	Year 1	**100**	100	100	10
3	Year 3	**100**	150	150	15
4	Year 5	**100**	200	200	15
5	Year 7	**100**	250	250	25
6					
7					
8					
9					
10		$5,500			
11		$6,000			

Step 7c

◉ Copy Cells
○ Fill Series
○ Fill Formatting Only
○ Fill Without Formatting

Figure 1.7 Project 2a

▲	A	B	C	D	E	F	G	H
1		January	February	March	April	May	June	
2	Year 1	**100**	100	100	100	125	125	
3	Year 3	**150**	150	150	150	175	175	
4	Year 5	**200**	200	200	150	150	150	
5	Year 7	**250**	250	250	250	250	250	
6								
7								
8								
9								
10	Qtr 1	$5,500	$6,250	$7,000	$8,500	$5,500	$4,500	
11	Qtr 2	$6,000	$7,250	$6,500	$9,000	$4,000	$5,000	
12	Qtr 3	$4,500	$8,000	$6,000	$7,500	$6,000	$5,000	
13	Qtr 4	$6,500	$8,500	$7,000	$8,000	$5,500	$6,000	
14								

Inserting Formulas

Excel is a powerful decision-making tool containing data that can be manipulated
to answer "what if" situations. Insert a formula in a worksheet and then manipulate
the data to make projections, answer specific questions, and use as a planning tool.
For example, the manager of a department might use an Excel worksheet to prepare
a department budget and then determine the impact on the budget of hiring a new
employee or increasing the volume of production.

Insert a formula in a worksheet to perform calculations on values. A formula
contains a mathematical operator, value, cell reference, cell range, and a function.
Formulas can be written that add, subtract, multiply, and/or divide values. Formulas
can also be written that calculate averages, percentages, minimum and maximum
values, and much more. Excel includes a Sum button in the Editing group in the
Home tab that inserts a formula to calculate the total of a range of cells.

Using the Sum Button to Add Numbers

You can use the Sum button in the Editing group in the Home tab to insert a
formula. The Sum button adds numbers automatically with the SUM function.
Make active the cell in which you want to insert the formula (this cell should be
empty) and then click the Sum button. Excel looks for a range of cells containing
numbers above the active cell. If no cell above contains numbers, then Excel looks
to the left of the active cell. Excel suggests the range of cells to be added. If the

QUICK STEPS

**Insert Formula Using
Sum Button**
1. Click in desired cell.
2. Click Sum button.
3. Check range identified
   and make changes if
   necessary.
4. Press Enter.

HINT

You can use the
keyboard shortcut,
Alt + = to insert the
SUM function in the
cell.

Σ ▾

Sum

suggested range is not correct, drag through the desired range with the mouse, and then press Enter. You can also just double-click the Sum button and this will insert the SUM function with the range Excel chooses.

Project 2b Adding Values with the Sum Button

1. With **ExcelL1_C1_P2.xlsx** open, make cell A6 active and then type **Total**.
2. Make cell B6 active and then calculate the sum of cells by clicking the Sum button in the Editing group in the Home tab.
3. Excel inserts the formula *=SUM(B2:B5)* in cell B6. This is the correct range of cells, so press Enter.

Step 2

	A	B	C	D	E	F	G	H	I	J	K	L	M	N
1		January	February	March	April	May	June							
2	Year 1	100	100	100	100	125	125							
3	Year 3	150	150	150	150	175	175							
4	Year 5	200	200	200	150	150	150							
5	Year 7	250	250	250	250	250	250							
6	Total	=SUM(B2:B5)												
7		SUM(number1, [number2], ...)												

Step 3

4. Make cell C6 active and then click the Sum button in the Editing group.
5. Excel inserts the formula *=SUM(C2:C5)* in cell C6. This is the correct range of cells, so press Enter.
6. Make cell D6 active.
7. Double-click the Sum button. (This inserts the formula *=SUM(D2:D5)* in cell D6 and inserts the sum *700*.)
8. Insert the sum in cells E6, F6, and G6.
9. Save **ExcelL1_C1_P2.xlsx**.

QUICK STEPS

Insert Average Formula Using Sum Button
1. Click in desired cell.
2. Click Sum button arrow.
3. Click *Average*.
4. Check range identified and make changes if necessary.
5. Press Enter.

Using the Sum Button to Average Numbers

A common function in a formula is the AVERAGE function. With this function, a range of cells is added together and then divided by the number of cell entries. The AVERAGE function is available on the Sum button. Click the Sum button arrow and a drop-down list displays with a number of common functions.

Using the Fill Handle to Copy a Formula

In a worksheet, you may want to insert the same basic formula in other cells. In a situation where a formula is copied to other locations in a worksheet, use a *relative cell reference*. Copy a formula containing relative cell references and the cell references change. For example, if you enter the formula *=SUM(A2:C2)* in cell D2 and then copy it relatively to cell D3, the formula in cell D3 displays as *=SUM(A3:C3)*. You can use the fill handle to copy a formula relatively in a worksheet. To do this, position the mouse pointer on the fill handle until the mouse pointer turns into a thin black cross. Hold down the left mouse button, drag and select the desired cells, and then release the mouse button.

QUICK STEPS

Copy Formula Using Fill Handle
1. Insert formula in cell.
2. Make active the cell containing formula.
3. Using fill handle, drag through cells you want to contain formula.

Project 2c — Inserting the AVERAGE Function and Copying a Formula Relatively

1. With **ExcelL1_C1_P2.xlsx** open, make cell A14 active, and then type **Average**.
2. Insert the average of cells B10 through B13 by completing the following steps:
   a. Make cell B14 active.
   b. Click the Sum button arrow and then click *Average* at the drop-down list.
   c. Excel inserts the formula *=AVERAGE(B10:B13)* in cell B14. This is the correct range of cells, so press Enter.
3. Copy the formula relatively to cells C14 through G14 by completing the following steps:
   a. Make cell B14 active.
   b. Position the mouse pointer on the fill handle, hold down the left mouse button, drag across to cell G14, and then release the mouse button.

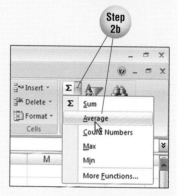

Step 2b

9						
10	Qtr 1	$5,500	$6,250	$7,000	$8,500	$5,500	$4,500
11	Qtr 2	$6,000	$7,250	$6,500	$9,000	$4,000	$5,000
12	Qtr 3	$4,500	$8,000	$6,000	$7,500	$6,000	$5,000
13	Qtr 4	$6,500	$8,500	$7,000	$8,000	$5,500	$6,000
14	Average	$5,625	$7,500	$6,625	$8,250	$5,250	$5,125
15							

Step 3b

4. Save **ExcelL1_C1_P2.xlsx**.

Selecting Cells

You can use a variety of methods for formatting cells in a worksheet. For example, you can change the alignment of data in cells or rows or add character formatting. To identify the cells that are to be affected by the formatting, select the specific cells.

Selecting Cells Using the Mouse

Select specific cells in a worksheet using the mouse or select columns or rows. Methods for selecting cells using the mouse display in Table 1.4.

Selected cells, except the active cell, display with a light blue background (this may vary) rather than a white background. The active cell is the first cell in the selection block and displays in the normal manner (white background with black data). Selected cells remain selected until you click a cell with the mouse or press an arrow key on the keyboard.

Table 1.4 Selecting with the Mouse

To select this	Do this
Column	Position the cell pointer on the column header (a letter) and then click the left mouse button.
Row	Position the cell pointer on the row header (a number) and then click the left mouse button.
Adjacent cells	Drag with mouse to select specific cells.
Nonadjacent cells	Hold down the Ctrl key while clicking column header, row header, or specific cells.
All cells in worksheet	Click Select All button (refer to Figure 1.2).

Selecting Cells Using the Keyboard

You can use the keyboard to select specific cells within a worksheet. Table 1.5 displays the commands for selecting specific cells.

Table 1.5 Selecting Cells Using the Keyboard

To select	Press
Cells in direction of arrow key	Shift + arrow key
To beginning of row	Shift + Home
To beginning of worksheet	Shift + Ctrl + Home
To last cell in worksheet containing data	Shift + Ctrl + End
An entire column	Ctrl + spacebar
An entire row	Shift + spacebar
An entire worksheet	Ctrl + A or Ctrl + Shift + spacebar

Selecting Data within Cells

The selection commands presented select the entire cell. You can also select specific characters within a cell. To do this with the mouse, position the cell pointer in the desired cell, and then double-click the left mouse button. Drag with the I-beam pointer through the data you want selected. Data selected within a cell displays in white with a black background. If you are using the keyboard to select data in a cell, hold down the Shift key, and then press the arrow key that moves the insertion point in the desired direction. Data the insertion point passes through will be selected. You can also press F8 to turn on the Extend Selection mode, move the insertion point in the desired direction to select the data, and then press F8 to turn off the Extend Selection mode. When the Extend Selection mode is on, the words *Extend Selection* display toward the left side of the Status bar.

Formatting with Predesigned Styles

An Excel worksheet contains default formatting. For example, letters and words are aligned at the left of a cell, numbers are aligned at the right, and data is set in 11-point Calibri. Excel provides predesigned styles you can use to apply formatting to cells in a worksheet. Apply table formatting styles with the Format as Table button or the Cell Styles button, both located in the Styles group in the Home tab.

Formatting with Table Styles

Apply table formatting styles to selected cells in a worksheet using the Format as Table button in the Styles group in the Home tab. When you select cells and then click the Format as Table button, a drop-down list displays as shown in Figure 1.8. Click the desired table style and the Format As Table dialog box displays. Click OK at this dialog box and the formatting is applied to the selected cells. Excel also inserts filtering arrows in each cell in the first row of selected cells. The filtering arrows do not print. You can turn off the display of the filtering arrows by clicking the Data tab and then clicking the Filter button in the Sort & Filter group. You will learn more about these filtering arrows in a later chapter.

Apply Table Formatting
1. Select desired cells.
2. Click Format as Table button.
3. Click desired table style.
4. Click OK at Format As Table dialog box.

Figure 1.8 Format as Table Drop-down List

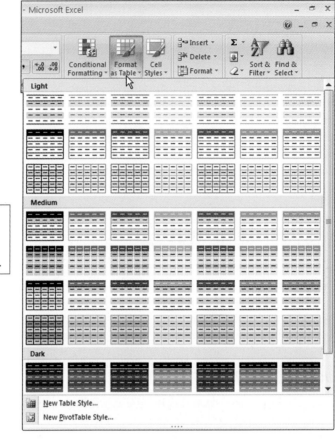

Choose an option at this drop-down list to apply predesigned formatting to selected cells in a worksheet.

Project **2d** **Formatting Cells with Table Styles**

1. With **ExcelL1_C1_P2.xlsx** open, apply a table style to specific cells by completing the following steps:
   a. Select cells A1 through G6.
   b. Click the Format as Table button in the Styles group in the Home tab.
   c. At the drop-down list, click the *Table Style Light 9* option (second style option from the left in the second row in the *Light* section).

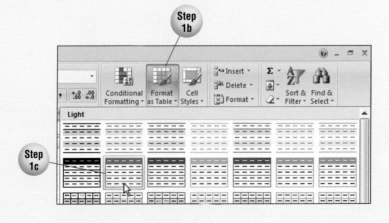

Step 1b

Step 1c

> d. At the Format As Table dialog box, click OK. (Excel inserts filtering arrows in the cells in the first row.)
>
> 2. Select cells A10 through G14 and then apply the Table Style Light 11 style (fourth style option from the left in the second row in the *Light* section). At the Format As Table dialog box, click OK.
>
> 3. Save **ExcelL1_C1_P2.xlsx**. (Excel inserts a row with filtering arrows.)

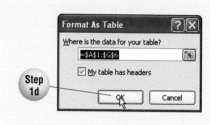

Step 1d

Formatting with Cell Styles

In some worksheets, you may want to highlight or accentuate certain cells. You can apply formatting to a cell or selected cells with cell styles. Click the Cell Styles button in the Styles group in the Home tab and a drop-down gallery of style options displays as shown in Figure 1.9. Hover your mouse pointer over a style option and the cell or selected cells display with the style formatting applied. You can hover your mouse over different style options to see how the style formatting affects the cell or selected cells. The Cell Styles button drop-down gallery is an example of the **live preview** feature, which allows you to see how the style formatting affects cells in your worksheet without having to return to the worksheet.

Apply Cell Style
1. Select desired cell(s).
2. Click Cell Styles button.
3. Click desired style option.

Cell Styles

Figure 1.9 Cell Styles Drop-down Gallery

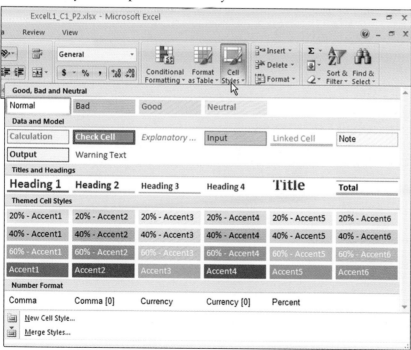

Choose an option at this drop-down gallery to apply a predesigned style to a cell or selected cells in a worksheet.

1. With **ExcelL1_C1_P2.xlsx** open, select cells B2 through G6.
2. Click the Cell Styles button in the Styles group in the Home tab.
3. At the drop-down gallery, hover your mouse over style options to see how the style formatting affects the selected cells.
4. Click the *Currency [0]* option (fourth option from the left in the *Number Format* section).

Step 2

Step 4

5. Select cells B6 through G6.
6. Click the Cell Styles button and then click the *Total* option (the last option in the *Titles and Headings* section).

Step 6

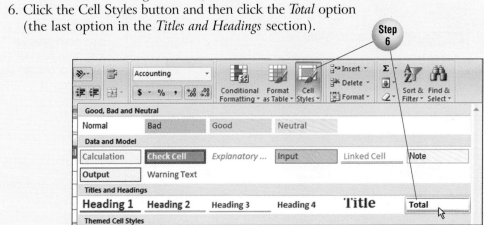

7. Select cells B15 through G15 and then apply the Total cell style.
8. Save, print, and then close **ExcelL1_C1_P2.xlsx**.

Project ③ Use the Help Feature

You will use the Help feature to learn more about entering data in cells and selecting text and saving a workbook. You will also customize Help to search for information offline and for Excel training.

Using Help

Excel's Help feature is an on-screen reference manual containing information about Excel features. Excel's Help feature is similar to the Windows Help and the Help features in Word, PowerPoint, and Access. Get help by clicking the Microsoft Office Excel Help button located in the upper right corner of the screen (a question mark in a circle) or by pressing the keyboard shortcut, F1. This displays the Excel Help window. In this window, type a topic, feature, or question in the *Search* text box and then press Enter. Topics related to the search text display in the Help window. Click a topic that interests you. If the topic window contains a <u>Show All</u> hyperlink in the upper right corner, click this hyperlink and the information expands to show all help information related to the topic. When you click the <u>Show All</u> hyperlink, it becomes the <u>Hide All</u> hyperlink.

QUICK STEPS

Use Help Feature
1. Click Microsoft Office Excel Help button.
2. Type help question.
3. Press Enter.

Help

Project ③a   Using the Help Feature

1. At a blank worksheet, click the Microsoft Office Excel Help button located in the upper right corner of the screen.
2. At the Excel Help window, type **enter data in cells** in the *Search* text box.
3. Press the Enter key.
4. When the list of topics displays, click the *Enter data manually in worksheet cells* hyperlink.
5. Click the <u>Show All</u> hyperlink that displays in the upper right corner of the window.

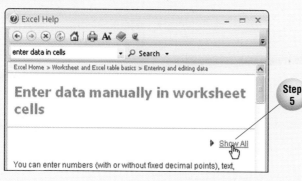

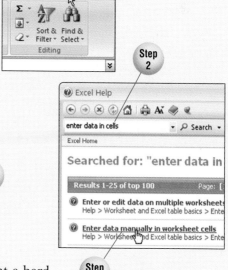

6. Read the information about entering data. (If you want a hard copy of the Help text, click the Print button located toward the top of the Excel Help window, and then click the Print button at the Print dialog box.)
7. Click the Close button to close the Excel Help window.

Getting Help in a Dialog Box

Dialog boxes contain a Help button you can click to display help in the Excel Help window that is specific to the dialog box. This button is located in the upper right corner of the dialog box and displays as a question mark inside a circle. Click this button and the Excel Help window displays with topics related to the dialog box.

Getting Help on a Button

When you position the mouse pointer on a button, a ScreenTip displays with information about the button. Some button ScreenTips display with the message "Press F1 for more help." that is preceded by an image of the Help button. With the ScreenTip visible, press the F1 function key and the Excel Help window opens and displays information about the specific button.

Project 3b Getting Help in a Dialog Box and Button ScreenTip

1. At a blank worksheet, click the Office button and then click *Save As* at the drop-down list.
2. At the Save As dialog box, click the Help button located in the upper right corner of the dialog box.
3. At the Excel Help window, click the *Save As* hyperlink.
4. In the Save As list box, click *Microsoft Office Excel*.
5. Read the information that displays about saving in Excel and then click the Close button to close the Excel Help window.
6. Close the Save As dialog box.
7. Position the mouse pointer on the Office button until the ScreenTip displays and then press F1.

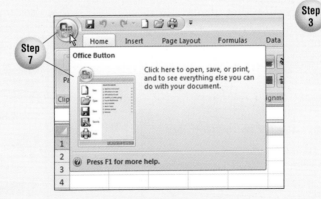

8. At the Excel Help window that displays, click a hyperlink that interests you. Read the information and then close the Excel Help window.

Customizing Help

By default, the Excel Help feature will search for an Internet connection and, if one is found, display help resources from Office Online. If you are connected online to help resources, the message "Connected to Office Online" displays in the lower right corner of the Excel Help window. If you are not connected to the Internet, the message displays as "Offline."

Office Online provides additional help resources such as training and templates. To view the resources, display the Excel Help window and then click the down-pointing arrow at the right side of the Search button. This displays a drop-down list similar to the one shown in Figure 1.10. Generally, the *All Excel* option in the *Content from Office Online* is selected. If you want to search only the Help resources available with your computer (offline), click the *Excel Help* option in the *Content from this computer* section. To access Office Online training, click the *Excel Training* option in the *Content from Office Online* section, type a training topic in the *Search* text box, and then click OK.

Figure 1.10 Excel Help Search Drop-down List

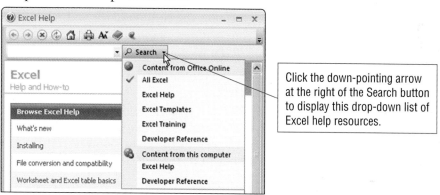

Click the down-pointing arrow at the right of the Search button to display this drop-down list of Excel help resources.

Project ③ᶜ Customizing Help

1. At a blank worksheet, click the Microsoft Office Excel Help button located toward the upper right corner of the screen.
2. Click the down-pointing arrow at the right side of the Search button in the Excel Help window.
3. At the drop-down list that displays, click *Excel Help* in the *Content from this computer* section.
4. Click in the *Search* text box, type **formulas** in the *Search* text box, and then press Enter.
5. Click a hyperlink that interests you and then read the information that displays.
6. Click the down-pointing arrow at the right side of the Search button and then click *Excel Training* in the *Content from Office Online* section.
7. Click in the *Search* text box (this will select *formulas*) and then press Enter.
8. Click the hyperlink of a training about formulas that interests you.
9. After completing the training, close Internet Explorer and then close the Excel Help window.

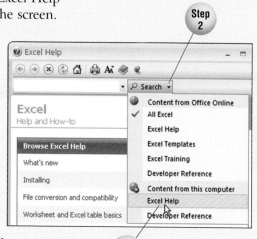

Step 2

Step 3

CHAPTER summary

- Use an Excel spreadsheet to create financial statements, prepare budgets, manage inventory, and analyze cash flow. Numbers and values can be easily manipulated in an Excel spreadsheet to answer "what if" questions.

- A file created in Excel is called a workbook. A workbook consists of individual worksheets. The intersection of columns and rows in a worksheet is referred to as a cell.

- An Excel window contains the following elements: Office button, Quick Access toolbar, Title bar, tabs, ribbon, Name box, Formula bar, scroll bars, sheet tabs, and Status bar.

- The horizontal and vertical lines that define cells in the worksheet area are called gridlines.

- When the insertion point is positioned in a cell, the cell name (also called the cell reference) displays in the Name box located at the left side of the Formula bar. The cell name includes the column letter and row number.

- To enter data in a cell, make the cell active and then type the data. To move the insertion point to the next cell, press the Tab key. To move the insertion point to the previous cell, press Shift + Tab. For other insertion point movement commands, refer to Table 1.2.

- Data being entered in a cell displays in the cell as well as in the Formula bar.

- If data entered in a cell consists of text (letters) and the text does not fit into the cell, it overlaps the cell to the right. However, if the data being entered are numbers and do not fit in the cell, the numbers are changed to number symbols (###).

- Save a workbook by clicking the Save button on the Quick Access toolbar or by clicking the Office button and then clicking *Save* at the drop-down list.

- To replace data in a cell, click the cell once and then type the new data. To edit data within a cell, double-click the cell and then make necessary changes.

- Print a workbook by clicking the Quick Print button on the Quick Access toolbar or by clicking the Office button, pointing to the *Print* option, and then clicking *Quick Print*.

- Close a workbook by clicking the Close Window button located in the upper right corner of the screen or by clicking the Office button and then clicking *Close* at the drop-down list.

- Exit Excel by clicking the Close button located in the upper right corner of the screen or by clicking the Office button and then clicking the Exit Excel button.

- The AutoComplete feature will automatically insert a previous entry if the character or characters being typed in a cell match a previous entry.

- The AutoCorrect feature corrects many common typographical errors.

- Use the AutoFill fill handle to fill a range of cells with the same or consecutive data.

- Open a workbook by clicking the Open button on the Quick Access toolbar or by clicking the Office button and then clicking the *Open* option at the drop-down list. At the Open dialog box, double-click the desired workbook.

- Use the Sum button in the Editing group in the Home tab to find the total or average of data in columns or rows.

- Select all cells in a column by clicking the column header. Select all cells in a row by clicking the row header. Select all cells in a worksheet by clicking the Select All button located immediately to the left of the column headers.
- To select cells with the mouse, refer to Table 1.4; to select cells using the keyboard, refer to Table 1.5.
- Use options from the Format as Table button drop-down gallery to apply predesigned table styles to selected cells.
- Use options from the Cell Styles button drop-down gallery to apply predesigned styles to a cell or selected cells.
- Excel's Help feature is an on-screen reference manual containing information about Excel features.
- Click the Microsoft Office Excel Help button or press F1 to display the Excel Help window. At this window, type a topic and then press Enter.
- Dialog boxes contain a Help button you can click to display the Excel Help window with information specific to the dialog box. The ScreenTip for some buttons displays with a message telling you to press F1. Press F1 and the Excel Help window opens with information about the button.
- Customize Help with options from the Search button drop-down list in the Excel Help window.

COMMANDS review

FEATURE	RIBBON TAB, GROUP	BUTTON	QUICK ACCESS TOOLBAR	OFFICE BUTTON DROP-DOWN LIST	KEYBOARD SHORTCUT
Close workbook		X		Close	Ctrl + F4
Exit Excel		X		Exit Excel	
Go To dialog box	Home, Editing	, Go To			Ctrl + G
Excel Help window		(?)			F1
Open workbook			📂	Open	Ctrl + O
Print workbook			🖨	Print, Quick Print	
Save workbook			💾	Save	Ctrl + S
Format as Table drop-down list	Home, Styles				
Cell Styles drop-down gallery	Home, Styles				
Sum button drop-down list	Home, Editing	Σ ▾			

CONCEPTS check

Test Your Knowledge

Completion: In the space provided at the right, indicate the correct term, symbol, or command.

1. Columns in a worksheet are labeled with this.

_____

2. Rows in a worksheet are labeled with this.

_____

3. The horizontal and vertical lines that define the cells in a worksheet area are referred to as this.

_____

4. Press this key on the keyboard to move the insertion point to the next cell.

_____

5. Press these keys on the keyboard to move the insertion point to the previous cell.

_____

6. If a number entered in a cell is too long to fit inside the cell, the number is changed to this.

_____

7. Data being typed in a cell displays in the cell as well as here.

_____

8. This is the name of the small black square that displays in the bottom right corner of the active cell.

_____

9. To select nonadjacent columns using the mouse, hold down this key on the keyboard while clicking the column headers.

_____

10. Use this button in the Editing group in the Home tab to insert a formula in a cell.

_____

11. With this function, a range of cells is added together and then divided by the number of cell entries.

_____

12. Click this button in the worksheet area to select all of the cells in the table.

_____

13. This feature allows you to see how style formatting affects cells in your worksheet without having to return to the worksheet.

_____

14. Press this function key to display the Excel Help window.

_____

SKILLS check

Demonstrate Your Proficiency

Assessment

1 CREATE AND FORMAT A WORKSHEET WITH A TABLE STYLE

1. Create the worksheet shown in Figure 1.11.
2. Select cells A1 through C5 and then apply the Table Style Medium 3 table style.
3. Save the workbook and name it **ExcelL1_C1_A1**.
4. Print and then close **ExcelL1_C1_A1.xlsx**.

Figure 1.11 Assessment 1

	A	B	C	D
1	Expense	Original	Current	
2	Labor	97000	98500	
3	Material	129000	153000	
4	Permits	1200	1350	
5	Tax	1950	2145	
6				

Assessment

2 CREATE A WORKSHEET USING AUTOCOMPLETE

1. Create the worksheet shown in Figure 1.12. To create the © symbol in cell A1, type (c). Type the misspelled words as shown and let the AutoCorrect feature correct the spelling. Use the AutoComplete feature to insert the second occurrence of *Category*, *Available*, and *Balance*.
2. Apply a table style of your choosing to cells A1 through B7. (Excel inserts a row with filtering arrows.)
3. Save the workbook and name it **ExcelL1_C1_A2**.
4. Print and then close **ExcelL1_C1_A2.xlsx**.

Figure 1.12 Assessment 2

	A	B	C
1	Premiere Plan©		
2	Plan A	Catagory	
3		Availalbe	
4		Balence	
5	Plan B	Category	
6		Available	
7		Balance	
8			

Assessment

3 CREATE A WORKSHEET USING THE FILL HANDLE

1. Create the worksheet shown in Figure 1.13. Type **Monday** in cell B2 and then use the fill handle to fill in the remaining days of the week. Use the fill handle to enter other repetitive data.
2. Apply a table style of your choosing to cells A1 through F4.
3. Save the workbook and name it **ExcelL1_C1_A3**.
4. Print and then close **ExcelL1_C1_A3.xlsx**.

Figure 1.13 Assessment 3

	A	B	C	D	E	F	G
1	CAPITAL INVESTMENTS						
2		Monday	Tuesday	Wednesday	Thursday	Friday	
3	Budget	350	350	350	350	350	
4	Actual	310	425	290	375	400	
5							

Assessment

4 INSERT FORMULAS IN A WORKSHEET

1. Open **ExcelC01Assessment04.xlsx** and then save the workbook and name it **ExcelL1_C1_A4**.
2. Insert a formula in cell B15 that totals the amounts in cells B4 through B14.
3. Use the fill handle to copy relatively the formula in cell B15 to cell C15.
4. Insert a formula in cell D4 that finds the average of cells B4 and C4.
5. Use the fill handle to copy relatively the formula in cell D4 down to cells D5 through D14.
6. Save, print, and then close **ExcelL1_C1_A4.xlsx**.

Assessment

5 USE HELP FEATURE TO LEARN ABOUT SCROLLING

1. Use the Help feature to learn more about how to scroll within an Excel worksheet.
2. Read and then print the information provided by Help.
3. Create a worksheet containing the information. Set this up as a worksheet with two columns (cells will contain only text—not numbers). Create a title for the worksheet.
4. Select the cells in your worksheet containing data and then apply a table style to the cells.
5. Save the completed workbook and name it **ExcelL1_C1_A5**.
6. Print and then close **ExcelL1_C1_A5.xlsx**.

CASE study

Apply Your Skills

You are the office manager for Deering Industries. One of your responsibilities is creating a monthly calendar containing information on staff meetings, training, and due dates for time cards. Open **DeeringCalendar.xlsx** and then insert the following information:

- Insert the text **September, 2010** in cell A2.
- Insert the days of the week (*Sunday*, *Monday*, *Tuesday*, *Wednesday*, *Thursday*, *Friday*, and *Saturday*) in cells A3 through G3.
- Insert the number *1* in cell D4, number *2* in cell E4, number *3* in cell F4, and number *4* in cell G4.
- Insert in the calendar the remaining numbers of the days (numbers 5-11 in cells A6 through G6, numbers 12 through 18 in cells A8 through G8, numbers 19 through 25 in cells A10 through G10, and numbers 26 through 30 in cells A12 through E12).
- Excel training will be held Thursday, September 2, from 9-11 a.m. Insert this information in cell E5. (Insert the text on two lines by typing Excel Training, pressing Alt + Enter to move the insertion point to the next line, and then typing 9-10 a.m.)
- A staff meeting is held the second and fourth Monday of each month from 9-10 a.m. Insert this information in cell B9 and cell B13.
- Time cards are due the first and third Fridays of the month. Insert in cells F5 and F9 information indicating that time cards are due.
- A production team meeting is scheduled for Tuesday, September 21, from 1-3 p.m. Insert this information in cell C11.

Save the workbook and name it **ExcelL1_C1_CS_P1**. Print and then close the workbook.

The manager of the Purchasing Department has asked you to prepare a worksheet containing information on quarterly purchases. Open **DeeringExpenditures.xlsx** and then insert the data as shown in Figure 1.14. After typing the data, insert in the appropriate cells formulas to calculate averages and totals. Save the workbook and name it **ExcelL1_C1_CS_P2**. Print and then close the workbook.

Figure 1.14 Case Study Part 2

	A	B	C	D	E	F	G
1				DEERING INDUSTRIES			
2		PURCHASING DEPARTMENT - EXPENDITURES					
3	Category	1st Qtr.	2nd Qtr.	3rd Qtr.	4th Qtr.	Average	
4	Supplies	$ 645.75	$ 756.25	$ 534.78	$ 78,950.00		
5	Equipment	$ 4,520.55	$ 10,789.35	$ 3,825.00	$ 12,890.72		
6	Furniture	$ 458.94	$ 2,490.72	$ 851.75	$ 743.20		
7	Training	$ 1,000.00	$ 250.00	$ 1,200.00	$ 800.00		
8	Software	$ 249.00	$ 1,574.30	$ 155.45	$ 3,458.70		
9	Total						
10							

Part 3

The manager of the Purchasing Department has asked you to prepare a note to the finances coordinator, Jennifer Strauss. In Word, type a note to Jennifer Strauss explaining that you have prepared an Excel worksheet with the Purchasing Department expenditures. You are including the cells from the worksheet containing the expenditure information. In Excel, open **ExcelL1_C1_CS_P2.xlsx**, copy cells A3 through F9, and then paste them in the Word document. Make any corrections to the table so the information is readable. Save the document and name it **WordExcelL1_C1_CS_P3**. Print and then close the document. Close **ExcelL1_C1_CS_P3.xlsx**.

Part 4

You will be ordering copy machines for several departments in the company and decide to research prices. Using the Internet, find three companies that sell copiers and write down information on different copier models. Open **DeeringCopiers.xlsx** and then type the company, model number, and price in the designated cells. Save the completed workbook and name it **ExcelL1_C1_CS_P4**. Print and then close **ExcelL1_C1_CS_P4.xlsx**.

Inserting Formulas in a Worksheet

PERFORMANCE OBJECTIVES

Upon successful completion of Chapter 2, you will be able to:

- Write formulas with mathematical operators
- Type a formula in the Formula bar
- Copy a formula
- Use the Insert Function feature to insert a formula in a cell
- Write formulas with the AVERAGE, MAX, MIN, COUNT, PMT, FV, DATE, NOW, and IF functions
- Create an absolute and mixed cell reference

Tutorial 2.1
Inserting and Editing Formulas
Tutorial 2.2
Working with Cell References

Excel is a powerful decision-making tool containing data that can be manipulated to answer "what if" situations. Insert a formula in a worksheet and then manipulate the data to make projections, answer specific questions, and use as a planning tool. For example, the owner of a company might prepare a worksheet on production costs and then determine the impact on company revenues if production is increased or decreased.

Insert a formula in a worksheet to perform calculations on values. A formula contains a mathematical operator, value, cell reference, cell range, and a function. Formulas can be written that add, subtract, multiply, and/or divide values. Formulas can also be written that calculate averages, percentages, minimum and maximum values, and much more. As you learned in Chapter 1, Excel includes a Sum button in the Editing group in the Home tab that inserts a formula to calculate the total of a range of cells and also includes some commonly used formulas. Along with the Sum button, Excel includes a Formulas tab that offers a variety of functions to create formulas.

Note: Before beginning computer projects, copy to your storage medium the Excel2007L1C2 subfolder from the Excel2007L1 folder on the CD that accompanies this textbook and make Excel2007L1C2 the active folder.

Project ① **Insert Formulas in a Worksheet**

You will open a worksheet containing data and then insert formulas to calculate differences, salaries, and percentages of budgets.

Writing Formulas with Mathematical Operators

As you learned in Chapter 1, the Sum button in the Editing group in the Home tab creates the formula for you. You can also write your own formulas using mathematical operators. Commonly used mathematical operators and their functions are displayed in Table 2.1. When writing your own formula, begin the formula with the equals (=) sign. For example, to create a formula that divides the contents of cell B2 by the contents of cell C2 and inserts the result in cell D2, you would make D2 the active cell and then type =B2/C2.

Table 2.1 Mathematical Operators

Operator	Function
+	Addition
-	Subtraction
*	Multiplication
/	Division
%	Percent
^	Exponentiation

If a formula contains two or more operators, Excel uses the same order of operations used in algebra. From left to right in a formula, this order, called the *order of operations*, is: negations (negative number—a number preceded by -) first, then percents (%), then exponentiations (^), followed by multiplications (*), divisions (/), additions (+), and finally subtractions (-). If you want to change the order of operations, use parentheses around the part of the formula you want calculated first.

Copying a Formula with Relative Cell References

In many worksheets, the same basic formula is used repetitively. In a situation where a formula is copied to other locations in a worksheet, use a **relative cell reference**. Copy a formula containing relative cell references and the cell references change. For example, if you enter the formula *=SUM(A2:C2)* in cell D2 and then copy it relatively to cell D3, the formula in cell D3 displays as *=SUM(A3:C3)*. (Additional information on cell references is discussed later in this chapter in the "Using an Absolute Cell Reference in a Formula" section.)

To copy a formula relatively in a worksheet, use the Fill button or the fill handle (you used the fill handle to copy a formula in Chapter 1). To use the Fill button, select the cell containing the formula as well as the cells to which you want the formula copied and then click the Fill button in the Editing group in the Home tab. At the Fill drop-down list, click the desired direction. For example, if you are copying the formula down cells, click the *Down* option.

QUICK STEPS

Copy Relative Formula
1. Insert formula in cell.
2. Select cell containing formula and all cells you want to contain formula.
3. Click Fill button.
4. Click desired direction.

Project 1a — Finding Differences by Inserting and Copying a Formula

1. Open **ExcelC02Project01.xlsx**.
2. Save the workbook with Save As and name it **ExcelL1_C2_P1**.
3. Insert a formula by completing the following steps:
   a. Make cell D3 active.
   b. Type the formula =C3-B3.
   c. Press Enter.
4. Copy the formula to cells D4 through D10 by completing the following steps:
   a. Select cells D3 through D10.
   b. Click the Fill button in the Editing group in the Home tab and then click *Down* at the drop-down list.
5. Save **ExcelL1_C2_P1.xlsx**.
6. With the worksheet open, make the following changes to cell contents:
   B4: Change *$48,290* to *46425*
   C6: Change *$61,220* to *60000*
   B8: Change *$55,309* to *57415*
   B9: Change *$12,398* to *14115*
7. Save **ExcelL1_C2_P1.xlsx**.

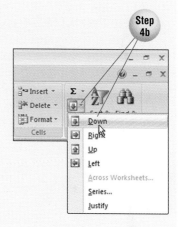

Step 4b

Copying Formulas with the Fill Handle

Use the fill handle to copy a formula up, down, left, or right within a worksheet. To use the fill handle, insert the desired data in the cell (text, value, formula, etc.). With the cell active, position the mouse pointer on the fill handle until the mouse pointer turns into a thin, black cross. Hold down the left mouse button, drag and select the desired cells, and then release the mouse button. If you are dragging a cell containing a formula, a relative version of the formula is copied to the selected cells.

HINT
Use the fill handle to copy a relative version of a formula.

1. With **ExcelL1_C2_P1.xlsx** open, insert a
   formula by completing the following steps:
   a. Make cell D15 active.
   b. Click in the Formula bar text box and then
      type =C15*B15.
   c. Click the Enter button on the Formula bar.
2. Copy the formula to cells D16 through D20
   by completing the following steps:
   a. Make sure cell D15 is the active cell.
   b. Position the mouse pointer on the fill
      handle that displays at the lower right
      corner of cell D15 until the pointer turns
      into a thin, black cross.
   c. Hold down the left mouse button, drag
      down to cell D20, and then release the
      mouse button.
3. Save **ExcelL1_C2_P1.xlsx**.
4. With the worksheet still open, make the
   following changes to cell contents:
   - B16: Change *20* to *28*
   - C17: Change *$18.75* to *19.10*
   - B19: Change *15* to *24*
5. Save **ExcelL1_C2_P1.xlsx**.

Step 1c   **Step 1b**

DATE   ▼   ✗ ✓ *fx*   =C15*B15

	A	B	C	D
1	**Highland Construction**			
2	Customer	Actual	Planned	Difference
3	Sellar Corporation	$30,349.00	$34,109.00	$3,760.00
4	Main Street Photos	$46,425.00	$48,100.00	$1,675.00
5	Sunset Automotive	$34,192.00	$32,885.00	-$1,307.00
6	Linstrom Enterprises	$63,293.00	$60,000.00	-$3,293.00
7	Morcos Media	$29,400.00	$30,500.00	$1,100.00
8	Green Valley Optics	$57,415.00	$58,394.00	$979.00
9	Detailed Designs	$14,115.00	$13,100.00	-$1,015.00
10	Arrowstar Company	$87,534.00	$86,905.00	-$629.00
11				
12				
13				
14	Name	Hours	Rate	Salary
15	Carolyn Bentley	35	$23.15	=C15*B15
16	Lindon Cassini	20	$19.00	

	Name	Hours	Rate	Salary
13				
14	Name	Hours	Rate	Salary
15	Carolyn Bentley	35	$23.15	$810.25
16	Lindon Cassini	20	$19.00	$380.00
17	Michelle DeFord	40	$18.75	$750.00
18	Javier Farias	24	$16.45	$394.80
19	Deborah Gould	15	$11.50	$172.50
20	William Jarman	15	$11.50	$172.50
21				
22				

Step 2c

Writing a Formula by Pointing

In Project 1a and Project 1b, you wrote formulas using cell references such as
=C3-B3. Another method for writing a formula is to "point" to the specific cells
that are to be part of the formula. Creating a formula by pointing is more accurate
than typing the cell reference since a mistake can happen when typing the cell
reference.

To write a formula by pointing, click the cell that will contain the formula, type
the equals sign to begin the formula, and then click the cell you want to reference
in the formula. This inserts a moving border around the cell and also changes the
mode from Enter to Point. (The word *Point* displays at the left side of the Status
bar.) Type the desired mathematical operator and then click the next cell reference.
Continue in this manner until all cell references are specified and then press the
Enter key. This ends the formula and inserts the result of the calculation of the
formula in the active cell. When writing a formula by pointing, you can also select
a range of cells you want included in a formula.

1. With **ExcelL1_C2_P1.xlsx** open, enter a formula by pointing that calculates the percentage of actual budget by completing the following steps:
   a. Make cell D25 active.
   b. Type the equals sign.
   c. Click cell C25. (This inserts a moving border around the cell and the mode changes from Enter to Point.)
   d. Type the forward slash symbol (/).
   e. Click cell B25.

	A	B	C	D	E
22					
23					
24	Expense	Actual	Budget	% of Actual	
25	Salaries	$126,000.00	$124,000.00	=C25/B25	
26	Commissions	$58,000.00	$54,500.00		
27	Media space	$8,250.00	$10,100.00		
28	Travel expenses	$6,350.00	$6,000.00		
29	Dealer display	$4,140.00	$4,500.00		
30	Payroll taxes	$2,430.00	$2,200.00		
31	Telephone	$1,450.00	$1,500.00		
32					

Steps
1a–1e

   f. Make sure the formula looks like this =C25/B25 and then press Enter.
2. Make cell D25 active, position the mouse pointer on the fill handle, drag down to cell D31, and then release the mouse button.
3. Save **ExcelL1_C2_P1.xlsx**.

	C	D	E
	Budget	% of Actual	
	$124,000.00	98%	
	$54,500.00	94%	
	$10,100.00	122%	
	$6,000.00	94%	
	$4,500.00	109%	
	$2,200.00	91%	
	$1,500.00	103%	

Step 2

Using the Trace Error Button

As you are working in a worksheet, you may occasionally notice a button pop up near the active cell. The general term for this button is *smart tag*. The display of the smart tag button varies depending on the action performed. In Project 1d, you will insert a formula that will cause a smart tag button, named the Trace Error button, to appear. When the Trace Error button appears, a small dark green triangle also displays in the upper left corner of the cell. Click the Trace Error button and a drop-down list displays with options for updating the formula to include specific cells, getting help on the error, ignoring the error, editing the error in the Formula bar, and completing an error check. In Project 1d, two of the formulas you insert return the desired results. You will click the Trace Error button, read information on what Excel perceives as the error, and then tell Excel to ignore the error.

Trace Error

1. With **ExcelL1_C2_P1.xlsx** open, enter a
   formula by pointing that computes the
   percentage of equipment down time by
   completing the following steps:
   a. Make cell B45 active.
   b. Type the equals sign followed by the
      left parenthesis (=().
   c. Click cell B37. (This inserts a moving
      border around the cell and the mode
      changes from Enter to Point.)
   d. Type the minus symbol (-).
   e. Click cell B43.
   f. Type the right parenthesis followed by
      the forward slash ()/).
   g. Click cell B37.
   h. Make sure the formula looks like
      this =(B37-B43)/B37 and then
      press Enter.

	A	B	C
33			
34			
35			EQUIPMENT
36	Hours	January	February
37	Total Hours Available	2,300	2,430
38	Avoidable Delays	19	12
39	Unavoidable Delays	9	8
40	Repairs	5	7
41	Servicing	6	13
42	Unassigned	128	95
43	In Use	2,040	2,105
44			
45	% of Down Time	=(B37-B43)/B37	
46	Jan - March Hours		
47	April - June Hours		
48			

Steps 1a–1g

2. Make cell B45 active, position the
   mouse pointer on the fill handle,
   drag across to cell G45, and then
   release the mouse button.
3. Enter a formula by dragging
   through a range of cells by
   completing the following steps:
   a. Click in cell B46 and then click
      the Sum button in the Editing
      group in the Home tab.
   b. Select cells B37 through D37.
   c. Click the Enter button on the
      Formula bar. (This inserts 7,260
      in cell B46.)

Step 3c

DATE ▾ ✗ ✓ fx =SUM(B37:D37)
Enter

	A	B	C	D	E
33					
34					
35			EQUIPMENT USAGE REPORT		
36	Hours	January	February	March	April
37	Total Hours Available	2,300	2,430	2,530	2,400
38	Avoidable Delays	19	12	16	20
39	Unavoidable Delays	9	8	6	12
40	Repairs	5	7	12	9
41	Servicing	6	13	7	6
42	Unassigned	128	95	85	135
43	In Use	2,040	2,105	2,320	2,180
44					
45	% of Down Time	11%	13%	8%	9%
46	Jan - March Hours	=SUM(B37:D37)			
47	April - June Hours	SUM(number1, [number2], ...)			

4. Click in cell B47 and then complete
   steps similar to those in Step 3 to create a
   formula that totals hours available from April
   through June (cells E37 through G37). (This
   inserts 7,080 in cell B47.)
5. Click in cell B46 and notice the Trace Error
   button that displays. Complete the following
   steps to read about the error and then tell Excel
   to ignore the error:
   a. Click the Trace Error button.
   b. At the drop-down list that displays, click the
      Help on this error option.
   c. Read the information that displays in the
      Excel Help window and then close the
      window.

Step 5a

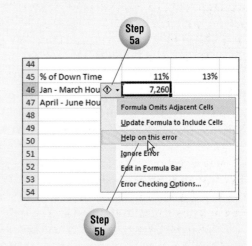

Step 5b

d. Click the Trace Error button again and then click *Ignore Error* at the drop-down list.

6. Remove the dark green triangle from cell B47 by completing the following steps:
   a. Click in cell B47.
   b. Click the Trace Error button and then click *Ignore Error* at the drop-down list.

7. Save, print, and then close **ExcelL1_C2_P1.xlsx**.

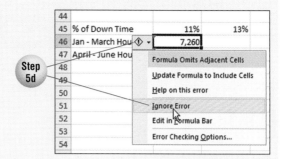

Step 5d

44			
45	% of Down Time	11%	13%
46	Jan - March Hou	7,260	
47	April - June Hou		

Formula Omits Adjacent Cells
Update Formula to Include Cells
Help on this error
Ignore Error
Edit in Formula Bar
Error Checking Options...

Project 2 Insert Formulas with Statistical Functions

You will use the AVERAGE function to determine average test scores, use the MINIMUM and MAXIMUM functions to determine lowest and highest averages, use the COUNT function to count number of students taking a test, and display formulas in a cell rather than the result of the formula.

Inserting Formulas with Functions

In Project 2a in Chapter 1, you used the Sum button to insert the formula =*SUM(B2:B5)* in a cell. The beginning section of the formula, =*SUM*, is called a *function*, which is a built-in formula. Using a function takes fewer keystrokes when creating a formula. For example, the =*SUM* function saved you from having to type each cell to be included in the formula with the plus (+) symbol between cell entries.

Excel provides other functions for writing formulas. A function operates on what is referred to as an *argument*. An argument may consist of a constant, a cell reference, or another function (referred to as a nested function). In the formula =*SUM(B2:B5)*, the cell range *(B2:B5)* is an example of a cell reference argument. An argument may also contain a *constant*. A constant is a value entered directly into the formula. For example, if you enter the formula =*SUM(B3:B9,100)*, the cell range *B3:B9* is a cell reference argument and *100* is a constant. In this formula, 100 is always added to the sum of the cells. If a function is included in an argument within a function, it is called a *nested function*. (You will learn about nested functions later in this chapter.)

When a value calculated by the formula is inserted in a cell, this process is referred to as *returning the result*. The term *returning* refers to the process of calculating the formula and the term *result* refers to inserting the value in the cell.

You can type a function in a cell in a worksheet or you can use the Insert Function button on the Formula bar or in the Formulas tab to help you write the formula. Figure 2.1 displays the Formulas tab. The Formulas tab provides the Insert Function button as well as other buttons for inserting functions in a worksheet. The Function Library group in the Formulas tab contains a number of buttons for inserting functions from a variety of categories such as Financial, Logical, Text, and Date & Time.

Insert Function

Figure 2.1 Formulas Tab

HINT

You can also display the Insert Function dialog box by clicking the down-pointing arrow at the right side of the Sum button and then clicking *More Functions.*

Click the Insert Function button on the Formula bar or in the Formulas tab and the Insert Function dialog box displays as shown in Figure 2.2. At the Insert Function dialog box, the most recently used functions display in the *Select a function* list box. You can choose a function category by clicking the down-pointing arrow at the right side of the *Or select a category* list box and then clicking the desired category at the drop-down list. Use the *Search for a function* option to locate a specific function.

Figure 2.2 Insert Function Dialog Box

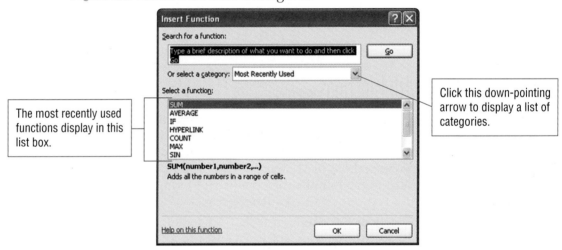

The most recently used functions display in this list box.

Click this down-pointing arrow to display a list of categories.

HINT

Click the down-pointing arrow at the right side of the Sum button in the Formulas tab and common functions display in a drop-down list.

With the desired function category selected, choose a function in the *Select a function* list box and then click OK. This displays a Function Arguments palette like the one shown in Figure 2.3. At this palette, enter in the *Number1* text box the range of cells you want included in the formula, enter any constants that are to be included as part of the formula, or enter another function. After entering a range of cells, a constant, or another function, click the OK button. You can include more than one argument in a function. If the function you are creating contains more than one argument, press the Tab key to move the insertion point to the *Number2* text box, and then enter the second argument. If you need to display a specific cell or cells behind the function palette, move the palette by clicking and dragging it.

Figure 2.3 Example Function Arguments Palette

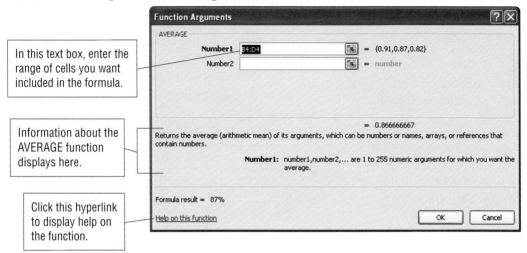

In this text box, enter the range of cells you want included in the formula.

Information about the AVERAGE function displays here.

Click this hyperlink to display help on the function.

Excel includes over 200 functions that are divided into 11 different categories including *Financial, Date & Time, Math & Trig, Statistical, Lookup & Reference, Database, Text, Logical, Information, Engineering,* and *Cube.* Clicking the Sum button in the Function Library group in the Formulas tab or the Editing group in the Home tab automatically adds numbers with the SUM function. The SUM function is included in the *Math & Trig* category. In some projects in this chapter, you will write formulas with functions in other categories including *Statistical, Financial, Date & Time,* and *Logical.*

Excel includes the Formula AutoComplete feature that displays a drop-down list of functions. To use this feature, click in the desired cell or click in the Formula bar text box, type the equals sign (=), and then type the first letter of the desired function. This displays a drop-down list with functions that begin with the letter. Double-click the desired function, enter the cell references, and then press Enter.

Writing Formulas with Statistical Functions

In this section, you will learn to write formulas with the statistical functions AVERAGE, MAX, MIN, and COUNT. The AVERAGE function returns the average (arithmetic mean) of the arguments. The MAX function returns the largest value in a set of values and the MIN function returns the smallest value in a set of values. Use the COUNT function to count the number of cells that contain numbers within the list of arguments.

Finding Averages

A common function in a formula is the AVERAGE function. With this function, a range of cells is added together and then divided by the number of cell entries. In Project 2a you will use the AVERAGE function, which will add all of the test scores for a student and then divide that number by the total number of tests. You will use the Insert Function button to simplify the creation of the formula containing an AVERAGE function.

One of the advantages to using formulas in a worksheet is the ability to easily manipulate data to answer certain questions. In Project 2a you will learn the impact of retaking certain tests on the final average score.

1. Open **ExcelC02Project02.xlsx**.
2. Save the workbook with Save As and name it **ExcelL1_C2_P2**.
3. Use the Insert Function button to find the average of test scores by completing the following steps:
   a. Make cell E4 active.
   b. Click the Insert Function button on the Formula bar.
   c. At the Insert Function dialog box, click the down-pointing arrow at the right side of the *Or select a category* list box and then click *Statistical* at the drop-down list.
   d. Click *AVERAGE* in the *Select a function* list box.
   e. Click OK.
   f. At the Function Arguments palette, make sure *B4:D4* displays in the *Number1* text box. (If not, type **B4:D4** in the *Number1* text box.)
   g. Click OK.

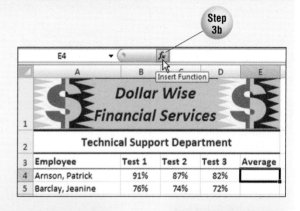

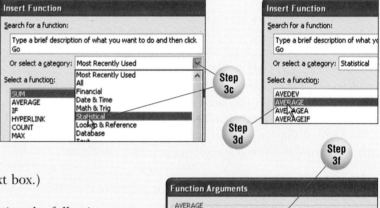

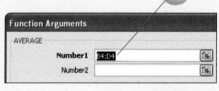

4. Copy the formula by completing the following steps:
   a. Make sure cell E4 is active.
   b. Position the mouse pointer on the fill handle until the pointer turns into a thin black cross.
   c. Hold down the left mouse button, drag down to cell E16, and then release the mouse button.
5. Save and then print **ExcelL1_C2_P2.xlsx**.
6. After viewing the averages of test scores, you notice that a couple of people have a low average. You decide to see what happens to the average score if students make up tests where they scored the lowest. You decide that a student can score a maximum of 70% on a retake of the test. Make the following changes to test scores to see how the changes will affect the test average.

   B9: Change *50 to 70*
   C9: Change *52 to 70*
   D9: Change *60 to 70*
   B10: Change *62 to 70*
   B14: Change *0 to 70*
   D14: Change *0 to 70*
   D16: Change *0 to 70*

7. Save and then print **ExcelL1_C2_P2.xlsx**. (Compare the test averages for Teri Fisher-Edwards, Stephanie Flanery, Claude Markovits, and Douglas Pherson to see what the effect of retaking the tests has on their final test averages.)

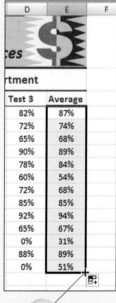

When a formula such as the AVERAGE formula you inserted in a cell in Project 2a calculates cell entries, it ignores certain cell entries. The AVERAGE function will ignore text in cells and blank cells (not zeros). For example, in the worksheet containing test scores, a couple of cells contained a *0%* entry. This entry was included in the averaging of the test scores. If you did not want that particular test to be included in the average, enter text in the cell such as *N/A* (for *not applicable*) or leave the cell blank.

Finding Maximum and Minimum Values

The MAX function in a formula returns the maximum value in a cell range and the MIN function returns the minimum value in a cell range. As an example, you could use the MAX and MIN functions in a worksheet containing employee hours to determine which employee worked the most number of hours and which worked the least. In a worksheet containing sales commissions, you could use the MAX and MIN functions to determine the salesperson who earned the most commission dollars and the one who earned the least.

Insert a MAX and MIN function into a formula in the same manner as an AVERAGE function. In Project 2b, you will use the Formula AutoComplete feature to insert the MAX function in cells to determine the highest test score average and the Insert Function button to insert the MIN function to determine the lowest test score average.

Project 2b Finding Maximum and Minimum Values in a Worksheet

1. With **ExcelL1_C2_P2.xlsx** open, type the following in the specified cells:
   A19: **Highest Test Average**
   A20: **Lowest Test Average**
   A21: **Average of All Tests**
2. Insert a formula to identify the highest test score average by completing the following steps:
   a. Make cell B19 active.
   b. Type **=M.** (This displays the Formula AutoComplete list.)
   c. Double-click *MAX* in the Formula AutoComplete list.
   d. Type **E4:E16)** and then press Enter.

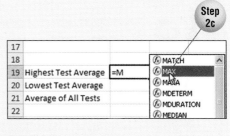

Step 2c

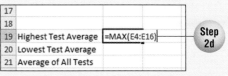

Step 2d

3. Insert a formula to identify the lowest test score average by completing the following steps:
   a. Make cell B20 active.
   b. Click the Insert Function button on the Formula bar.
   c. At the Insert Function dialog box, make sure *Statistical* is selected in the *Or select a category* list box, and then click *MIN* in the *Select a function* list box. (You will need to scroll down the list to display *MIN*.)
   d. Click OK.
   e. At the Function Arguments palette, type **E4:E16** in the *Number1* text box.
   f. Click OK.

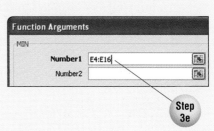

Step 3e

4. Insert a formula to determine the average of all test scores by completing the following steps:
   a. Make cell B21 active.
   b. Click the Formulas tab.
   c. Click the Insert Function button in the Function Library group.
   d. At the Insert Function dialog box, make sure *Statistical* is selected in the *Or select a category* list box and then click *AVERAGE* in the *Select a function* list box.
   e. Click OK.
   f. At the Function Arguments palette, type **E4:E16** in the *Number1* text box, and then click OK.
5. Save and then print **ExcelL1_C2_P2.xlsx**.
6. Change the *70%* values (which were previously *0%*) in cells B14, D14, and D16 to *N/A*. (This will cause the average of test scores for Claude Markovits and Douglas Pherson to increase and will change the minimum number and average of all test scores.)
7. Save and then print **ExcelL1_C2_P2.xlsx**.

Counting Numbers in a Range

Use the COUNT function to count the numeric values in a range. For example, in a range of cells containing cells with text and cells with numbers, you can count how many cells in the range contain numbers. In Project 2c, you will use the COUNT function to specify the number of students taking Test 2 and Test 3. In the worksheet, the cells containing the text N/A are not counted by the COUNT function.

Project 2c — Counting the Number of Students Taking Tests

1. With **ExcelL1_C2_P2.xlsx** open, make cell A22 active.
2. Type **Test 2 Completed**.
3. Make cell B22 active.
4. Insert a formula counting the number of students who have taken Test 2 by completing the following steps:
   a. With cell B22 active, click in the Formula bar text box.
   b. Type **=C**.
   c. At the Formula AutoComplete list that displays, scroll down the list until *COUNT* displays and then double-click *COUNT*.
   d. Type **C4:C16)** and then press Enter.
5. Count the number of students who have taken Test 3 by completing the following steps:
   a. Make cell A23 active.
   b. Type **Test 3 Completed**.

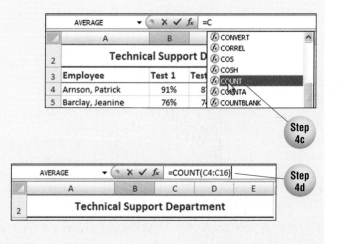

c. Make cell B23 active.

d. Click the Insert Function button on the Formula bar.

e. At the Insert Function dialog box, make sure *Statistical* is selected in the *Or select a category* list box.

f. Scroll down the list of functions in the *Select a function* list box until *COUNT* is visible and then double-click *COUNT*.

g. At the formula palette, type **D4:D16** in the *Value1* text box, and then click OK.

6. Save and then print **ExcelL1_C2_P2.xlsx**.

7. Add test scores by completing the following steps:

a. Make cell B14 active and then type **68**.

b. Make cell D14 active and then type **70**.

c. Make cell D16 active and then type **55**.

d. Press Enter.

8. Save and then print **ExcelL1_C2_P2.xlsx**.

Displaying Formulas

In some situations, you may need to display the formulas in a worksheet rather than the results of the formula. You may want to turn on formulas for auditing purposes or check formulas for accuracy. Display all formulas in a worksheet rather than the results by pressing Ctrl + ` (this is the grave accent). Press Ctrl + ` to turn off the display of formulas.

 Project **2d** Displaying Formulas

1. With **ExcelL1_C2_P2.xlsx** open, make cell A3 active.

2. Press Ctrl + ` to turn on the display of formulas.

3. Print the worksheet with the formulas.

4. Press Ctrl + ` to turn off the display of formulas.

5. Save and then close **ExcelL1_C2_P2.xlsx**.

 Project **3** Insert Formulas with Financial and Date and Time Functions

You will use the PMT financial function to calculate payments and the FV function to find the future value of an investment. You will also use the DATE function to return the serial number for a date and the NOW function to insert the current date and time as a serial number.

Writing Formulas with Financial Functions

In this section, you will learn to write formulas with the financial functions PMT and FV. The PMT function calculates the payment for a loan based on constant payments and a constant interest rate. Use the FV function to return the future value of an investment based on periodic, constant payments and a constant interest rate.

Finding the Periodic Payments for a Loan

The PMT function finds the periodic payment for a loan based on constant payments and a constant interest rate. The PMT function contains the arguments Nper, Pv, Fv, and Type. The Nper argument is the number of payments that will be made to an investment or loan, Pv is the current value of amounts to be received or paid in the future, Fv is the value of a loan or investment at the end of all periods, and Type determines whether calculations will be based on payments made in arrears (at the end of each period) or in advance (at the beginning of each period).

Project 3a — Calculating Payments

1. Open **ExcelC02Project03.xlsx**.
2. Save the workbook with Save As and name it **ExcelL1_C2_P3**.
3. The owner of Real Photography is interested in purchasing a new developer and needs to determine monthly payments on three different models. Insert a formula that calculates monthly payments and then copy that formula by completing the following steps:
   a. Make cell E5 active.
   b. Click the Formulas tab.
   c. Click the Financial button in the Function Library group, scroll down the drop-down list until *PMT* displays, and then click *PMT*.

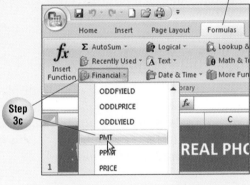

   d. At the Function Arguments palette, type **C5/12** in the *Rate* text box. (This tells Excel to divide the interest rate by 12 months.)
   e. Press the Tab key. (This moves the insertion point to the *Nper* text box).
   f. Type **D5**. (This is the total number of months in the payment period.)
   g. Press the Tab key. (This moves the insertion point to the *Pv* text box.)
   h. Type **-B5**. (Excel displays the result of the PMT function as a negative number since the loan represents a negative cash flow to the borrower. Insert a minus sign before *B5* to show the monthly payment as a positive number rather than a negative number.)
   i. Click OK. (This closes the palette and inserts the monthly payment of *$316.98* in cell E7.)
   j. Copy the formula in cell E5 down to cells E6 and E7.
4. Insert a formula in cell F5 that calculates the total amount of the payments by completing the following steps:
   a. Make cell F5 active.
   b. Type **=E5*D5** and then press Enter.
   c. Make cell F5 active and then copy the formula down to cells F6 and F7.
5. Insert a formula in cell G5 that calculates the total amount of interest paid by completing the following steps:
   a. Make cell G5 active.
   b. Type **=F5-B5** and then press Enter.
   c. Make cell G5 active and then copy the formula down to cells G6 and G7.
6. Save **ExcelL1_C2_P3.xlsx**.

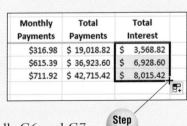

Monthly Payments	Total Payments	Total Interest
$316.98	$ 19,018.82	$ 3,568.82
$615.39	$ 36,923.60	$ 6,928.60
$711.92	$ 42,715.42	$ 8,015.42

Finding the Future Value of a Series of Payments

The FV function calculates the future value of a series of equal payments or an annuity. Use this function to determine information such as how much money can be earned in an investment account with a specific interest rate and over a specific period of time.

Project 3b — **Finding the Future Value of an Investment**

1. Make sure **ExcelL1_C2_P3.xlsx** is open.
2. The owner of Real Photography has decided to save money to purchase a new developer and wants to compute how much money can be earned by investing the money in an investment account that returns 9% annual interest. The owner determines that $1,200 per month can be invested in the account for three years. Complete the following steps to determine the future value of the investment account by completing the following steps:
   a. Make cell B15 active.
   b. Click the Financial button in the Function Library group in the Formulas tab.
   c. At the drop-down list that displays, scroll down the list until *FV* is visible and then click *FV*.
   d. At the Function Arguments palette, type **B12/12** in the *Rate* text box.
   e. Press the Tab key.
   f. Type **B13** in the *Nper* text box.
   g. Press the Tab key.
   h. Type **B14** in the *Pmt* text box.
   i. Click OK. (This closes the palette and also inserts the future value of *$49,383.26* in cell B15.)
3. Save and then print **ExcelL1_C2_P3.xlsx**.
4. The owner decides to determine the future return after two years. To do this, change the amount in cell B13 from *36* to *24* and then press Enter. (This recalculates the future investment amount in cell B15.)
5. Save and then print **ExcelL1_C2_P3.xlsx**.

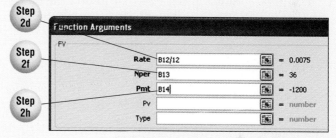

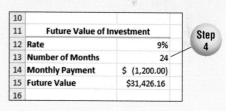

10		
11	**Future Value of Investment**	
12	**Rate**	9%
13	**Number of Months**	24
14	**Monthly Payment**	$ (1,200.00)
15	**Future Value**	$31,426.16
16		

Writing Formulas with Date and Time Functions

In this section, you will learn to write formulas with the date and time functions NOW and DATE. The NOW function returns the serial number of the current date and time. The DATE function returns the serial number that represents a particular date. Excel can make calculations using dates because the dates are represented as serial numbers. To calculate a date's serial number, Excel counts the days since the beginning of the twentieth century. The date serial number for January 1, 1900, is 1. The date serial number for January 1, 2000, is 36,526. To access the DATE and NOW functions, click the Date & Time button in the Function Library group in the Formulas tab.

HINT

Ctrl + ; is the keyboard shortcut to insert the current date in the active cell.

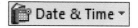

Project **Using the DATE and NOW Functions**

1. Make sure **ExcelL1_C2_P3.xlsx** is open.
2. Certain cells in this worksheet establish overdue dates for Real Photography accounts. Enter a formula in cell D20 that returns the serial number for the date March 17, 2010, by completing the following steps:
   a. Make cell D20 active.
   b. Click the Formulas tab.
   c. Click the Date & Time button in the Function Library group.
   d. At the drop-down list that displays, click *DATE*.
   e. At the Function Arguments palette, type **2010** in the *Year* text box.
   f. Press the Tab key and then type **03** in the *Month* text box.
   g. Press the Tab key and then type **17** in the *Day* text box.
   h. Click OK.

3. Complete steps similar to those in Step 2 to enter the following dates as serial numbers in the specified cells:

   D21 = March 24, 2010
   D22 = March 31, 2010
   D23 = April 7, 2010

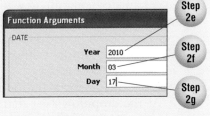

Step 2e

Step 2f

Step 2g

4. Enter a formula in cell F20 that inserts the due date (the purchase date plus the number of days in the *Terms* column) by completing the following steps:
   a. Make cell F20 active.
   b. Type **=D20+E20** and then press Enter.
   c. Make cell F20 active and then copy the formula down to cells F21, F22, and F23.
5. Make cell A26 active and then type your name.
6. Insert the current date and time as a serial number by completing the following steps:
   a. Make cell A27 active.
   b. Click the Date & Time button in the Function Library group in the Formulas tab and then click *NOW* at the drop-down list.
   c. At the Function Arguments palette telling you that the function takes no argument, click OK.
7. Save, print, and then close **ExcelL1_C2_P3.xlsx**.

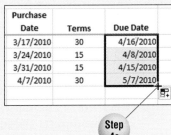

Step 4c

Project ④ **Insert Formulas with the IF Logical Function**

You will use the IF logical function to calculate sales bonuses, determine letter grades based on test averages, and identify discounts and discount amounts.

Writing a Formula with the IF Logical Function

The IF function is considered a *conditional function*. With the IF function you can perform conditional tests on values and formulas. A question that can be answered with true or false is considered a *logical test*. The IF function makes a logical test and then performs a particular action if the answer is true and another action if the answer is false.

For example, an IF function can be used to write a formula that calculates a salesperson's bonus as 10% if the quota of $100,000 is met or exceeded, and zero if the quota is less than $100,000. That formula would look like this: =IF(quota=>100000,quota*0.1,0). The formula contains three parts—the condition or logical test IF(quota=>100000), action taken if the condition or logical test is true (quota*0.1), and the action taken if the condition or logical test is false (0). Commas separate the condition and the actions. In the bonus formula, if the quota is equal to or greater than $100,000, then the quota is multiplied by 10%. If the quota is less than $100,000, then the bonus is zero.

In Project 4a, you will write a formula with cell references rather than cell data. The formula in Project 4a is =IF(C5>B5,C5*0.15,0). In this formula the condition or logical test is whether or not the number in cell C5 is greater than the number in cell B5. If the condition is true and the number is greater, then the number in cell C5 is multiplied by 0.15 (providing a 15% bonus). If the condition is false and the number in cell C5 is less than the number in cell B5, then nothing happens (no bonus). Notice how commas are used to separate the logical test from the actions.

Editing a Formula

Edit a formula by making active the cell containing the formula and then editing the formula in the cell or in the Formula bar text box. After editing the formula, press Enter or click the Enter button on the Formula bar and Excel will recalculate the result of the formula.

Enter

Project 4a   **Writing a Formula with an IF Function and Editing the Formula**

1. Open **ExcelC02Project04.xlsx**.
2. Save the workbook with Save As and name it **ExcelL1_C2_P4**.
3. Write a formula with the IF function by completing the following steps. (The formula will determine if the quota has been met and, if it has, will insert the bonus [15% of the actual sales]. If the quota has not been met, the formula will insert a zero.)
   a. Make cell D5 active.
   b. Type =IF(C5>B5,C5*0.15,0) and then press Enter.
   c. Make cell D5 active and then use the fill handle to copy the formula to cells D6 through D10.
4. Print the worksheet.
5. Revise the formula so it will insert a 25% bonus if the quota has been met by completing the following steps:
   a. Make cell D5 active.
   b. Click in the Formula bar, edit the formula so it displays as =IF(C5>B5,C5*0.25,0), and then click the Enter button on the Formula bar.
   c. Copy the formula down to cells D6 through D10.
6. Save and then print **ExcelL1_C2_P4.xlsx**.

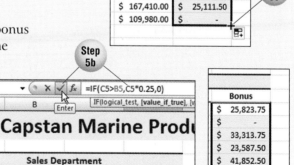

Writing a Nested IF Condition

In Project 4a, the IF function had only two possible actions—the actual sales times 15% or a zero. In a formula where more than two actions are required, use nested IF functions. For example, in Project 4b, you will write a formula with IF conditions that has four possible actions—a letter grade of A, B, C, or D. When writing nested IF conditions, insert symbols such as commas, quotation marks, and parentheses in the proper locations. If you want an IF condition to insert text, insert quotation marks before and after the text. The formula you will be writing in Project 4b is shown below.

$$=IF(E16>89,"A",IF(E16>79,"B",IF(E16>69,"C",IF(E16>59, "D"))))$$

This formula begins with the condition *=IF(E16>89, "A",*. If the number in cell E16 is greater than 89, then the condition is met and the grade of A is returned. The formula continues with a nested condition, *IF(E16>79, "B",*. If the number in cell E16 does not meet the first condition (greater than 89), then Excel looks to the next condition—is the number in cell E16 greater than 79? If it is, then the grade of B is inserted in cell E16. The formula continues with another nested condition, *IF(E16>69, "C",*. If the number in cell E16 does not match the first condition, Excel looks to the second condition, and if that condition is not met, then Excel looks to the third condition. If the number in cell E16 is greater than 69, then the grade of C is inserted in cell E16. The final nested condition is *IF(E16>59, "D"*. If the first three conditions are not met but this one is, then the grade of D is inserted in cell E16. The four parentheses at the end of the formula end each condition in the formula.

Project 4b — Writing a Formula with Nested IF Conditions

1. With **ExcelL1_C2_P4.xlsx** open, insert a formula to average the scores by completing the following steps:
   a. Make cell E16 active.
   b. Type **=AVERAGE(B16:D16)** and then press Enter.
   c. Make cell E16 active and then copy the formula down to cells E17 through E20.
2. Insert a formula with nested IF conditions by completing the following steps:
   a. Make cell F16 active.
   b. Type **=IF(E16>89,"A",IF(E16>79,"B",IF(E16>69,"C",IF(E16>59,"D"))))** and then press Enter.

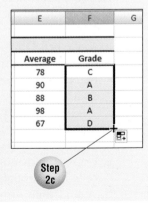

D	E	F	G	H	I
Orientation					
Quiz 3	Average	Grade			
=IF(E16>89,"A", IF(E16>79,"B",IF(E16>69,"C",IF(E16>59,"D"))))					
86	90				

Step 2b

	E	F	G
	Average	Grade	
	78	C	
	90	A	
	88	B	
	98	A	
	67	D	

Step 2c

   c. Make cell F16 active and then use the fill handle to copy the formula down to cells F17 through F20.
3. Save **ExcelL1_C2_P4.xlsx**.

As you typed the formula with nested IF conditions in Step 2b of Project 4b, did you notice that the parentheses were different colors? Each color represents a condition. The four right parentheses at the end of the formula ended each of the conditions and each matched in color a left parenthesis. If an average in column E in **ExcelL1_C2_P4.xlsx** is less than 59, the nested formula inserts *FALSE* in the cell. If you want the formula to insert a letter grade, such as *F,* instead of *FALSE,* include another nested IF condition in the formula. Up to 64 levels of functions can be nested.

You can use the IF function from the Logical button drop-down list in the Function Library in the Formulas tab to write an IF statement. The IF statement you write using the IF function from the Logical button checks whether a condition is met and returns one value if the condition is met and another if the condition is not met. For example, in Project 4c you will insert an IF statement that identifies whether or not a part receives a discount. Parts that sell for more than $499 receive a discount and parts that sell for less do not. If the condition is met (the amount is greater than $499), then the statement will return a *YES* and if the condition is not met, the statement will return a *NO.*

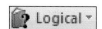

In Project 4c, you will type the second IF statement in the cell rather than using the IF function from the Logical button drop-down list. The IF statement you write will reduce the price by five percent for parts that sell from $500 up to $749, seven percent for parts that sell from $750 up to $999, and ten percent for parts that sell for at least $1,000.

Project 4c Writing IF Statements Identifying Discounts and Discount Amounts

1. With **ExcelL1_C2_P4.xlsx** open, insert an IF statement by completing the following steps:
   a. Make cell C26 active.
   b. Click the Logical button in the Function Library group in the Formulas tab and then click IF at the drop-down list.
   c. At the Function Arguments palette, type B26>499 in the *Logic_test* text box.
   d. Press the Tab key to move the insertion point to the *Value_if_true* text box and then type YES.
   e. Press the Tab key to move the insertion point to the *Value_if_false* text box and then type NO.
   f. Click OK to close the Function Arguments palette.
2. Copy the formula in cell C26 down to cells C27 through C38.
3. Make cell D26 active.
4. Insert the following IF statement in the cell:
   =IF(B26>999,B26*0.1,IF(B26>749,B26*0.07,IF(B26>499,B26*0.05,IF(B26>0,"N/A"))))
5. Copy the formula in cell D26 down to cells D27 through D38.
6. Save, print, and then close **ExcelL1_C2_P4.xlsx**.

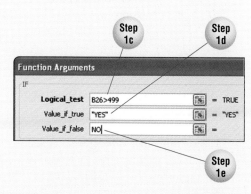

Project 5 — Insert Formulas Using Absolute and Mixed Cell References

You will insert a formula containing an absolute cell reference that determines the effect on earnings with specific increases, insert a formula with multiple absolute cell references that determine the weighted average of scores, and use mixed cell references to determine simple interest.

Using Absolute and Mixed Cell References in Formulas

A reference identifies a cell or a range of cells in a worksheet and can be relative, absolute, or mixed. Relative cell references refer to cells relative to a position in a formula. Absolute references refer to cells in a specific location. When a formula is copied, a relative cell reference adjusts while an absolute cell reference remains constant. A mixed cell reference does both—either the column remains absolute and the row is relative or the column is relative and the row is absolute. Distinguish between relative, absolute, and mixed cell references using the dollar sign ($). Type a dollar sign before the column and/or row cell reference in a formula to specify that the column or row is an absolute cell reference.

Using an Absolute Cell Reference in a Formula

In this chapter you have learned to copy a relative formula. For example, if the formula =SUM(A2:C2) in cell D2 is copied relatively to cell D3, the formula changes to =SUM(A3:C3). In some situations, you may want a formula to contain an absolute cell reference, which always refers to a cell in a specific location. In Project 5a, you will add a column for projected job earnings and then perform "what if" situations using a formula with an absolute cell reference. To identify an absolute cell reference, insert a $ symbol before the row and the column. For example, the absolute cell reference C12 would be typed as $C$12 in a formula.

Project 5a — Inserting and Copying a Formula with an Absolute Cell Reference

1. Open **ExcelC02Project05.xlsx**.
2. Save the workbook with Save As and name it **ExcelL1_C2_P5**.
3. Determine the effect on actual job earnings with a 20% increase by completing the following steps:
   a. Make cell C3 active, type the formula =B3*$B$12, and then press Enter.
   b. Make cell C3 active and then use the fill handle to copy the formula to cells C4 through C10.
4. Save and then print **ExcelL1_C2_P5.xlsx**.

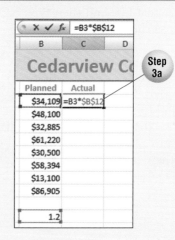

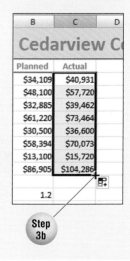

5. With the worksheet still open, determine the effect on actual job earnings with a 10% decrease by completing the following steps:
   a. Make cell B12 active.
   b. Type **0.9** and then press Enter.
6. Save and then print the **ExcelL1_C2_P5.xlsx**.
7. Determine the effects on actual job earnings with a 10% increase. (To do this, type 1.1 in cell B12.)
8. Save and then print **ExcelL1_C2_P5.xlsx**.

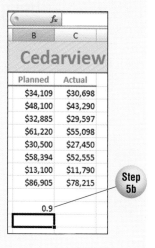

Step 5b

In Project 5a, you created a formula with one absolute cell reference. You can also create a formula with multiple absolute cell references. For example, in Project 5b you will create a formula that contains both relative and absolute cell references to determine the average of training scores based on specific weight percentages.

Project 5b Inserting and Copying a Formula with Multiple Absolute Cell References

1. With **ExcelL1_C2_P5.xlsx** open, insert the following formulas:
   a. Insert a formula in cell B23 that averages the percentages in cells B17 through B22.
   b. Copy the formula in cell B23 to the right to cells C23 and D23.
2. Insert a formula that determines the weighted average of training scores by completing the following steps:
   a. Make cell E17 active.
   b. Type the following formula:
      =$B$24*B17+$C$24*C17+$D$24*D17
   c. Press the Enter key.
   d. Copy the formula in cell E17 down to cells E18 through E22.
3. Save and then print the **ExcelL1_C2_P5.xlsx**.
4. With the worksheet still open, determine the effect on weighted training scores if the weighted values change by completing the following steps:
   a. Make cell B24 active, type **30**, and then press Enter.
   b. Make cell D24 active, type **40**, and then press Enter.
5. Save and then print **ExcelL1_C2_P5.xlsx**.

15	Employee Training				
16	Name	Plumbing	Electrical	Carpentry	Weighted Average
17	Allesandro	76%	80%	84%	89%
18	Ellington	66%	72%	64%	73%
19	Goodman	90%	88%	94%	100%
20	Huntington	76%	82%	88%	91%
21	Kaplan-Downing	90%	84%	92%	98%
22	Larimore	58%	62%	60%	66%
23	Training Averages	76%	78%	80%	
24	Training Weights	30%	30%	50%	
25					

Step 4a

Using a Mixed Cell Reference in a Formula

The formula you created in Step 3a in Project 5a contained a relative cell reference (B3) and an absolute cell reference ($B$12). A formula can also contain a mixed cell reference. In a mixed cell reference either the column remains absolute and the row is relative or the column is relative and the row is absolute. In Project 5c you will insert a number of formulas, two of which will contain mixed cell references. You will insert the formula $=E29*E\$26$ to calculate withholding tax and $=E29*H\$36$ to calculate Social Security tax. The dollar sign before the rows indicates that the row is an absolute cell reference.

Project 5c   **Determining Payroll Using Formulas with Absolute and Mixed Cell References**

1. With **ExcelL1_C2_P5.xlsx** open, make cell E29 active and then insert the following formula containing mixed cell references:
   =(B29*C29+(B29*$B$36*D29))
2. Copy the formula in cell E29 down to cells E30 through E34.
3. Make cell F29 active and then insert the following formula that calculates the amount of withholding tax:
   =E29*E$36
4. Copy the formula in cell F29 down to cells F30 through F34.
5. Make cell G29 active and then insert the following formula that calculates the amount of Social Security tax:
   =E29*H$36
6. Copy the formula in cell G29 down to cells G30 through G34.
7. Make cell H29 active and then insert the following formula that calculates net pay:
   =E29-(F29+G29)
8. Copy the formula in cell H29 down to cells H30 through H34.
9. Save **ExcelL1_C2_P5.xlsx**.

As you learned in Project 5c, a formula can contain a mixed cell reference. In a mixed cell reference either the column remains absolute and the row is relative or the column is relative and the row is absolute. In Project 5d, you will create the formula $=\$A41*B\$40$. In the first cell reference in the formula, $\$A41$, the column is absolute and the row is relative. In the second cell reference, $B\$40$, the column is relative and the row is absolute. The formula containing the mixed cell references allows you to fill in the column and row data using only one formula.

Identify an absolute or mixed cell reference by typing a dollar sign before the column and/or row reference or press the F4 function key to cycle through the various cell references. For example, type $=A41$ in a cell, press F4, and the cell reference changes to $=\$A\$41$. Press F4 again and the cell reference changes to $=A\$41$. The next time you press F4, the cell reference changes to $=\$A41$ and press it again to change the cell reference back to $=A41$.

Determining Simple Interest Using a Formula with Mixed Cell References

1. With **ExcelL1_C2_P5.xlsx** open, make cell B41 the active cell and then insert a formula containing mixed cell references by completing the following steps:
   a. Type **=A41** and then press the F4 function key three times. (This changes the cell reference to *$A41*.)
   b. Type ***B40** and then press the F4 function key twice. (This changes the cell reference to *B$40*.)
   c. Make sure the formula displays as *=$A41*B$40* and then press Enter.

39	SIMPLE INTEREST LOAN TABLE					
40		$ 1,000	$ 2,000	$ 3,000	$ 4,000	$ 5,000
41	5%	=$A41*B$40				
42	6%					
43	7%					

Step 1c

2. Copy the formula to the right by completing the following steps:
   a. Make cell B41 active and then use the fill handle to copy the formula right to cell F41.

39	SIMPLE INTEREST LOAN TABLE					
40		$ 1,000	$ 2,000	$ 3,000	$ 4,000	$ 5,000
41	5%	$ 50	$ 100	$ 150	$ 200	$ 250
42	6%					
43	7%					

Step 2a

   b. With cells B41 through F41 selected, use the fill handle to copy the formula down to cell F51.

39	SIMPLE INTEREST LOAN TABLE					
40		$ 1,000	$ 2,000	$ 3,000	$ 4,000	$ 5,000
41	5%	$ 50	$ 100	$ 150	$ 200	$ 250
42	6%	$ 60	$ 120	$ 180	$ 240	$ 300
43	7%	$ 70	$ 140	$ 210	$ 280	$ 350
44	8%	$ 80	$ 160	$ 240	$ 320	$ 400
45	9%	$ 90	$ 180	$ 270	$ 360	$ 450
46	10%	$ 100	$ 200	$ 300	$ 400	$ 500
47	11%	$ 110	$ 220	$ 330	$ 440	$ 550
48	12%	$ 120	$ 240	$ 360	$ 480	$ 600
49	13%	$ 130	$ 260	$ 390	$ 520	$ 650
50	14%	$ 140	$ 280	$ 420	$ 560	$ 700
51	15%	$ 150	$ 300	$ 450	$ 600	$ 750
52						

Step 2b

3. Save, print, and then close **ExcelL1_C2_P5.xlsx**. (This worksheet will print on two pages.)

CHAPTER summary

- Type a formula in a cell and the formula displays in the cell as well as in the Formula bar. If cell entries are changed, a formula will automatically recalculate the values and insert the result in the cell.

- Create your own formula with commonly used operators such as addition (+), subtraction (-), multiplication (*), division (/), percent (%), and exponentiation (^). When writing a formula, begin with the equals (=) sign.

- Copy a formula to other cells in a row or column with the Fill button in the Editing group in the Home tab or with the fill handle that displays in the bottom right corner of the active cell.

- Another method for writing a formula is to point to specific cells that are part of the formula.

- If Excel detects an error in a formula, a Trace Error button appears and a dark green triangle displays in the upper left corner of the cell containing the formula.

- Excel includes over 200 functions that are divided into eleven categories. Use the Insert Function feature to create formulas using built-in functions.

- A function operates on an argument, which may consist of a cell reference, a constant, or another function. When a value calculated by a formula is inserted in a cell, this is referred to as returning the result.

- The AVERAGE function returns the average (arithmetic mean) of the arguments. The MAX function returns the largest value in a set of values, and the MIN function returns the smallest value in a set of values. The COUNT function counts the number of cells containing numbers within the list of arguments.

- Use the keyboard shortcut, Ctrl + ` (grave accent) to turn on the display of formulas in a worksheet.

- The PMT function calculates the payment for a loan based on constant payments and a constant interest rate. The FV function returns the future value of an investment based on periodic, constant payments and a constant interest rate.

- The NOW function returns the serial number of the current date and time and the DATE function returns the serial number that represents a particular date.

- Use the IF function, considered a conditional function, to perform conditional tests on values and formulas.

- Use nested IF functions in a formula where more than two actions are required.

- A reference identifies a cell or a range of cells in a worksheet and can be relative, absolute, or mixed. Identify an absolute cell reference by inserting a $ symbol before the column and row. Cycle through the various cell reference options by typing the cell reference and then pressing F4.

COMMANDS review

FEATURE	RIBBON TAB, GROUP	BUTTON	KEYBOARD SHORTCUT
SUM function	Home, Editing OR Formulas, Function Library	Σ AutoSum ▾	Alt + =
Insert Function dialog box	Formulas, Function Library	fx	Shift + F3
Display formulas			Ctrl + `

CONCEPTS check

Test Your Knowledge

Completion: In the space provided at the right, indicate the correct term, symbol, or command.

1. When typing a formula, begin the formula with this sign. _____

2. This is the operator for division that is used when writing a formula. _____

3. This is the operator for multiplication that is used when writing a formula. _____

4. This is the name of the small black box located at the bottom right corner of a cell that can be used to copy a formula to adjacent cells. _____

5. A function operates on this, which may consist of a constant, a cell reference, or other function. _____

6. This function returns the largest value in a set of values. _____

7. This is the keyboard shortcut to display formulas in a worksheet. _____

8. This function finds the periodic payment for a loan based on constant payments and a constant interest rate. _____

9. This function returns the serial number of the current date and time. _____

10. This function is considered a conditional function. _____

11. To identify an absolute cell reference, type this symbol before the column and row. _____

12. Suppose that cell B2 contains the budgeted amount and cell C2 contains the actual amount. Write the formula (including the IF conditions) that would insert the word *under* if the actual amount was less than the budgeted amount and insert the word *over* if the actual amount was greater than the budgeted amount. _____

SKILLS check
Demonstrate Your Proficiency

Assessment

1 ### INSERT AVERAGE, MAX, AND MIN FUNCTIONS

1. Open **ExcelC02Assessment01.xlsx**.
2. Save the workbook with Save As and name it **ExcelL1_C2_A1**.
3. Use the AVERAGE function to determine the monthly sales (cells H4 through H9).
4. Total each monthly column including the Average column (cells B10 through H10).
5. Use the MAX function to determine the highest monthly total (for cells B4 through G9) and insert the amount in cell B11.
6. Use the MIN function to determine the lowest monthly total (for cells B4 through G9) and insert the amount in cell B12.
7. Save, print, and then close **ExcelL1_C2_A1.xlsx**.

Assessment

2 ### INSERT PMT FUNCTION

1. Open **ExcelC02Assessment02.xlsx**.
2. Save the workbook with Save As and name it **ExcelL1_C2_A2**.
3. The manager of Clearline Manufacturing is interested in refinancing a loan for either $125,000 or $300,000 and wants to determine the monthly payments, total payments, and total interest paid. Insert a formula with the following specifications:
   a. Make cell E5 active.
   b. Use the Insert Function button on the Formula bar to insert a formula using the PMT function. At the formula palette, enter the following:

   Rate = C5/12
   Nper = D5
   Pv = -B5

   c. Copy the formula in cell E5 down to cells E6 through E8.
4. Insert a formula in cell F5 that multiplies the amount in E5 by the amount in D5.

5. Copy the formula in cell F5 down to cells F6 through F8.
6. Insert a formula in cell G5 that subtracts the amount in B5 from the amount in F5. (The formula is =F5-B5.)
7. Copy the formula in cell G5 down to cells G6 through G8.
8. Save, print, and then close **ExcelL1_C2_A2.xlsx**.

Assessment

3 INSERT FV FUNCTION

1. Open **ExcelC02Assessment03.xlsx**.
2. Save the workbook with Save As and name it **ExcelL1_C2_A3**.
3. Make the following changes to the worksheet:
   a. Change the percentage in cell B3 from *9%* to *10%*.
   b. Change the number in cell B4 from *36* to *60*.
   c. Change the amount in cell B5 from *($1,200)* to *-500*.
   d. Use the FV function to insert a formula that calculates the future value of the investment. *Hint: For help with the formula, refer to Project 3b.*
4. Save, print, and then close **ExcelL1_C2_A3.xlsx**.

Assessment

4 WRITE IF STATEMENT FORMULAS

1. Open **ExcelC02Assessment04.xlsx**.
2. Save the workbook with Save As and name it **ExcelL1_C2_A4**.
3. Insert a formula in cell C4 that contains an IF statement with the following details:

   If the contents of cell B4 are greater than 150000, then insert the word Platinum.
   If the contents of cell B4 are greater than 100000, then insert the word Gold.
   If the contents of cell B4 are greater than 75000, then insert the word Silver.
   If the contents of cell B4 are greater than 0 (zero), then insert the word Bronze.

   When writing the IF statement, make sure you insert quotes around the words *Platinum, Gold, Silver,* and *Bronze.* Copy the formula in cell C4 down to cell C14.
4. Insert a formula in cell D4 that contains in IF statement with the following details:

   If the content of cell C4 is Bronze, then insert the word None.
   If the content of cell C4 is Silver, then insert $3,000.
   If the content of cell C4 is Gold, then insert $5,000.
   If the content of cell C4 is Platinum, then insert $10,000.

   When writing the IF statement, you will need to insert quotes around the words *Platinum, Gold, Silver, Bronze,* and *None* as well as the amounts *$3,000, $5,000,* and *$10,000.* Copy the formula in cell D4 down to cell D14.
5. Save and then print **ExcelL1_C2_A4.xlsx**.

6. Display the formulas in the worksheet.
7. Print **ExcelL1_C2_A4.xlsx**.
8. Turn off the display of the formulas.
9. Save and then close **ExcelL1_C2_A4.xlsx**.

Assessment

5   WRITE FORMULAS WITH ABSOLUTE CELL REFERENCES

1. Open **ExcelC02Assessment05.xlsx**.
2. Save the workbook with Save As and name it **ExcelL1_C2_A5**.
3. Make the following changes to the worksheet:
   a. Insert a formula using an absolute reference to determine the projected quotas at 10% of the current quotas.
   b. Save and then print **ExcelL1_C2_A5.xlsx**.
   c. Determine the projected quotas at 15% of the current quota by changing cell A15 to *15% Increase* and cell B15 to *1.15*.
   d. Save and then print **ExcelL1_C2_A5.xlsx**.
   e. Determine the projected quotas at 20% of the current quota.
4. Save, print, and then close **ExcelL1_C2_A5.xlsx**.

Assessment

6   USE HELP TO LEARN ABOUT EXCEL OPTIONS

1. Learn about specific options in the Excel Options dialog box by completing the following steps:
   a. Display the Excel Options dialog box by clicking the Office button and then clicking the Excel Options button that displays in the lower right corner of the drop-down list.
   b. At the Excel Options dialog box, click the *Advanced* option located in the left panel.
   c. Click the Help button that displays in the upper right corner of the dialog box, read the information that displays about advanced features, and then close the Excel Help window.
   d. Write down the check box options available in the *Display options for this workbook* section and the *Display options for this worksheet* section of the dialog box and identify whether or not the check box contains a check mark. (Record only check box options and ignore buttons and options preceded by circles.)
2. With the information you wrote down about the options, create an Excel spreadsheet with the following information:
   a. In column C, type each option you wrote down. (Include an appropriate heading.)
   b. In column B, insert an X in the cell that precedes any option that contains a check mark in the check box. (Include an appropriate heading.)
   c. In column A, write a formula with the IF function that inserts the word ON in the cell if the cell in column B contains an X and inserts the word OFF if it does not (the cell is blank). (Include an appropriate heading.)
   d. Apply formatting to improve the visual appeal of the worksheet.

3. Save the workbook and name it **ExcelL1_C2_A6**.
4. Turn on the display of formulas.
5. Print the worksheet.
6. Turn off the display of formulas.
7. Save, print, and then close **ExcelL1_C2_A6.xlsx**.

CASE study

Apply Your Skills

Part 1

You are a loan officer for Dollar Wise Financial Services and work in the department that specializes in home loans. You have decided to prepare a sample home mortgage worksheet to show prospective clients. This sample home mortgage worksheet will show the monthly payments on variously priced homes with varying interest rates. Open the **DollarWise.xlsx** worksheet and then complete the home mortgage worksheet by inserting the following formulas:

- Since many homes in your area sell for at least $400,000, you decide to add that amount to the worksheet with a 5%, 10%, 15%, and 20% down payment.
- In column C, insert a formula that determines the down payment amount.
- In column D, insert a formula that determines the loan amount.
- In column G, insert a formula using the PMT function (the monthly payment will display as a negative number).

Save the worksheet and name it **ExcelL1_C2_CS_P1**.

Part 2

If home buyers put down less than twenty percent of the home's purchase price, mortgage insurance is required. With **ExcelL1_C2_C1.xlsx** open, insert an IF statement in the cells in column H that inserts the word "No" if the percentage in column B is equal to or greater than 20% or inserts the word "Yes" if the percentage in column B is less than 20%. Save and then print **ExcelL1_C2_CS_P1.xlsx**.

Part 3

Interest rates fluctuate on a regular basis. Using the resources available to you, determine a current interest rate in your area. Delete the interest rate of 7% in the Dollar Wise worksheet and insert the interest rate for your area. Save and then print **ExcelL1_C2_CS_P1.xlsx**.

Part 4

When a client is required to purchase mortgage insurance, you would like to provide information to the client concerning this insurance. Use the Help feature to learn about creating hyperlinks in Excel. Locate a helpful Web site that specializes in private mortgage insurance. Create a hyperlink in the worksheet that will display the Web site. Save, print, and then close **ExcelL1_C2_CS_P1.xlsx**.

Part 5

Once a loan has been approved and finalized, a letter is sent to the client explaining the details of the loan. Use a letter template in Word to create a letter that is sent to the client. Copy and link the information in the **ExcelL1_C2_CS_P1.xlsx** worksheet to the client letter. Save the letter document and name it **WordDollarWiseLetter**. Print and then close **WordDollarWiseLetter.docx**.

Formatting an Excel Worksheet

PERFORMANCE OBJECTIVES

Upon successful completion of Chapter 3, you will be able to:

- Change column widths
- Change row heights
- Insert rows and columns in a worksheet
- Delete cells, rows, and columns in a worksheet
- Clear data in cells
- Apply formatting to data in cells
- Apply formatting to selected data using the Mini toolbar
- Preview a worksheet
- Apply a theme and customize the theme font and color
- Format numbers
- Repeat the last action
- Automate formatting with Format Painter
- Hide and unhide rows and columns

excel Chapter 3

Tutorial 3.1
Working with Excel
Tutorial 3.2
Enhancing the Appearance of a
Worksheet

The appearance of a worksheet on the screen and how it looks when printed is called the *format*. In Chapter 1, you learned how to apply formatting to a table with the Format as Table button in the Styles group in the Home tab and apply formatting to a cell or selected cells with the Cell Styles button. Other types of formatting you may want to apply to a worksheet include changing column width and row height; applying character formatting such as bold, italics, and underlining; specifying number formatting; inserting and deleting rows and columns; and applying borders, shading, and patterns to cells. You can also apply formatting to a worksheet with a theme. A theme is a set of formatting choices that include colors and fonts.

Note: Before beginning computer projects, copy to your storage medium the Excel2007L1C3 subfolder from the Excel2007L1 folder on the CD that accompanies this textbook and then make Excel2007L1C3 the active folder.

Project ① Format a Product Pricing Worksheet

You will open a workbook containing a worksheet with product pricing data, and then format the worksheet by changing column widths and row heights, inserting and deleting rows and columns, deleting rows and columns, and clearing data in cells. You will also apply font and alignment formatting to data in cells and then preview the worksheet.

Changing Column Width

Columns in a worksheet are the same width by default. In some worksheets you may want to change column widths to accommodate more or less data. You can change column width using the mouse on column boundaries or at a dialog box.

Changing Column Width Using Column Boundaries

You can use the mouse to change the width of a column or selected columns. For example, to change the width of column B, you would position the mouse pointer on the blue boundary line between columns B and C in the column header until the mouse pointer turns into a double-headed arrow pointing left and right and then drag the boundary to the right to increase the size or to the left to decrease the size.

HINT

To change the width of all columns in a worksheet, click the Select All button and then drag a column boundary to the desired position.

You can change the width of selected adjacent columns at the same time. To do this, select the columns and then drag one of the column boundaries within the selected columns. As you drag the boundary the column width changes for all selected columns. To select adjacent columns, position the cell pointer on the first desired column header (the mouse pointer turns into a black, down-pointing arrow), hold down the left mouse button, drag the cell pointer to the last desired column header, and then release the mouse button.

As a column boundary is being dragged, the column width displays in a box above the mouse pointer. The column width number that displays represents the average number of characters in the standard font that can fit in a cell.

A column width in an existing worksheet can be adjusted to fit the longest entry in the column. To automatically adjust a column width to the longest entry, position the cell pointer on the column boundary at the right side of the column and then double-click the left mouse button.

Project ⓛ Changing Column Width Using a Column Boundary

1. Open **ExcelC03Project01.xlsx**.
2. Save the workbook with Save As and name it **ExcelL1_C3_P1**.
3. Insert a formula in cell D2 that multiplies the price in cell B2 with the number in cell C2. Copy the formula in cell D2 down to cells D3 through D14.

4. Change the width of column D by completing the following steps:
   a. Position the mouse pointer on the column boundary in the column header between columns D and E until it turns into a double-headed arrow pointing left and right.
   b. Hold down the left mouse button, drag the column boundary to the right until *Width: 11.00 (82 pixels)* displays in the box, and then release the mouse button.

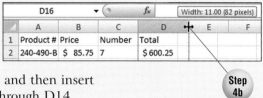

5. Make cell D15 active and then insert the sum of cells D2 through D14.

Step 4b

6. Change the width of columns A and B by completing the following steps:
   a. Select columns A and B. To do this, position the cell pointer on the column A header, hold down the left mouse button, drag the cell pointer to the column B header, and then release the mouse button.
   b. Position the cell pointer on the column boundary between columns A and B until it turns into a double-headed arrow pointing left and right.
   c. Hold down the left mouse button, drag the column boundary to the right until *Width: 10.14 (76 pixels)* displays in the box, and then release the mouse button.

Step 6c

7. Adjust the width of column C to accommodate the longest entry in the column by completing the following steps:
   a. Position the cell pointer on the column boundary between columns C and D until it turns into a double-headed arrow pointing left and right.
   b. Double-click the left mouse button.
8. Save **ExcelL1_C3_P1.xlsx**.

Changing Column Width at the Column Width Dialog Box

At the Column Width dialog box shown in Figure 3.1, you can specify a column width number. Increase the column width number to make the column wider or decrease the column width number to make the column narrower.

To display the Column Width dialog box, click the Format button in the Cells group in the Home tab and then click *Column Width* at the drop-down list. At the Column Width dialog box, type the number representing the average number of characters in the standard font that you want to fit in the column, and then press Enter or click OK.

Figure 3.1 Column Width Dialog Box

QUICK STEPS

Change Column Width
Drag column boundary line.
OR
Double-click column boundary.
OR
1. Click Format button.
2. Click *Column Width* at drop-down list.
3. Type desired width.
4. Click OK.

Type the column width in this text box.

Project 1b **Changing Column Width at the Column Width Dialog Box**

1. With **ExcelL1_C3_P1.xlsx** open, change the width of column A by completing the following steps:
   a. Make any cell in column A active.
   b. Click the Format button in the Cells group in the Home tab and then click *Column Width* at the drop-down list.
   c. At the Column Width dialog box, type **12.75** in the *Column width* text box.
   d. Click OK to close the dialog box.
2. Make any cell in column B active and then change the width of column B to *12.75* by completing steps similar to those in Step 1.
3. Make any cell in column C active and then change the width of column C to *8* by completing steps similar to those in Step 1.
4. Save **ExcelL1_C3_P1.xlsx**.

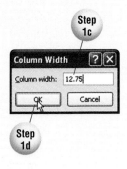

Step 1c

Step 1d

QUICK STEPS

Change Row Height
Drag row boundary line.
OR
1. Click Format button.
2. Click *Row Height* at drop-down list.
3. Type desired height.
4. Click OK.

Changing Row Height

Row height can be changed in much the same manner as column width. For example, you can change the row height using the mouse on a row boundary, or at the Row Height dialog box. Change row height using a row boundary in the same manner as you learned to change column width. To do this, position the cell pointer on the boundary between rows in the row header until it turns into a double-headed arrow pointing up and down, hold down the left mouse button, drag up or down until the row is the desired height, and then release the mouse button.

The height of selected rows that are adjacent can be changed at the same time. (The height of nonadjacent rows will not all change at the same time.) To do this, select the rows and then drag one of the row boundaries within the selected rows. As the boundary is being dragged the row height changes for all selected rows.

As a row boundary is being dragged, the row height displays in a box above the mouse pointer. The row height number that displays represents a point measurement. A vertical inch contains approximately 72 points. Increase the point size to increase the row height; decrease the point size to decrease the row height.

At the Row Height dialog box shown in Figure 3.2, you can specify a row height number. To display the Row Height dialog box, click the Format button in the Cells group in the Home tab and then click *Row Height* at the drop-down list.

HINT

To change the height of all rows in a worksheet, click the Select All button and then drag a row boundary to the desired position.

Figure 3.2 Row Height Dialog Box

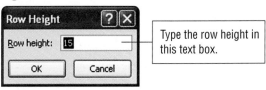

Type the row height in this text box.

1. With **ExcelL1_C3_P1.xlsx** open, change the height of row 1 by completing the following steps:
   a. Position the cell pointer in the row header on the row boundary between rows 1 and 2 until it turns into a double-headed arrow pointing up and down.
   b. Hold down the left mouse button, drag the row boundary down until *Height: 19.50 (26 pixels)* displays in the box, and then release the mouse button.
2. Change the height of rows 2 through 14 by completing the following steps:
   a. Select rows 2 through 14. To do this, position the cell pointer on the number 2 in the row header, hold down the left mouse button, drag the cell pointer to the number 14 in the row header, and then release the mouse button.
   b. Position the cell pointer on the row boundary between rows 2 and 3 until it turns into a double-headed arrow pointing up and down.
   c. Hold down the left mouse button, drag the row boundary down until *Height: 16.50 (22 pixels)* displays in the box, and then release the mouse button.
3. Change the height of row 15 by completing the following steps:
   a. Make cell A15 active.
   b. Click the Format button in the Cells group in the Home tab and then click *Row Height* at the drop-down list.
   c. At the Row Height dialog box, type 20 in the *Row height* text box, and then click OK.
4. Save **ExcelL1_C3_P1.xlsx**.

Step 1b

Step 2c

Step 3c

Inserting/Deleting Cells, Rows, and Columns

New data may need to be included in an existing worksheet. For example, a row or several rows of new data may need to be inserted into a worksheet, or data may need to be removed from a worksheet.

Inserting Rows

After you create a worksheet, you can add (insert) rows to the worksheet. Insert a row with the Insert button in the Cells group in the Home tab or with options at the Insert dialog box. By default, a row is inserted above the row containing the active cell. To insert a row in a worksheet, select the row below where the row is to be inserted, and then click the Insert button. If you want to insert more than one row, select the number of rows in the worksheet that you want inserted and then click the Insert button.

HINT

When you insert rows in a worksheet, all references affected by the insertion are automatically adjusted.

Insert Row
Click Insert button.
OR
1. Click Insert button arrow.
2. Click *Insert Sheet Rows* at drop-down list.
OR
1. Click Insert button arrow.
2. Click *Insert Cells.*
3. Click *Entire row* in dialog box.
4. Click OK.

You can also insert a row by making a cell active in the row below where the row is to be inserted, clicking the Insert button arrow, and then clicking *Insert Sheet Rows*. Another method for inserting a row is to click the Insert button arrow and then click *Insert Cells*. This displays the Insert dialog box as shown in Figure 3.3. At the Insert dialog box, click *Entire row*. This inserts a row above the active cell.

Figure 3.3 Insert Dialog Box

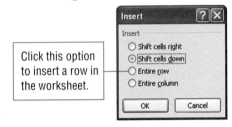

Click this option to insert a row in the worksheet.

Project ⑩ Inserting Rows

1. With **ExcelL1_C3_P1.xlsx** open, insert two rows at the beginning of the worksheet by completing the following steps:
   a. Make cell A1 active.
   b. Click the Insert button arrow in the Cells group in the Home tab.
   c. At the drop-down list that displays, click *Insert Sheet Rows*.
   d. With cell A1 active, click the Insert button arrow and then click *Insert Sheet Rows* at the drop-down list.

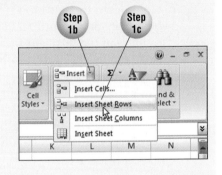

2. Type the text **Capstan Marine Products** in cell A1.
3. Make cell A2 active and then type **Purchasing Department**.
4. Change the height of row 1 to *42.00 (56 pixels)*.
5. Change the height of row 2 to *21.00 (28 pixels)*.
6. Insert two rows by completing the following steps:
   a. Select rows 7 and 8 in the worksheet.
   b. Click the Insert button in the Cells group in the Home tab.

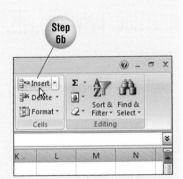

7. Type the following data in the specified cells (you do not need to type the dollar sign in cells containing money amounts):

   A7 = 855-495
   B7 = 42.75
   C7 = 5
   A8 = ST039
   B8 = 12.99
   C8 = 25

8. Make D6 the active cell and then use the fill handle to copy the formula down to cells D7 and D8.
9. Save **ExcelL1_C3_P1.xlsx**.

Inserting Columns

Insert columns in a worksheet in much the same way as rows. Insert a column with options from the Insert button drop-down list or with options at the Insert dialog box. By default, a column is inserted immediately to the left of the column containing the active cell. To insert a column in a worksheet, make a cell active in the column immediately to the right of where the new column is to be inserted, click the Insert button arrow and then click *Insert Sheet Columns* at the drop-down list. If you want to insert more than one column, select the number of columns in the worksheet that you want inserted, click the Insert button arrow and then click *Insert Sheet Columns*.

You can also insert a column by making a cell active in the column immediately to the right of where the new column is to be inserted, clicking the Insert button arrow, and then clicking *Insert Cells* at the drop-down list. This causes the Insert dialog box to display. At the Insert dialog box, click *Entire column*. This inserts an entire column immediately to the left of the active cell.

Excel includes an especially helpful and time-saving feature related to inserting columns. When you insert columns in a worksheet, all references affected by the insertion are automatically adjusted.

QUICK STEPS

Insert Column
Click Insert button.
OR
1. Click Insert button arrow.
2. Click *Insert Sheet Columns* at drop-down list.
OR
1. Click Insert button arrow.
2. Click *Insert Cells*.
3. Click *Entire column*.
4. Click OK.

Project 1e   Inserting a Column

1. With **ExcelL1_C3_P1.xlsx** open, insert a column by completing the following steps:
   a. Click in any cell in column A.
   b. Click the Insert button arrow in the Cells group in the Home tab and then click *Insert Sheet Columns* at the drop-down list.
2. Type the following data in the specified cell:
   A3 = Company
   A4 = RD Manufacturing
   A8 = Smithco, Inc.
   A11 = Sunrise Corporation
   A15 = Geneva Systems
3. Make cell A1 active and then adjust the width of column A to accommodate the longest entry.
4. Insert another column by completing the following steps:
   a. Make cell B1 active.
   b. Click the Insert button arrow and then click *Insert Cells* at the drop-down list.
   c. At the Insert dialog box, click *Entire column*.
   d. Click OK.
5. Type **Date** in cell B3 and then press Enter.
6. Save **ExcelL1_C3_P1.xlsx**.

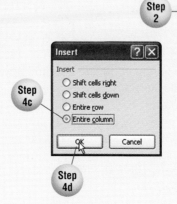

Deleting Cells, Rows, or Columns

You can delete specific cells in a worksheet or rows or columns in a worksheet. To delete a row, select the row and then click the Delete button in the Cells group in the Home tab. To delete a column, select the column and then click the Delete button. Delete a specific cell by making the cell active, clicking the Delete button arrow, and then clicking *Delete Cells* at the drop-down list. This displays the Delete dialog box shown in Figure 3.4. At the Delete dialog box, specify what you want deleted, and then click OK. You can also delete adjacent cells by selecting the cells and then displaying the Delete Cells dialog box.

Figure 3.4 Delete Dialog Box

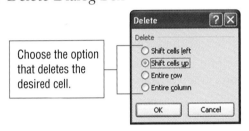

Choose the option that deletes the desired cell.

Clear

Clearing Data in Cells

If you want to delete cell contents but not the cell, make the cell active or select desired cells and then press the Delete key. A quick method for clearing the contents of a cell is to right-click the cell and then click *Clear Contents* at the shortcut menu. Another method for deleting cell contents is to make the cell active or select desired cells, click the Clear button in the Editing group in the Home tab, and then click *Clear Contents* at the drop-down list.

With the options at the Clear button drop-down list you can clear the contents of the cell or selected cells as well as formatting and comments. Click the *Clear Formats* option to remove formatting from cells or selected cells while leaving the data. You can also click the *Clear All* option to clear the contents of the cell or selected cells as well as the formatting.

Project ⑪ Deleting and Clearing Rows in a Worksheet

1. With **ExcelL1_C3_P1.xlsx** open, delete column B in the worksheet by completing the following steps:
   a. Click in any cell in column B.
   b. Click the Delete button arrow in the Cells group in the Home tab and then click *Delete Sheet Columns* at the drop-down list.
2. Delete row 5 by completing the following steps:
   a. Select row 5.
   b. Click the Delete button in the Cells group.

Step 1b

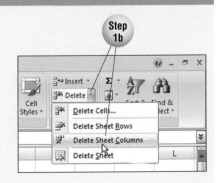

3. Clear row contents by completing the following steps:
   a. Select rows 7 and 8.
   b. Click the Clear button in the Editing group in the Home tab and then click *Clear Contents* at the drop-down list.

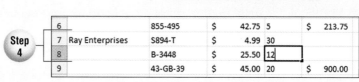

4. Type the following data in the specified cell:

A7	=	**Ray Enterprises**
B7	=	**S894-T**
C7	=	**4.99**
D7	=	**30**
B8	=	**B-3448**
C8	=	**25.50**
D8	=	**12**

6		855-495	$	42.75	5	$	213.75
7	Ray Enterprises	S894-T	$	4.99	30		
8		B-3448	$	25.50	12		
9		43-GB-39	$	45.00	20	$	900.00

5. Make cell E6 active and then copy the formula down to cells E7 and E8.
6. Save **ExcelL1_C3_P1.xlsx**.

Applying Formatting

With many of the groups in the Home tab you can apply formatting to text in the active cells or selected cells. Use buttons in the Font group to apply font formatting to text and use buttons in the Alignment group to apply alignment formatting to text.

Applying Font Formatting

You can apply a variety of formatting to cells in a worksheet with buttons in the Font group in the Home tab. With buttons in the Font group shown in Figure 3.5, you can change the font, font size, and font color; bold, italicize, and underline data in cells; change the text color; and apply a border or add fill to cells.

Figure 3.5 Font Group

Use buttons in the font group to apply formatting to cells or data in cells.

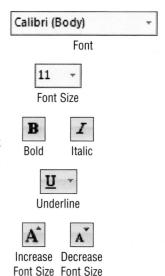

Use the Font button in the Font group to change the font of text in a cell and use the Font Size button to specify size for the text. Apply bold formatting to text in a cell with the Bold button, italic formatting with the Italic button, and underlining with the Underline button.

Click the Increase Font Size button and the text in the active cell or selected cells increases from 11 points to 12 points. Click the Increase Font Size button again and the font size increases to 14. Each additional time you click the button, the font size increases by two points. Click the Decrease Font Size button and text in the active cell or selected cells decreases in point size.

Border

Fill Color

Font Color

With the Borders button in the Font group, you can insert a border on any or all sides of the active cell or any or all sides of selected cells. The name of the button changes depending on the most recent border applied to a cell or selected cells. Use the Fill Color button to insert color in the active cell or in selected cells. With the Font Color button, you can change the color of text within a cell.

Formatting with the Mini Toolbar

Double-click in a cell and then select data within the cell and the Mini toolbar displays in a dimmed fashion above the selected data. Hover the mouse pointer over the Mini toolbar and it becomes active. The Mini toolbar contains buttons for applying font formatting such as font, font size, and font color as well as bold and italic formatting. Click a button on the Mini toolbar to apply formatting to selected text.

Applying Alignment Formatting

Merge & Center

Orientation

Wrap Text

The alignment of data in cells depends on the type of data entered. Enter words or text combined with numbers in a cell and the text is aligned at the left edge of the cell. Enter numbers in a cell and the numbers are aligned at the right side of the cell. Use options in the Alignment group to align text at the left, center, or right side of the cell; align text at the top, center, or bottom of the cell; increase and/or decrease the indent of text; and change the orientation of text in a cell. Click the Merge & Center button to merge selected cells and center data within the merged cells. If you have merged cells and want to split them again, select the cells and then click the Merge & Center button.

Click the Orientation button to rotate data in a cell. Click the Orientation button and a drop-down list displays with options for rotating text in a cell. If data typed in a cell is longer than the cell, it overlaps the next cell to the right. If you want data to remain in a cell and wrap to the next line within the same cell, click the Wrap Text button in the Alignment group.

Project **1g** | **Applying Font and Alignment Formatting**

1. With **ExcelL1_C3_P1.xlsx** open, make cell B1 active and then click the Wrap Text button in the Alignment group in the Home tab. (This wraps the company name within the cell.)
2. Make cell B2 active and then click the Wrap Text button.
3. Instead of wrapping text within cells, you decide to spread out the text over several cells and vertically align text in cells by completing the following steps:
   a. Select cells A1 through E1.
   b. Click the Merge & Center button in the Alignment group in the Home tab.
   c. Click the Middle Align button in the Alignment group.
   d. Select cells A2 through E2, click the Merge & Center button, and then click the Middle Align button.

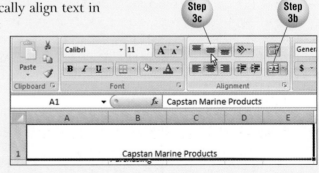

4. Rotate text in the third row by completing the following steps:
   a. Select cells A3 through E3.
   b. Click the Orientation button in the Alignment group and then click *Angle Counterclockwise* at the drop-down list.
   c. After looking at the rotated text, you decide to return the orientation back to the horizontal by clicking the Undo button on the Quick Access toolbar.
5. Change the font, font size, and font color for text in specific cells by completing the following steps:
   a. Make cell A1 active.
   b. Click the Font button arrow in the Font group in the Home tab, scroll down the drop-down gallery, and then click *Bookman Old Style*.

Step 4b

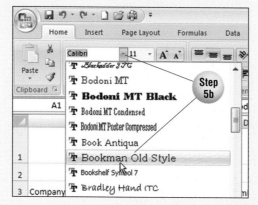

Step 5b

   c. Click the Font Size button arrow in the Font group and then click *22* at the drop-down gallery.
   d. Click the Font Color button arrow and then click *Dark Blue* in the *Standard* section of the drop-down color palette.
6. Make cell A2 active and then complete steps similar to those in Step 5 to change the font to Bookman Old Style, the font size to 16, and the font color to Dark Blue.
7. Select cells A3 through E3 and then click the Center button in the Alignment group.
8. With cells A3 through E3 still selected, click the Bold button in the Font group and then click the Italic button.
9. Select cells A3 through E18 and then change the font to Bookman Old Style.
10. Apply formatting to selected data using the Mini toolbar by completing the following steps:
    a. Double-click cell A4.
    b. Select the letters *RD*. (This displays the dimmed Mini toolbar above the selected word.)
    c. Click the Increase Font Size button on the Mini toolbar.

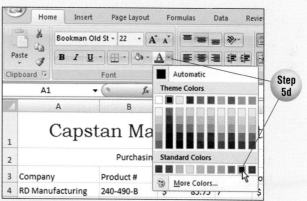

Step 5d

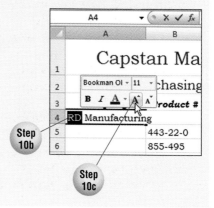

Step 10b

Step 10c

   d. Double-click cell A14.

   e. Select the word *Geneva* and then click the Italic button on the Mini toolbar.

11. Adjust columns A through E to accommodate the longest entry in each column.

12. Select cells D4 through D17 and then click the Center button in the Alignment group.

13. Add a double-line bottom border to cell A2 by completing the following steps:

   a. Make cell A2 active.

   b. Click the Borders button arrow in the Font group in the Home tab.

   c. Click the *Bottom Double Border* option at the drop-down list.

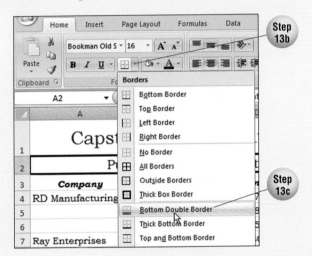

14. Add a single-line bottom border to cells A3 through E3 by completing the following steps:

   a. Select cells A3 through E3.

   b. Click the Borders button arrow and then click the *Bottom Border* option.

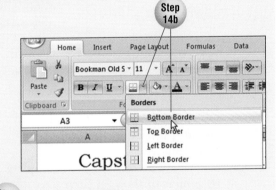

15. Apply fill color to specific cells by completing the following steps:

   a. Select cells A1 through E3.

   b. Click the Fill Color button arrow in the Font group.

   c. Click the *Aqua, Accent 5, Lighter 80%* color option.

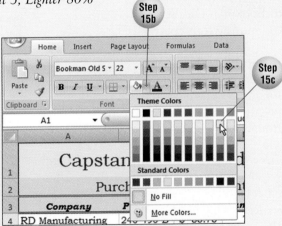

16. Save **ExcelL1_C3_P1.xlsx**.

Previewing a Worksheet

Before printing a worksheet, consider previewing it to see how it will appear when printed. To preview a worksheet, click the Office button, point to the *Print* option, and then click the *Print Preview* option. You can also display a worksheet in Print Preview by clicking the Preview button that displays in the lower left corner of the Print dialog box. A document displays in Print Preview as it will appear when printed. Figure 3.6 displays the **ExcelL1_C3_P1.xlsx** worksheet in Print Preview. Notice that the gridlines in the worksheet do not print.

Figure 3.6 Worksheet in Print Preview

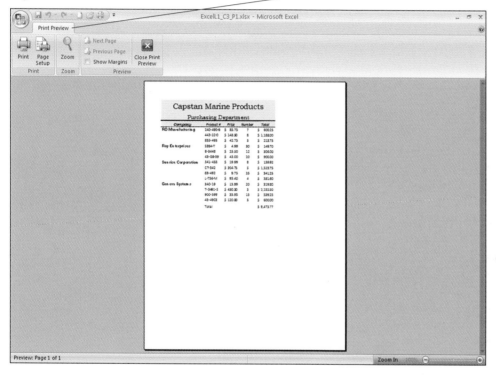

To zoom in on the worksheet, position the mouse pointer (displays as a magnifying glass) in the worksheet text and then click the left mouse button. You can also click the Zoom In option located at the left slide of the Zoom slider bar located at the right side of the Status bar (lower right corner of the Excel window). Click the Print button in the Print Preview tab to send the worksheet to the printer. Click the Page Setup button in the Print Preview tab and the Page Setup dialog box displays with options for changing the paper size and orientation of the page. Insert a check mark in the *Show Margins* check box and margin boundary lines display around the worksheet. Insert a check mark in the *Show Margins* check box and you can change worksheet margins by dragging margin borders. Close Print Preview by clicking the Close Print Preview button.

Preview a Worksheet
1. Click Office button.
2. Point to *Print*.
3. Click *Print Preview*.

Changing the Zoom Setting

HINT

Click the zoom percentage at the left side of the Zoom slider bar to display the Zoom dialog box.

Zoom Out   Zoom In

In Print Preview, you can zoom in on the worksheet and make the display bigger. You can also change the size of worksheet display in Normal view using the Zoom slider bar that displays at the right side of the Status bar. To change the percentage of display, drag the button on the Zoom slider bar to increase or decrease the percentage of display. You can also click the Zoom Out button located at the left side of the slider bar to decrease the percentage of display or click the Zoom In button located at the right side of the slider bar to increase the percentage of display.

Project 1h   Previewing a Worksheet

1. With **ExcelL1_C3_P1.xlsx** open, click the Office button, point to the *Print* option, and then click the *Print Preview* option.
2. At the print preview screen, click in the worksheet. (This increases the display of the worksheet cells.)
3. After viewing the worksheet, click the Close Print Preview button.
4. At the worksheet, drag the button on the Zoom slider bar to the right until the zoom displays as 190%. (The percentage amount displays at the left side of the slider.)
5. After viewing the worksheet at 190% display, click the Zoom Out button located at the left side of the slider until the display percentage is 100%.

6. Save, print, and then close **ExcelL1_C3_P1.xlsx**.

Project 2   Apply a Theme to a Payroll Worksheet

You will open a workbook containing a worksheet with payroll information and then insert text, apply formatting to cells and cell contents, apply a theme, and then change the theme font and colors.

Applying a Theme

Excel provides a number of themes you can use to format text and cells in a worksheet. A theme is a set of formatting choices that include a color theme (a set of colors), a font theme (a set of heading and body text fonts), and an effects theme (a set of lines and fill effects). To apply a theme, click the Page Layout tab and then click the Themes button in the Themes group. At the drop-down gallery that displays, click the desired theme. Position the mouse pointer over a theme and the *live preview* feature will display the worksheet with the theme formatting applied. With the live preview feature you can see how the theme formatting affects your worksheet before you make your final choice.

Project ❷ Applying a Theme

1. Open **ExcelC03Project02.xlsx** and then save it and name it **ExcelL1_C3_P2**.
2. Make G4 the active cell and then insert a formula that calculates the amount of Social Security tax (multiply the gross pay amount in E4 with the Social Security rate in cell H11 [you will need to use the mixed cell reference H$11 when writing the formula]).
3. Copy the formula in cell G4 down to cells G5 through G9.
4. Make H4 the active cell and then insert a formula that calculates the net pay (gross pay minus withholding and Social Security tax).
5. Automatically adjust the width of column H.
6. Copy the formula in H4 down to cells H5 through H9.
7. Increase the height of row 1 to 36.00.
8. Make A1 the active cell, click the Middle Align button in the Alignment group, click the Font Size button arrow and click *18* at the drop-down list, and then click the Bold button.
9. Type **Stanton & Barnett Associates** in cell A1.
10. Select cells A2 through H3 and then click the Bold button in the Font group.
11. Apply a theme and customize the font and colors by completing the following steps:
    a. Click the Page Layout tab.
    b. Click the Themes button in the Themes group and then click *Aspect* at the drop-down gallery. (You might want to point the mouse to various themes to see how the theme formatting affects the worksheet).

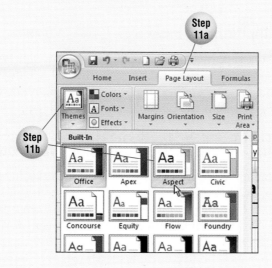

c. Click the Colors button in the Themes group and then click *Flow* at the drop-down gallery.
d. Click the Fonts button in the Themes group, scroll down the drop-down gallery, and then click *Opulent*.

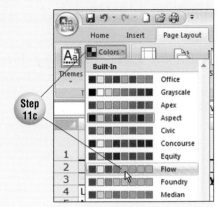

Step 11c

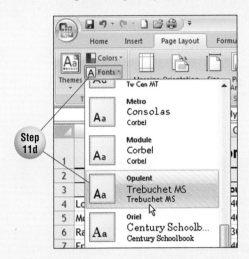

Step 11d

12. Select columns A through H and then adjust the width of the columns to accommodate the longest entries.
13. Save, print, and then close **ExcelL1_C3_P2.xlsx**.

Project 3 Format an Invoices Worksheet

You will open a workbook containing an invoice worksheet and apply number formatting to numbers in cells.

Formatting Numbers

Numbers in a cell, by default, are aligned at the right and decimals and commas do not display unless they are typed in the cell. Change the format of numbers with buttons in the Number group in the Home tab or with options at the Format Cells dialog box with the Number tab selected.

Formatting Numbers Using Number Group Buttons

Format symbols you can use to format numbers include a percent sign (%), a comma (,), and a dollar sign ($). For example, if you type the number *$45.50* in a cell, Excel automatically applies Currency formatting to the number. If you type *45%*, Excel automatically applies the Percent formatting to the number. The Number group in the Home tab contains five buttons you can use to format numbers in cells. The five buttons are shown and described in Table 3.1.

Table 3.1 Number Formatting Buttons on Formatting Toolbar

	Click this button	To do this
$\boxed{\$\ \blacktriangledown}$	Accounting Number Format	Add a dollar sign, any necessary commas, and a decimal point followed by two decimal digits, if none are typed; right-align number in cell
$\boxed{\%}$	Percent Style	Multiply cell value by 100 and display result with a percent symbol; right-align number in cell
$\boxed{,}$	Comma Style	Add any necessary commas and a decimal point followed by two decimal digits, if none are typed; right-align number in cell
$\boxed{{}^{+.0}_{.00}}$	Increase Decimal	Increase number of decimal places displayed after decimal point in selected cells
$\boxed{{}^{.00}_{\to.0}}$	Decrease Decimal	Decrease number of decimal places displayed after decimal point in selected cells

Specify the formatting for numbers in cells in a worksheet before typing the numbers, or format existing numbers in a worksheet. The Increase Decimal and Decrease Decimal buttons in the Number group in the Home tab will change decimal places for existing numbers only.

Increase Decrease
Decimal Decimal

The Number group in the Home tab also contains the Number Format button. Click the Number Format button arrow and a drop-down list displays of common number formats. Click the desired format at the drop-down list to apply the number formatting to the cell or selected cells.

Number Format

Project ③a Formatting Numbers with Buttons in the Number Group

1. Open **ExcelC03Project03.xlsx**.
2. Save the workbook with Save As and name it **ExcelL1_C3_P3**.
3. Make the following changes to column widths:
   a. Change the width of column C to 17.00.
   b. Change the width of column D to 10.00.
   c. Change the width of column E to 7.00.
   d. Change the width of column F to 12.00.
4. Select row 1 and then click the Insert button in the Cells group.
5. Change the height of row 1 to 42.00.
6. Select cells A1 through F1 and then make the following changes:
   a. Click the Merge & Center button in the Alignment group.
   b. With cell A1 active, change the font size to 24 points.
   c. Click the Fill Color button arrow in the Font group and then click *Olive Green, Accent 3, Lighter 80%*.

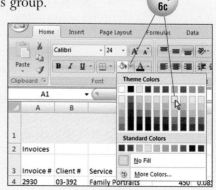

Step 6c

d. Click the Borders button arrow in the Font group and then click the *Top and Thick Bottom Border* option.

e. With cell A1 active, type **REAL PHOTOGRAPHY** and then press Enter.

7. Change the height of row 2 to 24.00.

8. Select cells A2 through F2 and then make the following changes:

a. Click the Merge & Center button in the Alignment group.

b. With cell A2 active, change the font size to 18.

c. Click the Fill Color button in the Font group. (This will fill the cell with light green color.)

d. Click the Borders button arrow in the Font group and then click the *Bottom Border* option.

9. Make the following changes to row 3:

a. Change the height of row 3 to 18.00.

b. Select cells A3 through F3, click the Bold button in the Font group, and then click the Center button in the Alignment group.

c. With the cells still selected, click the Borders button arrow and then click the *Bottom Border* option.

10. Make the following number formatting changes:

a. Select cells E4 through E16 and then click the *Percent Style* button in the Number group.

b. With the cells still selected, click once on the Increase Decimal button in the Number group. (The percent numbers should contain one decimal place.)

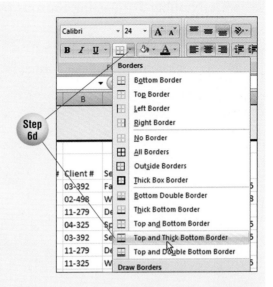

Step 6d

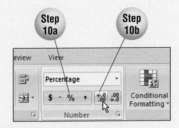

Step 10a   Step 10b

c. Select cells A4 through B16.

d. Click the Number Format button arrow, scroll down the drop-down list, and then click *Text*.

e. With A4 through B16 still selected, click the Center button in the Alignment group.

11. Save **ExcelL1_C3_P3.xlsx**.

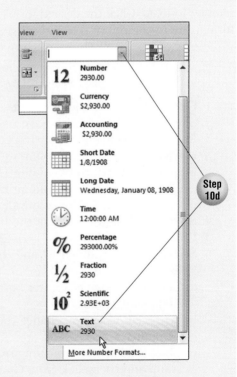

Step 10d

Formatting Numbers Using the Format Cells Dialog Box

Along with buttons in the Number group, you can format numbers with options at the Format Cells dialog box with the Number tab selected as shown in Figure 3.7. Display this dialog box by clicking the Number group dialog box launcher or by clicking the Number Format button arrow and then clicking *More Number Formats* at the drop-down list. The left side of the dialog box displays number categories with a default category of *General*. At this setting no specific formatting is applied to numbers except right-aligning numbers in cells. The other number categories are described in Table 3.2.

Figure 3.7 Format Cells Dialog Box with Number Tab Selected

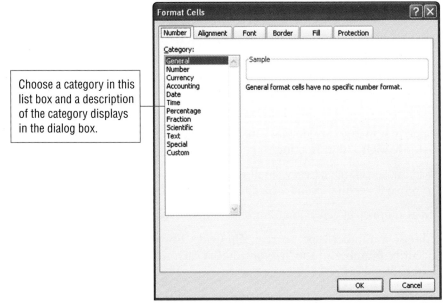

Choose a category in this list box and a description of the category displays in the dialog box.

Table 3.2 Number Categories at the Format Cells Dialog Box

Click this category	To apply this number formatting
Number	Specify number of decimal places and whether or not a thousand separator should be used; choose the display of negative numbers; right-align numbers in cell.
Currency	Apply general monetary values; dollar sign is added as well as commas and decimal points, if needed; right-align numbers in cell.
Accounting	Line up the currency symbol and decimal points in a column; add dollar sign and two digits after a decimal point; right-align numbers in cell.
Date	Display date as date value; specify the type of formatting desired by clicking an option in the *Type* list box; right-align date in cell.
Time	Display time as time value; specify the type of formatting desired by clicking an option in the *Type* list box; right-align time in cell.
Percentage	Multiply cell value by 100 and display result with a percent symbol; add decimal point followed by two digits by default; number of digits can be changed with the *Decimal places* option; right-align number in cell.
Fraction	Specify how fraction displays in cell by clicking an option in the *Type* list box; right-align fraction in cell.
Scientific	Use for very large or very small numbers. Use the letter *E* to tell Excel to move a decimal point a specified number of positions.
Text	Treat number in cell as text; number is displayed in cell exactly as typed.
Special	Choose a number type, such as Zip Code, Phone Number, or Social Security Number in the *Type* option list box; useful for tracking list and database values.
Custom	Specify a numbering type by choosing an option in the *Type* list box.

Project 3b Formatting Numbers at the Format Cells Dialog Box

1. With **ExcelL1_C3_P3.xlsx** open, make cell F4 active and then insert the following formula: =(D4*E4)+D4.
2. Make cell F4 active and then copy the formula down to cells F5 through F16.
3. Change number formatting by completing the following steps:
   a. Select cells D4 through D16.
   b. Click the Number group dialog box launcher.

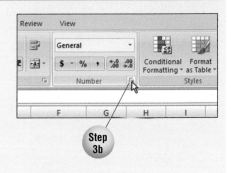

Step 3b

c. At the Format Cells dialog box with the Number tab selected, click *Accounting* in the *Category* section.

d. Make sure a *2* displays in the *Decimal places* option box and a dollar sign *$* displays in the *Symbol* option box.

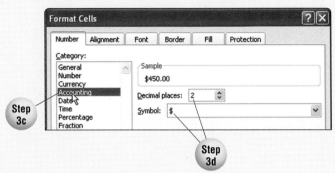

e. Click OK.

4. Apply Accounting formatting to cells F4 through F16 by completing steps similar to those in Step 3.

5. Save, print, and then close **ExcelL1_C3_P3.xlsx**.

Project 4 Format a Company Budget Worksheet

You will open a workbook containing a company budget worksheet and then apply formatting to cells with options at the Format Cells dialog box, use the Format Painter to apply formatting, and hide and unhide rows and columns in the worksheet.

Formatting Cells Using the Format Cells Dialog Box

In the previous section, you learned how to format numbers with options at the Format Cells dialog box with the Number tab selected. This dialog box contains a number of other tabs you can select to format cells.

Aligning and Indenting Data

You can align and indent data in cells using buttons in the Alignment group in the Home tab or with options at the Format Cells dialog box with the Alignment tab selected as shown in Figure 3.8. Display this dialog box by clicking the Alignment group dialog box launcher.

Figure 3.8 Format Cells Dialog Box with Alignment Tab Selected

Specify horizontal and vertical alignment with options in this section.

Use options in this section to control how text fits in a cell.

Rotate text in a cell by clicking a point on the arc or by entering a number in the *Degrees* text box.

In the *Orientation* section, you can choose to rotate data. A portion of the *Orientation* section shows points on an arc. Click a point on the arc to rotate the text along that point. You can also type a rotation degree in the *Degrees* text box. Type a positive number to rotate selected text from the lower left to the upper right of the cell. Type a negative number to rotate selected text from the upper left to the lower right of the cell.

If data typed in a cell is longer than the cell, it overlaps the next cell to the right. If you want data to remain in a cell and wrap to the next line within the same cell, click the *Wrap text* option in the *Text control* section of the dialog box. Click the *Shrink to fit* option to reduce the size of the text font so all selected data fits within the column. Use the *Merge cells* option to combine two or more selected cells into a single cell.

If you want to enter data on more than one line within a cell, enter the data on the first line and then press Alt + Enter. Pressing Alt + Enter moves the insertion point to the next line within the same cell.

Project 4a Aligning and Rotating Data in Cells

1. Open **ExcelC03Project04.xlsx**.
2. Save the workbook with Save As and name it **ExcelL1_C3_P4**.
3. Make the following changes to the worksheet:
   a. Insert a new row at the beginning of the worksheet.
   b. Change the height of row 1 to 66.00.
   c. Merge and center cells A1 through E1.
   d. Type **Harris & Briggs** in cell A1 and then press Alt + Enter. (This moves the insertion point down to the next line in the same cell.)
   e. Type **Construction** and then press Enter.
   f. With cell A2 active, type **Preferred**, press Alt + Enter, type **Customer**, and then press Enter.

g. Change the width of column A to 20.00.

h. Change the width of column B to 7.00.

i. Change the width of columns C, D, and E to 10.00.

4. Change number formatting for specific cells by completing the following steps:

a. Select cells C3 through E11.

b. Click the Number group dialog box launcher.

c. At the Format Cells dialog box with the Number tab selected, click *Accounting* in the *Category* section.

d. Click the down-pointing arrow at the right side of the *Decimal places* option until *0* displays.

e. Make sure a dollar sign *$* displays in the *Symbol* option box.

f. Click OK.

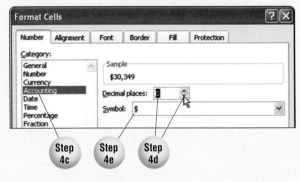

Step 4c Step 4e Step 4d

5. Make cell E3 active and then insert a formula that subtracts the *Planned* amount from the *Actual* amount. Copy this formula down to cells E4 through E11.

6. Change the orientation of data in cells by completing the following steps:

a. Select cells B2 through E2.

b. Click the Alignment group dialog box launcher.

c. At the Format Cells dialog box with the Alignment tab selected, select *0* in the *Degrees* text box and then type 45.

d. Click OK.

7. Change the vertical alignment of text in cells by completing the following steps:

a. Select cells A1 through E2.

b. Click the Alignment group dialog box launcher.

c. At the Format Cells dialog box with the Alignment tab selected, click the down-pointing arrow at the right side of the *Vertical* alignment option.

d. Click *Center* at the drop-down list.

e. Click OK.

8. Change the horizontal alignment of text in cells by completing the following steps:

a. Select cells A2 through E2.

b. Click the Alignment group dialog box launcher.

c. At the Format Cells dialog box with the Alignment tab selected, click the down-pointing arrow at the right side of the *Horizontal* alignment option.

d. Click *Center* at the drop-down list.

e. Click OK.

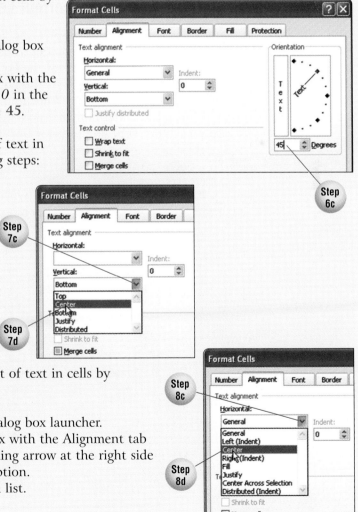

Step 6c

Step 7c

Step 7d

Step 8c

Step 8d

9. Change the horizontal alignment and indent of
   text in cells by completing the following steps:
   a. Select cells B3 through B11.
   b. Click the Alignment group dialog box launcher.
   c. At the Format Cells dialog box with the
      Alignment tab selected, click the down-pointing
      arrow at the right side of the *Horizontal*
      alignment option and then click *Right (Indent)* at
      the drop-down list.
   d. Click once on the up-pointing arrow at the right
      side of the *Indent* option box (this displays *1* in
      the box).
   e. Click OK.
10. Save **ExcelL1_C3_P4.xlsx**.

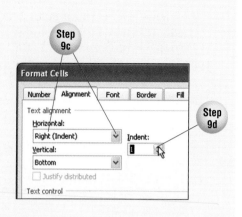

Changing the Font at the Format Cells Dialog Box

As you learned earlier in this chapter, the Font group in the Home tab contains
buttons for applying font formatting to data in cells. You can also change the
font for data in cells with options at the Format Cells dialog box with the Font tab
selected as shown in Figure 3.9. At the Format Cells dialog box with the Font
tab selected, you can change the font, font style, font size, and font color. You
can also change the underlining method and add effects such as superscript and
subscript. Click the Font group dialog box launcher to display this dialog box.

Figure 3.9 Format Cells Dialog Box with Font Tab Selected

1. With **ExcelL1_C3_P4.xlsx** open,
   change the font and font color by
   completing the following steps:
   a. Select cells A1 through E11.
   b. Click the Font group dialog box
      launcher.
   c. At the Format Cells dialog
      box with the Font tab
      selected, click *Garamond* in
      the *Font* list box (you will need
      to scroll down the list to make
      this font visible).
   d. Click *12* in the *Size* list box.
   e. Click the down-pointing arrow at
      the right of the *Color* option box.
   f. At the palette of color choices
      that displays, click the *Dark Red*
      color (first color option from the
      left in the *Standard Colors*
      section).
   g. Click OK to close the dialog box.
2. Make cell A1 active and then change the font to
   24-point Garamond bold.
3. Select cells A2 through E2 and then apply bold formatting.
4. Save and then print **ExcelL1_C3_P4.xlsx**.

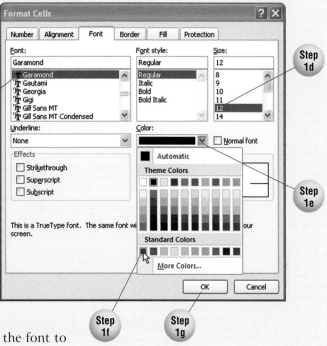

Adding Borders to Cells

The gridlines that display in a worksheet do not print. As you learned earlier in
this chapter, you can use the Borders button in the Font group to add borders to
cells that will print. You can also add borders to cells with options at the Format
Cells dialog box with the Border tab selected as shown in Figure 3.10. Display this
dialog box by clicking the Borders button arrow in the Font group and then clicking
More Borders at the drop-down list.

With options in the *Presets* section, you can remove borders with the *None*
option, add only outside borders with the *Outline* option, or click the *Inside* option
to add borders to the inside of selected cells. In the *Border* section of the dialog box,
specify the side of the cell or selected cells to which you want to apply a border.
Choose the style of line desired for the border with the options that display in the
Style list box. Add color to border lines with choices from the color palette that
displays when you click the down-pointing arrow located at the right side of the
Color option box.

QUICK STEPS

Add Borders to Cells
1. Select cells.
2. Click Borders button
   arrow.
3. Click desired border.
OR
1. Select cells.
2. Click Borders button
   arrow.
3. Click *More Borders*.
4. Use options in dialog
   box to apply desired
   border.
5. Click OK.

Figure 3.10 Format Cells Dialog Box with Border Tab Selected

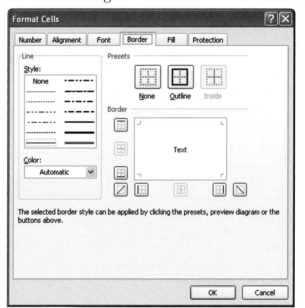

Project 4c Adding Borders to Cells

1. With **ExcelL1_C3_P4.xlsx** open, remove the 45 degrees orientation you applied in Project 4a by completing the following steps:
   a. Select cells B2 through E2.
   b. Click the Alignment group dialog box launcher.
   c. At the Format Cells dialog box with the Alignment tab selected, select *45* in the *Degrees* text box and then type 0.
   d. Click OK.

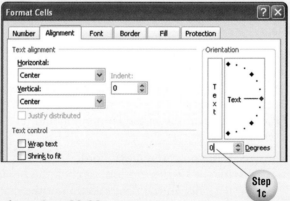

Step 1c

2. Change the height of row 2 to 33.00.
3. Add a thick, dark red border line to cells by completing the following steps:
   a. Select cells A1 through E11 (cells containing data).
   b. Click the Border button arrow in the Font group and then click the *More Borders* option at the drop-down list.

c. At the Format Cells dialog box with the Border tab selected, click the down-pointing arrow at the right side of the *Color* option and then click *Dark Red* at the color palette (first color option from the left in the *Standard Colors* section).

d. Click the thick single line option located in the second column (sixth option from the top) in the *Style* option box in the *Line* section.

e. Click the *Outline* option in the *Presets* section.

f. Click OK.

4. Add a border above and below cells by completing the following steps:

a. Select cells A2 through E2.

b. Click the Border button arrow in the Font group and then click *More Borders* at the drop-down list.

c. At the Format Cells dialog box with the Border tab selected, make sure the color is Dark Red.

d. Make sure the thick single line option (sixth option from the top in the second column) is selected in the *Style* option box in the *Line* section.

e. Click the top border of the sample cell in the *Border* section of the dialog box.

f. Click the double-line option (bottom option in the second column) in the *Style* option box.

g. Click the bottom border of the sample cell in the *Border* section of the dialog box.

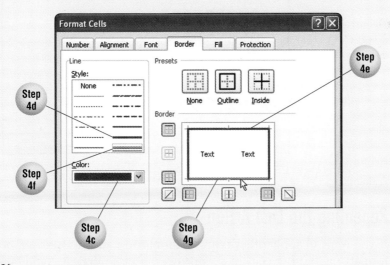

h. Click OK.

5. Save **ExcelL1_C3_P4.xlsx**.

Adding Fill and Shading to Cells

Add Shading to Cells
1. Select cells.
2. Click Fill Color button arrow.
3. Click desired color.
OR
1. Select cells.
2. Click Format button.
3. Click *Format Cells* at drop-down list.
4. Click Fill tab.
5. Use options in dialog box to apply desired shading.
6. Click OK.

To enhance the visual display of cells and data within cells, consider adding fill and/or shading to cells. As you learned earlier in this chapter, you can add fill color to cells with the Fill Color button in the Font group. You can also add fill color and/or shading to cells in a worksheet with options at the Format Cells dialog box with the Fill tab selected as shown in Figure 3.11. Display the Format Cells dialog box by clicking the Format button in the Cells group and then clicking *Format Cells* at the drop-down list. You can also display the dialog box by clicking the Font group, Alignment group, or Number group dialog box launcher. At the Format Cells dialog box, click the Fill tab.

Choose a fill color for a cell or selected cells by clicking a color choice in the *Color* palette. To add shading to a cell or selected cells, click the Fill Effects button, and then click the desired shading style at the Fill Effects dialog box.

Figure 3.11 Format Cells Dialog Box with Fill Tab Selected

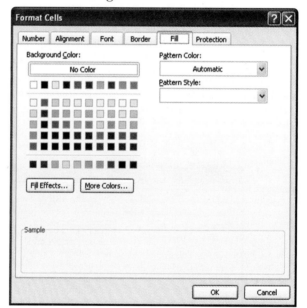

Repeating the Last Action

If you want to apply other types of formatting, such as number, border, or shading formatting to other cells in a worksheet, use the Repeat command by pressing F4 or Ctrl + Y. The Repeat command repeats the last action performed.

1. With **ExcelL1_C3_P4.xlsx** open, add fill color to cell A1 and repeat the formatting by completing the following steps:
   a. Make cell A1 active.
   b. Click the Format button in the Cells group and then click *Format Cells* at the drop-down list.
   c. At the Format Cells dialog box, click the Fill tab.
   d. Click a light purple color in the *Color* section (click the eighth color from the left in the second row).

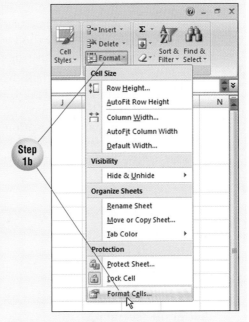

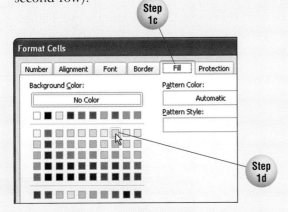

   e. Click OK.
   f. Select cells A2 through E2 and then press the F4 function key. (This repeats the light purple fill.)
2. Select row 2, insert a new row, and then change the width of the new row to 12.00.
3. Add shading to cells by completing the following steps:
   a. Select cells A2 through E2.
   b. Click the Format button in the Cells group and then click *Format Cells* at the drop-down list.
   c. At the Format Cells dialog box, if necessary, click the Fill tab.
   d. Click the Fill Effects button.
   e. At the Fill Effects dialog box, click the down-pointing arrow at the right side of the *Color 2* option box and then click *Purple, Accent 4* (eighth color from the left in the top row).
   f. Click *Horizontal* in the *Shading styles* section of the dialog box.
   g. Click OK to close the Fill Effects dialog box.
   h. Click OK to close the Format Cells dialog box.
4. Save **ExcelL1_C3_P4.xlsx**.

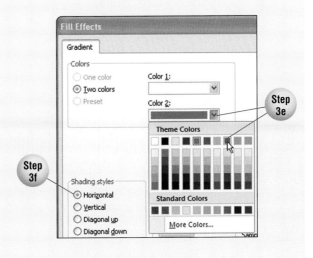

Formatting with Format Painter

Format with Format Painter
1. Select cells with desired formatting.
2. Double-click Format Painter button.
3. Select cells.
4. Click Format Painter button.

Format Painter

The Clipboard group in the Home tab contains a button you can use to copy formatting to different locations in the worksheet. This button is the Format Painter button and displays in the Clipboard group as a paintbrush. To use the Format Painter button, make a cell or selected cells active that contain the desired formatting, click the Format Painter button, and then click the cell or selected cells to which you want the formatting applied.

When you click the Format Painter button, the mouse pointer displays with a paintbrush attached. If you want to apply formatting a single time, click the Format Painter button once. If, however, you want to apply the character formatting in more than one location in the worksheet, double-click the Format Painter button. If you have double-clicked the Format Painter button, turn off the feature by clicking the Format Painter button once.

Project 4e Formatting with Format Painter

1. With **ExcelL1_C3_P4.xlsx** open, select cells A5 through E5.
2. Click the Font group dialog box launcher.
3. At the Format Cells dialog box, click the Fill tab.
4. Click the light green color (seventh color from the left in the second row).
5. Click OK to close the dialog box.
6. Use Format Painter to "paint" formatting to rows by completing the following steps:
   a. With A5 through E5 selected, double-click the Format Painter button in the Clipboard group.
   b. Select cells A7 through E7.
   c. Select cells A9 through E9.
   d. Select cells A11 through E11.
   e. Turn off Format Painter by clicking the Format Painter button in the Clipboard group.
7. Save and then print **ExcelL1_C3_P4.xlsx**.

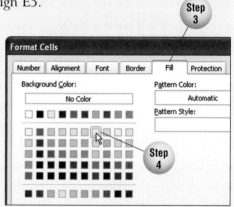

Hiding and Unhiding Columns/Rows

If a worksheet contains columns and/or rows of sensitive data or data that you are not using or do not want to view, consider hiding the columns and/or rows. To hide columns in a worksheet, select the columns to be hidden, click the Format button in the Cells group in the Home tab, point to *Hide & Unhide*, and then click *Hide Columns*. To hide selected rows, click the Format button in the Cells group, point to *Hide & Unhide*, and then click *Hide Rows*. To make a hidden column visible, select the column to the left and the column to the right of the hidden column, click the Format button in the Cells group, point to *Hide & Unhide*, and then click *Unhide Columns*. To make a hidden row visible, select the row above and the row below the hidden row, click the Format button in the Cells group, point to *Hide & Unhide*, and then click *Unhide Rows*.

If the first row or column is hidden, use the Go To feature to make the row or column visible. To do this, click the Find & Select button in the Editing group in the Home tab and then click *Go To* at the drop-down list. At the Go To dialog box, type A1 in the *Reference* text box, and then click OK. At the worksheet, click the Format button in the Cells group, point to *Hide & Unhide*, and then click *Unhide Columns* or click *Unhide Rows*.

You can also unhide columns or rows using the mouse. If a column or row is hidden, the light blue boundary line in the column or row header displays as a slightly thicker blue line. To unhide a column, position the mouse pointer on the slightly thicker blue line that displays in the column header until the mouse pointer changes to left- and right-pointing arrows with a double line between. (Make sure the mouse pointer displays with two lines between the arrows. If a single line displays, you will simply change the size of the visible column.) Hold down the left mouse button, drag to the right until the column displays at the desired width, and then release the mouse button. Unhide a row in a similar manner. Position the mouse pointer on the slightly thicker blue line in the row header until the mouse pointer changes to up- and down-pointing arrows with a double line between. Drag down to display the row and then release the mouse button. If two or more adjacent columns or rows are hidden, you will need to unhide each column or row separately.

Project ④ **Hiding/Unhiding Columns and Rows**

1. With **ExcelL1_C3_P4.xlsx** open, hide the row for Linstrom Enterprises and the row for Summit Services by completing the following steps:
   a. Click the row 7 header to select the entire row.
   b. Hold down the Ctrl key and then click the row 11 header to select the entire row.
   c. Click the Format button in the Cells group in the Home tab, point to *Hide & Unhide*, and then click *Hide Rows*.
2. Hide the column containing the planned amounts by completing the following steps:
   a. Click cell D3 to make it the active cell.
   b. Click the Format button in the Cells group, point to *Hide & Unhide*, and then click *Hide Columns*.
3. Save and then print **ExcelL1_C3_P4.xlsx**.

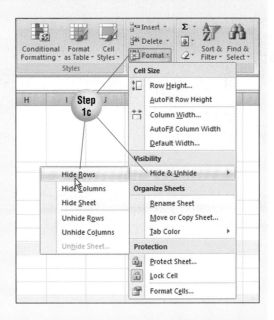

4. Unhide the rows by completing the following steps:
   a. Select rows 6 through 12.
   b. Click the Format button in the Cells group, point to *Hide & Unhide*, and then click *Unhide Rows*.
   c. Click in cell A4.

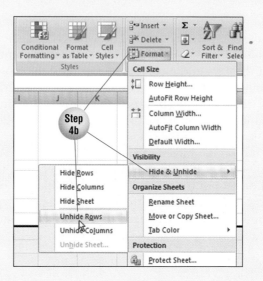

5. Unhide column D by completing the following steps:
   a. Position the mouse pointer on the thicker blue line that displays between columns C and E in the column header until the pointer turns into arrows pointing left and right with a double line between.
   b. Hold down the left mouse button, drag to the right until *Width: 12.57 (93 pixels)* displays in a box above the mouse pointer, and then release the mouse button.

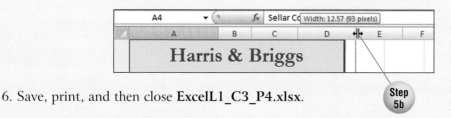

6. Save, print, and then close **ExcelL1_C3_P4.xlsx**.

CHAPTER summary

- Change column width using the mouse on column boundaries or with options at the Column Width dialog box.
- To automatically adjust a column to accommodate the longest entry in the column, double-click the column header boundary on the right.
- Change row height using the mouse on row boundaries or with options at the Row Height dialog box.
- Insert a row in a worksheet with the Insert button in the Cells group in the Home tab or with options at the Insert dialog box.
- Insert a column in a worksheet with the Insert button in the Cells group or with options at the Insert dialog box.
- Delete a specific cell by clicking the Delete button arrow and then clicking *Delete Cells* at the drop-down list. At the Delete dialog box, specify if you want to delete just the cell or an entire row or column.
- Delete a selected row(s) or column(s) by clicking the Delete button in the Cells group.
- Delete cell contents by pressing the Delete key or clicking the Clear button in the Editing group and then clicking *Clear Contents* at the drop-down list.
- Apply font formatting with buttons in the Font group in the Home tab.
- Use the Mini toolbar to apply font formatting to selected data in a cell.
- Apply alignment formatting with buttons in the Alignment group in the Home tab.
- Preview a worksheet by clicking the Office button, pointing to *Print*, and then clicking *Print Preview*.
- Change the size of the worksheet display with the Zoom button in the Print Preview tab or with the Zoom slider bar that displays at the right side of the Status bar.
- Use the Themes button in the Themes group in the Page Layout tab to apply a theme to cells in a worksheet that applies formatting such as color, font, and effects. Use the other buttons in the Themes group to customize the theme.
- Format numbers in cells with the Accounting Number Format, Percent Style, Comma Style, Increase Decimal, and Decrease Decimal buttons in the Number group in the home tab. You can also apply number formatting with options at the Format Cells dialog box with the Number tab selected.
- Apply formatting to cells in a worksheet with options at the Format Cells dialog box. This dialog box includes the following tabs for formatting cells: Number, Alignment, Font, Border, and Fill.
- Press F4 or Ctrl + Y to repeat the last action performed.
- Use the Format Painter button in the Clipboard group in the Home tab to apply formatting to different locations in a worksheet.
- Hide selected columns or rows in a worksheet by clicking the Format button in the Cells group in the Home tab, pointing to *Hide & Unhide*, and then clicking *Hide Columns* or *Hide Rows*.

- To make a hidden column visible, select the column to the left and right, click the Format button in the Cells group, point to *Hide & Unhide*, and then click *Unhide Columns*.
- To make a hidden row visible, select the row above and below, click the Format button in the Cells group, point to *Hide & Unhide*, and then click *Unhide Rows*.

COMMANDS review

FEATURE	RIBBON TAB, GROUP	BUTTON	KEYBOARD SHORTCUT
Format	Home, Cells	Format	
Insert cells, rows, columns	Home, Cells	Insert	
Delete cells, rows, columns	Home, Cells	Delete	
Clear cell or cell contents	Home, Editing		
Font	Home, Font	Calibri	
Font size	Home, Font	11	
Increase Font Size	Home, Font	A	
Decrease Font Size	Home, Font	A	
Bold	Home, Font	B	Ctrl + B
Italic	Home, Font	I	Ctrl + I
Underline	Home, Font	U	Ctrl + U
Borders	Home, Font		
Fill Color	Home, Font		
Font Color	Home, Font	A	
Top Align	Home, Alignment		
Middle Align	Home, Alignment		
Bottom Align	Home, Alignment		
Orientation	Home, Alignment		
Align Text Left	Home, Alignment		

continued

FEATURE	RIBBON TAB, GROUP	BUTTON	KEYBOARD SHORTCUT
Center	Home, Alignment		
Align Text Right	Home, Alignment		
Decrease Indent	Home, Alignment		Ctrl + Alt + Shift + Tab
Increase Indent	Home, Alignment		Ctrl + Alt + Tab
Wrap Text	Home, Alignment		
Merge & Center	Home, Alignment		
Print Preview		, Print, Print Preview	Ctrl + F2
Themes	Page Layout, Themes		
Number Format	Home, Number	General	
Accounting Number Format	Home, Number	$	
Percent Style	Home, Number	%	Ctrl + Shift + %
Increase Decimal	Home, Number		
Decrease Decimal	Home, Number		
Format Painter	Home, Clipboard		
Repeat			F4 or Ctrl + Y

CONCEPTS check

Test Your Knowledge

Completion: In the space provided at the right, indicate the correct term, symbol, or command.

1. To automatically adjust a column width to accommodate the longest entry in the cell, do this with the mouse on the column boundary.

   _____

2. By default, a column is inserted in this direction from the column containing the active cell.

   _____

3. To delete a row, select the row and then click the Delete button in this group in the Home tab.

   _____

4. With the options at this button drop-down list, you can clear the contents of the cell or selected cells.

_____

5. Use this button to insert color in the active cell or selected cells.

_____

6. By default, numbers are aligned at this side of a cell.

_____

7. Click this button to merge selected cells and center data within the merged cells.

_____

8. Select data in a cell and this displays in a dimmed fashion above the selected text.

_____

9. Click this button in the Alignment group in the Home tab to rotate data in a cell.

_____

10. Use this bar, located at the right side of the Status bar, to zoom the display of the worksheet.

_____

11. The Themes button is located in this tab.

_____

12. If you type a number with a dollar sign, such as $50.25, Excel automatically applies this formatting to the number.

_____

13. If you type a number with a percent sign, such as 25%, Excel automatically applies this formatting to the number.

_____

14. Align and indent data in cells using buttons in the Alignment group in the Home tab or with options at this dialog box with the Alignment tab selected.

_____

15. You can repeat the last action performed with the command Ctrl + Y or pressing this function key.

_____

16. The Format Painter button is located in this group in the Home tab.

_____

17. To hide a column, select the column, click this button in the Cells group in the Home tab, point to *Hide & Unhide*, and then click *Hide Columns*.

_____

SKILLS check
Demonstrate Your Proficiency

1 FORMAT A SALES AND BONUSES WORKSHEET

1. Open **ExcelC03Assessment01.xlsx**.
2. Save the workbook with Save As and name it **ExcelL1_C3_A1**.
3. Change the width of columns as follows:

   Column A   =   14.00
   Columns B - E   =   10.00
   Column F   =   6.00

4. Select row 2 and then insert a new row.
5. Merge and center cells A2 through F2.
6. Type **Sales Department** in cell A2 and then press Enter.
7. Increase the height of row 1 to 33.00.
8. Increase the height of row 2 to 21.00.
9. Increase the height of row 3 to 18.00.
10. Make the following formatting changes to the worksheet:
    a. Make cell A1 active, change the font size to 18 points, and turn on bold.
    b. Make cell A2 active, change the font size to 14 points, and turn on bold.
    c. Select cells A3 through F3, click the Bold button in the Font group, and then click the Center button in the Alignment group.
    d. Select cells A1 through F3, change the vertical alignment to Middle Align.
    e. Select cells B4 through E11 and then change the number formatting to Accounting with 0 decimal places and a dollar sign.
11. Insert the following formulas in the worksheet:
    a. Insert a formula in D4 that adds the amounts in B4 and C4. Copy the formula down to cells D5 through D11.
    b. Insert a formula in E4 that averages the amounts in B4 and C4. Copy the formula down to cells E5 through E11.
    c. Insert an IF statement in cell F4 that says that if the amount in cell E4 is greater than 74999, then insert the word "Yes" and if the amount is less than 75000, then insert the word "No." Copy this formula down to cells F5 through F11.
12. Make the following changes to the worksheet:
    a. Select cells F4 through F11 and then click the Center button in the Alignment group.
    b. Add a double-line border around cells A1 through F11.
    c. Select cells A1 and A2 and then apply a light orange fill color.
    d. Select cells A3 through F3 and then apply an orange fill color.
13. Save and then print the worksheet.
14. Apply the Verve theme to the worksheet.
15. Save, print, and then close **ExcelL1_C3_A1.xlsx**.

2 FORMAT AN OVERDUE ACCOUNTS WORKSHEET

1. Open **ExcelC03Assessment02.xlsx**.
2. Save the workbook with Save As and name it **ExcelL1_C3_A2**.
3. Change the width of columns as follows:

    Column A   =   21.00
    Column B   =   10.00
    Column C   =   10.00
    Column D   =   12.00
    Column E   =   7.00
    Column F   =   12.00

4. Make cell A1 active and then insert a new row.
5. Merge and center cells A1 through F1.
6. Type **Compass Corporation** in cell A1 and then press Enter.
7. Increase the height of row 1 to 42.00.
8. Increase the height of row 2 to 24.00.
9. Make the following formatting changes to the worksheet:
    a. Select cells A1 through F11 and then change the font to 10-point Bookman Old Style.
    b. Make cell A1 active, change the font size to 24 points, and turn on bold.
    c. Make cell A2 active, change the font size to 18 points, and turn on bold.
    d. Select cells A3 through F3, click the Bold button in the Font group and then click the Center button in the Alignment group.
    e. Select cells A1 through F3, click the Middle Align button in the Alignment group.
    f. Select cells B4 through C11 and then click the Center button in the Alignment group.
    g. Select cells E4 through E11 and then click the Center button in the Alignment group.
10. Use the DATE function in the following cells to enter a formula that returns the serial number for the following dates:

    D4   =   September 1, 2010
    D5   =   September 3, 2010
    D6   =   September 8, 2010
    D7   =   September 22, 2010
    D8   =   September 15, 2010
    D9   =   September 30, 2010
    D10 =   October 6, 2010
    D11 =   October 13, 2010

11. Enter a formula in cell F4 that inserts the due date (the purchase date plus the number of days in the Terms column). Copy the formula down to cells F5 through F11.
12. Apply the following borders and fill color:
    a. Add a thick line border around cells A1 through F11.
    b. Make cell A2 active and then add a double-line border at the top and bottom of the cell.
    c. Select cells A3 through F3 and then add a single line border to the bottom of the cells.
    d. Select cells A1 and A2 and then apply a light blue fill color.
13. Save, print, and then close **ExcelL1_C3_A2.xlsx**.

3 FORMAT A SUPPLIES AND EQUIPMENT WORKSHEET

1. Open **ExcelC03Assessment03.xlsx**.
2. Save the workbook with Save As and name it **ExcelL1_C3_A3**.
3. Select cells A1 through D19 and then change the font to Garamond and the font color to dark blue.
4. Select and then merge and center cells A1 through D1.
5. Select and then merge and center cells A2 through D2.
6. Make cell A1 active and then change the font size to 22 points and turn on bold.
7. Make cell A2 active and then change the font size to 12 points and turn on bold.
8. Change the height of row 1 to 36.00.
9. Change the height of row 2 to 21.00.
10. Change the width of column A to 15.00.
11. Select cells A3 through A17, turn on bold, and then click the Wrap Text button in the Alignment group.
12. Select cells A1 and A2 and then click the Middle Align button in the Alignment group.
13. Make cell B3 active and then change the number formatting to Currency with no decimal places.
14. Select cells C6 through C19 and then change the number formatting to Percentage with one decimal place.
15. Automatically adjust the width of column B.
16. Make cell D6 active and then type a formula that multiplies the absolute cell reference $B$3 with the percentage in cell C6. Copy the formula down to cells D7 through D19.
17. With cells D6 through D19 selected, change the number formatting to Currency with no decimal places.
18. Make cell D8 active and then clear the cell contents. Use the Repeat command, F4, to clear the contents from cells D11, D14, and D17.
19. Add light green fill color to the following cells: A1, A2, A5–D5, A8–D8, A11–D11, A14–D14, and A17–D17.
20. Add borders and/or shading of your choosing to enhance the visual appeal of the worksheet.
21. Save, print, and then close **ExcelL1_C3_A3.xlsx**.

4 FORMAT A FINANCIAL ANALYSIS WORKSHEET

1. Use the Help feature to learn how to use the shrink to fit option to show all data in a cell (with an option at the Format Cells dialog box with the Alignment tab selected).
2. Open **ExcelC03Assessment04.xlsx**.
3. Save the workbook with Save As and name it **ExcelL1_C3_A4**.
4. Make cell B9 active and then insert a formula that averages the percentages in cells B3 through B8. Copy the formula to the right to cells C9 and D9.

5. Select cells B3 through D9, display the Format Cells dialog box with the Alignment tab selected, change the horizontal alignment to Right (Indent) and the indent to *2*, and then close the dialog box.
6. Select cells A1 through D9 and then change the font size to 14.
7. Select cells B2 through D2 and then change the orientation to 45 degrees.
8. With cells B2 through D2 still selected, shrink the font size to show all data in the cells.
9. Save, print, and then close **ExcelL1_C3_A4.xlsx**.

CASE study
Apply Your Skills

Part 1

You are the office manager for HealthWise Fitness Center and you decide to prepare an Excel worksheet that displays the various plans offered by the health club. In this worksheet, you want to include yearly dues for each plan as well as quarterly and monthly payments. Open the **HealthWise.xlsx** workbook and then save it and name it **ExcelL1_C3_CS_P1A**. Make the following changes to the worksheet:

- Select cells B3 through D8 and then change the number formatting to Accounting with two decimal places and a dollar sign.
- Make cell B3 active and then insert *500.00*.
- Make cell B4 active and then insert a formula that adds the amount in B3 with the product (multiplication) of B3 multiplied by 10%. (The formula should look like this: **=B3+(B3*10%)**. The Economy plan is the base plan and each additional plan costs 10% more than the previous plan.)
- Copy the formula in cell B4 down to cells B5 through B8.
- Insert a formula in cell C3 that divides the amount in cell B3 by 4 and then copy the formula down to cells C4 through C8.
- Insert a formula in cell D3 that divides the amount in cell B3 by 12 and then copy the formula down to cells D4 through D8.
- Apply formatting to enhance the visual display of the worksheet.

Save and print the completed worksheet.

With **ExcelL1_C3_CS_P1A.xlsx** open, save the workbook with Save As and name it **ExcelL1_C3_CS_P1B**, and then make the following changes:

- You have been informed that the base rate for yearly dues has increased from $500.00 to $600.00. Change this amount in cell B3 of the worksheet.
- If clients are late with their quarterly or monthly dues payments, a late fee is charged. You decide to add the late fee information to the worksheet. Insert a new column to the right of Column C. Type **Late Fees** in cell D2 and also in cell F2.
- Insert a formula in cell D3 that multiplies the amount in C3 by 5%. Copy this formula down to cells D4 through D8.
- Insert a formula in cell F3 that multiplies the amount in E3 by 7%. Copy this formula down to cells F4 through F8. If necessary, change the number formatting for cells F3 through F8 to Accounting with two decimal places and a dollar sign.
- Apply any additional formatting to enhance the visual display of the worksheet.

Save, print, and then close **ExcelL1_C3_CS_P1B.xlsx**.

Prepare a payroll sheet for the employees of the fitness center and include the following information:

HealthWise Fitness Center

Weekly Payroll

Employee	Hourly Wage	Hours	Weekly Salary	Benefits
Heaton, Kelly	$26.50	40		
Severson, Joel	$25.00	40		
Turney, Amanda	$20.00	15		
Walters, Leslie	$19.65	30		
Overmeyer, Jean	$18.00	20		
Haddon, Bonnie	$16.00	20		
Baker, Grant	$15.00	40		
Calveri, Shannon	$12.00	15		
Dugan, Emily	$10.50	10		
Joyner, Daniel	$10.50	10		
Lee, Alexander	$10.50	10		

Insert a formula in the *Weekly Salary* column that multiplies the hourly wage by the number of hours. Insert an IF statement in the *Benefits* column that states that if the number in the *Hours* column is greater than 19, then insert "Yes" and if the number is less than 20, then insert "No." Apply formatting to enhance the visual display of the worksheet. Save the workbook and name it **ExcelL1_C3_CS_P2**. Print **ExcelL1_C3_CS_P2.xlsx**. Press Ctrl + ` to turn on the display of formulas, print the worksheet, and then press Ctrl + ` to turn off the display of formulas.

Make the following changes to the worksheet:

- Change the hourly wage for Amanda Turney to $22.00.
- Increase the hours for Emily Dugan to 20.
- Remove the row for Grant Baker.
- Insert a row between Jean Overmeyer and Bonnie Haddon and then type the following information in the cells in the new row: Employee: Tonya McGuire; Hourly Wage: $17.50; Hours: 15.

Save and then print **ExcelL1_C3_CS_P2.xlsx**. Press Ctrl + ` to turn on the display of formulas and then print the worksheet. Press Ctrl + ` to turn off the display of formulas and then save and close **ExcelL1_C3_CS_P2.xlsx**.

Your boss is interested in ordering new equipment for the health club. She is interested in ordering three elliptical machines, three recumbent bikes, and three upright bikes. She has asked you to use the Internet to research models and prices for this new equipment. She then wants you to prepare a worksheet with the information. Using the Internet, search for the following equipment:

- Search for elliptical machines for sale. Locate two different models and, if possible, find at least two companies that sell each model. Make a note of the company names, model numbers, and prices.

- Search for recumbent bikes for sale. Locate two different models and, if possible, find at least two companies that sell each model. Make a note of the company names, model numbers, and prices.
- Search for upright bikes for sale. Locate two different models and, if possible, find at least two companies that sell each model. Make a note of the company names, model numbers, and prices.

Using the information you found on the Internet, prepare an Excel worksheet with the following information:

- Equipment name
- Equipment model
- Price
- A column that multiplies the price by the number required (which is 3).

Include the fitness center name, HealthWise Fitness Center, and any other information you determine is necessary to the worksheet. Apply formatting to enhance the visual display of the worksheet. Save the workbook and name it **ExcelL1_C3_CS_P3**. Print and then close **ExcelL1_C3_CS_P3.xlsx**.

Part

4

When a prospective client contacts HealthWise about joining, you send a letter containing information about the fitness center, the plans offered, and the dues amounts. Use a letter template in Word to create a letter to send to a prospective client (you determine the client's name and address). Copy the cells in **ExcelL1_C3_CS_P1B.xlsx** containing data and paste them into the body of the letter. Make any formatting changes to make the data readable. Save, print, and then close the letter.

CHAPTER 4

Enhancing a Worksheet

PERFORMANCE OBJECTIVES

Upon successful completion of Chapter 4, you will be able to:

- Change worksheet margins
- Center a worksheet horizontally and vertically on the page
- Insert a page break in a worksheet
- Print gridlines and row and column headings
- Set and clear a print area
- Insert headers and footers
- Customize print jobs
- Complete a spelling check on a worksheet
- Find and replace data and cell formatting in a worksheet
- Sort data in cells in ascending and descending order
- Filter a list using AutoFilter
- Plan and create a worksheet

excel Chapter 4

Tutorial 4.1
Printing Worksheets
Tutorial 4.2
Finding, Sorting, and Filtering
Data

Excel contains features you can use to enhance and control the formatting of a worksheet. In this chapter, you will learn how to change worksheet margins, orientation, size, and scale; print column and row titles; print gridlines; and center a worksheet horizontally and vertically on the page. You will also learn how to complete a spell check on text in a worksheet, find and replace specific data and formatting in a worksheet, sort and filter data, and plan and create a worksheet.

Note: Before beginning computer projects, copy to your storage medium the Excel2007L1C4 subfolder from the Excel2007L1 folder on the CD that accompanies this textbook and make Excel2007L1C4 the active folder.

Project 1 Format a Yearly Budget Worksheet

You will format a yearly budget worksheet by inserting formulas; changing margins, page orientation, and page size; inserting a page break; printing column headings on multiple pages; scaling data to print on one page; inserting a background picture; inserting headers and footers; and identifying a print area and customizing print jobs.

QUICK STEPS

Change Worksheet Margins
1. Click Page Layout tab.
2. Click Margins button.
3. Click desired predesigned margin.
OR
1. Click Page Layout tab.
2. Click Margins button.
3. Click *Custom Margins* at drop-down list.
4. Change the top, left, right, and/or bottom measurements.
5. Click OK.

Margins

Formatting a Worksheet Page

An Excel worksheet contains default page formatting. For example, a worksheet contains left and right margins of 0.7 inch and top and bottom margins of 0.75 inch, a worksheet prints in portrait orientation, and the worksheet page size is 8.5 inches by 11 inches. These default settings as well as additional options can be changed and/or controlled with options in the Page Layout tab.

Changing Margins

The Page Setup group in the Page Layout tab contains buttons for changing margins, the page orientation and size, as well as buttons for establishing a print area, inserting a page break, applying a picture background, and printing titles.

Change the worksheet margins by clicking the Margins button in the Page Setup group in the Page Layout tab. This displays a drop-down list of predesigned margin choices. If one of the predesigned choices is what you want to apply to the worksheet, click the option. If you want to customize margins, click the *Custom Margins* option at the bottom of the Margins drop-down list. This displays the Page Setup dialog box with the Margins tab selected as shown in Figure 4.1.

Figure 4.1 Page Setup Dialog Box with Margins Tab Selected

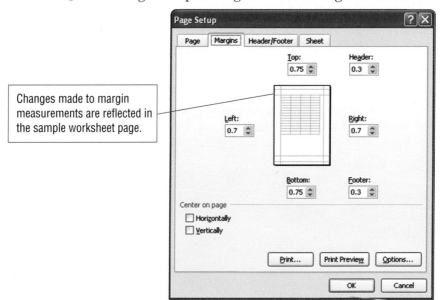

Changes made to margin measurements are reflected in the sample worksheet page.

A worksheet page showing the cells and margins displays in the dialog box. As you increase or decrease the top, bottom, left, or right margin measurements, the sample worksheet page reflects the change. You can also increase or decrease the measurement from the top of the page to the header with the *Header* option or the measurement from the footer to the bottom of the page with the *Footer* option. (You will learn about headers and footers later in this chapter.)

QUICK STEPS

Center Worksheet Horizontally/ Vertically
1. Click Page Layout tab.
2. Click *Custom Margins* at drop-down list.
3. Click *Horizontally* option and/or click *Vertically* option.
4. Click OK.

Centering a Worksheet Horizontally and/or Vertically

By default, worksheets print in the upper left corner of the page. You can center a worksheet on the page by changing the margins; however, an easier method for centering a worksheet is to use the *Horizontally* and/or *Vertically* options that display at the bottom of the Page Setup dialog box with the Margins tab selected. If you choose one or both of these options, the worksheet page in the preview section displays how the worksheet will print on the page.

Project 1a   **Changing Margins and Horizontally and Vertically Centering a Worksheet**

1. Open **ExcelC04Project01.xlsx**.
2. Save the workbook with Save As and name it **ExcelL1_C4_P1**.
3. Insert the following formulas in the worksheet:
   a. Insert formulas in column N, rows 5 through 10 that sum the totals for each income item.
   b. Insert formulas in row 11, columns B through N that sum the income as well as the total for all income items.
   c. Insert formulas in column N, rows 14 through 19 that sum the totals for each expense item.
   d. Insert formulas in row 20, columns B through N that sum the expenses as well as the total of expenses.
   e. Insert formulas in row 21, columns B through N that subtract the total expenses from the income. (To begin the formula, make cell B21 active and then type the formula *=B11-B20*. Copy this formula to columns C through N.)
4. Click the Page Layout tab.
5. Click the Margins button in the Page Setup group and then click *Custom Margins* at the drop-down list.

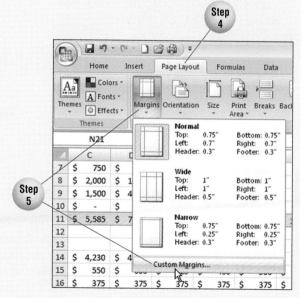

6. At the Page Setup dialog box with the Margins tab selected, click the up-pointing arrow at the right side of the *Top* text box until *3.5* displays.
7. Click the up-pointing arrow at the right side of the *Bottom* text box until *1.5* displays.
8. Preview the worksheet by clicking the Print Preview button located toward the bottom of the Page Setup dialog box. The worksheet appears to be a little low on the page so you decide to horizontally and vertically center it by completing the following steps:
   a. Click the Close Print Preview button.
   b. Click the Margins button in the Page Setup group and then click *Custom Margins* at the drop-down list.
   c. At the Page Setup dialog box with the Margins tab selected, change the *Top* and *Bottom* measurements to *1*.
   d. Click the *Horizontally* option. (This inserts a check mark.)
   e. Click the *Vertically* option. (This inserts a check mark.)
   f. Click OK to close the dialog box.
9. Save **ExcelL1_C4_P1.xlsx**.

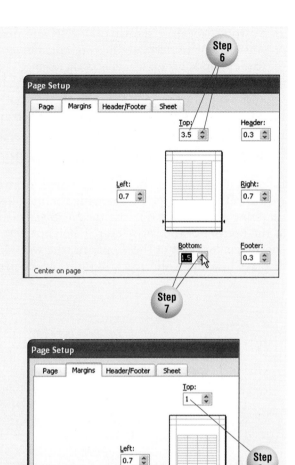

Changing Page Orientation

Change Page Orientation
1. Click Page Layout tab.
2. Click Orientation button.
3. Click desired orientation at drop-down list.

Click the Orientation button in the Page Setup group and a drop-down list displays with two choices, *Portrait* and *Landscape*. The two choices are represented by sample pages. A sample page that is taller than it is wide shows how the default orientation (*Portrait*) prints data on the page. The other choice, *Landscape*, will rotate the data and print it on a page that is wider than it is tall.

Changing the Page Size

An Excel worksheet page size, by default, is set at 8.5 × 11 inches. You can change this default page size by clicking the Size button in the Page Setup group. At the drop-down list that displays, notice that the default setting is *Letter* and the measurement *8.5″ × 11″* displays below *Letter*. This drop-down list also contains a number of page sizes such as *Executive*, *Legal*, and a number of envelope sizes.

Change Page Size
1. Click Page Layout tab.
2. Click Size button.
3. Click desired size at drop-down list.

Project 1b Changing Page Orientation and Size

1. With **ExcelL1_C4_P1.xlsx** open, click the Orientation button in the Page Setup group in the Page Layout tab and then click *Landscape* at the drop-down list.

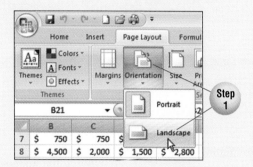

2. Click the Size button in the Page Setup group and then click *Legal* at the drop-down list.

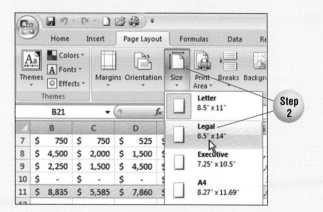

3. Preview the worksheet by clicking the Office button, pointing to *Print*, and then clicking *Print Preview*. After viewing the worksheet in Print Preview, click the Close Print Preview button.
4. Save **ExcelL1_C4_P1.xlsx**.

Inserting and Removing Page Breaks

The default left and right margins of 0.7 inch allow approximately 7 inches of cells across the page (8.5 inches minus 1.4 inches equals 7.1 inches). If a worksheet contains more than 7 inches of cells across the page, a page break is inserted in the worksheet and the remaining columns are moved to the next page. A page break displays as a broken line along cell borders. Figure 4.2 shows the page break in **ExcelL1_C4_P1.xlsx**.

Figure 4.2 Page Break

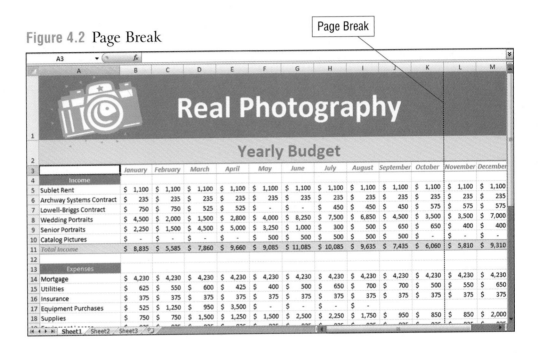

Page Break

Insert Page Break
1. Select column or row.
2. Click Page Layout tab.
3. Click Breaks button.
4. Click *Insert Page Break* at drop-down list.

Breaks

A page break also displays horizontally in a worksheet. By default, a worksheet can contain approximately 9.5 inches of cells vertically down the page. This is because the paper size is set by default at 11 inches. With the default top and bottom margins of 0.75 inch, this allows 9.5 inches of cells to print on one page.

Excel automatically inserts a page break in a worksheet. You can insert your own if you would like more control over what cells print on a page. To insert your own page break, select the column or row, click the Breaks button in the Page Setup group in the Page Layout tab, and then click *Insert Page Break* at the drop-down list. A page break is inserted immediately left of the selected column or immediately above the selected row.

If you want to insert both a horizontal and vertical page break at the same time, make a cell active, click the Breaks button in the Page Setup group and then click *Insert Page Break*. This causes a horizontal page break to be inserted immediately above the active cell, and a vertical page break to be inserted at the left side of the active cell. To remove a page break, select the column or row or make the desired cell active, click the Breaks button in the Page Setup group, and then click *Remove Page Break* at the drop-down list.

The page break automatically inserted by Excel may not be visible initially in a worksheet. One way to display the page break is to preview the worksheet. When you close Print Preview, the page break will display in the worksheet.

Displaying a Worksheet in Page Break Preview

Excel provides a page break view that displays worksheet pages and page breaks. To display this view, click the Page Break Preview button located in the view area at the right side of the Status bar or click the View tab and then click the Page Break Preview button in the Workbook Views group. This causes the worksheet to display similar to the worksheet shown in Figure 4.3. The word *Page* along with the page number is displayed in gray behind the cells in the worksheet. A solid blue line indicates a page break inserted by Excel and a dashed blue line indicates a page break inserted manually.

You can move the page break by positioning the arrow pointer on the blue line, holding down the left mouse button, dragging the line to the desired location, and then releasing the mouse button. To return to the Normal view, click the Normal button in the view area on the Status bar or click the View tab and then click the Normal button in the Workbook Views group.

HINT
You can edit a worksheet in Page Break Preview.

Page Break Preview

Normal

Figure 4.3 Worksheet in Page Break Preview

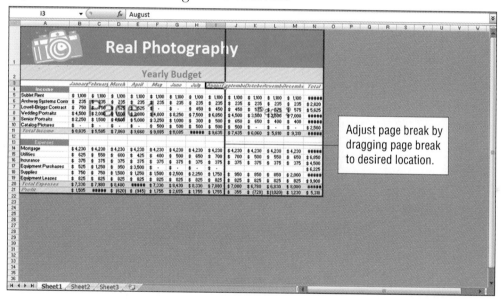

Adjust page break by dragging page break to desired location.

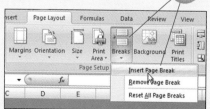

Project 1c Inserting a Page Break in a Worksheet

1. With **ExcelL1_C4_P1.xlsx** open, click the Size button in the Page Setup group in the Page Layout tab and then click *Letter* at the drop-down list.
2. Click the Margins button and then click *Custom Margins* at the drop-down list.
3. At the Page Setup dialog box with the Margins tab selected, click *Horizontally* to remove the check mark, click *Vertically* to remove the check mark, and then click OK to close the dialog box.
4. Insert a page break between columns I and J by completing the following steps:
   a. Select column J.
   b. Click the Breaks button in the Page Setup group and then click *Insert Page Break* at the drop-down list. Click in any cell in column I.

5. View the worksheet in Page Break Preview by completing the following steps:

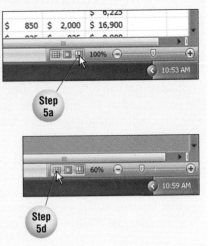

Step 5a

a. Click the Page Break Preview button located in the view area on the Status bar. (If a welcome message displays, click OK.)

b. View the pages and page breaks in the worksheet.

c. You decide to include the first six months of the year on one page. To do this, position the arrow pointer on the vertical blue line, hold down the left mouse button, drag the line to the left so it is positioned between columns G and H, and then release the mouse button.

d. Click the Normal button located in the view area on the Status bar.

Step 5d

6. Save **ExcelL1_C4_P1.xlsx**.

Printing Column and Row Titles on Multiple Pages

Print
Titles

Columns and rows in a worksheet are usually titled. For example, in **ExcelL1_C4_P1.xlsx**, column titles include *Income, Expenses, January, February, March,* and so on. Row titles include the income and expenses categories. If a worksheet prints on more than one page, having column and/or row titles printing on each page can be useful. To do this, click the Print Titles button in the Page Setup group in the Page Layout tab. This displays the Page Setup dialog box with the Sheet tab selected as shown in Figure 4.4.

Figure 4.4 Page Setup Dialog Box with Sheet Tab Selected

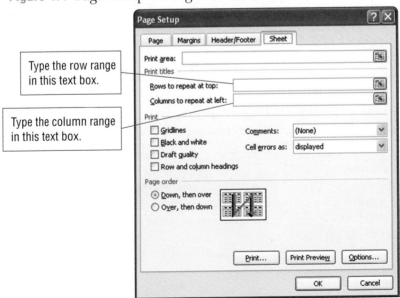

Type the row range in this text box.

Type the column range in this text box.

At the Page Setup dialog box with the Sheet tab selected, specify the range of row cells you want to print on every page in the *Rows to repeat at top* text box. Type a cell range using a colon. For example, if you want cells A1 through J1 to print on every page, you would type **A1:J1** in the *Rows to repeat at top* text box. Type the range of column cells you want to print on every page in the *Columns to repeat at left* text box. To make rows and columns easier to identify on the printed page, specify that row and/or column headings print on each page.

QUICK STEPS

Print Column and Row Titles
1. Click Page Layout tab.
2. Click Print Titles button.
3. Type row range in *Rows to repeat at top* option.
4. Type column range in *Columns to repeat at left* option.
5. Click OK.

Project 10 Printing Column Titles on Each Page of a Worksheet

1. With **ExcelL1_C4_P1.xlsx** open, click the Page Layout tab and then click the Print Titles button in the Page Setup group.
2. At the Page Setup dialog box with the Sheet tab selected, click in the *Columns to repeat at left* text box.
3. Type **A1:A21**.

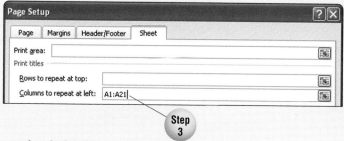

Step 3

4. Click OK to close the dialog box.
5. Save, preview, and then print **ExcelL1_C4_P1.xlsx**.

Scaling Data

With buttons in the Scale to Fit group in the Page Layout tab, you can adjust the printed output by a percentage to fit the number of pages specified. For example, if a worksheet contains too many columns to print on one page, click the down-pointing arrow at the right side of the *Width* box in the Scale to Fit group in the Page Layout tab and then click *1 page*. This causes the data to shrink so all columns display and print on one page.

Project **1e**   **Scaling Data to Fit on One Page**

1. With **ExcelL1_C4_P1.xlsx** open, click the down-pointing arrow at the right side of the *Width* box in the Scale to Fit group in the Page Layout tab.
2. At the drop-down list that displays, click the *1 page* option.

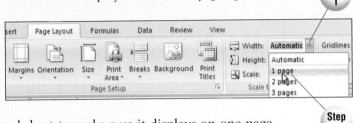

Step 1

Step 2

3. Preview the worksheet to make sure it displays on one page.
4. Save and then print **ExcelL1_C4_P1.xlsx**.

Inserting a Background Picture

Insert Background Picture
1. Click Page Layout tab.
2. Click Background button.
3. Navigate to desired picture and double-click picture.

With the Background button in the Page Setup group in the Page Layout tab you can insert a picture as a background to the worksheet. The picture displays only on the screen and does not print. To insert a picture, click the Background button in the Page Setup group. At the Sheet Background dialog box navigate to the folder containing the desired picture and then double-click the picture. To remove the picture from the worksheet, click the Delete Background button.

Project **1f**   **Inserting a Background Picture**

1. With **ExcelL1_C4_P1.xlsx** open, change the scaling back to the default by completing the following steps:
   a. Click the down-pointing arrow at the right side of the *Width* box in the Scale to Fit group and then click *Automatic* at the drop-down list.
   b. Click the up-pointing arrow at the right side of the *Scale* measurement box until *100%* displays in the box.
2. Remove titles from printing on second and subsequent pages by completing the following steps:
   a. Click the Print Titles button in the Page Setup group.
   b. At the Page Setup dialog box with the Sheet tab selected, select the text that displays in the *Columns to repeat at left* text box and then press the Delete key.
   c. Click OK to close the dialog box.
3. Insert a background picture by completing the following steps:
   a. Click the Background button in the Page Setup group.
   b. At the Sheet Background dialog box, navigate to the Excel2007L1C4 folder, and then double-click **Mountain.jpg**.
4. Preview the worksheet. (Notice that the picture does not display in Print Preview.)
5. Remove the picture by clicking the Delete Background button in the Page Setup group.
6. Save **ExcelL1_C4_P1.xlsx**.

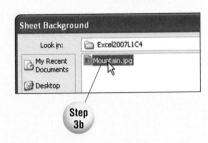

Step 3b

Printing Gridlines and Row and Column Headings

By default, the gridlines that create the cells in a worksheet and the row numbers and column letters do not print. The Sheet Options group in the Page Layout tab contain check boxes for gridlines and headings. The *View* check boxes for Gridlines and Headings contain check marks. At these settings, gridlines and row and column headings display on the screen but do not print. If you want them to print, insert check marks in the *Print* check boxes. Complex worksheets may be easier to read with the gridlines printed.

You can also control the display and printing of gridlines and headings with options at the Page Setup dialog box with the Sheet tab selected. Display this dialog box by clicking the Sheet Options dialog box launcher. To print gridlines and headings, insert check marks in the check boxes located in the *Print* section of the dialog box. The *Print* section contains two additional options—*Black and white* and *Draft quality*. If you are printing with a color printer, you can print the worksheet in black and white by inserting a check mark in the *Black and white* check box. Insert a check mark in the *Draft* option if you want to print a draft of the worksheet. With this option checked, some formatting such as shading and fill are not printed.

QUICK STEPS

Print Gridlines
1. Click Page Layout tab.
2. Click *Print* check box in Gridlines section in Sheet Options group.
OR
1. Click Page Layout tab.
2. Click Sheet Options dialog box launcher.
3. Click *Gridlines* option.
4. Click OK.

Print Row and Column Headings
1. Click Page Layout tab.
2. Click *Print* check box in Headings section in Sheet Options group.
OR
1. Click Page Layout tab.
2. Click Sheet Options dialog box launcher.
3. Click *Row and column headings* option.
4. Click OK.

Project 1g Printing Gridlines and Row and Column Headings

1. With **ExcelL1_C4_P1.xlsx** open, click in the *Print* check box below Gridlines in the Sheet Options group to insert a check mark.
2. Click in the *Print* check box below Headings in the Sheet Options group to insert a check mark.

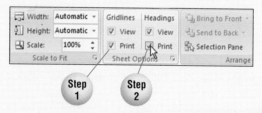

3. Click the Margins button in the Page Setup group and then click *Custom Margins* at the drop-down list.
4. At the Page Setup dialog box with the Margins tab selected, click in the *Horizontally* check box to insert a check mark.
5. Click in the *Vertically* check box to insert a check mark.
6. Click OK to close the dialog box.
7. Save, preview, and then print **ExcelL1_C4_P1.xlsx**.
8. Click in the *Print* check box below Headings in the Sheet Options group to remove the check mark.
9. Click in the *Print* check box below Gridlines in the Sheet Options group to remove the check mark.
10. Save **ExcelL1_C4_P1.xlsx**.

Printing a Specific Area of a Worksheet

With the Print Area button in the Page Setup group in the Page Layout tab you can select and print specific areas in a worksheet. To do this, select the cells you want to print, click the Print Area button in the Page Setup group in the Page Layout tab, and then click *Set Print Area* at the drop-down list. This inserts a border around the selected cells. Click the Quick Print button on the Quick Access toolbar and the cells within the border are printed.

You can specify more than one print area in a worksheet. To do this, select the first group of cells, click the Print Area button in the Page Setup group, and then click *Set Print Area*. Select the next group of cells, click the Print Area button, and then click *Add to Print Area*. Clear a print area by clicking the Print Area button in the Page Setup group and then clicking *Clear Print Area* at the drop-down list.

Each area specified as a print area will print on a separate page. If you want nonadjacent print areas to print on the same page, consider hiding columns and/or rows in the worksheet to bring the areas together.

Project ⓗ Printing Specific Areas

1. With **ExcelL1_C4_P1.xlsx** open, print the first half expenses by completing the following steps:
   a. Select cells A3 through G21.
   b. Click the Print Area button in the Page Setup group in the Page Layout tab and then click *Set Print Area* at the drop-down list.

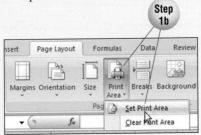

Step 1b

   c. With the border surrounding the cells A3 through G21, click the Quick Print button on the Quick Access toolbar.
   d. Clear the print area by clicking the Print Area button in the Page Setup group and then clicking *Clear Print Area* at the drop-down list.
2. Suppose you want to print the income and expenses information as well as the totals for the month of April. To do this, hide columns and select a print area by completing the following steps:
   a. Select columns B through D.
   b. Click the Home tab.
   c. Click the Format button in the Cells group, point to *Hide & Unhide*, and then click *Hide Columns*.
   d. Click the Page Layout tab.
   e. Select cells A3 through E21. (Columns A and E are now adjacent.)
   f. Click the Print Area button in the Page Setup group and then click *Set Print Area* at the drop-down list.

3. Click the Quick Print button on the Quick Access toolbar.

4. Clear the print area by making sure cells A3 through E21 are selected, clicking the Print Area button in the Page Setup group, and then clicking *Clear Print Area* at the drop-down list.

5. Unhide the columns by completing the following steps:
   a. Click the Home tab.
   b. Select columns A and E (these columns are adjacent).
   c. Click the Format button in the Cells group, point to *Hide & Unhide*, and then click *Unhide Columns*.
   d. Deselect the text by clicking in any cell containing data in the worksheet.

6. Save **ExcelL1_C4_P1.xlsx**.

Inserting Headers/Footers

Text that prints at the top of each worksheet page is called a ***header*** and text that prints at the bottom of each worksheet page is called a ***footer***. You can create a header and/or footer with the Header & Footer button in the Text group in the Insert tab, in Page Layout View, or with options at the Page Setup dialog box with the Header/Footer tab selected.

To create a header with the Header & Footer button, click the Insert tab and then click the Header & Footer button in the Text group. This displays the worksheet in Page Layout view and displays the Header & Footer Tools Design tab. Use buttons in this tab, shown in Figure 4.5, to insert predesigned headers and/or footers or insert header and footer elements such as the page number, date, time, path name, and file name. You can also create a different header or footer on the first page of the worksheet or create a header or footer for even pages and another for odd pages.

QUICK STEPS

Insert a Header or Footer
1. Click Insert tab.
2. Click Header & Footer button.
3. Click Header button and then click predesigned header or click Footer button and then click predesigned footer.

OR

1. Click Insert tab.
2. Click Header & Footer button.
3. Click desired header or footer elements.

HINT
Close the header or footer pane by clicking in the worksheet or pressing Esc.

Figure 4.5 Header & Footer Tools Design Tab

1. With **ExcelL1_C4_P1.xlsx** open, create a header by completing the following steps:
   a. Click the Insert tab.
   b. Click the Header & Footer button in the Text group.

Step 1a

Step 1b

c. Click the Header button located at the left side of the Header & Footer Tools Design tab and then click *Page 1, ExcelL1_C4_P1.xlsx* at the drop-down list. (This inserts the page number in the middle header box and the workbook name in the right header box.)
2. Click in any cell in the worksheet containing data.
3. Click the Normal view button located in the view area on the Status bar.
4. Save **ExcelL1_C4_P1.xlsx**.

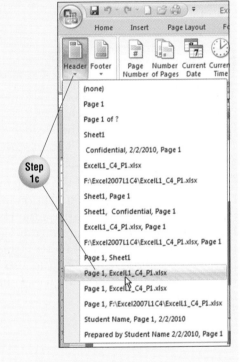

Step 1c

You also can insert a header and/or footer by switching to Page Layout view. In Page Layout view, the top of the worksheet page displays with the text *Click to add header*. Click this text and the insertion point is positioned in the middle header box. Type the desired header in this box or click in the left box or the right box and then type the header. Create a footer in a similar manner. Scroll down the worksheet until the bottom of the page displays and then click the text *Click to add footer*. Type the footer in the center footer box or click the left or right box and then type the footer.

1. With **ExcelL1_C4_P1.xlsx** open, click the Page Layout button located in the view area on the Status bar.
2. Scroll down the worksheet until the text *Click to add footer* displays and then click the text.

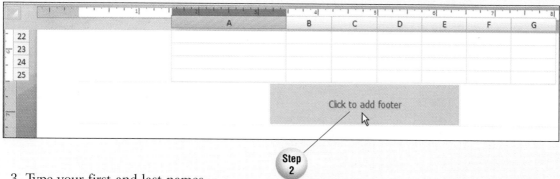

Step 2

3. Type your first and last names.
4. Click in the left footer box and then click the Current Date button in the Header & Footer Elements group in the Header & Footer Tools Design tab.
5. Click in the right footer box and then click the Current Time button in the Header & Footer Elements group.
6. Click in a cell in the worksheet.
7. Save and then print **ExcelL1_C4_Pl.xlsx**.
8. Modify the header by completing the following steps:
   a. Scroll to the beginning of the worksheet and display the header text.
   b. Click the page number in the middle header box. (This displays the Header & Footer Tools Design tab, changes the header to a field, and selects the field.)
   c. Press the Delete key to delete the header.
   d. Click the header text that displays in the right header box and then press the Delete key.
   e. Insert the page number by clicking the Page Number button in the Header & Footer Elements group.
   f. Click in the left header box and then click the File Name button in the Header & Footer Elements group.

Step 8f

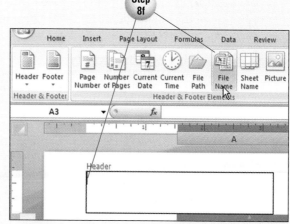

9. Click in any cell in the worksheet containing data.
10. Click the Normal button in the view area on the Status bar.
11. Preview the worksheet to determine how the header and footer print on each page.
12. Save and then print **ExcelL1_C4_P1.xlsx**.

Customizing Print Jobs

The Print dialog box provides options for customizing a print job. Display the Print dialog box shown in Figure 4.6 by clicking the Office button and then clicking *Print* at the drop-down list or by pressing the keyboard shortcut Ctrl + P. Use options at the Print dialog box to print a specific range of cells, selected cells, or multiple copies of a workbook.

Figure 4.6 Print Dialog Box

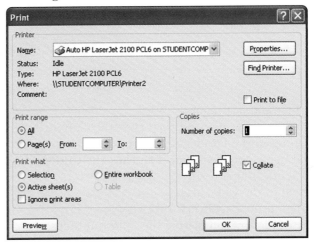

At the Print dialog box, the currently selected printer name displays in the *Name* option box. If other printers are installed, click the down-pointing arrow at the right side of the *Name* option box to display a list of printers.

The *Active sheet(s)* option in the *Print what* section is selected by default. At this setting, the currently active worksheet will print. If you want to print an entire workbook that contains several worksheets, click *Entire workbook* in the *Print what* section. Click the *Selection* option in the *Print what* section to print the currently selected cells.

If you want more than one copy of a worksheet or workbook printed, change the desired number of copies with the *Number of copies* option in the *Copies* section. If you want the copies collated, make sure the *Collate* check box in the *Copies* section contains a check mark.

A worksheet within a workbook can contain more than one page. If you want to print specific pages of a worksheet within a workbook, click *Page(s)* in the *Print range* section, and then specify the desired page numbers in the *From* and *To* text boxes.

If you want to preview the worksheet before printing, click the Preview button that displays at the bottom left corner of the dialog box. This displays the worksheet as it will appear on the printed page. After viewing the worksheet, click the Close Print Preview button that displays at the right side of the Print Preview tab.

Project 1k   Printing Specific Cells in a Worksheet

1. With **ExcelL1_C4_P1.xlsx** open, print selected cells by completing the following steps:
   a. Select cells A3 through G11.
   b. Click the Office button and then click *Print* at the drop-down list.
   c. At the Print dialog box, click *Selection* in the *Print what* section.
   d. Click OK.
2. Close **ExcelL1_C4_P1.xlsx**.

Project 2   Format a May Sales and Commissions Worksheet

You will format a sales commission worksheet by inserting a formula, completing a spelling check, and finding and replacing data and cell formatting.

Completing a Spelling Check

Excel includes a spelling checker you can use to check the spelling of text in a worksheet. Before checking the spelling in a worksheet, make the first cell active. The spell checker checks the worksheet from the active cell to the last cell in the worksheet that contains data.

To use the spelling checker, click the Review tab and then click the Spelling button. Figure 4.7 displays the Spelling dialog box. At this dialog box, you can click a button to tell Excel to ignore a word or you can replace a misspelled word with a word from the *Suggestions* list box.

QUICK STEPS

Complete a Spelling Check
1. Click Review tab.
2. Click Spelling button.
3. Replace or ignore selected words.

HINT
Customize spell checking options at the Excel Options dialog box with Proofing selected.

Figure 4.7 Excel Spelling Dialog Box

The word in the worksheet not found in the spell check dictionary displays here.

Suggested spellings display in the *Suggestions* list box.

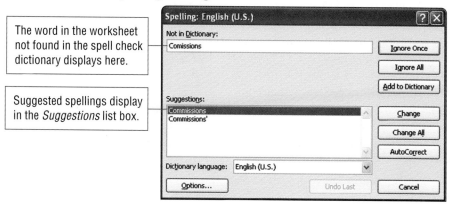

Using Undo and Redo

HINT

Ctrl + Z is the keyboard shortcut to undo a command.

Undo

Redo

Excel includes an Undo button on the Quick Access toolbar that will reverse certain commands or delete the last data typed in a cell. For example, if you apply an autoformat to selected cells in a worksheet and then decide you want the autoformatting removed, click the Undo button on the Quick Access toolbar. If you decide you want the autoformatting back again, click the Redo button on the Quick Access toolbar.

Excel maintains actions in temporary memory. If you want to undo an action performed earlier, click the down-pointing arrow at the right side of the Undo button and a drop-down list displays containing the actions performed on the worksheet. Click the desired action at the drop-down list. Any actions preceding a chosen action are also undone. You can do the same with the Redo drop-down list. Multiple actions must be undone or redone in sequence.

Project 2a   Spell Checking and Formatting a Worksheet

1. Open **ExcelC04Project02.xlsx**.
2. Save the workbook with Save As and name it **ExcelL1_C4_P2**.
3. Complete a spelling check on the worksheet by completing the following steps:
   a. Make sure cell A1 is the active cell.
   b. Click the Review tab.
   c. Click the Spelling button.
   d. Click the Change button as needed to correct misspelled words in the worksheet. (When the spell checker stops at proper names *Pirozzi, Valona,* and *Yonemoto,* click the Ignore All button.)
   e. At the message telling you the spelling check is completed, click OK.

Step 3c

Step 3b

4. Make cell G4 active and then insert a formula that multiplies the sale price by the commission percentage. Copy the formula down to cells G5 through G26.
5. Make cell G27 active and then insert the sum of cells G4 through G26.
6. Apply a theme by clicking the Page Layout button, clicking the Themes button, and then clicking *Civic* at the drop-down gallery.
7. After looking at the worksheet with the Civic theme applied, you decide you want to return to the original formatting. To do this, click the Undo button on the Quick Access toolbar.
8. You realize that copying the formula in cell G4 down to cells G5 through G26 caused the yellow fill to be removed from certain cells and you decide to insert the shading. To do this, complete the following steps:
   a. Make cell G5 active.
   b. Click the Home tab.

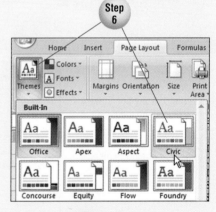

Step 6

Step 7

c. Click the Fill Color button arrow and then click *More Colors* at the drop-down gallery.

d. At the Colors dialog box with the Standard tab selected, click the yellow color as shown at the right.

e. Click OK to close the dialog box.

f. Make cell G7 active and then press F4 (the Repeat command).

g. Use F4 to apply yellow shading to cells G9, G11, G13, G15, G17, G19, G21, G23, and G25.

9. Save **ExcelL1_C4_P2.xlsx**.

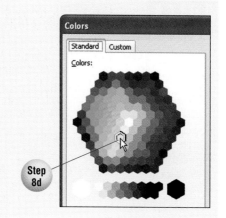

Step 8d

Finding and Replacing Data in a Worksheet

Excel provides a Find feature you can use to look for specific data and either replace it with nothing or replace it with other data. This feature is particularly helpful in a large worksheet with data you want to find quickly. Excel also includes a find and replace feature. Use this to look for specific data in a worksheet and replace it with other data.

To find specific data in a worksheet, click the Find & Select button located in the Editing group in the Home tab and then click *Find* at the drop-down list. This displays the Find and Replace dialog box with the Find tab selected as shown in Figure 4.8. Type the data you want to find in the *Find what* text box and then click the Find Next button. Continue clicking the Find Next button to move to the next occurrence of the data. If the Find and Replace dialog box obstructs your view of the worksheet, use the mouse pointer on the title bar to drag the box to a different location.

QUICK STEPS

Find Data
1. Click Find & Select button.
2. Click *Find* at drop-down list.
3. Type data in *Find what* text box.
4. Click Find Next button.

Find & Select ▾

Figure 4.8 Find and Replace Dialog Box with Find Tab Selected

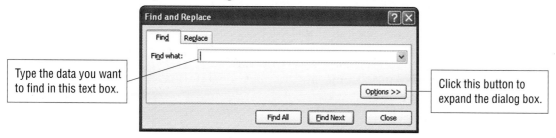

Type the data you want to find in this text box.

Click this button to expand the dialog box.

Find and Replace Data
1. Click Find & Select button.
2. Click *Replace* at drop-down list.
3. Type data in *Find what* text box.
4. Type data in *Replace with* text box.
5. Click Replace button or Replace All button.

To find specific data in a worksheet and replace it with other data, click the Find & Select button in the Editing group in the Home tab and then click *Replace* at the drop-down list. This displays the Find and Replace dialog box with the Replace tab selected as shown in Figure 4.9. Enter the data for which you are looking in the *Find what* text box. Press the Tab key or click in the *Replace with* text box and then enter the data that is to replace the data in the *Find what* text box.

Figure 4.9 Find and Replace Dialog Box with Replace Tab Selected

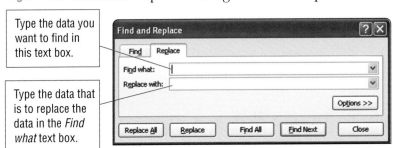

Type the data you want to find in this text box.

Type the data that is to replace the data in the *Find what* text box.

Click the Find Next button to tell Excel to find the next occurrence of the data. Click the Replace button to replace the data and find the next occurrence. If you know that you want all occurrences of the data in the *Find what* text box replaced with the data in the *Replace with* text box, click the Replace All button. Click the Close button to close the Replace dialog box.

Display additional find and replace options by clicking the Options button. This expands the dialog box as shown in Figure 4.10. By default, Excel will look for any data that contains the same characters as the data in the *Find what* text box, without concern for the characters before or after the entered data. For example, in Project 2b, you will be looking for sale prices of $450,000 and replacing with $475,000. If you do not specify to Excel that you want to find cells that contain only *450000,* Excel will stop at any cell containing *450000.* In this example, Excel would stop at a cell containing *$1,450,000* or a cell containing *$2,450,000.* To specify that the only data that should be contained in the cell is what is entered in the *Find what* text box, click the Options button to expand the dialog box, and then insert a check mark in the *Match entire cell contents* check box.

Figure 4.10 Expanded Find and Replace Dialog Box

Search the active worksheet or the entire workbook with the *Within* option.

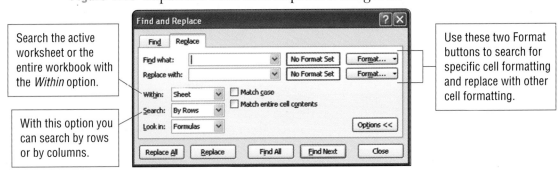

Use these two Format buttons to search for specific cell formatting and replace with other cell formatting.

With this option you can search by rows or by columns.

If the *Match case* option is active (contains a check mark), Excel will look for only that data that exactly matches the case of the data entered in the *Find what* text box. Remove the check mark from this check box if you do not want Excel to find exact case matches. Excel will search in the current worksheet. If you want Excel to search an entire workbook, change the *Within* option to *Workbook*. Excel, by default, searches by rows in a worksheet. You can change this to *By Columns* with the *Search* option.

Project 2b Finding and Replacing Data

1. With **ExcelL1_C4_P2.xlsx** open, find all occurrences of *Land* in the worksheet and replace with *Acreage* by completing the following steps:
   a. Click the Find & Select button in the Editing group in the Home tab and then click *Replace* at the drop-down list.
   b. At the Find and Replace dialog box with the Replace tab selected, type **Land** in the *Find what* text box.
   c. Press the Tab key (this moves the insertion point to the *Replace with* text box).
   d. Type **Acreage**.
   e. Click the Replace All button.
   f. At the message telling you that four replacements were made, click OK.
   g. Click the Close button to close the Find and Replace dialog box.

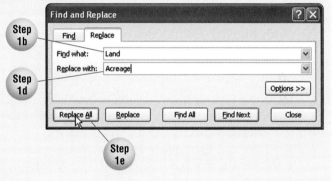

2. Find all occurrences of *$450,000* and replace with *$475,000* by completing the following steps:
   a. Click the Find & Select button in the Editing group and then click *Replace* at the drop-down list.
   b. At the Find and Replace dialog box with the Replace tab selected, type **450000** in the *Find what* text box.
   c. Press the Tab key.
   d. Type **475000**.
   e. Click the Options button to display additional options. (If additional options already display, skip this step.)
   f. Click the *Match entire cell contents* option to insert a check mark in the check box.
   g. Click Replace All.
   h. At the message telling you that two replacements were made, click OK.
   i. At the Find and Replace dialog box, click the *Match entire cell contents* option to remove the check mark.
   j. Click the Close button to close the Find and Replace dialog box.
3. Save **ExcelL1_C4_P2.xlsx**.

Finding and Replacing Cell Formatting

Use the Format buttons at the expanded Find and Replace dialog box (see Figure 4.10) to search for specific cell formatting and replace with other formatting. Click the down-pointing arrow at the right side of the Format button and a drop-down list displays. Click the *Format* option and the Find Format dialog box displays with the Number, Alignment, Font, Border, Fill, and Protection tabs. Specify formatting at this dialog box. Click the *Choose Format From Cell* option and the mouse pointer displays with a pointer tool attached. Click in the cell containing the desired formatting and the formatting displays in the *Preview* box to the left of the Format button. Click the *Clear Find Format* option and any formatting in the *Preview* box is removed.

Project 2c Finding and Replacing Cell Formatting

1. With **ExcelL1_C4_P2.xlsx** open, search for light turquoise fill color and replace with a purple fill color by completing the following steps:
   a. Click the Find & Select button in the Editing group and then click *Replace* at the drop-down list.
   b. At the Find and Replace dialog box with the Replace tab selected, make sure the dialog box is expanded. (If not, click the Options button.)
   c. Select and then delete any text that displays in the *Find what* text box.
   d. Select and then delete any text that displays in the *Replace with* text box.
   e. Make sure the boxes immediately preceding the two Format buttons display with the text *No Format Set*. (If not, click the down-pointing arrow at the right of the Format button, and then click the *Clear Find Format* option at the drop-down list. Do this for each Format button.)
   f. Click the top Format button.
   g. At the Find Format dialog box, click the Fill tab.
   h. Click the More Colors button.
   i. At the Colors dialog box with the Standard tab selected, click the light turquoise color shown at the right.
   j. Click OK to close the Colors dialog box.
   k. Click OK to close the Find Format dialog box.
   l. Click the bottom Format button.
   m. At the Replace Format dialog box with the Fill tab selected, click the purple color shown at the right.
   n. Click OK to close the dialog box.
   o. At the Find and Replace dialog box, click the Replace All button.
   p. At the message telling you that ten replacements were made, click OK.

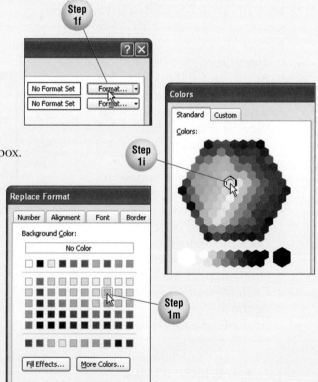

2. Search for yellow fill color and replace with a green fill color by completing the following steps:

   a. At the Find and Replace dialog box, click the top Format button.
   b. At the Find Format dialog box, click the Fill tab.
   c. Click the More Colors button.
   d. At the Colors dialog box with the Standard tab selected, click the yellow color as shown at the right.
   e. Click OK to close the Colors dialog box.
   f. Click OK to close the Find Format dialog box.
   g. Click the bottom Format button.
   h. At the Replace Format dialog box with the Fill tab selected, click the green color shown at the right.
   i. Click OK to close the dialog box.
   j. At the Find and Replace dialog box, click the Replace All button.
   k. At the message telling you that 78 replacements were made, click OK.

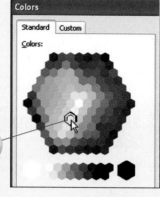

Step 2d

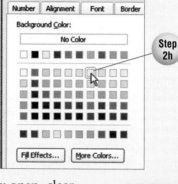

Step 2h

3. Search for 11-point Calibri formatting and replace with 10-point Arial formatting by completing the following steps:

   a. With the Find and Replace dialog box open, clear formatting from the top Format button by clicking the down-pointing arrow and then clicking the *Clear Find Format* option at the drop-down list.
   b. Clear formatting from the bottom Format button by clicking the down-pointing arrow and then clicking *Clear Replace Format*.
   c. Click the top Format button.
   d. At the Find Format dialog box, click the Font tab.
   e. Click *Calibri* in the *Font* list box (you may need to scroll down the list to display this typeface).
   f. Click *11* in the *Size* text box.
   g. Click OK to close the dialog box.
   h. Click the bottom Format button.
   i. At the Replace Format dialog box with the Font tab selected, click *Arial* in the *Font* list box (you may need to scroll down the list to display this typeface).
   j. Click *10* in the *Size* list box.
   k. Click OK to close the dialog box.
   l. At the Find and Replace dialog box, click the Replace All button.
   m. At the message telling you that 174 replacements were made, click OK.
   n. At the Find and Replace dialog box, remove formatting from both Format buttons.
   o. Click the Close button to close the Find and Replace dialog box.

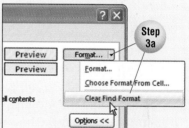

Step 3a

4. Save, print, and then close **ExcelL1_C4_P2.xlsx**.

Project ③ Format a Billing Worksheet

You will insert a formula in a weekly billing worksheet and then sort and filter specific data in the worksheet.

QUICK STEPS

Sort Data
1. Select cells.
2. Click Sort & Filter button.
3. Click desired sort option at drop-down list.

HINT
If you are not satisfied with the results of the sort, immediately click the Undo button.

Sorting Data

Excel is primarily a spreadsheet program, but it also includes some basic database functions. With a database program, you can alphabetize information or arrange numbers numerically. Data can be sorted by columns in a worksheet. Sort data in a worksheet with the Sort & Filter button in the Editing group in the Home tab.

To sort data in a worksheet, select the cells containing data you want to sort, click the Sort & Filter button in the Editing group and then click the option representing the desired sort. The sort option names vary depending on the data in selected cells. For example, if the first column of selected cells contains text, the sort options in the drop-down list display as *Sort A to Z* and *Sort Z to A*. If the selected cells contain dates, the sort options in the drop-down list display as *Sort Oldest to Newest* and *Sort Newest to Oldest* and if the cells contain numbers or values, the sort options display as *Sort Smallest to Largest* and *Sort Largest to Smallest*. If you select more than one column in a worksheet, Excel will sort the data in the first selected column.

Project ③ | Sorting Data

1. Open **ExcelC04Project03.xlsx** and save it and name it **ExcelL1_C4_P3**.
2. Insert a formula in cell F4 that multiplies the rate by the hours. Copy the formula down to cells F5 through F29.
3. Sort the data in the first column in descending order by completing the following steps:
   a. Make cell A4 active.
   b. Click the Sort & Filter button in the Editing group.
   c. Click the *Sort Largest to Smallest* option at the drop-down list.
4. Sort in ascending order by clicking the Sort & Filter button and then clicking *Sort Smallest to Largest* at the drop-down list.
5. Save and then print **ExcelL1_C4_P3.xlsx**.

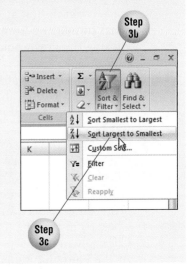

Step 3b

Step 3c

Completing a Custom Sort

If you want to sort data in a column other than the first column, use the Sort dialog box. If you select just one column in a worksheet, click the Sort & Filter button, and then click the desired sort option, only the data in that column is sorted. If this data is related to data to the left or right of the data in the sorted column, that relationship is broken. For example, if you sort cells C4 through C29 in **ExcelL1_C4_P3.xlsx**, the client number, treatment, hours, and total would no longer match the date.

Use the Sort dialog box to sort data and maintain the relationship of all cells. To sort using the Sort dialog box, select the cells you want sorted, click the Sort & Filter button, and then click *Custom Sort*. This displays the Sort dialog box shown in Figure 4.11.

The data displayed in the *Sort by* option box will vary depending on what you have selected. Generally, the data that displays is the title of the first column of selected cells. If the selected cells do not have a title, the data may display as *Column A*. Use this option to specify what column you want sorted. Using the Sort dialog box to sort data in a column maintains the relationship of the data.

Figure 4.11 Sort Dialog Box

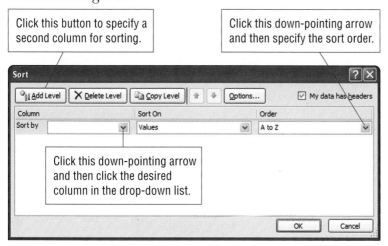

Click this button to specify a second column for sorting.

Click this down-pointing arrow and then specify the sort order.

Click this down-pointing arrow and then click the desired column in the drop-down list.

Project ③b Sorting Data Using the Sort Dialog Box

1. With **ExcelL1_C4_P3.xlsx** open, sort the rates in cells E4 through E29 in ascending order and maintain the relationship to the other data by completing the following steps:
   a. Select cells A3 through F29.
   b. Click the Sort & Filter button and then click *Custom Sort*.
   c. At the Sort dialog box, click the down-pointing arrow at the right of the *Sort by* option box, and then click *Rate* at the drop-down list.
   d. Click the down-pointing arrow at the right of the *Order* option box and then click *Largest to Smallest* at the drop-down list.
   e. Click OK to close the Sort dialog box.
   f. Deselect the cells.

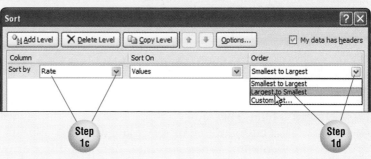

Step 1c

Step 1d

2. Save and then print **ExcelL1_C4_P3.xlsx**.
3. Sort the dates in ascending order (oldest to newest) by completing steps similar to those in Step 1.
4. Save and then print **ExcelL1_C4_P3.xlsx**.

Sorting More Than One Column

When sorting data in cells, you can sort in more than one column. For example, in Project 3c you will be sorting the date from oldest to newest and then sorting client numbers from lowest to highest. In this sort, the dates are sorted first and then client numbers are sorted in ascending order within the same date.

To sort in more than one column, select all columns in the worksheet that need to remain relative and then display the Sort dialog box. At the Sort dialog box, specify the first column you want sorted in the *Sort by* option box, click the *Add Level* button, and then specify the second column in the first *Then by* option box. In Excel, you can sort on multiple columns. Add additional *Then by* option boxes by clicking the *Add Level* button.

Project  **Sorting Data in Two Columns**

1. With **ExcelL1_C4_P3.xlsx** open, select cells A3 through F29.
2. Click the Sort & Filter button and then click *Custom Sort*.
3. At the Sort dialog box, click the down-pointing arrow at the right side of the *Sort by* option box, and then click *Date* in the drop-down list.
4. Make sure *Oldest to Newest* displays in the *Order* option box.
5. Click the *Add Level* button.
6. Click the down-pointing arrow at the right of the first *Then by* option box and then click *Client #* in the drop-down list.
7. Click OK to close the dialog box.
8. Deselect the cells.
9. Save and then print **ExcelL1_C4_P3.xlsx**.

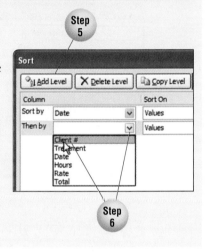

Step 5

Step 6

QUICK STEPS

Filter a List
1. Select cells.
2. Click Filter & Sort button.
3. Click *Filter* at drop-down list.
4. Click down-pointing arrow of heading to filter.
5. Click desired option at drop-down list.

Filtering Data

You can place a restriction, called a *filter*, on data in a worksheet to isolate temporarily specific data. To turn on filtering, make a cell containing data active, click the Filter & Sort button in the Editing group in the Home tab, and then click *Filter* at the drop-down list. This turns on filtering and causes a filter arrow to appear in each column label in the worksheet as shown in Figure 4.12. You do not need to select before turning on filtering because Excel automatically searches for column labels in a worksheet.

To filter data in a worksheet, click the filter arrow in the heading you want to filter. This causes a drop-down list to display with options to filter all records, create a custom filter, or select an entry that appears in one or more of the cells in the column. When you filter data, the filter arrow changes to a funnel icon. The funnel icon indicates that rows in the worksheet have been filtered. To turn off filtering, click the Sort & Filter button and then click *Filter*.

If a column contains numbers, click the filter arrow, point to *Number Filters*, and a side menu displays with options for filtering numbers. For example, you can filter numbers that are equal to, greater than, or less than a number you specify; filter the top ten numbers; and filter numbers that are above or below a specified number.

Figure 4.12 Filtering Data

Turn on the filter feature and filter arrows display in column headings.

Click the filter in the Client # heading, click the *(Select All)* check box to remove the check mark, and then click the *3102* check box to display only those rows containing Client # 3102.

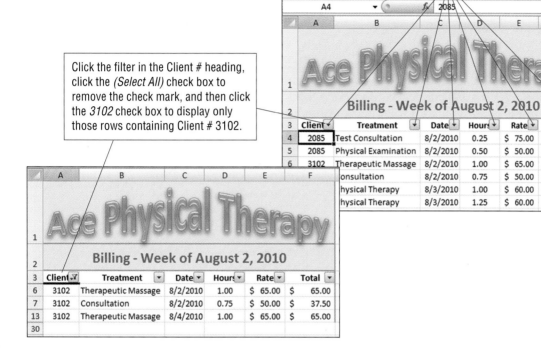

Client ▾	Treatment	Date ▾	Hours ▾	Rate ▾	Total ▾
2085	Test Consultation	8/2/2010	0.25	$ 75.00	$ 18.75
2085	Physical Examination	8/2/2010	0.50	$ 50.00	$ 25.00
3102	Therapeutic Massage	8/2/2010	1.00	$ 65.00	$ 65.00
	onsultation	8/2/2010	0.75	$ 50.00	$ 37.50
	hysical Therapy	8/3/2010	1.00	$ 60.00	$ 60.00
	hysical Therapy	8/3/2010	1.25	$ 60.00	$ 75.00

Billing - Week of August 2, 2010

Client ▾	Treatment	Date ▾	Hours ▾	Rate ▾	Total ▾
3102	Therapeutic Massage	8/2/2010	1.00	$ 65.00	$ 65.00
3102	Consultation	8/2/2010	0.75	$ 50.00	$ 37.50
3102	Therapeutic Massage	8/4/2010	1.00	$ 65.00	$ 65.00

Project 3d Filtering Data

1. With **ExcelL1_C4_P3.xlsx** open, click in cell A4.
2. Turn on filtering by clicking the Sort & Filter button in the Editing group in the Home tab and then clicking *Filter* at the drop-down list.
3. Filter and then print rows for client number 3102 by completing the following steps:
   a. Click the filter arrow in the *Client #* heading.
   b. Click the *(Select All)* check box to remove the check mark.
   c. Scroll down the list box and then click *3102* to insert a check mark in the check box.
   d. Click OK.
   e. Print the worksheet by clicking the Quick Print button on the Quick Access toolbar.
4. Redisplay all rows containing data by completing the following steps:
   a. Click the funnel icon in the *Client #* heading.
   b. Click the *(Select All)* check box to insert a check mark (this also inserts a check mark for all items in the list).
   c. Click OK.

Step 3a

Step 3b

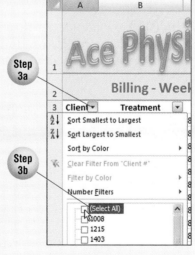

5. Filter and then print a list of clients receiving physical therapy by completing the following steps:
   a. Click the filter arrow in the *Treatment* heading.
   b. Click the *(Select All)* check box.
   c. Click the *Physical Therapy* check box.
   d. Click OK.
   e. Click the Quick Print button on the Quick Access toolbar.
6. Redisplay all rows containing data by completing the following steps:
   a. Click the funnel icon in the *Treatment* heading.
   b. Click the *(Select All)* check box to insert a check mark (this also inserts a check mark for all items in the list).
   c. Click OK.
7. Display the top two highest rates by completing the following steps:
   a. Click the filter arrow in the *Rate* heading.
   b. Point to *Number Filters* and then click *Top 10* at the side menu.
   c. At the Top 10 AutoFilter dialog box, select the *10* that displays in the middle text box and then type *2*.
   d. Click OK to close the dialog box.
   e. Click the Quick Print button on the Quick Access toolbar.
8. Redisplay all rows containing data by completing the following steps:
   a. Click the funnel icon in the *Rate* heading.
   b. Click the *(Select All)* check box to insert a check mark (this also inserts a check mark for all items in the list).
   c. Click OK.

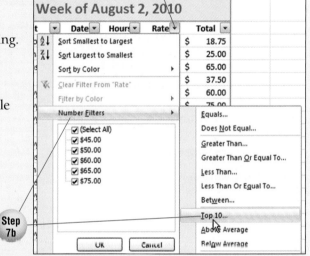

9. Display totals greater than $60 by completing the following steps:
   a. Click the filter arrow in the *Total* heading.
   b. Point to *Number Filters* and then click *Greater Than*.
   c. At the Custom AutoFilter dialog box, type *60* and then click OK.

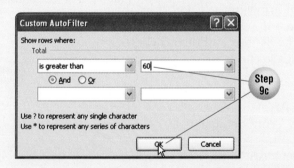

   d. Click the Quick Print button on the Quick Access toolbar.
10. Turn off the filtering feature by clicking the Sort & Filter button and then clicking *Filter* at the drop-down list.
11. Save and then close **ExcelL1_C4_P3.xlsx**.

Project ④ Plan and Create a Worksheet

You will use steps presented to plan a worksheet and then create, save, print, and then close the worksheet.

Planning a Worksheet

The worksheets you have worked with so far basically have already been planned. If you need to plan a worksheet yourself, some steps you can follow are listed below. These are basic steps—you may think of additional steps or additional information to help you plan a worksheet.

- **Step 1: Identify the purpose of the worksheet.** The more definite you are about your purpose, the easier organizing your data into an effective worksheet will be. Consider things such as the purpose of the worksheet, the intended audience, the desired output or results, and the data required.

- **Step 2: Design the worksheet.** To do this, you need to determine how the data is to be organized, the titles of columns and rows, and how to emphasize important information. Designing the worksheet also includes determining any calculations that need to be performed.

- **Step 3: Create a sketch of the worksheet.** A diagram or sketch can help create a logical and well-ordered worksheet. With a sketch, you can experiment with alternative column and row configurations and titles and headings. When creating a sketch, start with the heading or title of the worksheet, which should provide a quick overview of what the data represents in the worksheet. Determine appropriate column and row titles that clearly identify the data.

- **Step 4: Enter the data in the worksheet.** Type the data in the worksheet, including the worksheet title, column titles, row titles, and data within cells. Enter any required formulas into the worksheet and then format the worksheet to make it appealing and easy to read.

- **Step 5: Test the worksheet data.** After preparing the worksheet and inserting any necessary formulas, check the data to be sure that the calculations are performed correctly. Consider verifying the formula results by completing the formula on a calculator.

Project ④ Planning and Creating a Worksheet

1. Look at the data shown in Figure 4.13. (The first paragraph is simply a description of the data—do not include this in the worksheet.) After reviewing the data, complete the following steps:
   a. Create a sketch of how you think the worksheet should be organized.
   b. Create a worksheet from the sketch. (Be sure to include the necessary formula to calculate the total costs.)
   c. Apply formatting to enhance the appearance of the worksheet.
2. Save the workbook and name it **ExcelL1_C4_P4**.
3. Print and then close **ExcelL1_C4_P4.xlsx**.

Figure 4.13 **Project 4**

The following data itemizes budgeted direct labor hours and dollars by department for planning purposes. This data is prepared quarterly and sent to the plant manager and production manager.

DIRECT LABOR BUDGET

	Labor Rate	Total Hours	Total Costs
April			
Assembly	12.75	723	
Electronics	16.32	580	
Machining	27.34	442	
May			
Assembly	12.75	702	
Electronics	16.32	615	
Machining	27.34	428	
June			
Assembly	12.75	694	
Electronics	16.32	643	
Machining	27.34	389	

CHAPTER summary

- The Page Setup group in the Page Layout tab contains buttons for changing margins, page orientation and size, and buttons for establishing a print area, inserting page break, applying a picture background, and printing titles.

- The default left and right margins are 0.7 inch and the default top and bottom margins are 0.75 inch. Change these default margins with the Margins button in the Page Setup group in the Page Layout tab.

- Display the Page Setup dialog box with the Margins tab selected by clicking the Margins button and then clicking *Custom Margins* at the drop-down list.

- Center a worksheet on the page with the *Horizontally* and *Vertically* options at the Page Setup dialog box with the Margins tab selected.

- Click the Orientation button in the Page Setup group in the Page Layout tab to display the two orientation choices—*Portrait* and *Landscape*.

- Insert a page break by selecting the column or row, clicking the Breaks button in the Page Setup group in the Page Layout tab, and then clicking *Insert Page Break* at the drop-down list.

- To insert both a horizontal and vertical page break at the same time, make a cell active, click the Breaks button, and then click *Insert Page Break* at the drop-down list.

- Display a worksheet in page break preview by clicking the Page Break Preview button in the view area on the Status bar or clicking the View tab and then clicking the Page Break Preview button.

- Use options at the Page Setup dialog box with the Sheet tab selected to specify that you want column or row titles to print on each page. Display this dialog box by clicking the Print Titles button in the Page Setup group in the Page Layout tab.

- Use options in the Scale to Fit group in the Page Layout tab to scale data to fit on a specific number of pages.

- Use the Background button in the Page Setup group in the Page Layout tab to insert a worksheet background picture. A background picture displays on the screen but does not print.

- Use options in the Sheet Options group in the Page Layout tab to specify if you want gridlines and headings to view and/or print.

- Specify a print area by selecting the desired cells, clicking the Print Area button in the Page Setup group in the Page Layout tab and then clicking *Set Print Area* at the drop-down list. Add another print area by selecting the desired cells, clicking the Print Area button, and then clicking *Add to Print Area* at the drop-down list.

- Create a header and/or footer with the Header & Footer button in the Text group in the Insert tab, in Page Layout view, or with options at the Page Setup dialog box with the Header/Footer tab selected.

- Customize print jobs with options at the Print dialog box.

- To check spelling in a worksheet, click the Review tab and then click the Spelling button.

- Click the Undo button on the Quick Access toolbar to reverse the most recent action and click the Redo button to redo a previously reversed action.
- Use options at the Find and Replace dialog box with the Find tab selected to find specific data and/or formatting in a worksheet.
- Use options at the Find and Replace dialog box with the Replace tab selected to find specific data and/or formatting and replace with other data and/or formatting.
- Sort data in a worksheet with options from the Sort & Filter button in the Editing group in the Home tab.
- Create a custom sort with options at the Sort dialog box. Display this dialog box by clicking the Sort & Filter button and then clicking *Custom Sort* at the drop-down list.
- Use the filter feature to temporarily isolate specific data. Turn on the filter feature by clicking the Sort & Filter button in the Editing group in the Home tab and then clicking *Filter* at the drop-down list. This inserts filter arrows in each column label. Click a filter arrow and then use options at the drop-down list that displays to specify the filter data.
- Plan a worksheet by completing these basic steps: identify the purpose of the worksheet, design the worksheet, create a sketch of the worksheet, enter the data in the worksheet, and test the worksheet data.

COMMANDS review

FEATURE	RIBBON TAB, GROUP	BUTTON, OPTION	KEYBOARD SHORTCUT
Margins	Page Layout, Page Setup		
Page Setup dialog box with Margins tab selected	Page Layout, Page Setup	, Custom Margins	
Orientation	Page Layout, Page Setup		
Size	Page Layout, Page Setup		
Insert page break	Page Layout, Page Setup	, Insert Page Break	
Remove page break	Page Layout, Page Setup	, Remove Page Break	
Page Break Preview	View, Workbook Views		
Page Setup dialog box with Sheet tab selected	Page Layout, Page Setup		
Scale width	Page Layout, Scale to Fit	Width: Automatic	
Scale height	Page Layout, Scale to Fit	Height: Automatic	
Scale	Page Layout, Scale to Fit	Scale: 100%	
Background picture	Page Layout, Page Setup		
Print Area	Page Layout, Page Setup		
Header and footer	Insert, Text		
Page Layout view	View, Workbook Views		
Spelling	Review, Proofing		F7
Find and Replace dialog box with Find tab selected	Home, Editing	, Find	Ctrl + F
Find and Replace dialog box with Replace tab selected	Home, Editing	, Replace	Ctrl + H
Sort data	Home, Editing		
Filter data	Home, Editing		

CONCEPTS check

Test Your Knowledge

Completion: In the space provided at the right, indicate the correct term, symbol, or command.

1. This is the default left and right margin measurement. _____

2. This is the default top and bottom margin measurement. _____

3. The Margins button is located in this tab. _____

4. By default, a worksheet prints in this orientation on a page. _____

5. Click the Print Titles button in the Page Setup group in the Page Layout tab and the Page Setup dialog box displays with this tab selected. _____

6. Use options in this group in the Page Layout tab to adjust the printed output by a percentage to fit the number of pages specified. _____

7. Use this button in the Page Setup group in the Page Layout tab to select and print specific areas in a worksheet. _____

8. Click the Header & Footer button in the Text group in the Insert tab and the worksheet displays in this view. _____

9. This tab contains options for formatting and customizing a header and/or footer. _____

10. Click this tab to display the Spelling button. _____

11. The Undo and Redo buttons are located on this toolbar. _____

12. Click this button in the Find and Replace dialog box to expand the dialog box. _____

13. Use these two buttons at the expanded Find and Replace dialog box to search for specific cell formatting and replace with other formatting. _____

14. Use this button in the Home tab to sort data in a worksheet. _____

15. Use this feature to isolate temporarily a specific data in a worksheet. _____

SKILLS check

Demonstrate Your Proficiency

1 FORMAT A DATA ANALYSIS WORKSHEET

1. Open **ExcelC04Assessment01.xlsx**.
2. Save the workbook with Save As and name it **ExcelL1_C4_A1**.
3. Make the following changes to the worksheet:
   a. Insert a formula in cell H4 that averages the amounts in cells B4 through G4.
   b. Copy the formula in cell H4 down to cells H5 through H9.
   c. Insert a formula in cell B10 that adds the amounts in cells B4 through B9.
   d. Copy the formula in cell B10 over to cells C10 through H10. (Click the AutoFill Options button and then click *Fill With Formatting* at the drop-down list.)
   e. Change the orientation of the worksheet to landscape.
   f. Change the top margin to 3 inches and the left margin to 1.5 inches.
4. Save and then print **ExcelL1_C4_A1.xlsx**.
5. Make the following changes to the worksheet:
   a. Change the top margin to 1 inch and the left margin to 0.7 inch.
   b. Change the orientation back to portrait.
   c. Horizontally and vertically center the worksheet on the page.
   d. Scale the worksheet so it fits on one page.
6. Save, print, and then close **ExcelL1_C4_A1.xlsx**.

2 FORMAT A TEST RESULTS WORKSHEET

1. Open **ExcelC04Assessment02.xlsx**.
2. Save the workbook with Save As and name it **ExcelL1_C4_A2**.
3. Make the following changes to the worksheet.
   a. Insert a formula in cell N4 that averages the test scores in cells B4 through M4.
   b. Copy the formula in cell N4 down to cells N5 through N21.
   c. Type **Average** in cell A22.
   d. Insert a formula in cell B22 that averages the test scores in cells B4 through B21.
   e. Copy the formula in cell B22 across to cells C22 through N22.
   f. Insert a page break between columns G and H.
4. View the worksheet in Page Break Preview.
5. Change back to the Normal view.
6. Specify that the column row titles (A3 through A22) are to print on each page.
7. Create a header that prints the page number at the right side of the page.
8. Create a footer that prints your name at the left side of the page and the workbook file name at the right side of the page.
9. Save and then print the worksheet.
10. Set a print area for cells N4 through N22 and then print the cells.
11. Clear the print area.
12. Save and then close **ExcelL1_C4_A2.xlsx**.

3 FORMAT AN EQUIPMENT RENTAL WORKSHEET

1. Open **ExcelC04Assessment03.xlsx**.
2. Save the workbook with Save As and name it **ExcelL1_C4_A3**.
3. Insert a formula in cell H3 that multiplies the rate in cell G3 by the hours in cell F3. Copy the formula in cell H3 down to cells H4 through H16.
4. Insert a formula in cell H17 that sums the amounts in cells H3 through H16.
5. Complete the following find and replaces:
    a. Find all occurrences of cells containing *75* and replace with *90*.
    b. Find all occurrences of cells containing *55* and replace with *60*.
    c. Find all occurrences of *Barrier Concrete* and replace with *Lee Sand and Gravel*.
    d. Find all occurrences of 11-point Calibri and replace with 10-point Cambria.
6. Insert a header that prints the date at the left side of the page and the time at the right side of the page.
7. Insert a footer that prints your name at the left side of the page and the workbook name at the right side of the page.
8. Print the worksheet horizontally and vertically centered on the page.
9. Save and then close **ExcelL1_C4_A3.xlsx**.

4 FORMAT AN INVOICES WORKSHEET

1. Open **ExcelC04Assessment04.xlsx**.
2. Save the workbook with Save As and name it **ExcelL1_C4_A4**.
3. Search for the light green fill (the lightest fill in the worksheet that fills cells in every other row beginning with row 5) and replace it with no fill. (Do this at the Find and Replace dialog box with the Replace tab selected.)
4. Insert a formula in G4 that multiplies the amount in E4 with the percentage in F4 and then adds the product to cell E4. (If you write the formula correctly, the result in G4 will display as *$488.25*.)
5. Copy the formula in cell G4 down to cells G5 through G17.
6. Complete a spelling check on the worksheet.
7. Find all occurrences of *Picture* and replace with *Portrait*. (Do not type a space after *Picture* or *Portrait* because you want to find occurrences that end with an "s.")
8. Sort the records by invoice number in ascending order (smallest to largest).
9. Sort the records by client number in ascending order (A to Z) and then by date in ascending order (oldest to newest).
10. Insert a footer in the worksheet that prints your name at the left side of the page and the current date at the right side of the page.
11. Center the worksheet horizontally and vertically on the page.
12. Save and then print **ExcelL1_C4_A4.xlsx**.
13. Select cells A3 through G3 and then turn on the filter feature and complete the following filters:
    a. Filter and then print a list of rows containing client number 11-279.

b. Filter and then print a list of rows containing the top three highest amounts due.

c. Filter and then print a list of rows containing amounts due that are less than $500.

14. Save and then close **ExcelL1_C4_A4.xlsx**.

5 CREATE A WORKSHEET CONTAINING SORT ORDER INFORMATION

1. Use Excel's Help feature and learn about the default sort order. After reading and printing the information presented, create a worksheet containing a summary of the information. Create the worksheet with the following features:

   a. Create a title for the worksheet.

   b. Set the data in cells in a serif typeface and change the data color.

   c. Add borders to the cells (you determine the border style).

   d. Add a color shading to cells (you determine the color—make it complementary to the data color).

   e. Create a footer that prints your name at the left margin and the file name at the right margin.

2. Save the workbook and name it **ExcelL1_C4_A5**.

3. Print and then close **ExcelL1_C4_A5.xlsx**.

CASE study

Part 1

Apply Your Skills

You are the sales manager for Macadam Realty. You decide that you want to display sample mortgage worksheets in the reception area display rack. Open the **MacadamMortgages.xlsx** workbook, save it with Save As and name it **ExcelL1_C4_CS_P1A**, and then add the following information and make the following changes:

- In column C, insert a formula that determines the down payment amount.
- In column D, insert a formula that determines the loan amount.
- In column G, insert a formula using the PMT function (enter the *Pv* as a negative).
- Insert the date and time as a header and your name and the workbook name (**ExcelL1_C4_CS_P1A.xlsx**) as a footer.
- Find 11-point Calibri formatting and replace with 11-point Candara formatting.
- Scale the worksheet so it prints on one page.

Save and then print **ExcelL1_C4_CS_P1A.xlsx**. After looking at the printed worksheet, you decide that you need to make the following changes:

- Sort the *Price of Home* column from smallest to largest.
- Change the percentage amount in column E from 6% to 7%.
- Shade the cells in row 4 in the light yellow color that matches the fill in cell A2. Copy this shading to every other row of cells in the worksheet (stopping at row 46).

Save the edited worksheet with Save As and name it **ExcelL1_C4_CS_P1B**. Edit the footer to reflect the workbook name change (from *ExcelL1_C4_CS_P1A.xlsx* to *ExcelL1_C4_CS_P1B.xlsx*). Save, print and then close **ExcelL1_C4_CS_P1B.xlsx**. (Make sure the worksheet prints on one page.)

Part 2

You are preparing for a quarterly sales meeting during which you will discuss retirement issues with the sales officers. You want to encourage them to consider opening an Individual Retirement Account (IRA) to supplement the retirement contributions made by Macadam Realty. You have begun an IRA worksheet but need to complete it. Open **MacadamIRA.xlsx** and then save it with Save As and name it **ExcelL1_C4_CS_P2A**. Make the following changes to the worksheet:

- Insert in cell C6 a formula that calculates the future value of an investment. Use the FV function to write the formula. You must use absolute and mixed cell references for the formula. When entering the *Rate* (percentage), the column letter is variable but the row number is fixed; when entering the *Nper* (years), the column letter is fixed but the row number is variable; and when entering the *Pmt* (the contribution amount), both the column letter and row number are absolute.
- Copy the formula in cell C6 down to cells C7 through C19. Copy the formula in cell C6 across to cells D6 through K6. Continue in this manner until the amounts are entered in all the appropriate cells.
- Select and then merge and center cells A6 through A19. Type the text **Number of Years** and then rotate the text up. Make sure the text is centered in the merged cell. Apply 12-point Calibri bold formatting to the text.
- Adjust the column widths so all text is visible in the cells.
- Change the page orientation to landscape.
- Vertically and horizontally center the worksheet.
- Include a header that prints the page number and insert a footer that prints your name.

Save the worksheet and then print it so that the row titles print on both pages. After looking at the worksheet, you decide to make the following changes:

- Remove the header containing the page number.
- Edit the footer so the date prints at the left margin and your name prints at the right margin.
- Scale the worksheet so it prints on one page.

Save the workbook and name it **ExcelL1_C4_CS_P2B** and then print the worksheet. Change the amount in cell D3 to *$2,500* and then print the worksheet again. Change the amount in cell D3 to *$3,000* and then print the worksheet again. Save and then close **ExcelL1_C4_CS_P2B.xlsx**.

You have clients living in Canada that are interested in purchasing real estate in the United States. For those clients, you like to keep a conversion worksheet available. Using the Internet, search for the MS MoneyCentral Investor Currency Rates site. Determine the current currency exchange rate for Canada and then create a worksheet with the following specifications:

- Apply formatting that is similar to the formatting in the worksheets you worked with in the first two parts of the case study.
- Create the following columns:
  - Column for home price in American dollars.
  - Column for home price in Canadian dollars.
  - Column for amount of down payment.
  - Column for loan total.
  - Column for monthly payment.
- In the column for home prices, insert home amounts beginning with $100,000, incrementing every $50,000, and ending with $1,000,000.
- Insert a formula in the home price in the Canadian dollars column that displays the home price in Canadian dollars.
- Insert a formula in the down payment column that multiplies the Canadian home price by 20%.
- Insert a formula in the loan total column that subtracts the down payment from the Canadian home price.
- Insert a formula in the monthly payment column that determines the monthly payment using the PMT function. Use 6% as the rate (be sure to divide by 12 months), 360 as the number of payments, and the loan amount as a negative as the present value.
- Apply any other formatting you feel necessary to improve the worksheet.

Save the completed workbook and name it **ExcelL1_C4_CS_P3**. Display formulas and then print the worksheet. Redisplay the formulas and then save and close the workbook.

After working with the commissions worksheet, you decide to maintain the information in an Access table. Before importing the information to an Access table, open **MacadamCommissions.xlsx** and then save the workbook with Save As and name it **ExcelL1_C4_CS_P4**. Insert a formula in G4 that multiplies the sale price by the commission percentage. Copy the formula down to cells G5 through G24. Insert a formula in cell G25 that totals the commissions and then adjust the column width so the entire total is visible. Select cells A3 through G25 and then save the selected cells in a separate workbook named **ExcelMacadamComm**. Create a database in Access named **Macadam** and then import the **ExcelMacadamComm.xlsx** Excel workbook as an Access table. Save the database and print the newly imported table.

Preparing and Formatting a Worksheet

ASSESSING proficiency

In this unit, you have learned to create, save, print, edit, and format Excel worksheets; create and insert formulas; and enhance worksheets with features such as headers and footers, page numbering, sorting, and filtering.

Note: Before beginning computer assessments, copy to your storage medium the Excel2007L1U1 subfolder from the Excel2007L1 folder on the CD that accompanies this textbook and then make Excel2007L1U1 the active folder.

Assessment 1 Create Sales Bonuses Workbook

1. Create the Excel worksheet shown in Figure U1.1. Format the cells as you see them in the figure. Format the money amounts in Accounting format with no decimal places.
2. Insert an IF statement in cell C4 that inserts *7%* if B4 is greater than 99999 and inserts *5%* if B4 is less than 100000.
3. Format the number in cell C4 so it displays as a percentage with no decimal places. Copy the formula in cell C4 down to cells C5 through C11.
4. Insert a formula in cell D4 that multiplies the amount in B4 with the percentage in cell C4. Copy the formula in D4 down to cells D5 through D11.
5. Insert a footer that contains your first and last names and the current date.
6. Print the worksheet horizontally and vertically centered on the page.
7. Save the workbook and name it **ExcelL1_U1_A1**.
8. Close **ExcelL1_U1_A1.xlsx**.

Figure U1.1 Assessment 1

	A	B	C	D	E
1	**Capstan Marine Products**				
2		Sales Department			
3	Salesperson	Sales	Bonus	Bonus Amount	
4	Allejandro, Eduardo	$ 105,345			
5	Crispin, Juliette	$ 96,345			
6	Frankel, Hayden	$ 89,234			
7	Hiesmann, Denae	$ 120,455			
8	Jarvis, Robert	$ 131,095			
9	Littleman, Marcus	$ 99,850			
10	Weisen, George	$ 103,125			
11	Schoenfeld, Allie	$ 78,495			
12					

Assessment 2 Format Equipment Purchase Plan Workbook

1. Open **ExcelU01Assessment02.xlsx** and then save the workbook and name it **ExcelL1_U1_A2**.
2. The owner of Hilltop Equipment Rental is interested in purchasing a new tractor and needs to determine monthly payments on three different models. Insert a formula in cell E4 that uses the PMT function to calculate monthly payments. Copy the formula down to cells E5 and E6.
3. Insert a formula in cell F4 that multiplies the amount in E4 by the amount in D4.
4. Copy the formula in cell F4 down to cells F5 and F6.
5. Insert a formula in cell G4 that subtracts the amount in B4 from the amount in F4.
6. Copy the formula in cell G4 down to cells G5 and G6.
7. Change the vertical alignment of cell A2 to Middle Align.
8. Change the vertical alignment of cells A3 through G3 to Bottom Align.
9. Save, print, and then close **ExcelL1_U1_A2.xlsx**.

Assessment 3 Format Accounts Due Workbook

1. Open **ExcelU01Assessment03.xlsx** and then save the workbook and name it **ExcelL1_U1_A3**.
2. Using the DATE function, enter a formula in each of the specified cells that returns the serial number for the specified date:

C4	=	**October 26, 2010**
C5	=	**October 27, 2010**
C6	=	**October 27, 2010**
C7	=	**October 29, 2010**
C8	=	**November 3, 2010**
C9	=	**November 5, 2010**
C10	=	**November 5, 2010**
C11	=	**November 12, 2010**
C12	=	**November 12, 2010**

3. Enter a formula in cell E4 that inserts the due date (date of service plus the number of days in the *Terms* column).
4. Copy the formula in cell E4 down to cells E5 through E12.
5. Make cell A14 active and then type your name.
6. Make cell A15 active and then use the NOW function to insert the current date as a serial number.
7. Save, print, and then close **ExcelL1_U1_A3.xlsx**.

Assessment 4 Format First Quarter Sales Workbook

1. Open **ExcelU01Assessment04.xlsx** and then save the workbook and name it **ExcelL1_U1_A4**.
2. Insert a formula in cell E4 that totals the amounts in B4, C4, and D4. Copy the formula in cell E4 down to cells E5 through E18.
3. Insert an IF statement in cell F4 that inserts *10%* if E4 is greater than 99999 and inserts *7%* if E4 is greater than 49999 and inserts *5%* if E4 is greater than 24999 and inserts *0%* if E4 is greater than 0.
4. Make sure the result of the IF formula displays in cell F4 as a percentage with no decimal points and then copy the formula down to cells F5 through F18.

5. Select cells A5 through F5 and then insert the same yellow fill as cell A2. Apply the same yellow fill to cells A7 through F7, A9 through F9, A11 through F11, A13 through F13, A15 through F15, and cells A17 through F17.

6. Insert a footer that prints your name at the left, the current date at the middle, and the current time at the right.

7. Print the worksheet horizontally and vertically centered on the page.

8. Save, print, and then close **ExcelL1_U1_A4.xlsx**.

Assessment 5 **Format Weekly Payroll Workbook**

1. Open **ExcelU01Assessment05.xlsx** and then save the workbook and name it **ExcelL1_U1_A5**.

2. Insert a formula in cell E4 that multiplies the hourly wage by the hours and then adds that to the multiplication of the hourly wage by the overtime pay rate (1.5) and then overtime hours. (Use parentheses in the formula and use an absolute cell reference for the overtime pay rate (1.5). Refer to Chapter 2, Project 5c.) Copy the formula down to cells E5 through E17.

3. Insert a formula in cell F4 that multiplies the gross pay by the withholding tax rate (W/H Rate). (Use a mixed cell reference for the cell containing the withholding rate. Refer to Chapter 2, Project 5c.) Copy the formula down to cells F5 through F17.

4. Insert a formula in cell G4 that multiplies the gross pay by the Social Security rate (SS Rate). (Use a mixed cell reference for the cell containing the Social Security rate. Refer to Chapter 2, Project 5c.) Copy the formula down to cells G5 through G17.

5. Insert a formula in cell H4 that adds together the Social Security tax and the withholding tax and subtracts that from the gross pay. Copy the formula down to cells H5 through H17.

6. Sort the employee last names alphabetically in ascending order (A to Z).

7. Center the worksheet horizontally and vertically on the page.

8. Insert a footer that prints your name at the left side of the page and the worksheet name at the right side of the page.

9. Save, print, and then close **ExcelL1_U1_A5.xlsx**.

Assessment 6 **Format Customer Sales Analysis Workbook**

1. Open **ExcelU01Assessment06.xlsx** and then save the workbook and name it **ExcelL1_U1_A6**.

2. Insert formulas and drag down formulas to complete the worksheet.

3. Change the orientation to landscape.

4. Insert a header that prints the page number at the right side of the page.

5. Insert a footer that prints your name at the right side of the page.

6. Horizontally and vertically center the worksheet on the page.

7. Specify that the column headings in cells A3 through A9 print on both pages.

8. Save, print, and then close **ExcelL1_U1_A6.xlsx**.

Assessment 7 **Format Invoices Workbook**

1. Open **ExcelU01Assessment07.xlsx** and then save the workbook and name it **ExcelL1_U1_A7**.

2. Insert a formula in cell G4 that multiplies the amount in E4 by the percentage in F4 and then adds that total to the amount in E4. (Use parentheses in this formula.)

3. Copy the formula in cell G4 down to cells G5 through G18.

4. Find all occurrences of cells containing *11-279* and replace with *10-005*.
5. Find all occurrences of cells containing *8.5* and replace with *9.0*.
6. Search for the Calibri font and replace with the Candara font (do not specify a type size so that Excel replaces all sizes of Calibri with Candara).
7. Print **ExcelL1_U1_A7.xlsx**.
8. Filter and then print a list of rows containing only the client number *04-325*. (After printing, return the list to *(All)*.)
9. Filter and then print a list of rows containing only the service *Development*. (After printing, return the list to *(All)*.)
10. Filter and then print a list of rows containing the top three highest totals in the *Amount Due* column. (After printing, turn off the filter feature.)
11. Save and then close **ExcelL1_U1_A7.xlsx**.

WRITING activities

The following activities give you the opportunity to practice your writing skills along with demonstrating an understanding of some of the important Excel features you have mastered in this unit. Use correct grammar, appropriate word choices, and clear sentence construction.

Activity 1 Plan and Prepare Orders Summary Workbook

Plan and prepare a worksheet with the information shown in Figure U1.2. Apply formatting of your choosing to the worksheet either with a cell or table style or with formatting at the Format Cells dialog box. Save the completed worksheet and name it **ExcelL1_U1_Act01**. Print and then close **ExcelL1_U1_Act01.xlsx**.

Figure U1.2 Activity 1

Prepare a weekly summary of orders taken that itemizes the products coming into the company and the average order size.

The products and average order size include:

Black and gold wall clock—$2,450 worth of orders, average order size of $125
Traveling alarm clock—$1,358 worth of orders, average order size of $195
Water-proof watch—$890 worth of orders, average order size of $90
Dashboard clock—$2,135 worth of orders, average order size of $230
Pyramid clock—$3,050 worth of orders, average order size of $375
Gold chain watch—$755 worth of orders, average order size of $80

In the worksheet, total the amount ordered and also calculate the average weekly order size. Sort the data in the worksheet by the order amount in descending order.

Activity 2 Prepare Depreciation Workbook

Assets within a company, such as equipment, can be depreciated over time. Several methods are available for determining the amount of depreciation such as the straight-line depreciation method, fixed-declining balance method, and the double-declining method. Use Excel's Help feature to learn about two depreciation methods—straight-line and double-declining depreciation. After reading about the two methods, create an Excel worksheet with the following information:

- An appropriate title
- A heading for straight-line depreciation
- The straight-line depreciation function
- The name and a description for each straight-line depreciation function argument category
- A heading for double-declining depreciation
- The double-declining depreciation function
- The name and a description for each double-declining depreciation function argument category

Apply formatting of your choosing to the worksheet. Save the completed workbook and name it **ExcelL1_U1_Act02**. Print the worksheet horizontally and vertically centered on the page. Close **ExcelL1_U1_Act02.xlsx**.

Activity 3 Insert Straight-Line Depreciation Formula

Open **ExcelU01Activity03.xlsx** and then save the workbook and name it **ExcelL1_U1_Act03**. Insert the function to determine straight-line depreciation in cell E3. Copy the formula down to cells E4 through E10. Apply formatting of your choosing to the worksheet. Print the worksheet horizontally and vertically centered on the page. Save and then close **ExcelL1_U1_Act03.xlsx**.

Optional: Briefly research the topic of straight-line and double-declining depreciation to find out why businesses depreciate their assets. What purpose does it serve? Locate information about the topic on the Internet or in your school library. Then use Word 2007 to write a half-page, single-spaced report explaining the financial reasons for using depreciation methods. Save the document and name it **ExcelL1_U1_Act03Report**. Print and then close the document.

Create a Travel Planning Worksheet

Make sure you are connected to the Internet. Use a search engine of your choosing to look for information on traveling to a specific country that interests you. Find sites that provide cost information for airlines, hotels, meals, entertainment, and car rentals. Create a travel planning worksheet for the country that includes the following:

- appropriate title
- appropriate headings
- airline costs

- hotel costs (off-season and in-season rates if available)
- estimated meal costs
- entertainment costs
- car rental costs

Save the completed workbook and name it **ExcelL1_U1_Act04**. Print and then close the workbook.

Microsoft®

Unit 2: Enhancing the Display of Workbooks

➤ Moving Data within and between Workbooks

➤ Maintaining Workbooks

➤ Creating a Chart in Excel

➤ Adding Visual Interest to Workbooks

Benchmark Microsoft® Excel 2007 Level 1

Microsoft Certified Application Specialist Skills—Unit 2

Reference No.	Skill	Pages
1	**Creating and Manipulating Data**	
1.3	Modify cell contents and formats	
1.3.1	Cut, copy, and paste data and cell contents	158-164, 181-182
1.4	Change worksheet views	
1.4.1	Change views within a single window	171-174
1.4.2	Split windows	171-174
1.4.3	Open and arrange new windows	177-180
1.5	Manage worksheets	
1.5.1	Copy worksheets	167-168, 207-208
1.5.2	Reposition worksheets within workbooks	167-168
1.5.3	Rename worksheets	167-168
1.5.4	Hide and unhide worksheets	169-170
1.5.5	Insert and delete worksheets	164-166
2	**Formatting Data and Content**	
2.1	Format worksheets	
2.1.3	Add color to worksheet tabs	167-168
2.1.4	Format worksheet backgrounds	291-292
2.3	Format cells and cell content	
2.3.8	Insert, modify, and remove hyperlinks	275-277
4	**Presenting Data Visually**	
4.1	Create and format charts	
4.1.1	Select appropriate data sources for charts	239-243
4.1.2	Select appropriate chart types to represent data sources	243-245
4.1.3	Format charts using Quick Styles	246-248, 257-259
4.2	Modify charts	
4.2.1	Add and remove chart elements	249-253
4.2.2	Move and size charts	241-243, 260-261
4.2.3	Change chart types	243-245
4.4	Insert and modify illustrations	
4.4.1	Insert and modify pictures from files (not clip art files)	255-256, 288-289
4.4.2	Insert and modify SmartArt graphics	292-297
4.4.3	Insert and modify shapes	284-287
5	**Collaborating and Securing Data**	
5.1	Manage changes to workbooks	
5.1.2	Insert, display, modify, and delete comments	222-226
5.4	Save workbooks	
5.4.1	Save workbooks for use in a previous version of Excel	211-212
5.4.2	Using the correct format, save a workbook as a template, a Web page, a macro-enabled document, or another appropriate format	213-214, 272-274

Note: The Level 1 and Level 2 texts each address approximately half of the Microsoft Certified Application Specialist skills. Complete coverage of the skills is offered in the combined Level 1 and Level 2 text titled *Benchmark Series Microsoft® Excel 2007: Levels 1 and 2*, which has been approved as certified courseware and which displays the Microsoft Certified Application Specialist logo on the cover.

Moving Data within and between Workbooks

PERFORMANCE OBJECTIVES

Upon successful completion of Chapter 5, you will be able to:

- Create a workbook with multiple worksheets
- Move, copy, and paste cells within a worksheet
- Split a worksheet into windows and freeze panes
- Name a range of cells and use a range in a formula
- Open multiple workbooks
- Arrange, size, and move workbooks
- Copy and paste data between workbooks
- Link data between worksheets
- Link worksheets with a 3-D reference
- Copy and paste a worksheet between programs

excel Chapter 5

Tutorial 5.1
Managing Worksheets and Workbooks
Tutorial 5.2
Working with Multiple Worksheets

Up to this point, the workbooks in which you have been working have consisted of only one worksheet. In this chapter, you will learn to create a workbook with several worksheets and complete tasks such as copying and pasting data within and between worksheets. Moving and pasting or copying and pasting selected cells in and between worksheets is useful for rearranging data or for saving time. You will also work with multiple workbooks and complete tasks such as arranging, sizing, and moving workbooks, and opening and closing multiple workbooks.

Note: Before beginning computer projects, copy to your storage medium the Excel2007L1C5 subfolder from the Excel2007L1 folder on the CD that accompanies this textbook and then make Excel2007L1C5 the active folder.

Project  Manage Data in a Multiple-Worksheet Account Workbook

You will open an account workbook containing three worksheets and then move, copy, and paste data between the worksheets. You will also hide and unhide worksheets, and format and print multiple worksheets in the workbook.

Creating a Workbook with Multiple Worksheets

An Excel workbook can contain multiple worksheets. You can create a variety of worksheets within a workbook for related data. For example, a workbook may contain a worksheet for the expenses for each salesperson in a company and another worksheet for the monthly payroll for each department within the company. Another example is recording sales statistics for each quarter in individual worksheets within a workbook.

By default, a workbook contains three worksheets named *Sheet1*, *Sheet2*, and *Sheet3*. (Later in this chapter, you will learn how to change these default names.) Display various worksheets in the workbook by clicking the desired tab.

Project 1a — Displaying Worksheets in a Workbook

1. Open **ExcelC05Project01.xlsx** and then save the workbook and name it **ExcelL1_C5_P1**.
2. This workbook contains three worksheets. Display the various worksheets by completing the following steps:
   a. Display the second worksheet by clicking the Sheet2 tab that displays immediately above the Status bar.
   b. Display the third worksheet by clicking the Sheet3 tab that displays immediately above the Status bar.
   c. Return to the first worksheet by clicking the Sheet1 tab.
3. Make the following changes to worksheets in the workbook:
   a. Click the Sheet2 tab and then change the column width for columns E, F, and G to 11.00.
   b. Click the Sheet3 tab and then change the column width for columns E, F, and G to 11.00.
   c. Click the Sheet1 tab to display the first worksheet.
4. Save **ExcelL1_C5_P1.xlsx**.

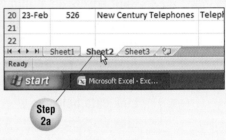

Step 2a

Cutting, Copying, and Pasting Selected Cells

Situations may arise where you need to move cells to a different location within a worksheet, or you may need to copy repetitive data in a worksheet. You can perform these actions by selecting cells and then using the Cut, Copy, and/or Paste buttons in the Clipboard group in the Home tab. You can also perform these actions with the mouse.

Moving Selected Cells

Cut

Paste

You can move selected cells and cell contents in a worksheet and between worksheets. Move selected cells with the Cut and Paste buttons in the Clipboard group in the Home tab or by dragging with the mouse.

To move selected cells with buttons in the Home tab, select the cells and then click the Cut button in the Clipboard group. This causes a moving dashed line border (called a marquee) to display around the selected cells. Click the cell where you want the first selected cell inserted and then click the Paste button in the Clipboard group. If you change your mind and do not want to move the selected cells, press the Esc key to remove the moving dashed line border or double-click in any cell.

To move selected cells with the mouse, select the cells and then position the mouse pointer on any border of the selected cells until the pointer turns into an arrow pointer with a four-headed arrow attached. Hold down the left mouse button, drag the outline of the selected cells to the desired location, and then release the mouse button.

Move and Paste Cells
1. Select cells.
2. Click Cut button.
3. Click desired cell.
4. Click Paste button.

HINT

Ctrl + X is the keyboard shortcut to cut selected data. Ctrl + V is the keyboard shortcut to paste data.

Project 1b   Moving Selected Cells

1. With **ExcelL1_C5_P1.xlsx** open, you realize that the sublet rent deposit was recorded on the wrong day. The correct day is January 11. To move the cells containing information on the deposit, complete the following steps:
   a. Make cell A13 active and then insert a row. (The new row should display above the row containing information on *Rainer Suppliers*.)
   b. Select cells A7 through F7.
   c. Click the Cut button in the Clipboard group in the Home tab.

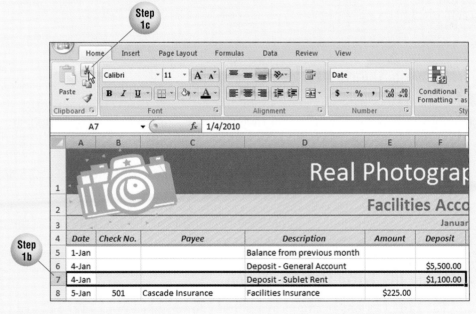

   d. Click cell A13 to make it active.
   e. Click the Paste button in the Clipboard group.

f. Change the date of the deposit from January 4 to January 11.

g. Select row 7 and then delete it.

2. Click the Sheet2 tab and then complete steps similar to those in Step 1 to move the sublet deposit row so it is positioned above the *Rainier Suppliers* row and below the *Clear Source* row. Change the date of the deposit to February 11 and make sure you delete row 7.

3. Move cells using the mouse by completing the following steps:

a. Click the Sheet3 tab.

b. Make cell A13 active and then insert a new row.

c. Using the mouse, select cells A7 through F7.

d. Position the mouse pointer on any boundary of the selected cells until it turns into an arrow pointer with a four-headed arrow attached.

e. Hold down the left mouse button, drag the outline of the selected cells to row 13, and then release the mouse button.

	Date	Check No.	Payee	Description	Amount	Deposit
5	1-Mar			Balance from previous month		
6	1-Mar			Deposit - General Account		$5,500.00
7	1-Mar			Deposit - Sublet Rent		$1,100.00
8	2-Mar	527				
9	3-Mar	528				
10	3-Mar	529				
11	8-Mar	530	Stationery Plus	Paper Supplies	$113.76	
12	9-Mar	531	Clear Source	Developer Supplies	$251.90	
13						
14	10-Mar	532	Rainier S A13:F13	Camera Supplies	$119.62	
15	11-Mar	533	A1 Wedding Supplies	Photo Albums	$323.58	

Step 3c

Step 3e

f. Change the date of the deposit to March 10.

g. Delete row 7.

4. Save **ExcelL1_C5_P1.xlsx**.

Copying Selected Cells

Copying selected cells can be useful in worksheets that contain repetitive data. To copy cells, select the cells, and then click the Copy button in the Clipboard group in the Home tab. Click the cell where you want the first selected cell copied and then click the Paste button in the Clipboard group.

You can also copy selected cells using the mouse and the Ctrl key. To do this, select the cells you want to copy and then position the mouse pointer on any border around the selected cells until it turns into an arrow pointer. Hold down the Ctrl key and the left mouse button, drag the outline of the selected cells to the desired location, release the left mouse button, and then release the Ctrl key.

Copy and Paste Cells
1. Select cells.
2. Click Copy button.
3. Click desired cell.
4. Click Paste button.

HINT
Ctrl + C is the keyboard shortcut to copy selected data.

Copy

Paste Options

Using the Paste Options Button

The Paste Options button displays in the lower right corner of the pasted cell(s) when you paste a cell or cells. Hover the mouse over this button until it displays with a down-pointing arrow and then click the left mouse button. This causes a drop-down list to display as shown in Figure 5.1. With the options from this list you can specify what you want pasted. You can specify that you want to keep source formatting or use destination themes or destination formatting. You can also keep the column widths of the source worksheet.

Figure 5.1 Paste Options Button Drop-down List

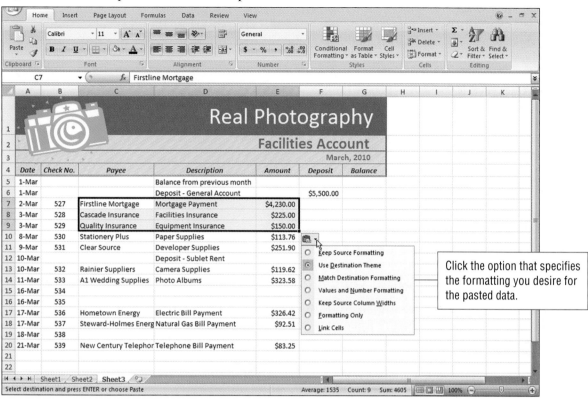

Click the option that specifies the formatting you desire for the pasted data.

Project 1c Copying Selected Cells in a Worksheet

1. With **ExcelL1_C5_P1.xlsx** open, make Sheet2 active.
2. Select cells C7 through E9.
3. Click the Copy button in the Clipboard group in the Home tab.

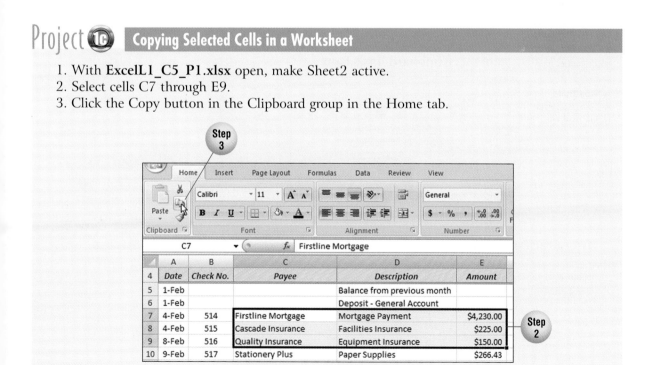

4. Make Sheet3 active.
5. Make cell C7 active.
6. Click the Paste button in the Clipboard group.
7. Click the Paste Options button that displays in the lower right corner of the pasted cells and then click *Keep Source Column Widths* at the drop-down list.
8. Make Sheet2 active and then press the Esc key to remove the moving marquee.
9. Save **ExcelL1_C5_P1.xlsx**.

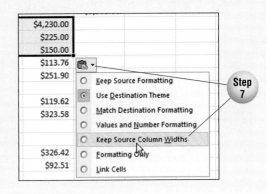

Using the Office Clipboard

Use the Office Clipboard feature to collect and paste multiple items. To use the Office Clipboard, display the Clipboard task pane by clicking the Clipboard group dialog box launcher. This button is located in the lower right corner of the Clipboard group in the Home tab. The Clipboard task pane displays at the left side of the screen in a manner similar to what you see in Figure 5.2.

Figure 5.2 Clipboard Task Pane

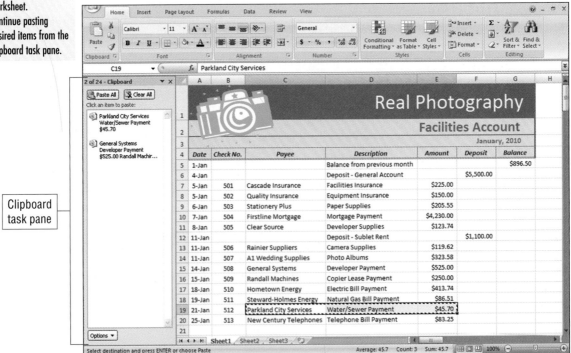

Clipboard task pane

Select data or an object you want to copy and then click the Copy button in the Clipboard group. Continue selecting text or items and clicking the Copy button. To insert an item, position the insertion point in the desired location and then click the item in the Clipboard task pane. If the copied item is text, the first 50 characters display. When all desired items are inserted, click the Clear All button to remove any remaining items. Sometimes, you may have a situation in which you want to copy all of the selected items to a single location. If so, position the insertion point in the desired location and then click the Paste All button in the Clipboard task pane.

Project ⑩ Copying and Pasting Cells Using the Office Clipboard

1. With **ExcelL1_C5_P1.xlsx** open, select cells for copying by completing the following steps:
   a. Display the Clipboard task pane by clicking the Clipboard group dialog box launcher. (If the Clipboard contains any copied data, click the Clear All button.)
   b. Click the Sheet1 tab.
   c. Select cells C15 through E16.
   d. Click the Copy button in the Clipboard group.
   e. Select cells C19 through E19.
   f. Click the Copy button in the Clipboard group.
2. Paste the copied cells by completing the following steps:
   a. Click the Sheet2 tab.
   b. Make cell C15 active.
   c. Click the item in the Clipboard task pane representing *General Systems Developer*.
   d. Click the Sheet3 tab.
   e. Make C15 active.
   f. Click the item in the Clipboard task pane representing *General Systems Developer*.
   g. Make cell C19 active.
   h. Click the item in the Clipboard task pane representing *Parkland City Services*.
3. Click the Clear All button located toward the top of the Clipboard task pane.
4. Close the Clipboard task pane by clicking the Close button (contains an X) located in the upper right corner of the task pane.
5. Save **ExcelL1_C5_P1.xlsx**.

Pasting Values Only

When you copy and then paste a cell containing a value as well as a formula, the Paste Options button contains the options shown in Figure 5.1 as well as the additional option *Values Only*. Click this option if you want to copy only the value and not the formula.

Project **1e** **Copying and Pasting Values**

1. With **ExcelL1_C5_P1.xlsx** open, make Sheet1 active.
2. Make cell G6 active, insert the formula =(F6-E6)+G5, and then press Enter.
3. Copy the formula in cell G6 down to cells G7 through G20.
4. Copy the final balance amount from Sheet1 to Sheet2 by completing the following steps:
   a. Make cell G20 active.
   b. Click the Copy button in the Clipboard group.
   c. Click the Sheet2 tab.
   d. Make cell G5 active and then click the Paste button in the Clipboard group.
   e. Hover the mouse over the Paste Options button until the button displays with a down-pointing arrow and then click the left mouse button.
   f. At the drop-down list, click the *Values Only* option. (This inserts the value and not the formula.)

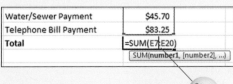

February, 2010

Deposit	Balance
◇	#VALUE!
$5,500.00	
$1,100.00	

Step 4e

○ Keep Source Formatting
◉ Use Destination Theme
○ Match Destination Formatting
○ Values Only
○ Values and Number Formatting
○ Values and Source Formatting
○ Keep Source Column Widths
○ Formatting Only
○ Link Cells

Step 4f

5. Make cell G6 active, insert a formula that determines the balance, and then copy the formula down to cells G7 through G20.
6. Copy the amount in cell G20 and then paste the value only into cell G5 in Sheet3.
7. With Sheet3 active, make cell G6 active, insert a formula that determines the balance, and then copy the formula down to cells G7 through G20.
8. Save **ExcelL1_C5_P1.xlsx**.

QUICK STEPS

Insert Worksheet
Click Insert Worksheet tab.
OR
Press Shift + F11.

Inserting a Worksheet

A workbook, by default, contains three worksheets. You can insert additional worksheets in a workbook. To do this, click the Insert Worksheet tab located to the right of the Sheet3 tab. This inserts a new worksheet labeled *Sheet4* at the right of the Sheet3 tab. You can also press Shift + F11 to insert a new worksheet. Or, you can insert a worksheet by clicking the Insert button arrow in the Cells group in the Home tab and then clicking *Insert Sheet*.

Project **1f** **Inserting a Worksheet**

1. With **ExcelL1_C5_P1.xlsx** open, make the following changes:
   a. Make Sheet1 active.
   b. Make cell D21 active, turn on bold, and then type Total.
   c. Make cell E21 active and then click once on the Sum button located in the Editing group in the Home tab. (This inserts the formula =SUM(E13:E20).)
   d. Change the formula to =SUM(E7:E20) and then press Enter.

Water/Sewer Payment	$45.70
Telephone Bill Payment	$83.25
Total	=SUM(E7:E20)

SUM(number1, [number2], ...)

Step 1d

e. Make cell F21 active and then click once on the Sum button in the Editing group. (This inserts the formula =SUM(F12:F20).)

f. Change the formula to =SUM(F6:F20) and then press Enter.

2. Make Sheet2 active and then complete the steps in Step 1 to insert the totals of the *Amount* and *Deposit* columns.

3. Make Sheet3 active and then complete the steps in Step 1 to insert the totals of the *Amount* and *Deposit* columns.

4. Insert a new worksheet by clicking the Insert Worksheet tab located to the right of the Sheet3 tab.

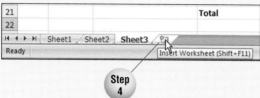

Step 4

5. Make Sheet1 active, copy cells A1 through G3, make Sheet4 active (with cell A1 active), and then paste the cells. (When copying the cells, position the cell pointer to the right of the image, make sure the pointer displays as a white plus symbol, and then drag to select the cells.)

6. Make the following changes to the worksheet:

a. Make cell A3 active and then type **First Quarter Summary, 2010**.

b. Change the width of column A to 20.00.

c. Change the width of columns B, C, and D to 12.00.

d. Select cells B4 through D4, click the Bold button in the Font group in the Home tab, and then click the Center button in the Alignment group.

e. Select cells B5 through D7 and then change the number formatting to Currency with two decimal places and include the dollar sign symbol.

f. Type the following text in the specified cells:

B4	=	January
C4	=	February
D4	=	March
A5	=	Checks Amount
A6	=	Deposit Amount
A7	=	End-of-month Balance

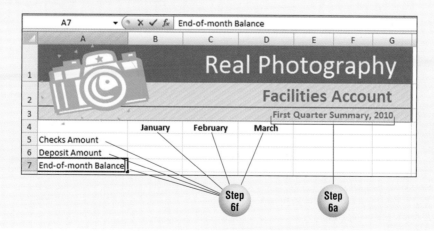

Step 6f

Step 6a

7. Copy a value by completing the following steps:
   a. Make Sheet1 active.
   b. Make cell E21 active and then click the Copy button in the Clipboard group in the Home tab.
   c. Make Sheet4 active.
   d. Make cell B5 active and then click the Paste button in the Clipboard group.
   e. Click the Paste Options button and then click *Values Only* at the drop-down list.

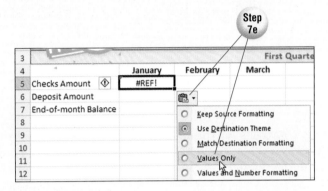

   f. Make Sheet1 active.
   g. Press the Esc key to remove the moving marquee.
   h. Make cell F21 active and then click the Copy button.
   i. Make Sheet4 active.
   j. Make cell B6 active and then click the Paste button.
   k. Click the Paste Options button and then click *Values Only* at the drop-down list.
   l. Make Sheet1 active.
   m. Press the Esc key to remove the moving marquee.
   n. Make cell G20 active and then click the Copy button.
   o. Make Sheet4 active.
   p. Make cell B7 active and then click the Paste button.
   q. Click the Paste Options button and then click *Values Only* at the drop-down list.
8. Complete steps similar to those in Step 7 to insert amounts and balances for February and March.
9. Save **ExcelL1_C5_P1.xlsx**.

Managing Worksheets

Right-click a sheet tab and a shortcut menu displays as shown in Figure 5.3 with the options for managing worksheets. For example, remove a worksheet by clicking the *Delete* option. Move or copy a worksheet by clicking the *Move or Copy* option. Clicking this option causes a Move or Copy dialog box to display where you specify before what sheet you want to move or copy the selected sheet. By default, Excel names worksheets in a workbook *Sheet1, Sheet2, Sheet3,* and so on. To rename a worksheet, click the *Rename* option (this selects the default sheet name) and then type the desired name.

Figure 5.3 Sheet Tab Shortcut Menu

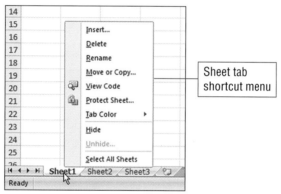

Sheet tab
shortcut menu

In addition to the shortcut menu options, you can use the mouse to move or copy worksheets. To move a worksheet, position the mouse pointer on the worksheet tab, hold down the left mouse button (a page icon displays next to the mouse pointer), drag the page icon to the desired position, and then release the mouse button. For example, to move Sheet2 tab after Sheet3 tab you would position the mouse pointer on the Sheet2 tab, hold down the left mouse button, drag the page icon so it is positioned after the Sheet3 tab, and then release the mouse button. To copy a worksheet, hold down the Ctrl key while dragging the sheet tab.

Use the *Tab Color* option at the shortcut menu to apply a color to a worksheet tab. Right-click a worksheet tab, point to *Tab Color* at the shortcut menu, and then click the desired color at the color palette.

Move or Copy a Worksheet
1. Right-click sheet tab.
2. Click *Move or Copy*.
3. At Move or Copy dialog box, click desired worksheet name in *Before sheet* list box.
4. Click OK.
OR
Drag worksheet tab to the desired position (to copy, hold down Ctrl key while dragging).

HINT

Use the tab scroll buttons, located to the left of the sheet tabs, to bring into view any worksheet tabs not currently visible.

Recolor Sheet Tab
1. Right-click sheet tab.
2. Point to *Tab Color*.
3. Click desired color at color palette.

1. With **ExcelL1_C5_P1.xlsx** open, move Sheet4 by completing the following steps:
   a. Right-click Sheet4 and then click *Move or Copy* at the shortcut menu.

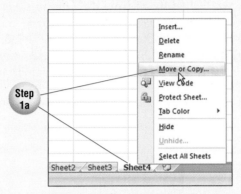

   b. At the Move or Copy dialog box, make sure *Sheet1* is selected in the *Before sheet* section, and then click OK.

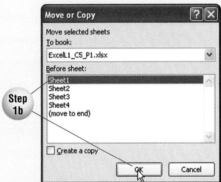

2. Rename Sheet4 by completing the following steps:
   a. Right-click the Sheet4 tab and then click *Rename*.
   b. Type **Summary** and then press Enter.

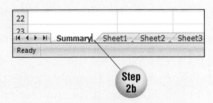

3. Complete steps similar to those in Step 2 to rename Sheet1 to *January*, Sheet2 to *February*, and Sheet3 to *March*.
4. Change the color of the Summary sheet tab by completing the following steps:
   a. Right-click the Summary sheet tab.
   b. Point to *Tab Color* at the shortcut menu.
   c. Click a red color of your choosing at the color palette.
5. Follow steps similar to those in Step 4 to change the January sheet tab to a blue color, the February sheet tab to a purple color, and the March sheet tab to a green color.
6. Save **ExcelL1_C5_P1.xlsx**.

Hiding a Worksheet in a Workbook

In a workbook containing multiple worksheets, you can hide a worksheet that may contain sensitive data or data you do not want to display or print with the workbook. To hide a worksheet in a workbook, click the Format button in the Cells group in the Home tab, point to *Hide & Unhide*, and then click *Hide Sheet*. You can also hide a worksheet by right-clicking a worksheet tab and then clicking the *Hide* option at the shortcut menu. To make a hidden worksheet visible, click the Format button in the Cells group, point to *Hide & Unhide*, and then click *Unhide Sheet*, or right-click a worksheet tab and then click *Unhide* at the shortcut menu. At the Unhide dialog box shown in Figure 5.4, double-click the name of the hidden worksheet you want to display.

Figure 5.4 Unhide Dialog Box

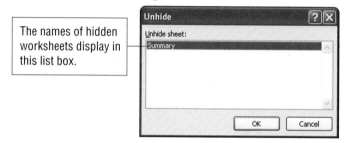

The names of hidden worksheets display in this list box.

Formatting Multiple Worksheets

When you apply formatting to a worksheet, such as changing margins, orientation, or inserting a header or footer, and so on, the formatting is applied only to the active worksheet. If you want formatting to apply to multiple worksheets in a workbook, select the tabs of the desired worksheets and then apply the formatting. For example, if a workbook contains three worksheets and you want to apply formatting to the first and second worksheets only, select the tabs for the first and second worksheets and then apply the formatting.

To select adjacent worksheet tabs, click the first tab, hold down the Shift key, and then click the last tab. To select nonadjacent worksheet tabs, click the first tab, hold down the Ctrl key, and then click any other tabs you want selected.

Hide a Worksheet
1. Click Format button.
2. Point to *Hide & Unhide*.
3. Click *Hide Sheet*.
OR
1. Right-click worksheet tab.
2. Click *Hide* at shortcut menu.

Unhide a Worksheet
1. Click Format button.
2. Point to *Hide & Unhide*.
3. Click *Unhide Sheet*.
4. Double-click desired hidden worksheet in Unhide dialog box.
OR
1. Right-click worksheet tab.
2. Click *Unhide* at shortcut menu.
3. Double-click desired hidden worksheet in Unhide dialog box.

HINT
If the *Hide* option is unavailable, the workbook is protected from change.

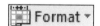

1. With **ExcelL1_C5_P1.xlsx** open, hide the Summary worksheet by completing the following steps:
   a. Click the Summary tab.
   b. Click the Format button in the Cells group in the Home tab, point to *Hide & Unhide*, and then click *Hide Sheet*.

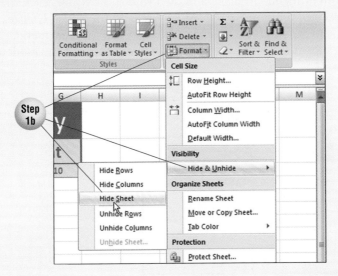

2. Unhide the worksheet by completing the following steps:
   a. Click the Format button in the Cells group, point to *Hide & Unhide*, and then click *Unhide Sheet*.
   b. At the Unhide dialog box, make sure *Summary* is selected and then click OK.

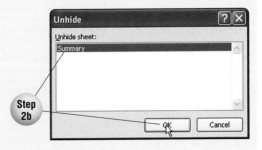

3. Insert a header for each worksheet by completing the following steps:
   a. Click the Summary tab.
   b. Hold down the Shift key and then click the March tab. (This selects all four tabs.)
   c. Click the Insert tab.
   d. Click the Header & Footer button in the Text group.
   e. Click the Header button in the Header & Footer group in the Header & Footer Tools Design tab and then click the option at the drop-down list that prints your name at the left side of the page, the page number in the middle, and the date at the right side of the page.
4. With all the sheet tabs selected, horizontally and vertically center each worksheet on the page. *Hint: Do this at the Page Setup dialog box with the Margins tab selected.*
5. With all of the sheet tabs still selected, change the page orientation to landscape. *Hint: Do this with the Orientation button in the Page Layout tab.*
6. Save **ExcelL1_C5_P1.xlsx**.

Printing a Workbook Containing Multiple Worksheets

**Print all Worksheets
in a Workbook**
1. Click Office button,
   Print.
2. Click *Entire workbook*.
3. Click OK.

By default, Excel prints the currently displayed worksheet. If you want to print all worksheets in a workbook, display the Print dialog box by clicking the Office button and then clicking *Print*. At the Print dialog box, click *Entire workbook* in the *Print what* section, and then click OK. You can also print specific worksheets in a workbook by selecting the tabs of the worksheets you want to print.

Project 1 **Printing All Worksheets in a Workbook**

1. With **ExcelL1_C5_P1.xlsx** open, click the Office button and then click *Print*.
2. At the Print dialog box, click the *Entire workbook* option in the *Print what* section.
3. Click OK.
4. Close **ExcelL1_C5_P1.xlsx**.

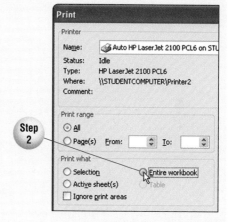

Step 2

Project 2 Write Formulas Using Ranges in an Equipment Usage Workbook

You will open an equipment usage workbook and then split the window and edit cells. You will also name ranges and then use the range names to write formulas in the workbook.

Splitting a Worksheet into Windows and Freezing and Unfreezing Panes

Split a Worksheet
1. Click View tab.
2. Click Split button.
OR
Drag horizontal and/or
vertical split bars.

In some worksheets, not all cells display at one time in the worksheet area (such as ExcelC05Project02.xlsx). When working in worksheets with more cells than can display at one time, you may find splitting the worksheet window into panes helpful. Split the worksheet window into panes with the Split button in the Window group in the View tab or with the split bars that display at the top of the vertical scroll bar and at the right side of the horizontal scroll bar. Figure 5.5 identifies these split bars.

Figure 5.5 Split Bars

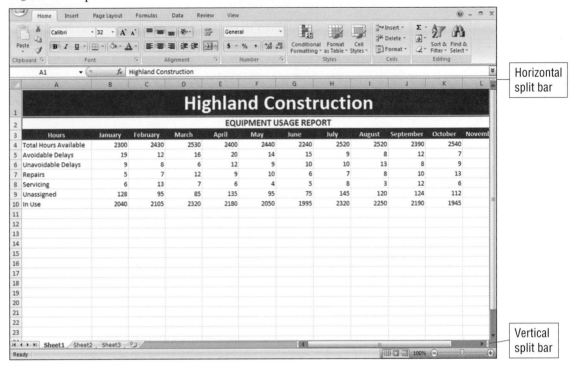

Horizontal split bar

Vertical split bar

HINT

Restore a split window by double-clicking anywhere on the split bar that divides the panes.

To split a window with the split bar located at the top of the vertical scroll bar, position the mouse pointer on the split bar until it turns into a double-headed arrow with a short double line in the middle. Hold down the left mouse button, drag down the thick gray line that displays until the pane is the desired size, and then release the mouse button. Split the window vertically with the split bar at the right side of the horizontal scroll bar.

To split a worksheet window with the Split button, click the View tab, and then click the Split button. This causes the worksheet to split into four window panes as shown in Figure 5.6. The windows are split by thick, light blue lines (with a three-dimensional look). To remove a split from a worksheet click the Split button to deactivate it or drag the split bars to the upper left corner of the worksheet.

Figure 5.6 Split Window

| | Home | Insert | Page Layout | Formulas | Data | Review | View | | | | | | | |

Cell reference: A1 — fx — Highland Construction

	A	B	C	D	E	F	G	H	I	J	K	L
1					Highland Construction							
2					EQUIPMENT USAGE REPORT							
3	Hours	January	February	March	April	May	June	July	August	September	October	Novem
4	Total Hours Available	2300	2430	2530	2400	2440	2240	2520	2520	2390	2540	
5	Avoidable Delays	19	12	16	20	14	15	9	8	12	7	
6	Unavoidable Delays	9	8	6	12	9	10	10	13	8	9	
7	Repairs	5	7	12	9	10	6	7	8	10	13	
8	Servicing	6	13	7	6	4	5	8	3	12	6	
9	Unassigned	128	95	85	135	95	75	145	120	124	112	
10	In Use	2040	2105	2320	2180	2050	1995	2320	2250	2190	1945	

Sheet1 / Sheet2 / Sheet3

A window pane will display the active cell. As the insertion point is moved through the pane, another active cell with a blue background may display. This additional active cell displays when the insertion point passes over one of the light blue lines that creates the pane. As you move through a worksheet, you may see both active cells—one with a normal background and one with a blue background. If you make a change to the active cell, the change is made in both. If you want only one active cell to display, freeze the window panes by clicking the Freeze Panes button in the Window group in the View tab and then clicking *Freeze Panes* at the drop-down list. You can maintain the display of column headings while editing or typing text in cells by clicking the Freeze Panes button and then clicking *Freeze Top Row*. Maintain the display of row headings by clicking the Freeze Panes button and then clicking *Freeze First Column*. Unfreeze window panes by clicking the Freeze Panes button and then clicking *Unfreeze Panes* at the drop-down list.

Using the mouse, you can move the thick, light blue lines that divide the window into panes. To do this, position the mouse pointer on the line until the pointer turns into a double-headed arrow with a double line in the middle. Hold down the left mouse button, drag the outline of the light blue line to the desired location, and then release the mouse button. If you want to move both the horizontal and vertical lines at the same time, position the mouse pointer on the intersection of the thick, light blue lines until it turns into a four-headed arrow. Hold down the left mouse button, drag the thick, light blue lines in the desired direction, and then release the mouse button.

1. Open **ExcelC05Project02.xlsx** and then save the workbook and name it **ExcelL1_C5_P2**.
2. Make sure cell A1 is active and then split the window by clicking the View tab and then clicking the Split button in the Window group. (This splits the window into four panes.)
3. Drag the vertical light blue line by completing the following steps:
   a. Position the mouse pointer on the vertical split line until the pointer turns into a double-headed arrow pointing left and right with a double-line between.
   b. Hold down the left mouse button, drag to the left until the vertical light blue line is immediately to the right of the first column, and then release the mouse button.

	A	B	C	D	E	F
						Highla|nd C(
1						
2						**EQU|IPMENT U**
3	Hours	January	February	March	April	May
4	Total Hours Available	2300	2430	2530	2400	2440
5	Avoidable Delays	19	12	16	20	14
6	Unavoidable Delays	9	8	6	12	9

A1 · fx Highland Construction

Step 3b

4. Freeze the window panes by clicking the Freeze Panes button in the Window group in the View tab and then clicking *Freeze Panes* at the drop-down list.

Step 4

View — Zoom 100% Zoom to Selection — New Window Split — Arrange All Hide — Freeze Panes Unhide — Save Workspace Switch Windows

Freeze Panes
Keep rows and columns visible while the rest of the worksheet scrolls (based on current selection).

Freeze Top Row
Keep the top row visible while scrolling through the rest of the worksheet.

Freeze First Column
Keep the first column visible while scrolling through the rest of the worksheet.

5. Make cell L4 active and then type the following data in the specified cells:

L4	=	2310	M4	=	2210
L5	=	12	M5	=	5
L6	=	5	M6	=	7
L7	=	9	M7	=	8
L8	=	11	M8	=	12
L9	=	95	M9	=	120
L10	=	2005	M10	=	1830

6. Unfreeze the window panes by clicking the Freeze Panes button and then clicking *Unfreeze Panes* at the drop-down list.
7. Remove the panes by clicking the Split button in the Window group to deactivate it.
8. Save **ExcelL1_C5_P2.xlsx**.

Working with Ranges

A selected group of cells is referred to as a *range*. A range of cells can be formatted, moved, copied, or deleted. You can also name a range of cells and then move the insertion point to the range or use a named range as part of a formula.

To name a range, select the cells, and then click in the Name box located at the left of the Formula bar. Type a name for the range (do not use a space) and then press Enter. To move the insertion point to a specific range and select the range, click the down-pointing arrow at the right side of the Name box and then click the range name.

You can also name a range using the Define Name button in the Formulas tab. To do this, click the Formulas tab and then click the Define Name button in the Defined Names group. At the New Name dialog box, type a name for the range and then click OK.

You can use a range name in a formula. For example, if a range is named *Profit* and you want to insert the average of all cells in the *Profit* range, you would make the desired cell active and then type =AVERAGE(Profit). You can use a named range in the current worksheet or in another worksheet within the workbook.

HINT

Another method for moving to a range is to click the Find & Select button in the Editing group in the Home tab and then click *Go To*. At the Go To dialog box, double-click the range name.

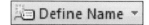

Project 2b — Naming a Range and Using a Range in a Formula

1. With **ExcelL1_C5_P2.xlsx** open, click the Sheet2 tab and then type the following text in the specified cells:

   A1 = EQUIPMENT USAGE REPORT
   A2 = Yearly Hours
   A3 = Avoidable Delays
   A4 = Unavoidable Delays
   A5 = Total Delay Hours
   A6 = (leave blank)
   A7 = Repairs
   A8 = Servicing
   A9 = Total Repair/Servicing Hours

   Step 1

	A	B	C	D
1	EQUIPMENT USAGE REPORT			
2	Yearly Hours			
3	Avoidable Delays			
4	Unavoidable Delays			
5	Total Delay Hours			
6				
7	Repairs			
8	Servicing			
9	Total Repair/Servicing Hours			
10				

2. Make the following formatting changes to the worksheet:
   a. Automatically adjust the width of column A.
   b. Center and bold the text in cells A1 and A2.
3. Select a range of cells in worksheet 1, name the range, and use it in a formula in worksheet 2 by completing the following steps:
   a. Click the Sheet1 tab.
   b. Select cells B5 through M5.
   c. Click in the Name box located to the left of the Formula bar.
   d. Type adhours (for Avoidable Delays Hours) and then press Enter.
   e. Click the Sheet2 tab.
   f. Make cell B3 active.
   g. Type the equation =SUM(adhours) and then press Enter.

   Step 3d

   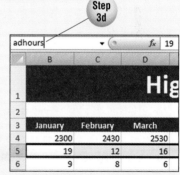

adhours			f_x	19
	B	C	D	
1			**Hig**	
2				
3	January	February	March	
4	2300	2430	2530	
5	19	12	16	
6	9	8	6	

4. Click the Sheet1 tab and then complete the following steps:
   a. Select cells B6 through M6.
   b. Click the Formulas tab.
   c. Click the Define Name button in the Defined Names group.

   Step 3g

   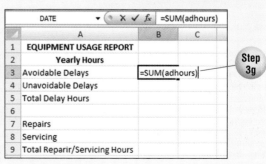

DATE			f_x	=SUM(adhours)
	A		B	C
1	EQUIPMENT USAGE REPORT			
2	Yearly Hours			
3	Avoidable Delays		=SUM(adhours)	
4	Unavoidable Delays			
5	Total Delay Hours			
6				
7	Repairs			
8	Servicing			
9	Total Repairir/Servicing Hours			

d. At the New Name dialog box, type **udhours** and
   then click OK.
e. Make worksheet 2 active, make cell B4 active, and
   then insert the equation =SUM(udhours).

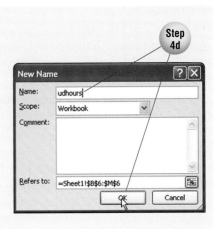

Step
4d

5. Make worksheet 1 active and then complete the
   following steps:
   a. Select cells B7 through M7 and then name the
      range *rhours*.
   b. Make worksheet 2 active, make cell B7 active, and
      then insert the equation =SUM(rhours).
   c. Make worksheet 1 active.
   d. Select cells B8 through M8 and then name the
      range *shours*.
   e. Make worksheet 2 active, make cell B8 active, and
      then insert the equation =SUM(shours).
6. With worksheet 2 still active, make the following changes:
   a. Make cell B5 active.
   b. Double-click the Sum button in the Editing group in the Home tab.
   c. Make cell B9 active.
   d. Double-click the Sum button in the Editing group in the
      Home tab.
7. Make worksheet 1 active and then move to the range *adhours* by
   clicking the down-pointing arrow at the right side of the Name
   box and then clicking *adhours* at the drop-down list.
8. Select both sheet tabs, change the orientation to landscape, scale
   the contents to fit on one page (in Page Layout tab, change
   width to *1 page*), and insert a custom footer with your name,
   page number, and date.
9. Print both worksheets in the workbook.
10. Save and then close **ExcelL1_C5_P2.xlsx**.

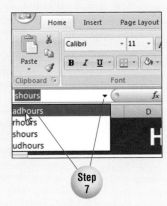

Step
7

Project ③ **Arrange, Size, and Copy Data between Workbooks**

You will open, arrange, hide, unhide, size, and move multiple workbooks. You will
also copy cells from one workbook and paste in another workbook.

Working with Windows

You can open multiple workbooks in Excel and arrange the open workbooks in
the Excel window. With multiple workbooks open, you can cut and paste or copy
and paste cell entries from one workbook to another using the same techniques
discussed earlier in this chapter with the exception that you activate the destination
workbook before executing the Paste command.

Opening Multiple Workbooks

With multiple workbooks open, you can move or copy information between workbooks or compare the contents of several workbooks. When you open a new workbook, it is placed on top of the original workbook. Once multiple workbooks are opened, you can resize the workbooks to see all or a portion of them on the screen.

Open multiple workbooks at one time at the Open dialog box. If workbooks are adjacent, display the Open dialog box, click the first workbook name to be opened, hold down the Shift key, and then click the last workbook name to be opened. If the workbooks are nonadjacent, click the first workbook name to be opened and then hold down the Ctrl key while clicking the remaining desired workbook names. Release the Shift key or the Ctrl key and then click the Open button.

To see what workbooks are currently open, click the View tab and then click the Switch Windows button in the Window group. The names of the open workbooks display in a drop-down list and the workbook name preceded by a check mark is the active workbook. To make one of the other workbooks active, click the desired workbook name at the drop-down list.

Arrange Workbooks
1. Click View tab.
2. Click Arrange All button.
3. At Arrange Windows dialog box, click desired arrangement.
4. Click OK.

Arranging Workbooks

If you have more than one workbook open, you can arrange the workbooks at the Arrange Windows dialog box shown in Figure 5.7. To display this dialog box, open several workbooks, and then click the Arrange All button in the Window group in the View tab. At the Arrange Windows dialog box, click *Tiled* to display a portion of each open workbook. Figure 5.8 displays four tiled workbooks.

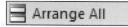

Figure 5.7 Arrange Windows Dialog Box

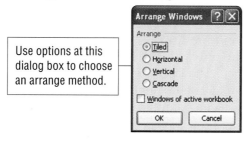

Use options at this dialog box to choose an arrange method.

Figure 5.8 Tiled Workbooks

Choose the *Horizontal* option at the Arrange Windows dialog box and the open workbooks display across the screen. The *Vertical* option displays the open workbooks up and down the screen. The last option, *Cascade*, displays the Title bar of each open workbook. Figure 5.9 shows four cascaded workbooks.

The option you select for displaying multiple workbooks depends on which part of the workbooks is most important to view simultaneously. For example, the tiled workbooks in Figure 5.8 allow you to view the company logos and the first few rows and columns of each workbook.

Figure 5.9 Cascaded Workbooks

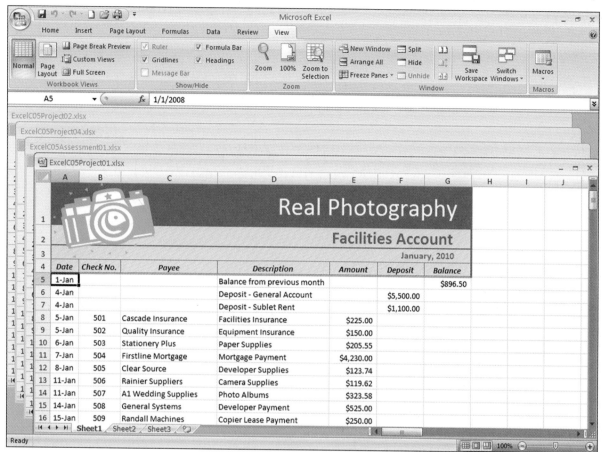

Hiding/Unhiding Workbooks

With the Hide button in the Window group in the View tab, you can hide the active workbook. If a workbook has been hidden, redisplay the workbook by clicking the Unhide button in the Window group in the View tab. At the Unhide dialog box, make sure the desired workbook is selected in the list box, and then click OK.

Project 3a   **Opening, Arranging, and Hiding/Unhiding Workbooks**

1. Open several workbooks at the same time by completing the following steps:
    a. Display the Open dialog box.
    b. Click the workbook named ***ExcelC05Project01.xlsx***.
    c. Hold down the Ctrl key, click ***ExcelC05Project02.xlsx***, click ***ExcelC05Project04.xlsx***, and click ***ExcelC05Assessment01.xlsx***.
    d. Release the Ctrl key and then click the Open button in the dialog box.

2. Make **ExcelC05Assessment01.xlsx** the active workbook by clicking the View tab, clicking the Switch Windows button in the Window group, and then clicking *4* at the drop-down list.

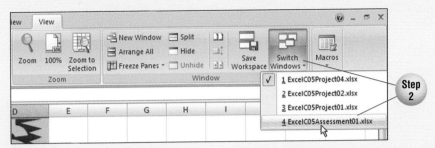

Step 2

3. Make **ExcelC05Project01.xlsx** the active workbook by clicking the Switch Windows button and then clicking *ExcelC05Project01.xlsx* at the drop-down list.
4. Tile the workbooks by completing the following steps:
   a. Click the Arrange All button in the Window group in the View tab.
   b. At the Arrange Windows dialog box, make sure *Tiled* is selected and then click OK.

Step 4b

5. Tile the workbooks horizontally by completing the following steps:
   a. Click the Arrange All button.
   b. At the Arrange Windows dialog box, click *Horizontal*.
   c. Click OK.
6. Cascade the workbooks by completing the following steps:
   a. Click the Arrange All button.
   b. At the Arrange Windows dialog box, click *Cascade*.
   c. Click OK.
7. Hide and unhide workbooks by completing the following steps:
   a. Make sure **ExcelC05Project01.xlsx** is the active workbook (displays on top of the other workbooks).
   b. Click the Hide button in the Window group in the View tab.
   c. Make sure **ExcelC05Assessment01.xlsx** is the active workbook (displays on top of the other workbooks).
   d. Click the Hide button.
   e. Click the Unhide button.
   f. At the Unhide dialog box, click *ExcelC05Project01.xlsx* in the list box, and then click OK.

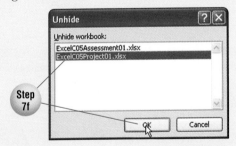

Step 7f

   g. Click the Unhide button.
   h. At the Unhide dialog box, make sure **ExcelC05Assessment01.xlsx** is selected in the list box and then click OK.
8. Close all of the open workbooks without saving changes.

Sizing and Moving Workbooks

You can use the Maximize and Minimize buttons located in the upper right corner of the active workbook to change the size of the window. The Maximize button is the button in the upper right corner of the active workbook immediately to the left of the Close button. (The Close button is the button containing the *X*.) The Minimize button is located immediately to the left of the Maximize button.

Maximize Minimize

Close Restore

If you arrange all open workbooks and then click the Maximize button in the active workbook, the active workbook expands to fill the screen. In addition, the Maximize button changes to the Restore button. To return the active workbook back to its size before it was maximized, click the Restore button.

Clicking the Minimize button causes the active workbook to be reduced and positioned as a button on the Taskbar. In addition, the Minimize button changes to the Restore button. To maximize a workbook that has been reduced, click the button on the Taskbar representing the workbook.

Project 3b Minimizing, Maximizing, and Restoring Workbooks

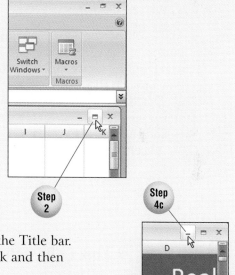

1. Open **ExcelC05Project01.xlsx**.
2. Maximize **ExcelC05Project01.xlsx** by clicking the Maximize button at the right side of the workbook Title bar. (The Maximize button is the button at the right side of the Title bar, immediately to the left of the Close button.)
3. Open **ExcelC05Project02.xlsx** and **ExcelC05Project03.xlsx**.
4. Make the following changes to the open workbooks:
   a. Tile the workbooks.
   b. Make **ExcelC05Project01.xlsx** the active workbook (Title bar displays with a light blue background [the background color may vary depending on how Windows is customized]).
   c. Minimize **ExcelC05Project01.xlsx** by clicking the Minimize button that displays at the right side of the Title bar.
   d. Make **ExcelC05Project02.xlsx** the active workbook and then minimize it.
   e. Minimize **ExcelC05Project03.xlsx**.
5. Close all workbooks.

Moving, Copying, and Pasting Data

With more than one workbook open, you can move, copy, and/or paste data from one workbook to another. To move, copy, and/or paste data between workbooks, use the cutting and pasting options you learned earlier in this chapter, together with the information about windows in this chapter.

1. Open **ExcelC05Project03.xlsx**.
2. If you just completed Project 3b, click the Maximize button so the worksheet fills the entire worksheet window.
3. Save the workbook and name it **ExcelL1_C5_P3**.
4. With **ExcelL1_C5_P3.xlsx** open, open **ExcelC05Deering.xlsx**.
5. Select and then copy text from **ExcelC05Deering.xlsx** to **ExcelL1_C5_P3.xlsx** by completing the following steps:
   a. With **ExcelC05Deering.xlsx** the active workbook, select cells A3 through D10.
   b. Click the Copy button in the Clipboard group in the Home tab.
   c. Click the button on the Taskbar representing **ExcelL1_C5_P3.xlsx**.

Step
5c

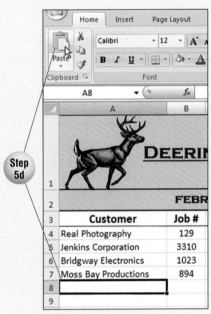

Step
5d

   d. Make cell A8 the active cell and then click the Paste button in the Clipboard group in the Home tab.
   e. Make cell E7 active and then drag the fill handle down to cell E15.
6. Print **ExcelL1_C5_P3.xlsx** horizontally and vertically centered on the page.
7. Save and then close **ExcelL1_C5_P3.xlsx**.
8. Close **ExcelC05Deering.xlsx**.

P roject **4** **Link Cells between Quarterly Expenses Worksheets**

You will open a workbook containing worksheets with quarterly expenses data and then link cells between the worksheets.

Linking Data between Worksheets

You may want to create a link between worksheets or workbooks with data in cells in related workbooks or workbooks containing multiple worksheets. When data is linked, a change made in a linked cell is automatically made to the other cells in the link. You can make links with individual cells or with a range of cells.

Linking cells between worksheets creates what is called a *dynamic link*. Dynamic links are useful in worksheets or workbooks that need to maintain consistency and control over critical data. The worksheet that contains the original data is called the *source* worksheet and the worksheet relying on the source worksheet for the data in the link is called the *dependent* worksheet.

To create a link, make active the cell containing the data to be linked (or select the cells), and then click the Copy button in the Clipboard group in the Home tab. Make active the worksheet where you want to paste the cell or cells, click the Paste button arrow, and then click *Paste Link* at the drop-down list. When a change is made to the cell or cells in the source worksheet, the change is automatically made to the linked cell or cells in the dependent worksheet. You can also create a link by clicking the Paste button, clicking the Paste Options button, and then clicking the *Link Cells* option.

You can also link cells with options at the Paste Special dialog box. Display this dialog box by clicking the Paste button arrow and then clicking *Paste Special* at the drop-down list. At the Paste Special dialog box, specify what in the cell you want to copy and what operators you want to include and then click the Paste Link button.

QUICK STEPS

Link Data between Worksheets
1. Select cells.
2. Click Copy button.
3. Click desired worksheet tab.
4. Click in desired cell.
5. Click Paste button arrow.
6. Click *Paste Link* at drop-down list.

Project ④ Linking Cells between Worksheets

1. Open **ExcelC05Project04.xlsx** and then save the workbook and name it **ExcelL1_C5_P4**.
2. Link cells in the first quarter worksheet to the other three worksheets by completing the following steps:
   a. Select cells C4 through C10.
   b. Click the Copy button in the Clipboard group in the Home tab.
   c. Click the 2nd Qtr. tab.
   d. Make cell C4 active.
   e. Click the Paste button arrow and then click *Paste Link* at the drop-down list.
   f. Click the 3rd Qtr. tab.
   g. Make cell C4 active.
   h. Click the Paste button.
   i. Click the Paste Options button that displays in the lower right corner of the pasted cell and then click *Link Cells* at the drop-down list.
   j. Click the 4th Qtr. tab.
   k. Make cell C4 active.
   l. Click the Paste button arrow and then click *Paste Link*.
   m. Click the 1st Qtr. tab and then press the Esc key to remove the moving marquee.

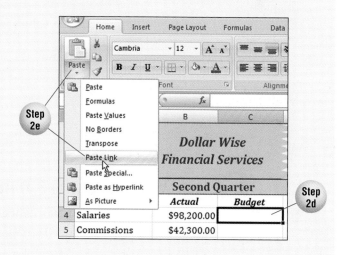

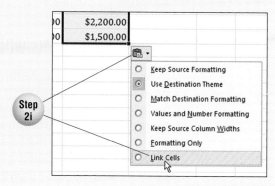

3. Insert a formula in all worksheets that subtracts the Budget amount from the Variance amount by completing the following steps:

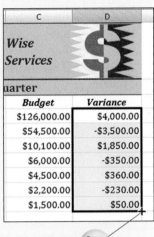

a. Make sure the first quarter worksheet displays.
b. Hold down the Shift key and then click the 4th Qtr. tab. (This selects all four tabs.)
c. Make cell D4 active and then insert the formula =C4-B4.
d. Copy the formula in cell D4 down to cells D5 through D10.
e. Click the 2nd Qtr. tab and notice that the formula was inserted and copied in this worksheet.
f. Click the other worksheet tabs and notice the formula.
g. Click the 1st Qtr. tab.

	C	D
	Wise Services	
	uarter	
	Budget	**Variance**
	$126,000.00	$4,000.00
	$54,500.00	-$3,500.00
	$10,100.00	$1,850.00
	$6,000.00	-$350.00
	$4,500.00	$360.00
	$2,200.00	-$230.00
	$1,500.00	$50.00

Step 3d

4. With the first quarter worksheet active, make the following changes to some of the linked cells:
   C4: Change $126,000 to 128,000
   C5: Change $54,500 to 56,000
   C9: Change $2,200 to 2,400
5. Click the 2nd Qtr. tab and notice that the values in cells C4, C5, and C9 automatically changed (because they are linked to the first quarter worksheet).
6. Click the 3rd Qtr. tab and notice that the values in cells C4, C5, and C9 automatically changed.
7. Click the 4th Qtr. tab and notice that the values in cells C4, C5, and C9 automatically changed.
8. Save **ExcelL1_C5_P4.xlsx** and then print all the worksheets in the workbook.
9. Close **ExcelL1_C5_P4.xlsx**.

 **roject ⑤ Link Worksheets with 3-D References**

You will open a workbook containing worksheets with quarterly sales data and then link the sales data in the worksheets with a 3-D reference.

Linking Worksheets with a 3-D Reference

In multiple worksheet workbooks, you can use a 3-D reference to analyze data in the same cell or range of cells. A 3-D reference includes the cell or range of cells, preceded by a range of worksheet names. For example, you can add all of the values contained in cells in B2 through B5 in worksheets 1 and 2 in a workbook using a 3-D reference. To do this, you would complete these basic steps:

1. Make active the cell where you want to enter the function.
2. Type =SUM(and then click the Sheet1 tab.
3. Hold down the Shift key and then click the Sheet2 tab.
4. Select cells B2 through B5 in the worksheet.
5. Type) (this is the closing parenthesis that ends the formula) and then press Enter.

Project ⑤ Linking Worksheets with a 3-D Reference

1. Open **ExcelC05Project05.xlsx** and then save the workbook and name it **ExcelL1_C5_P5**.
2. Make sure Sales 2007 is the active worksheet.
3. Make the following changes to the Sales 2007 worksheet:
   a. Make cell B12 active.
   b. Click the Center button in the Alignment group and then click the Bold button in the Font group.
   c. Type **January Sales** and then press Alt + Enter.
   d. Type **2007-2009** and then press Enter.
4. Link the Sales 2007, Sales 2008, and Sales 2009 worksheets with a 3-D reference by completing the following steps:
   a. With cell B13 active, type **=SUM(**.
   b. Hold down the Shift key, click the Sales 2009 sheet tab, and then release the Shift key. (This selects all three sheet tabs.)
   c. Select cells B5 through B10.
   d. Type **)** and then press Enter.

3	FIRST-QUARTER SALES - 2007					
4	Customer	January		February		March
5	Lakeside Trucking	$	84,231	$	73,455	$ 97,549
6	Gresham Machines	$	33,199	$	40,390	$ 50,112
7	Real Photography	$	30,891	$	35,489	$ 36,400
8	Genesis Productions	$	72,190	$	75,390	$ 83,219
9	Landower Company	$	22,188	$	14,228	$ 38,766
10	Jewell Enterprises	$	19,764	$	50,801	$ 32,188
11						
12	January Sales 2007-2009					
13	=SUM('Sales 2007:Sales 2009'!B5:B10)					
14						

Steps 4a–4d

5. Complete steps similar to those in Step 3 to add *February Sales 2007-2009* (on two lines) in cell C12 and complete steps similar to those in Step 4 to insert the formula with the 3-D reference in cell C13. (Select cells C5 through C10.)
6. Complete steps similar to those in Step 3 to add *March Sales 2007-2009* (on two lines) in cell D12 and complete steps similar to those in Step 4 to insert the formula with the 3-D reference in cell D13. (Select cells D5 through D10.)
7. Save the workbook.
8. Print only the Sales 2007 worksheet.
9. Close **ExcelL1_C5_P5.xlsx**.

Project ⑥ Copy and Paste a Worksheet in a Word Document

You will copy cells in a worksheet and paste the cells in a Word letter document. You will then edit some of the data in cells in the Word document.

Copying and Pasting a Worksheet between Programs

Microsoft Office is a suite that allows integration, which is the combining of data from two or more programs into one file. Integration can occur by copying and pasting data between programs. The program containing the data to be copied is called the *source* program and the program where the data is pasted is called the *destination* program. For example, you can create a worksheet in Excel and then

copy it to a Word document. The steps to copy and paste between programs are basically the same as copying and pasting within the same program.

When copying data between worksheets or from one program to another, you can copy and paste, copy and link, or copy and embed the data. Consider the following when choosing a method for copying data:

- Copy data in the source program and paste it in the destination program when the data will not need to be edited.
- Copy data in the source program and then link it in the destination program when the data is updated regularly in the source program and you want the update reflected in the destination program.
- Copy data in the source program and then embed it in the destination program when the data will be edited in the destination program (with the tools of the source program).

Earlier in this chapter, you copied and pasted cells within and between worksheets and you also copied and linked cells between worksheets. You can also copy and link data between programs. Copy and embed data using options at the Paste Special dialog box. In Project 6, you will copy cells in a worksheet and then embed the cells in a Word document. With the worksheet embedded in a Word document, double-click the worksheet and Excel tools display in the document for editing the worksheet.

Project ⑥ Copying and Pasting a Worksheet into a Word Document

1. Open the Word program and then open **WordC05_Letter01.docx**.
2. Save the document and name it **WordExcelL1_C5_P6**.
3. With **WordExcelL1_C5_P6.docx** open, make Excel the active program.
4. Open **ExcelC05Project06.xlsx** and then save the workbook and name it **ExcelL1_C5_P6**.
5. Copy the worksheet to the letter by completing the following steps:
   a. Select cells A1 through D8.
   b. Click the Copy button in the Clipboard group in the Home tab.
   c. Click the button on the Taskbar representing the Word document **WordExcelL1_C5_P6.docx**.
   d. Position the insertion point on the blank line below the first paragraph of text in the body of the letter.
   e. Click the Paste button arrow in the Clipboard group in the Home tab and then click *Paste Special* at the drop-down list.
   f. At the Paste Special dialog box, click *Microsoft Office Excel Worksheet Object* in the *As* list box, and then click OK.

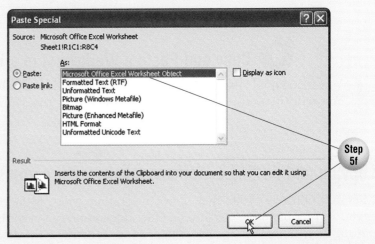

Step 5f

6. Edit a few of the cells in the worksheet by completing the following steps:
   a. Double-click anywhere in the worksheet. (This displays the Excel ribbon for editing.)
   b. Click in each of the following cells and make the change indicated:
      B6: Change *196%* to *110%*.
      C6: Change *190%* to *104%*.
      D6: Change *187%* to *101%*.

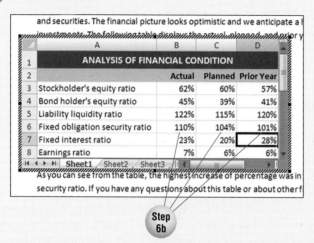

Step 6b

   c. Click outside the worksheet to remove the Excel tools (and deselect the worksheet).
7. Save, print, and then close **WordExcelL1_C5_P6.docx**.
8. Exit Word.
9. With Excel the active program, close **ExcelL1_C5_P6.xlsx**.

CHAPTER summary

- An Excel workbook, by default, contains three worksheets. Click a worksheet tab to display the worksheet.
- Move selected cells and cell contents in and between worksheets using the Cut, Copy, and Paste buttons in the Clipboard group in the Home tab or by dragging with the mouse.
- Move selected cells with the mouse by dragging the outline of the selected cells to the desired position.
- Copy selected cells with the mouse by holding down the Ctrl key and the left mouse button, dragging the outline of the selected cells to the desired location, releasing the left mouse button, and then releasing the Ctrl key.
- When pasting data, use the Paste Options button to specify what you want pasted. Click the Paste Options button and a drop-down list displays with options to specify that you want to keep source formatting, use destination themes, use destination formatting, or keep the column widths of the source worksheet. If you are pasting a cell containing a value as well as a formula, the Paste Options button drop-down list also includes the *Values Only* option.
- Use the Clipboard task pane to collect and paste data within and between worksheets and workbooks. Display the Clipboard task pane by clicking the Clipboard group dialog box launcher.
- Insert a worksheet in a workbook by clicking the Insert Worksheet tab located to the right of the Sheet3 tab or pressing Shift + F11.
- Perform maintenance activities, such as deleting and renaming, on worksheets within a workbook by clicking the *right* mouse button on a sheet tab and then clicking the desired option at the shortcut menu.
- You can use the mouse to move or copy worksheets. To move a worksheet, drag the worksheet tab with the mouse. To copy a worksheet, hold down the Ctrl key and then drag the worksheet tab with the mouse.
- Use the *Tab Color* option at the sheet tab shortcut menu to apply a color to a worksheet tab.
- Hide and unhide a worksheet by clicking the Format button in the Cells group and then clicking the desired option at the drop-down list, or by right-clicking the worksheet tab and then clicking the desired option at the shortcut menu.
- Manage more than one worksheet at a time by first selecting the worksheets. Use the mouse together with the Shift key to select adjacent worksheet tabs and use the mouse together with the Ctrl key to select nonadjacent worksheet tabs.
- If you want formatting to apply to multiple worksheets in a workbook, select the tabs of the desired worksheets and then apply the formatting.
- To print all worksheets in a workbook, click *Entire workbook* in the *Print what* section of the Print dialog box. You can also print specific worksheets by selecting the tabs of the worksheets you want to print.
- Split the worksheet window into panes with the Split button in the Window group in the View tab or with the split bars on the horizontal and vertical scroll bars.

CONCEPTS check

Completion: In the space provided at th

1. By default, a workbook contains th

2. To copy selected cells with the mous
   dragging the outline of the selected

3. The Cut, Copy, and Paste buttons a
   the Home tab.

4. This button displays in the lower ri

5. Use this task pane to collect and pa

6. Click this tab to insert a new works

7. Click this option at the sheet tab sh
   color to a worksheet tab.

8. To select adjacent worksheet tabs, cli
   this key, and then click the last tab.

9. To select nonadjacent worksheet tab
   down this key, and then click any oth

10. Click this option in the *Print what* se
    box to print all worksheets in a work

11. The Split button is located in this ta

12. Display the Arrange Windows dialog b
    in the Window group in the View tab

13. Click this button to make the active
    the screen.

14. Click this button to reduce the active
    the Taskbar.

15. When copying and pasting data betwee
    containing the original data is called t

- To remove a split from a worksheet, click the Split button to deactivate it or drag the split bars to the upper left corner of the worksheet.

- Freeze window panes by clicking the Freeze Panes button in the Window group in the View tab and then clicking *Freeze Panes* at the drop-down list. Unfreeze window panes by clicking the Freeze Panes button and then clicking *Unfreeze Panes* at the drop-down list.

- A selected group of cells is referred to as a range. A range can be named and used in a formula. Name a range by typing the name in the Name box located to the left of the Formula bar or at the New Name dialog box.

- To open multiple workbooks that are adjacent, display the Open dialog box, click the first workbook, hold down the Shift key, click the last workbook, and then click the Open button. If workbooks are nonadjacent, click the first workbook, hold down the Ctrl key, click the desired workbooks, and then click the Open button.

- To see a list of open workbooks, click the View tab and then click the Switch Windows button in the Window group.

- Arrange multiple workbooks in a window with options at the Arrange Windows dialog box.

- Hide the active workbook by clicking the Hide button and unhide a workbook by clicking the Unhide button in the Window group in the View tab.

- Click the Maximize button located in the upper right corner of the active workbook to make the workbook fill the entire window area. Click the Minimize button to shrink the active workbook to a button on the Taskbar. Click the Restore button to return the workbook to its previous size.

- You can move, copy, and/or paste data between workbooks.

- Copy and then link data if you make changes in the source worksheet and you want the changes reflected in the destination worksheet. The worksheet containing the original data is called the source worksheet and the worksheet relying on the source worksheet for data in the link is called the dependent worksheet.

- Copy and link data using the Paste Special dialog box or the *Link Cells* option at the Paste Options button drop-down list.

- You can copy data from a file in one program (called the source program) and paste the data into a file in another program (called the destination program).

- Use a 3-D reference to analyze data in the same cell or range of cells.

- You can copy and then paste, link, or embed data between programs in the Office suite. Integrating is the combining of data from two or more programs in the Office suite.

COMMANDS

FEATURE	
Cut selected cells	
Copy selected cells	
Paste selected cells	
Clipboard task pane	
Insert worksheet	
Hide worksheet	
Unhide worksheet	
Split window into pane	
Freeze window panes	
Unfreeze window panes	
New Name dialog box	
Arrange Windows dialog box	
Maximize window	
Restore	
Minimize window	
Paste Special dialog box	

SKILLS check
Demonstrate Your Proficiency

Assessment

1 COPY AND PASTE DATA BETWEEN WORKSHEETS IN A SALES WORKBOOK

1. Open **ExcelC05Assessment01.xlsx** and then save the workbook and name it **ExcelL1_C5_A1**.
2. Turn on the display of the Clipboard task pane, click the Clear All button to clear any content, and then complete the following steps:
   a. Select and copy cells A7 through C7.
   b. Select and copy cells A10 through C10.
   c. Select and copy cells A13 through C13.
   d. Display the second worksheet, make cell A7 active, and then paste the *Avalon Clinic* cells.
   e. Make cell A10 active and then paste the *Stealth Media* cells.
   f. Make A13 active and then paste the *Danmark Contracting* cells.
   g. Make the third worksheet active and then complete similar steps to paste the cells in the same location as the second worksheet.
   h. Clear the contents of the Clipboard task pane and then close the task pane.
3. Change the name of the Sheet1 tab to *2007 Sales*, the name of the Sheet2 tab to *2008 Sales*, and the name of the Sheet3 tab to *2009 Sales*.
4. Change the color of the 2007 Sales tab to blue, the color of the 2008 Sales tab to green, and the color of the 2009 Sales tab to yellow.
5. Display the 2007 Sales worksheet, select all three tabs, and then insert a formula in cell D4 that sums the amounts in cells B4 and C4. Copy the formula in cell D4 down to cells D5 through D14.
6. Make cell D15 active and then insert a formula that sums the amounts in cells D4 through D14.
7. Insert a footer on all three worksheets that prints your name at the left side and the current date at the right.
8. Save, print, and then close **ExcelL1_C5_A1.xlsx**.

Assessment

2 COPY, PASTE, AND FORMAT WORKSHEETS IN AN INCOME STATEMENT WORKBOOK

1. Open **ExcelC05Assessment02.xlsx** and then save the workbook and name it **ExcelL1_C5_A2**.
2. Copy cells A1 through B17 in Sheet1 and paste them into Sheet2. (Click the Paste Options button and then click *Keep Source Column Widths* at the drop-down list.)
3. Make the following changes to the Sheet2 worksheet:
   a. Adjust the row heights so they match the heights in the Sheet1 worksheet.
   b. Change the month from *January* to *February*.
   c. Change the amount in B4 to *97,655*.
   d. Change the amount in B5 to *39,558*.
   e. Change the amount in B11 to *1,105*.

4. Select both sheet tabs and then insert the following formulas:
   a. Insert a formula in B6 that subtracts the Cost of Sales from the Sales Revenue (=B4-B5).
   b. Insert a formula in B16 that sums the amounts in B8 through B15.
   c. Insert a formula in B17 that subtracts the Total Expenses from the Gross Profit (=B6-B16).
5. Change the name of the Sheet1 tab to *January* and the name of the Sheet2 tab to *February*.
6. Change the color of the January tab to blue and the color of the February tab to red.
7. Insert a custom footer on both worksheets that prints your name at the left side, the date in the middle, and the file name at the right side.
8. Save, print, and then close **ExcelL1_C5_A2.xlsx**.

Assessment

3 FREEZE AND UNFREEZE WINDOW PANES IN A TEST SCORES WORKBOOK

1. Open **ExcelC05Assessment03.xlsx** and then save the workbook and name it **ExcelL1_C5_A3**.
2. Make cell A1 active and then split the window by clicking the View tab and then clicking the Split button in the Window group. (This causes the window to split into four panes.)
3. Drag both the horizontal and vertical gray lines up and to the left until the horizontal gray line is immediately below the second row and the vertical gray line is immediately to the right of the first column.
4. Freeze the window panes.
5. Add two rows immediately above row 18 and then type the following text in the specified cells:

A18	=	Nauer, Sheryl		A19	=	Nunez, James
B18	=	75		B19	=	98
C18	=	83		C19	=	96
D18	=	85		D19	=	100
E18	=	78		E19	=	90
F18	=	82		F19	=	95
G18	=	80		G19	=	93
H18	=	79		H19	=	88
I18	=	82		I19	=	91
J18	=	92		J19	=	89
K18	=	90		K19	=	100
L18	=	86		L19	=	96
M18	=	84		M19	=	98

6. Insert a formula in cell N3 that averages the percentages in cells B3 through M3 and then copy the formula down to cells N4 through N22.
7. Unfreeze the window panes.
8. Remove the split.
9. Save the worksheet and then print it in landscape orientation.
10. Close **ExcelL1_C5_A3.xlsx**.

4 CREATE, COPY, PASTE, AND FORMAT CELLS IN AN EQUIPMENT USAGE WORKBOOK

1. Create the worksheet shown in Figure 5.10 (change the width of column A to 21.00).
2. Save the workbook and name it **ExcelL1_C5_A4**.
3. With **ExcelL1_C5_A4.xlsx** open, open **ExcelC05Project02.xlsx**.
4. Select and copy the following cells from **ExcelC05Project02.xlsx** to **ExcelL1_C5_A4.xlsx**:
   a. Copy cells A4 through G4 in **ExcelC05Project02.xlsx** and paste them into **ExcelL1_C5_A4.xlsx** beginning with cell A12.
   b. Copy cells A10 through G10 in **ExcelC05Project02.xlsx** and paste them into **ExcelL1_C5_A4.xlsx** beginning with cell A13.
5. With **ExcelL1_C5_A4.xlsx** the active workbook, make cell A1 active and then apply the following formatting:
   a. Change the height of row 1 to 25.50.
   b. Change the font size of the text in cell A1 to 14 points.
   c. Insert Olive Green, Accent 3, Lighter 60% fill color to cell A1.
6. Select cells A2 through G2 and then insert Olive Green, Accent 3, Darker 50% fill color.
7. Select cells B2 through G2 and then change to right alignment, change the text color to white, and turn on italics.
8. Select cells A3 through G3 and then insert Olive Green, Accent 3, Lighter 80% fill color.
9. Select cells A7 through G7 and then insert Olive Green, Accent 3, Lighter 80% fill color.
10. Select cells A11 through G11 and then insert Olive Green, Accent 3, Lighter 80% fill color.
11. Change the orientation to landscape.
12. Print the worksheet centered horizontally and vertically on the page.
13. Save and then close **ExcelL1_C5_A4.xlsx**.
14. Close **ExcelC05Project02.xlsx** without saving the changes.

Figure 5.10 Assessment 4

	A	B	C	D	E	F	G	H
1	EQUIPMENT USAGE REPORT							
2		January	February	March	April	May	June	
3	Machine #12							
4	Total Hours Available	2300	2430	2530	2400	2440	2240	
5	In Use	2040	2105	2320	2180	2050	1995	
6								
7	Machine #25							
8	Total Hours Available	2100	2240	2450	2105	2390	1950	
9	In Use	1800	1935	2110	1750	2215	1645	
10								
11	Machine #30							
12								

5 LINK WORKSHEETS IN A SALES WORKBOOK WITH 3-D REFERENCES

1. Open **ExcelC05Assessment05.xlsx** and then save the workbook and name it **ExcelL1_C5_A5**.
2. Change the color of the Sales 2007 tab to purple, the color of the Sales 2008 tab to blue, and the color of the Sales 2009 tab to green.
3. Make the following changes to the workbook:
   a. Make Sales 2007 the active worksheet.
   b. Select columns B, C, and D and then change the width to 16.00.
   c. Insert the heading *Average January Sales 2007-2009* (on multiple lines) in cell B11, centered and bolded.
   d. Insert a formula in cell B12 with a 3-D reference that averages the total in cells B4 through B9 in the Sales 2007, Sales 2008, and Sales 2009 worksheets.
   e. Insert the heading *Average February Sales 2007-2009* (on multiple lines) in cell C11, centered and bolded.
   f. Insert a formula in cell C12 with a 3-D reference that averages the total in cells C4 through C9 in the Sales 2007, Sales 2008, and Sales 2009 worksheets.
   g. Insert the heading *Average March Sales 2007-2009* (on multiple lines) in cell D11, centered and bolded.
   h. Insert a formula in cell D12 with a 3-D reference that averages the total in cells D4 through D9 in the Sales 2007, Sales 2008, and Sales 2009 worksheets.
4. Save the workbook and then print only the Sales 2007 worksheet.
5. Close **ExcelL1_C5_A5.xlsx**.

6 LINK DATA BETWEEN A WORD LETTER AND AN EXCEL WORKSHEET

1. Use Excel's Help feature to learn about linking data between programs.
2. After locating and reading the information on linking, open the Word program and then open **WordC05_Letter02.docx**.
3. Save the document and name it **WordExcelL1_C5_A6**.
4. Make Excel the active program and then open **ExcelC05Assessment06.xlsx**.
5. Save the workbook with Save As and name it **ExcelL1_C5_A6**.
6. In column G, insert a formula using the PMT function.
7. Save and then print the worksheet.
8. Select cells A2 through G10 and then copy and link the cells to **WordExcelL1_C5_A6.docx** (between the two paragraphs in the body of the letter).
9. Save, print, and then close **WordExcelL1_C5_A6.docx**.
10. Click the button on the Taskbar representing the Excel workbook **ExcelL1_C5_A6.xlsx** and then change the percentages in cells E3 through E6 to 7.5% and the percentages in cells E7 through E10 to 8.5%.
11. Save, print, and then close **ExcelL1_C5_A6.xlsx**.
12. Make Word the active program and then open **WordExcelL1_C5_A6.docx**.
13. At the message that displays, click Yes.
14. Save, print, and then close **WordExcelL1_C5_A6.docx**.
15. Exit Word.

CASE study

Apply Your Skills

You are an administrator for Gateway Global, an electronics manufacturing corporation. You are gathering information on money spent on supplies and equipment purchases. You have gathered information for the first quarter of the year and decide to create a workbook containing worksheets for monthly information. To do this, create a worksheet that contains the following information:

- Company name is Gateway Global.
- Create the title *January Expenditures*.
- Create the following columns:

Department	Supplies	Equipment	Total
Production	$25,425	$135,500	
Research and Development	$50,000	$125,000	
Technical Support	$14,500	$65,000	
Finance	$5,790	$22,000	
Sales and Marketing	$35,425	$8,525	
Facilities	$6,000	$1,200	
Total			

- Insert a formula in the *Total* column that sums the amounts in the *Supplies* and *Equipment* columns and insert a formula in the *Total* row that sums the Supplies amounts, Equipment amounts, and Total amounts.
- Apply formatting such as fill color, borders, font color, and shading to enhance the visual appeal of the worksheet.

After creating and formatting the worksheet, complete the following:

- Copy the worksheet data to Sheet2 and then to Sheet3.
- Make the following changes to data in Sheet2:
  - Change *January Expenditures* to *February Expenditures*.
  - Change the Production Department Supplies amount to *$38,550* and the Equipment amount to *$88,500*.
  - Change the Technical Support Department Equipment amount to *$44,250*.
  - Change the Finance Department Supplies amount to *$7,500*.
- Make the following changes to data in Sheet3:
  - Change *January Expenditures* to *March Expenditures*.
  - Change the Research and Development Department Supplies amount to *$65,000* and the Equipment amount to *$150,000*.
  - Change the Technical Support Department Supplies amount to *$21,750* and the Equipment amount to *$43,525*.
  - Change the Facilities Department Equipment amount to *$18,450*.

Create a new worksheet that summarizes the Supplies and Equipment totals for January, February, and March. Apply the same formatting to the worksheet as applied to the other three. Change the tab name for Sheet1 to *Jan. Expenditures*, the tab name for Sheet2 to *Feb. Expenditures*, the tab name for Sheet3 to *Mar. Expenditures*, and the tab name for Sheet4 to *Qtr. Summary*. Change the color of each tab (you determine the colors).

Insert a footer that prints your name at the left side of each worksheet and the current date at the right side of each worksheet. Save the workbook and name it **ExcelL1_C5_CS_P1**. Print all the worksheets in the workbook and then close the workbook.

Part

2

Employees of Gateway Global have formed two intramural co-ed softball teams and you have volunteered to keep statistics for the players. Open **ExcelGGStats.xlsx** and then make the following changes to both worksheets in the workbook:

- Insert a formula that calculates a player's batting average (Hits divided by At Bats).
- Insert a formula that calculates a player's on-base percentage (Walks + Hits divided by At Bats plus Walks). Make sure you insert parentheses in the formula.
- Insert the company name.
- Apply formatting to enhance the visual appeal of the worksheets.
- Horizontally and vertically center the worksheets.
- Insert a footer that prints on both worksheets and prints your name at the left side of the worksheet and the date at the right of the worksheet.

Using Help, learn how to apply conditional formatting to data in a worksheet. Select both worksheets and then apply conditional formatting that inserts red fill and changes text color to dark red for cells in the *Batting Average* column with an average over .400. Save the workbook and name it **ExcelL1_C5_CS_P2**. Print and then close **ExcelL1_C5_CS_P2.xlsx**.

Part

3

Many of the suppliers for Gateway Global are international and use different length, weight, and volume measurements. The purchasing manager has asked you to prepare a conversion chart in Excel that displays conversion tables for length, weight, volume, and temperature. Use the Internet to locate conversion tables for length, weight, and volume. When preparing the workbook, create a worksheet with the following information:

- Include the following length conversions:
  ○ 1 inch to centimeters
  ○ 1 foot to centimeters
  ○ 1 yard to meters
  ○ 1 mile to kilometers
- Include the following weight conversions:
  ○ 1 ounce to grams
  ○ 1 pound to kilograms
  ○ 1 ton to metric tons
- Include the following volume conversions:
  ○ 1 fluid ounce to milliliters
  ○ 1 pint to liters
  ○ 1 quart to liters
  ○ 1 gallon to liters

Locate a site on the Internet that provides the formula for converting Fahrenheit temperatures to Celsius temperatures and then create another worksheet in the workbook with the following information:

- Insert Fahrenheit temperatures beginning with zero, continuing to 100, and incrementing by 5 (for example, 0, 5, 10, 15, and so on).
- Insert a formula that converts the Fahrenheit temperature to a Celsius temperature.

Include the company name, Gateway Global, in both worksheets. Apply additional formatting to improve the visual appeal of both worksheets. Rename both sheet names and apply a color to each tab (you determine the names and colors). Save the workbook and name it **ExcelL1_C5_CS_P3**. Print both worksheets centered horizontally and vertically on the page and then close **ExcelL1_C5_CS_P3.xlsx**.

Part
4

Open Microsoft Word and then create a letterhead document that contains the company name *Gateway Global*, the address (you decide the address including street address, city, state, and ZIP code or street address, city, province, and postal code), and the telephone number (you determine the telephone number). Apply formatting to improve the visual display of the letterhead. Save the document and name it **WordGGLtrhd**. Save the document again with Save As and name it **WordL1_C5_CS_P4A**. In Excel, open **ExcelL1_C5_CS_P3.xlsx**. In the first worksheet, copy the cells containing data and then paste them in **WordL1_C5_CS_P4A.docx** using Paste Special. Save, print, and then close **WordL1_C5_CS_P4A.docx**. In Word, open **WordGGLtrd.docx**. Save the document with Save As and name it **WordL1_C5_CS_P4B**. In Excel, make the worksheet active that contains the Fahrenheit conversion information, copy the cells containing data, and then paste them in the Word document using Paste Special. Save, print, and then close **WordL1_C5_CS_P4B.docx**. Close Microsoft Word and then, in Excel, close **ExcelL1_C5_CS_P3.xlsx**.

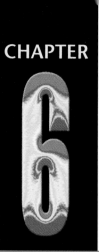

Maintaining Workbooks

PERFORMANCE OBJECTIVES

Upon successful completion of Chapter 6, you will be able to:

- Create and rename a folder
- Delete workbooks and folders
- Copy and move workbooks within and between folders
- Copy, move, and rename worksheets within a workbook
- Save a workbook in a variety of formats
- Maintain consistent formatting with styles
- Use comments for review and response
- Create financial forms using templates

excel Chapter 6

Tutorial 6.1
Managing Folders and
Workbooks
Tutorial 6.2
Advanced Formatting Techniques

Once you have been working with Excel for a period of time you will have accumulated several workbook files. Workbooks should be organized into folders to facilitate fast retrieval of information. Occasionally you should perform file maintenance activities such as copying, moving, renaming, and deleting workbooks to ensure the workbook list in your various folders is manageable. You will learn these file management tasks in this chapter along with creating and applying styles, inserting and printing comments, and using Excel templates to create a workbook.

Note: Before beginning computer projects, copy to your storage medium the Excel2007L1C6 subfolder from the Excel2007L1 folder on the CD that accompanies this textbook and then make Excel2007L1C6 the active folder.

roject ① Manage Workbooks

You will perform a variety of file management tasks including creating and renaming a folder; selecting and then deleting, copying, cutting, pasting, and renaming workbooks; deleting a folder; and opening, printing, and closing a workbook.

Maintaining Workbooks

You can complete many workbook management tasks at the Open and Save As dialog boxes. These tasks can include copying, moving, printing, and renaming workbooks; opening multiple workbooks; and creating and renaming a new folder. Some file maintenance tasks such as creating a folder and deleting files are performed by using buttons on the Open dialog box or Save As dialog box toolbar. Figure 6.1 displays the Open dialog box toolbar buttons.

Figure 6.1 Open Dialog Box Toolbar Buttons

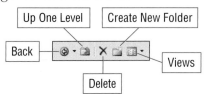

Creating a Folder

QUICK STEPS

Create a Folder
1. Click Office button, *Open*.
2. Click Create New Folder button.
3. Type folder name.
4. Press Enter.

In Excel, you should logically group and store workbooks in folders. For example, you could store all of the workbooks related to one department in one folder with the department name being the folder name. You can create a folder within a folder (called a **subfolder**). If you create workbooks for a department by individuals, each individual name could have a subfolder within the department folder. The main folder on a disk or drive is called the root folder. You create additional folders as branches of this root folder.

At the Open or Save As dialog boxes, workbook file names display in the list box preceded by a workbook icon and a folder name displays preceded by a folder icon. Create a new folder by clicking the Create New Folder button located on the dialog box toolbar at the Open dialog box or Save As dialog box. At the New Folder dialog box shown in Figure 6.2, type a name for the folder in the *Name* text box, and then click OK or press Enter. The new folder becomes the active folder.

If you want to make the previous folder the active folder, click the Up One Level button on the dialog box toolbar. After clicking the Up One Level button, the Back button becomes active. Click this button and the previously active folder becomes active again.

A folder name can contain a maximum of 255 characters. Numbers, spaces, and symbols can be used in the folder name, except those symbols explained in Chapter 1 in the "Saving a Workbook" section.

> **HINT**
> Change the default folder with the *Default file location* option at the Excel Options dialog box with Save selected.

Create New Folder

Up One Level

Figure 6.2 New Folder Dialog Box

Type the new folder name in the *Name* text box.

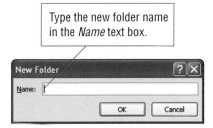

1. Create a folder named *Payroll* on your storage medium. To begin, display the Open dialog box.
2. Double-click the *Excel2007L1C6* folder name to make it the active folder.
3. Click the Create New Folder button (located on the dialog box toolbar).
4. At the New Folder dialog box, type Payroll.
5. Click OK. (The Payroll folder is now the active folder.)

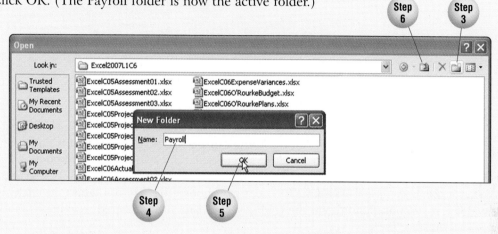

6. Click the Up One Level button on the dialog box toolbar to change back to the Excel2007L1C6 folder.

Renaming a Folder

As you organize your files and folders, you may decide to rename a folder. Rename a folder using the Tools button in the Open dialog box or using a shortcut menu. To rename a folder using the Tools button, display the Open dialog box, click in the list box the folder you want to rename, click the Tools button located in the lower left corner of the dialog box, and then click *Rename* at the drop-down list. This selects the folder name and inserts a border around the name. Type the new name for the folder and then press Enter. To rename a folder using a shortcut menu, display the Open dialog box, right-click the folder name in the list box, and then click *Rename* at the shortcut menu. Type a new name for the folder and then press Enter.

A tip to remember when you are organizing files and folders is to be sure that your system is set up to display all of the files in a particular folder and not just the Excel files, for example. You can display all files in a folder by changing the *Files of type* option at the Open dialog box to *All Files (*.*)*.

QUICK STEPS

Rename a Folder
1. Click Office button, *Open.*
2. Click desired folder.
3. Click Tools button, *Rename.*
4. Type new name.
5. Press Enter.
OR
1. Click Office button, *Open.*
2. Right-click folder name.
3. Click *Rename.*
4. Type new name.
5. Press Enter.

Tools ▾

Project 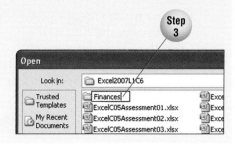 Renaming a Folder

1. At the Open dialog box, right-click the *Payroll* folder name in the Open dialog box list box.
2. Click *Rename* at the shortcut menu.
3. Type **Finances** and then press Enter.

Selecting Workbooks

You can complete workbook management tasks on one workbook or selected workbooks. To select one workbook, display the Open dialog box, and then click the desired workbook. To select several adjacent workbooks (workbooks that display next to each other), click the first workbook, hold down the Shift key, and then click the last workbook. To select workbooks that are not adjacent, click the first workbook, hold down the Ctrl key, click any other desired workbooks, and then release the Ctrl key.

Delete Workbook/ Folder
1. Click Office button, *Open*.
2. Click workbook or folder name.
3. Click Delete button.
4. Click Yes.

Deleting Workbooks and Folders

At some point, you may want to delete certain workbooks from your storage medium or any other drive or folder in which you may be working. To delete a workbook, display the Open or Save As dialog box, select the workbook, and then click the Delete button on the dialog box toolbar. At the dialog box asking you to confirm the deletion, click Yes. To delete a workbook using a shortcut menu, display the Open dialog box, right-click the workbook name in the list box, and then click *Delete* at the shortcut menu. Click Yes at the confirmation dialog box.

Delete

Deleting to the Recycle Bin

Workbooks deleted from the hard drive are automatically sent to the Windows Recycle Bin. You can easily restore a deleted workbook from the Recycle Bin. To free space on the drive, empty the Recycle Bin on a periodic basis. Restoring a workbook from or emptying the contents of the Recycle Bin is completed at the Windows desktop (not in Excel). To display the Recycle Bin, minimize the Excel window, and then double-click the *Recycle Bin* icon located on the Windows desktop. At the Recycle Bin, you can restore file(s) and empty the Recycle Bin.

Project Selecting and Deleting Workbooks

1. At the Open dialog box, open **ExcelC05Project01.xlsx** (located in the Excel2007L1C6 folder).
2. Save the workbook with Save As and name it **ExcelL1_C6_P1**.
3. Close **ExcelL1_C6_P1.xlsx**.

4. Delete **ExcelL1_C6_P1.xlsx** by completing the following steps:
   a. Display the Open dialog box with Excel2007L1C6 the active folder.
   b. Click **ExcelL1_C6_P1.xlsx** to select it.
   c. Click the Delete button on the dialog box toolbar.

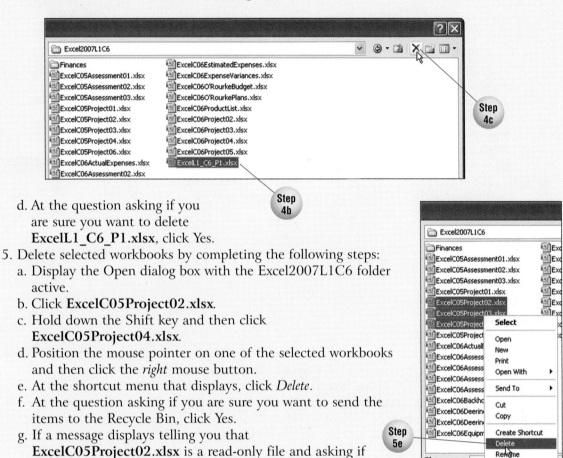

Step 4c

Step 4b

   d. At the question asking if you are sure you want to delete **ExcelL1_C6_P1.xlsx**, click Yes.
5. Delete selected workbooks by completing the following steps:
   a. Display the Open dialog box with the Excel2007L1C6 folder active.
   b. Click **ExcelC05Project02.xlsx**.
   c. Hold down the Shift key and then click **ExcelC05Project04.xlsx**.
   d. Position the mouse pointer on one of the selected workbooks and then click the *right* mouse button.
   e. At the shortcut menu that displays, click *Delete*.
   f. At the question asking if you are sure you want to send the items to the Recycle Bin, click Yes.
   g. If a message displays telling you that **ExcelC05Project02.xlsx** is a read-only file and asking if you want to delete it, click the Yes to All button.
6. Close the Open dialog box.

Step 5e

Copying Workbooks

In previous chapters, you have been opening a workbook from your storage medium and saving it with a new name in the same location. This process makes an exact copy of the workbook, leaving the original on your storage medium. You have been copying workbooks and saving the new workbook in the same folder as the original workbook. You can also copy a workbook into another folder.

Project **1d** **Saving a Copy of an Open Workbook**

1. Open **ExcelC05Assessment01.xlsx**.
2. Save the workbook with Save As and name it **TotalSales**. (Make sure Excel2007L1C6 is the active folder.)
3. Save a copy of the **TotalSales.xlsx** workbook in the Finances folder you created in Project 1a by completing the following steps:
   a. With **TotalSales.xlsx** open, display the Save As dialog box.
   b. At the Save As dialog box, change to the Finances folder. To do this, double-click *Finances* at the beginning of the list box (folders are listed before workbooks).
   c. Click the Save button located in the lower right corner of the dialog box.
4. Close **TotalSales.xlsx**.
5. Change back to the Excel2007L1C6 folder by completing the following steps:
   a. Display the Open dialog box.
   b. Click the Up One Level button located on the dialog box toolbar.
   c. Close the Open dialog box.

Step
5b

Copy a Workbook
1. Click Office button, *Open*.
2. Right-click workbook name.
3. Click *Copy*.
4. Navigate to desired folder.
5. Right-click white area in list box.
6. Click *Paste*.

You can copy a workbook to another folder without opening the workbook first. To do this, use the *Copy* and *Paste* options from a shortcut menu at the Open (or Save As) dialog box. You can also copy a workbook or selected workbooks into the same folder. When you do this, Excel names the workbook(s) "Copy of xxx" (where *xxx* is the current workbook name). You can copy one workbook or selected workbooks into the same folder.

Project **1e** **Copying a Workbook at the Open Dialog Box**

1. Copy **ExcelC05Assessment02.xlsx** to the Finance folder. To begin, display the Open dialog box with the Excel2007L1C6 folder active.
2. Position the arrow pointer on **ExcelC05Assessment02.xlsx**, click the right mouse button, and then click *Copy* at the shortcut menu.
3. Change to the Finance folder by double-clicking *Finances* at the beginning of the list box.
4. Position the arrow pointer in any white area (not on a workbook name) in the list box, click the right mouse button, and then click *Paste* at the shortcut menu.
5. Change back to the Excel2007L1C6 folder by clicking the Up One Level button located on the dialog box toolbar.
6. Close the Open dialog box.

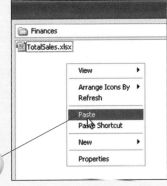

Step
4

Sending Workbooks to a Different Drive or Folder

Copy workbooks to another folder or drive with the *Copy* and *Paste* options from the shortcut menu at the Open or Save As dialog box. With the *Send To* option, you can send a copy of a workbook to another drive or folder. To use this option, position the arrow pointer on the workbook you want copied, click the *right* mouse button, point to *Send To* (this causes a side menu to display), and then click the desired drive or folder.

Cutting and Pasting a Workbook

You can remove a workbook from one folder and insert it in another folder using the *Cut* and *Paste* options from the shortcut menu at the Open dialog box. To do this, display the Open dialog box, position the arrow pointer on the workbook to be removed (cut), click the *right* mouse button, and then click *Cut* at the shortcut menu. Change to the desired folder or drive, position the arrow pointer in a white area in the list box, click the *right* mouse button, and then click *Paste* at the shortcut menu.

QUICK STEPS

Move a Workbook
1. Click Office button, *Open.*
2. Right-click workbook name.
3. Click *Cut.*
4. Navigate to desired folder.
5. Right-click white area in list box.
6. Click *Paste.*

Project 11   Cutting and Pasting a Workbook

1. Move a workbook to a different folder. To begin, display the Open dialog box with the Excel2007L1C6 folder active.
2. Position the arrow pointer on **ExcelC05Project06.xlsx**, click the right mouse button, and then click *Cut* at the shortcut menu.
3. Double-click *Finances* to make it the active folder.
4. Position the arrow pointer in the white area in the list box, click the right mouse button, and then click *Paste* at the shortcut menu.
5. If a Confirm File Move dialog box displays asking if you are sure you want to move the file, click Yes. (This dialog box usually does not appear when you cut and paste. Since the files you copied from your student CD-ROM are read-only files, this warning message appears.)
6. Click the Up One Level button to make the Excel2007L1C6 folder the active folder.

Renaming Workbooks

At the Open dialog box, use the *Rename* option from the Tools button drop-down list or the shortcut menu to give a workbook a different name. The *Rename* option changes the name of the workbook and keeps it in the same folder. To use *Rename*, display the Open dialog box, click once on the workbook to be renamed, click the Tools button located in the lower left corner of the dialog box, and then click *Rename*. This causes a thin black border to surround the workbook name and the name to be selected. Type the new name and then press Enter.

You can also rename a workbook by right-clicking the workbook name at the Open dialog box and then clicking *Rename* at the shortcut menu. Type the new name for the workbook and then press the Enter key.

QUICK STEPS

Rename Workbook
1. Click Office button, *Open.*
2. Click desired workbook.
3. Click Tools button, *Rename.*
4. Type new name.
5. Press Enter.
OR
1. Click Office button, *Open.*
2. Right-click workbook name.
3. Click *Rename.*
4. Type new name.
5. Press Enter.

Project 1g Renaming a Workbook

1. Rename a workbook located in the Finances folder. To begin, make sure the Open dialog box displays with Excel2007L1C6 the active folder.
2. Double-click *Finances* to make it the active folder.
3. Click once on **ExcelC05Project06.xlsx** to select it.
4. Click the Tools button that displays in the lower left corner of the dialog box.
5. Click *Rename* at the drop-down list.
6. Type **Analysis.xlsx** and then press the Enter key.
7. If a message displays asking if you are sure you want to change the name of the read-only file, click Yes.
8. Complete steps similar to those in Steps 3 through 6 to rename **ExcelC05Assessment02.xlsx** to *SoftwareTests.xlsx*.
9. Click the Up One Level button.

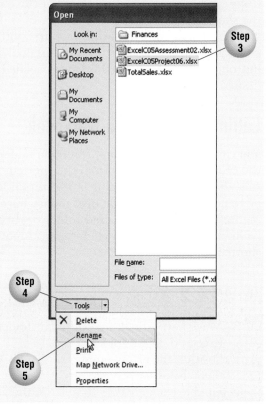

Deleting a Folder and Its Contents

As you learned earlier in this chapter, you can delete a workbook or selected workbooks. In addition to workbooks, you can delete a folder and all of its contents. Delete a folder in the same manner as you delete a workbook.

Project 1h Deleting a Folder and Its Contents

1. Delete the Finances folder and its contents. To begin, make sure the Open dialog box displays with the Excel2007L1C6 folder active.
2. Right-click on the *Finances* folder.
3. Click *Delete* at the shortcut menu.
4. At the Confirm Folder Delete dialog box, click Yes.
5. If the Confirm File Delete dialog box displays, click the Yes to All button.

Printing Workbooks

Up to this point, you have opened a workbook and then printed it. With the *Print* option from the Tools button drop-down list or the *Print* option from the shortcut menu at the Open dialog box, you can print a workbook or several workbooks without opening them.

Project ⑪ Printing Workbooks

1. At the Open dialog box with the Excel2007L1C6 folder active, select **ExcelC05Assessment01.xlsx** and **ExcelC05Assessment02.xlsx**.
2. Click the Tools button located in the lower left corner of the dialog box.
3. Click *Print* at the drop-down list.

Project ② Copy and Move Worksheets into an Equipment Rental Workbook

You will open an equipment rental workbook, open two other workbooks containing equipment rental information, and then copy and move worksheets between the workbooks.

Managing Worksheets

You can move or copy individual worksheets within the same workbook or to another existing workbook. Exercise caution when moving sheets since calculations or charts based on data on a worksheet might become inaccurate if you move the worksheet. To make a duplicate of a worksheet in the same workbook, hold down the Ctrl key and then drag the worksheet tab to the desired position.

Copying a Worksheet to Another Workbook

To copy a worksheet to another existing workbook, open both the source and the destination workbooks. Right-click the sheet tab and then click *Move or Copy* at the shortcut menu. At the Move or Copy dialog box shown in Figure 6.3, select the destination workbook name from the *To book* drop-down list, select the worksheet that you want the copied worksheet placed before in the *Before sheet* list box, click the *Create a copy* check box, and then click OK.

QUICK STEPS

Copy a Worksheet to Another Workbook
1. Right-click desired sheet tab.
2. Click *Move or Copy*.
3. Select desired destination workbook.
4. Select desired worksheet location.
5. Click *Create a copy* check box.
6. Click OK.

Figure 6.3 Move or Copy Dialog Box

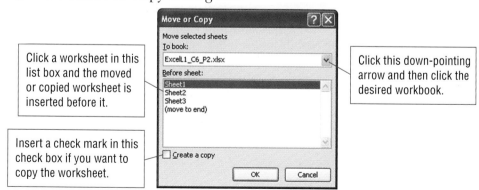

Click a worksheet in this list box and the moved or copied worksheet is inserted before it.

Click this down-pointing arrow and then click the desired workbook.

Insert a check mark in this check box if you want to copy the worksheet.

1. Open **ExcelC06Project02.xlsx** and then save the
   workbook and name it **ExcelL1_C6_P2**.
2. With **ExcelL1_C6_P2.xlsx** open, open
   ExcelC06Equipment.xlsx.
3. Copy the Front Loader worksheet by completing the
   following steps:
   a. With **ExcelC06Equipment.xlsx** the active
      workbook, right-click the Front Loader tab and
      then click *Move or Copy* at the shortcut menu.
   b. Click the down-pointing arrow next to the *To book*
      option box and then click **ExcelL1_C6_P2.xlsx** at
      the drop-down list.
   c. Click *Sheet2* in the *Before sheet* list box.
   d. Click the *Create a copy* check box to insert a
      check mark.
   e. Click OK. (Excel switches to the
      ExcelL1_C6_P2.xlsx workbook and inserts the
      copied Front Loader worksheet between Sheet1
      and Sheet2.)
4. Complete steps similar to those in Step 3 to copy
   the Tractor worksheet to the **ExcelL1_C6_P2.xlsx**
   workbook. (Insert the Tractor worksheet between
   Front Loader and Sheet2.)
5. Complete steps similar to those in Step 3 to copy
   the Forklift worksheet to the **ExcelL1_C6_P2.xlsx**
   workbook. (Insert the Forklift worksheet between
   Tractor and Sheet2.)
6. Save **ExcelL1_C6_P2.xlsx**.
7. Make **ExcelC06Equipment.xlsx** the active
   workbook and then close it.

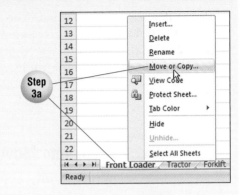

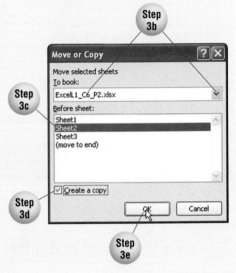

Step 3a

Step 3b

Step 3c

Step 3d

Step 3e

Moving a Worksheet to Another Workbook

To move a worksheet to another existing workbook, open both the source and the
destination workbooks. Make active the sheet you want to move in the source
workbook, right-click the sheet tab and then click *Move or Copy* at the shortcut
menu. At the Move or Copy dialog box shown in Figure 6.3, select the destination
workbook name from the *To book* drop-down list, select the worksheet that you
want the worksheet placed before in the *Before sheet* list box, and then click OK.
If you need to reposition a worksheet tab, drag the tab to the desired position.

Be careful when moving a worksheet to another workbook file. If formulas
exist in the workbook that depend on the contents of the cells in the worksheet
that is moved, they will no longer calculate properly.

1. With **ExcelL1_C6_P2.xlsx** open, open **ExcelC06Backhoe.xlsx**.
2. Move Sheet1 from **ExcelC06Backhoe.xlsx** to **ExcelL1_C6_P2.xlsx** by completing the following steps:

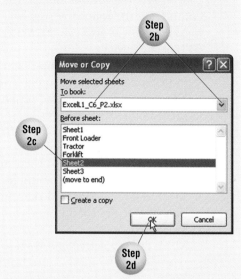

   a. With **ExcelC06Backhoe.xlsx** the active workbook, right-click the Sheet1 tab and then click *Move or Copy* at the shortcut menu.
   b. Click the down-pointing arrow next to the *To book* option box and then click **ExcelL1_C6_P2.xlsx** at the drop-down list.
   c. Click *Sheet2* in the *Before sheet* list box.
   d. Click OK.
3. Make **ExcelC06Backhoe.xlsx** the active workbook and then close it without saving the changes.
4. With **ExcelL1_C6_P2.xlsx** open, make the following changes:
   a. Delete Sheet2 and Sheet3 tabs. (These worksheets are blank.)
   b. Rename Sheet1 to **Equipment Hours**.
   c. Rename Sheet1 (2) to **Backhoe**.
5. Create a range for the Forklift total hours available by completing the following steps:
   a. Click the Front Loader tab.
   b. Select cells B4 through E4.
   c. Click in the Name box.
   d. Type **FrontLoaderHours**.

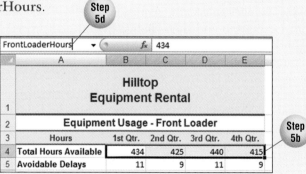

   e. Press Enter.
6. Complete steps similar to those in Step 5 to create the following ranges:
   a. In the Front Loader worksheet, create a range with cells B10 through E10 and name it *FrontLoaderHoursInUse*.
   b. Click the Tractor tab and then create a range with cells B4 through E4 and name it *TractorHours* and create a range with cells B10 through E10 and name it *TractorHoursInUse*.
   c. Click the Forklift tab and then create a range with cells B4 through E4 and name it *ForkliftHours* and create a range with cells B10 through E10 and name it *ForkliftHoursInUse*.
   d. Click the Backhoe tab and then create a range with cells B4 through E4 and name it *BackhoeHours* and create a range with cells B10 through E10 and name it *BackhoeHoursInUse*.

7. Click the EquipmentHours tab to make it the active worksheet and then insert a formula that inserts the total hours for the Front Loader by completing the following steps:

a. Make cell C4 active.

b. Type =SUM(Fr.

c. When you type *Fr* a drop-down list displays with the Front Loader ranges. Double-click *FrontLoaderHours*.

d. Type) (the closing parenthesis).

e. Press Enter.

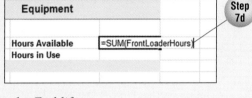

8. Complete steps similar to those in Step 7 to insert ranges in the following cells:

a. Make cell C5 active and then insert a formula that inserts the total in-use hours for the Front Loader.

b. Make cell C8 active and then insert a formula that inserts the total hours available for the Tractor.

c. Make cell C9 active and then insert a formula that inserts the total in-use hours for the Tractor.

d. Make cell C12 active and then insert a formula that inserts the total hours available for the Forklift.

e. Make cell C13 active and then insert a formula that inserts the total in-use hours for the Forklift.

f. Make cell C16 active and then insert a formula that inserts the total hours available for the Backhoe.

g. Make cell C17 active and then insert a formula that inserts the total in-use hours for the Backhoe.

9. Make the following changes to specific worksheets:

a. Click the Front Loader tab and then change the number in cell E4 from *415* to *426* and change the number in cell C6 from *6* to *14*.

b. Click the Forklift tab and then change the number in cells E4 from *415* to *426* and change the number in cell D8 from *4* to *12*.

10. Select all of the worksheet tabs and then create a footer that prints your name at the left side of each worksheet, the page number in the middle, and the current date at the right side of each worksheet.

11. Save, print, and then close **ExcelL1_C6_P2.xlsx**.

 roject ③ **Save Workbooks in Various Formats**

You will open a workbook and then save it in a previous version of Excel, in text format, and in PDF format.

Saving a Workbook in a Different Format

When you save a workbook, the workbook is automatically saved as an Excel workbook with the *.xlsx* file extension. If you need to share a workbook with someone who is using a different version of Excel, or someone who will open it in an application other than Excel, save the workbook in another format. You can also save an Excel workbook as a Web page and in text format. Save a workbook in a different format with options from the Office button Save As side menu or with the *Save as type* option at the Save As dialog box.

Saving a Workbook in a Previous Version of Excel

If you create workbooks that others will open in a previous version of Excel, consider saving the workbook in the Excel 97-2003 format. If you save a workbook in a previous version, the workbook name displays in the title bar followed by the words *[Compatibility Mode]*. In this mode, some Excel 2007 features may not be available.

You can save a workbook in a previous version with the Office button Save As side menu or with the *Save as type* option at the Save As dialog box. To save using the side menu, click the Office button, point to the *Save As* option, and then click *Excel 97-2003 Workbook* at the side menu as shown in Figure 6.4. At the Save As dialog box, type the name for the workbook, and then click the Save button. Note also that some file formats save the active worksheet and others save the entire workbook. If you want to save a specific worksheet, hide the other worksheets and then save.

Figure 6.4 Save As Side Menu

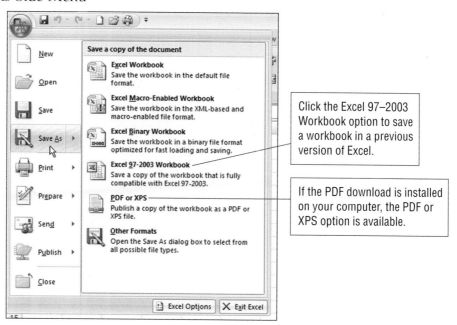

Click the Excel 97–2003 Workbook option to save a workbook in a previous version of Excel.

If the PDF download is installed on your computer, the PDF or XPS option is available.

1. Open **ExcelC06Project03.xlsx**.
2. Click the Office button, point to the *Save As* option, and then click the *Excel 97-2003 Workbook* option that displays in the side menu.
3. At the Save As dialog box with the *Save as type* option changed to *Excel 97-2003 Workbook (*.xls)*, type **ExcelL1_C6_P3_xlsformat** in the *File name* text box and then press Enter.

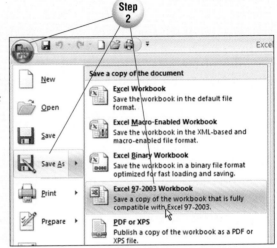

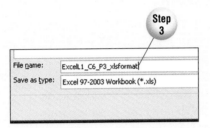

4. At the Compatibility Checker dialog box, click Continue.
5. Close **ExcelL1_C6_P3_xlsformat.xls**.
6. Open **ExcelL1_C6_P3_xlsformat.xls** and then notice that *[Compatibility Mode]* displays after the workbook title at the top of the screen.
7. Close **ExcelL1_C6_P3_xlsformat.xls**.

Saving a Workbook in Text Format

Along with the Save As side menu, you can also save workbooks in different formats with options at the *Save as type* drop-down list at the Save As dialog box. In Project 3b, you will save an Excel worksheet as a text file with tab delimiters.

1. Open **ExcelC06Project03.xlsx**.
2. Click the Office button and then click *Save As*.
3. At the Save As dialog box, type **ExcelL1_C6_P3tab** in the *File name* text box.
4. Click the down-pointing arrow at the right side of the *Save as type* list box and then click *Text (Tab delimited) (*.txt)* at the drop-down list. (You will need to scroll down the list box to display this option.)

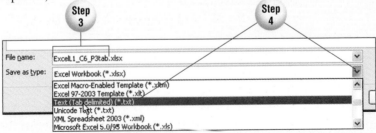

5. Click the Save button.
6. At the message telling you that the selected file type does not support workbooks that contain multiple worksheets, click OK.
7. At the message telling you that the file may contain features that are not compatible with Text (Tab delimited) and asking if you want to keep the workbook in the format, click Yes.
8. Close the workbook. (At the message asking if you want to save the changes, click Yes. At the message asking if you want to keep the workbook in the format, click Yes.)
9. Open Microsoft Word.
10. Display the Open dialog box, change the *Files of type* to *All Files (*.*)* and then open **ExcelL1_C6_P3tab.txt**.
11. Close **ExcelL1_C6_P3tab.txt** and then exit Word.

Saving in PDF Format

The portable document format (PDF) was developed by Adobe Systems and is a format that captures all of the elements of a file as an electronic image. You can view a PDF file on any application on any computer making this format the most widely used for transferring files to other users. A workbook saved in PDF format is printer friendly and most, if not all, of the workbook's original appearance is maintained.

Before saving an Excel workbook in PDF format, you must install an add-in download from the Microsoft Web site. To determine whether or not the download is installed, click the Office button and then point to the *Save As* option. If the add-in is installed, you will see the option *PDF or XPS* in the side menu with the following text below the option: *Publish a copy of the document as a PDF or XPS file.* If the add-in is not downloaded, you will see the option *Find add-ins for other file formats* in the side menu with the following text below the option: *Learn about add-ins to save to other formats such as PDF or XPS.*

If the add-in is not downloaded and you want to download it, click the *Find add-ins for other file formats* option at the side menu. This displays the Excel Help window with information on how to download the add-in. The steps in Project 3c assume that the PDF add-in is downloaded and installed and available on your computer. Before completing Project 3c, check with your instructor.

When you click the *PDF or XPS* option at the Save As side menu, the Save As dialog box displays with *PDF (*.pdf)* specified as the *Save as type* option. At this dialog box, type a name in the *File name* text box and then click the Publish button. By default, the workbook will open in PDF format in Adobe Reader. The Adobe Reader application is designed to view your workbook. You will be able to navigate in the workbook but you will not be able to make any changes to the workbook. After viewing the workbook in Adobe Reader, click the Close button located in the upper right corner of the Adobe Reader window. This closes the workbook and also closed Adobe Reader.

You can open your PDF file in Adobe Reader or in your browser window. To open a PDF workbook in your browser window, click File on the browser Menu bar and then click *Open*. (If the Menu bar is not visible, click the Tools button located in the upper right corner of the window and then click *Menu Bar* at the drop-down list.) At the Open dialog box, browse to the folder containing your PDF workbook and then double-click the workbook. You may need to change the *Files of type* option to *All Files (*.*)*.

1. Open **ExcelC06Project03.xlsx**.
2. Save the workbook in PDF file format by completing the following steps:
   a. Click the Office button and then point to the *Save As* option.
   b. Click *PDF or XPS* in the side menu. (If this option does not display, the PDF add-in download has not been installed.)

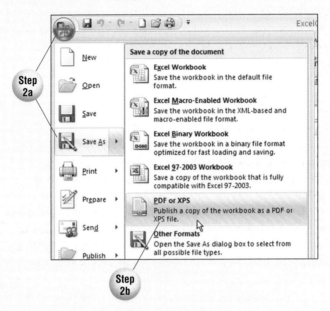

c. At the Save As dialog box with the *Save as type* option set at *PDF (*.pdf)*, click the Publish button.

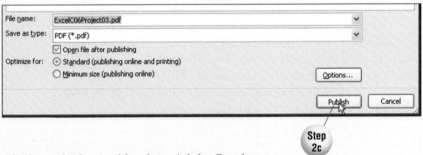

3. Scroll through the workbook in Adobe Reader.
4. Click the Close button located in the upper right corner of the window to close Adobe Reader.
5. Close **ExcelC06Project03.xlsx**.

Project ④ Create and Apply Styles to a Payroll Workbook

You will open a payroll workbook, define styles and apply styles and then modify the styles. You will also copy the styles to another workbook and then apply the styles in the new workbook.

Formatting with Cell Styles

In Chapter 1 you learned how to apply formatting to cells with the Cell Styles button in the Styles group in the Home tab. A style is a predefined set of formatting attributes such as font, font size, alignment, borders, shading, and so forth. You can apply the styles from the Cell Styles drop-down gallery or create your own style. Using a style to apply formatting has several advantages. A style helps to ensure consistent formatting from one worksheet to another. Once you define all attributes for a particular style, you do not have to redefine them again. If you need to change the formatting, change the style and all cells formatted with that style automatically reflect the change.

Defining a Cell Style

Two basic methods are available for defining your own cell style. You can define a style with formats already applied to a cell or you can display the Style dialog box, click the Format button, and then choose formatting options at the Format Cells dialog box. Styles you create are only available in the workbook in which they are created. To define a style with existing formatting, select the cell or cells containing the desired formatting, click the Cell Styles button in the Styles group in the Home tab, and then click the *New Cell Style* option located toward the bottom of the drop-down gallery. At the Style dialog box, shown in Figure 6.5, type a name for the new style in the *Style name* text box, and then click OK to close the dialog box.

Figure 6.5 Style Dialog Box

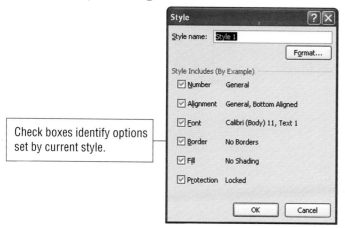

Check boxes identify options set by current style.

QUICK STEPS

Define a Cell Style with Existing Formatting
1. Select cell containing formatting.
2. Click Cell Styles button.
3. Click *New Cell Style*.
4. Type name for new style.
5. Click OK.

Define a Style
1. Click in a blank cell.
2. Click Cell Styles button.
3. Click *New Cell Style*.
4. Type name for new style.
5. Click Format button.
6. Choose formatting options.
7. Click OK to close Format Cells dialog box.
8. Click OK to close Style dialog box.

HINT

Cell styles are based on the workbook theme.

Cell Styles

Project 4a — Defining a Style

1. Open **ExcelC06Project04.xlsx** and then save the workbook and name it **ExcelL1_C6_P4**.
2. Make Sheet1 the active worksheet and then insert the necessary formulas to calculate gross pay, withholding tax amount, Social Security tax amount, and net pay. *Hint: Refer to Project 5c in Chapter 2 for assistance.*
3. Make Sheet2 the active worksheet and then insert a formula that calculates the amount due.

4. Make Sheet3 the active worksheet and then insert a formula in the *Due Date* column that inserts the purchase date plus the number of days in the *Terms* column. **Hint: Refer to Project 3c in Chapter 2 for assistance.**
5. Define a style named *C06Title* with the formatting in cell A1 by completing the following steps:
    a. Make *Sheet1* active and then make cell A1 active.
    b. Click the Cell Styles button in the Styles group in the Home tab and then click the *New Cell Style* option located toward the bottom of the drop-down gallery.

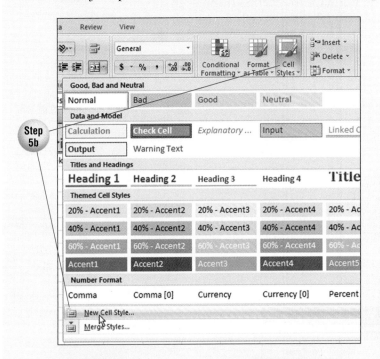

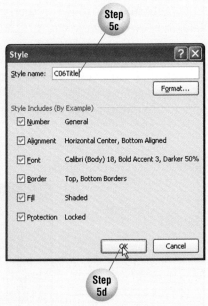

Step 5b

Step 5c

Step 5d

    c. At the Style dialog box, type **C06Title** in the *Style name* text box.
    d. Click OK.
6. Save **ExcelL1_C6_P4.xlsx**.

Applying a Style

To apply a style, select the cells you want to format, click the Cell Styles button in the Styles group, and then click the desired style at the drop-down gallery. The styles you create display at the top of the drop-down gallery.

Project 4b Applying a Style

1. With **ExcelL1_C6_P4.xlsx** open, apply the C06Title style to cell A1 by completing the following steps:
   a. Make sure cell A1 is the active cell. (Even though cell A1 is already formatted, the style has not been applied to it. Later, you will modify the style and the style must be applied to the cell for the change to affect it.)
   b. Click the Cell Styles button in the Styles group in the Home tab.
   c. Click the *C06Title* style in the *Custom* section located toward the top of the drop-down gallery.

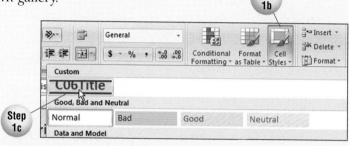

2. Apply the C06Title style to other cells by completing the following steps:
   a. Click the Sheet2 tab.
   b. Make cell A1 active.
   c. Click the Cell Styles button in the Styles group and then click the *C06Title* style at the drop-down gallery. (Notice that the style did not apply the row height formatting. The style applies only cell formatting.)
   d. Click the Sheet3 tab.
   e. Make cell A1 active.
   f. Click the Cell Styles button and then click the *C06Title* style at the drop-down gallery.
   g. Click the Sheet1 tab.
3. Save **ExcelL1_C6_P4.xlsx**.

In addition to defining a style based on cell formatting, you can also define a new style without first applying the formatting. To do this, you would display the Style dialog box, type a name for the new style, and then click the Format button. At the Format Cells dialog box, apply any desired formatting and then click OK to close the dialog box. At the Style dialog box, remove the check mark from any formatting that you do not want included in the style and then click OK to close the Style dialog box.

Project 4c Defining a Style without First Applying Formatting

1. With **ExcelL1_C6_P4.xlsx** open, define a new style named *C06Subtitle* without first applying the formatting by completing the following steps:
   a. With Sheet1 active, click in any empty cell.
   b. Click the Cell Styles button in the Styles group and then click *New Cell Style* at the drop-down gallery.

c. At the Style dialog box, type **C06Subtitle** in the *Style name* text box.

d. Click the Format button in the Style dialog box.

e. At the Format Cells dialog box, click the Font tab.

f. At the Format Cells dialog box with the Font tab selected, change the font to Candara, the font style to bold, the size to 12, and the color to white.

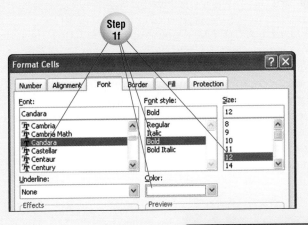

g. Click the Fill tab.

h. Click the bottom color in the green column as shown at the right.

i. Click the Alignment tab.

j. Change the Horizontal alignment to Center.

k. Click OK to close the Format Cells dialog box.

l. Click OK to close the Style dialog box.

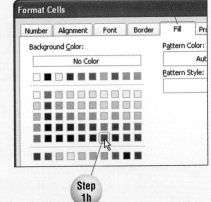

2. Apply the C06Subtitle style by completing the following steps:

   a. Make cell A2 active.

   b. Click the Cell Styles button and then click the *C06Subtitle* style located toward the top of the drop-down gallery in the *Custom* section.

   c. Click the Sheet2 tab.

   d. Make cell A2 active.

   e. Click the Cell Styles button and then click the *C06Subtitle* style.

   f. Click the Sheet3 tab.

   g. Make cell A2 active.

   h. Click the Cell Styles button and then click the *C06Subtitle* style.

   i. Click the Sheet1 tab.

3. Apply the following predesigned cell styles:

   a. Select cells A3 through G3.

   b. Click the Cell Styles button and then click the *Heading 3* style at the drop-down gallery.

   c. Select cells A5 through G5.

   d. Click the Cell Styles button and then click the *20% - Accent3* style.

   e. Apply the 20% - Accent3 style to cells A7 through G7 and cells A9 through G9.

   f. Click the Sheet2 tab.

   g. Select cells A3 through F3 and then apply the Heading 3 style.

   h. Select cells A5 through F5 and then apply the 20% - Accent3 style.

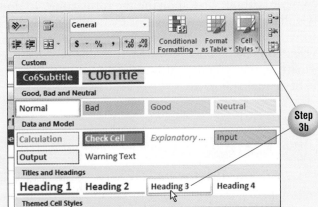

    i. Apply the 20% - Accent3 style to every other row of cells (A7 through F7, A9 through F9, and so on, finishing with A17 through F17).

    j. Click the Sheet3 tab.

    k. Select cells A3 through F3 and then apply the Heading 3 style.

    l. Apply the 20% - Accent3 style to A5 through F5, A7 through F7, and A9 through F9.

4. Make Sheet2 active and then change the height of row 1 to 36.00 (48 pixels).

5. Make Sheet3 active and then change the height of row 1 to 36.00 (48 pixels).

6. Make Sheet1 active.

7. Save **ExcelL1_C6_P4.xlsx** and then print only the first worksheet.

Modifying a Style

One of the advantages to formatting with a style is that you can modify the formatting of the style and all cells formatted with that style automatically reflect the change. You can modify a style you create or one of the predesigned styles provided by Word. When you modify a predesigned style, only the style in the current workbook is affected. If you open a blank workbook, the cell styles available are the default styles.

    To modify a style, click the Cell Styles button in the Styles group in the Home tab and then right-click the desired style at the drop-down gallery. At the shortcut menu that displays, click *Modify*. At the Style dialog box, click the Format button. Make the desired formatting changes at the Format Cells dialog box and then click OK. Click OK to close the Style dialog box and any cells formatted with the specific style are automatically updated.

QUICK STEPS

Modify a Style
1. Click Cell Styles button.
2. Right-click desired style at drop-down gallery.
3. Click *Modify*.
4. Click Format button.
5. Make desired formatting changes.
6. Click OK to close Format Cells dialog box.
7. Click OK to close Style dialog box.

Project 4d   **Modifying Styles**

1. With **ExcelL1_C6_P4.xlsx** open, modify the C06Title style by completing the following steps:

    a. Click in any empty cell.

    b. Click the Cell Styles button in the Styles group.

    c. At the drop-down gallery, right-click on the *C06Title* style located toward the top of the gallery in the *Custom* section, and then click Modify.

    d. At the Style dialog box, click the Format button.

    e. At the Format Cells dialog box, click the Font tab, and then change the font to Candara.

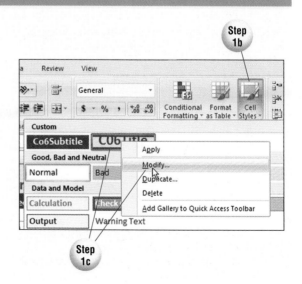

f. Click the Alignment tab.

g. Click the down-pointing arrow to the right of the *Vertical* option box, and then click *Center* at the drop-down list.

h. Click the Fill tab.

i. Click the light turquoise fill color as shown at the right.

j. Click OK to close the Format Cells dialog box.

k. Click OK to close the Style dialog box.

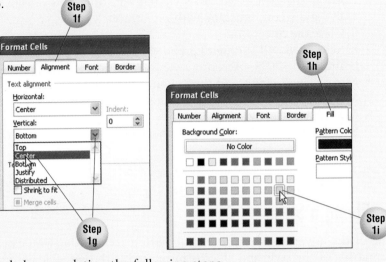

Step 1f

Step 1h

Step 1g

Step 1i

2. Modify the C06Subtitle style by completing the following steps:

a. Click in any empty cell.

b. Click the Cell Styles button in the Styles group.

c. At the drop-down gallery, right-click on the *C06Subtitle* style located toward the top of the gallery in the *Custom* section, and then click *Modify*.

d. At the Style dialog box, click the Format button.

e. At the Format Cells dialog box, click the Font tab, and then change the font to Calibri.

f. Click the Fill tab.

g. Click the dark turquoise fill color as shown at the right.

h. Click OK to close the Format Cells dialog box.

i. Click OK to close the Style dialog box.

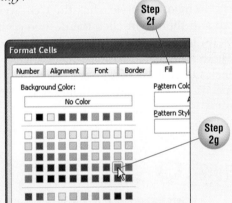

Step 2f

Step 2g

3. Modify the predefined 20% - Accent3 style by completing the following steps:

a. Click the Cell Styles button in the Styles group.

b. At the drop-down gallery, right-click on the 20% - Accent3 style and then click *Modify*.

c. At the Style dialog box, click the Format button.

d. At the Format Cells dialog box, click the Fill tab.

e. Click the light turquoise fill color as shown at the right.

f. Click OK to close the Format Cells dialog box.

g. Click OK to close the Style dialog box.

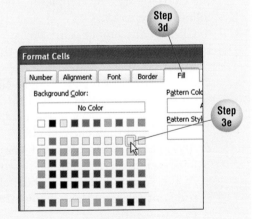

Step 3d

Step 3e

4. Click each sheet tab and notice the formatting changes made by the modified styles.

5. Change the name of Sheet1 to *Weekly Payroll*, the name of Sheet2 to *Invoices*, and the name of Sheet3 to *Overdue Accounts*.

6. Apply a different color to each of the three worksheet tabs.

7. Save and then print all the worksheets in **ExcelL1_C6_P4.xlsx**.

Copying Styles to Another Workbook

Styles you define are saved with the workbook in which they are created. You can, however, copy styles from one workbook to another. To do this, open the workbook containing the styles you want to copy and open the workbook into which you want to copy the styles. Click the Cell Styles button in the Styles group in the Home tab, and then click the *Merge Styles* option located at the bottom of the drop-down gallery. At the Merge Styles dialog box shown in Figure 6.6, double-click the name of the workbook that contains the styles you want to copy, and then click OK.

Figure 6.6 Merge Styles Dialog Box

Removing a Style

If you apply a style to text and then decide you do not want the formatting applied, return the formatting to Normal, which is the default formatting. To do this, select the cells formatted with the style you want to remove, click the Cell Styles button, and then click *Normal* at the drop-down gallery.

Deleting a Style

To delete a style, click the Cell Styles button in the Styles group in the Home tab. At the drop-down gallery that displays, right-click the style you want to delete, and then click *Delete* at the shortcut menu. Formatting applied by the deleted style is removed from cells in the workbook.

Project ④ⓔ **Copying and Removing Styles**

1. With **ExcelL1_C6_P4.xlsx** open, open **ExcelC06O'RourkePlans.xlsx**.
2. Save the workbook with Save As and name it **ExcelL1_C6_P4b**.

QUICK STEPS

Copy Styles to Another Workbook
1. Open workbook containing desired styles.
2. Click Cell Styles button.
3. Click *Merge Styles* option.
4. Double-click name of workbook that contains styles you want to copy.

Remove a Style
1. Select cells formatted with style you want removed.
2. Click Cell Styles button.
3. Click *Normal* at drop-down gallery.

Delete a Style
1. Click Cell Styles button.
2. Right-click desired style to delete.
3. Click *Delete* at shortcut menu.

HINT
The Undo command will not reverse the effects of the Merge Styles dialog box.

HINT
You cannot delete the Normal style.

3. Copy the styles in **ExcelL1_C6_P4.xlsx** into **ExcelL1_C6_P4b.xlsx** by completing the following steps:
   a. Click the Cell Styles button in the Styles group in the Home tab.
   b. Click the *Merge Styles* option located toward the bottom of the drop-down gallery.
   c. At the Merge Styles dialog box, double-click **ExcelL1_C6_P4.xlsx** in the *Merge styles from* list box.
   d. At the message that displays asking if you want to merge styles that have the same names, click Yes.

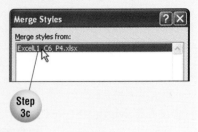

Step 3c

4. Apply the C06Title style to cell A1 and the C06Subtitle style to cell A2.
5. Increase the height of row 1 to 36.00 (48 pixels).
6. Insert the required formulas in the workbook. **Hint: Refer to Project 3a of Chapter 2 for assistance.**
7. If neccessary, adjust column widths so all text is visible in cells.
8. Save, print, and then close **ExcelL1_C6_P4b.xlsx**.
9. Close **ExcelL1_C6_P4.xlsx**.

roject ⑤ **Insert, Modify, and Print Comments in an Equipment Rental Workbook**

You will open an equipment rental workbook and then insert, edit, delete and print comments.

Inserting Comments

If you want to make comments in a worksheet, or if a reviewer wants to make comments in a worksheet prepared by someone else, insert a comment. A comment is useful for providing specific instructions, identifying critical information, or for multiple individuals reviewing the same worksheet to insert comments. Some employees in a company may be part of a ***workgroup***, which is a networked collection of computers sharing files, printers, and other resources. In a workgroup, you may collaborate with coworkers on a specific workbook. Comments provide a method for reviewing the workbook and responding to others in the workgroup.

Inserting a Comment

Insert a comment by clicking the Review tab and then clicking the New Comment button in the Comments group. This displays a color shaded box with the user's name inside. Type the desired information or comment in this comment box and then click outside the comment box. A small, red triangle appears in the upper right corner of a cell containing a comment. You can also insert a comment by right-clicking a cell and then clicking *Insert Comment* at the shortcut menu.

Displaying a Comment

Hover the mouse over a cell containing a comment and the comment box displays. You can also display comments by right-clicking the cell containing a comment and then clicking *Show/Hide Comments* at the shortcut menu. Turn on the display of all comments by clicking the Show All Comments button in the Comments group in the Review tab. Turn on the display of an individual comment by making the cell active and then clicking the Show/Hide Comment button in the Comments group in the Review tab. Hide the display of an individual comment by clicking the same button. Move to comments in a worksheet by clicking the Next or Previous buttons in the Comments group in the Review tab.

Project 5a — Inserting and Displaying Comments

1. Open **ExcelC06Project05.xlsx**.
2. Save the workbook with Save As and name it **ExcelL1_C6_P5**.
3. Insert a formula in cell H3 that multiplies the rate by the hours and then copy the formula down to cells H4 through H16. (When you copy the formula, click the Auto Fill Options button and then click *Fill Without Formatting* at the drop-down list.)
4. Make cell H17 active and then insert a formula that sums the amounts in cells H3 through H16.
5. Insert a comment by completing the following steps:
   a. Click cell F3 to make it active.
   b. Click the Review tab.
   c. Click the New Comment button in the Comments group.
   d. In the comment box, type Bill Lakeside Trucking for only 7 hours for the backhoe and front loader on May 1.
   e. Click outside the comment box.
6. Insert another comment by completing the following steps:
   a. Click cell C6 to make it active.
   b. Click the New Comment button in the Comments group.
   c. In the comment box, type I think Country Electrical has changed their name to Northwest Electrical.
   d. Click outside the comment box.

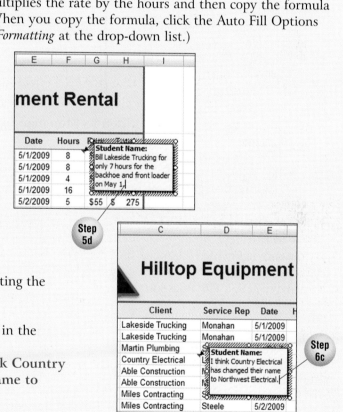

7. Assume that more than one person is reviewing and commenting on this worksheet. Change the user name and then insert additional comments by completing the following steps:

   a. Click the Office button and then click the Excel Options button located toward the bottom of the drop-down list.

   b. At the Excel Options dialog box make sure *Popular* is selected in the left panel.

   c. Select the current name in the *User name* text box (remember the name you are selecting) and then type **Jean Coen**.

   d. Click OK to close the dialog box.

   e. Click cell D11 to make it active.

   f. Click the New Comment button in the Comments group.

Step 7b

Excel Options

- Popular — Change the most popular options in Excel.
- Formulas
- Proofing
- Save
- Advanced
- Customize
- Add-Ins
- Trust Center
- Resources

Top options for working with Excel

- ☑ Show Mini Toolbar on selection ⓘ
- ☑ Enable Live Preview ⓘ
- ☐ Show Developer tab in the Ribbon ⓘ
- ☑ Always use ClearType

Color scheme: Blue ▾

ScreenTip style: Show feature descriptions in ScreenTips

Create lists for use in sorts and fill sequences: Edit Custom

When creating new workbooks

Use this font: Body Font
Font size: 11 ▾
Default view for new sheets: Normal View ▾
Include this many sheets: 3 ⬍

Personalize your copy of Microsoft Office

User name: Jean Coen

Choose the languages you want to use with Microsoft Office:

Step 7c

   g. In the comment box, type **This rental should be credited to Monahan instead of Leuke.**

   h. Click outside the comment box.

   i. Click cell G11 to make it active.

   j. Click the New Comment button in the Comments group.

   k. In the comment box, type **The hourly rental for the pressure sprayer is $25.**

   l. Click outside the comment box.

8. Complete steps similar to those in Steps 7a through 7d to return the user name back to the original name (the name that displayed before you changed it to *Jean Coen*).

9. Click the Show All Comments button to turn on the display of all comments.

10. Save **ExcelL1_C6_P5.xlsx**.

H I N T — Printing a Comment

Display the document in Print Preview to view how comments will print.

By default, comments do not print. If you want comments to print, use the *Comments* option at the Page Setup dialog box with the Sheet tab selected. Display this dialog box by clicking the Page Layout tab, clicking the Page Setup group dialog box launcher, and then clicking the Sheet tab. Click the down-pointing arrow at the right side of the *Comments* option box. At the drop-down list that displays, choose *At end of sheet* to print comments on the page after cell contents, or choose the *As displayed on sheet* option to print the comments in the comment box in the worksheet.

1. With **ExcelL1_C6_P5.xlsx** open, click the Page Layout tab.
2. Click the Orientation button in the Page Setup group and then click *Landscape* at the drop-down list.
3. Click the Page Setup group dialog box launcher.
4. At the Page Setup dialog box, click the Sheet tab.
5. Click the down-pointing arrow at the right side of the *Comments* option box and then click *As displayed on sheet*.
6. Click the Print button that displays toward the bottom of the dialog box and then click OK at the Print dialog box.
7. Turn off the display of comments by clicking the Review tab and then clicking the Show All Comments button.
8. Save **ExcelL1_C6_P5.xlsx**.

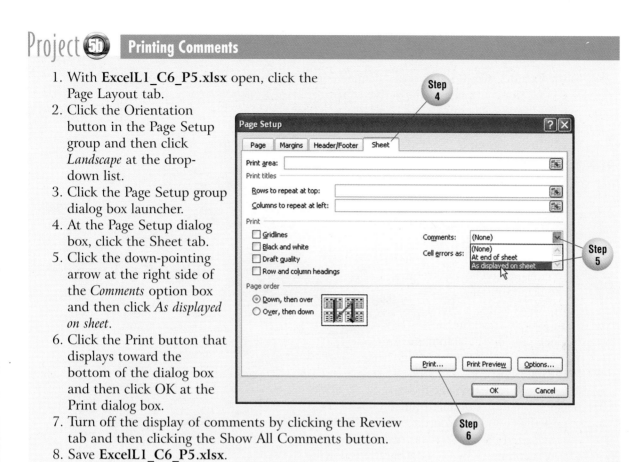

Step 4

Step 5

Step 6

Editing a Comment

To edit a comment, click the cell containing the comment and then click the Edit Comment button in the Comments group in the Review tab. (The New Comment button changes to the Edit Comment button when the active cell contains a comment.) You can also edit a comment by right-clicking the cell containing the comment and then clicking *Edit Comment* at the shortcut menu.

Edit Comment

Deleting a Comment

Cell comments exist in addition to data in a cell. Deleting data in a cell does not delete the comment. To delete a comment, click the cell containing the comment and then click the Delete button in the Comments group in the Review tab. You can also delete a comment by right-clicking the cell containing the comment and then clicking *Delete Comment* at the shortcut menu.

Delete

1. With **ExcelL1_C6_P5.xlsx** open, display comments by completing the following steps:
   a. Click cell A3 to make it the active cell.
   b. Click the Review tab.
   c. Click the Next button in the Comments group.
   d. Read the comment and then click the Next button.
   e. Continue clicking the Next button until a message displays telling you that Microsoft Excel has reached the end of the workbook and asking if you want to continue reviewing from the beginning of the workbook. At this message, click the Cancel button.
   f. Click outside the comment box.

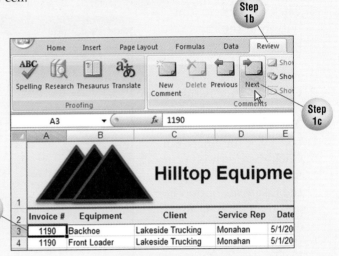

2. Edit a comment by completing the following steps:
   a. Click cell D11 to make it active.
   b. Click the Edit Comment button.
   c. Edit the comment so it displays as *This rental should be credited to Steele instead of Leuke.*
3. Delete a comment by completing the following steps:
   a. Click cell C6 to make it active.
   b. Click the Delete button in the Comments group.
4. Respond to the comments by making the following changes:
   a. Change the contents of F3 from *8* to *7*.
   b. Change the contents of F4 from *8* to *7*.
   c. Change the contents of D11 from *Leuke* to *Steele*.
   d. Change the contents of G11 from *$20* to *$25*.
5. Print the worksheet and the comments by completing the following steps:
   a. Click the Page Layout tab.
   b. Click the Page Setup group dialog box launcher.
   c. At the Page Setup dialog box, click the Sheet tab.
   d. Click the down-pointing arrow at the right side of the *Comments* option and then click *At end of sheet*.
   e. Click the Print button that displays toward the bottom of the dialog box.
   f. At the Print dialog box, click OK. (The worksheet will print on one page and the comments will print on a second page.)
6. Save and then close **ExcelL1_C6_P5.xlsx**.

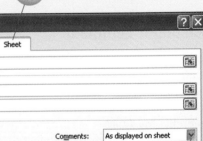

roject **6** **Create a Billing Statement Workbook Using a Template**

You will open a Billing Statement template provided by Excel, add data, save it as an Excel workbook, and then print the workbook.

Using Excel Templates

Excel has included a number of *template* worksheet forms formatted for specific uses. For example, Excel has provided template forms for a balance sheet, billing statement, loan amortization, sales invoice, and timecard. To view the templates available, click the Office button and then click *New* at the drop-down list. At the New Workbook dialog box shown in Figure 6.7, click the *Installed Templates* option in the *Templates* section. This displays the installed templates in the middle panel of the dialog box. Note that the first time you download a template, Microsoft checks to determine if you are using a genuine Office product.

Use an Excel Template
1. Click Office button, *New*.
2. Click *Installed Templates* option.
3. Double-click desired template.

Figure 6.7 New Workbook Dialog Box

Click the *Installed Templates* option to display available templates.

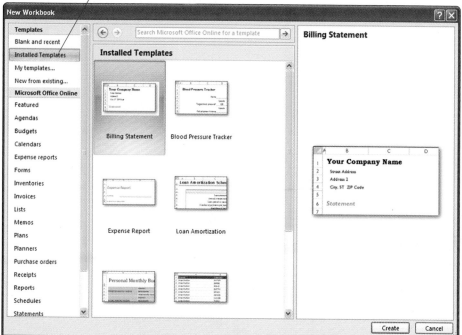

Entering Data in a Template

Templates contain unique areas where information is entered at the keyboard. For example, in the Billing Statement template shown in Figure 6.8, you enter information such as the customer name, address, and telephone number, and also the date, time, description, amount, payment, and balance of items. To enter information in the appropriate location, position the mouse pointer (white plus sign) in the location where you want to type data and then click the left mouse button. After typing the data, click the next location. You can also move the insertion point to another cell using the commands learned in Chapter 1. For example, press the Tab key to make the next cell active, press Shift + Tab to make the previous cell active.

Figure 6.8 Billing Statement Template

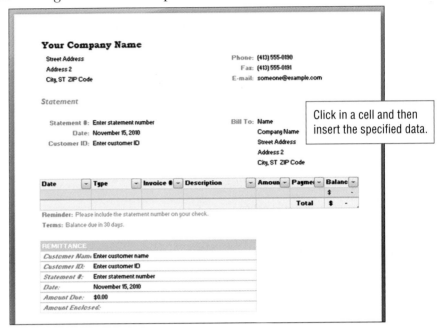

Click in a cell and then insert the specified data.

Project ⑥ **Preparing a Billing Statement Using a Template**

1. Click the Office button and then click *New* at the drop-down list.
2. At the New Workbook dialog box, click the *Installed Templates* option in the *Templates* section.
3. Double-click the *Billing Statement* template in the *Installed Templates* section of the dialog box.

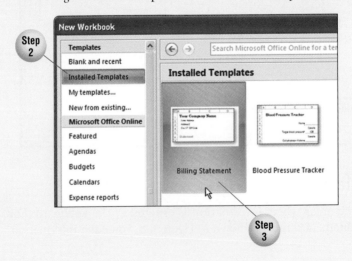

4. With cell B1 active, type **IN-FLOW SYSTEMS**.
5. Click the text *Street Address* (cell B2) and then type 320 Milander Way.
6. Click in the specified location (cell) and then type the text indicated:

  Address 2 (cell B3) = P.O. Box 2300
  City, ST ZIP Code (cell B4) = Boston, MA 02188
  Phone (cell F2) = (617) 555-3900
  Fax (cell F3) = (617) 555-3945
  Statement # (cell C8) = 5432
  Customer ID (cell C10) = 25-345
  Name (cell F8) = Aidan Mackenzie
  Company Name (cell F9) = Stanfield Enterprises
  Street Address (cell F10) = 9921 South 42nd Avenue
  Address 2 (cell F11) = P.O. Box 5540
  City, ST ZIP Code (cell F12) = Boston, MA 02193
  Date (cell B15) = (insert current date in numbers as ##/##/####)
  Type (cell C15) = System Unit
  Invoice # (cell D15) = 7452
  Description (cell E15) = Calibration Unit
  Amount (cell F15) = 950
  Payment (cell G15) = 200
  Customer Name (cell C21) = Stanfield Enterprises
  Amount Enclosed (C26) = 750

Steps 4–6

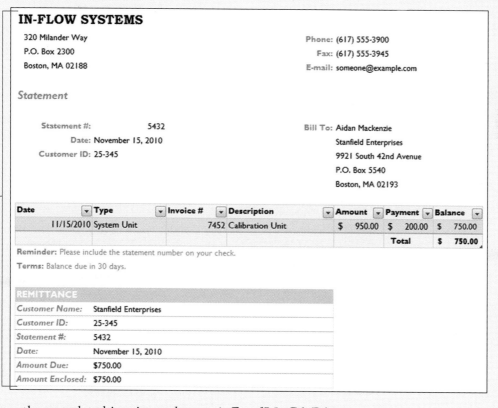

7. Save the completed invoice and name it **ExcelL1_C6_P6**.
8. Print and then close **ExcelL1_C6_P6.xlsx**.

CHAPTER summary

- Perform file management tasks such as copying, moving, printing, and renaming workbooks and creating a new folder and renaming a folder at the Open or Save As dialog boxes.

- Create a new folder by clicking the Create New Folder button located on the dialog box toolbar at the Open dialog box or Save As dialog box.

- Rename a folder with the *Rename* option from the Tools button drop-down list or with a shortcut menu.

- To select adjacent workbooks in the Open dialog box, click the first workbook, hold down the Shift key, and then click the last workbook. To select nonadjacent workbooks, click the first workbook, hold down the Ctrl key, and then click any desired workbooks.

- To delete a workbook, use the Delete button on the Open or Save As dialog box toolbar, the *Delete* option at the Tools button drop-down list, or with a shortcut menu option.

- Workbooks deleted from the hard drive are automatically sent to the Windows Recycle Bin where they can be restored or permanently deleted.

- Create a copy of an existing workbook by opening the workbook and then using the *Save As* command to assign the workbook a different file name.

- Use the *Copy* and *Paste* options from the shortcut menu at the Open (or Save As) dialog box to copy a workbook from one folder to another folder or drive.

- When you copy a workbook into the same folder from which it originates, Excel names the duplicated workbook(s) "Copy of xxx" (where *xxx* is the original workbook name).

- Use the *Send To* option from the shortcut menu to send a copy of a workbook to another drive or folder.

- Remove a workbook from a folder or drive and insert it in another folder or drive using the *Cut* and *Paste* options from the shortcut menu.

- Use the *Rename* option from the Tools button drop-down list or the shortcut menu to give a workbook a different name.

- Print multiple workbooks by selecting the desired workbooks at the Print dialog box, clicking the Tools button, and then clicking *Print* at the drop-down list.

- To move or copy a worksheet to another existing workbook, open both the source and the destination workbook and then open the Move or Copy dialog box.

- Save a workbook in a different format with options from the Office button Save As side menu or with the *Save as type* option at the Save As dialog box. Click the down-pointing arrow at the right side of the *Save as type* option and a drop-down list displays with the available formats.

- Automate the formatting of cells in a workbook by defining and then applying styles. A style is a predefined set of formatting attributes.

- A style helps to ensure consistent formatting from one worksheet to another. All formatting attributes for a particular style are defined only once. Define a style with formats already applied to a cell or display the Style dialog box, click the Format button, and then choose formatting options at the Format Cells dialog box.

- To apply a style, select the desired cells, click the Cell Styles button in the Styles group in the Home tab, and then click the desired style at the drop-down gallery.

- Modify a style and all cells to which the style is applied automatically reflect the change. To modify a style, click the Cell Styles button in the Styles group in the Home tab, right-click the desired style, and then click *Modify* at the shortcut menu.

- Styles are saved in the workbook in which they are created. Styles can be copied, however, to another workbook. Do this with options at the Merge Styles dialog box.

- Insert comments in a worksheet to provide specific instructions, identify critical information, review a workbook, and respond to others in a workgroup about the workbook.

- Insert, display, edit, and delete comments using buttons in the Comments group in the Review tab.

- By default, comments do not print. To print comments, display the Page Setup dialog box with the Sheet tab selected, and then choose the printing location with the *Comments* option.

- Excel provides preformatted templates for creating forms such as a balance sheet, billing statement, loan amortization, sales invoice, and timecard. Display the available templates by clicking the *Installed Templates* option in the *Templates* section of the New Workbook dialog box.

- Templates contain unique areas where information is entered at the keyboard. These areas vary depending on the template.

COMMANDS review

FEATURE	RIBBON TAB, GROUP	BUTTON, OPTION	OFFICE BUTTON DROP-DOWN LIST	KEYBOARD SHORTCUT
Open dialog box			Open	Ctrl + O
Save As dialog box			Save As	Ctrl + S
Print dialog box			Print	Ctrl + P
Save in PDF format			Save As, PDF or XPS	
Style dialog box	Home, Styles	, New Cell Style		
Merge Styles dialog box	Home, Styles	, Merge Styles		
Insert comment	Review, Comments			Shift + F2
Display all comments	Review, Comments	Show All Comments		
Delete comment	Review, Comments			
Display next comment	Review, Comments			
Display previous comment	Review, Comments			
New Workbook dialog box			New	

CONCEPTS check

Test Your Knowledge

Completion: In the space provided at the right, indicate the correct term, symbol, or command.

1. Perform file management tasks such as copying, moving, or deleting workbooks with options at the Open dialog box or this dialog box. _____

2. Click this button on the Open dialog box toolbar to display the folder that is up a level from the current folder. _____

3. At the Open dialog box, hold down this key while selecting nonadjacent workbooks.

_____

4. Workbooks deleted from the hard drive are automatically sent to this location.

_____

5. Click the down-pointing arrow at the right side of this option at the Save As dialog box to display a drop-down list of available workbook formats.

_____

6. If the PDF format is installed, this option for saving a workbook in PDF file format displays at the Office button Save As side menu.

_____

7. The Cell Styles button is located in this group in the Home tab.

_____

8. Click the *New Cell Style* option at the Cell Styles button drop-down gallery and this dialog box displays.

_____

9. A style you create displays in this section of the Cell Styles button drop-down gallery.

_____

10. Copy styles from one workbook to another with options at this dialog box.

_____

11. This displays in the upper right corner of a cell containing a comment.

_____

12. The New Comment button is located in the Comments group in this tab.

_____

13. Print comments by choosing the desired printing location with the *Comments* option at the Page Setup dialog box with this tab selected.

_____

14. Click this button in the Comments group to display all comments in the worksheet.

_____

15. Click this option at the New Workbook dialog box to display available templates.

_____

SKILLS check

Demonstrate Your Proficiency

Assessment

1 MANAGE WORKBOOKS

1. Display the Open dialog box with Excel2007L1C6 the active folder.
2. Create a new folder named *O'Rourke* in the Excel2007L1C6 folder.
3. Copy **ExcelC06O'RourkeBudget.xlsx**, **ExcelC06O'RourkePlans.xlsx**, and **ExcelC06Project04.xlsx** to the O'Rourke folder.
4. Display the contents of the O'Rourke folder and then rename **ExcelC06O'RourkeBudget.xlsx** to **EquipmentBudget.xlsx**.
5. Rename **ExcelC06O'RourkePlans.xlsx** to **PurchasePlans.xlsx** in the O'Rourke folder.
6. Change the active folder back to Excel2007L1C6.
7. Delete all of the workbooks in the Excel2007L1C6 folder that begin with *ExcelC05*.
8. Close the Open dialog box.

Assessment

2 MOVE AND COPY WORKSHEETS BETWEEN SALES ANALYSIS WORKBOOKS

1. Open **ExcelC06Assessment02.xlsx**.
2. Save the workbook with Save As and name it **ExcelL1_C6_A2**.
3. Rename Sheet1 to *1st Qtr.*
4. Rename Sheet2 to *Yearly Summary*.
5. Move the Yearly Summary sheet before the 1st Qtr. sheet.
6. Open **ExcelC06DeeringQtrs.xlsx**.
7. Rename Sheet1 to *2nd Qtr.* and then copy it to **ExcelL1_C6_A2.xlsx** (following the 1st Qtr. worksheet).
8. Make **ExcelC06DeeringQtrs.xlsx** active, rename Sheet2 to *3rd Qtr.* and then copy it to **ExcelL1_C6_A2.xlsx** (following the 2nd Qtr. worksheet).
9. Make **ExcelC06DeeringQtrs.xlsx** active and then close it without saving the changes.
10. Open **ExcelC06DeeringFourthQtr.xlsx**.
11. Rename Sheet1 to *4th Qtr.* and then move it to **ExcelL1_C6_A2.xlsx** (following the 3rd Qtr. worksheet).
12. Make **ExcelC06DeeringFourthQtr.xlsx** active and then close it without saving the changes.
13. With **ExcelL1_C6_A2.xlsx** active, make the following changes:
    a. Make 1st Qtr. the active worksheet and then insert a formula to calculate the averages and another to calculate the totals. (Use the Auto Fill Options button to fill without formatting.)
    b. Make 2nd Qtr. the active worksheet and then insert a formula to calculate the averages and another to calculate the totals. (Use the Auto Fill Options button to fill without formatting.)

c. Make 3rd Qtr. the active worksheet and then insert a formula to calculate the averages and another to calculate the totals. (Use the Auto Fill Options button to fill without formatting.)

d. Make 4th Qtr. the active worksheet and then insert a formula to calculate the averages and another to calculate the totals. (Use the Auto Fill Options button to fill without formatting.)

e. Make Yearly Summary the active worksheet and then insert a formula that inserts in cell B4 the average of the amounts in cell E4 for the 1st Qtr., 2nd Qtr., 3rd Qtr., and 4th Qtr. worksheets.

f. Copy the formula in cell B4 down to cells B5 through B9.

g. Make cell B10 active and then insert a formula that calculates the total of cells B4 through B9.

14. Delete the Sheet3 tab.

15. Insert a footer on all worksheets that prints your name at the left, the page number in the middle, and the current date at the right.

16. Horizontally and vertically center the worksheets.

17. Save and then print all of the worksheets in **ExcelL1_C6_A2.xlsx**.

18. Close **ExcelL1_C6_A2.xlsx**.

Assessment

3 DEFINE AND APPLY STYLES TO A PROJECTED EARNINGS WORKBOOK

1. At a blank worksheet, define a style named *C06Heading* that contains the following formatting:
   a. 14-point Cambria bold in dark blue color
   b. Horizontal alignment of Center
   c. Top and bottom border in a dark red color
   d. Light purple fill

2. Define a style named *C06Subheading* that contains the following formatting:
   a. 12-point Cambria bold in dark blue color
   b. Horizontal alignment of Center
   c. Top and bottom border in dark red color
   d. Light purple fill

3. Define a style named *C06Column* that contains the following formatting:
   a. 12-point Cambria in dark blue color
   b. Light purple fill

4. Save the workbook and name it **ExcelL1_C6_A3_Styles**.

5. With **ExcelL1_C6_A3_Styles.xlsx** open, open **ExcelC06Assessment03.xlsx**.

6. Save the workbook with Save As and name it **ExcelL1_C6_A3**.

7. Make cell C6 active and then insert a formula that multiplies the content of cell B6 with the amount in cell B3. (When writing the formula, identify cell B3 as an absolute reference.) Copy the formula down to cells C7 through C17.

8. Copy the styles from **ExcelL1_C6_A3_Styles.xlsx** into **ExcelL1_C6_A3.xlsx**. *Hint: Do this at the Merge Styles dialog box.*

9. Apply the following styles:
   a. Select cells A1 and A2 and then apply the C06Heading style.
   b. Select cells A5 through C5 and then apply the C06Subheading style.
   c. Select cells A6 through A17 and then apply the C06Column style.

10. Save the workbook again and then print **ExcelL1_C6_A3.xlsx**.

11. With **ExcelL1_C6_A3.xlsx** open, modify the following styles:
  a. Modify the C06Heading style so it changes the font color to dark purple (instead of dark blue), changes the vertical alignment to Center, and inserts a top and bottom border in dark purple (instead of dark red).
  b. Modify the C06Subheading style so it changes the font color to dark purple (instead of dark blue) and inserts a top and bottom border in dark purple (instead of dark red).
  c. Modify the C06Column style so it changes the font color to dark purple (instead of dark blue). Leave all of the other formatting attributes.
12. Save the workbook and then print **ExcelL1_C6_A3.xlsx**.
13. Close **ExcelL1_C6_A3.xlsx** and then close **ExcelL1_C6_A3_Styles.xlsx** without saving the changes.

Assessment

4 INSERT, DELETE AND PRINT COMMENTS IN A TRAVEL WORKBOOK

1. Open **ExcelC06Asessment04.xlsx**.
2. Save the workbook with Save As and name it **ExcelL1_C6_A4.xlsx**.
3. Insert the following comments in the specified cells:
   B7   =   Should we include Sun Valley, Idaho, as a destination?
   B12   =   Please include the current exchange rate.
   G8   =   What other airlines fly into Aspen, Colorado?
4. Save **ExcelL1_C6_A4.xlsx**.
5. Turn on the display of all comments.
6. Print the worksheet in landscape orientation with the comments as displayed on the worksheet.
7. Turn off the display of all comments.
8. Delete the comment in cell B12.
9. Print the worksheet again with the comments printed at the end of the worksheet. (The comments will print on a separate page from the worksheet.)
10. Save and then close **ExcelL1_C6_A4.xlsx**.

Assessment

5 APPLY CONDITIONAL FORMATTING TO A SALES WORKBOOK

1. Use Excel Help files to learn more about conditional formatting.
2. Open **ExcelC06Assessment05.xlsx** and then save the workbook and name it **ExcelL1_C6_A5**.
3. Select cells D5 through D19 and then use conditional formatting to display the amounts as data bars.
4. Insert a footer that prints your name, a page number, and the current date.
5. Save, print, and then close **ExcelL1_C6_A5.xlsx**.

CASE study

Apply Your Skills

You are the office manager for Leeward Marine and you decide to consolidate into one workbook worksheets containing information on expenses. Copy **ExcelC06EstimatedExpenses.xlsx**, **ExcelC06ActualExpenses.xlsx**, and **ExcelC06ExpenseVariances.xlsx** into one workbook. Apply appropriate formatting to numbers and insert necessary formulas. Include the company name, Leeward Marine, in each worksheet. Create styles and apply the styles to cells in each worksheet to maintain consistent formatting. Rename and recolor the three worksheet tabs (you determine the names and colors). Save the workbook and name it **ExcelC06LeewardExpenses**.

As you look at the information in each worksheet in the **ExcelC06LeewardExpenses.xlsx** workbook, you decide that the information should be summarized for easy viewing. Include a new worksheet in the workbook that summarizes each category in Employee Costs, Facilities Costs, and Marketing Costs by estimated costs, actual costs, and expense variances. Insert formulas in the summary worksheet that insert the appropriate totals from each of the three other worksheets. Insert an appropriate header or footer in the workbook. Scale the worksheets so each print on one page. Save, print (all of the worksheets in the workbook), and then close **ExcelC06LeewardExpenses.xlsx**.

You are not happy with the current product list form so you decide to look at template forms available at the Microsoft online site. Display the New Workbook dialog box and then download the Product price list template located in the *Lists* category. Open **ExcelC06ProductList.xlsx** and then copy the product information into the Produce price list template. Insert the following company information as required by the template:

> Leeward Marine
> 4500 Shoreline Drive,
> Ketchikan, AK 99901
> (907) 555-2200
> (907) 555-2595 (fax)
> www.emcp.com/leewardmarine

Format the product list form with formatting similar to the formatting you applied to the **ExcelC06LeewardExpenses.xlsx** workbook. Save the completed products list form and name it **ExcelC06ProductsList**. Print and then close the workbook.

You need to print a number of copies of the product list and you want the company letterhead to print at the top of the page. You decide to use the letterhead you created in Word and copy the product list information from Excel into the Word letterhead document. To do this, open Word and then open the document named **LeewardMarineLtrhd.docx**. Open **ExcelC06ProductList.xlsx** and then copy the cells containing data and paste them into the Word letterhead document using *Paste Special*. When the product list information is pasted into the Word document, apply blue font color to the data in the cells. Apply any other formatting you think will enhance the cells in the document. Save the Word document with *Save As* and name it **WordC06ProductList**. Print and then close **WordC06ProductList.docx** and then close **ExcelC06ProductList.xlsx**.

CHAPTER 7

Creating a Chart in Excel

PERFORMANCE OBJECTIVES

Upon successful completion of Chapter 7, you will be able to:

- Create a chart with data in an Excel worksheet
- Size, move, and delete charts
- Print a selected chart and print a worksheet containing a chart
- Preview a chart
- Choose a chart style, layout, and formatting
- Change chart location
- Insert, move, size, and delete chart labels, shapes, and pictures

excel Chapter 7

SNAP

Tutorial 7.1
Creating and Formatting Charts

In the previous Excel chapters, you learned to create data in worksheets. While a worksheet does an adequate job of representing data, you can present some data more visually by charting the data. A chart is sometimes referred to as a *graph* and is a picture of numeric data. In this chapter, you will learn to create and customize charts in Excel.

Note: Before beginning computer projects, copy to your storage medium the Excel2007L1C7 subfolder from the Excel2007L1 folder on the CD that accompanies this textbook and then make Excel2007L1C7 the active folder.

Project Create a Quarterly Sales Column Chart

You will open a workbook containing quarterly sales data and then use the data to create a column chart. You will decrease the size of the chart, move it to a different location in the worksheet and then make changes to sales numbers.

Creating a Chart

In Excel, create a chart with buttons in the Charts group in the Insert tab as shown in Figure 7.1. With buttons in the Charts group you can create a variety of charts such as a column chart, line chart, pie chart, and much more. Excel provides 11

basic chart types as described in Table 7.1. To create a chart, select cells in a worksheet that you want to chart, click the Insert tab, and then click the desired chart button in the Charts group. At the drop-down gallery that displays, click the desired chart style. You can also create a chart by selecting the desired cells and then pressing Alt + F1. This keyboard shortcut, by default, inserts the data in a 2-D column chart (unless the default chart type has been changed).

Create a Chart
1. Select cells.
2. Click Insert tab.
3. Click desired chart button.
4. Click desired chart style at drop-down list.

Create Chart as Default Chart Type
1. Select cells.
2. Press Alt + F1.

Figure 7.1 Chart Group Buttons

These buttons display in the Insert tab and you can use them to create a variety of charts.

Table 7.1 Types of Charts

Chart	Description
Area	An Area chart emphasizes the magnitude of change, rather than time and the rate of change. It also shows the relationship of parts to a whole by displaying the sum of the plotted values.
Bar	A Bar chart shows individual figures at a specific time, or shows variations between components but not in relationship to the whole.
Bubble	A Bubble chart compares sets of three values in a manner similar to a scatter chart, with the third value displayed as the size of the bubble marker.
Column	A Column chart compares separate (noncontinuous) items as they vary over time.
Doughnut	A Doughnut chart shows the relationship of parts of the whole.
Line	A Line chart shows trends and change over time at even intervals. It emphasizes the rate of change over time rather than the magnitude of change.
Pie	A Pie chart shows proportions and relationships of parts to the whole.
Radar	A Radar chart emphasizes differences and amounts of change over time and variations and trends. Each category has its own value axis radiating from the center point. Lines connect all values in the same series.
Stock	A Stock chart shows four values for a stock—open, high, low, and close.
Surface	A Surface chart shows trends in values across two dimensions in a continuous curve.
XY (Scatter)	A Scatter chart either shows the relationships among numeric values in several data series or plots the interception points between x and y values. It shows uneven intervals of data and is commonly used in scientific data.

Sizing, Moving, and Deleting a Chart

When you create a chart, the chart is inserted in the same worksheet as the selected cells. Figure 7.2 displays the worksheet and chart you will create in Project 1a. The chart is inserted in a box which you can size and/or move in the worksheet.

To size the worksheet, position the mouse pointer on the four dots located in the middle of the border you want to size until the pointer turns into a two-headed arrow, hold down the left mouse button, and then drag to increase or decrease the size of the chart. To increase or decrease the height and width of the chart at the same time, position the mouse pointer on the three dots that display in a chart border corner until the pointer displays as a two-headed arrow, hold down the left mouse button, and then drag to the desired size. To increase or decrease the size of the chart and maintain the proportions of the chart, hold down the Shift key while dragging a chart corner border.

To move the chart, make sure the chart is selected (light turquoise box displays around the chart), position the mouse pointer on a border until it turns into a four-headed arrow, hold down the left mouse button, and then drag to the desired position.

Figure 7.2 Project 1a Chart

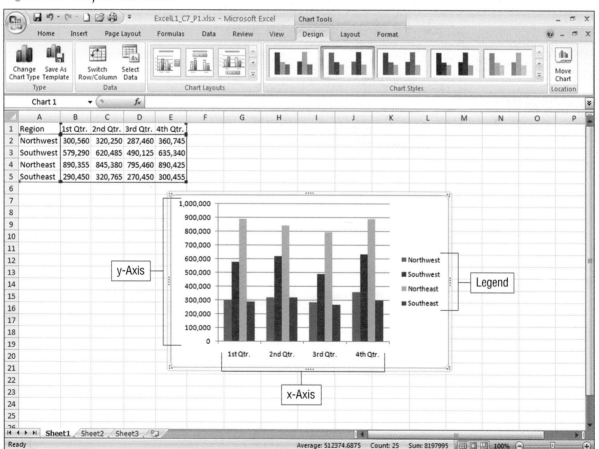

Editing Data

The cells you select to create the chart are linked to the chart. If you need to change data for a chart, edit the data in the desired cell and the corresponding section of the chart is automatically updated.

Project ⓐ Creating a Chart

1. Open **ExcelC07Project01.xlsx** and then save the workbook and name it **ExcelL1_C7_P1**.
2. Select cells A1 through E5.
3. Press Alt + F1.
4. Slightly increase the size of the chart and maintain the proportions of the chart by completing the following steps:
   a. Position the mouse pointer on the bottom right corner of the chart border until the pointer turns into a two-headed arrow pointing diagonally.
   b. Hold down the Shift key and then hold down the left mouse button.
   c. Drag out approximately one-half inch and then release the mouse button and then the Shift key.

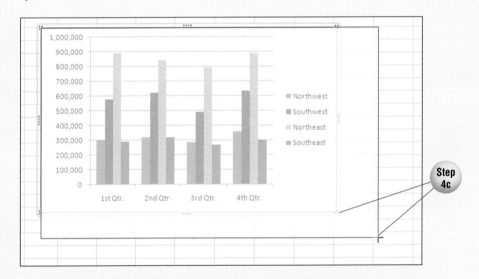

Step 4c

5. Move the chart below the cells containing data by completing the following steps:
   a. Make sure the chart is selected (light turquoise border surrounds the chart).

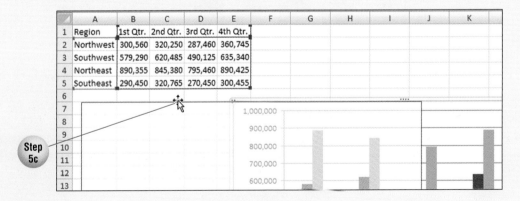

Step 5c

b. Position the mouse pointer on the chart border until the pointer turns into a four-headed arrow.

c. Hold down the left mouse button, drag the chart so it is positioned below the cells containing data, and then release the mouse button.

6. Make the following changes to the specified cells:
   a. Make cell B2 active and then change *300,560* to *421,720*.
   b. Make cell C2 active and then change *320,250* to *433,050*.
   c. Make cell D2 active and then change *287,460* to *397,460*.
   d. Make cell E2 active and then change *360,745* to *451,390*.

7. Save **ExcelL1_C7_P1.xlsx**.

Printing Only the Chart

In a worksheet containing data in cells as well as a chart, you can print only the chart. To do this, click the chart to select it and then display the Print dialog box. At the Print dialog box, *Selected Chart* will automatically be selected in the *Print what* section. Click OK to print only the selected chart.

Previewing a Chart

Preview a chart by clicking the Office button, pointing to the *Print* option, and then clicking *Print Preview*. After previewing the chart, click the Close Preview button, or print the worksheet by clicking the Print button in the Print Preview tab.

Project ① Previewing and Printing the Chart

1. With **ExcelL1_C7_P1.xlsx** open, make sure the chart displays.
2. Preview the chart by completing the following steps:
   a. Click the Office button.
   b. Point to the *Print* option.
   c. Click *Print Preview*.
   d. After viewing the chart in Print Preview, click the Close Print Preview button.
3. Print the worksheet by clicking the Quick Print button in the Quick Access toolbar.
4. Save and then close **ExcelL1_C7_P1.xlsx**.

Project ② Create a Technology Purchases Bar Chart and Column Chart

You will open a workbook containing technology purchases data by department and then create a bar chart with the data. You will then change the chart type, layout, and style and move the chart to a new sheet.

Changing the Chart Design

When you insert a chart in a worksheet, the Chart Tools Design tab displays as shown in Figure 7.3. With options in this tab, you can change the chart type, specify a different layout or style for the chart, and change the location of the chart so it displays in a separate worksheet.

Figure 7.3 Chart Tools Design Tab

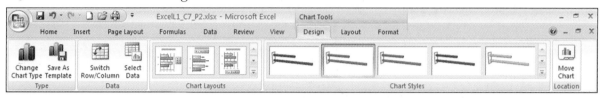

Choosing a Custom Chart Style

The chart feature offers a variety of preformatted custom charts and offers varying styles for each chart type. You can choose a chart style with buttons in the Charts group by clicking a chart button and then choosing from the styles offered at the drop-down list. You can also choose a chart style with the Change Chart Type button in the Chart Tools Design tab. Click this button and the Change Chart Type dialog box displays as shown in Figure 7.4. Click the desired chart type in the panel at the left side of the dialog box and then click the desired chart style at the right. If you create a particular chart type on a regular basis, you may want to set that chart type as the default. To do this, click the Set as Default Chart button in the Change Chart Type dialog box.

Change Chart Type

Figure 7.4 Change Chart Type Dialog Box

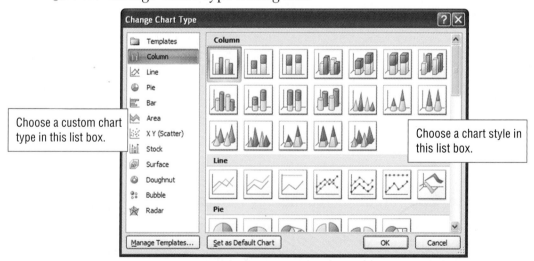

Choose a custom chart type in this list box.

Choose a chart style in this list box.

Changing the Data Series

A data series is information represented on the chart by bars, lines, columns, pie slices, and so on. When Excel creates a chart, the data in the first column (except the first cell) is used to create the x-axis (the information along the bottom of the chart) and the data in the first row (except the first cell) is used to create the legend. You can switch the data in the axes by clicking the Switch Row/Column button in the Data group in the Chart Tools Design tab. This moves the data on the x-axis to the y-axis and the y-axis data to the x-axis.

QUICK STEPS

Change Chart Data Series
1. Make the chart active.
2. Click Chart Tools Design tab.
3. Click Switch Row/Column button.

Switch Row/Column

Project 2a — Creating a Chart and Changing the Design

1. Open **ExcelC07Project02.xlsx** and then save the workbook and name it **ExcelL1_C7_P2**.
2. Create a bar chart by completing the following steps:
   a. Select cells A3 through B9.
   b. Click the Insert tab.
   c. Click the Bar button in the Charts group.
   d. Click the first option from the left in the *Cylinder* section (*Clustered Horizontal Cylinder*).
3. With the chart selected and the Chart Tools Design tab displayed, change the data series by clicking the Switch Row/Column button located in the Data group.

Step 3

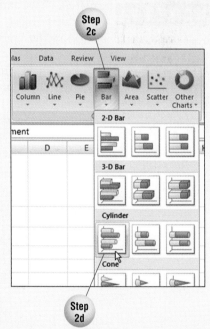

Step 2c

Step 2d

4. Change the chart type and style by completing the following steps:
   a. Click the Change Chart Type button located in the Type group.
   b. At the Change Chart Type dialog box, click the *Column* option in the left panel.
   c. Click the *3-D Cylinder* option in the *Column* section (fourth chart style from the left in the second row of the *Column* section).
   d. Click OK to close the Change Chart Type dialog box.
5. Save **ExcelL1_C7_P2.xlsx**.

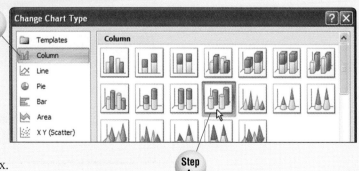

Step 4b

Step 4c

Changing Chart Layout and Style

The Chart Tools Design tab contains options for changing the chart layout and style. The Chart Layouts group in the tab contains preformatted chart layout options. Click the More button (contains an underline and a down-pointing arrow) to display a drop-down list of layout options. Hover the mouse pointer over an option and a ScreenTip displays with the option name. You can also scroll through layout options by clicking the up-pointing arrow or the down-pointing arrow located at the right side of the Chart Layouts group.

Use options in the Chart Styles group to apply a particular style of formatting to a chart. Click the More button located at the right side of the Chart Styles group to display a drop-down list with all the style options or click the up-pointing or down-pointing arrow at the right of the group to scroll through the options.

Changing Chart Location

Create a chart and the chart is inserted in the currently open worksheet as an embedded object. You can change the location of a chart with the Move Chart button in the Location group. Click this button and the Move Chart dialog box displays as shown in Figure 7.5. Click the *New sheet* option to move the chart to a new sheet within the workbook. Excel automatically names the sheet *Chart1*. Click the down-pointing arrow at the right side of the *Object in* option box and then click the desired location. The drop-down list will generally display the names of the worksheets within the open workbook. You can use the keyboard shortcut, F11, to create a default chart type (usually a column chart) and Excel automatically inserts the chart in a separate sheet.

If you have moved a chart to a separate sheet, you can move it back to the original sheet or move it to a different sheet within the workbook. To move a chart to a sheet, click the Move Chart button in the Location group in the Chart Tools Design tab. At the Move Chart dialog box, click the down-pointing arrow at the right side of the *Object in* option and then click the desired sheet at the drop-down list. Click OK and the chart is inserted in the specified sheet as an object that you can move, size, and format.

Figure 7.5 Move Chart Dialog Box

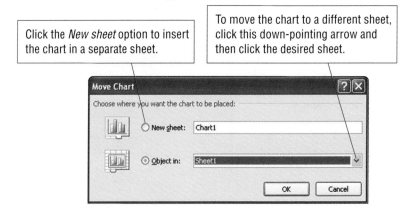

Click the *New sheet* option to insert the chart in a separate sheet.

To move the chart to a different sheet, click this down-pointing arrow and then click the desired sheet.

Deleting a Chart

QUICK STEPS

Delete a Chart
1. Click once in chart.
2. Press Delete key.
OR
1. Right-click chart tab.
2. Click Cut.

Delete a chart created in Excel by clicking once in the chart to select it and then pressing the Delete key. If you move a chart to a different worksheet in the workbook and then delete the chart, the chart is deleted but not the worksheet. To delete the chart as well as the worksheet, position the mouse pointer on the Chart1 tab, click the *right* mouse button, and then click *Delete* at the shortcut menu. At the message box telling you that selected sheets will be permanently deleted, click Delete.

Project 2b Changing Chart Layout, Style, and Location

1. With **ExcelL1_C7_P2.xlsx** open, make sure the Chart Tools Design tab displays. (If it does not, make sure the chart is selected and then click the Chart Tools Design tab.)
2. Change the chart type by completing the following steps:
   a. Click the Change Chart Type button in the Type tab.
   b. Click *3-D Clustered Column* (fourth column style from the left in the top row).
   c. Click OK to close the dialog box.

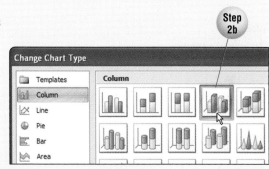

Step 2b

3. Change the chart layout by clicking the *Layout 1* option in the Chart Layouts group (first option from the left). This layout inserts the words *Chart Title* at the top of the chart.

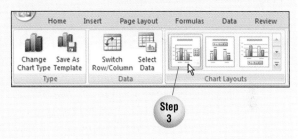

Step 3

4. Change the chart style by clicking the More button located at the right side of the Chart Styles group and the clicking *Style 34* (second option from the left in the fifth row).

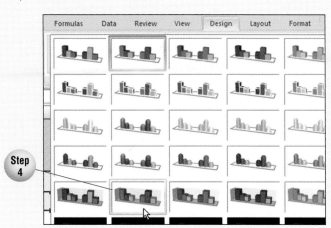

Step 4

5. Move the chart to a new location by completing the following steps:
   a. Click the Move Chart button in the Location group.
   b. At the Move Chart dialog box, click the *New sheet* option and then click OK. (The chart is inserted in a worksheet named *Chart1*.)
6. Save **ExcelL1_C7_P2.xlsx**.
7. Print the Chart1 worksheet containing the chart.
8. Move the chart from Chart1 to Sheet2 by completing the following steps:
   a. Make sure Chart1 is the active sheet and that the chart is selected (not an element in the chart).
   b. Make sure the Chart Tools Design tab is active.
   c. Click the Move Chart button in the Location group.
   d. At the Move Chart dialog box, click the down-pointing arrow at the right side of the *Object in* option and then click *Sheet2* at the drop-down list.

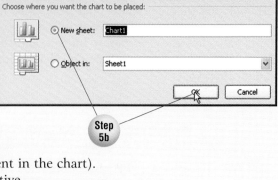

Step 5b

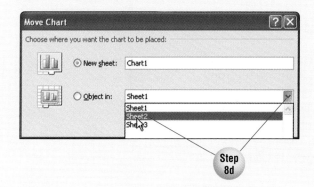

Step 8d

   e. Click OK.
9. Increase the size of the chart and maintain the proportions by completing the following steps:
   a. Click inside the chart but outside any chart elements. (This displays a light turquoise border around the chart.)
   b. Hold down the Shift key.
   c. Position the mouse pointer on the upper left border corner until the pointer turns into a double-headed arrow pointing diagonally.
   d. Hold down the left mouse button, drag left approximately one inch and then release the mouse button and then the Shift key.
   e. Display the worksheet in Print Preview to determine if the chart will print on one page. If the chart does not fit on the page, close Print Preview and then decrease the size of the chart until it fits on one page.
10. Change amounts in Sheet1 by completing the following steps:
   a. Click Sheet1.
   b. Make cell B4 active and then change the number from *$33,500* to *$12,750*.
   c. Make cell B9 active and then change the number from *$19,200* to *$5,600*.
   d. Make cell A2 active.
   e. Click the Sheet2 tab and notice that the chart displays the updated amounts.
11. Print the active worksheet (Sheet2).
12. Save and then close **ExcelL1_C7_P2.xlsx**.

roject ③ **Create a Population Comparison Bar Chart**

You will open a workbook containing population comparison data for Seattle and Portland and then create a bar chart with the data. You will also add chart labels and shapes and move, size, and delete labels/shapes.

Changing the Chart Layout

Customize the layout of labels in a chart with options in the Chart Tools Layout tab as shown in Figure 7.6. With buttons in this tab, you can change the layout and/or insert additional chart labels. Certain chart labels are automatically inserted in a chart including a chart legend and labels for the x-axis and y-axis. Add chart labels to an existing chart with options in the Labels group in the Chart Tools Layout tab. In addition to chart labels, you can also insert shapes, pictures, and/or clip art and change the layout of 3-D chart labels.

Figure 7.6 Chart Tools Layout Tab

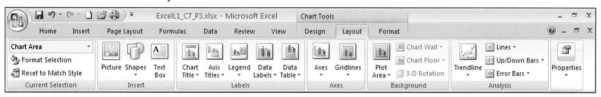

Inserting, Moving, and Deleting Chart Labels

Certain chart labels are automatically inserted in a chart, including a chart legend and labels for the x-axis and y-axis. The legend identifies which data series is represented by which data marker. Insert additional chart labels with options in the Labels group in the Chart Tools Layout tab. For example, click the Chart Title button in the Labels group and a drop-down list displays with options for inserting a chart title in a specific location in the chart.

You can move and/or size a chart label. To move a chart label, click the label to select it and then move the mouse pointer over the border line until the pointer turns into a four-headed arrow. Hold down the left mouse button, drag the label to the desired location, and then release the mouse button. To size a chart label, use the sizing handles that display around the selected label to increase or decrease the size. To delete a chart label, click the label to select it and then press the Delete key. You can also delete a label by right-clicking the label and then clicking *Delete* at the shortcut menu.

Add Chart Labels
1. Make the chart active.
2. Click Chart Tools Layout tab.
3. Click desired chart labels button.
4. Choose desired option at drop-down list.

Chart Title ▾

1. Open **ExcelC07Project03.xlsx** and then save the workbook and name it **ExcelL1_C7_P3**.
2. Create a Bar chart by completing the following steps:
    a. Select cells A2 through H4.
    b. Click the Insert tab.
    c. Click the Bar button in the Charts group and then click the *Clustered Horizontal Cylinder* option in the *Cylinder* section.
3. Change to a Line chart by completing the following steps:
    a. Click the Change Chart Type button in the Type group.
    b. At the Change Chart Type dialog box, click *Line* located at the left side of the dialog box.
    c. Click the *Line with Markers* option in the *Line* section (fourth option from the left).

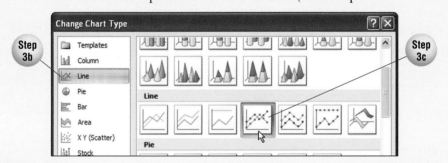

    d. Click OK to close the Change Chart Type dialog box.
4. Click the More button in the Chart Styles group in the Chart Tools Design tab and then click *Style 18* at the drop-down gallery (second option from left in the third row).

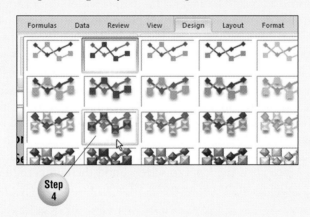

5. Change the layout of the chart by completing the following steps:
   a. Click the Chart Tools Layout tab.
   b. Click the Legend button in the Labels group.
   c. At the drop-down list, click the *Show Legend at Bottom* option.

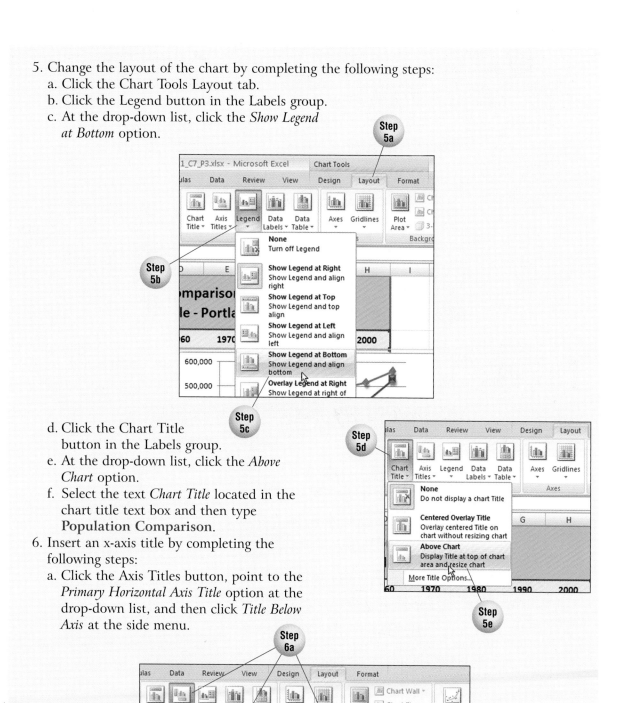

   d. Click the Chart Title button in the Labels group.
   e. At the drop-down list, click the *Above Chart* option.
   f. Select the text *Chart Title* located in the chart title text box and then type **Population Comparison**.
6. Insert an x-axis title by completing the following steps:
   a. Click the Axis Titles button, point to the *Primary Horizontal Axis Title* option at the drop-down list, and then click *Title Below Axis* at the side menu.

   b. Select the text *Axis Title* located in the title text box and then type **Decades**.

7. Insert a y-axis title by completing the following steps:
   a. Click the Axis Titles button, point to the *Primary Vertical Axis Title* option at the drop-down list, and then click *Rotated Title* at the side menu. (This inserts a rotated title at the left side of the chart containing the text *Axis Title*).

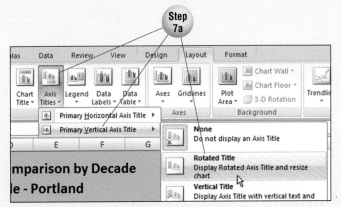

   b. Select the text *Axis Title* located in the axis title text box and then type **Total Population**.
8. Click the Gridlines button in the Axes group, point to *Primary Vertical Gridlines*, and then click the *Major & Minor Gridlines* option at the side menu.

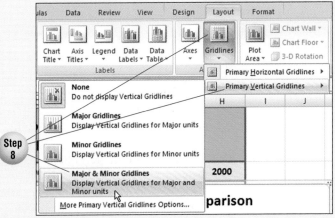

9. Click the Data Table button in the Labels group and then click the *Show Data Table* option. (This inserts cells toward the bottom of the chart containing cell data.)

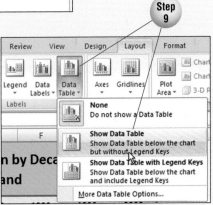

10. Click the Lines button in the Analysis group and then click *Drop Lines* at the drop-down list.

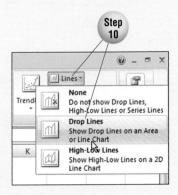

11. Drag the bottom right corner of the chart border to increase the size by approximately one inch.
12. Drag the chart so it is positioned below the data in cells but not overlapping the data.
13. Click the x-axis title (*Decades*) to select the title text box and then drag the box so it is positioned as shown below.

	1940	1950	1960	1970	1980	1990	2000
Seattle	368,302	467,591	557,087	530,831	493,846	516,259	563,374
Portland	305,394	373,628	372,676	376,967	366,383	437,319	529,121

Decades

—— Seattle —— Portland

Step 13

14. Print only the selected chart.
15. Delete the horizontal axis title by clicking the axis title *Decades* and then pressing the Delete key.
16. Save **ExcelL1_C7_P3.xlsx**.

Inserting Shapes

The Insert group in the Chart Tools Layout tab contains three buttons with options for inserting shapes or images in a chart. Click the Shapes button in the Insert group and a drop-down list displays with a variety of shape options as shown in Figure 7.7. Click the desired shape at the drop-down list and the mouse pointer turns into a thin, black plus symbol. Drag with this pointer symbol to create the shape in the chart. The shape is inserted in the chart with default formatting. You can change this formatting with options in the Drawing Tools Format tab. This tab contains many of the same options as the Chart Tools Format tab. For example, you can insert a shape, apply a shape or WordArt style, and arrange and size the shape.

Moving, Sizing, and Deleting Shapes

Move, size, and delete shapes in the same manner as moving, sizing, and deleting chart elements. To move a shape, select the shape, position the mouse pointer over the border line until the pointer turns into a four-headed arrow. Hold down the left mouse button, drag the shape to the desired location, and then release the mouse button. To size a shape, select the shape and then use the sizing handles that display around the shape to increase or decrease the size. Delete a selected shape by clicking the Delete key or right-clicking the shape and then clicking *Cut* at the shortcut menu.

Insert Shape
1. Make the chart active.
2. Click Chart Tools Layout tab.
3. Click Shapes button.
4. Click desired shape at drop-down list.
5. Drag pointer symbol to create shape in chart.

Shapes

HINT
Chart elements can be repositioned for easier viewing.

Figure 7.7 Shapes Button Drop-down List

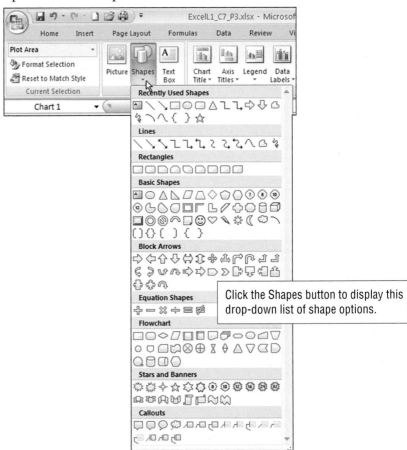

Click the Shapes button to display this drop-down list of shape options.

Project ③D Inserting and Customizing a Shape

1. With **ExcelL1_C7_P3.xlsx** open, make sure the Chart Tools Layout tab displays.
2. Create a shape similar to the shape shown in Figure 7.8. Begin by clicking the Shapes button in the Insert group.
3. Click the *Up Arrow Callout* shape in the *Block Arrows* section (last shape in the second row).
4. Drag in the chart to create the shape.

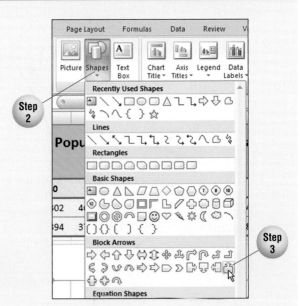

5. Click the More button in the Shapes Styles group (located at the right side of the three shapes) and then click *Subtle Effect - Accent 1* at the drop-down gallery.

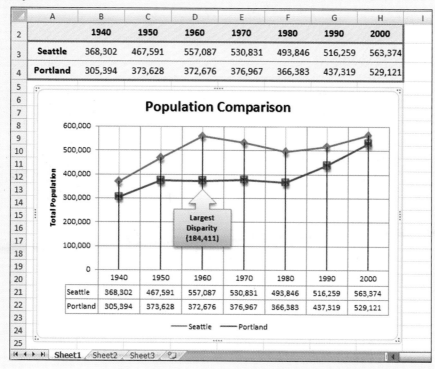

6. With the shape selected, use the sizing handles around the shape to increase and/or decrease the size so it displays as shown in Figure 7.8.

7. Type **Largest Disparity** in the shape box, press Enter, and then type (184,411).

8. Select the text you just typed and then complete the following steps:
   a. Click the Home tab.
   b. Click the Center button in the Alignment group.
   c. Click the Bold button in the Font group.
   d. Click the Font Size button arrow and then click *10*.

9. With the shape selected, drag the shape so it is positioned as shown in Figure 7.8.

10. Save **ExcelL1_C7_P3.xlsx**.

Figure 7.8 **Project 3b Chart**

	A	B	C	D	E	F	G	H	I
2		1940	1950	1960	1970	1980	1990	2000	
3	**Seattle**	368,302	467,591	557,087	530,831	493,846	516,259	563,374	
4	**Portland**	305,394	373,628	372,676	376,967	366,383	437,319	529,121	

Population Comparison

	1940	1950	1960	1970	1980	1990	2000
Seattle	368,302	467,591	557,087	530,831	493,846	516,259	563,374
Portland	305,394	373,628	372,676	376,967	366,383	437,319	529,121

Largest Disparity (184,411)

Inserting Images

Click the Picture button in the Insert group in the Chart Tools Layout tab and the Insert Picture dialog box displays. If you have a picture or image file saved in a folder, navigate to the desired folder and then double-click the file name. This inserts the picture or image in the chart. Drag the picture or image to the desired position in the chart and use the sizing handles to change the size.

Project 3c Inserting a Picture in a Chart

1. With **ExcelL1_C7_P3.xlsx** open, make sure the chart is selected and then click the Chart Tools Layout tab.
2. Insert the company logo by completing the following steps:
   a. Click the Picture button in the Insert group.
   b. At the Insert Picture dialog box, navigate to the Excel2007L1C7 folder on your storage medium and then double-click *WELogo.jpg* in the list box.

Step 2b

3. With the logo image inserted in the chart, use the sizing handles to decrease the size of the image and then move the image so it displays in the upper left corner of the chart area as shown in Figure 7.9.
4. Print only the selected chart.
5. Save and then close **ExcelL1_C7_P3.xlsx**.

Figure 7.9 Project 3c Chart

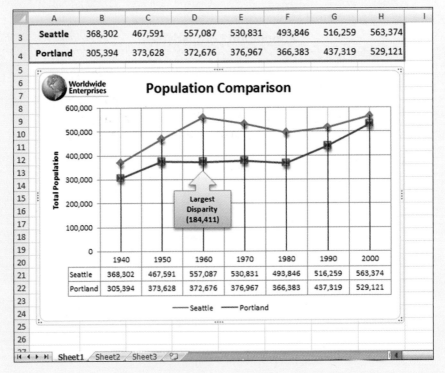

roject ④ **Create a Costs Percentage Pie Chart**

You will open a workbook containing percentage of costs for company departments and then create a pie chart with the data. You will apply formatting to the chart and then move the chart to a new worksheet.

Changing the Chart Formatting

Customize the format of the chart and chart elements with options in the Chart Tools Format tab as shown in Figure 7.10. With buttons in the Current Selection group you can identify a specific element in the chart and then apply formatting to that element. You can also click the Reset to Match Style button in the Current Selection group to return the formatting of the chart back to the original layout.

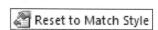

Figure 7.10 Chart Tools Format Tab

With options in the Shape Styles group, you can apply formatting styles to specific elements in a chart. Identify the desired element either by clicking the element to select it or by clicking the down-pointing arrow at the right side of the Chart Elements button in the Current Selection group and then clicking the desired element name at the drop-down list. With the chart element specified, apply formatting by clicking a style button in the Shape Styles group. You can also apply a style from a drop-down gallery. Display this gallery by clicking the More button located at the right side of the shape styles. Click the up-pointing or the down-pointing arrow at the right of the shape styles to cycle through the available style options.

H I N T
Apply a WordArt style to make numbers stand out.

Chart Elements

1. Open **ExcelC07Project04.xlsx** and then save the workbook and name it **ExcelL1_C7_P4**.
2. Create the pie chart as shown in Figure 7.11 by completing the following steps:
   a. Select cells A3 through B10.
   b. Click the Insert tab.
   c. Click the Pie button in the Charts group and then click the first pie option in the *2-D Pie* section.
3. Click the More button located at the right side of the Chart Styles group.
4. At the drop-down gallery, click the *Style 32* option (last option in the fourth row).

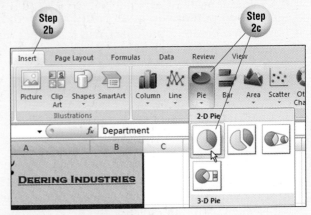

Step 2b

Step 2c

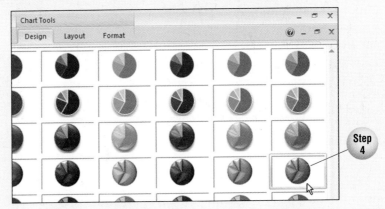

Step 4

5. Click the Chart Tools Layout tab.
6. Insert data labels by clicking the Data Labels button in the Labels group and then clicking *Outside End* at the drop-down list.
7. Format chart elements by completing the following steps:
   a. Click the Chart Tools Format tab.
   b. Click the down-pointing arrow at the right side of the Chart Elements button in the Current Selection group and then click *Legend* at the drop-down list.
   c. Click the More button in the Shape Styles group and then click the last option in the fourth row (*Subtle Effect - Accent 6*).
   d. Click the down-pointing arrow at the right side of the Chart Elements button in the Current Selection group and then click *Chart Title*.

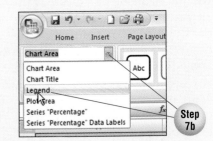

Step 7b

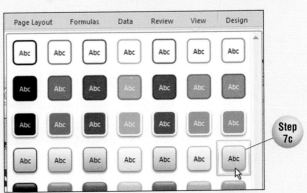

Step 7c

e. Click the More button at the right side of the WordArt styles in the WordArt Styles group and then click the *Gradient Fill - Accent 6, Inner Shadow* (second option from the left in the fourth row).

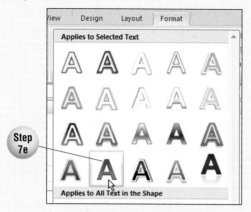

8. Insert the chart in a new sheet by completing the following steps:
   a. With the chart selected, click the Chart Tools Design tab.
   b. Click the Move Chart button in the Location group.
   c. At the Move Chart dialog box, click the *New sheet* option.
   d. Click OK.
9. Print only the worksheet containing the chart.
10. Save and then close **ExcelL1_C7_P4.xlsx**.

Figure 7.11 **Project 4**

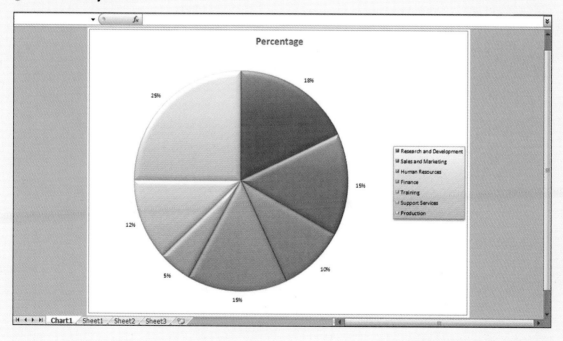

Project ⑤ Create a Regional Sales Column Chart

You will create a column chart using regional sales data, change the layout of the chart, apply formatting, and change the height and width of the chart.

QUICK STEPS

Change Chart Height and/or Width
1. Make the chart active.
2. Click Chart Tools Format tab.
3. Insert desired height and/or width with *Shape Height* and/or *Shape Width* text boxes.

Changing the Chart Height and Width

You can size a chart by selecting the chart and then dragging a sizing handle. You can also size a chart to specific measurements with the *Shape Height* and *Shape Width* measurement boxes in the Size group in the Chart Tools Format tab. Change the height or width by clicking the up- or down-pointing arrows that display at the right side of the button or select the current measurement in the measurement box and then type a specific measurement.

Project ⑤ Changing the Height and Width of a Chart

1. Open **ExcelC07Project05.xlsx**.
2. Save the workbook with Save As and name it **ExcelL1_C7_P5**.
3. Create a Column chart by completing the following steps:
   a. Select cells A3 through B8.
   b. Click the Insert tab.
   c. Click the Column button in the Charts group.
   d. Click the *3-D Clustered Column* option (first option in the *3-D Column* section).
   e. Click the Switch Row/Column button located in the Data group to change the data series.
   f. Click the *Layout 1* option in the Chart Layouts group (first option from the left in the group).
   g. Select the text *Chart Title* and then type **Northeast Regional Sales**.
   h. Click the More button located at the right side of the Chart Styles group and then click *Style 32* at the drop-down gallery (last option in fourth row).

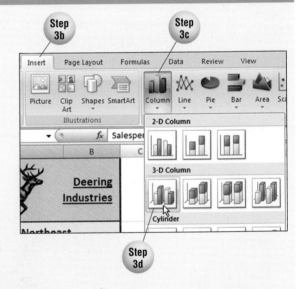

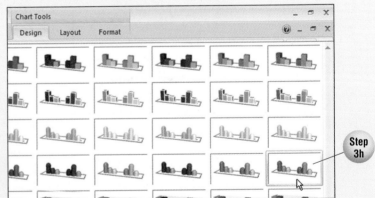

4. Change a series color by completing the following steps:
   a. Click the Chart Tools Format tab.
   b. Click the down-pointing arrow at the right side of the Chart Elements button and then click *Series "Newman, Jared"* at the drop-down list.

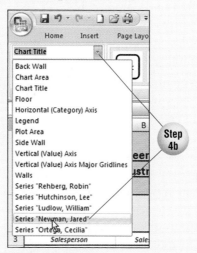

c. Click the Shape Fill button arrow in the Shape Styles group and then click the dark red color *Red, Accent 2, Darker 25%*.

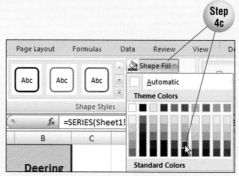

5. Change a series color by completing the following steps:
   a. With the Chart Tools Format tab active, click the down-pointing arrow at the right side of the Chart Elements button and then click *Series "Hutchinson, Lee"* at the drop-down list.
   b. Click the Shape Fill button arrow in the Shape Styles group and then click the dark green color *Olive Green, Accent 3, Darker 25%*.
6. Drag the chart down below the cells containing data.
7. Click the Chart Tools Format tab.
8. Click in the *Shape Height* measurement box in the Size group and then type 3.8.
9. Click the up-pointing arrow at the right side of the *Shape Width* measurement box in the Size group until *5.5* displays in the text box.

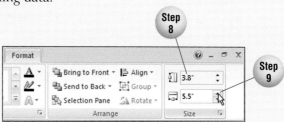

10. Print only the chart.
11. Save and then close **ExcelL1_C7_P5.xlsx**.

CHAPTER summary

- Create a chart with data in an Excel worksheet. A chart is a visual presentation of data.

- Excel provides 11 basic chart types: Area, Bar, Bubble, Column, Doughnut, Line, Pyramid, Radar, Stock, Surface, and XY (Scatter).

- To create a chart, select cells containing data you want to chart, click the Insert tab, and then click the desired chart button in the Charts group.

- A chart you create is inserted in the same worksheet as the selected cells.

- You can increase or decrease the size of a chart by positioning the mouse pointer on the four dots located in the middle of each border line or the three dots at each corner, and then dragging to the desired size.

- Move a chart by positioning the mouse pointer on the chart border until it turns into a four-headed arrow and then dragging with the mouse.

- Data in cells used to create the chart are linked to the chart. If you change the data in cells, the chart reflects the changes.

- Print by selecting the chart and then displaying the Print dialog box. At the Print dialog box, make sure *Selected Chart* is selected and then click OK.

- Preview a chart by clicking the Office button, pointing to *Print*, and then clicking *Print Preview* at the side menu.

- When you insert a chart in a worksheet, the Chart Tools Design tab is active. Use options in this tab to change the chart type, specify a different layout or style, and change the location of the chart.

- Choose a chart style with buttons in the Charts group in the Insert tab or at the Change Chart Type dialog box. Display this dialog box by clicking the Change Chart Type button in the Type group in the Chart Tools Design tab.

- The Chart Layouts group in the Chart Tools Design tab contains preformatted chart layout options. Use options in the Chart Styles group to apply a particular style of formatting to a chart.

- By default, a chart is inserted in the active worksheet. You can move the chart to a new sheet within the workbook with the *New sheet* option at the Move Chart dialog box. Display this dialog box by clicking the Move Chart button in the Location group in the Chart Tools Design tab.

- To delete a chart in a worksheet, click the chart to select it, and then press the Delete key. To delete a chart created in a separate sheet, position the mouse pointer on the chart tab, click the *right* mouse button, and then click Delete.

- Use options in the Chart Tools Layout tab to change the layout and/or insert additional chart labels, shapes, pictures, or clip art images.

- Insert additional chart labels with options in the Labels group in the Chart Tools Layout tab.

- Use buttons in the Insert group in the Chart Tools Layout tab to insert shapes, pictures, or text boxes.

- To move a chart label, click the label to select it and then drag the label with the mouse. To delete a label, click the label and then press the Delete key.

- Use options in the Chart Tools Format tab to customize the format of the chart and chart elements.
- Change the chart size by dragging the chart sizing handles or by entering a measurement in the *Shape Height* and *Shape Width* measurement boxes in the Size group in the Chart Tools Format tab.

COMMANDS review

FEATURE	RIBBON TAB, GROUP	BUTTON, OPTION	KEYBOARD SHORTCUT
Default chart in worksheet			Alt + F1
Default chart in separate sheet			F11
Change Chart Type dialog box	Chart Tools Design, Type		
Move Chart dialog box	Chart Tools Design, Location		
Shapes button drop-down list	Chart Tools Layout, Insert		
Insert Picture dialog box	Chart Tools Layout, Insert		

CONCEPTS check

Test Your Knowledge

Completion: In the space provided at the right, indicate the correct term, symbol, or command.

1. This is the keyboard shortcut to create a chart with the default chart type.

   _____

2. This type of chart shows proportions and relationships of parts to the whole.

   _____

3. The Charts group contains buttons for creating charts and is located in this tab.

   _____

4. When you create a chart, the chart is inserted in this location by default.

   _____

5. Select a chart in a worksheet, display the Print dialog box, and this option is automatically selected in the *Print what* section.

   _____

6. When Excel creates a chart, the data in the first row (except the first cell) is used to create this.

   _____

7. Click the Picture button in the Chart Tools Layout tab and this dialog box displays.

   _____

8. Click this option at the Move Chart dialog box to move the chart to a separate sheet.

   _____

9. Use buttons in the Insert group in this tab to insert shapes, pictures, or text boxes.

   _____

10. Change the chart size by entering measurements in these text boxes in the Size group in the Chart Tools Format tab.

    _____

SKILLS check
Demonstrate Your Proficiency

Assessment

1 CREATE A COMPANY SALES COLUMN CHART

1. Open **ExcelC07Assessment01.xlsx** and then save the workbook and name it **ExcelL1_C7_A1**.
2. Select cells A3 through C15 and then create a Column chart with the following specifications:
   a. Choose the *3-D Clustered Column* chart at the Chart button drop-down list.
   b. At the Chart Tools Design tab, click the *Layout 3* option in the Chart Layouts group.
   c. Change the chart style to *Style 26*.
   d. Select the text *Chart Title* and then type **Company Sales**.
   e. Move the location of the chart to a new sheet.
3. Print only the worksheet containing the chart.
4. Save and then close **ExcelL1_C7_A1.xlsx**.

Assessment

2 CREATE QUARTERLY DOMESTIC AND FOREIGN SALES BAR CHART

1. Open **ExcelC07Assessment02.xlsx** and then save the workbook and name it **ExcelL1_C7_A2**.
2. Select cells A3 through E5 and then create a Bar chart with the following specifications:
   a. Click the *Clustered Bar in 3-D* option at the Bar button drop-down list.
   b. At the Chart Tools Design tab choose the *Layout 2* option in the Chart Layouts group.
   c. Choose the *Style 23* option in the Chart Styles group.
   d. Select the text *Chart Title*, type **Quarterly Sales**, and then click in the chart but outside any chart elements.
   e. Display the Chart Tools Layout tab and then insert primary vertical minor gridlines. (Do this with the Gridlines button.)
   f. Display the Chart Tools Format tab and then apply to the chart the *Subtle Effect - Accent 3* option in the Shape Styles group.
   g. Select the *Domestic* series (using the Chart Elements button) and then apply a purple fill (Purple, Accent 4, Darker 25%) using the Shape Fill button in the Shape Styles group.
   h. Select the Foreign series and then apply a dark aqua fill (Aqua, Accent 5, Darker 25%) using the Shape Fill button in the Shape Styles group.
   i. Select the chart title and then apply the *Gradient Fill - Accent 6, Inner Shadow* option with the WordArt Styles button.
   j. Increase the height of the chart to 4 inches and the width to 6 inches.
   k. Move the chart below the cells containing data and make sure the chart fits on the page with the data. (**Hint: Display the worksheet in Print Preview.**)
3. Print only the worksheet.
4. Save and then close **ExcelL1_C7_A2.xlsx**.

3 CREATE AND FORMAT A CORPORATE SALES COLUMN CHART

1. Open **ExcelC07Assessment03.xlsx** and then save the workbook and name it **ExcelL1_C7_A3**.
2. Create a column chart and format the chart so it displays as shown in Figure 7.12.
3. Print only the worksheet containing the chart.
4. Save and then close **ExcelL1_C7_A3.xlsx**.

Figure 7.12 Assessment 3

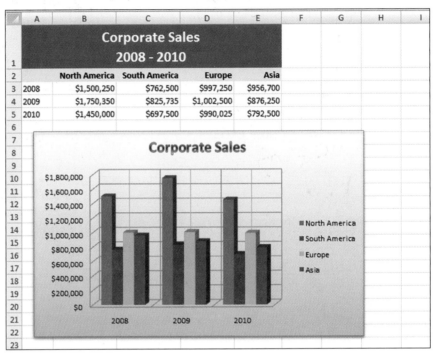

4 CREATE A FUNDS ALLOCATIONS PIE CHART

1. At a blank worksheet, create a worksheet with the following data:

   Fund Allocations

Fund	Percentage
Annuities	23%
Stocks	42%
Bonds	15%
Money Market	20%

2. Using the data above, create a pie chart as a separate worksheet with the following specifications:
   a. Create a title for the pie chart.
   b. Add data labels to the chart.
   c. Add any other enhancements that will improve the visual presentation of the data.

3. Save the workbook and name it **ExcelL1_C7_A4**.
4. Print only the sheet containing the chart.
5. Close **ExcelL1_C7_A4.xlsx**.

Assessment

5 CREATE AN ACTUAL AND PROJECTED SALES CHART

1. Open **ExcelC07Assessment05.xlsx** and then save the workbook and name it **ExcelL1_C7_A5**.
2. Look at the data in the worksheet and then create a chart to represent the data. Add a title to the chart and add any other enhancements to improve the visual display of the chart.
3. Save the workbook and then print the chart.
4. Close **ExcelL1_C7_A5.xlsx**.

Assessment

6 CREATE AN ATTENDANCE SCATTER CHART

1. Use Excel's Help feature to learn more about chart types and then create a worksheet with the data shown in Figure 7.13. Create a scatter chart from the data in a separate sheet and create an appropriate title for the chart. Use the DATE function to enter the dates in the first column and enter the current year for the date.
2. Save the completed workbook and name it **ExcelL1_C7_A6**.
3. Print both sheets of the workbook (the sheet containing the data in cells and the sheet containing the chart).
4. Close **ExcelL1_C7_A6.xlsx**.

Figure 7.13 Assessment 6

HIGHLAND PARK ATTENDANCE

Week	Projected	Actual
July 1	35,000	42,678
July 8	33,000	41,065
July 15	30,000	34,742
July 22	28,000	29,781
July 29	28,000	26,208

CASE study

Apply Your Skills

You are an administrator for Dollar Wise Financial Services and you need to prepare charts indicating home loan and commercial loan amounts for the past year. Use the information below to prepare two charts in Excel. You determine the type and style of chart and the layout and formatting of the chart. Insert a shape in the Commercial Loans chart that contains the text *All-time High* and points to the second quarter amount (*$6,785,250*).

Home Loans
1st Qtr. = $2,675,025
2nd Qtr. = $3,125,750
3rd Qtr. = $1,975,425
4th Qtr. = $875,650

Commercial Loans
1st Qtr. = $5,750,980
2nd Qtr. = $6,785,250
3rd Qtr. = $4,890,625
4th Qtr. = $2,975,900

Save the workbook containing the two charts and name it **ExcelL1_C7_CS_P1**. Print only the two charts and then close **ExcelL1_C7_CS_P1.xlsx**.

You need to present information on the budget for the company. You have the dollar amounts and need to convert the amounts to a percentage of the entire budget. Use the information below to calculate the percentage of the budget for each item and then create a pie chart with the information. You determine the chart style, layout, and formatting.

Total Budget: $6,000,000

Building Costs	=	$720,000
Salaries	=	$2,340,000
Benefits	=	$480,000
Advertising	=	$840,000
Marketing	=	$600,000
Client Expenses	=	$480,000
Equipment	=	$420,000
Supplies	=	$120,000

Save the workbook containing the pie chart and name it **ExcelL1_C7_CS_P2**. Print only the chart and then close **ExcelL1_C7_CS_P2.xlsx**.

One of your clients owns a number of stocks and you like to prepare a daily chart of the stocks' high, low, and close price. Use the Help feature to learn about stock charts and then create a stock chart with the following information (the company stock symbols are fictitious):

	IDE	POE	QRR
High	$23.75	$18.55	$34.30
Low	$18.45	$15.00	$31.70
Close	$19.65	$17.30	$33.50

Save the workbook containing the stock chart and name it **ExcelL1_C7_CS_P3**. Print only the chart and then close **ExcelL1_C7_CS_P3.xlsx**.

You need to prepare information on mortgage rates for a community presentation. You decide to include the information on mortgage rates in a chart for easy viewing. Use the Internet to search for historical data on the national average for mortgage rates. Determine the average mortgage rate for a 30-year FRM (fixed-rate mortgage) for each January and July beginning with the year 2005 and continuing to the current year. Also include the current average rate. Use this information to create the chart. Save the workbook and name it **ExcelL1_C7_CS_P4**. Print only the chart and then close **ExcelL1_C7_CS_P4.xlsx**.

You will be presenting information at an upcoming meeting on the information in the previous challenges for which you created a chart. You decide to include the charts in a PowerPoint presentation so you can display the charts on a screen while presenting. Open PowerPoint and then open the presentation named **ExcelC07Presentation.pptx**. Copy the chart you created in Part 1 to the second slide, copy the chart for Part 2 into the third slide, and then copy the chart for Part 4 into the fourth slide. Increase the size of the charts to better fill the slides. Save the presentation and name it **PPL1_C7_CS_P5**. Print the three slides containing charts. Close **PPL1_C7_CS_P5.pptx**.

Project ③ **Insert a Clip Art Image and Shapes in a Financial Analysis Workbook**

You will open a financial analysis workbook and then insert, move, size, and format a clip art image in the workbook. You will also insert an arrow shape, type and format text in the shape, and then copy the shape.

QUICK STEPS

Insert Symbol
1. Click in desired cell.
2. Click the Insert tab.
3. Click Symbol button.
4. Double-click desired symbol.
5. Click Close.

Insert Special Character
1. Click in desired cell.
2. Click Insert tab.
3. Click Symbol button.
4. Click Special Characters tab.
5. Double-click desired special character.
6. Click Close.

HINT
You can increase and/or decrease the size of the Symbol dialog box by positioning the mouse pointer on the lower right corner until the pointer displays as a two-headed arrow and then dragging with the mouse.

Symbol

Inserting Symbols and Special Characters

You can use the Symbol button in the Insert tab to insert special symbols in a worksheet. Click the Symbol button in the Text group in the Insert tab and the Symbol dialog box displays as shown in Figure 8.4. At the Symbol dialog box, double-click the desired symbol, and then click Close; or click the desired symbol, click the Insert button, and then click Close. At the Symbol dialog box with the Symbols tab selected, you can change the font with the *Font* option. When you change the font, different symbols display in the dialog box. Click the Special Characters tab at the Symbol dialog box and a list of special characters displays along with keyboard shortcuts to create the special character.

Figure 8.4 Symbol Dialog Box with Symbols Tab Selected

Use the *Font* option to select the desired set of characters.

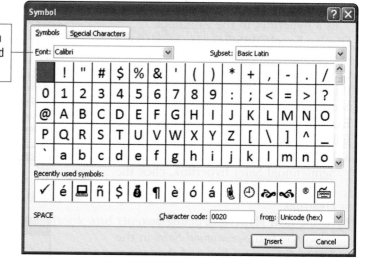

1. Open **ExcelC08Project03.xlsx** and then save the workbook and name it **ExcelL1_C8_P3**.
2. Insert a symbol by completing the following steps:
   a. Double-click cell A2.
   b. Delete the *e* that displays at the end of *Qualite*.
   c. With the insertion point positioned immediately right of the *t* in *Qualit*, click the Insert tab.
   d. Click the Symbol button in the Text group.
   e. At the Symbol dialog box, scroll down the list box and then click the *é* symbol (ninth symbol from the left in the eleventh row).
   f. Click the Insert button and then click the Close button.

3. Insert a special character by completing the following steps:
   a. With cell A2 selected and in Edit mode, move the insertion point so it is positioned immediately right of *Group*.
   b. Click the Symbol button in the Text group.
   c. At the Symbol dialog box, click the Special Characters tab.
   d. Double-click the ® symbol (tenth option from the top).
   e. Click the Close button.

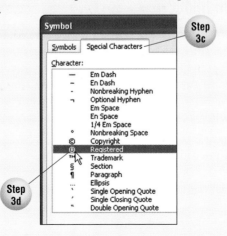

4. Insert a symbol by completing the following steps:
   a. With cell A2 selected and in Edit mode, move the insertion point so it is positioned immediately left of the *Q* in *Qualité*.
   b. Click the Symbol button in the Text group.
   c. At the Symbol dialog box, click the down-pointing arrow at the right side of the *Font* option box and then click *Wingdings* at the drop-down list. (You will need to scroll down the list to display this option.)
   d. Click the ❖ symbol (seventh option from the left in the sixth row).
   e. Click the Insert button and then click the Close button.

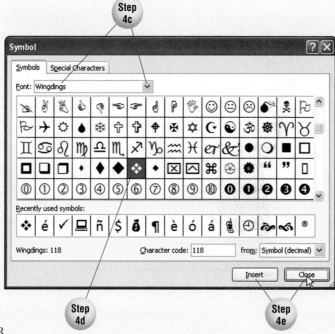

Step 4c

Step 4d

Step 4e

5. Click in cell A3.
6. Save **ExcelL1_C8_P3.xlsx**.

Inserting an Image

  You can insert an image such as a picture or clip art in an Excel workbook with buttons in the Illustrations group in the Insert tab. Click the Picture button to display the Insert Picture dialog box where you can specify the desired picture file, or click the Clip Art button and then choose from a variety of images available at the Clip Art task pane. When you insert a picture or a clip art image in a worksheet, the Picture Tools Format Tab displays as shown in Figure 8.5.

Figure 8.5 Picture Tools Format Tab

Customizing and Formatting an Image

With options in the Adjust group in the Picture Tools Format tab you can recolor the picture or clip art image and change the brightness and contrast of the image. You can also reset the picture or clip art back to its original color or change to a different image. Use the Compress Pictures button to compress the size of the image file. Apply predesigned styles with options in the Picture Styles group. Use options in the Arrange group to position the image on the page, specify text wrapping in relation to the image, align the image with other objects in the worksheet, and rotate the image. Use the Crop button in the Size group to remove any unnecessary parts of the image and specify the image size with the *Shape Height* and *Shape Width* measurement boxes.

Sizing and Moving an Image

You can change the size of an image with the *Shape Height* and *Shape Width* measurement boxes in the Size group in the Picture Tools Format tab or with the sizing handles that display around the selected image. To change size with a sizing handle, position the mouse pointer on a sizing handle until the pointer turns into a double-headed arrow and then hold down the left mouse button. Drag the sizing handle in or out to decrease or increase the size of the image and then release the mouse button. Use the middle sizing handles at the left or right side of the image to make the image wider or thinner. Use the middle sizing handles at the top or bottom of the image to make the image taller or shorter. Use the sizing handles at the corners of the image to change both the width and height at the same time. Hold down the Shift key while dragging a sizing handle to maintain the proportions of the image.

HINT

You can use arrow keys on the keyboard to move a selected object. To move the image in small increments, hold down the Ctrl key while pressing one of the arrow keys.

Move an image by positioning the mouse pointer on the image border until the pointer displays with a four-headed arrow attached. Hold down the left mouse button, drag the image to the desired position, and then release the mouse button. Rotate the image by positioning the mouse pointer on the green, round rotation handle until the pointer displays as a circular arrow. Hold down the left mouse button, drag in the desired direction, and then release the mouse button.

Inserting a Clip Art Image

Microsoft Office includes a gallery of media images you can insert in a worksheet such as clip art, photographs, and movie images, as well as sound clips. To insert an image in a worksheet, click the Insert tab and then click the Clip Art button in the Illustrations group. This displays the Clip Art task pane at the right side of the screen as shown in Figure 8.6.

Insert Clip Art Image
1. Click Insert tab.
2. Click Clip Art button.
3. Type desired word or topic in *Search for* text box.
4. Click Go button or press Enter.
5. Click desired image.

Figure 8.6 Clip Art Task Pane

Type in this text box the word or topic for which you are searching.

Use these options to specify where to search and the media types.

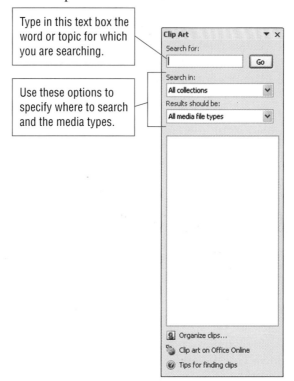

HINT

You can insert a clip art image by dragging the image from the Clip Art task pane into the worksheet.

HINT

Insert multiple clip art images by holding down the Ctrl key, clicking each desired clip art in the Clip Art task pane, and then dragging the images into the worksheet.

To view all picture, sound, and motion files, make sure the *Search for* text box in the Clip Art task pane does not contain any text and then click the Go button. When the desired image is visible, click the image to insert it in the worksheet. Use buttons in the Picture Tools Format tab shown in Figure 8.5 to format and customize the clip art image.

By default (unless it has been customized), the Clip Art task pane looks for all media images and sound clips found in all locations. You can narrow the search to specific locations and to specific images. The *Search in* option at the Clip Art task pane has a default setting of *All collections*. This can be changed to *My Collections*, *Office Collections*, and *Web Collections*. The *Results should be* option has a default setting of *Selected media file types*. Click the down-pointing arrow at the right side of this option to display media types. To search for a specific media type, remove the check mark before all options at the drop-down list but the desired type. For example, if you are searching only for photograph images, remove the check mark before Clip Art, Movies, and Sound.

If you are searching for specific images, click in the *Search for* text box, type the desired topic, and then click the Go button. For example, if you want to find images related to business, click in the *Search for* text box, type **business**, and then click the Go button. Clip art images related to *business* display in the viewing area of the task pane. If you are connected to the Internet, Word will search for images at the Office Online Web site matching the topic.

 Project ⓷ⓑ **Inserting an Image**

1. With **ExcelL1_C8_P3.xlsx** open, insert a clip art image by completing the following steps:
   a. Click the Insert tab.
   b. Click the Clip Art button in the Illustrations group.
   c. At the Clip Art task pane, click the down-pointing arrow at the right side of the *Results should be* option box and then click the *Photographs*, *Movies*, and *Sounds* check boxes at the drop-down list to remove the check marks. Click in the task pane to remove the drop-down list.

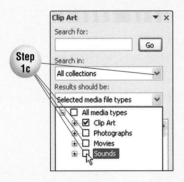

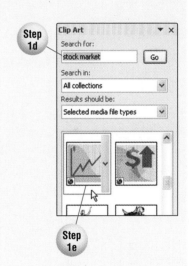

   d. Select any text that displays in the *Search for* text box, type **stock market**, and then press Enter.
   e. Click the image in the list box as shown at the right. (If you are not connected to the Internet and this image is not available, click a similar image.)
   f. Click the down-pointing at the right side of the *Results should be* option box and then click the *Photographs*, *Movies*, and *Sounds* check boxes at the drop-down list to insert check marks.
   g. Close the Clip Art task pane by clicking the Close button (contains an X) located in the upper right corner of the task pane.
2. Size and move the clip art image by completing the following steps:
   a. Click in the *Shape Width* measurement box, type 2.52, and then press Enter.

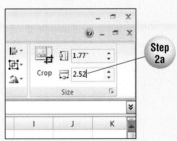

b. Position the mouse pointer on a border of the clip art image until the mouse pointer displays with a four-headed arrow attached. Hold down the left mouse button, drag the upper left corner of the clip art image so it is positioned in the upper left corner of cell A1, and then release the mouse button.

c. Change the height of the clip art image by positioning the mouse pointer on the bottom middle sizing handle until the mouse pointer displays as a double-headed arrow pointing up and down. Hold down the left mouse button, drag up until the bottom of the clip art image is aligned with the bottom of cell A1, and then release the mouse button.

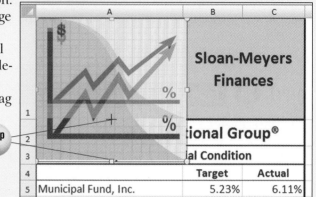

3. Click outside the clip art image to deselect it.

4. Save **ExcelL1_C8_P3.xlsx**.

QUICK STEPS

Insert Shape
1. Click Insert tab.
2. Click Shapes button.
3. Click desired shape at drop-down list.
4. Drag in worksheet to create shape.

Inserting a Shape

In Chapter 7, you learned how to insert shapes in a chart. With the Shapes button in the Illustrations group in the Insert tab, you can also insert shapes in a worksheet. Use the Shapes button in the Insert tab to draw shapes in a worksheet including lines, basic shapes, block arrows, flow chart shapes, callouts, stars, and banners. Click a shape and the mouse pointer displays as crosshairs (plus sign). Position the crosshairs where you want the shape to begin, hold down the left mouse button, drag to create the shape, and then release the mouse button. This inserts the shape in the worksheet and also displays the Drawing Tools Format tab shown in Figure 8.7. Use buttons in this tab to change the shape, apply a style to the shape, arrange the shape, and change the size of the shape.

If you choose a shape in the *Lines* section of the drop-down list, the shape you draw is considered a *line drawing*. If you choose an option in the other sections of the drop-down list, the shape you draw is considered an *enclosed object*. When drawing an enclosed object, you can maintain the proportions of the shape by holding down the Shift key while dragging with the mouse to create the shape. You can type text in an enclosed object and then use buttons in the WordArt Styles group to format the text.

Figure 8.7 Drawing Tools Format Tab

Copying Shapes

If you have drawn or inserted a shape, you may want to copy it to other locations in the worksheet. To copy a shape, select the shape and then click the Copy button in the Clipboard group in the Home tab. Position the insertion point at the location where you want the copied image and then click the Paste button. You can also copy a selected shape by holding down the Ctrl key while dragging the shape to the desired location.

Project 3c   Drawing Arrow Shapes

1. With **ExcelL1_C8_P3.xlsx** open, create the tallest arrow shown in Figure 8.8 by completing the following steps:
   a. Click the Insert tab.
   b. Click the Shapes button and then click the *Up Arrow* shape (third option from the left in the top row of the *Block Arrows* section).
   c. Position the mouse pointer (displays as a thin, black cross) near the upper left corner of cell D1, hold down the left mouse button, drag down and to the right to create the shape as shown below, and then release the mouse button.

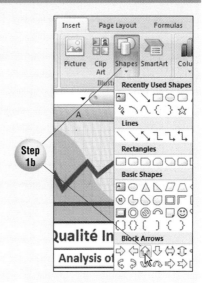

Step 1b

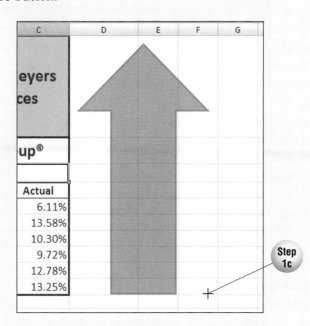

Step 1c

   d. Click in the *Shape Height* measurement box and then type 3.9.
   e. Click in the *Shape Width* measurement box, type 2.2, and then press Enter.

f. If necessary, drag the arrow so it is positioned as shown in Figure 8.8. (To drag the arrow, position the mouse pointer on the border of the selected arrow until the pointer turns into a four-headed arrow, hold down the left mouse button, drag the arrow to the desired position, and then release the mouse button.)

g. Click the More button at the right side of the shapes in the Shape Styles group and then click the *Intense Effect - Accent 1* option (second option from the left in the bottom row).

h. Click the Shape Effects button in the Shape Styles group, point to *Glow*, and then click the last option in the bottom row (*Accent color 6, 18 pt glow*).

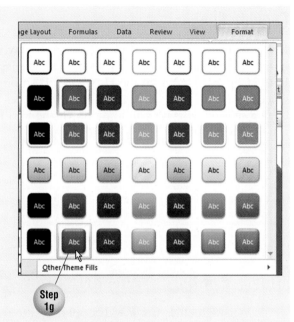

Step 1g

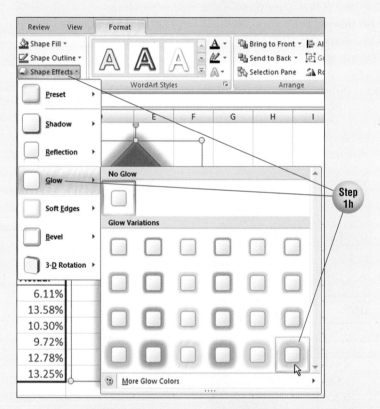

Step 1h

2. Insert text in the arrow shape by completing the following steps:
   a. With the arrow shape selected, type **McGuire Mutual Shares 5.33%**.
   b. Select the text you just typed (*McGuire Mutual Shares 5.33%*).

c. Click the More button at the right side of the styles in the WordArt Styles group and then click the second option from the left in the second row (*Fill - None, Outline - Accent 6, Glow - Accent 6*).

d. Click the Home tab.

e. Click the Top Align button in the Alignment group.

3. With the arrow selected, copy the arrow by completing the following steps:

a. Hold down the Ctrl key.

b. Position the mouse pointer on the arrow border until the pointer displays with a square box and plus symbol attached.

c. Hold down the left mouse button and drag to the right so the outline of the arrow is positioned at the right side of the existing arrow.

d. Release the mouse button and then release the Ctrl key.

4. Format the second arrow by completing the following steps:

a. With the second arrow selected, click the Drawing Tools Format tab.

b. Click in the *Shape Height* measurement box and then type 2.

c. Click in the *Shape Width* measurement box, type 1.7, and then press Enter

d. Select the text *McGuire Mutual Shares 5.33%* and then type **SR Linus Fund 0.22%**.

e. Drag the arrow so it is positioned as shown in Figure 8.8.

5. Change the orientation to landscape. (Make sure the cells containing data and the arrows will print on the same page.)

6. Save, print, and then close **ExcelL1_C8_P3.xlsx**.

Figure 8.8 Project 3c

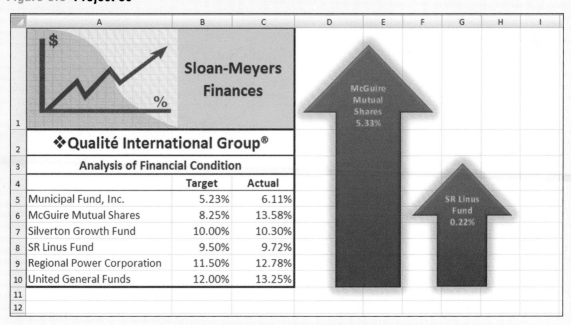

Project ④ Insert a Picture and Text Box in a Division Sales Workbook

You will open a division sales workbook and then insert, move, and size a picture. You will also insert a text box and then format the text.

Insert Picture
1. Click Insert tab.
2. Click Picture button.
3. Navigate to desired folder.
4. Double-click desired picture.

Inserting a Picture

To insert a picture in a worksheet, click the Insert tab and then click the Picture button in the Illustrations group. At the Insert Picture dialog box, navigate to the folder containing the desired picture and then double-click the picture. Use buttons in the Picture Tools Format tab to format and customize the picture.

Project ④a Inserting and Customizing a Picture

1. Open **ExcelC08Project04.xlsx** and then save the workbook and name it **ExcelL1_C8_P4**.
2. Make the following changes to the bird clip art image:
   a. Click the bird clip art image to select it.
   b. Click the Picture Tools Format tab.
   c. Click the Rotate button in the Arrange group and then click *Flip Horizontal* at the drop-down list.

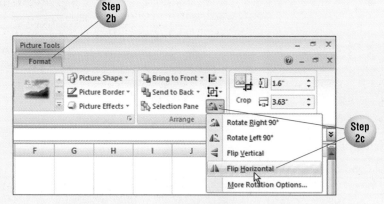

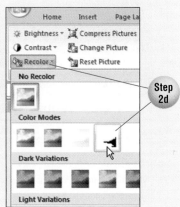

   d. Click the Recolor button in the Adjust group and then click the *Black and White* option in the *Color Modes* section.

e. Click in the *Shape Height* measurement box and
   then type 0.6.
f. Click in the *Shape Width* measurement box, type
   1.3, and then press Enter.

3. Insert and format a picture by completing the
   following steps:
   a. Click in cell A1 outside of the bird image.
   b. Click the Insert tab.
   c. Click the Picture button in the Illustrations group.
   d. At the Insert Picture dialog box, navigate to the
      Excel2007L1C8 folder on your storage medium and then
      double-click *Ocean.jpg*.
   e. With the picture selected, click the Send to Back button in
      the Arrange group in the Picture Tools Format tab.
   f. Use the sizing handles that display around the picture image
      to move and size it so it fills cell A1 as shown in Figure 8.9.
   g. Click the bird clip art image and then drag the image so it is
      positioned as shown in Figure 8.9.

4. Save **ExcelL1_C8_P4.xlsx**.

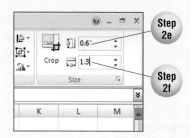

Step
2e

Step
2f

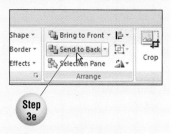

Step
3e

Drawing and Formatting a Text Box

Use the Text Box button in the Insert tab to draw a text box in a worksheet. To
draw a text box, click the Insert tab and then click the Text Box button in the Text
group. This causes the mouse pointer to display as a thin, down-pointing arrow.
Position the arrow in the worksheet and then drag to create the text box. When
a text box is selected, the Drawing Tools Format tab displays with options for
customizing the text box.

Click a text box to select it and a dashed border and sizing handles display
around the text box. If you want to delete the text box, click the text box border
again to change the dashed border lines to solid border lines and then press the
Delete key.

QUICK STEPS

Draw Text Box
1. Click Insert tab.
2. Click Text Box button.
3. Drag in worksheet to
   create text box.

Text
Box

Project 4D Inserting and Formatting a Text Box

1. With **ExcelL1_C8_P4.xlsx** open,
   draw a text box by completing the
   following steps:
   a. Click the Insert tab.
   b. Click the Text Box button in the
      Text group.
   c. Drag in cell A1 to draw a text box
      the approximate size and shape
      shown at the right.

Step
1c

2. Format the text box by completing the
   following steps:
   a. Make sure the Drawing Tools Format tab
      is active.
   b. Click the Shape Fill button arrow in the
      Shape Styles group and then click *No Fill*
      at the drop-down gallery.
   c. Click the Shape Outline button arrow in
      the Shape Styles group and then click *No
      Outline* at the drop-down gallery.

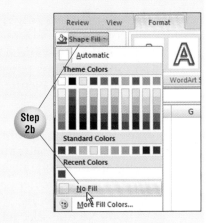

Step
2b

3. Insert text in the text box by completing the
   following steps:
   a. With the text box selected, click the
      Home tab.
   b. Click the Font button arrow and then click *Lucida Calligraphy* at the drop-down gallery.
      (You will need to scroll down the gallery to display this font.)
   c. Click the Font Size button arrow and then click *32* at the drop-down gallery.
   d. Click the Font Color button arrow and then click *White, Background 1* (first option in the
      first row in the *Theme Colors* section).
   e. Type **Seabird Productions**.
4. Move the text box so the text is positioned in cell A1 as shown in Figure 8.9. If necessary,
   move the bird clip art image. (To move the bird image, you may need to move the text box
   so you can select the image. Move the text box back to the desired location after moving
   the bird image.)
5. Save, print, and then close **ExcelL1_C8_P4.xlsx**.

Figure 8.9 Projects 4a and 4b

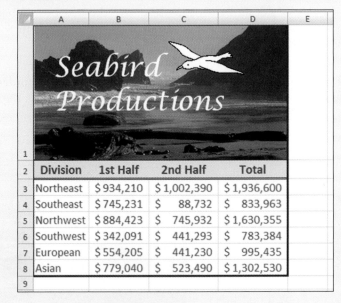

Division	1st Half	2nd Half	Total
Northeast	$934,210	$1,002,390	$1,936,600
Southeast	$745,231	$ 88,732	$ 833,963
Northwest	$884,423	$ 745,932	$1,630,355
Southwest	$342,091	$ 441,293	$ 783,384
European	$554,205	$ 441,230	$ 995,435
Asian	$779,040	$ 523,490	$1,302,530

Project ⑤ Insert a Watermark in an Equipment Usage Workbook

You will open an equipment usage report workbook and then insert a picture watermark that prints on both pages of the worksheet.

Inserting a Picture as a Watermark

A watermark is a lightened image that displays behind data in a file. You can create a watermark in a Word document but the watermark functionality is not available in Excel. You can, however, insert a picture in a header or footer and then resize and format the picture to display behind each page of the worksheet.

To create a picture watermark in a worksheet, click the Insert tab and then click the Header & Footer button in the Text group. With the worksheet in Print Layout view, click the Picture button in the Header & Footer Elements group in the Header & Footer Tools Design tab. At the Insert Picture dialog box, navigate to the desired folder and then double-click the desired picture. This inserts &[Picture] in the header. Resize and format the picture by clicking the Format Picture button in the Header & Footer Elements group. Use options at the Format Picture dialog box with the Size tab selected to specify the size of the picture and use options in the dialog box with the Picture tab selected to specify brightness and contrast.

QUICK STEPS

Insert Picture as Watermark
1. Click Insert tab.
2. Click Header & Footer button.
3. Click Picture button.
4. Navigate to desired folder.
5. Double-click desired picture.

Picture

Format Picture

Project ⑤ Inserting a Picture as a Watermark

1. Open **ExcelC08Project05.xlsx** and then save the workbook and name it **ExcelL1_C8_P5**.
2. Insert a picture as a watermark by completing the following steps:
   a. Click the Insert tab.
   b. Click the Header & Footer button in the Text group.
   c. Click the Picture button in the Header & Footer Elements group in the Header & Footer Tools Design tab.
   d. At the Insert Picture dialog box, navigate to the Excel2007L1C8 folder on your storage medium and then double-click *Olympics.jpg*.
   e. Click the Format Picture button in the Header & Footer Elements group.
   f. At the Format Picture dialog box with the Size tab selected, click the *Lock aspect ratio* in the *Scale* section to remove the check mark.
   g. Select the current measurement in the *Height* measurement box in the *Size and rotate* section and then type 10.
   h. Select the current measurement in the *Width* measurement box in the *Size and rotate* section and then type 7.5.

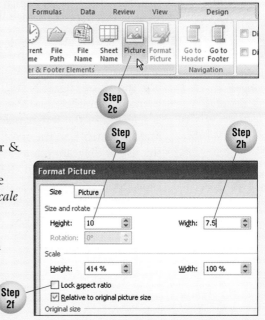

i. Click the Picture tab.
j. At the Format Picture dialog box with the Picture tab selected, select the current percentage number in the *Brightness* option box in the *Image control* section and then type 75.
k. Select the current percentage number in the *Contrast* option box and then type 25.
l. Click OK to close the Format Picture dialog box.
3. Click in the worksheet.
4. Display the worksheet in Print Preview to view how the image will print on page 1 and page 2 and then close Print Preview.
5. Save, print, and then close **ExcelL1_C8_P5.xlsx**. (If you are printing on a laser printer, the text may not print in the worksheet. Check with your instructor before printing this worksheet.)

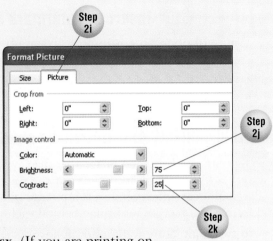

Step 2i

Step 2j

Step 2k

Project ⑥ Insert and Format Diagrams in a Company Sales Workbook

You will open a workbook that contains two company sales worksheets. You will insert and format a cycle diagram in one worksheet and insert and format a relationship diagram in the other. You will also create and format WordArt text.

Inserting a SmartArt Diagram

QUICK STEPS

Insert SmartArt Diagram
1. Click Insert tab.
2. Click SmartArt button.
3. Double-click desired diagram.

HINT
Generally, you would use a SmartArt diagram to represent text and a chart to represent numbers.

SmartArt

Excel includes the SmartArt feature you can use to insert diagrams and organizational charts in a worksheet. SmartArt offers a variety of predesigned diagrams and organizational charts that are available at the Choose a SmartArt Graphic dialog box shown in Figure 8.10. Display this dialog box by clicking the Insert tab and then clicking the SmartArt button in the Illustrations group. At the dialog box, *All* is selected in the left panel and all available predesigned diagrams display in the middle panel. Use the scroll bar at the right side of the middle panel to scroll down the list of diagram choices. Click a diagram in the middle panel and the name of the diagram displays in the right panel along with a description of the diagram type. SmartArt includes diagrams for presenting a list of data; showing data processes, cycles, and relationships; and presenting data in a matrix or pyramid. Double-click a diagram in the middle panel of the dialog box and the diagram is inserted in the worksheet.

Figure 8.10 Choose a SmartArt Graphic Dialog Box

Double-click the desired SmartArt graphic in this panel.

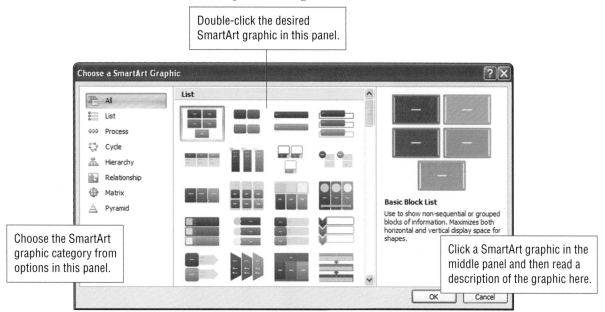

Choose the SmartArt graphic category from options in this panel.

Click a SmartArt graphic in the middle panel and then read a description of the graphic here.

Entering Data in a Diagram

Some diagrams are designed to include text. You can type text in a diagram by selecting the shape and then typing text in the shape or you can display a text pane and then type text in the pane. Display the text pane by clicking the Text Pane button in the Create Graphic group in the SmartArt Tools Design tab. Turn off the display of the pane by clicking the Text Pane button or by clicking the Close button that displays in the upper right corner of the text pane.

Sizing, Moving, and Deleting a Diagram

Increase or decrease the size of a diagram by dragging the diagram border. Increase or decrease the width of the diagram by positioning the mouse pointer on the set of four dots that displays in the middle of the left and right borders until the pointer turns into a left- and right-pointing arrow, hold down the left mouse button and then drag the border to the desired size. Increase or decrease the height of the diagram in a similar manner using the set of four dots that displays in the middle of the top and bottom borders. To increase or decrease both the height and the width of the diagram, drag one of the sets of three dots that displays in each corner of the border.

To move a diagram, select the diagram and then position the mouse pointer on the diagram border until the pointer turns into a four-headed arrow. Hold down the left mouse button, drag the diagram to the desired position, and then release the mouse button. Delete a diagram by selecting the diagram and then pressing the Delete key.

1. Open **ExcelC08Project06.xlsx** and then save the workbook and name it **ExcelL1_C8_P6**.
2. Create the diagram shown in Figure 8.11. To begin, click the Insert tab.
3. Click the SmartArt button in the Illustrations group.
4. At the Choose a SmartArt Graphic dialog box, click *Cycle* in the left panel.
5. Double-click *Radial Cycle* as shown at the right.
6. If the text pane is not open, click the Text Pane button in the Create Graphic group. (The text pane will display at the left side of the diagram.)
7. With the insertion point positioned after the top bullet in the text pane, type **Evergreen Products**.
8. Click the *[Text]* box below *Evergreen Products* and then type **Seattle**.
9. Click the next *[Text]* box and then type **Olympia**.
10. Click the next *[Text]* box and then type **Portland**.
11. Click the next *[Text]* box and then type **Spokane**.
12. Click the Text Pane button to turn off the display of the text pane.
13. Drag the diagram so it is positioned as shown in Figure 8.11. To drag the diagram, position the mouse pointer on the diagram border until the pointer turns into a four-headed arrow. Hold down the left mouse button, drag the diagram to the desired position, and then release the mouse button.
14. Increase or decrease the size of the diagram so it displays as shown in Figure 8.11. Use the sets of dots on the diagram border to drag the border to the desired size.
15. Save **ExcelL1_C8_P6.xlsx**.

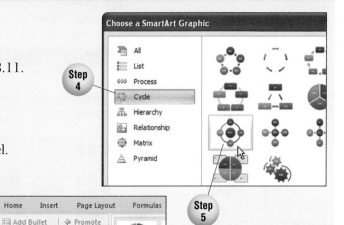

Step 4

Step 5

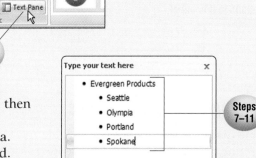

Step 6

Steps 7–11

HINT

To restore the SmartArt default layout and color, click the Reset Graphic button in the Reset group in the SmartArt Tools Design tab.

Changing the Diagram Design

When you double-click a diagram at the dialog box, the diagram is inserted in the worksheet and the SmartArt Tools Design tab is active. With options and buttons in this tab, you can add objects, change the diagram layout, apply a style to the diagram, and reset the diagram back to the original formatting.

Project ⑥ᵇ Changing the Diagram Design

1. With **ExcelL1_C8_P6.xlsx** open, make sure the SmartArt Tools Design tab is active and the *Spokane* circle shape is selected.
2. Click the Right to Left button in the Create Graphic group. (This switches *Olympia* and *Spokane*.)
3. Click the More button located at the right side of the SmartArt Styles group and then click the *Polished* option at the drop-down list (first option from the left in the top row of the *3-D* section).

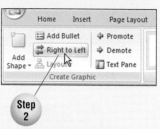

Step 2

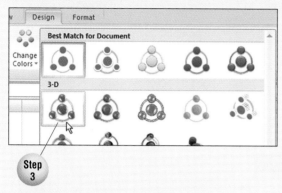

Step 3

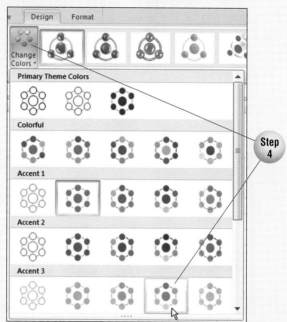

Step 4

4. Click the Change Colors button in the SmartArt Styles group and then click the fourth option from the left in the *Accent 3* section (*Gradient Loop - Accent 3*).
5. Click outside the diagram to deselect it.
6. Change the orientation to landscape. (Make sure the diagram fits on the first page.)
7. Save **ExcelC1_C8_P6.xlsx** and then print the Total Sales worksheet.

Figure 8.11 **Projects 6a and 6b**

	A	B	C	D	E	F	G	H	I
1	**Evergreen Products**								
2	2010 Company Sales								
3	Division	First Half	Second Half	Total Sales					
4	Seattle	$ 1,250,360	$ 1,345,200	$ 2,595,560					
5	Spokane	$ 905,250	$ 987,550	$ 1,892,800					
6	Portland	$ 1,125,000	$ 1,200,500	$ 2,325,500					
7	Olympia	$ 705,610	$ 789,450	$ 1,495,060					
8	Total	$ 3,986,220	$ 4,322,700	$ 8,308,920					
9									

Changing the Diagram Formatting

Click the SmartArt Tools Format tab and options display for formatting a diagram. Use buttons in this tab to insert and customize shapes; apply a shape quick style; customize shapes; insert WordArt quick styles; and specify the position, alignment, rotation, wrapping style, height, and width of the diagram.

Project **6c** **Changing the Diagram Formatting**

1. With **ExcelL1_C8_P6.xlsx** open, click the Seattle Sales worksheet tab.
2. Create the diagram shown in Figure 8.12. To begin, click the Insert tab and then click the SmartArt button in the Illustrations group.
3. At the Choose a SmartArt Graphic dialog box, click *Relationship* in the left panel and then double-click *Gear* in the middle panel.

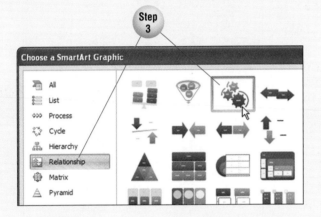

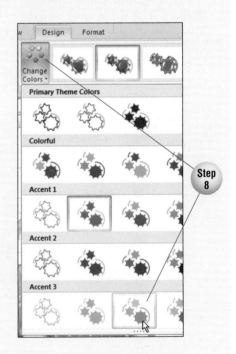

4. Click *[Text]* that appears in the bottom gear and then type **Quality Products**.
5. Click *[Text]* that appears in the left gear and then type **Customized Plans**.
6. Click *[Text]* that appears in the top gear and then type **Exemplary Service**.
7. Click the More button that displays at the right side of the SmartArt Styles group and then click the *Inset* option (second option from the left in the top row of the *3-D* section).
8. Click the Change Colors button in the SmartArt Styles group and then click the third option from the left in the *Accent 3* section (*Gradient Range - Accent 3*).
9. Click the SmartArt Tools Format tab.

10. Click the Size button located at the right side of the tab.
11. Click in the *Height* text box and then type 3.75.
12. Click in the *Width* text box, type 5.25, and then press Enter.

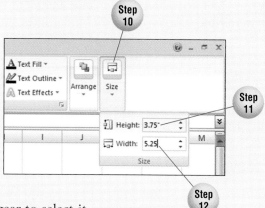

Step 10

Step 11

Step 12

13. Click the bottom gear to select it.
14. Click the Shape Fill button arrow in the Shape Styles group and then click the bottom dark green color (*Olive Green, Accent 3, Darker 50%*) that displays in the *Theme Colors* section.
15. Click the top gear to select it.
16. Click the Shape Fill button arrow and then click the dark green color (*Olive Green, Accent 3, Darker 25%*) that displays in the *Theme Colors* section.
17. Change the orientation to landscape.
18. Move the diagram so it fits on the first page and displays as shown in Figure 8.12.
19. Save **ExcelL1_C8_P6.xlsx** and then print the Seattle Sales worksheet.

Step 14

Figure 8.12 Project 6c

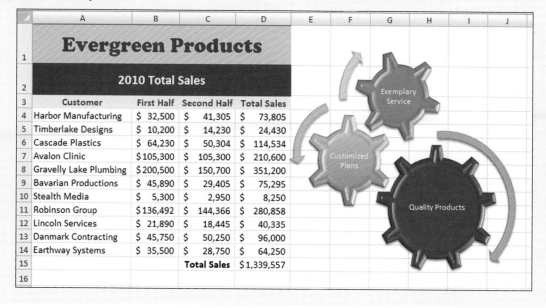

Creating WordArt

With the WordArt application, you can distort or modify text to conform to a variety of shapes. This is useful for creating company logos and headings. With WordArt, you can change the font, style, and alignment of text. You can also use different fill patterns and colors, customize border lines, and add shadow and three-dimensional effects.

To insert WordArt in an Excel worksheet, click the Insert tab, click the WordArt button in the Text group, and then click the desired option at the drop-down list. This displays *Your Text Here* inserted in the worksheet in the WordArt option you selected at the gallery. Type the desired text and then use the buttons on the Drawing Tools Format tab to format the WordArt.

Sizing and Moving WordArt

WordArt text inserted in a worksheet is surrounded by white sizing handles. Use the white sizing handles to change the height and width of the WordArt text. To move WordArt text, position the arrow pointer on the border of the WordArt until the pointer displays with a four-headed arrow attached. Hold down the left mouse button, drag the outline of the WordArt text box to the desired position, and then release the mouse button. When you change the shape of the WordArt text, the WordArt border displays with a purple diamond shape. Use this shape to change the slant of the WordArt text.

Project 6d Inserting and Formatting WordArt

1. With **ExcelL1_C8_P6.xlsx** open, click the Total Sales worksheet tab.
2. Make cell A1 active and then press the Delete key. (This removes the text from the cell.)
3. Increase the height of row 1 to 136.50.
4. Click the Insert tab.
5. Click the WordArt button in the Text group and then click the last option in the top row (*Fill - Accent 3, Outline - Text 2*).

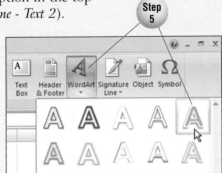

6. Type **Evergreen**, press the Enter key, and then type **Products**.
7. Position the mouse pointer on the WordArt border until the pointer displays with a four-headed arrow attached and then drag the WordArt inside cell A1.

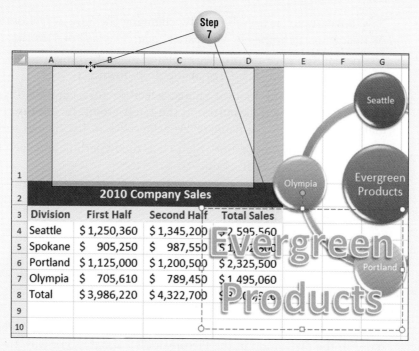

Step 7

8. Click the Text Fill button arrow in the WordArt Styles group and then click the dark green color (*Olive Green, Accent 3, Darker 25%*).
9. Click the Text Outline button arrow in the WordArt Styles group and then click the dark green color (*Olive Green, Accent 3, Darker 50%*).
10. Resize the chart and position it so it prints on one page with the data.
11. Click the Seattle Sales worksheet tab and then complete steps similar to those in Steps 2 through 10 to insert *Evergreen Products* as WordArt.
12. Save **ExcelL1_C8_P6.xlsx** and then print both worksheets.
13. Close **ExcelL1_C8_P6.xlsx**.

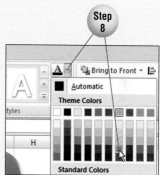

Step 8

CHAPTER summary

- Save a workbook as a Web page by changing the *Save as type* option at the Save As dialog box to *Single File Web Page (*.mht; *.mhtml)* or *Web Page (*.htm; *.html)*.

- To open a Web page in Internet Explorer, open the browser, click File on the Menu bar, and then click *Open* at the drop-down list.

- To create a hyperlink in a workbook, select the text, click the Insert tab, and then click the Hyperlink button in the Links group. At the Insert Hyperlink dialog box, type the file name or Web site URL in the *Address* text box.

- To modify or edit a hyperlink, right-click the hyperlink and then click *Edit Hyperlink* at the shortcut menu.

- Insert symbols with options at the Symbol dialog box with the Symbols tab or the Special Characters tab selected. Click the Insert tab and then click the Symbol button to display the dialog box.

- With buttons in the Illustrations group in the Insert tab, you can insert a picture, clip art image, shapes, or a SmartArt diagram.

- When you insert a picture or clip art image in a worksheet, the Picture Tools Format tab is active and includes options for adjusting the image, applying preformatted styles, and arranging and sizing the image.

- Change the size of an image with the *Shape Height* and *Shape Width* measurement boxes in the Size group in the Picture Tools Format tab or with the sizing handles that display around the selected image.

- Move an image by positioning the mouse pointer on the image border until the pointer displays with a four-headed arrow attached and then drag the image to the desired location.

- Delete a selected image by pressing the Delete key.

- Rotate an image by positioning the mouse pointer on the green rotation handle until the pointer displays as a circular arrow and then dragging in the desired direction.

- Insert an image in a workbook with options at the Clip Art task pane. Display this task pane by clicking the Insert tab and then clicking the Clip Art button in the Illustrations group.

- With options at the Clip Art task pane, you can narrow the search for images to specific locations and to specific images.

- To draw shapes in a workbook, click the Insert tab, click the Shapes button in the Illustrations group, and then click the desired shape at the drop-down list. Drag in the worksheet to draw the shape. To maintain the proportions of the shape, hold down the Shift key while dragging in the worksheet.

- Copy a shape with the Copy and Paste buttons in the Clipboard group in the Home tab or by holding down the Ctrl key while dragging the shape.

- You can type text in an enclosed drawn object.

- To insert a picture in a worksheet, click the Insert tab and then click the Picture button in the Illustrations group. At the Insert Picture dialog box, navigate to the desired folder and then double-click the file name.

- Draw a text box in a worksheet by clicking the Insert tab, clicking the Text Box button in the Text group and then dragging in the worksheet. Use options at the Drawing Tools Format tab to format and customize the text box.
- A watermark is a lightened image that displays behind data in a file. You can create a picture watermark in a worksheet by inserting a picture in a header or footer and then changing the size and formatting of the picture.
- Insert a SmartArt diagram in a worksheet by clicking the Insert tab, clicking the SmartArt button in the Illustrations group, and then double-clicking the desired diagram at the Choose a SmartArt Graphic dialog box. Customize a diagram with options in the SmartArt Tools Design tab or the SmartArt Tools Format tab.
- Use WordArt to create, distort, modify, and/or conform text to a variety of shapes. Insert WordArt in a worksheet by clicking the Insert tab, clicking the WordArt button in the Text group, and then clicking the desired option at the drop-down list.
- Customize WordArt text with options in the Drawing Tools Format tab.
- Size WordArt using the sizing handles that display around selected WordArt text and move selected WordArt by dragging it to the desired location using the mouse.

COMMANDS review

FEATURE	RIBBON TAB, GROUP	BUTTON	KEYBOARD SHORTCUT
Insert Hyperlink dialog box	Insert, Links		Ctrl + K
Symbol dialog box	Insert, Text		
Clip Art task pane	Insert, Illustrations		
Shapes drop-down list	Insert, Illustrations		
Insert Picture dialog box	Insert, Illustrations		
Text box	Insert, Text		
Choose a SmartArt Graphic dialog box	Insert, Illustrations		
WordArt drop-down list	Insert, Text		

CONCEPTS check

Test Your Knowledge

Completion: In the space provided at the right, indicate the correct term, symbol, or command.

1. Change the *Save as type* option at the Save As dialog box to this to save the open workbook as a single Web page. _____

2. Click the Insert tab and then click the Hyperlink button and this dialog box displays. _____

3. The Symbol button is located in this tab. _____

4. The *Font* option is available at the Symbol dialog box with this tab selected. _____

5. Insert a picture, clip art image, shape, or SmartArt diagram with buttons in this group in the Insert tab. _____

6. When you insert a picture or clip art image in a worksheet, this tab is active. _____

7. Maintain the proportions of the image by holding down this key while dragging a sizing handle. _____

8. To move an image, position the mouse pointer on the image border until the mouse pointer displays with this attached and then drag the image to the desired location. _____

9. To copy a shape, hold down this key while dragging the shape. _____

10. When you draw a text box in a worksheet and then release the mouse button, this tab is active. _____

11. This term refers to a lightened image that displays behind data in a file. _____

12. Click the SmartArt button in the Illustrations group in the Insert tab and this dialog box displays. _____

SKILLS check

Demonstrate Your Proficiency

Assessment

1 INSERT A TEXT BOX IN AND SAVE A BOOK CLUB WORKBOOK AS A WEB PAGE

1. Display the Open dialog box with Excel2007L1C8 the active folder.
2. Open **ExcelC08Assessment01.xlsx** and then save the workbook and name it **ExcelL1_C8_A1**.
3. Draw a text box at the right side of the Books Galore clip art image with the following specifications:
   a. Change the height to 1.7″ and the width to 2.7″.
   b. Remove the text box outline.
   c. Click the Middle Align button and the Center button in the Alignment group in the Home tab.
   d. Change the font to 32-point Forte and change the font color to blue.
   e. Type **Book of the Month Club News, 2010** in the text box.
4. Change the orientation to landscape.
5. Save and then print **ExcelL1_C8_A1.xlsx**.
6. Save **ExcelL1_C8_A1.xlsx** as a single Web page in the ExcelWebPages folder (you created this folder in Project 8a) on your storage medium and name it **BooksGaloreWebPage**.
7. Open Internet Explorer and then open **BooksGaloreWebPage.mht**.
8. Close Internet Explorer.
9. Print **BooksGaloreWebPage.mht** in landscape orientation.
10. Select E12 and hyperlink it to *www.microsoft.com*.
11. Select E13 and hyperlink it to *www.symantec.com*.
12. Select E14 and hyperlink it to *www.nasa.gov*.
13. Select E15 and hyperlink it to *www.cnn.com*.
14. Make sure you are connected to the Internet and then click the hyperlink to NASA.
15. Jump to a link from the NASA Web page that interests you.
16. Print the page you viewed from NASA and then close the browser application window.
17. Jump to each of the remaining links in the Web page. At each Web page, jump to a link that interests you, print the page, and then close the browser application window.
18. Save (click Yes at the compatibility dialog box) and then close **BooksGaloreWebPage.mht**.

2 INSERT A CLIP ART IMAGE AND WORDART IN AN EQUIPMENT PURCHASE WORKBOOK

1. Open **ExcelC08Assessment02.xlsx** and then save the workbook and name it **ExcelL1_C8_A2**.
2. Insert a formula in cell E4 using the PMT function that calculates monthly payments. *Hint: Refer to Chapter 2, Project 3a.*
3. Copy the formula in cell E4 down to cells E5 and E6.
4. Insert a formula in cell F4 that calculates the total amount of the payments. *Hint: Refer to Chapter 2, Project 3a.*
5. Copy the formula in cell F4 down to cells F5 and F6.
6. Insert a formula in cell G4 that calculates to the total amount of interest paid. *Hint: Refer to Chapter 2, Project 3a.*
7. Copy the formula in cell G4 down to cells G5 and G6.
8. Increase the height of row 1 to 75.00.
9. Delete *BAYSIDE TRAVEL* in cell A1.
10. Insert the clip art image shown in Figure 8.13 (search for this clip art by searching only for clip art images [remove check marks from *Photographs, Movies,* and *Sound*] and typing **travel** in the *Search for* text box). If this clip art image is not available, choose another image related to travel. (Before closing the Clip Art task pane, reinsert check marks in the *Photographs, Movies,* and *Sound* check boxes at the *Results should be* option drop-down list.)
11. Size and move the clip art image so it is positioned as shown in Figure 8.13.
12. Insert the company name as WordArt as shown in Figure 8.13 with the following specifications:
    a. Create the WordArt with the second option from the left in the bottom row of the WordArt drop-down list (*Fill - Accent 6, Warm Matte Bevel*).
    b. Select the WordArt text, click the Text Fill button arrow in the WordArt Styles group, and then click the light blue color (in the *Standard Colors* section) at the drop-down gallery.
13. Change the worksheet orientation to landscape
14. Save, print, and then close **ExcelL1_C8_A2.xlsx**.

Figure 8.13 Assessment 2

	Equipment	Purchase Price	Interest Rate	Term in Months	Monthly Payments	Total Payments	Total Interest
4	Photocopier, Model C120	$ 8,500.00	8.80%	60			
5	Photocopier, Model C150	$12,750.00	8.80%	60			
6	Photocopier, Model C280	$19,250.00	8.80%	60			

Assessment 3

INSERT AND FORMAT SHAPES IN A COMPANY SALES WORKBOOK

1. Open **ExcelC08Assessment03.xlsx** and then save the workbook and name it **ExcelL1_C8_A3**.
2. In cell A1, type **Mountain**, press Alt + Enter, and then type **Systems**.
3. Select *Mountain Systems* and then change the font to 24-point Calibri bold.
4. Change the horizontal alignment of cell A1to left and the vertical alignment to center.
5. Display the Format Cells dialog box with the Alignment tab selected and then change the *Indent* measurement to *1*. ***Hint: Display the Format Cells dialog box by clicking the Alignment group dialog box launcher in the Home tab.***
6. Click outside cell A1.
7. Use the *Isosceles Triangle* shape located in the *Basic Shapes* section of the Shapes drop-down palette to draw a triangle as shown in Figure 8.14.
8. Copy the triangle three times. Add green fill, dark green outline color, and a shadow effect of your choosing to the triangles so they appear in a similar manner to the triangles in Figure 8.14. Position the triangles as shown in the figure.
9. Save, print, and then close **ExcelL1_C8_A3.xlsx**.

Figure 8.14 Assessment 3

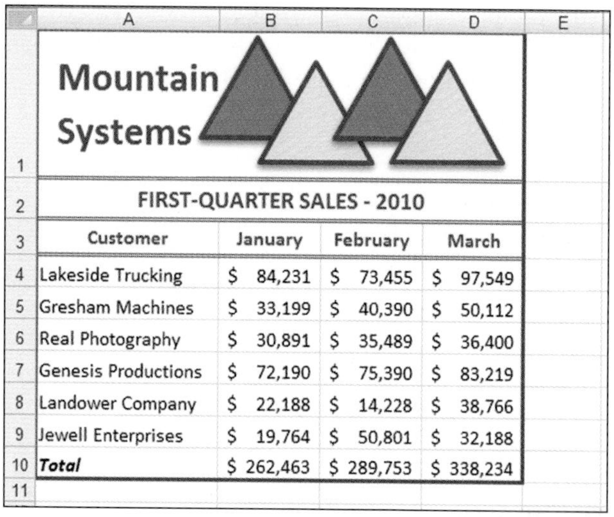

	A	B	C	D	E
1	Mountain Systems				
2	FIRST-QUARTER SALES - 2010				
3	Customer	January	February	March	
4	Lakeside Trucking	$ 84,231	$ 73,455	$ 97,549	
5	Gresham Machines	$ 33,199	$ 40,390	$ 50,112	
6	Real Photography	$ 30,891	$ 35,489	$ 36,400	
7	Genesis Productions	$ 72,190	$ 75,390	$ 83,219	
8	Landower Company	$ 22,188	$ 14,228	$ 38,766	
9	Jewell Enterprises	$ 19,764	$ 50,801	$ 32,188	
10	*Total*	$ 262,463	$ 289,753	$ 338,234	
11					

Assessment 4

INSERT AND FORMAT A SMARTART DIAGRAM IN A SALES WORKBOOK

1. Open **ExcelC08Assessment04.xlsx** and then save the workbook and name it **ExcelL1_C8_A4**.
2. Change the orientation to landscape.
3. Insert a pyramid shape at the right side of the worksheet data using the *Basic Pyramid* SmartArt diagram and insert the following information in the pyramid:
   a. In the bottom shape, type **Red Level**, press Enter, and then type **$25,000 - $49,999**.

b. In the middle shape, type **Blue Level**, press Enter, and then type $50,000 - $99,999.

c. In the top shape, type **Gold Level**, press Enter, and then type $100,000+.

d. Change the font size and/or move the text so the text displays in each shape.

e. Change the color of the shapes to match the color level.

f. If necessary, change the color of the text inside the shapes so it is easy to read.

g. Size and/or move the diagram so it displays attractively at the right side of the worksheet data. (Make sure the entire diagram will print on the same page as the worksheet data.)

4. Save, print, and then close **ExcelL1_C8_A4.xlsx**.

Assessment

5 APPLY CONDITIONAL FORMATTING TO CELLS IN A SALES WORKBOOK

1. Using the Help feature, learn about applying conditional formatting to numbers in cells that match a specific range.

2. Open **ExcelL1_C8_A4.xlsx** and then save the workbook and name it **ExcelL1_C8_A5**.

3. Using the conditional formatting feature, apply the following formatting to amounts in the *Total* column:

a. Apply red color formatting to numbers between $25,000 and $49,999.

b. Apply blue color formatting to numbers between $50,000 and $99,999.

c. Apply gold color formatting to numbers between $100,000 and $500,000.

4. Save, print, and then close **ExcelL1_C8_A5.xlsx**.

CASE study

Apply Your Skills

Part 1

You are the office manager for Ocean Truck Sales and are responsible for maintaining a spreadsheet of the truck and SUV inventory. Open **ExcelC08Ocean.xlsx** and then save the workbook and name it **ExcelL1_C8_CS_P1**. Apply formatting to improve the appearance of the worksheet and insert at least one clip art image (related to "truck" or "ocean"). Save **ExcelL1_C8_CS_P1.xlsx** and then print the worksheet.

Part 2

You have been asked to save the inventory worksheet as a Web page for viewing online and also to insert hyperlinks to various sites. With **ExcelL1_C8_CS_P1.xlsx** open, locate at least one financial institution in your area that will finance an automobile and then insert in the worksheet a hyperlink to that site. Locate another site that provides information on book value of a used automobile and then insert in the worksheet a hyperlink to that site. Save the workbook as a single Web page with the name **ExcelC08OceanWebPage**. Open your Internet browser and then open the Web page. Click each hyperlink to make sure it takes you to the proper Web site. Close your Internet browser and then close **ExcelC08OceanWebPage.mht**.

Open **ExcelL1_C8_CS_P1.xlsx** and then save it with Save As and name it **ExcelL1_C8_CS_P3**. You make the inventory workbook available to each salesperson at the beginning of the week. For easier viewing, you decide to divide the workbook into two worksheets with one worksheet containing all Ford vehicles and the other worksheet containing all Chevrolet vehicles. Rename the worksheet tabs to reflect the contents. Sort each worksheet by price from the most expensive to the least expensive. The owner offers incentives each week to help motivate the sales force. Insert in the first worksheet a SmartArt diagram of your choosing that contains the following information:

Small-sized truck = $100
2WD Regular Cab = $75
SUV 4x4 = $50

Copy the diagram in the first worksheet and then paste it into the second worksheet. Change the orientation to landscape and then save, print, and close **ExcelL1_C8_CS_P3.xlsx**.

As part of your weekly duties, you need to post the incentive diagram in various locations throughout the company. You decide to insert the diagram in PowerPoint for easy printing. Open **ExcelL1_C8_CS_P3.xlsx** and then open PowerPoint. Change the slide layout in PowerPoint to Blank. Copy the diagram in the first worksheet and paste it into the PowerPoint blank slide. Increase and/or move the diagram so it better fills the slide. Print the slide and then close PowerPoint without saving the presentation. Close **ExcelL1_C8_CS_P3.xlsx**.

Maintaining and Enhancing Workbooks

ASSESSING proficiency

In this unit, you have learned how to work with multiple windows; move, copy, link, and paste data between workbooks and applications; create and customize charts with data in a worksheet; save a workbook as a Web page; insert hyperlinks; and insert and customize pictures, clip art images, shapes, SmartArt diagrams, and WordArt.

Note: Before beginning computer assessments, copy to your storage medium the Excel2007L1U2 subfolder from the Excel2007L1 folder on the CD that accompanies this textbook and then make Excel2007L1U2 the active folder.

Assessment 1 **Copy and Paste Data and Insert WordArt in a Training Scores Workbook**

1. Open **ExcelU02Assessment01.xlsx** and then save the workbook and name it **ExcelL1_U2_A1**.
2. Delete row 15 (the row for *Kwieciak, Kathleen*).
3. Insert a formula in cell D4 that averages the percentages in cells B4 and C4.
4. Copy the formula in cell D4 down to cells D5 through D20.
5. Make cell A22 active, turn on bold, and then type Highest Averages.
6. Display the Clipboard task pane and make sure it is empty.
7. Select and then copy each of the following rows (individually): row 7, 10, 14, 16, and 18.
8. Make cell A23 active and then paste row 14 (the row for *Jewett, Troy*).
9. Make cell A24 active and then paste row 7 (the row for *Cumpston, Kurt*).
10. Make cell A25 active and then paste row 10 (the row for *Fisher-Edwards, Theresa*).
11. Make cell A26 active and then paste row 16 (the row for *Mathias, Caleb*).
12. Make cell A27 active and then paste row 18 (the row for *Nyegaard, Curtis*).
13. Click the Clear All button in the Clipboard task pane and then close the task pane.
14. Insert in cell A1 the text *Roseland* as WordArt. Format the WordArt text to add visual appeal to the worksheet.
15. Save, print, and then close **ExcelL1_U2_A1.xlsx**.

Assessment 2 Manage Multiple Worksheets in a Projected Earnings Workbook

1. Open **ExcelU02Assessment02.xlsx** and then save the workbook and name it **ExcelL1_U2_A2**.
2. Delete *Roseland* in cell A1. Open **ExcelL1_U2_A1.xlsx** and then copy the *Roseland* WordArt text and paste it into cell A1 in **ExcelL1_U2_A2.xlsx**. If necessary, increase the height of row 1 to accommodate the WordArt text.
3. Notice the fill color in cells in **ExcelL1_U2_A1.xlsx** and then apply the same fill color to cells of data in **ExcelL1_U2_A2.xlsx**. Close **ExcelL1_U2_A1.xlsx**.
4. Select cells A1 through C11 and then copy and paste the cells to Sheet2 keeping the source column widths.
5. With Sheet2 displayed, make the following changes:
   a. Increase the height of row 1 to accommodate the WordArt text.
   b. Delete the contents of cell B2.
   c. Change the contents of the following cells:
   - A6: Change *January* to *July*
   - A7: Change *February* to *August*
   - A8: Change *March* to *September*
   - A9: Change *April* to *October*
   - A10: Change *May* to *November*
   - A11: Change *June* to *December*
   - B6: Change *8.30%* to *8.10%*
   - B8: Change *9.30%* to *8.70%*
6. Make Sheet1 active and then copy cell B2 and paste link it to cell B2 in Sheet2.
7. Rename Sheet1 to *First Half* and rename Sheet2 to *Second Half*.
8. Make the First Half worksheet active and then determine the effect on projected monthly earnings if the projected yearly income is increased by 10% by changing the number in cell B2 to *$1,480,380*.
9. Save the workbook (two worksheets) again and then print both worksheets of the workbook so they are horizontally and vertically centered on each page.
10. Determine the effect on projected monthly earnings if the projected yearly income is increased by 20% by changing the number in cell B2 to *$1,614,960*.
11. Save the workbook again and then print both worksheets of the workbook so they are horizontally and vertically centered on each page.
12. Close **ExcelL1_U2_A2.xlsx**.

Assessment 3 Create Charts in Worksheets in a Sales Totals Workbook

1. Open **ExcelU02Assessment03** and then save the workbook and name it **ExcelL1_U2_A3**.
2. Insert the heading **Average Sales 2008-2010** (on multiple lines) in cell A13.
3. Insert a formula in cell B13 with a 3-D reference that averages the total in cells B4 through B11 in Sheet1, Sheet2, and Sheet3.
4. Insert a formula in cell C13 with a 3-D reference that averages the total in cells C4 through C11 in Sheet1, Sheet2, and Sheet3.
5. Rename Sheet1 to *2008 Sales*, rename Sheet2 to *2009 Sales*, and rename Sheet3 to *2010 Sales*.
6. Make the 2008 Sales worksheet active, select cells A3 through C11 and create a column chart. Click the Switch Row/Column button at the Chart Tools Design tab. Apply formatting to increase the visual appeal of the chart. Drag the chart below the worksheet data. (Make sure the chart fits on the page.)

7. Make the 2009 Sales worksheet active and then create the same type of chart you created in Step 6.
8. Make the 2010 Sales worksheet active and then create the same type of chart you created in Step 6.
9. Save the workbook and then print the entire workbook.
10. Close **ExcelL1_U2_A3.xlsx**.

Assessment 4 Create and Format a Line Chart

1. Type the following information in a worksheet:

Country	Total Sales
Denmark	$85,345
Finland	$71,450
Norway	$135,230
Sweden	$118,895

2. Using the data just entered in the worksheet, create a line chart with the following specifications:
   a. Apply a chart style of your choosing.
   b. Insert major and minor primary vertical gridlines.
   c. Insert drop lines. (Do this with the Lines button in the Analysis group in the Chart Tools Layout tab.)
   d. Apply any other formatting to improve the visual appeal of the chart.
   e. Move the chart to a new sheet.
3. Save the workbook and name it **ExcelL1_U2_A4**.
4. Print only the sheet containing the chart.
5. Change the line chart to a bar chart of your choosing.
6. Save the workbook and then print only the sheet containing the chart.
7. Close **ExcelL1_U2_A4.xlsx**.

Assessment 5 Create and Format a Pie Chart

1. Open **ExcelU02Assessment05.xlsx** and then save the workbook and name it **ExcelL1_U2_A5**.
2. Create a pie chart as a separate sheet with the data in cells A3 through B10. You determine the type of pie. Include an appropriate title for the chart and include percentage labels.
3. Print only the sheet containing the chart.
4. Save and then close **ExcelL1_U2_A5.xlsx**.

Assessment 6 Insert a Text Box in and Save a Travel Workbook as a Web Page

1. Open **ExcelU02Assessment06.xlsx** and then save the workbook and name it **ExcelL1_U2_A6**.
2. Insert a text box in the workbook with the following specifications:
   a. Draw the text box at the right side of the clip art image.
   b. Remove the fill in the text box and the outline around the text box.
   c. Type Call 1-888-555-1288 for last-minute vacation specials!
   d. Select the text and then change the font to 20-point Bradley Hand ITC in blue color and turn on bold.
   e. Size and position the text box so it appears visually balanced with the travel clip art image.
3. Make sure you are connected to the Internet and then search for sites that might be of interest to tourists for each of the cities in the worksheet. Write down the URL for the best Web page you find for each city.

4. Create a hyperlink for each city to jump to the URL you wrote down in Step 3. (Select the hyperlink text in each cell and change the font size to 18 points.)
5. Save **ExcelL1_U2_A6.xlsx** and then print the worksheet.
6. Create a new folder named TravelWebPages in the Excel2007L1U2 folder.
7. Save **ExcelL1_U2_A6.xlsx** as a single file Web page in the TravelWebPages folder with the following specifications:
   a. Name the Web page **TravelAdvantageWebPage**.
   b. Change the title to *Winter Getaway Destinations!*
8. Open Internet Explorer and then open **TravelAdvantageWebPage.mht**.
9. Test the hyperlinks to make sure you entered the URLs correctly by clicking each hyperlink and then closing the Web browser.
10. Close **TravelAdvantageWebPage.mht** and then close Internet Explorer.
11. Save and then close **ExcelL1_U2_A6.xlsx**.

Assessment 7 Insert Clip Art Image and Smart Diagram in a Projected Quotas Workbook

1. Open **ExcelU02Assessment07.xlsx** and then save the workbook and name it **ExcelL1_U2_A7**.
2. Insert a formula in cell C3 using an absolute reference to determine the projected quotas at 10% of the current quotas.
3. Copy the formula in cell C3 down to cells C4 through C12.
4. Insert a clip art image in row 1 related to money. You determine the size and position of the clip art image. If necessary, increase the height of the row.
5. Apply the following conditional formatting to the values in cells C3 through C12:
   Apply green color to values from $50,000 to $99,999.
   Apply blue color to values from $100,000 to $149,999.
   Apply red color to values from $150,000 to $200,000.
6. Insert a SmartArt diagram at the right side of the chart that contains three shapes. Insert the quota ranges in the shapes as identified in Step 5 and apply color fill to match the conditional formatting. (For example, type $50,000 to $99,999 in a shape and then apply green fill color to the shape.)
7. Change the orientation to landscape and make sure the diagram fits on the page.
8. Save, print, and then close **ExcelL1_U2_A7.xlsx**.

Assessment 8 Insert Symbol, Clip Art, and Comments in a Sales Workbook

1. Open **ExcelU02Assessment08.xlsx** and then save the workbook and name it **ExcelL1_U2_A8**.
2. Delete the text *Landower Company* and then type **Económico** in the cell. (Use the Symbol dialog box to insert *ó*.)
3. Insert a new row at the beginning of the worksheet.
4. Select and then merge cells A1 through D1.
5. Increase the height of row 1 to approximately 100.50.
6. Insert the text *Custom Interiors* as WordArt in cell A1. You determine the formatting of the WordArt. Move and size the WordArt so it fits in cell A1.
7. Insert the following comments in the specified cells:
   D4 = Increase amount to $100,000.
   A5 = Change the name to Gresham Technology.
   A9 = Decrease amounts for this company by 5%.

8. Turn on the display of all comments.
9. Print the worksheet with the comments as displayed on the worksheet.
10. Turn off the display of all comments.
11. Delete the comment in A5.
12. Print the worksheet again with the comments printed at the end of the worksheet. (The comments will print on a separate page from the worksheet.)
13. Save and then close **ExcelL1_U2_A8.xlsx**.

Assessment 9 Insert and Format a Shape in a Budget Workbook

1. Open **ExcelU02Assessment09.xlsx** and then save the workbook and name it **ExcelL1_U2_A9**.
2. Make the following changes to the worksheet so it displays as shown in Figure U2.1:
   a. Select and then merge cells A1 through D1.
   b. Add fill to the cells as shown in Figure U2.1.
   c. Increase the height of row 1 to the approximate size shown in Figure U2.1.
   d. Insert the text **SOLAR ENTERPRISES** in cell A1 set in 20-point Calibri bold, center and middle aligned, and set in aqua (Aqua, Accent 5, Darker 25%).
   e. Insert the sun shape (located in the *Basic Shapes* section of the Shapes button drop-down list). Apply orange shape fill and change the shape outline to aqua (Aqua, Accent 5, Darker 25%)
3. Save, print, and then close **ExcelL1_U2_A9.xlsx**.

Figure U2.1 Assessment 9

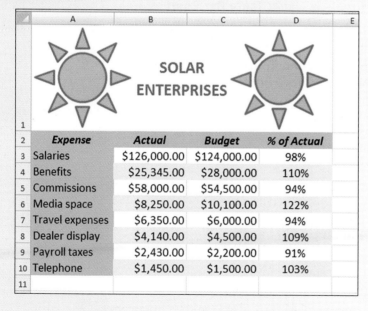

WRITING
activities

The following activities give you the opportunity to practice your writing skills along with demonstrating an understanding of some of the important Excel features you have mastered in this unit. Use correct grammar, appropriate word choices, and clear sentence constructions.

Activity 1 Prepare a Projected Budget

You are the accounting assistant in the financial department of McCormack Funds and you have been asked to prepare a yearly proposed department budget. The total amount for the department is $1,450,000. You are given the percentages for the proposed budget items, which are: Salaries, 45%; Benefits, 12%; Training, 14%; Administrative Costs, 10%; Equipment, 11%; and Supplies, 8%. Create a worksheet with this information that shows the projected yearly budget, the budget items in the department, the percentage of the budget, and the amount for each item. After the worksheet is completed, save the workbook and name it **ExcelL1_U2_Act01**. Print and then close the workbook.

Optional: Using Word 2007, write a memo to the McCormack Funds Finance Department explaining that the proposed annual department budget is attached for their review. Comments and suggestions are to be sent to you within one week. Save the file and name it **ExcelL1_U2_Act01_Memo**. Print and then close the file.

Activity 2 Create a Travel Tours Bar Chart

Prepare a worksheet in Excel for Carefree Travels that includes the following information:

Scandinavian Tours

Country	Tours Booked
Norway	52
Sweden	62
Finland	29
Denmark	38

Use the information in the worksheet to create and format a bar chart as a separate sheet. Save the workbook and name it **ExcelL1_U2_Act02**. Print only the sheet containing the chart and then close **ExcelL1_U2_Act02.xlsx**.

Activity 3 Prepare a Ski Vacation Worksheet

Prepare a worksheet for Carefree Travels that advertises a snow skiing trip. Include the following information in the announcement:

- At the beginning of the worksheet, create a company logo that includes the company name *Carefree Travels* and a clip art image related to travel.
- Include the heading *Whistler Ski Vacation Package* in the worksheet.
- Include the following below the heading:
  - Round-trip air transportation: $395
  - Seven nights' hotel accommodations: $1,550
  - Four all-day ski passes: $425

- Compact rental car with unlimited mileage: $250
- Total price of the ski package: (calculate the total price)
- Include the following information somewhere in the worksheet:
  - Book your vacation today at special discount prices.
  - Two-for-one discount at many of the local ski resorts.

Save the workbook and name it **ExcelL1_U2_Act03**. Print and then close **ExcelL1_U2_Act03.xlsx**.

Find Information on Excel Books and Present the Data in a Worksheet

Locate two companies on the Internet that sell new books. At the first new book company site, locate three books on Microsoft Excel. Record the title, author, and price for each book. At the second new book company site, locate the same three books and record the prices. Create an Excel worksheet that includes the following information:

- Name of each new book company
- Title and author of the three books
- Prices for each book from the two book company sites

Create a hyperlink for each book company to the URL on the Internet. Then save the completed workbook and name it **ExcelL1_U2_InternetResearch**. Print and then close the workbook.

Create a Customized Time Card for a Landscaping Company

You are the manager of a landscaping company and are responsible for employee time cards. Locate the time card template that is available with *Installed Templates* selected in the New Workbook dialog box. Use the template to create a customized time card for your company. With the template open, delete the Company Name that displays in the middle header pane. Insert additional blank rows to increase the spacing above the Employee row. Insert a clip art image related to landscaping or gardening and position and size it attractively in the form. Include a text box with the text Lawn and Landscaping Specialists inside the box. Format, size, and position the text attractively in the form. Fill in the form for the current week with the following employee information:

Employee = Jonathan Holder
Address = 12332 South 152nd Street, Baton Rouge, LA 70804
Manager = (Your name)
Employee phone = (225) 555-3092
Employee e-mail = None

Regular hours = 8 hours for Monday, Tuesday, Wednesday, and Thursday
Overtime = 2 hours on Wednesday
Sick hours = None
Vacation = 8 hours on Friday
Rate per hour = $20.00
Overtime pay = $30.00

Save the completed form and name it **ExcelL1_U2_JobStudy**. Print and then close **ExcelL1_U2_JobStudy.xlsx**.

Microsoft Office
    Excel Help button, 27, 31
    gallery of media images with, 281
    integration allowed by, 185, 189
Microsoft Web site: installing PDF
    add-in download from, 213
Middle Align button, 100
MIN function, 47, 60
Minimize button, 181, 189, 190
Minimum values
    finding, 47–48
    formulas for calculation of, 19,
        37
Mini toolbar: formatting with, 76,
    99
Misspelled words: correcting, 15,
    125
Mixed cell references
    simple interest determined,
        using formula with, 59
    using in formulas, 56, 58, 59
More button, 246, 286, 287, 296
Motion files: viewing, 282
Mouse
    activating cells with, 11
    changing column width with, 68
    copying selected cells with, 160,
        188
    diagrams sized with, 293
    editing data in cells with, 13
    hiding/unhiding columns or
        rows with, 97
    moving or copying worksheets
        with, 167
    moving selected cells with, 159,
        188
    row height changed with, 70, 99
    selecting cells with, 22, 31
    shapes inserted with, 284
Move Chart button, 246, 262
Move Chart dialog box, 246, 262
Move or Copy dialog box, 167,
    207, 208
Moving
    chart labels, 249, 262
    charts, 241
    data, 181
    diagrams, 293
    images, 281, 300
    selected cells, 158–160
    shapes in charts, 253
    WordArt, 298
    workbooks, 181, 199, 200
Multiple absolute cell references:
    inserting and copying
        formulas with, 57
Multiple actions: undoing/redoing,
    126
Multiple worksheets: creating
    workbooks with, 158

Multiplication operator (*):
    formulas written with, 38, 60

N

Name box, 10, 175, 189
    in Excel window, 30
    in Excel worksheet, 8, 9
Name option box: in Print dialog
    box, 124
Names: for workbook files, 11
Name text box: at New Folder
    dialog box, 200
N/A (not applicable) text in cell,
    47, 48
Nested functions, 43
Nested IF condition
    writing, 54–55
    writing a formula with, 54
Nested IF functions: using, 60
New Comment button, 222
New Folder dialog box, 200
New Name dialog box, 175, 189,
    190
New sheet option: in Move Chart
    dialog box, 246, 262
New Workbook dialog box, 227,
    230, 232
Next button, 223
None option: of Format Cells
    dialog box, 91
Normal button, 115
Normal view, 115
    changing size of worksheet
        display in, 80
NOW function, 51, 60
    using, 52
Nper argument: in PMT function,
    50
Number category: in Format Cells
    dialog box, 86
Number Format button, 83, 101
Number formatting: specifying, 67
Number group, 82, 83, 99
Number group buttons: formatting
    numbers with, 82–84
Number group dialog box launcher,
    85, 94
Number of copies option: in Print
    dialog box, 124
Numbers
    automatically inserting in a
        series, 14
    counting in a range, 48
    entering in cells, 11, 30
    filtering, 134
    in folder names, 200
    formatting, 82–87, 99
    formatting, at Format Cells
        dialog box, 85, 86–87

formatting, with Number group
    buttons, 82–84
Number symbols: in cells, 11, 30
Number tab
    in Find Format dialog box, 130
    in Format Cells dialog box, 99

O

Odd pages: headers or footers for,
    121
Office button, 14, 15, 30, 79, 99,
    124, 211, 227, 243, 275
    in Excel window, 30
    in Excel worksheet, 8, 9
Office Clipboard feature
    copying and pasting cells with,
        163
    using, 162–163
Office Online: help resources from,
    29
Office Online Web site: image
    searches at, 283
Offline message, 29
Open button, 177
Open dialog box, 177, 189, 200,
    201, 202, 230, 232, 274
    copying workbook at, 204
    displaying, 18
    toolbar buttons, 200
Options button, 128
Organizational charts: predesigned,
    292
Orientation
    changing, 79
    changing, in worksheets, 110,
        138
Orientation button, 76, 100, 112,
    138, 141
Orientation section: in Format
    Cells dialog box, 88
Or select a category list box: in
    Insert Function dialog box, 44

P

Page Break Preview: worksheets
    displayed in, 115, 120, 139,
        141
Page Break Preview button, 115, 139
Page breaks
    inserting and removing, 114,
        115–116, 141
    inserting in worksheets, 110,
        138
Page formatting: default, for Excel
    worksheets, 110
Page icon, 167
Page Layout group, 99, 138
Page Layout tab, 81, 110, 114,
    116, 118, 119, 120, 139

Level 2

Microsoft® excel

Making Excel Work for You!

Complex analysis of numerical data is made easier with the advanced features in Microsoft Office Excel 2007. Learn to use functions with conditional logic and apply various tools to assist with projecting, analyzing, consolidating, and managing data. By getting accurate results more efficiently, you can use your time to focus on the meaning of the numbers, which will lead to sound decision making and, in the final analysis, a competitive edge for you and your company.

Organizing Information

Naming ranges means you can assign user-friendly names to cells for use in formulas. Using the range name in a calculation makes it clear how a result was obtained. Consider how much easier it is to read and understand the formula *=HoursWorked*PayRate* than to read *=D22*$E$12*. The significance of the formula quickly becomes clear, thanks to the name.

The expression "No one is perfect" fits more often than we like to admit, but with the error checking tools in Excel, perfect work is more attainable. When Excel detects an error in a cell,

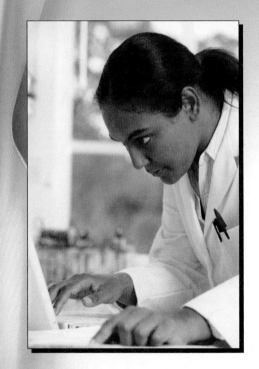

Instruct Excel to circle cells that do not meet the test of a validation rule so that you can check the source data.

Display tracer arrows to help solve a formula error using buttons in the Formula Auditing group in the Formulas tab.

the Trace Error button becomes active with options for helping you find the source of the problem. The Trace Precedents and Trace Dependents buttons can assist with troubleshooting by drawing arrows between cells that reference each other.

Finding specific information in a long worksheet can become cumbersome and time consuming. Using the Table feature makes it easier to manipulate long lists of data. A table range expands automatically to include new rows or columns added to the worksheet. Use Excel's Data features to consolidate data, find duplicate records, or enforce data validation rules to ensure accuracy in the worksheet. The Outline command organizes the worksheet by displaying only the summary rows. Check the summaries and then expand groups that you want to review. Groups can be added or removed to the outline. With Excel's Table, Outline, and Subtotal features, those long worksheets are now much easier to navigate.

Analyzing Information

The conditional formatting feature allows you to use the what-if decision making capability for applying formats to cells. For example, assume you have an insurance claim worksheet with data organized by client including number of claims, number of automobiles, rating, liability limits, and so on. At a glance, you want to see clients with more than two claims reported. Rather than pore over the data yourself, use conditional formatting to instruct Excel to apply a different color and/or fill to highlight the clients with more frequent claims. You can also visually organize the number of autos covered in a policy using icons, or apply data bars formatting to make higher claim cost clients stand out in the worksheet. Within seconds, the visual clues added to the worksheet allow you to pinpoint the higher risk clients.

Today's employers often require that two or more people at the same or different workplace work together on financial

Click the outline level number or individual show detail or hide detail buttons to view billings by individual attorney, view subtotals by attorney, or view only the grand total.

This worksheet is outlined with three levels of detail. Subtotals have been added to view the billings associated with individual attorneys.

Use data bar conditional formatting to visually compare numbers.

This column is conditionally formatted with an icon set to visually organize like items.

This column is conditionally formatted to highlight cells with more than two claims.

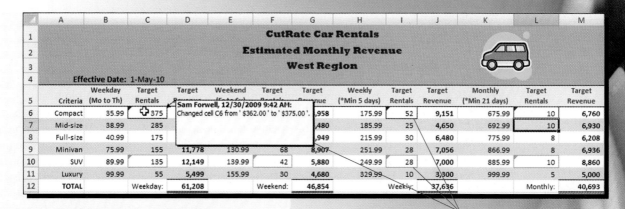

	A	B	C	D	E	F	G	H	I	J	K	L	M
1						**CutRate Car Rentals**							
2						**Estimated Monthly Revenue**							
3						**West Region**							
4	**Effective Date:**	1-May-10											
5	Criteria	Weekday (Mo to Th)	Target Rentals	Target Revenue	Weekend (Fr to Su)	Target Rentals	Target Revenue	Weekly (*Min 5 days)	Target Rentals	Target Revenue	Monthly (*Min 21 days)	Target Rentals	Target Revenue
6	Compact	35.99	375	Sam Forwell, 12/30/2009 9:42 AM: Changed cell C6 from ' $362.00 ' to ' $375.00 '.	,958		175.99	52	9,151	675.99	10	6,760	
7	Mid-size	38.99	285		,480		185.99	25	4,650	692.99	10	6,930	
8	Full-size	40.99	175		,949		215.99	30	6,480	775.99	8	6,208	
9	Minivan	75.99	155	11,778	130.99	68	8,907	251.99	28	7,056	866.99	8	6,936
10	SUV	89.99	135	12,149	139.99	42	5,880	249.99	28	7,000	885.99	10	8,860
11	Luxury	99.99	55	5,499	155.99	30	4,680	329.99	10	3,300	999.99	5	5,000
12	**TOTAL**		Weekday:	61,208		Weekend:	46,854		Weekly:	37,636		Monthly:	40,693

Excel tracks changes made to a shared workbook automatically. Display an individual's change by pointing to a cell, and/or create a History sheet to view a summary of all changes made. Excel uses different colored boxes for different authors.

worksheets, research data, or other tracking of columnar information. Excel features that accommodate this collaboration among workers include the ability to share a workbook, track changes, and accept or reject changes made by multiple authors.

While using these tools to help facilitate a team project, you and your managers can rest assured that the confidential information is secure by protecting cells, worksheets, and workbooks, assigning passwords, or attaching a digital signature for authentication.

Excel's Goal Seek, Data Table, and Scenario Manager tools assist decision makers by calculating solutions or displaying multiple what-if alternatives. In each case you specify the cells containing the constraints or variables and instruct Excel on how to arrive at the result you are looking for. Use Goal Seek to calculate a value when you have only one changing variable. When more than one factor affects your decision, or you want to view a variety of outcomes based on changing cells to different inputs, consider using Scenario Manager to define every set of circumstances and then view how each scenario affects the final outcome. Scenario Manager can also produce a summary worksheet that provides an easy comparison of the stored variables and the impact on the target cell. One-variable or two-variable data tables allow you to create an array of alternative outcomes to a formula. Help with those difficult decisions is just a few mouse clicks away!

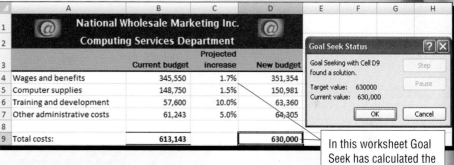

	A	B	C	D
1		**National Wholesale Marketing Inc.**		
2		**Computing Services Department**		
3		Current budget	Projected increase	New budget
4	Wages and benefits	345,550	1.7%	351,354
5	Computer supplies	148,750	1.5%	150,981
6	Training and development	57,600	10.0%	63,360
7	Other administrative costs	61,243	5.0%	64,305
8				
9	Total costs:	613,143		630,000

Goal Seek Status [?][X]

Goal Seeking with Cell D9 found a solution.

Target value: 630000
Current value: 630,000

[Step] [Pause] [OK] [Cancel]

In this worksheet Goal Seek has calculated the projected increase in Wages and benefits that makes the new budget total equal $630,000.

Scenario Summary

	Current Values:	Low_Inflation	High_Inflation	Original_Forecast
Changing Cells:				
WageIncrease	3.5%	2.0%	4.5%	3.5%
SuppliesIncrease	1.5%	1.0%	3.0%	1.5%
TrainingIncrease	10.0%	5.0%	11.0%	10.0%
AdminIncrease	5.0%	1.5%	6.0%	5.0%
Result Cells:				
$D$9	636,291	625,340	643,166	636,291

Notes: Current Values column represents [values at] time Scenario Summary Report was create[d. Changing cells for each] scenario are highlighted in gray.

This summary report, generated by Scenario Manager, compares the impact on a total budget value based on changing variables in three scenarios named: *Low_Inflation*, *High_Inflation*, and *Original_Forecast*.

Presenting Information

PivotTables and PivotCharts present information by condensing and summarizing a large number of cells into a smaller table or chart. A PivotTable or PivotChart summarizes the data based on the rows and columns you specify that you want consolidated. For example, assume a worksheet contains a long list of equipment sales by region, by salesperson, and by item sold. You want to view summaries of the total value of sales by region and/or by salesperson. To do this on your own would take a significant effort. However, by creating a PivotTable or PivotChart, the summary is created in seconds!

Excel 2007 includes new themes and cell styles that allow you to create professional-quality worksheets using designs in the drop-down galleries. You can also choose to customize a theme by changing the colors, fonts, or effects to suit your preferences. Several colorful table styles are also available for ranges defined as a table.

The features described in Microsoft Office Excel are invaluable tools with which to manage the deluge of information that workers face each day. Learning how to use these features will save time and effort—a worthwhile goal at which you will want to *excel*!

Premium Fitness Equipment Sales Ltd.
January Sales

Region	Salesperson	Product	Manufacturer	Model	SalePrice
North	Kazmarek	Treadmill	Cybex	CX500	1575
North	Fernandez	Elliptical	Vision	VS3000	3250
West	Clarke	Treadmill	Vision	VS5000	2250
West					1575
West					2588
North					2345
North					875
North					2499
North					1295
West					1199
West					999
Central					3250
Central					3250
Central					1150
Central					875
South	Clarke	Stepper	Cybex	CX700	2499
South	Clarke	CrossTrainer	SportArt	SA3450	2245
East	Adams	Treadmill	SportArt	SA5010	1249
East	Adams	Treadmill	SportArt	SA5000	1500
South	Fernandez	Elliptical	TrueFit	TF150	2500
East	Fernandez	Elliptical	TrueFit	TF100	2345
East	Clarke	CrossTrainer	TrueFit	TF910	1199
Central	Adams	Stepper	SportArt	SA4000	1295
North	Kazmarek	Elliptical	Cybex	CX324	3150
West	Kazmarek	Treadmill	TrueFit	TF250	999
South	Fernandez	Treadmill	TrueFit	TF280	1150
East	Fernandez	Stepper	Vision	VS2200	1745
Central	Adams	Bike	Vision	VS1000	975
Central	Clarke	CrossTrainer	Cybex	CX410	3595
North	Clarke	Bike	Cybex	CX850	1150
North	Clarke	Elliptical	TrueFit	TF150	2500

A long list of data can be grouped and summarized by more than one column and presented as a PivotTable or a PivotChart. Once created, the PivotTable and PivotChart can be easily manipulated to show different results by *pivoting* the table on a different criterion. For example, the table or chart shown could be easily changed to show sales by region and by salesperson by a specific model number.

Model	(All)				
Sum of SalePrice	Column Labels				
Row Labels	Adams	Clarke	Fernandez	Kazmarek	Grand Total
Central	5,520	4,470		8,474	18,464
East	7,682	1,199	4,090	3,540	16,511
North	2,250	7,120	4,545	8,099	22,014
South		4,744	6,295		11,039
West	3,974	4,838	2,944	2,574	14,330
Grand Total	19,426	22,371	17,874	22,687	82,358

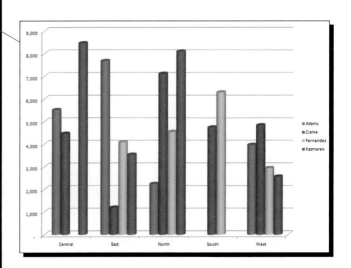

Microsoft®

excel

Unit 1: Advanced Formatting, Formulas, and Data Management

> Advanced Formatting Techniques

> Advanced Functions and Formulas

> Working with Tables and Data Features

> Summarizing and Consolidating Data

Benchmark Microsoft® Excel 2007 Level 2

Microsoft Certified Application Specialist Skills—Unit 1

Reference No.	Skill	Pages
1	**Creating and Manipulating Data**	
1.2	Ensure data integrity	
1.2.1	Restrict data using data validation	83-88
1.2.2	Remove duplicate rows from spreadsheets	82-83
2	**Formatting Data and Content**	
2.3	Format cells and cell content	
2.3.2	Create custom cell formats	20-22
2.3.4	Format text in cells	22-23
2.3.5	Convert text to columns	80-81
2.4	Format data as a table	
2.4.1	Apply Quick Styles to tables	74-75
2.4.2	Add rows to a table	76-78
2.4.3	Insert and delete rows and columns in tables	75-76
3	**Creating and Modifying Formulas**	
3.1	Reference data in formulas	
3.1.2	Create formulas that reference data from other worksheets or workbooks	110-115
3.1.3	Manage named ranges	36-37, 47
3.1.4	Use named ranges in formulas	36-37, 119-120
3.2	Summarize data using a formula	
3.2.1	Use SUM, COUNT, COUNTA, AVERAGE, MIN, and MAX	37-44
3.3	Summarize data using subtotals	
3.3.1	Create and modify list ranges	88-94, 98-99
3.4	Conditionally summarize data using a formula	
3.4.1	Using SUMIF, SUMIFS, COUNTIF, COUNTIFS, AVERAGEIF, and AVERAGEIFS	38-46
3.5	Look up data using a formula	
3.5.1	Using VLOOKUP and HLOOKUP	48-51
3.6	Use conditional logic in a formula	
3.6.1	Using IF, AND, OR, NOT, and IFERROR	56-61
3.7	Format or modify text using formulas	
3.7.1	Format text by using formulas	62-64
3.7.2	Convert text to columns	80-81
4	**Presenting Data Visually**	
4.3	Apply conditional formatting	
4.3.1	Manage conditional formats by using the Conditional Formatting Rules Manager	8-14
4.3.2	Allow more than one rule to be true	10-12
4.3.3	Apply conditional formats	8-16
4.5	Outline data	
4.5.1	Group and ungroup data	93-94
4.5.2	Subtotal data	88-93
4.6	Sort and filter data	
4.6.1	Sort data using single or multiple criteria	23-27
4.6.2	Filter data using AutoFilter	23-25
4.6.3	Filter and sort data using conditional formatting	25-27
4.6.4	Filter and sort data using cell attributes	25-27

Note: The Level 1 and Level 2 texts each address approximately half of the Microsoft Certified Application Specialist skills. Complete coverage of the skills is offered in the combined Level 1 and Level 2 text titled *Benchmark Series Microsoft® Excel 2007: Levels 1 and 2*, which has been approved as certified courseware and which displays the Microsoft Certified Application Specialist logo on the cover.

CHAPTER 1

Advanced Formatting Techniques

PERFORMANCE OBJECTIVES

Upon successful completion of Chapter 1, you will be able to:

- Apply conditional formatting by entering parameters for a rule
- Apply conditional formatting using a predefined rule
- Create and apply a new rule for conditional formatting
- Edit and delete a conditional formatting rule
- Apply conditional formatting using an icon set, data bars, and color scale
- Apply fraction and scientific formatting
- Apply a special format for a number
- Create a custom number format
- Apply wrap text and shrink to fit text control options
- Filter a worksheet using a custom AutoFilter
- Filter and sort a worksheet using conditional formatting
- Filter and sort a worksheet using cell attributes

Tutorial 1.1
Formatting an Excel Worksheet

Although many worksheets can be formatted using buttons available in the Font, Alignment, and Number groups in the Home tab of the ribbon or in the Mini toolbar, some situations require format categories that are not represented with a button. In other worksheets you may want to make use of Excel's advanced formatting techniques to format based on a condition. In this chapter you will learn how to apply advanced formatting and filtering techniques.

Note: Before beginning computer projects, copy to your storage medium the Excel2007L2C1 subfolder from the Excel2007L2 folder on the CD that accompanies this textbook and make Excel2007L2C1 the active folder. Steps on how to copy a folder are presented on the inside of the back cover of this textbook. Do this every time you start a chapter's projects.

 **Format Cells Based on Values**

Working with a payroll worksheet, you will change the appearance of cells based on criteria related to overtime hours and gross pay.

Conditional Formatting

Apply Conditional Formatting Using Predefined Rule
1. Select desired range.
2. Click Conditional Formatting button.
3. Point to desired rule category.
4. Click desired rule.
5. If necessary, enter parameter value.
6. If necessary, change format options.
7. Click OK.

Conditional formatting applies format changes to a range of cells for those cells within the selection that meet a condition. Cells that do not meet the condition remain unformatted. Changing the appearance of a cell based on a condition allows you to quickly identify values that are high, low, or that represent a trend. Formatting can be applied based on a specific value, a value that falls within a range, or by using a comparison operator such as equals (=), greater than (>), or less than (<). Conditional formats can also be based on date, text entries, or duplicated values. Consider using conditional formatting to analyze a question such as *Which store locations earned sales above their target?* Using a different color and/or shading the cells that exceeded a sales target easily identifies the top performers. Excel 2007 provides predefined conditional formatting rules accessed from the Conditional Formatting drop-down list shown in Figure 1.1. You can also create your own conditional formatting rules.

Figure 1.1 Conditional Formatting Drop-down List

Project 1a   Formatting Cells Based on a Value Comparison

1. Start Excel.
2. Open **VantagePayroll-Oct24.xlsx**. (This workbook is located in the Excel2007L2C1 folder you copied to your storage medium.)
3. Save the workbook with Save As and name it **ExcelL2_C1_P1**.
4. Apply conditional formatting to highlight overtime hours that exceeded 5 for the week by completing the following steps:
   a. Select K6:K23.
   b. Click the Conditional Formatting button in the Styles group of the Home tab.
   c. Point to *Highlight Cells Rules* and then click *Greater Than* at the drop-down list.
   d. At the Greater Than dialog box, with the text already selected in the *Format cells that are GREATER THAN* text box, type 5.

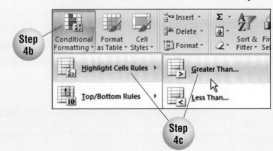

Step 4b

Step 4c

e. Click the down-pointing arrow next to the list box to the right of *with* (currently displays *Light Red Fill with Dark Red Text*) and then click *Red Text* at the drop-down list.

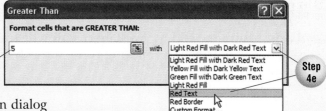

Step 4d

Step 4e

f. Click OK to close the Greater Than dialog box and apply the conditional format.

g. Click in any cell to deselect the range.

h. Review the cells that have been conditionally formatted. Notice that cells with overtime hours greater than 5 are formatted with red text.

5. Save **ExcelL2_C1_P1.xlsx**.

Using the Top/Bottom Rules list you can elect to highlight cells based on a top ten or bottom ten value or percent, or by above average or below average values.

Project 1b   Formatting Cells Based on Top/Bottom Rules

1. With **ExcelL2_C1_P1.xlsx** open, apply conditional formatting to the Gross Pay values to identify employees who earned above average wages for the week by completing the following steps:

a. Select M6:M23.

b. Click the Conditional Formatting button in the Styles group of the Home tab.

c. Point to *Top/Bottom Rules* and then click *Above Average* at the drop-down list.

d. At the Above Average dialog box, with *Light Red Fill with Dark Red Text* selected in the *Format cells that are ABOVE AVERAGE* list box, click OK.

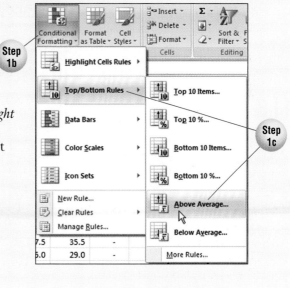

Step 1b

Step 1c

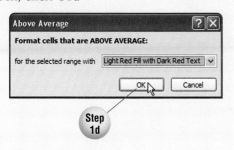

Step 1d

e. Click in any cell to deselect the range.

f. Review the cells that have been conditionally formatted.

2. Change the page orientation to landscape and print the worksheet.

3. Save and then close **ExcelL2_C1_P1.xlsx**.

In an insurance claims worksheet you will format cells by creating, editing, and deleting conditional formatting rules and classify the number of cars into categories using an icon set.

Creating a New Formatting Rule

Create and Apply New Formatting Rule
1. Select desired range.
2. Click Conditional Formatting button.
3. Click *Manage Rules.*
4. Click New Rule button.
5. Click desired rule type.
6. Add criteria as required.
7. Click Format button.
8. Select desired formatting attributes.
9. Click OK to close Format Cells dialog box.
10. Click OK to close New Formatting Rule dialog box.
11. Click Apply button.
12. Click OK.

Cells are conditionally formatted based on a rule that defines the criterion by which the cell is selected for formatting and includes the formatting attributes that are applied to the cells that meet the conditional test. The predefined rules that you used in Project 1a and Project 1b allowed you to use the feature without having to specify each component in the rule's parameters. At the New Formatting Rule dialog box shown in Figure 1.2, you can create your own custom conditional formatting rule in which you define all parts of the criterion and the formatting. The *Edit the Rule Description* section of the dialog box varies depending on the active option in the *Select a Rule Type* section.

Figure 1.2 New Formatting Rule Dialog Box

H I N T
You can create a rule to format cells based on cell values, specific text, dates, blank, or error values.

Begin creating a new rule by choosing the type of condition you want Excel to check before formatting.

This section varies depending on the option selected in the *Select a Rule Type* section.

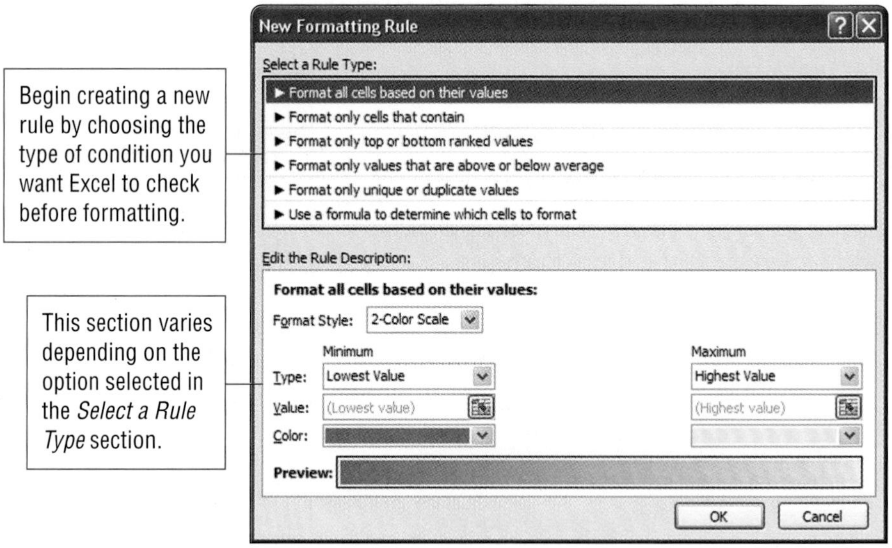

1. Open **AllClaims-Policies.xlsx**.
2. Save the workbook with Save As and name it **ExcelL2_C1_P2**.
3. The owner of AllClaims Insurance Brokers is considering changing the discount plan for those customers with no claims or with only one claim. The owner would like to see the two claim criteria formatted in color to provide a reference for how many customers this discount would affect. Create a formatting rule that will change the appearance of cells in the claims columns for those values that equal 0 by completing the following steps:

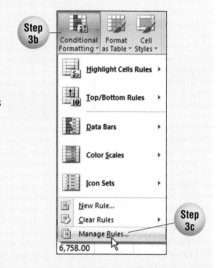

   a. Select H4:H20.
   b. Click the Conditional Formatting button.
   c. Click *Manage Rules* at the drop-down list.
   d. At the Conditional Formatting Rules Manager dialog box, click the New Rule button.
   e. At the New Formatting Rule dialog box, click *Format only cells that contain* in the *Select a Rule Type* section.

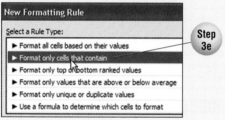

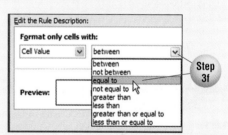

   f. Click the down-pointing arrow located at the right of the second list box from the left in the *Format only cells with* section (currently displays *between*) and then click *equal to* at the drop-down list.

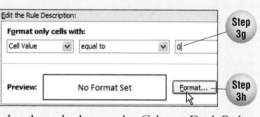

   g. Click in the blank text box next to *equal to* and then type 0.
   h. Click the Format button in the *Preview* section.
   i. At the Format Cells dialog box with the Font tab selected, change the *Color* to *Dark Red*, turn on bold, and then click OK.
   j. Click OK at the New Formatting Rule dialog box.
4. Create a second formatting rule that will change the appearance of cells in the claims columns for those values that equal 1 by completing the following steps:
   a. At the Conditional Formatting Rules Manager dialog box, click the New Rule button.
   b. At the New Formatting Rule dialog box, click *Format only cells that contain* in the *Select a Rule Type* section.
   c. Click the down-pointing arrow located at the right end of the second list box from the left in the *Format only cells with* section (currently displays *between*) and then click *equal to* at the drop-down list.
   d. Click in the blank text box next to *equal to* and then type 1.
   e. Click the Format button.
   f. At the Format Cells dialog box with the Font tab selected, change the *Color* to *Red*, turn on bold, and then click OK.

g. Click OK at the New Formatting Rule dialog box.

5. At the Conditional Formatting Rules Manager dialog box, click the Apply button to apply the rules to the selected range.

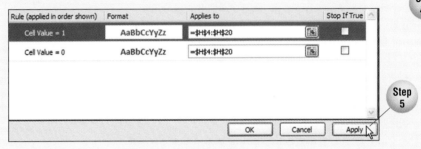

Preview of red bold text formatting that will be applied to cells that meet the condition.

Edit the Rule Description:
Format only cells with:

| Cell Value | equal to | 1 |

Preview: AaBbCcYyZz   Format...

OK

Step 4g

Rule (applied in order shown)	Format	Applies to	Stop If True
Cell Value = 1	AaBbCcYyZz	=$H$4:$H$20	☐
Cell Value = 0	AaBbCcYyZz	=$H$4:$H$20	☐

OK   Cancel   Apply

Step 5

6. Click OK to close the Conditional Formatting Rules Manager dialog box.
7. Click in any cell to deselect the range.
8. Save **ExcelL2_C1_P2.xlsx**.

QUICK STEPS

Edit Formatting Rule
1. Select range.
2. Click Conditional Formatting button.
3. Click *Manage Rules.*
4. Click desired rule.
5. Click Edit Rule button.
6. Make desired changes to parameters and/or formatting options.
7. Click OK twice.

Delete Formatting Rule
1. Click Conditional Formatting button.
2. Click *Manage Rules.*
3. Change *Show formatting rules for* to *This Worksheet.*
4. Click desired rule.
5. Click Delete Rule button.
6. Click OK.

Editing and Deleting Conditional Formatting Rules

Edit the comparison rule criteria and/or formatting options for a conditional formatting rule by opening the Conditional Formatting Rules Manager dialog box. Click to select the rule that you want to change and then click the Edit Rule button. At the Edit Formatting Rule dialog box, make the desired changes and then click OK twice. By default, *Show formatting rules for* is set to *Current Selection* when you open the Conditional Formatting Rules Manager. If necessary, click the down-pointing arrow to the right of the list box and select *This Worksheet* to show all formatting rules in the current sheet.

To remove conditional formatting from a range, select the range, click the Conditional Formatting button, point to *Clear Rules* at the drop-down list, and then click either *Clear Rules from Selected Cells* or *Clear Rules from Entire Sheet*. You can also delete a custom rule at the Conditional Formatting Rules Manager dialog box. Formatting options applied to the cells by the rule that was deleted are removed.

Project 2b | **Creating, Editing, and Deleting a Formatting Rule**

1. With **ExcelL2_C2_P2.xlsx** open, create a new formatting rule to add a fill color to the cells in the *No. of Autos* column for those policies that have more than two cars by completing the following steps:
   a. Select C4:C20.
   b. Click the Conditional Formatting button and then click *New Rule* at the drop-down list.
   c. Click *Format only cells that contain* in the *Select a Rule Type* section of the New Formatting Rule dialog box.
   d. In the *Edit the Rule Description* section, change the rule's parameters to format only cells with a *Cell Value greater than 2*.
   e. Click the Format button and then click the Fill tab at the Format Cells dialog box.
   f. Click the *Yellow* color square (fourth from left in last row) in the *Background Color* palette and then click OK.
   g. Click OK to close the New Formatting Rule dialog box and apply the rule to the selected cells.

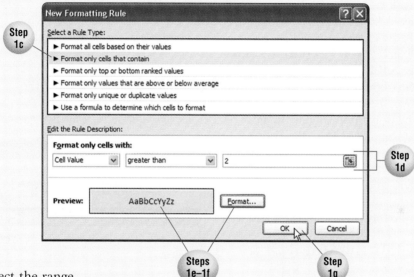

h. Deselect the range.
2. After reviewing the formatted cells, you decide that cells should be formatted for all policies with 2 or more cars. Edit the formatting rule by completing the following steps:
   a. Select C4:C20.
   b. Click the Conditional Formatting button and then click *Manage Rules* at the drop-down list.
   c. Click to select *Cell Value > 2* in the Conditional Formatting Rules Manager dialog box and then click the Edit Rule button.

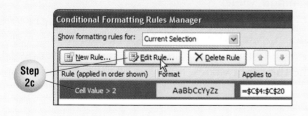

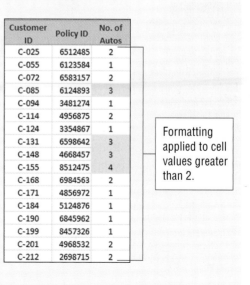

Customer ID	Policy ID	No. of Autos
C-025	6512485	2
C-055	6123584	1
C-072	6583157	2
C-085	6124893	3
C-094	3481274	1
C-114	4956875	2
C-124	3354867	1
C-131	6598642	3
C-148	4668457	3
C-155	8512475	4
C-168	6984563	2
C-171	4856972	1
C-184	5124876	1
C-190	6845962	1
C-199	8457326	1
C-201	4968532	2
C-212	2698715	2

Formatting applied to cell values greater than 2.

d. Click the down-pointing arrow next to the second list box (currently displays *greater than*) and then click *greater than or equal to* at the drop-down list.

e. Click OK.

f. Click OK to close the Conditional Formatting Rules Manager dialog box and apply the revised rule to the selected cells.

g. Deselect the range.

3. Save and print the worksheet.

4. After reviewing the printed copy of the formatted worksheet, you decide to experiment with another method of formatting the data that classifies the policies by the number of cars. You will do this in the next project. In preparation for the next project, save the revised worksheet under a new name and then delete the formatting rule in the original worksheet by completing the following steps:

a. Use Save As to name the workbook **ExcelL2_C1_P2-Autos2+**. By saving the workbook under a new name you will have a copy of the conditional formatting applied in this project.

b. Close **ExcelL2_C1_P2-Autos2+.xlsx**.

c. Open **ExcelL2_C1_P2.xlsx**.

d. Click the Conditional Formatting button and then click *Manage Rules* at the drop-down list.

e. Click the down-pointing arrow next to the *Show formatting rules for* list box and then click *This Worksheet*.

f. Click to select *Cell Value >= 2* and then click the Delete Rule button.

g. Click OK to close the Conditional Formatting Rules Manager dialog box. Notice the formatting has been removed from the cells in column C.

5. Save **ExcelL2_C1_P2.xlsx**.

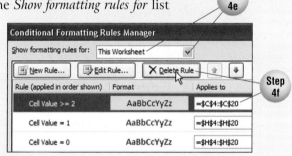

QUICK
STEPS

Apply Conditional Formatting Using Icon Set

1. Select desired range.
2. Click Conditional Formatting button.
3. Point to *Icon Sets*.
4. Click desired icon set.
5. Deselect range.

Green Up Arrow

Red   Yellow
Down   Sideways
Arrow   Arrow

Conditional Formatting Using Icon Sets

Format a range of values using an icon set to classify data into three to five categories. Icons are assigned to cells based on threshold values for the selected range. For example, if you choose the *3 Arrows (Colored)* icon set, icons are assigned as follows:

• Green up arrow for higher values

• Red down arrow for lower values

• Yellow sideways arrow for middle values

The available icon sets are shown in Figure 1.3. Choose the icon set that best represents the number of different categories within the range and the desired symbol type such as flags, arrows, traffic lights, and so on. To create your own icon set where you can set the threshold values, open the Manage Rules dialog box and add a new rule.

Figure 1.3 Conditional Formatting Icon Sets Gallery

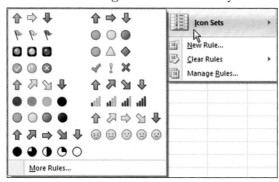

Project 2c — Conditionally Formatting Using an Icon Set

1. With **ExcelL2_C1_P2.xlsx** open, select C4:C20.
2. Classify the number of automobiles into categories using an icon set by completing the following steps:
   a. Click the Conditional Formatting button.
   b. Point to *Icon Sets*.
   c. Click *Red To Black* at the Icon Sets drop-down gallery (sixth from the top in the left column).

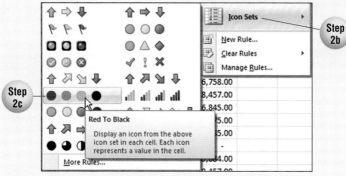

Step 2b

Step 2c

Step 2d

   d. Click in any cell to deselect the range. Notice that Excel assigns an icon to each cell that correlates the icon with the value group. For example, all cells containing the value 1 have the same icon, all cells containing the value 2 have the same icon, and so on.
3. Save, print, and then close **ExcelL2_C1_P2.xlsx**.

Conditional Formatting Using Data Bars and Color Scales

Excel 2007 also provides the ability to conditionally format cells using two-color scales, three-color scales, or data bars to provide visual guides to identify distributions or variations within a range. Use a data bar to easily see the higher and lower values within the range. A bar is added to the background of the cell with the length of the bar dependent on the value within the cell. A longer bar represents a higher value within the range and a shorter bar represents a lower value within the range.

Color scales format the range using either a two-color or three-color palette. The gradation of color applied to a cell illustrates the cell's value in comparison to higher or lower values within the range. Color scales are useful to view the distribution of the data. In a two-color scale, you specify the shade of color that represents higher and lower values. In a three-color scale you specify the shade of color that represents higher, middle, or lower values. Figure 1.4 displays the payroll worksheet for Vantage Video Rentals with data bar and color scale conditional formatting applied. In column M, data bars depict the gross pay distribution. Notice the length of the colored bars in the background of the cells for various gross pay amounts. In column J, the Green-Yellow two-color scale has been applied to show the distribution of total hours. Cells with higher values are displayed in gradations of green, while cells with lower values are displayed in gradations of yellow.

Figure 1.4 Data Bar and Color Scale Conditional Formatting Applied to Payroll Worksheet

	A	B	C	D	E	F	G	H	I	J	K	L	M
1							Vantage Video Rentals						
2							Payroll						
3							Week Ended: October 24, 2009						
4										Total	Overtime	Pay	Gross
5				Sun	Mon	Tue	Wed	Thu	Fri	Sat	Hours	Hours	Rate	Pay
6	Andrew	Gridzak	-	5.0	7.0	8.0	8.0	9.0	9.5	46.5	6.5	8.35	415.41
7	Derrick	MacLean	8.0	-	6.5	8.0	8.0	8.5	9.0	48.0	8.0	9.25	481.00
8	Priya	Bhardwaj	8.0	-	4.0	8.0	8.0	8.5	6.5	43.0	3.0	8.25	367.13
9	Emil	Cehajic	8.0	8.0	8.0	5.5	8.0	-	8.0	45.5	5.5	9.75	470.44
10	Dana	Sparling	-	6.0	7.5	8.0	8.0	-	8.0	37.5	-	8.25	309.38
11	Irene	O'Rourke	4.0	-	8.0	-	6.5	9.5	7.5	35.5	-	8.25	292.88
12	Ruthann	Goldstein	3.5	-	8.0	-	4.0	7.5	6.0	29.0	-	9.25	268.25
13	Stefan	Kominek	-	6.0	8.0	-	8.0	8.5	4.5	35.0	-	8.35	292.25
14	Alex	Spivak	-	5.0	8.0	8.5	7.5	9.0	8.0	46.0	6.0	8.35	409.15
15	Erica	Wilkins	-	7.0	-	6.0	-	6.0	6.4	25.4	-	8.25	209.55
16	Carmon	Vanderhoek	8.0	7.0	-	8.0	-	5.5	5.0	33.5	-	8.25	276.38
17	Ashley	Castillo	4.0	8.0	-	7.5	8.0	4.0	8.5	40.0	-	8.25	330.00
18	Susan	Anez	-	3.0	5.5	-	-	7.0	7.0	22.5	-	9.25	208.13
19	Dana	Ivanowski	-	4.0	6.0	-	8.5	6.8	-	25.3	-	9.25	234.03
20	Linda	Lanczos	-	7.0	4.5	-	7.5	7.5	-	26.5	-	8.25	218.63
21	Gilbert	Yee	9.0	-	9.0	8.0	7.5	8.0	-	41.5	1.5	8.25	348.56
22	Annette	Frishette	8.0	-	-	6.5	5.0	7.5	7.0	34.0	-	8.35	283.90
23	Randy	Brown	4.0	-	-	5.5	4.0	6.0	4.0	23.5	-	9.25	217.38
24	TOTAL		64.5	66.0	90.0	87.5	106.5	118.8	104.9	638.2	30.5		5,632.41

Gross Pay column with data bar conditional formatting applied.

Total Hours column with *Green-Yellow* color scale conditional formatting applied.

roject **3** **Use Fraction and Scientific Formatting Options**

Using two lesson plan worksheets for a math tutor, you will format cells in a solution column to the appropriate format to display the answers for the tutor.

Fraction and Scientific Formatting

While most worksheets have values that are formatted using the Accounting Number Format, Percent Style, or Comma Style buttons in the Number group of the Home tab, some worksheets contain values that require other number formats. The *Number Format* list box in the Number group of the Home tab displays a drop-down list with additional format options including date, time, fraction, scientific, and text options. Click *More Number Formats* at the Number Format drop-down list to open the Format Cells dialog box with the Number tab selected shown in Figure 1.5. At this dialog box you can specify additional parameters for the number format categories. For example, with the *Fractions* category you can choose the type of fraction you want displayed.

Scientific formatting converts a number to exponential notation. Part of the number is replaced with E + *n* where E means Exponent and *n* represents the power. For example, the number *1,500,000.00* formatted in scientific number format displays as *1.50E+06*. In this example, *+06* means add 6 zeros to the right of the number left of E and then move the decimal point 6 positions to the right. Scientists, mathematicians, engineers, and statisticians often use exponential notation to write very large numbers or very small numbers in a more manageable way.

QUICK STEPS

Apply Fraction Formatting
1. Select desired range.
2. Click *Number Format* list arrow.
3. Click *More Number Formats*.
4. Click *Fraction* in *Category* list box.
5. Click desired option in *Type* list box.
6. Click OK.
7. Deselect range.

Apply Scientific Notation Formatting
1. Select desired range.
2. Click *Number Format* list box arrow.
3. Click *Scientific*.
4. Deselect range.

Figure 1.5 Format Cells Dialog Box with Number Tab Selected and Fraction Category Active

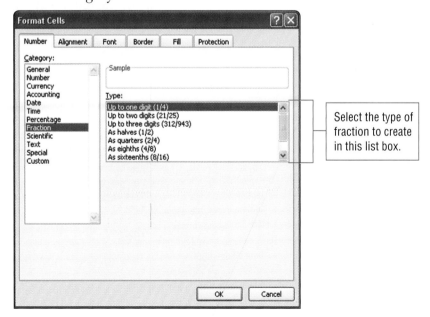

Select the type of fraction to create in this list box.

1. Open **JanelleTutoring-MathLessons.xlsx**.
2. Save the workbook with Save As and name it **ExcelL2_C1_P3**.
3. Make sure Fractions is the active worksheet. If necessary, click the Fractions sheet tab located at the bottom of the worksheet area just above the Status bar.
4. Apply fraction formatting to the values in column D in a fractions lesson to create the solution column for Janelle by completing the following steps:
   a. Select D11:D20.
   b. Click the down-pointing arrow at the right side of the *Number Format* list box in the Number group of the Home tab.
   c. Click *More Number Formats* at the drop-down list.
   d. At the Format Cells dialog box with the Number tab selected, click *Fraction* in the *Category* list box.
   e. Click *Up to two digits (21/25)* in the *Type* list box.

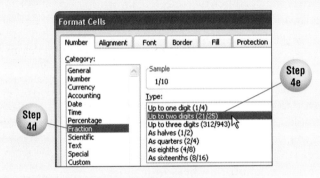

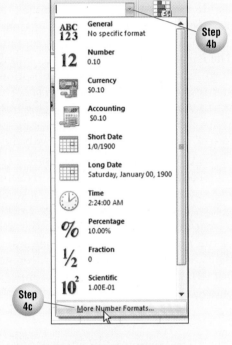

   f. Click OK.
   g. Click in any cell to deselect the range.
5. Save **ExcelL2_C1_P3**.
6. Print the worksheet in landscape orientation.
7. Apply scientific notation formatting to the values in column D in a scientific notation lesson to create the solution column for Janelle by completing the following steps:
   a. Click the Exponents sheet tab located at the bottom of the worksheet area just above the Status bar.
   b. Select D11:D24.
   c. Click the down-pointing arrow at the right side of the *Number Format* list box in the Number group of the Home tab and then click *Scientific* at the drop-down list.
   d. Click in any cell to deselect the range.

10	Examples		Converted to Scientific Notation	
11	1,000,000,000		1.00E+09	
12	100,000,000		1.00E+08	
13	10,000,000		1.00E+07	
14	1,000,000		1.00E+06	
15	100,000		1.00E+05	
16	10,000		1.00E+04	
17	1,000		1.00E+03	
18	100		1.00E+02	
19	10		1.00E+01	
20	1		1.00E+00	
21	0.01		1.00E-02	
22	0.001		1.00E-03	
23	0.0001		1.00E-04	
24	0.00001		1.00E-05	

Scientific formatting applied to D11:D24 in Steps 7a–7d.

8. Print the worksheet in landscape orientation.
9. Save and then close **ExcelL2_C1_P3.xlsx**.

roject **4** **Apply Advanced Formatting Options**

You will update a product worksheet by formatting telephone numbers, creating a custom number format to add descriptive characters before and after a value, and applying text alignment options for long labels.

Special Number Formats

At the Format Cells dialog box with the Number tab active, Excel provides special number formats that are specific to a country and language. For example, in a worksheet with social security numbers you can format the range that will contain the numbers and then type the data without the hyphens. Typing *000223456* converts the entry to *000-22-3456* in the cell with special formatting applied. As shown in Figure 1.6, four *Type* options are available for the *English (U.S.)* location: *Zip Code, Zip Code + 4, Phone Number,* and *Social Security Number*. Changing the location to *English (Canada)* displays two *Type* options: *Phone Number* and *Social Insurance Number*.

QUICK STEPS

Apply Special Number Format
1. Select desired range.
2. Click Format Cells: Number dialog box launcher button.
3. Click *Special* in *Category* list box.
4. Click desired option in *Type* list box.
5. Click OK.
6. Deselect range.

HINT
By applying a special number format you save typing keystrokes and ensure consistency in the data.

Figure 1.6 Format Cells Dialog Box with Number Tab Selected and Special Category Active

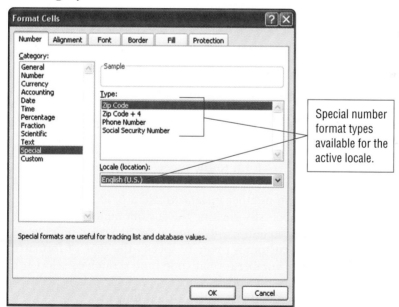

Special number format types available for the active locale.

1. Open **Precision-BulkProductList.xlsx**.
2. Save the workbook with Save As and name it **ExcelL2_C1_P4**.
3. Format the range that will contain telephone numbers to include brackets around the area code and a hyphen between the first three and last four digits of the number by completing the following steps:
   a. Select C15:C19.
   b. Click the Format Cells: Number dialog box launcher button 🔲 located at the bottom right of the Number group in the Home tab.
   c. At the Format Cells dialog box with the Number tab selected and with *Locale (location)* set to *English (U.S.)*, click *Special* in the *Category* list box.
   d. Click *Phone Number* in the *Type* list box.
   e. Click OK.
   f. Click C15 to deselect the range and make the first cell to contain a telephone number active.

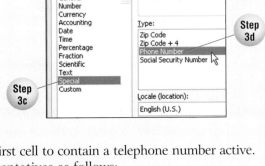

4. Type the telephone numbers for the sales representatives as follows:

C15	8005553429
C16	8005553439
C17	8005553449
C18	8005553459
C19	8005553469

14	Divisional Sales Representatives		
15	Northeast	Jordan Fellowes	(800) 555-3429
16	Northwest	Sandra Berkelmans	(800) 555-3439
17	Central	Pietr Doering	(800) 555-3449
18	Southeast	Karsten Das	(800) 555-3459
19	Southwest	Milton Strickland	(800) 555-3469

Step 4

5. Save **ExcelL2_C1_P4.xlsx**.

Creating a Custom Number Format

You can create a custom number format for a worksheet in which you want to enter values that do not conform to the predefined number formats or values for which you want to add punctuation or text to the number. For example, in Project 4b you will create a custom number format to add a product category letter preceding all of the model numbers. By creating the custom number format, Excel adds the letter automatically. You can also specify a font color in a custom number format. Formatting codes are used in custom formats to specify the type of formatting to apply. You can type a custom number format code from scratch or select from a list of custom formats and modify the codes as necessary. Table 1.1 displays commonly used format codes along with examples of their usage.

Once the custom format is created you can apply the format elsewhere within the workbook by opening the Format Cells dialog box with the Number tab selected, selecting the *Custom* category, scrolling down to the bottom of the *Type* list box, clicking to select the custom format code, and then clicking OK.

Table 1.1 Custom Number Format Code Examples

Format Code	Description	Custom Number Format Example	Display Result
#	Represents a digit; type one for each digit. Excel will round if necessary to fit the number of decimals	####.###	Typing *145.0068* displays *145.007*
0	Also used for digits. Excel rounds numbers to fit the number of decimals but also fills in leading zeros	000.00	Typing *50.45* displays *050.45*
?	Rounds numbers to fit the number of decimals but also aligns the numbers vertically on the decimal point by adding spaces	???.???	Typing *123.5, .8,* and *55.356* one below each other in a column aligns the numbers vertically on the decimal point
"text"	Adds the characters between quotation symbols to the entry	"Model No. " ###	Typing *587* displays *Model No. 587*
[color]	Applies the font color specified in square brackets to the cell entry	[Blue]##.##	Typing *55.346* displays **55.35**
;	Separates the positive value format from the negative value format	[Blue];[Red]	Positive numbers are displayed in blue while negative numbers are displayed in red.

Project 4b   Creating a Custom Number Format

1. With **ExcelL2_C1_P4.xlsx** open, select A5:A12.
2. Create a custom number format to insert the characters *PD-* in front of each model number by completing the following steps:
   a. Click the Format Cells: Number dialog box launcher button located at the bottom right of the Number group in the Home tab.
   b. Click *Custom* in the *Category* list box.
   c. Scroll down the list of custom formats in the *Type* list box noting the various combinations of format codes for numbers, dates, and times.
   d. Select *General* in the *Type* text box, press Delete, and then type **"PD-"####**.

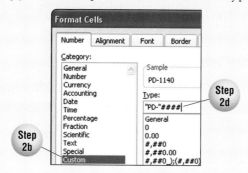

e. Click OK.

f. With the range A5:A12 still selected, click the Center button in the Alignment group of the Home tab.

g. Deselect the range.

3. Create a custom number format to insert the characters *lbs* after the weights in columns D and E by completing the following steps:

a. Select D5:E12.

b. Click the Format Cells: Number dialog box launcher button.

c. Click *Custom* in the *Category* list box.

d. Select *General* in the *Type* text box, press Delete, and then type ### "lbs". Make sure to include one space after ###.

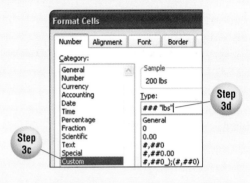

e. Click OK.

f. Deselect the range.

4. Save **ExcelL2_C1_P4.xlsx**.

To delete a custom number format, open the workbook in which you created the custom format code, open the Format Cells dialog box with the Number tab selected, click *Custom* in the *Category* list box, scroll down the list of custom formats in the *Type* list box to the bottom of the list, click the custom format code that you created, and then click the Delete button. Cells within the workbook that had the format code applied have the custom formatting removed when the format is deleted.

Wrapping and Shrinking Text to Fit within a Cell

Several options exist for formatting long labels that do not fit within the column width. The column width can be expanded, the font can be reduced to a smaller size, a group of cells can be merged, or you can allow the text to spill over into adjacent unused columns. Additional options available in the Format Cells dialog box with the Alignment tab selected include *Wrap text* and *Shrink to Fit* in the *Text control* section. Text wrapped within a cell causes the row height to automatically increase to accommodate the number of lines needed to display the text within the cell. Alternatively, shrinking the text to fit within the cell causes Excel to scale the font size down to the size required to fit all text within one line. Consider widening the column width before wrapping text or shrinking to fit to ensure the column is a reasonable width in which to display multiple lines of text or a smaller font size.

1. With **ExcelL2_C1_P4.xlsx** open, wrap text within cells by completing the following steps:
   a. Select B21:B22.
   b. Click the Wrap Text button in the Alignment group of the Home tab.

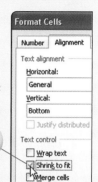

Step 1b

   c. Print the worksheet.
2. You decide to try the Shrink to Fit option on the same cells to see if a better result is produced. Press Ctrl + Z or click the Undo button on the Quick Access toolbar to restore the cells back to their original state.
3. Shrink the text to fit within the cells by completing the following steps:
   a. With B21:B22 still selected, click the Format Cells: Alignment dialog box launcher button located at the bottom right of the Alignment group in the Home tab.
   b. At the Format Cells dialog box with the Alignment tab selected, click the *Shrink to fit* check box in the *Text control* section to insert a check mark.

Step 3b

   c. Click OK.
   d. Deselect the range.
4. Save, print, and then close **ExcelL2_C1_P4.xlsx**.

Step 3d

18	Southeast	Karsten Das	(800) 555-3459
19	Southwest	Milton Strickland	(800) 555-3469
20			
21		Minimum order quantity of 5 applies	
22		Preferred carriers are UPS and DHL	

Project 5 — Filter and Sort Data Based on Values, Icon Set, and Font Color

You will filter an insurance policy worksheet to show policies based on a range of liability limits and by number of claims, filter policies based on the number of automobiles, and filter and sort a payroll worksheet by font and cell colors.

Filtering a Worksheet Using a Custom AutoFilter

The AutoFilter feature is used to display only the rows that meet specified criteria defined using the filter arrow at the top of each column. Rows that do not meet the criteria are temporarily hidden from view. For each column in the selected range or table, the filter arrow button includes in the drop-down list each unique field value that exists within the column. Display the Custom AutoFilter dialog box shown in Figure 1.7 in a worksheet where you want to filter values by more than one criterion using a comparison operator. You can use the ? and * wildcard characters in a custom filter. For example, you could filter a list of products by a product number beginning with P using P* as the criteria.

QUICK STEPS

Filter Using a Custom AutoFilter
1. Select range.
2. Click Sort & Filter button.
3. Click *Filter*.
4. Deselect range.
5. Click filter arrow button in desired column.
6. Point to *Number Filters*.
7. Click desired filter category.
8. Enter criteria at Custom AutoFilter dialog box.
9. Click OK.

Sort & Filter ▾

Figure 1.7 Custom AutoFilter Dialog Box

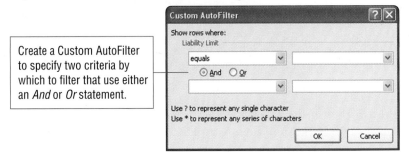

Create a Custom AutoFilter to specify two criteria by which to filter that use either an *And* or *Or* statement.

Project 5a Filtering Policy Information

1. Open **AllClaims-Policies.xlsx**.
2. Save the workbook with Save As and name it **ExcelL2_C1_P5**.
3. The owner of AllClaims Insurance Brokers wants to review policies with liability limits between $500 thousand and $1 million and with claims greater than 1 to determine if customers should increase their coverage. Filter the policy information to produce the list of policies that meet the owner's request by completing the following steps:

    a. Select A3:I20.

    b. Click the Sort & Filter button in the Editing group of the Home tab.

    c. Click *Filter* at the drop-down list to display a filter arrow button at the top of each column.

    d. Deselect the range.

    e. Click the filter arrow button ▾ next to *Liability Limit* in E3.

    f. Point to *Number Filters* and then click *Between* at the drop-down list.

    g. At the Custom AutoFilter dialog box, with the insertion point positioned in the blank text box next to *is greater than or equal to*, type 500000.

    h. Notice *And* is the option selected between criteria. This is correct since the owner wants a list of policies with the liability limit greater than or equal to 500,000 *and* less than or equal to 1,000,000.

    i. Click in the blank text box next to *is less than or equal to* and type 1000000.

    j. Click OK to close the Custom AutoFilter dialog box. The range is filtered to display the rows with liability limits between $500 thousand and $1 million.

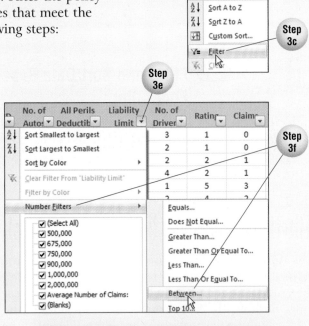

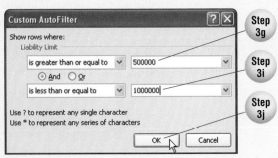

Step 3b

Step 3c

Step 3e

Step 3f

Step 3g

Step 3i

Step 3j

k. Click the filter arrow button next to *Claims* in H3.

l. Point to *Number Filters* and then click *Greater Than* at the drop-down list.

m. At the Custom AutoFilter dialog box with the insertion point positioned in the blank text box next to *is greater than*, type 1 and then click OK.

4. Print the filtered worksheet.

5. Save and then close **ExcelL2_C1_P5.xlsx**.

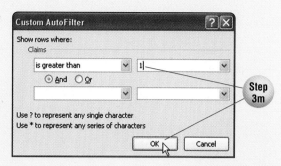

Step 3m

Filtering and Sorting Data Using Conditional Formatting or Cell Attributes

A worksheet with cells that have been formatted manually or by conditional formatting to change the cell or font color can be filtered by the colors. As well, a worksheet conditionally formatted by icon sets can be filtered by a cell icon. Click the filter arrow button in the column by which you want to filter and then point to *Filter by Color* at the drop-down list. Depending on the formatting that has been applied, the list contains the cell colors, font colors, or icon sets that have been applied to cells within the column. Click the desired color square to filter the column.

The filter drop-down list also contains a *Sort by Color* option with which you can choose to sort rows within the range or table by a specified cell color, font color, or cell icon. To sort by color, select the range. Then right-click within the range, point to *Sort*, and click the desired sort by color option.

QUICK STEPS

Filter by Icon Set
1. Select range.
2. Click Sort & Filter button.
3. Click *Filter*.
4. Deselect range.
5. Click filter arrow button in desired column.
6. Point to *Filter by Color*.
7. Click desired icon.

Filter by Color
1. Select range.
2. Click Sort & Filter button.
3. Click *Filter*.
4. Deselect range.
5. Click filter arrow button in desired column.
6. Point to *Filter by Color*.
7. Click desired color.
OR
1. Select range.
2. Right-click within range.
3. Point to *Filter*.
4. Click *Filter by Selected Cell's Font Color*.

Project 5b   **Filtering Data by Icon Set**

1. Open **ExcelL2_C1_P2.xlsx**.

2. Filter the worksheet to display the policies that have coverage for only one automobile by completing the following steps:

a. Select A3:I20.

b. Click the Sort & Filter button in the Editing group of the Home tab.

c. Click *Filter* at the drop-down list to display a filter arrow button at the top of each column.

d. Deselect the range. Note that the black circle represents the *1* data set.

e. Click the filter arrow button next to *No. of Autos* in C3.

f. Point to *Filter by Color* at the drop-down list.

g. Click the black circle icon in the *Filter by Cell Icon* list.

3. Print the filtered worksheet.

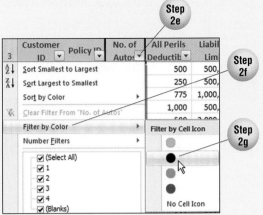

Step 2e

Step 2f

Step 2g

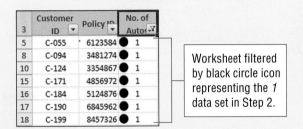

Worksheet filtered by black circle icon representing the *1* data set in Step 2.

4. Click the filter arrow button next to *No. of Autos* in C3 and then click *Clear Filter From "No. of Autos"* at the drop-down list to redisplay all rows.

5. Save and then close **ExcelL2_C1_P2.xlsx**.

Project 5c Filtering by Font Color

1. Open **ExcelL2_C1_P1.xlsx**.

2. The store manager wants a list of employees who worked more than five overtime hours during the pay period. You recall conditionally formatting the overtime hours by applying red font color to cells greater than 5. Filter the worksheet by the conditional formatting by completing the following steps:

a. Select K6:K23.

b. Right-click within the selected range.

c. Point to *Filter* and then click *Filter by Selected Cell's Font Color* at the shortcut menu.

3. Print the filtered worksheet.

4. Click the filter arrow button at the top of the column and then clear the filter.

5. Click the Sort & Filter button in the Editing group of the Home tab and then click *Filter* at the drop-down list to remove the filter arrow button in K6.

6. Deselect the range.

7. Save **ExcelL2_C1_P1.xlsx**.

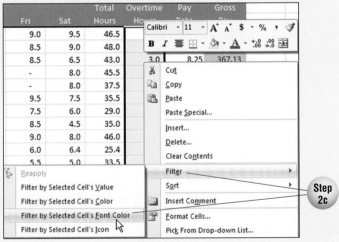

Step 2c

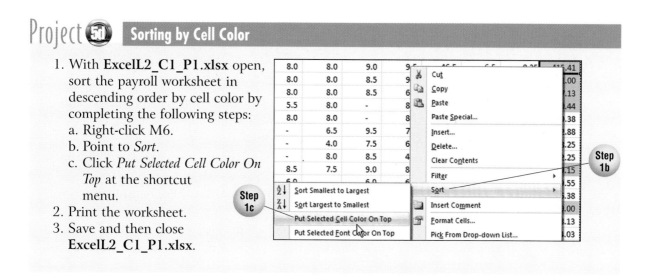

Project 5d Sorting by Cell Color

1. With **ExcelL2_C1_P1.xlsx** open, sort the payroll worksheet in descending order by cell color by completing the following steps:
   a. Right-click M6.
   b. Point to *Sort*.
   c. Click *Put Selected Cell Color On Top* at the shortcut menu.
2. Print the worksheet.
3. Save and then close **ExcelL2_C1_P1.xlsx**.

A default sort order for sorting by color is not available in Excel. In a worksheet with more than one cell or font color applied to a column you would have to define a custom sort. Click the Sort & Filter button in the Editing group of the Home tab and then click *Custom Sort* at the drop-down list. At the Sort dialog box, define the color to sort first and then add a level for each other color in the order in which you want sorting by color to occur. Figure 1.8 shows an example of a sort definition for a column in which three cell colors have been used.

Figure 1.8 Sort Dialog Box with Three Color Sort Defined

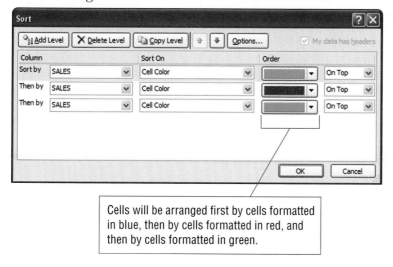

Cells will be arranged first by cells formatted in blue, then by cells formatted in red, and then by cells formatted in green.

CHAPTER summary

- Conditional formatting applies format changes to cells based on a condition; cells that meet the condition have the formatting applied whereas cells that do not meet the condition remain unformatted.
- Conditional formats can be based on values, dates, text entries, or duplicated values.
- Use the *Highlight Cells Rules* option at the Conditional Formatting drop-down list to conditionally format based on a value comparison.
- Use the *Top/Bottom Rules* option at the Conditional Formatting drop-down list to conditionally format based on the top ten or bottom ten percent values or on average values.
- Conditional formats are based on rules which specify the criterion by which the cells are tested and the formatting attributes to apply to cells that meet the condition.
- Create your own conditional formatting rules by selecting *Manage Rules* or *New Rule* at the Conditional Formatting drop-down list.
- Edit or delete a rule at the Conditional Formatting Rules Manager dialog box.
- In addition to formatting changes to cells, you can conditionally format using data bars, color scales, or icon sets.
- Fraction formatting converts decimal values to fractions.
- To choose the type of fraction you want to convert, open the Format Cells dialog box with the Number tab selected.
- Scientific formatting displays numbers in exponential notation where part of the number that is formatted is replaced with E + *n* where E stands for Exponent and *n* represents the power.
- Excel provides special number formats specific to countries and language to format entries such as telephone numbers, social security numbers, or ZIP codes.
- In a worksheet with numbers that do not conform to the standard formats available in the Number group of the Home tab, you can create your own custom number format.
- Custom number formats use formatting codes to create the format definition.
- A custom number format can be used to add text or punctuation to a value entered into a cell.
- Long labels can be formatted to fit within a cell by either wrapping the text within the cell or shrinking the font size to fit the cell.
- Display the Custom AutoFilter dialog box to filter values by more than one criterion using a comparison operator such as greater than or equal to.
- A worksheet that has been formatted manually or by conditional formatting can be filtered by the colors or icons.
- A worksheet that has been formatted manually or by conditional formatting can also be sorted by the colors.
- Define a custom sort if the worksheet contains more than one cell or font color and you want to specify the order of the colors to sort.

COMMANDS review

FEATURE	RIBBON TAB, GROUP	BUTTON	KEYBOARD SHORTCUT
Conditional formatting	Home, Styles		
Custom AutoFilter	Home, Editing		Ctrl + Shift + L
Custom number format	Home, Number		Ctrl + 1
Fraction number format	Home, Number	General ▾	Ctrl + 1
Scientific number format	Home, Number	General ▾	Ctrl + 1
Shrink to Fit	Home, Alignment		
Special number format	Home, Number		Ctrl + 1
Wrap text	Home, Alignment		

CONCEPTS check

Test Your Knowledge

Completion: In the space provided at the right, indicate the correct term, command, or number.

1. Point to this option from the Conditional Formatting drop-down list to format cells based on a comparison operator such as *Greater Than*. _____.

2. To conditionally format a range using the Above Average condition, click this option from the Conditional Formatting drop-down list. _____

3. Open this dialog box to create, edit, or delete a formatting rule. _____

4. Excel uses threshold values to classify data into three to five categories when conditionally formatting by this option. _____

5. Open this dialog box to format a selected range using a fraction and select the type of fraction to display. _____

6. Scientific formatting is used by scientists or others who need to write very large numbers using this notation. _____

7. The special number format options displayed in the *Type* list box are dependent on this other setting. _____

8. What would display in a cell in which you typed *156.3568* for which the custom number format code ###.## applied? _____

9. Use either of these two text control options to format a long label within the existing column width. _____

10. Open this dialog box to filter by more than one criterion using a comparison operator. _____

11. A worksheet can be filtered by a cell color that has been applied manually or by this feature. _____

12. Open this dialog box to arrange cells in a worksheet by more than one color. _____

SKILLS check
Demonstrate Your Proficiency

Assessment

1 USE CONDITIONAL AND FRACTION FORMATTING

1. Open **RSR-ServiceReport.xlsx**.
2. Save the workbook with Save As and name it **ExcelL2_C1_A1**.
3. Apply the following formatting changes to the worksheet:
   a. Format C6:C23 to fractions using the type *As quarters (2/4)*.
   b. Format the rate codes in D6:D22 with icon set *3 Traffic Lights (Unrimmed)*. This is the second option from the top in the right column at the icon set side menu.
   c. Format the parts values in F6:F22 to color the cell with *Yellow Fill with Dark Yellow Text* for those cells that are equal to zero.
   d. Bold the values in G6:G22.
   e. Format the total invoice values in G6:G22 using an orange data bar from the Conditional Formatting drop-down list.
4. Print the worksheet in landscape orientation.
5. Save and then close **ExcelL2_C1_A1.xlsx**.

Assessment

2 APPLY CUSTOM NUMBER FORMATTING

1. Open **ExcelL2_C1_A1.xlsx**.
2. Save the workbook with Save As and name it **ExcelL2_C1_A2**.
3. Create and apply the following custom number formats:
   a. Create a custom number format that displays *hrs* one space after the values in C6:C23.
   b. Create a custom number format that displays *RSR-* in front of each work order number in B6:B22.
4. Save, print, and then close **ExcelL2_C1_A2.xlsx**.

Assessment

3 USE CUSTOM AUTOFILTER; FILTER AND SORT BY COLOR

1. Open **ExcelL2_C1_A2.xlsx**.
2. Save the workbook with Save As and name it **ExcelL2_C1_A3.xlsx**.
3. Select A5:G22 and turn on the Filter feature.
4. Filter the worksheet as follows:
   a. Using the filter arrow button in the *Hours Billed* column, display those invoices where the hours billed is between 1.75 and 3.75 hours.
   b. Print the filtered worksheet.
   c. Clear the filter from the *Hours Billed* column.

d. Filter the *Parts* column by color to show only those invoices for which no parts were billed.

e. Print the filtered worksheet.

f. Clear the filter from the *Parts* column.

g. Filter the worksheet by the icon associated with rate code 3.

h. Print the filtered worksheet.

i. Clear the filter from the *Rate Code* column.

5. Remove the filter arrow buttons from the worksheet.

6. Define a custom sort to sort the invoices by the rate code icon set as follows:

a. Make any cell active within the invoice list.

b. Open the Sort dialog box.

c. Define three sort levels as follows:

Sort by	*Sort On*	*Order*
Rate Code	Cell Icon	Red Circle (On Top)
Rate Code	Cell Icon	Yellow Circle (On Top)
Rate Code	Cell Icon	Green Circle (On Top)

7. Print the sorted worksheet.

8. Save and then close **ExcelL2_C1_A3.xlsx**.

Assessment

4 CREATE, EDIT, AND DELETE FORMATTING RULES

1. Open **VantagePayroll-Oct24.xlsx**.

2. Save the workbook with Save As and name it **ExcelL2_C1_A4**.

3. Create and apply two formatting rules for the values in the *Pay Rate* column as follows:

a. Apply a light purple fill color to the values between 8.00 and 9.00.

b. Apply a light green fill color to the values greater than 9.00.

4. Change the page orientation to landscape and print the worksheet.

5. Edit the formatting rule for *Cell Value > 9* by changing the fill color to bright yellow and apply bold to the font.

6. Delete the formatting rule for *Cell Value between 8.00 and 9.00*.

7. Print the revised worksheet.

8. Save and then close **ExcelL2_C1_A4.xlsx**.

CASE study

Apply Your Skills

You work as a market research assistant at NuTrends Market Research. Yolanda Robertson has provided you with data from the U.S. Census Bureau related to estimated 2005 median annual income for two-person families by state. Open the file named **USIncomeStats.xlsx**. Save the workbook and name it **ExcelL2_C1_CS_P1**. Yolanda is working with a new client who is developing a marketing strategy for a new product launch. In preparation for the marketing plan, Yolanda has asked for your help to format the report to make it easy for her to spot significant data. Specifically Yolanda wants you to format the worksheet using colors to assist her with marketing strategies by income level. She has proposed the following categories for which she would like you to apply color formatting.

> *Median Income Range*
> Less than 40,000
> Between 40,000 and 50,000
> Between 50,000 and 60,000
> Greater than 60,000

Create new formatting rules using the Conditional Formatting Rules Manager for this request since Yolanda may change these salary ranges later after she reviews the data, and you want the ability to edit the rule if that happens. Choose color formats that will be easy to distinguish from each other. To help Yolanda easily read the worksheet, create a reference table starting in D1 that provides Yolanda with a legend to read the colors. For example, in D1 type **Less than 40,000** and in G1 type a sample value and format the cell to the color that represents the formatting you applied to the rule category. Save and then print the worksheet. ***Note: If you do not have access to a color printer, write on the printout the color format options you applied to each category***.

Yolanda has reviewed the worksheet from Part 1 and has requested some further work to help refine the marketing plan. Before you begin modifying the file, you decide to keep the original file intact in case this data can be used for another client. Use Save As to save the workbook using the name **ExcelL2_C1_CS_P2**. Yolanda would like the worksheet sorted in descending order from the highest income level to the lowest. After sorting the worksheet, filter the median incomes to display the top 20 states. Yolanda will be sending the file electronically to the client. She wants you to put contact telephone numbers in the worksheet next to the top 20 state data. Set up a contact telephone reference list with the telephone numbers provided. Apply the special number format for phone numbers to ensure the data is displayed consistently. Apply formatting options to the telephone reference list to make the contact numbers stand out separately from the data. For example, add borders and change the fill color for each contact number. Save and then print the worksheet.

Yolanda (cell)	800 555 3117
Yolanda (office)	800 555 4629
Yolanda (home)	800 555 2169
Yolanda (fax)	800 555 6744

Part 3

While working with conditional formatting you noticed the option on the drop-down list to format using color scales. Continuing with the worksheet formatted in Part 2 of this Case Study, you decide to experiment with the filtered census data worksheet to see if formatting using color scales will highlight the spread between the highest and lowest median incomes more distinctly. Use the Help feature to learn how Excel applies color gradation to illustrate data in two-color and three-color scales with conditional formatting. Use Save As to name the workbook **ExcelL2_C1_P3**. Using the information you learned in Help, format the filtered median incomes using either a two-color or a three-color scale. Save and then print the worksheet. Write on your printout the reason you selected a two-color or a three-color scale to portray the data.

Part 4

Yolanda is preparing a seminar for new market researchers hired at NuTrends Market Research. For background material for the section on statistics available from the U.S. Census Bureau, Yolanda has asked you to research the history of the bureau. Using the Internet, go to the URL http://www.census.gov/ and find the page that describes the history of the Census Bureau. In a new sheet in the same file as the median income data, type in column A five to seven interesting facts you learned about the bureau from their Web site. Adjust the width of column A and apply wrap text or shrink to fit formatting to improve the appearance. Save the revised workbook and name it **ExcelL2_C1_CS_P4**. Print the worksheet and then close the workbook.

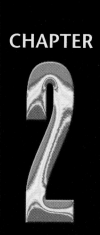

Advanced Functions and Formulas

PERFORMANCE OBJECTIVES

Upon successful completion of Chapter 2, you will be able to:

- Use named ranges in formulas
- Use functions COUNTA, COUNTIF, COUNTIFS
- Use functions AVERAGEIF, AVERAGEIFS
- Use functions SUMIF, SUMIFS
- Delete a range name
- Look up data using the lookup functions VLOOKUP and HLOOKUP
- Analyze financial data using PPMT, PV, and NPV
- Use conditional logic functions IF, AND, OR, NOT, and IFERROR
- Modify text using the text functions PROPER, UPPER, LOWER, and SUBSTITUTE

Tutorial 2.1
Using Financial, Math, and Statistical Functions
Tutorial 2.2
Working with Ranges

Excel includes numerous built-in functions grouped by function category. Eleven categories contain preprogrammed formulas to facilitate complex calculations for worksheets containing statistical, financial, scientific, database, and other data. The Insert function dialog box assists with locating and building function formulas. The structure of a function formula begins with the equals sign (=), followed by the name of the function, and then the function argument. Argument is the term given to the values to be included in the calculation. The structure of the argument is dependent on the type of function being used and can include a single cell, a range, multiple ranges, or any combination of the preceding.

Note: Before beginning computer projects, copy to your storage medium the Excel2007L2C2 subfolder from the Excel2007L2 folder on the CD that accompanies this textbook and then make Excel2007L2C2 the active folder.

You will create and manage range names in an insurance claims worksheet and use the range names in statistical formulas that count, find averages, and sum based on single and multiple criteria.

Naming Ranges

Assigning a name to a cell or a range of cells allows you to reference the source by a descriptive label rather than the cell address or range address when creating formulas, printing, or navigating a worksheet. Referencing by name makes the task of managing a complex formula easier. Another person editing the worksheet experiences clarity more quickly as to the formula's purpose. To demonstrate the use of names for clarity read the formula examples in Table 2.1. Each row provides two formulas that reference the same source cells; however, the formula on the right is meaningful to you more quickly than the formula on the left. The formulas in the left column might require that you locate the source cell in the worksheet to figure out the calculation steps while the formula on the right provides comprehension almost immediately.

Table 2.1 Standard Formulas and Formulas with Named Ranges

Standard Formula	Same Formula Using Named Ranges
=D3-D13	=Sales-Expenses
=J5*K5	=Hours*PayRate
=G10/J10	=ThisYear/LastYear
=IF(E4-B2>0,E4*D2,0)	=IF(Sales-Target>0,Sales*Bonus,0)

Create a range name by selecting a single cell or range, clicking in the Name box located at the left end of the formula bar, typing the name, and then pressing Enter. The Name box displays the active cell address or the cell name when one has been defined. When creating a name for a cell or a range of cells, the following naming rules apply:

- Names can be a combination of letters, numbers, underscore characters, or periods up to 255 characters.
- The first character must be a letter, an underscore, or a backslash (\).
- Spaces are not valid within a range name. Use underscore characters or periods to separate words.
- A valid cell address cannot become a range name.
- Range names are not case sensitive.

1. Open **AllClaims-VehicleRptOct09.xlsx**.
2. Save the workbook with Save As and name it **ExcelL2_C2_P1**.
3. Assign names to ranges by completing the following steps:
   a. Select D4:D23.
   b. Click in the Name box located at the left end of the Formula bar, type **Auto_No**, and then press Enter.
   c. Select E4:E23, click in the Name box, type **Driver_No**, and then press Enter.
   d. Select F4:F23, click in the Name box, type **Rating**, and then press Enter.
   e. Select H4:H23, click in the Name box, type **Claim_Estimate**, and then press Enter.
   f. Select I4:I23, click in the Name box, type **Repair_Shop**, and then press Enter.
4. View the range names by clicking the down-pointing arrow at the right end of the Name box.
5. Click *Auto_No* at the drop-down list to move the selected range to column D. One reason for creating a range name is to quickly move the active cell to navigate a large worksheet.

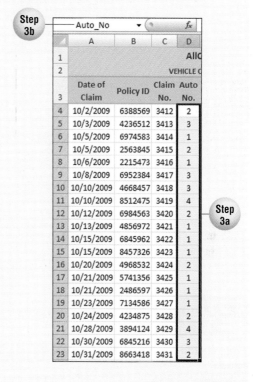

6. Deselect the range.
7. Save **ExcelL2_C2_P1.xlsx**.

Statistical Functions

Commonly used statistical functions include AVERAGE, MAX, and MIN where AVERAGE returns the arithmetic mean, MAX returns the largest value, and MIN returns the smallest value in the range. Another function used often is COUNT, which returns the number of cells that contain numbers or dates. Empty cells, text labels, or error values in the range are ignored. Excel provides additional AVERAGE and COUNT functions that are used to count text entries and count and find averages for a range based on a criterion.

COUNTA

In a worksheet that requires cells containing text, or cells containing a combination of text and numbers (such as *Model-2146*) to be counted, Excel provides the COUNTA function. COUNTA returns the number of cells that are not empty; therefore, this formula can be used to count a range of cells other than values. As shown in the worksheet in Figure 2.1, when the regular COUNT function is used in E8 to count parts in the range A2:A6, Excel returns a value of 0. However, in E9, when the same range is counted using COUNTA, Excel returns the value of 5.

Figure 2.1 COUNTA Example

	A	B	C	D	E
1	Part Number	Qty	Price		
2	Part#-134A	55	2.10		
3	Part#-112S	21	3.15		
4	Part#-874T	47	4.58		
5	Part#784U	65	3.68		
6	Part#546C	85	4.85		
7					
8	Count of column A using COUNT function:				0
9	Count of column A using COUNTA function:				5

Formula =COUNT(A2:A6) returns zero.

Formula =COUNTA(A2:A6) returns the correct result.

QUICK STEPS

Create COUNTIF formula
1. Make desired cell active.
2. Click Insert Function button.
3. Change category to *Statistical.*
4. Select *COUNTIF.*
5. Click OK.
6. Enter range address or range name to select by in *Range* text box.
7. Enter condition expression or text in *Criteria* text box.
8. Click OK.

COUNTIF and COUNTIFS

Use the COUNTIF function to count cells within a range that meet a single criterion. For example, in a grades worksheet you might use a COUNTIF function to count the number of students who achieved greater than 75 percent. This function combines an operation with conditional logic where the criterion defines the conditional test and only those cells that meet the test are selected for action. The structure of a COUNTIF function is *=COUNTIF(range,criteria)*. For the grades worksheet example the function to count the cells of students who achieved greater than 75 percent would be =COUNTIF(grades," >75") assuming the range name *grades* has been defined. Notice the syntax of the argument requires criteria to be enclosed in quotation symbols. Use the Insert function dialog box to create formulas and Excel adds the required syntax automatically.

COUNTIFS is used to count cells that meet multiple criteria. The formula uses the same structure as COUNTIF with additional ranges and criteria within the argument. The structure of a COUNTIFS function is *=COUNTIFS(range1,criteria1,range2,criteria2 . . .)*. Figure 2.2 illustrates the use of a single criterion COUNTIF to count the number of pizza franchises that met a sales target and a multiple criteria COUNTIFS to count the number of pizza franchises established before 2008 that met a sales target.

Create COUNTIFS formula
1. Make desired cell active.
2. Click Insert Function button.
3. Change category to *Statistical*.
4. Select *COUNTIFS*.
5. Click OK.
6. Enter range address or range name to select by in *Criteria_range1* text box.
7. Enter condition expression or text in *Criteria1* text box.
8. Enter range address or range name to select by in *Criteria_range2* text box.
9. Enter condition expression or text in *Criteria2* text box.
10. Continue adding criteria range expressions and criteria as needed.
11. Click OK.

Figure 2.2 COUNTIF and COUNTIFS Formulas

Formula
=COUNTIF(sales,">500000")

	A	B	C	D	E	F
1				**Pizza by Mario Franchise Sales**		
2	Store_No	State	Year_Est.	Gross_Sales	Number of franchises	
3	101	Michigan	2004	652,458		
4	102	Michigan	2004	324,125	With sales greater than $500 thousand	10
5	103	Ohio	2004	845,612		
6	104	Ohio	2005	354,268	Established before 2008 and with sales	
7	105	Ohio	2005	856,412	greater than $500 thousand	7
8	106	Wisconsin	2006	512,463		
9	107	Minnesota	2006	325,496		
10	108	Minnesota	2006	845,621		
11	109	Minnesota	2007	451,236		
12	110	Wisconsin	2007	554,168		
13	111	Kentucky	2007	715,683		
14	112	Kentucky	2008	864,123		
15	113	Kentucky	2008	942,315		
16	114	Michigan	2009	458,321		
17	115	Michigan	2009	612,475		
18	TOTAL GROSS SALES			9,314,776		

Formula
=COUNTIFS(Year_Est.,"<2008",sales,">500000")

1. With **ExcelL2_C2_P1.xlsx** open, make L4 the active cell.
2. Create a COUNTIF function to count the number of claims where A+ Paint & Body is the repair shop by completing the following steps:

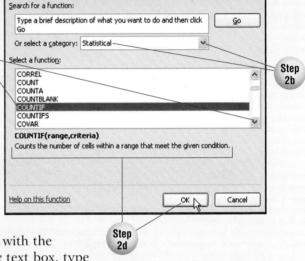

Step 2c

Step 2b

Step 2d

   a. Click the Insert Function button f_x in the Formula bar.
   b. At the Insert Function dialog box, click the down-pointing arrow to the right of the *Or select a category* list box and then click *Statistical* at the drop-down list.
   c. Scroll down the *Select a function* list box and then click *COUNTIF*.
   d. Read the formula description below the function list box and then click OK.
   e. At the Function Arguments dialog box with the insertion point positioned in the *Range* text box, type **Repair_Shop** and then press Tab. Recall from Project 1a that you defined a range name for the entries in column I. ***Note: If necessary, drag the Function Arguments dialog box to the bottom of the screen if the dialog box is obscuring your view of the worksheet.***

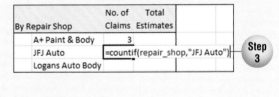

Step 2e

Step 2f

   f. With the insertion point positioned in the *Criteria* text box, type **A+ Paint & Body** and then press Tab. When you press Tab, Excel adds the quotation symbols to the criteria text.
   g. Click OK. Excel returns the value *3* in L4.
   h. Look at the formula in the Formula bar created by the Function Arguments dialog box =*COUNTIF(Repair_Shop,"A+ Paint & Body")*.
3. Make L5 the active cell, type the formula =countif(repair_shop,"JFJ Auto"), and then press Enter.
4. Enter the following COUNTIF formulas in the cells indicated using either the Insert Function dialog box or by typing the formula directly into the cell.

By Repair Shop	No. of Claims	Total Estimates	
A+ Paint & Body	3		
JFJ Auto	=countif(repair_shop,"JFJ Auto")		
Logans Auto Body			

Step 3

   L6   =COUNTIF(Repair_Shop,"Logans Auto Body")
   L7   =COUNTIF(Repair_Shop,"West Collision")

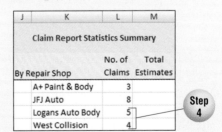

J	K	L	M
Claim Report Statistics Summary			
By Repair Shop	No. of Claims	Total Estimates	
A+ Paint & Body	3		
JFJ Auto	8		
Logans Auto Body	5		
West Collision	4		

Step 4

5. Save **ExcelL2_C2_P1.xlsx**.

1. With **ExcelL2_C2_P1.xlsx** open, make L10 the active cell.
2. Create a COUNTIFS function to count the number of claims where the repair shop is JFJ Auto and the claims estimate is greater than $5 thousand by completing the following steps:
   a. Click the Insert Function button in the Formula bar.
   b. With *Statistical* the category in the *Or select a category* list box, scroll down the *Select a function* list box and then click *COUNTIFS*.
   c. Read the formula description below the function list box and then click OK.
   d. At the Function Arguments dialog box with the insertion point positioned in the *Criteria_range1* text box, type **Repair_Shop** and then press Tab. After you press Tab, a *Criteria_range2* text box is added to the dialog box.
   e. With the insertion point positioned in the *Criteria1* text box, type **JFJ Auto** and then press Tab.
   f. With the insertion point positioned in the *Criteria_range2* text box, type **Claim_Estimate** and then press Tab.
   g. With the insertion point positioned in the *Criteria2* text box, type **>5000** and then press Tab.
   h. Click OK. Excel returns the value *5* in L10.

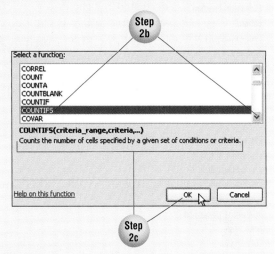

Step 2b

Step 2c

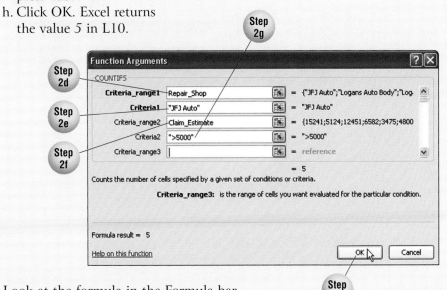

Step 2d
Step 2e
Step 2f
Step 2g
Step 2h

3. Look at the formula in the Formula bar created by the Function Arguments dialog box =COUNTIFS(Repair_Shop,"JFJ Auto",Claim_Estimate,">5000").
4. Enter the following COUNTIFS formula in L13 using either the Insert Function dialog box or by typing the formula directly into the cell:
   =COUNTIFS(Repair_Shop,"JFJ Auto",Rating," >3")
5. Save **ExcelL2_C2_P1.xlsx**.

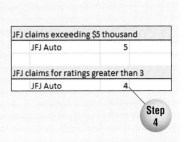

JFJ claims exceeding $5 thousand	
JFJ Auto	5

JFJ claims for ratings greater than 3	
JFJ Auto	4

Step 4

AVERAGEIF and AVERAGEIFS

Create AVERAGEIF formula

1. Make desired cell active.
2. Click Insert Function button.
3. Change category to *Statistical*.
4. Select *AVERAGEIF*.
5. Click OK.
6. Enter range address or range name to select by in *Range* text box.
7. Enter condition expression or text in *Criteria* text box.
8. Enter range address or range name to average in *Average_range* text box.
9. Click OK.

Create AVERAGEIFS formula

1. Make desired cell active.
2. Click Insert Function button.
3. Change category to *Statistical*.
4. Select *AVERAGEIFS*.
5. Click OK.
6. Enter range address or range name to average in *Average_range* text box.
7. Enter range address or range name to select by in *Criteria_range1* text box.
8. Enter condition expression or text in *Criteria1* text box.
9. Enter range address or range name to select by in *Criteria_range2* text box.
10. Enter condition expression or text in *Criteria2* text box.
11. Continue adding criteria range expressions and criteria as needed.
12. Click OK.

The AVERAGEIF function is used to find the arithmetic mean of the cells within the specified range that meet a single criterion. The structure of an AVERAGEIF function is *=AVERAGEIF(range,criteria,average_range)* where *range* is the cells to be tested for the criterion, *criteria* is the conditional statement used to select cells, and *average_range* is the range containing the values you want to average.

AVERAGEIFS is used to average cells that meet multiple criteria using the formula *=AVERAGEIFS(average_range,criteria_range1,criteria1,criteria_range2,criteria2 . . .)*. Figure 2.3 continues with the pizza franchise example to illustrate the use of a single criterion AVERAGEIF to average the sales of pizza franchises established before 2008 and a multiple criteria AVERAGEIFS to average the sales of pizza franchises established before 2008 located in the state of Michigan.

Figure 2.3 AVERAGEIF and AVERAGEIFS Formulas

Formula
=AVERAGEIF(Year_Est,"<2008",sales)

	A	B	C	D	E	F
1			Pizza by Mario Franchise Sales			
2	Store_No	State	Year_Est.	Gross_Sales	Number of franchises	
3	101	Michigan	2004	652,458		
4	102	Michigan	2004	324,125	With sales greater than $500 thousand	10
5	103	Ohio	2004	845,612		
6	104	Ohio	2005	354,268	Established before 2008 and with sales	
7	105	Ohio	2005	856,412	greater than $500 thousand	7
8	106	Wisconsin	2006	512,463	Average Sales	
9	107	Minnesota	2006	325,496		
10	108	Minnesota	2006	845,621	For franchises established before 2008	585,231
11	109	Minnesota	2007	451,236		
12	110	Wisconsin	2007	554,168	For franchises established before 2008	
13	111	Kentucky	2007	715,683	in Michigan	488,292
14	112	Kentucky	2008	864,123		
15	113	Kentucky	2008	942,315		
16	114	Michigan	2009	458,321		
17	115	Michigan	2009	612,475		
18	TOTAL GROSS SALES			9,314,776		

Formula
=AVERAGEIFS(sales,Year_Est,"<2008",state,"=Michigan")

1. With **ExcelL2_C2_P1.xlsx** open, make M16 the active cell.
2. Create an AVERAGEIF function to calculate the average claim estimate for those claims with a rating of 1 by completing the following steps:

   a. Click the Insert Function button in the Formula bar.

   b. With *Statistical* the category in the *Or select a category* list box, click *AVERAGEIF* in the *Select a function* list box.

   c. Read the formula description below the function list box and then click OK.

   d. At the Function Arguments dialog box with the insertion point positioned in the *Range* text box, type **Rating** and then press Tab.

   e. With the insertion point positioned in the *Criteria* text box, type **1** and then press Tab.

   f. With the insertion point positioned in the *Average_range* text box, type **Claim_Estimate** and then press Tab.

   g. Click OK. Excel returns the value *2691* in M16.

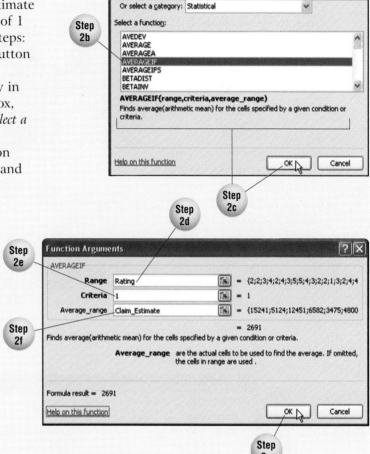

   h. Look at the formula in the Formula bar created by the Function Arguments dialog box =*AVERAGEIF(Rating,1,Claim_Estimate)*.

3. Format M16 to Comma Style number format with zero decimals.
4. Make M17 the active cell, type the formula =**averageif(rating,2,claim_estimate)**, and then press Enter.
5. Format M17 to Comma Style number format with zero decimals.
6. Make M17 the active cell and then drag the fill handle down to M18:M20.
7. Edit the formulas in M18, M19, and M20 by changing the rating criterion value from *2* to *3*, *4*, and *5*, respectively. When completed, the AVERAGEIF formulas will be as follows:

M18	=AVERAGEIF(Rating,3,Claim_Estimate)
M19	=AVERAGEIF(Rating,4,Claim_Estimate)
M20	=AVERAGEIF(Rating,5,Claim_Estimate)

By Rating	Avg. Est.
1	2,691
2	6,987
3	9,014
4	8,901
5	14,564

   Step 7

8. Save **ExcelL2_C2_P1.xlsx**.

1. With **ExcelL2_C2_P1.xlsx** open, make M22 the active cell.
2. Create an AVERAGEIFS function to calculate the average claim estimate for those claims with a rating of 2 and driver number 1 by completing the following steps:
   a. Click the Insert Function button in the Formula bar.
   b. With *Statistical* the category in the *Or select a category* list box, click *AVERAGEIFS* in the *Select a function* list box.
   c. Read the formula description below the function list box and then click OK.
   d. At the Function Arguments dialog box with the insertion point positioned in the *Average_range* text box, type **Claim_Estimate** and then press Tab.

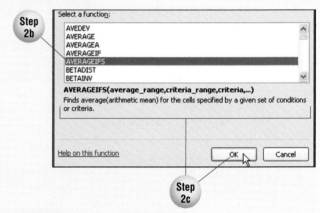

   e. Type **Rating** in the *Criteria_range1* text box and then press Tab.
   f. Type **2** in the *Criteria1* text box and then press Tab.
   g. Type **Driver_No** in the *Criteria_range2* text box and then press Tab.
   h. Type **1** in the *Criteria2* text box and then click OK. Excel returns the value *6272.6667* in the cell.

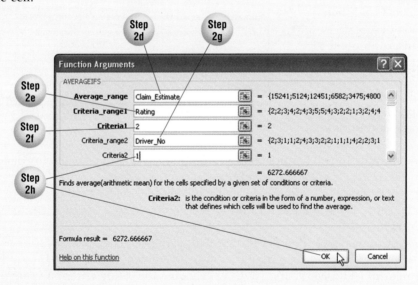

   i. Format M22 to Comma Style number format with zero decimals.
3. Copy the AVERAGEIFS formula in M22 and paste to M23.
4. Edit the formula in M23 to change the rating criterion from *2* to *3*. When completed, the AVERAGEIFS formula will be: *=AVERAGEIFS(Claim_Estimate,Rating,3,Driver_No,1)*.
5. If necessary, format M23 to Comma Style number format with zero decimals.
6. Save **ExcelL2_C2_P1.xlsx**.

Math and Trigonometry Functions

Excel includes several math and trigonometry functions such as ABS to return the absolute value of a number, SQRT to find the square root of a number, and RAND to return a random number between 0 and 1, to name a few. At the Insert Function dialog box change the *Or select a category* option to *Math & Trig* to scroll the list of available functions in the category.

SUMIF and SUMIFS

Within the math and trigonometry function category, Excel includes SUMIF to add the cells within a range that meet a single criterion and SUMIFS to add the cells within a range that meet multiple criteria. The structure of the SUMIF formula is =*SUMIF(range,criteria,sum_range)* where *range* is the cells to be tested for the criterion, *criteria* is the conditional statement used to select cells, and *sum_range* is the range containing the values to add.

SUMIFS is used to add cells that meet multiple criteria using the formula =*SUMIFS(sum_range,criteria_range1,criteria1,criteria_range2,criteria2 . . .)*. Figure 2.4 continues with the pizza franchise example to illustrate the use of a single criterion SUMIF to add the sales of pizza franchises established before 2008 and a multiple criteria SUMIFS to add the sales of pizza franchises established before 2008 located in the state of Michigan.

QUICK STEPS

Create SUMIF formula
1. Make desired cell active.
2. Click Insert Function button.
3. Change category to *Math & Trig.*
4. Select *SUMIF.*
5. Click OK.
6. Enter range address or range name to select by in *Range* text box.
7. Enter condition expression or text in *Criteria* text box.
8. Enter range address or range name to add in *Sum_range* text box.
9. Click OK.

🔒 Math & Trig ▾

Figure 2.4 SUMIF and SUMIFS Formulas

	A	B	C	D	E	F
1				Pizza by Mario Franchise Sales		
2	Store_No	State	Year_Est.	Gross_Sales	Number of franchises	
3	101	Michigan	2004	652,458		
4	102	Michigan	2004	324,125	With sales greater than $500 thousand	10
5	103	Ohio	2004	845,612		
6	104	Ohio	2005	354,268	Established before 2008 and with sales	
7	105	Ohio	2005	856,412	greater than $500 thousand	7
8	106	Wisconsin	2006	512,463	Average Sales	
9	107	Minnesota	2006	325,496		
10	108	Minnesota	2006	845,621	For franchises established before 2008	585,231
11	109	Minnesota	2007	451,236		
12	110	Wisconsin	2007	554,168	For franchises established before 2008	
13	111	Kentucky	2007	715,683	in Michigan	488,292
14	112	Kentucky	2008	864,123	Total Sales	
15	113	Kentucky	2008	942,315		
16	114	Michigan	2009	458,321	For franchises established before 2008	6,437,542
17	115	Michigan	2009	612,475		
18	TOTAL GROSS SALES			9,314,776	For franchises established before 2008	
19					in Michigan	976,583

Formula
=SUMIF(Year_Est,"<2008",sales)

Formula
=SUMIFS(sales,Year_Est,"<2008",state,"=Michigan")

Note: At Step 5 you will print the worksheet. Check with your instructor before printing to see if you need to print two copies of the worksheets for all projects in this chapter: one as displayed and another displaying cell formulas. Save the worksheet before displaying formulas (Ctrl + ~) so that you can adjust column widths as necessary and then close without saving the changes.

1. With **ExcelL2_C2_P1.xlsx** open, make M4 the active cell.
2. Create a SUMIF function to sum the claim estimates for those claims being repaired at A+ Paint & Body by completing the following steps:
   a. Click the Insert Function button in the Formula bar.
   b. Click the down-pointing arrow to the right of the *Or select a category* list box and then click *Math & Trig* at the drop-down list.
   c. Scroll down the *Select a function* list box and then click *SUMIF*.
   d. Read the formula description below the function list box and then click OK.
   e. At the Function Arguments dialog box with the insertion point positioned in the *Range* text box, type **Repair_Shop** and then press Tab.
   f. Type **A+ Paint & Body** in the *Criteria* text box and then press Tab.
   g. Type **Claim_Estimate** in the *Sum_range* text box and then click OK. Excel returns the value *16656* in M4.
   h. Format M4 to Comma Style number format with zero decimals.

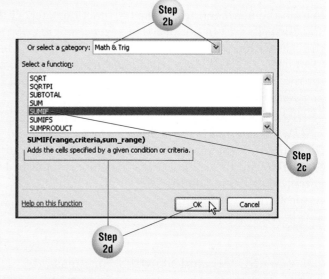

Step 2b

Step 2c

Step 2d

3. Enter the following SUMIF formulas in the cells indicated using either the Insert Function dialog box or by typing the formula directly into the cell.
   M5   =SUMIF(Repair_Shop,"JFJ Auto",Claim_Estimate)
   M6   =SUMIF(Repair_Shop,"Logans Auto Body",Claim_Estimate)
   M7   =SUMIF(Repair_Shop,"West Collision",Claim_Estimate)
4. Format M5:M7 to Comma Style number format with zero decimals.
5. Save and then print **ExcelL2_C2_P1.xlsx**. *Note: The worksheet will print in landscape orientation*.

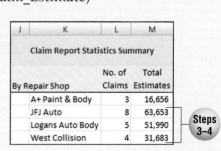

J	K	L	M
Claim Report Statistics Summary			
		No. of	Total
By Repair Shop		Claims	Estimates
A+ Paint & Body		3	16,656
JFJ Auto		8	63,653
Logans Auto Body		5	51,990
West Collision		4	31,683

Steps 3–4

Managing Range Names

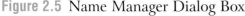

The Name Manager dialog box can be used to create, edit, or delete range names. A range name can be edited by changing the name or modifying the range address associated with the name. A range name can also be deleted if the name is not being used. Exercise caution when deleting a range name. If a range name used in a formula is deleted, cells that used the range name display the error #NAME? New range names can also be added to the workbook using the Name Manager dialog box shown in Figure 2.5.

Delete Range Name
1. Click Formulas tab.
2. Click Name Manager button.
3. Click desired range name.
4. Click Delete button.
5. Click OK.
6. Click Close.

Figure 2.5 Name Manager Dialog Box

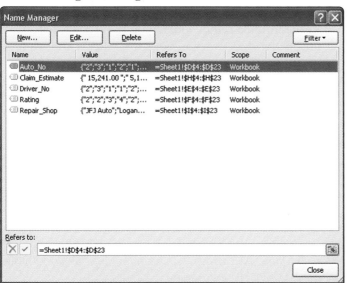

Project 1g Deleting a Range Name

1. With **ExcelL2_C2_P1.xlsx** open, click the Formulas tab in the ribbon.
2. Delete the range name *Auto_No* by completing the following steps:
   a. Click the Name Manager button in the Defined Names group.
   b. At the Name Manager dialog box, click *Auto_No* in the Name list box.
   c. Click the Delete button.
   d. At the Microsoft Office Excel message box asking you to confirm the deletion of the name *Auto_No*, click OK.
   e. Click the Close button located at the bottom right of the Name Manager dialog box.
3. Save and then close **ExcelL2_C2_P1.xlsx**.

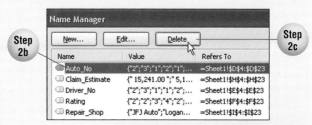

Step 2b

Step 2c

Step 2d

P roject ② **Populate Cells by Looking Up Data**

You will use a lookup formula to automatically enter discounts for containers and then calculate net prices.

Lookup Functions

The Lookup & Reference category of functions provides formulas that can be used to look up values in a range. For example, in a grades worksheet, the final numerical score for a student can be looked up in a range of cells that contain the letter grades with corresponding numerical scores for each grade. The letter grade can be returned in the formula cell by looking up the student's score. The ability to look up a value automates data entry in large worksheets and when used properly can avoid inaccuracies from data entry errors. Excel provides two lookup functions: VLOOKUP and HLOOKUP which refer to a vertical or horizontal lookup. The layout of the lookup range (referred to as a lookup table) determines whether to use VLOOKUP or HLOOKUP. VLOOKUP is more commonly used since most lookup tables are arranged with comparison data in columns which means Excel searches for the lookup value in a vertical order. HLOOKUP is used when the lookup range has placed comparison data in rows and Excel searches for the lookup value in a horizontal pattern.

VLOOKUP

QUICK STEPS

Create VLOOKUP formula
1. Make desired cell active.
2. Click Formulas tab.
3. Click Lookup & Reference button.
4. Click *VLOOKUP*.
5. Enter cell address or value in *Lookup_value* text box.
6. Enter range or range name in *Table_array* text box.
7. Type column number to return values from in *Col_index_num* text box.
8. Type **FALSE** or leave blank for *TRUE* in *Range_lookup* text box.
9. Click OK.

The structure of a VLOOKUP formula is =*VLOOKUP(lookup_value,table_array,col_index_num,range_lookup)*. Table 2.2 explains each section of the VLOOKUP argument.

VLOOKUP is easier to understand using an example. In the worksheet shown in Figure 2.6, VLOOKUP is used to return the starting salary for new hires. Each new hire is assigned a salary grid number that places his or her starting salary depending on their education and years of work experience. The lookup table contains the grid numbers with the corresponding starting salary. VLOOKUP formulas in column E automatically insert the starting salary for each new employee based on the employee's grid number in column D.

Table 2.2 VLOOKUP Argument Parameters

Argument parameter	Description
Lookup_value	The value that you want Excel to search for in the lookup table. You can enter a value or a cell reference to a value.
Table_array	The range address or range name for the lookup table that you want Excel to search. The first column of the table is the column Excel compares with the lookup_value.
Col_index_num	The column number from the lookup table that contains the data you want placed in the formula cell.
Range_lookup	Enter TRUE or FALSE to instruct Excel to find an exact match for the lookup value or an approximate match. If this parameter is left out of the formula, Excel assumes TRUE, which means if an exact match is not found, Excel returns the value for the next largest number that is less than the lookup value. For the formula to work properly, the first column of the lookup table must be sorted in ascending order.
	Enter FALSE to instruct Excel to return only exact matches to the lookup value.

Figure 2.6 VLOOKUP Example

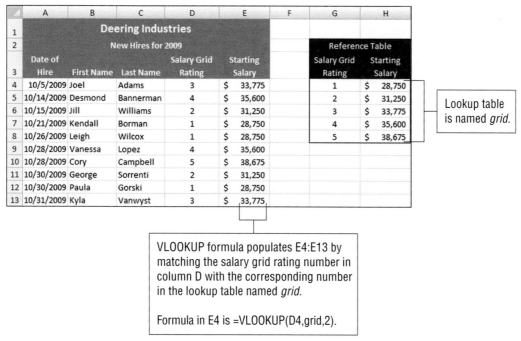

Lookup table is named *grid*.

VLOOKUP formula populates E4:E13 by matching the salary grid rating number in column D with the corresponding number in the lookup table named *grid*.

Formula in E4 is =VLOOKUP(D4,grid,2).

1. Open **Precision-BulkPriceList.xlsx**.
2. Save the workbook with Save As and name it **ExcelL2_C2_P2**.
3. Create a VLOOKUP formula to find the correct discount values for each product by completing the following steps:
   a. Make E4 the active cell.
   b. Click the Formulas tab.
   c. Click the Lookup & Reference button in the Function Library group.
   d. Click *VLOOKUP* at the drop-down list.
   e. If necessary, drag the Function Arguments dialog box down so that you can see the first few rows of the product list and the Discount Table data.
   f. With the insertion point positioned in the *Lookup_value* text box, type **c4** and then press Tab. Product discounts are categorized by letter codes. To find the correct discount, you need Excel to look for the matching category letter code for the product within the first column of the Discount table. Notice the letter codes in the Discount table are listed in ascending order.
   g. Type **Discount_Table** in the *Table_array* text box and then press Tab. The worksheet has the range name *Discount_Table* created, which references the cells $H$4:$I$8. Using a range name for a reference table is a good idea since the formula will be copied and absolute references are needed.
   h. Type **2** in the *Col_index_num* text box and then press Tab.
   i. Type **false** in the *Range_lookup* text box and then click OK. By typing *false*, you are instructing Excel to return a value for exact matches only. Should a discount category be typed into a cell in column C for which no entry exists in the Discount Table, Excel will return *#N/A* in the formula cell, which will alert you that an error has occurred in the data entry.

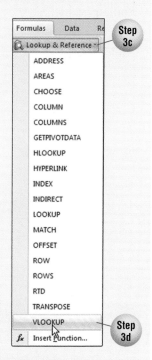

Step 3c

Step 3d

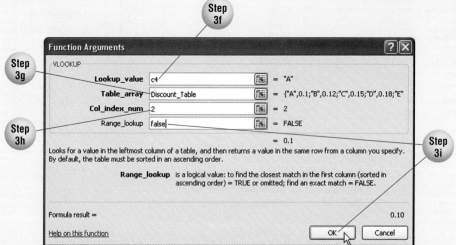

Step 3f

Step 3g

Step 3h

Step 3i

4. Look at the formula in the Formula bar =*VLOOKUP(C4,Discount_Table,2,FALSE)*.
5. Format E4 to Percent Style.

6. Make F4 the active cell, type the formula =d4-(d4*e4), and then press Enter.
7. Select E4:F4 and then drag the fill handle down to row 21.
8. Deselect the range.
9. Print the worksheet. *Note: The worksheet will print in landscape orientation*.
10. Save and then close **ExcelL2_C2_P2.xlsx**.

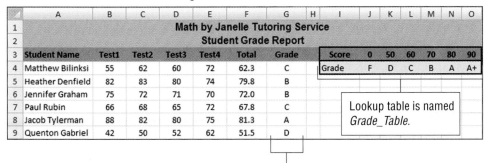

C	D	E	F	G	H	I
Packaging						
ts Price List					Discount Table	
Discount Category	List Price	Discount	Net Price		Discount Category	Discount Percent
A	18.67	10%	=d4-(d4*e4)		A	10%
C	22.50				B	12%
B	14.53				C	15%
D	5.25				D	18%
A	18.54				E	20%

Step 6

HLOOKUP

The HLOOKUP function uses the same argument parameters as VLOOKUP. Use HLOOKUP when the table in which you want to search for a comparison value is arranged in a horizontal arrangement similar to the one shown in Figure 2.7. Excel searches across the table in the first row for a matching value and then returns to the formula cell the value from the same column. The structure of an HLOOKUP formula is =*HLOOKUP(lookup_value,table_array,row_index_num,range_lookup)*. The argument parameters are similar to VLOOKUP's parameters described in Table 2.1. Excel searches the first row of the table for the lookup value. When a match is found, Excel returns the value from the same column in the row number specified in the *row_index_num* argument.

Figure 2.7 HLOOKUP Example

	A	B	C	D	E	F	G	H	I	J	K	L	M	N	O
1				Math by Janelle Tutoring Service											
2				Student Grade Report											
3	Student Name	Test1	Test2	Test3	Test4	Total	Grade		Score	0	50	60	70	80	90
4	Matthew Bilinksi	55	62	60	72	62.3	C		Grade	F	D	C	B	A	A+
5	Heather Denfield	82	83	80	74	79.8	B								
6	Jennifer Graham	75	72	71	70	72.0	B								
7	Paul Rubin	66	68	65	72	67.8	C								
8	Jacob Tylerman	88	82	80	75	81.3	A								
9	Quenton Gabriel	42	50	52	62	51.5	D								

Lookup table is named *Grade_Table*.

HLOOKUP formula populates G4:G9 by looking up the total value in column F with the first row in Grade_Table. Excel stops at the largest value in the table that does not go over the lookup value. Looking for 62.3 would cause Excel to stop at 60 because moving to the next value, 70, would be over the lookup value.

Formula in G4 is =HLOOKUP(F4,Grade_Table,2).

Project ③ Analyze an Expansion Project and Investment

You will use financial functions to calculate the principal portion of an expansion loan payment, the net present value of the proposed expansion project, and the present value of a proposed annuity investment plan.

QUICK STEPS

Create PPMT Formula
1. Make desired cell active.
2. Click Formulas tab.
3. Click Financial button.
4. Click *PPMT*.
5. Enter argument for interest rate in *Rate* text box.
6. Enter number representing payment to find principal for in *Per* text box.
7. Enter argument for total number of payments in *Nper* text box.
8. Enter cell address for amount borrowed in *Pv* text box.
9. Click OK.

Financial Functions

Financial functions can be used for a variety of financial analyses including loan amortizations, annuity payments, investment planning, depreciation, and so on. The PMT function is used to calculate a payment for a loan based on a constant interest rate and constant payments for a set period of time. Excel provides two related financial functions: PPMT, to calculate the principal portion of the loan payment; and IPMT, to calculate the interest portion.

PPMT

Knowing the principal portion of a loan payment is useful to determine the amount of the payment that is being used to reduce the principal balance owing. The difference between the loan payment and the PPMT value represents the interest cost. The function returns the principal portion of a specific payment for a loan. For example, you can calculate the principal on the first payment, the last payment, or any payment in between. The structure of a PPMT function is =PPMT(rate,per,nper,pv,fv,type) where:

- *rate* is the interest rate per period,
- *per* is the period for which you want to find the principal portion of the payment,
- *nper* is the number of payment periods,
- *pv* is the amount of money borrowed,
- *fv* is the balance at the end of the loan (if left blank, zero is assumed), and
- *type* is either 0 (payment at end of period) or 1 (payment at beginning of period).

Be careful to be consistent with the units for the interest rate and payment periods. If you divide the interest rate by 12 for a monthly rate, make sure the payment periods are also expressed monthly—for example, multiply the term by 12 if the amortization is entered in the worksheet in years.

Project ③a   Calculating Principal Portion of Loan Payments

1. Open **DeeringFinancials.xlsx**.
2. Save the workbook with Save As and name it **ExcelL2_C2_P3.xlsx**.
3. Calculate the principal portion of loan payments for two loan proposals to fund a building loan expansion project by completing the following steps:
   a. Make C10 the active cell.
   b. If necessary, click the Formulas tab.

c. Click the Financial button in the Function Library group.

d. Scroll down the Financial functions drop-down list and then click *PPMT*.

e. If necessary, move the Function Arguments dialog box to the right side of the screen so that you can see all of the values in column C.

f. With the insertion point positioned in the *Rate* text box, type **c4/12** and then press Tab. Since the interest rate is stated per annum, dividing the rate by 12 calculates the monthly rate.

g. Type **1** in the *Per* text box to calculate principal for the first loan payment and then press Tab.

h. Type **c5*12** in the *Nper* text box and then press Tab. Since loan payments are made each month, the number of payments is 12 times the amortization period.

i. Type **c6** in the *Pv* text box and then click OK. Pv refers to present value and in this example means the loan amount for which the payments are being calculated. Excel returns the value *-1,291.40* in C10. Payments are shown as negative numbers since they represent cash that would be paid out.

4. Copy and paste the formula from C10 to E10 and then press Esc to remove the moving marquee from C10.

5. Make C12 the active cell, type **=c8*12*c5**, and then press Enter.

6. Copy and paste the formula from C12 to E12. Press Esc to remove the moving marquee from C12 and then AutoFit the width of column E. Notice the loan from Dominion Trust is a better choice for Deering Industries provided the company can afford the higher monthly payments. Although the interest rate is higher than Victory Trust's loan, the shorter term means the loan is repaid faster at a lesser total cost.

7. Print the worksheet. *Note: The worksheet will print in landscape orientation.*

8. Save **ExcelL2_C2_P3.xlsx**.

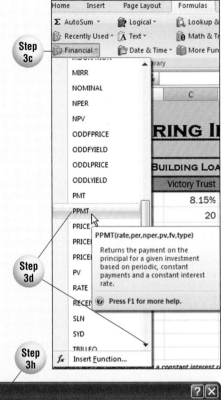

Step 3c

Step 3d

Step 3h

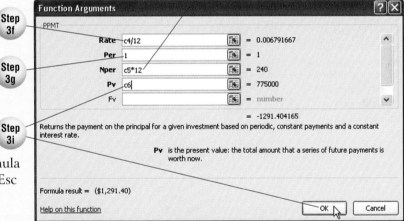

Step 3f

Step 3g

Step 3i

Step 5

Create PV Formula
1. Make desired cell active.
2. Click Formulas tab.
3. Click Financial button.
4. Click PV.
5. Enter argument for interest rate in *Rate* text box.
6. Enter argument for total number of payments in *Nper* text box.
7. Enter cell address or value for amount of payment in *Pmt* text box.
8. Click OK.

Create NPV Formula
1. Make desired cell active.
2. Click Formulas tab.
3. Click Financial button.
4. Click *NPV*.
5. Enter cell address or value for discount rate in *Rate* text box.
6. Enter cell address or value for first payment or income in *Value1* text box.
7. Continue entering in sequential order cell addresses or values for cash flows in *Value* text boxes.
8. Click OK.

PV

Present value returns the amount that a series of future payments is worth today. The PV function assumes a constant interest rate and a constant payment over the life of the annuity. The structure of a PV formula is *=PV(rate,nper,pmt,fv,type)*, where *rate* is the interest rate per period, *nper* is the number of payment periods, *pmt* is the payment made each period, *fv* is the balance at the end of the investment (if left blank, zero is assumed), and *type* is either 0 (payment at end of period) or 1 (payment at beginning of period).

NPV

Net present value returns the value of an investment today using a discount rate and incorporating a series of future cash inflows or outflows related to the investment. The discount rate used can be the rate of return on a competing investment or an inflation rate. Financial managers calculate net present value to determine if a capital project that requires a significant cash outflow will have a positive payback after a specific period of time. Generally speaking, if a project's NPV is negative, a company is better off using capital funds for another project or investment that provides positive payback. The structure of an NPV formula is *=NPV(rate,value1,value2 . . .)* where *rate* is the discount rate and *value1,value2 . . .* represent the future cash outflows and inflows from the investment at equally spaced time intervals. The difference between PV and NPV is that PV uses a constant payment whereas NPV allows you to vary the payments over the life of the investment.

Project 3b   **Calculating the NPV of a Capital Project and the PV of an Annuity**

1. With **ExcelL2_C2_P3.xlsx** open, click the NPV-ExpansionProject sheet tab located at the bottom of the screen above the Status bar. The worksheet contains financial data that managers at Deering Industries have prepared for the building expansion project. The cost of the expansion project is $775 thousand. Managers have forecasted additional revenues (net of additional costs) over 10 years in the range C8:C17. Using a discount rate of 4.5% (the rate of a competitive investment such as a government bond), management wants to find out if the expansion project has a positive net present value after 10 years.
2. Calculate the net present value of the building expansion project using the NPV function by completing the following steps:
   a. Make C19 the active cell.
   b. If necessary, click the Formulas tab.

c. Click the Financial button in the Function Library group.

d. Scroll down the Financial functions drop-down list and then click *NPV*.

e. With the insertion point positioned in the *Rate* text box, type **Discount_Rate** and then press Tab. Range names have already been defined in the workbook. The range name *Discount_Rate* references C4.

f. Type **Initial_Cost** in the *Value1* text box and then press Tab. The range name *Initial_Cost* references the cost of expansion value in C6.

g. Type **Future_Returns** in the *Value2* text box and then click OK. The range name *Future_Returns* refers to the Net Returns over 10 years in the range C8:C17.

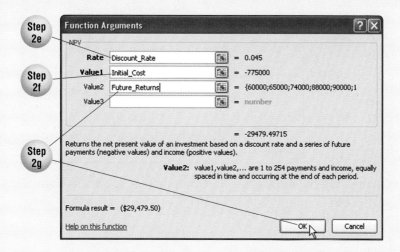

3. Excel returns the value -29,479.50 in C19, which means the project will not provide Deering Industries with a positive net present value after 10 years. The expansion project should be carefully reviewed to see if the project can proceed at a lower cost, at a lower discount rate, or if the company needs to consider a longer payback period.

4. Print the worksheet. ***Note: The worksheet will print in landscape orientation***.

5. Click the PV-Annuity sheet tab located at the bottom of the screen above the Status bar. In this worksheet, management has entered details regarding an annuity investment that will cost $1,000 to buy. Management wants to find out if the investment is worth $1,000. The investment will pay an annuity twice per year for 20 years. Calculate the present value of the investment using the PV function by completing the following steps:

a. Make C12 the active cell.

b. Click the Financial button, scroll down the drop-down list, and then click *PV*.

c. With the insertion point positioned in the *Rate* text box, type **Market_Rate/2** and then press Tab. *Market_Rate* is the range name that references the current market interest rate in C11. The rate is divided by 2 since the annuity is paid twice per year.

d. Type **Term*2** in the *Nper* text box and then press Tab. *Term* is the range name that references the time to maturity in C5 and is multiplied times 2 since the annuity payment is paid semiannually.

e. Type **Annuity** in the *Pmt* text box and then click OK. *Annuity* is the range name that references the annuity payment that will be received semiannually in C9.

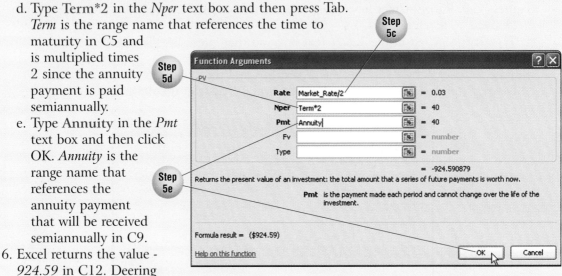

Step 5c

Step 5d

Step 5e

6. Excel returns the value -924.59 in C12. Deering Industries should only buy the annuity if they can purchase it for less than $924.59.

7. Print the worksheet. *Note: The worksheet will print in landscape orientation.*

8. Save and then close **ExcelL2_C2_P3.xlsx**.

Project ④ Calculate Benefit Costs Using Conditional Logic

You will create formulas to calculate the employee benefit costs for Vantage Video Rentals using logical functions to test multiple conditions.

Logical Functions

Create IF Formula
1. Make desired cell active.
2. Click Formulas tab.
3. Click Logical button.
4. Click *IF*.
5. Type conditional test argument in *Logical_test* text box.
6. Press Tab.
7. Type argument in *Value_if_true* text box.
8. Press Tab.
9. Type argument in *Value_if_false* text box.
10. Click OK.

Conditional logic in formulas requires Excel to perform a calculation based on the outcome of a conditional test where one calculation is performed if the test proves true and another calculation is performed if the test proves false. For example, an IF statement to calculate a sales bonus if sales exceed a target could be created similar to the following: *=IF(Sales>Target,Bonus,0)*. Excel first tests the value in the cell named Sales to see if the value is greater than the value in the cell named Target. If the condition proves true, Excel returns the value in the cell named Bonus; if Sales are not greater than Target the condition proves false and Excel places a 0 in the cell. The structure of the IF statement is *=IF(condition,value_if_true,value_if_false)*.

AND, OR, and NOT

Other logic functions offered in Excel include AND, OR, and NOT. These functions use Boolean logic to construct a conditional test in a formula. Table 2.3 describes how the three functions work to test a statement and provides an example for each.

Table 2.3 AND, OR, and NOT Logical Functions

Logical Function	Description	Example
AND	Excel returns *True* if all conditions test true. Excel returns *False* if any one of the conditions test false.	=AND(Sales>Target,NewClients>5) Returns *True* if both test true. If Sales>Target but NewClients<5, returns *False*. If Sales<Target but NewClients>5, returns *False*.
OR	Excel returns *True* if any condition tests true. Excel returns *False* if all conditions test false.	=OR(Sales>Target,NewClients>5) Returns *True* if either Sales>Target or NewClients>5. Returns *False* only if both Sales is not greater than Target and NewClients is not greater than 5.
NOT	Performs reverse logic. If the condition tests true, Excel returns *False* in the cell. If the condition tests false, Excel returns *True* in the cell.	=NOT(Age>65) If Age is 70, returns *False*. If Age is 60, returns *True*. If Age is 65, returns *True*.

QUICK STEPS

Create AND Formula
1. Make desired cell active OR nest formula in IF statement *Logical_test* text box.
2. Type **=AND(** OR **AND(** if nesting in IF statement.
3. Type first conditional test argument.
4. Type **,**.
5. Type second conditional test argument.
6. Repeat Steps 4–5 for remaining conditions.
7. Type **)**.

Create OR Formula
1. Make desired cell active OR nest formula in IF statement *Logical_test* text box.
2. Type **=OR(** OR **OR(** if nesting in IF statement.
3. Type first conditional test argument.
4. Type **,**.
5. Type second conditional test argument.
6. Repeat Steps 4–5 for remaining conditions.
7. Type **)**.

Create NOT Formula
1. Make desired cell active.
2. Type **=NOT(**.
3. Type argument or value to test.
4. Type **)**.
5. Press Enter.

HINT

You can nest an AND, OR, or NOT function with an IF function to test multiple conditions.

1. Open **VantageSalary&Benefits.xlsx**.
2. Save the workbook with Save As and name it **ExcelL2_C2_P4**.
3. Vantage Video Rentals contributes 5% of an employee's salary into a privately managed company retirement account if the employee is full-time and earns more than $45 thousand in salary. Calculate the pension benefit cost for eligible employees by completing the following steps:
   a. Make H6 the active cell.
   b. Click the Formulas tab.
   c. Click the Logical button in the Function Library group and then click *IF* at the drop-down list.
   d. If necessary, drag the Function Arguments dialog box down until you can see all of row 6 in the worksheet.
   e. With the insertion point positioned in the *Logical_test* text box, type **and(c6="FT",g6>45000)** and then press Tab. An AND function is required since both conditions must be true for the company to contribute to the pension plan. *Note: Excel requires quotation symbols around text when used in a conditional test formula*.
   f. Type **g6*5%** in the *Value_if_true* text box and then press Tab.
   g. Type **0** in the *Value_if_false* text box and then click OK.

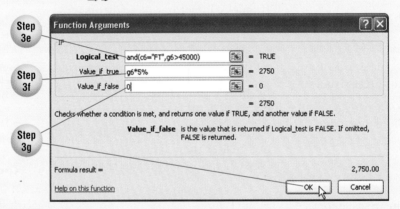

h. Look at the formula *=IF(AND(C6="FT",G6>45000),G6*5%,0)* in the Formula bar. Notice the AND function is nested within the IF function. Since both conditions for the first employee tested true, the pension cost is calculated.
i. Copy the formula in H6 to H7:H14 without copying the border formatting by completing the following steps:
   1) With H6 the active cell, click the Home tab and then click the Copy button in the Clipboard group.
   2) Select H7:H14.
   3) Click the Paste button arrow in the Clipboard group and then click *No Borders* at the drop-down list.
   4) Press the Esc key to remove the moving marquee from H6.
   5) Deselect the range.
4. Save **ExcelL2_C2_P4.xlsx**.

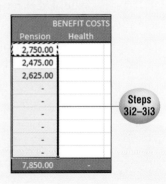

Project ⓵ⓑ **Calculating Health and Dental Costs Using Nested IF and OR Functions**

1. With **ExcelL2_C2_P4.xlsx** open, make I6 the active cell.
2. Vantage Video Rentals offers to pay the annual health premiums for employees who are not covered by any other medical plan. The company pays $2,100 per year per employee for family coverage and $1,380 per year for single coverage. Calculate the cost of the health benefit for those employees who opted into the plan by completing the following steps:
   a. This formula requires a nested IF statement since the result will be either *$2,180* or *$1,380* depending on the contents in cell D6. Type the formula shown below in I6 and then press Enter. (An OR statement will not work for this formula since two different values are used.)

   =if(d6="Family",2100,if(d6="Single",1380,0))

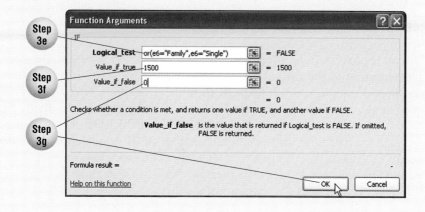

   b. Copy the formula in I6 to I7:I14. Notice the cells for which no value is entered. In column D, these employees show the text *Declined*. Excel returned zero since both conditions D6="Family" and D6="Single" proved false.
3. Vantage Video Rentals negotiated a flat fee with their dental benefit service provider. The company pays the same rate of $1,500 per year for all employees regardless of the type of coverage. The service provider requires Vantage to report each person's coverage as *Family* or *Single* for audit purposes. The dental plan is optional and some employees have declined the coverage. Calculate the dental plan cost by completing the following steps:
   a. Make J6 the active cell.
   b. Click the Formulas tab.
   c. Click the Logical button and then click *IF* at the drop-down list.
   d. If necessary, drag the Function Arguments dialog box down until you can see all of row 6 in the worksheet.
   e. With the insertion point positioned in the *Logical_test* text box, type or(e6="Family",e6="Single") and then press Tab. An OR function is suited to this benefit since either condition can be true for the company to contribute to the dental plan.
   f. Type **1500** in the *Value_if_true* text box and then press Tab.
   g. Type **0** in the *Value_if_false* text box and then click OK.

h. Look at the formula =IF(OR(E6="Family",E6="Single"),1500,0) in the Formula bar. Notice the OR function is nested within the IF function. Since E6 contained neither *Family* or *Single*, the OR statement tested false and the result of *0* is returned in J6.

i. Copy the formula in J6 and paste to J7:J14 without pasting the border formatting by completing the following steps:
   1) With J6 the active cell, click the Home tab and then click the Copy button in the Clipboard group.
   2) Select J7:J14.
   3) Click the Paste button arrow in the Clipboard group and then click *No Borders* at the drop-down list.
   4) Press the Esc key to remove the moving marquee from J6.
   5) Deselect the range.

BENEFIT COSTS		
Pension	Health	Dental
2,750.00	2,100.00	-
2,475.00	1,380.00	1,500.00
2,625.00	-	-
-	2,100.00	1,500.00
-	1,380.00	1,500.00
-	2,100.00	-
-	1,380.00	-
-	-	-
-	-	1,500.00
7,850.00	10,440.00	6,000.00

Step 3i

4. Save **ExcelL2_C2_P4.xlsx**.
5. Print and then close **ExcelL2_C2_P4.xlsx**. *Note: The worksheet will print in landscape orientation*.

Project 5 Flag Part-Time Employee Earnings Ceiling

You will add information to a worksheet to make sure the part-time senior employees at Vantage Video Rentals who are receiving a pension benefit payment are flagged for the payroll administrator since these employees have an earnings ceiling.

QUICK STEPS

Create IFERROR Formula
1. Make desired cell active.
2. Type =IFERROR(.
3. Type argument for *value* parameter.
4. Type ,.
5. Type argument for *value_if_error* parameter.
6. Type).
7. Press Enter.

IFERROR

Use an IFERROR function to alert the reader if an error condition occurs in a cell. The structure of the formula is *=IFERROR(value,value_if_error)*. In the worksheet shown in Figure 2.8, the IFERROR formula alerts the reader that an incorrect sales target value was entered in E7. Since it is not possible to divide by zero, an error occurs when the value is calculated. The IFERROR formula displays the message *Incorrect target* in the cell rather than *#DIV/0*, which is the normal error result. In E13 in the example worksheet, no value has been entered. The IFERROR formula in this case displays the message *Incorrect target* since the cell being divided contains two asterisks (**) instead of a value.

Figure 2.8 IFERROR Example

	A	B	C	D	E	F
1			Pizza by Mario Franchise Sales			
2	Store_No	State	Year_Est.	Gross_Sales	Target	Variance %
3	101	Michigan	2004	652,458	600,000	8.7%
4	102	Michigan	2004	324,125	400,000	-19.0%
5	103	Ohio	2004	845,612	800,000	5.7%
6	104	Ohio	2005	354,268	350,000	1.2%
7	105	Ohio	2005	856,412	-	Incorrect target
8	106	Wisconsin	2006	512,463	550,000	-6.8%
9	107	Minnesota	2006	325,496	315,000	3.3%
10	108	Minnesota	2006	845,621	850,000	-0.5%
11	109	Minnesota	2007	451,236	460,000	-1.9%
12	110	Wisconsin	2007	554,168	560,000	-1.0%
13	111	Kentucky	2007	715,683	**	Incorrect target
14	112	Kentucky	2008	864,123	875,000	-1.2%
15	113	Kentucky	2008	942,315	900,000	4.7%
16	114	Michigan	2009	458,321	400,000	14.6%
17	115	Michigan	2009	612,475	575,000	6.5%
18	TOTAL GROSS SALES			9,314,776	7,635,000	22.0%

Formula =IFERROR((D7-E7)/E7,"Incorrect target") returns *Incorrect target* since E7 contains 0 and you cannot divide by zero.

Project 5   Flagging Employees by Age for an Earnings Ceiling using NOT and IFERROR

1. Open **Vantage-PTRetirees.xlsx**.
2. Save the workbook with Save As and name it **ExcelL2_C2_P5.xlsx**.
3. The part-time employees at Vantage Video Rentals who are over 65 receive a pension benefit payment each month. The pension benefit payment is reduced if the employee earns over $12 thousand per year. The payroll administrator would like a report to flag those employees who receive a pension benefit to ensure the employees do not risk having their benefit reduced. Use a NOT function to flag those employees who are over 65 by completing the following steps:
   a. Make F6 the active cell.
   b. Type **=not(d6<65)** and then press Enter.

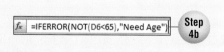

   Step 3b

Age	Receiving Pension?
28	=not(d6<65)

   c. Notice Excel returned the value *FALSE* in F6. The NOT function uses reverse logic. The employee's age in D6 is 28 and 28 is less than 65. The condition tested true; therefore, reverse logic means Excel returns *FALSE*. This result makes sense with the column title in the worksheet *Receiving Pension?* Since the employee is less than 65, the employee would not be receiving a pension benefit payment.
4. Notice some of the ages in column D display *#N/A* instead of a value. You discover that the payroll administrator is still waiting for birth certificates from some employees. Edit the formula in F6 to display a message for those employees where the age is missing by completing the following steps:
   a. Make F6 the active cell.
   b. Edit the formula in the Formula bar so that the formula reads as follows:

   f_x =IFERROR(NOT(D6<65),"Need Age")   Step 4b

   =IFERROR(NOT(D6<65),"Need Age")

Age	Receiving Pension?
28	FALSE
66	TRUE
45	FALSE
#N/A	Need Age
67	TRUE
65	TRUE
#N/A	Need Age
38	FALSE
47	FALSE
#N/A	Need Age
70	TRUE
55	FALSE
69	TRUE
22	FALSE

   Step 4d

   c. Copy the formula in F6 to F7:F19. Notice the IFERROR formula causes the text *Need Age* to appear in those cells where the age in column D contains the entry *#N/A*.
   d. If necessary, press the Esc key to remove the moving marquee from F6 and deselect the range.
5. Save, print, and then close **ExcelL2_C2_P5.xlsx**.

P roject ⑥ **Convert Text Using Text Functions**

You will open a worksheet with data downloaded from the U.S. Census Bureau and use text functions to modify a heading and convert state names to upper case.

QUICK STEPS

Substitute Text Formula
1. Make desired cell active.
2. Type **=SUBSTITUTE(**.
3. Type source text cell address.
4. Type **,**.
5. Type text to be changed in quotation symbols.
6. Type **,**.
7. Type replacement text in quotation symbols.
8. Type **)**.
9. Press Enter.

Convert Text to Uppercase
1. Make desired cell active.
2. Type **=UPPER(**.
3. Type source cell address OR
   Type text to convert in quotation symbols.
4. Type **)**.
5. Press Enter.

Text Functions

Text can be formatted or modified using a text function formula. For example, text can be converted from uppercase to lowercase or vice versa using the LOWER and UPPER functions. Text that has incorrect capitalization can be changed to initial case using the PROPER function. Substitute existing text with new text using the SUBSTITUTE function. Table 2.4 provides the structure of each of these functions, a description, and provides an example.

Table 2.4 Text Function Examples

Text Function	Description	Example
=PROPER(text)	Capitalizes the first letter of each word.	=PROPER("annual budget") returns *Annual Budget* in formula cell OR A3 holds the text *annual budget*; =PROPER(A3) entered in C3 causes C3 to display *Annual Budget*
=UPPER(text)	Converts text to uppercase.	=UPPER("annual budget") returns *ANNUAL BUDGET* in formula cell OR A3 holds the text *annual budget*; =UPPER(A3) entered in C3 causes C3 to display *ANNUAL BUDGET*
=LOWER(text)	Converts text to lowercase.	=LOWER("ANNUAL BUDGET") returns *annual budget* in formula cell OR A3 holds the text *ANNUAL BUDGET*; =LOWER(A3) entered in C3 causes C3 to display *annual budget*
=SUBSTITUTE(text)	New text is inserted in place of old text.	A3 holds the text *Annual Budget*; =SUBSTITUTE(A3,"Annual","2010") entered in C3 causes C3 to display *2010 Budget*

1. Open **USIncomeStats.xlsx**.
2. Save the workbook with Save As and name it **ExcelL2_C2_P6**.
3. The worksheet contains 2005 median income data downloaded from the U.S. Census Bureau. You want to estimate 2009 median income using a formula based on 2005 statistics. To begin, copy and substitute text at the top of the worksheet to create the layout for 2009 data by completing the following steps:
   a. Copy A1 and paste to D1. Click the Paste Options button and then click *Keep Source Column Widths* at the drop-down list.

   b. Press the ESC key to remove the moving marquee from A1.
   c. Make D2 the active cell, type **=substitute(a2,"2005","2009")** and then press Enter.

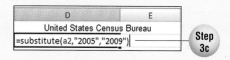

   d. Copy A3:B4, paste to D3, and then press the ESC key to remove the moving marquee from A3.
4. Copy the state names from column A to column D and convert the text to uppercase by completing the following steps:
   a. Make D5 the active cell.
   b. Type **=upper(a5)** and then press Enter. Excel returns the text *ALABAMA* in D5.

	D	E
	United States Census Bureau	
	Estimated 2009 Median Annual Income	
	2 person families by state	
	State	Median Income
	=upper(a5)	

Step 4b

   c. Press the Up Arrow key to move the active cell back to D5 and then drag the fill handle down to D55.
5. Enter the formula to estimate 2009 median income based on 2005 data plus 6.7 percent by completing the following steps:
   a. Make E5 the active cell.
   b. Type **=(b5*6.7%)+b5** and then press Enter.

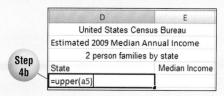

c. Press the Up Arrow key to move the active cell back to E5 and then format the cell to Comma Style number format with no decimals.

d. Drag the fill handle in E5 down to E55.

e. Deselect the range.

	A	B	C	D	E
1	United States Census Bureau			United States Census Bureau	
2	Estimated 2005 Median Annual Income			Estimated 2009 Median Annual Income	
3	2 person families by state			2 person families by state	
4	State	Median Income		State	Median Income
5	Alabama	46,086		ALABAMA	49,174
6	Alaska	60,983		ALASKA	65,069
7	Arizona	48,630		ARIZONA	51,888
8	Arkansas	39,463		ARKANSAS	42,107
9	California	57,237		CALIFORNIA	61,072

Rows 1–9 of completed worksheet.

6. Change the Page Setup to print the worksheet centered horizontally.

7. In the Scale to Fit group, set the width and height to *1 page*.

8. Save, print, and then close **ExcelL2_C2_P6.xlsx**.

In this chapter you learned how to use a small sampling of functions from the statistical, math and trigonometry, lookup, financial, logical, and text function lists. Excel includes over 300 functions in eleven categories. When you need to enter a complex formula and are not sure if Excel includes a preprogrammed function, open the Insert Function dialog box, type a description of the function in the *Search for a function* text box and then click the Go button.

CHAPTER summary

- Assign names to cells or ranges to reference by name in formulas or navigation.
- Using range names in formulas make formulas easier to comprehend.
- Create range names by selecting the source range and then typing a name in the Name text box.
- COUNTA is a statistical function that counts nonblank cells. Use the function to count cells containing text and a combination of text and numbers.
- The COUNTIF statistical function counts cells within a range based on a single criterion.
- Use COUNTIFS to count cells within a range based on multiple criteria.
- Find the arithmetic mean of a range of cells based on a single criterion using the statistical AVERAGEIF function.
- AVERAGEIFS finds the arithmetic mean for a range based on multiple criteria.
- The math function SUMIF adds cells within a range based on a single criterion.
- To add cells within a range based on multiple criteria, use the SUMIFS function.
- Open the Name Manager dialog box to create new range names, edit existing range names, or delete a range name.
- Lookup & Reference functions VLOOKUP and HLOOKUP look up data in a reference table and return in the formula cell a value from a column or row in the lookup table.
- The PPMT financial function returns the principal portion of a specified loan payment within the term based on an interest rate, total number of payments, and loan amount.
- Calculate present value and net present value of an investment using the PV and NPV financial functions.
- Conditional logic in a formula performs a calculation based on the outcome of a conditional test where one action is performed if the test proves true, or another action is performed if the test proves false.
- Use the AND logical function to test multiple conditions. Excel returns *TRUE* if all conditions test true and returns *FALSE* if any one of the conditions test false.
- The OR logical function also tests multiple conditions. The function returns *TRUE* if any one of the conditions tests true and *FALSE* if all of the conditions test false.
- Perform reverse logic using the NOT logical function. If the condition tests true, Excel returns *FALSE* in the cell. If the condition tests false, Excel returns *TRUE* to the cell.
- Use an IFERROR function to flag a cell in which an error condition has occurred.
- The text function =PROPER capitalizes the first letter of each word in the text source.
- Convert the case of text from lowercase to uppercase, or uppercase to lowercase, using the =UPPER and =LOWER text functions.
- Replace a text string with new text using the SUBSTITUTE text function.

COMMANDS review

FEATURE	RIBBON TAB, GROUP	BUTTON	KEYBOARD SHORTCUT
Financial functions	Formulas, Function Library	Financial ▾	
Insert Function dialog box	Formulas, Function Library	*fx*	Shift + F3
Logical functions	Formulas, Function Library	Logical ▾	
Lookup & Reference functions	Formulas, Function Library	Lookup & Reference ▾	
Math & Trigonometry functions	Formulas, Function Library	Math & Trig ▾	
Name Manager dialog box	Formulas, Defined Names		Ctrl + F3
Statistical functions	Formulas, Function Library	More Functions ▾	
Text functions	Formulas, Function Library	A Text ▾	

CONCEPTS check

Test Your Knowledge

Completion: In the space provided at the right, indicate the correct term, command, or number.

1. Assign a name to a selected range by typing the desired name in this text box.

   _____

2. A range name can be a combination of letters, numbers, underscore characters and this punctuation character.

   _____

3. This COUNTIF function would count the number of cells in a range named *sales* where the values are greater than $50 thousand.

   _____

4. Use this statistical function to find the mean of a range based on two criteria.

   _____

5. SUMIF is found in this function category.

   _____

6. Open this dialog box to delete a range name.

   _____

7. Use this lookup function to look up a value in a reference table where the comparison data in the table is arranged in rows.

   _____

8. This financial function returns the principal portion of a specified loan payment.

   _____

9. This financial function returns the value of an investment today using a discount rate and incorporating future cash inflows and outflows.

   _____

10. This logical function performs reverse logic.

    _____

11. Excel's AND and OR functions use this type of logic to construct a conditional test.

    _____

12. This logical function can be used to display a message in a cell if an error occurs when a value is calculated.

    _____

13. This text function can be used to capitalize the first letter of each word in a cell.

    _____

14. This formula converts text typed in lowercase within a cell to all uppercase characters.

    _____

15. Use this text function to change a text string in the source cell to new text in the formula cell.

    _____

SKILLS check
Demonstrate Your Proficiency

Assessment

1 CREATE RANGE NAMES AND USE THE LOOKUP FUNCTION

Note: Check with your instructor before printing assessments to see if you need to print two copies of each assessment; one as displayed and another with cell formulas displayed.

1. Open **RSR-OctLaborCost.xlsx**.
2. Save the workbook with Save As and name it **ExcelL2_C2_A1**.
3. Create the following range names:
   - C7:C22   *Hours*
   - D7:D22   *TechCode*
   - F7:F22   *LaborCost*
   - I3:J5   *RateChart*
4. In E7 create the VLOOKUP formula to return the correct hourly rate based on the technician code in D7. Use the range name *RateChart* within the formula to reference the hourly rate chart. Make sure Excel will return values for exact matches only.
5. Copy the VLOOKUP formula in E7 and paste to E8:E22.
6. In F7 create the formula to extend the labor cost by multiplying the hours in C7 times the hourly rate in E7.
7. Copy the formula in F7 and paste to F8:F22.
8. Create the formula in F23 to sum the column.
9. Preview and then print the worksheet.
10. Save and then close **ExcelL2_C2_A1.xlsx**.

Assessment

2 WORK WITH STATISTICAL FUNCTIONS

Note: For all functions in Assessment 2 with the exception of Step 3, use range names in the formulas to reference sources.

1. Open **ExcelL2_C2_A1.xlsx**.
2. Save the workbook with Save As and name it **ExcelL2_C2_A2**.
3. In I23 create a COUNTA formula to count the number of calls made in October using the dates in column A as the source range.
4. Create the COUNTIF formulas in the cells indicated below.
   - I9   Count the number of calls made by Technician 1
   - I10   Count the number of calls made by Technician 2
   - I11   Count the number of calls made by Technician 3

5. In I14 create a COUNTIFS formula to count the number of calls made by Technician 3 where the hours logged were greater than 3.
6. Create the SUMIF formulas in the cells indicated below.
    J9   Add the labor cost for calls made by Technician 1
    J10   Add the labor cost for calls made by Technician 2
    J11   Add the labor cost for calls made by Technician 3
7. Format J9:J11 to Comma Style number format.
8. In J14 create a SUMIFS formula to add the labor cost for calls made by Technician 3 where the hours logged were greater than 3.
9. Format J14 to Comma Style number format.
10. Create the AVERAGEIF formulas in the cells indicated below.
    J18   Average the labor cost for calls made by Technician 1
    J19   Average the labor cost for calls made by Technician 2
    J20   Average the labor cost for calls made by Technician 3
11. Format J18:J20 to Comma Style number format.
12. Save, print, and then close **ExcelL2_C2_A2.xlsx**.

Assessment

3   USE FINANCIAL FUNCTIONS

1. Open **Precision-NewWarehouse.xlsx**.
2. Save the workbook with Save As and name it **ExcelL2_C2_A3.xlsx**.
3. With the Financing tab active, create the PMT formula in D8 to calculate the monthly loan payment for the proposed loan from NewVentures Capital Inc.
4. Find the principal portion of the loan payment for the first loan payment in D10 and the last loan payment in D11.
5. In D13 create the formula to calculate the total cost of the loan by multiplying the monthly loan payment times 12 times the amortization period in years.
6. In D14 create the formula to calculate the interest cost of the loan by entering the formula **=d13+d6**. *Note: Normally, you would calculate interest cost on a loan by subtracting the amount borrowed from the total payments made; however, in this worksheet you have to add the two cells because the total cost of the loan is a negative number. Subtracting D6 from D13 would cause Excel to add the two values because two negative values create a positive.*
7. Print the Financing worksheet.
8. Make the NPV worksheet active.
9. In C22 create the formula to calculate the net present value of the new warehouse project using the discount rate in C3 and the values in C4 and C7:C21.
10. Print the NPV worksheet.
11. Save, print, and then close **ExcelL2_C2_A3.xlsx**.

Assessment

4 USE LOGICAL FUNCTIONS

1. Open **AllClaims-PremiumReview.xlsx**.
2. Save the workbook with Save As and name it **ExcelL2_C2_A4.xlsx**.
3. Create the formula in G4 to display the text *Yes* if the number of *AtFault Claims* is greater than 1 and the *Current Rating* is greater than 2. Both conditions must test true to display *Yes*; otherwise display *No* in the cell. **Hint: Use a nested IF and AND formula**.
4. Center the result in G4 and then copy the formula to G5:G23.
5. Create the formula in H4 to display the text *Yes* in the cell if either the number of claims is greater than 2 or the current deductible is less than $1,000.00. **Hint: Use a nested IF and OR formula**.
6. Center the result in H4 and then copy the formula to H5:H23. Deselect the range after copying.
7. Save, print, and then close **ExcelL2_C2_A4.xlsx**.

Assessment

5 WORK WITH THE HLOOKUP FUNCTION

1. Open **JanelleTutoring-ProgressRpt.xlsx**.
2. Save the workbook with Save As and name it **ExcelL2_C2_A5**.
3. Use the Name text box to scroll to the range named *Grade_Table*. Notice the range is located in the sheet labeled *ProgressComments*.
4. Deselect the range and then make StudentProgress the active sheet.
5. Create a formula in G4 that will look up the student's total score in column F in the range named *Grade_Table* and return the appropriate progress comment.
6. Copy the formula in G4 and paste to G5:G12.
7. Save, print, and then close **ExcelL2_C2_A5.xlsx**.

CASE study

Apply Your Skills

Yolanda Robertson of NuTrends Market Research was pleased with your previous work and has requested that you be assigned to assist with another new client. Yolanda is preparing a marketing plan for a franchise expansion for the owners of Pizza by Mario. The franchise was started in Michigan and has stores in Ohio, Wisconsin, and Iowa. The owners plan to double their locations within the next two years by expanding into neighboring states. The owners have provided a confidential franchise sales report to Yolanda in an Excel file named **PizzabyMario-FranchiseSales.xlsx**. Yolanda needs your help with Excel to extract some statistics and calculate franchise royalty payments. With this information, Yolanda can develop a franchise communication package for prospective franchisees. Open the workbook and name it **ExcelL2_C2_CS_P1**. Yolanda has asked for the following statistics:

- A count of the number of stores with gross sales greater than $500 thousand
- A count of the number of stores located in Michigan with sales greater than $500 thousand
- Average sales for the Detroit, Michigan stores
- Average sales for the Michigan stores established prior to 2004
- Total sales for stores established prior to 2008
- Total sales for the Michigan stores established prior to 2004

Yolanda created range names to help with the statistical formulas but does not know how to extract statistics using single and multiple criteria. Create the formulas for Yolanda in columns H and I using the range names she created. You determine the layout, labels, and other formats for the statistics section. Save and print the worksheet.

Yolanda is interested in calculating the royalty fees paid to the franchise head office. In the marketing package for new prospects, she plans to include sample sales figures and related franchise royalty payments. Pizza by Mario charges stores a percentage that is based on the store's annual sales. As sales increase, the royalty percentage increases. For example, a store that earns gross sales of $430 thousand pays a royalty of 2% on sales, while a store that earns gross sales of $765 thousand pays a royalty of 5% of gross sales. A royalty rate table is included in the worksheet and Yolanda created a range name for the table. Note that the royalty percentage the franchisee pays is the closest percentage to actual sales without going over the next highest sales value in the rate table. Create a lookup formula to insert the correct royalty percentage for each store in column F and then create a formula to calculate the royalty payment based on the store's gross sales times the percent value in column G. Save the revised workbook and name it **ExcelL2_C2_CS_P2**. Print the worksheet.

Part 3

Use the Help feature to learn about the MEDIAN and STDEV functions. Yolanda would like to calculate further statistics in a separate worksheet. Copy A2:E23 to Sheet2 keeping the source column widths. Using the sales data in column E, calculate the following statistics:

- Average sales
- Maximum store sales
- Minimum store sales
- Median store sales
- Standard deviation of the sales data

Create a comment box for the median and standard deviation values that explains to the reader what the numbers mean based on what you learned in Help. Print the worksheet making sure the printout fits on one page. Save the revised workbook and name it **ExcelL2_C2_CS_P3**.

Part 4

Choose two states that are in close proximity to Michigan, Ohio, Wisconsin, and Iowa and research statistics on the Internet that Yolanda can use to prepare a marketing plan. Within each state find population and income statistics for two to three cities. In a new worksheet within the Pizza by Mario franchise workbook, prepare a summary of your research findings. Include the URLs of the sites from which you obtained your data in the worksheet in case Yolanda wants to explore the links for further details. Print the worksheet making sure the printout fits on one page. Save the revised workbook and name it **ExcelL2_C2_CS_P4**. Close the workbook.

Working with Tables and Data Features

PERFORMANCE OBJECTIVES

Upon successful completion of Chapter 3, you will be able to:

- Create a table in a worksheet
- Expand a table to include new rows and columns
- Add a calculated column in a table
- Format a table by applying table styles and table style options
- Add a total row to a table and add formulas to total cells
- Sort and filter a table
- Split contents of a cell into separate columns
- Remove duplicate records
- Restrict data entry by creating validation criteria
- Convert a table to a normal range
- Create subtotals in groups of related data
- Ungroup data
- Summarize data using database functions DSUM and DAVERAGE
- Summarize data using the SUBTOTAL function formula

Tutorial 3.1
Working with Tables and
Extensive Data

In Excel 2007, the List feature from earlier versions was renamed *Table*. A table can be managed separately from other rows and columns in the worksheet so that you can sort, filter, calculate, and total data as a separate unit. A worksheet can contain more than one table so that multiple groups of data can be managed separately within the same workbook. While working with the table feature you will also use data tools such as validation, duplicate records, and converting text to a table. A table that no longer needs to be managed independently can be converted back to a normal range and data tools such as grouping related records, calculating subtotals, and database functions applied to the data.

Note: Before beginning computer projects, copy to your storage medium the Excel2007L2C3 subfolder from the Excel2007L2 folder on the CD that accompanies this textbook and then make Excel2007L2C3 the active folder.

Project 1 Create and Modify a Table

You will convert data in a billing summary worksheet to a table and then modify the table by applying Table Style options and sorting and filtering the data.

Create Table
1. Open worksheet.
2. Select range.
3. Click Insert tab.
4. Click Table button.
5. Click OK.
6. Deselect range.

Table

Creating Tables

A table in Excel is similar in structure to a database. Columns are called *fields* and are used to store a single unit of information about a person, place, or object. The first row of the table contains column headings and is called the *field names row* or *header row*. Each column heading in the table should be unique. Below the field names, data entered in rows are called *records*. A record contains all of the field values related to one person, place, or object that is the topic of the table. No blank rows exist within the table as shown in Figure 3.1. To create a table in Excel, enter the data in the worksheet and then define the range as a table using the Table button in the Tables group of the Insert tab. Before converting a range to a table, delete any blank rows between column headings and data or within the data range.

Figure 3.1 Excel Table

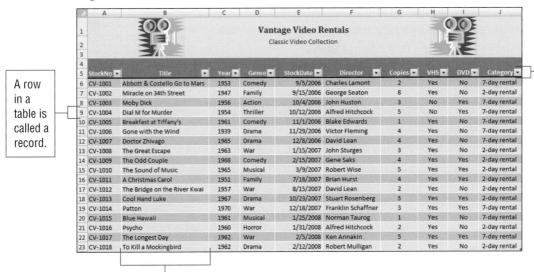

A row in a table is called a record.

A column in a table contains a single unit of information and is called a field.

The first row of a table contains field names and is called a header row.

Converting a Range to a Table

1. Open **O'Donovan&Sullivan-Billing.xlsx**.
2. Save the workbook with Save As and name it **ExcelL2_C3_P1**.
3. Convert the billing summary data to a table by completing the following steps:
   a. Select A4:I24.
   b. Click the Insert tab.
   c. Click the Table button in the Tables group.
   d. At the Create Table dialog box with *$A$4:$I$24* selected in the *Where is the data for your table?* text box and the *My table has headers* check box selected, click OK.
   e. Deselect the range.
4. Double-click each column boundary to AutoFit each column's width.
5. Save **ExcelL2_C3_P1**.

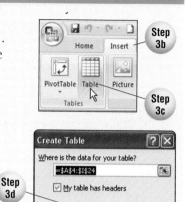

Step 3b

Step 3c

Step 3d

Modifying a Table

Once a table has been defined, typing new data in the row immediately below the last row of the table, or in the column immediately right of the last column causes the table to automatically expand to include the new entries. Excel displays the AutoCorrect Options button when the table is expanded. Click the button to display a drop-down list with the options *Undo Table AutoExpansion* and *Stop Automatically Expanding Tables*. If you need to add data near a table without having the table expand, leave a blank column or row between the table and the new data.

Typing a formula in the first row of a new table column creates a calculated column. In a calculated column, Excel copies the formula from the first cell to the remaining cells in the column automatically. The AutoCorrect Options button appears when Excel converts a column to a calculated column with the options *Undo Calculated Column* and *Stop Automatically Creating Calculated Columns* available in the drop-down list.

QUICK STEPS

Add Rows or Columns to Table
Type data in first row below table or first column to right of table.

Add Calculated Column
1. Type formula in first record in column.
2. Press Enter.

Adding a Row and a Calculated Column to a Table

1. With **ExcelL2_C3_P1.xlsx** open, add a new record to the table by completing the following steps:
   a. Make A25 the active cell, type **RE-522**, and then press Enter. Excel automatically expands the table to include the new row and displays the AutoCorrect Options button.
   b. Make B25 the active cell and then type the remainder of the record as follows:

ClientID	10512
Date	10/09/2009
Last_Name	Melanson
First_Name	Connie

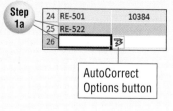

Step 1a

AutoCorrect Options button

Attorney	Kyle Williams
Area	**Real Estate**
Billable_Hrs	2.5
Rate	75.00

2. Add a calculated column to calculate Billable_Hrs times Rate by completing the following steps:
   a. Make J4 the active cell.
   b. Type **Fees_Due** and then press Enter. Excel automatically expands the table to include the new column.
   c. With J5 the active cell, type **=h5*i5** and then press Enter. Excel creates a calculated column and copies the formula to the rest of the rows in the table.
   d. Double-click the column J boundary to AutoFit the column.
3. Adjust the centering and fill color of the titles across the top of the table by completing the following steps:
   a. Make A1 the active cell.
   b. Click the Merge & Center button in the Alignment group in the Home tab to unmerge A1:I1.
   c. Select A1:J1 and then click the Merge & Center button.
   d. Make A2 the active cell and then repeat Steps 3b–3c to merge and center row 2 across columns A through J.
   e. Make A3 the active cell and then repeat Steps 3b–3c to merge and center row 3 across columns A through J.
4. Save **ExcelL2_C3_P1.xlsx**.

Rate	Fees_D
85.00	573.75
55.00	178.75
75.00	393.75
100.00	425.00
65.00	211.25
75.00	206.25
75.00	393.75
75.00	318.75
100.00	500.00
75.00	243.75
65.00	292.50
85.00	318.75
100.00	450.00
55.00	192.50
65.00	341.25
75.00	393.75
75.00	262.50
100.00	425.00
100.00	375.00
75.00	337.50
75.00	187.50

Steps 2a–2b

Step 2c

Table Styles and Table Style Options

The contextual Table Tools Design tab shown in Figure 3.2 contains options for formatting the table. Apply a different visual style to the table using the Table Styles gallery. Excel provides several table styles categorized by Light, Medium, and Dark color themes. By default, Excel bands the rows within the table, which means that even rows are formatted differently than odd rows. Banding rows or columns makes the task of reading data across a row or down a column in a large table easier. You can remove the banding from the rows and/or add banding to the columns. Use the *First Column* and *Last Column* check boxes in the Table Style Options group to add emphasis to the first or last column in the table by formatting the column separately from the rest of the table. The *Header Row* check box is used to show or hide the column headings row in the table.

Adding a total row to the table causes Excel to add the word *Total* in a new row at the bottom of the table in the leftmost cell. A Sum function is added automatically to the last numeric column in the table. Click in a cell in the total row to display a down-pointing arrow from which you can select a function formula in a pop-up list.

Figure 3.2 Table Tools Design Tab

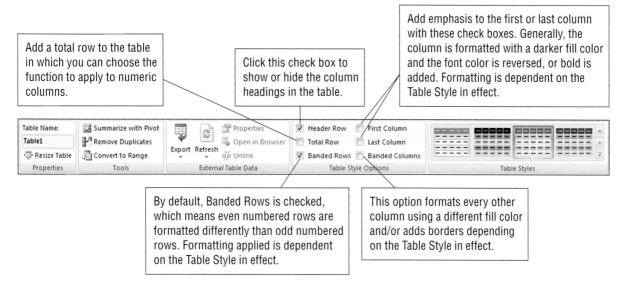

Add a total row to the table in which you can choose the function to apply to numeric columns.

Click this check box to show or hide the column headings in the table.

Add emphasis to the first or last column with these check boxes. Generally, the column is formatted with a darker fill color and the font color is reversed, or bold is added. Formatting is dependent on the Table Style in effect.

By default, Banded Rows is checked, which means even numbered rows are formatted differently than odd numbered rows. Formatting applied is dependent on the Table Style in effect.

This option formats every other column using a different fill color and/or adds borders depending on the Table Style in effect.

Project 1c   Formatting a Table and Adding a Total Row

1. With **ExcelL2_C3_P1.xlsx** open, change the table style by completing the following steps:
   a. Click any cell within the table to activate the table and the contextual Table Tools Design tab.
   b. Click the Table Tools Design tab.
   c. Click the More button located at the bottom of the vertical scroll bar in the Table Styles gallery.
   d. Click *Table Style Medium 14* at the drop-down gallery (last option in second row in *Medium* section).

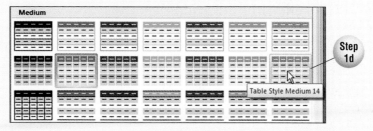

Step 1d

Table Style Medium 14

2. Change the Table Style options to remove the row banding, insert column banding, and emphasize the first column in the table by completing the following steps:
   a. Click the *Banded Rows* check box in the Table Style Options group in the Table Tools Design tab to clear the box. All of the rows in the table are now formatted the same.
   b. Click the *Banded Columns* check box in the Table Style Options group to insert a check mark. Every other column in the table is now formatted differently.
   c. Click the *First Column* check box in the Table Style Options group. Notice the first column has a darker fill color and reverse font color applied.

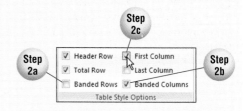

Step 2c

Step 2a

Step 2b

d. Click the *Header Row* check box in the Table Style Options group to clear the box. Notice the first row of the table containing the column headings disappears and is replaced with empty cells. The row is also removed from the table range definition.

e. Click the *Header Row* check box to insert a check mark and redisplay the column headings.

3. Add a total row and add function formulas to numeric columns by completing the following steps:

a. Click the *Total Row* check box in the Table Style Options group to add a total row to the bottom of the table. Excel formats row 26 as a total row, adds the label *Total* in A26, and automatically creates a Sum function in J26.

b. Make H26 the active cell.

c. Click the down-pointing arrow that appears in H26 and then click *Sum* at the pop-up list.

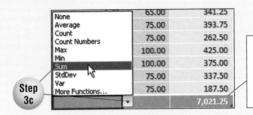

Step 3c

Fees_Due column totaled automatically when Total Row added to table in Step 3a.

d. Make I26 the active cell, click the down-pointing arrow that appears, and then click *Average* at the pop-up list.

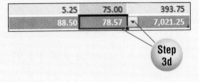

Step 3d

4. Click the Page Layout tab and scale the worksheet to 1 page width.

5. Preview and then print the worksheet. ***Note: The worksheet will print in landscape orientation.***

6. Save **ExcelL2_C3_P1.xlsx**.

QUICK STEPS

Sorting and Filtering a Table

Filter Table
1. Click desired filter arrow button.
2. Click desired filter options.
3. Click OK.

Sort Table
1. Click desired filter arrow button.
2. Click desired sort order.
OR
1. Click Sort & Filter button.
2. Click Custom Sort.
3. Define sort levels.
4. Click OK.

By default, Excel displays a filter arrow button next to each label in the table header row. Click the filter arrow button to display a drop-down list with the same sort and filter options you used in Chapter 1.

1. With **ExcelL2_C3_P1.xlsx** open, filter the table by attorney name to print a list of billable hours for Marty O'Donovan by completing the following steps:

   a. Click the filter arrow button located next to *Attorney* in F4.

   b. Click the *(Select All)* check box to clear the check mark from the box.

   c. Click the *Marty O'Donovan* check box to insert a check mark and then click OK. The table is filtered to display only those records with *Marty O'Donovan* in the *Attorney* field. The sum functions in columns H and J reflect the totals for the filtered records only.

   d. Print the filtered worksheet.

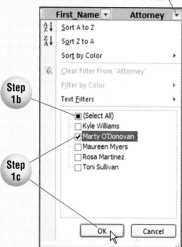

2. Redisplay all records by clicking the Attorney filter arrow button and then clicking *Clear Filter From "Attorney"* at the drop-down list.

3. Sort the table first by the attorney name, then by the area of law, and then by the client last name using the Sort dialog box by completing the following steps:

   a. With the active cell positioned anywhere within the table, click the Home tab.

   b. Click the Sort & Filter button in the Editing group and then click *Custom Sort* at the drop-down list.

   c. At the Sort dialog box, click the down-pointing arrow next to the *Sort by* list box in the *Column* section and then click *Attorney* at the drop-down list. The default options for *Sort On* and *Order* are correct since you want to sort by the column values in ascending order.

   d. Click the Add Level button.

   e. Click the down-pointing arrow next to the *Then by* list box and then click *Area* at the drop-down list.

   f. Click the Add Level button.

   g. Click the down-pointing arrow next to the second *Then by* list box and then click *Last_Name* at the drop-down list.

   h. Click OK.

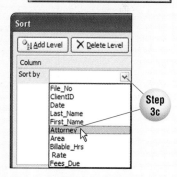

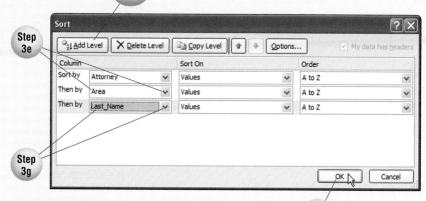

4. Print the sorted table.

5. Save and then close **ExcelL2_C3_P1.xlsx**.

Project ② Use Data Tools to Split Data and Ensure Data Integrity

You will use Excel's data tools to split the attorney first and last names into two separate columns, remove duplicate records, and restrict the type of data that can be entered into a field.

QUICK STEPS

Split Text into Multiple Columns
1. Insert blank column(s) next to source data.
2. Select data to be split.
3. Click Data tab.
4. Click Text to Columns button.
5. Click Next at first dialog box.
6. Select delimiter check box for character that separates data.
7. Click Next.
8. Click Finish.
9. Deselect range.

Data Tools

The Data Tools group in the Data tab shown in Figure 3.3 includes features useful for working with data in tables. A worksheet that has a column in which multiple data have been entered into the same column can be separated into multiple columns using the Text to Columns feature. For example, a worksheet with a column that has first and last names entered into the same cell can have the first name split into one column and the last name split into a separate column. Breaking up the data into separate columns facilitates sorting and other data management functions. Before using the Text to Columns feature, insert the number of blank columns you will need to separate the data immediately right of the column to be split. Next, select the column containing multiple data and then click the Text to Columns button to start the Convert Text to Columns Wizard. The wizard contains three dialog boxes to guide you through the steps of separating the data.

Figure 3.3 Data Tools Group in Data Tab

Project ②a Separating Attorney Names into Two Columns

1. Open **ExcelL2_C3_P1.xlsx**.
2. Save the workbook with Save As and name it **ExcelL2_C3_P2**.
3. Position the active cell anywhere within the table, click the Sort & Filter button in the Editing group of the Home tab, and then click *Clear* at the drop-down list to clear the existing sort criteria.
4. Create a custom sort to sort the table first by *Date* (Oldest to Newest) and then by *ClientID* (Smallest to Largest). Refer to Project 1d, Step 3 if you need assistance with this step.
5. Split the attorney first and last names in column F into two columns by completing the following steps:
   a. Right-click column letter G at the top of the worksheet area and then click *Insert* at the shortcut menu to insert a blank column between the *Attorney* and *Area* columns in the table.
   b. Select F5:F25.
   c. Click the Data tab.

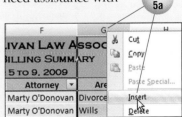

Step 5a

d. Click the Text to Columns button 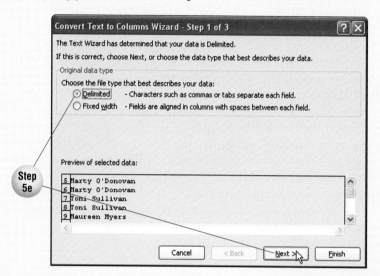 in the Data Tools group.
e. At the Convert Text to Columns Wizard - Step 1 of 3 dialog box, with *Delimited* selected in the *Choose the file type that best describes your data* section, click Next.

f. At the Convert Text to Columns Wizard - Step 2 of 3 dialog box, click the *Space* check box in the *Delimiters* section and then click Next. The *Data preview* section of the dialog box updates after you click the *Space* check box to show the names split into two columns.

g. Click Finish at the last Convert Text to Columns Wizard dialog box to accept the default *General* data format for both columns.

h. Deselect the range.

6. Make F4 the active cell, edit the label to **Attorney_FName**, and then AutoFit the column width.

7. Make G4 the active cell, edit the label to **Attorney_LName**, and then AutoFit the column width.

8. Save **ExcelL2_C3_P2.xlsx**.

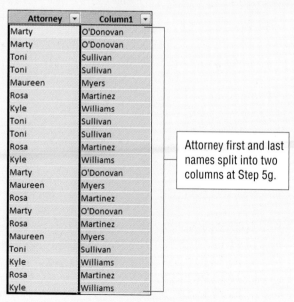

Attorney first and last names split into two columns at Step 5g.

QUICK STEPS

Remove Duplicate Rows
1. Select range or make cell active in table.
2. Click Data tab.
3. Click Remove Duplicates button.
4. Select columns to compare.
5. Click OK.
6. Click OK

Removing Duplicate Records

Excel can compare records within a worksheet and automatically delete duplicate rows based on the columns you select that might contain duplicate values. At the Remove Duplicates dialog box shown in Figure 3.4, by default all columns are selected when the dialog box is opened. Click the Unselect All button to remove the check marks from each column and then click the individual columns you want to compare if you do not want Excel to check for duplicates in every column. When you click OK, Excel performs an automatic deletion of rows containing duplicate values and displays a message box when the operation is completed informing you of the number of rows that were removed from the worksheet or table and the number of unique values that remain. Consider conditionally formatting duplicate values first to view the records that will be deleted. Use the *Duplicate Values* option in *Highlight Cells Rules* from the Conditional Formatting drop-down list. (Display the Conditional Formatting drop-down list by clicking the Conditional Formatting button in the Styles group in the Home tab.)

Excel includes the Remove Duplicates button in the Data Tools group in the Data tab and in the Tools group in the Table Tools Design tab. Click Undo if you remove duplicate rows by mistake.

Figure 3.4 Remove Duplicates Dialog Box

Choose the columns you want Excel to compare data within in order to flag a record as a duplicate entry in the table and remove it.

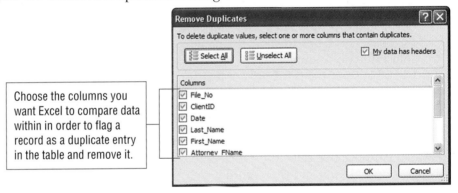

1. With **ExcelL2_C3_P2.xlsx** open, remove duplicate rows in the billing summary table by completing the following steps:

    a. With the active cell positioned anywhere within the table, click the Remove Duplicates button in the Data Tools group in the Data tab.

    b. At the Remove Duplicates dialog box with all columns selected in the *Columns* list box, click the Unselect All button.

    c. The billing summary table should have only one record per file per client per date since attorneys record once per day the total hours spent on each file. A record is a duplicate if the same values exist in the three columns that store the file number, client number, and date. Click the *File_No* check box to insert a check mark.

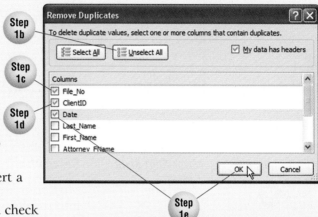

    d. Click the *ClientID* check box to insert a check mark.

    e. Click the *Date* check box to insert a check mark and then click OK.

    f. Click OK at the Microsoft Office Excel message box that says 1 duplicate value was found and removed and 20 unique values remain.

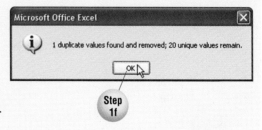

2. Scroll the worksheet to view the total in K25. Compare the total with your printout from Project 1d, Step 4. Notice the total in *Fees_Due* is now *6,627.50* compared to *7,021.25* in the printout.

3. Save **ExcelL2_C3_P2.xlsx**.

Validating and Restricting Data Entry

Excel's data validation feature allows you to control the type of data that is accepted for entry in a cell. You can specify the type of data that is allowed as well as parameters that validate whether the entry is within a certain range of acceptable values, dates, times, or text length. You can also set up a list of values that display in a drop-down list when the cell is made active. At the Data Validation dialog box shown in Figure 3.5, begin by choosing the type of data you want to validate in the *Allow* list box in the Settings tab. Additional list or text boxes appear in the dialog box depending on the option chosen in the *Allow* list.

As well as defining acceptable data entry parameters, you have the option of adding an input message and an error alert message to the range. You define the text that appears in these messages. The input message displays when the cell is made active for which data validation rules apply. These messages are informational in nature. Error alerts are messages that appear if incorrect data is entered in the cell. Three styles of error alerts are available. A description and example for each type of alert is described in Table 3.1.

QUICK STEPS

Create Data Validation Rule
1. Select desired range.
2. Click Data tab.
3. Click Data Validation button.
4. Specify validation criteria in Settings tab.
5. Click Input Message tab.
6. Type input message title and text.
7. Click Error Alert tab.
8. Select error style.
9. Type error alert title and message text.
10. Click OK.

Figure 3.5 Data Validation Dialog Box with Settings Tab Selected

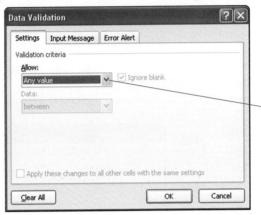

Specify the type of data you will allow to be entered into the cells within the range by specifying one of the following options: *Whole number, Decimal, List, Date, Time, Text Length, Custom.* Other parameter boxes appear depending on the selection made in *Allow.*

Table 3.1 Data Validation Error Alert Message Styles

Error Alert Icon	Error Alert Style	Description
✖	Stop	Stop error alerts prevent the data from being entered into the cell. The error alert message box provides three buttons to ensure new data is entered.
⚠	Warning	Warning error alerts do not prevent the data from being entered into the cell. The error alert message box provides four buttons displayed below the prompt *Continue?*
ⓘ	Information	Information error alerts do not prevent the data from being entered into the cell. The error alert message box provides three buttons displayed below the error message.

> **Date is outside accepted range**
> ✖ Please enter a date between October 5 and October 9, 2009
> [Retry] [Cancel] [Help]

> **Check number of hours**
> ⚠ The hours you have entered are greater than 8.
> Continue?
> [Yes] [No] [Cancel] [Help]

> **Verify hours entered**
> ⓘ The hours you have entered are outside the normal range.
> [OK] [Cancel] [Help]

If an error alert message has not been defined, Excel displays the Stop error alert with a default error message of *The value you entered is not valid. A user has restricted values that can be entered into this cell.*

1. With **ExcelL2_C3_P2.xlsx** open, create a validation rule, input message, and error alert for dates in the billing summary worksheet by completing the following steps:
   a. Select C5:C24.
   b. Click the Data Validation button in the Data Tools group in the Data tab.
   c. With Settings the active tab at the Data Validation dialog box, click the down-pointing arrow next to the *Allow* list box (currently displays *Any value*) and then click *Date* at the drop-down list. Validation options are dependent on the *Allow* setting. When you choose *Date*, Excel adds *Start date* and *End date* text boxes to the *Validation criteria* section.
   d. With *between* automatically selected in the *Data* list box, click in the *Start date* text box and then type **10/05/2009**.
   e. Click in the *End date* text box and then type **10/09/2009**. Since the billing summary worksheet is for the week of October 5 to 9, 2009, entering this validation criteria will ensure that only dates between the start date and end date are accepted.
   f. Click the Input Message tab.
   g. Click in the *Title* text box and then type **Billing Date**.
   h. Click in the *Input message* text box and then type **This worksheet is for the week of October 5 to October 9, 2009 only**.
   i. Click the Error Alert tab.

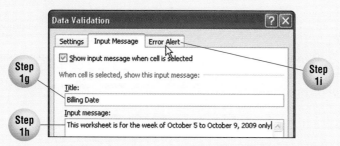

Step 1f
Step 1c
Step 1d
Step 1e

Step 1g
Step 1h
Step 1i

   j. With *Stop* selected in the *Style* list box, click in the *Title* text box and then type **Date is outside accepted range**.
   k. Click in the *Error message* text box and then type **Please enter a date between October 5 and October 9, 2009**.
   l. Click OK. Since the range is active for which the data validation rules apply, the input message box appears.
   m. Deselect the range.
2. Add a new record to the table to test the date validation rule by completing the following steps:
   a. Right-click row number 25 and then click *Insert* at the shortcut menu to insert a new row into the table.

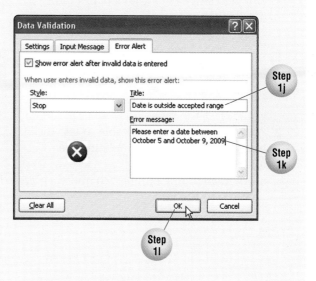

Step 1j
Step 1k
Step 1l

b. Make A25 the active cell, type **PL-348**, and then press Tab.

c. Type **10420** in *ClientID* and then press Tab. The input message title and text appear when the *Date* column is made active.

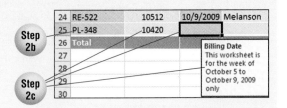

Step 2b

d. Type **10/12/2009** and then press Enter. Since the date entered is invalid, the error alert message box appears.

Step 2c

e. Click the Retry button.

f. Type **10/09/2009** and then press Tab.

g. Enter the data in the remaining fields as follows. Press Tab to move from column to column in the table.

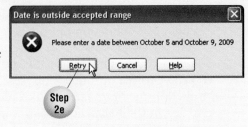

Last_Name	Torrez
First_Name	Alexander
Attorney_FName	Rosa
Attorney_LName	Martinez
Area	Patent
Billable_Hrs	2.25
Rate	100.00

Step 2e

3. Save **ExcelL2_C3_P2.xlsx**.

Project **2d**   **Restricting Data Entry to Values Within a List**

1. With **ExcelL2_C3_P2.xlsx** open, create a list of values that are allowed in a cell by completing the following steps:

   a. Select J5:J25.

   b. Click the Data Validation button in the Data Tools group.

   c. If necessary, click the Settings tab.

   d. Click the down-pointing arrow next to the *Allow* list box and then click *List* at the drop-down list.

   e. Click in the *Source* text box and then type **55.00,65.00,75.00,85.00,100.00**.

   f. Click OK.

   g. Deselect the range.

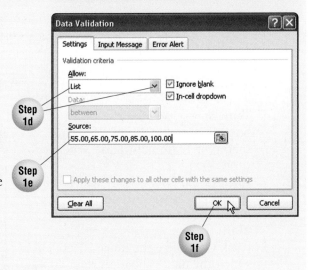

Step 1d

Step 1e

Step 1f

2. Add a new record to the table to test the rate validation list by completing the following steps:

   a. Right-click row number 26 and then click *Insert* at the shortcut menu to insert a new row into the table.

b. Make A26 the active cell and then type data in the fields as follows. Press Tab to move from column to column in the table.

File_No	IN-745
ClientID	10210
Date	10/09/2009
Last_Name	Boscovic
First_Name	Victor
Attorney_FName	Maureen
Attorney_LName	Myers
Area	Insurance
Billable_Hrs	1.75

c. At the *Rate* field, the validation list becomes active and a down-pointing arrow appears at the field. Type *125.00* and then press Tab to test the validation rule. Since no error alert message was entered, the default message appears.

d. Click the Cancel button. The value is cleared from the field.

e. Click the down-pointing arrow at the end of the field, click *100.00* at the drop-down list, and then press Tab.

3. Save **ExcelL2_C3_P2.xlsx**.

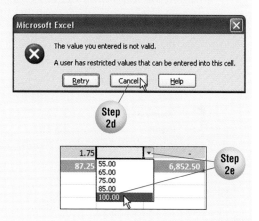

Step 2d

Step 2e

Project **2e**   **Ensuring Data Entered Is a Specified Text Length**

1. With **ExcelL2_C3_P2.xlsx** open, create a validation rule to ensure that all client identification numbers are five characters in length to coincide with the firm's accounting system by completing the following steps:

a. Select B5:B26 and click the Data Validation button.

b. Click the down-pointing arrow next to the *Allow* list box and then click *Text length* at the drop-down list.

c. Click the down-pointing arrow next to *Data* and then click *equal to* at the drop-down list.

d. Click in the *Length* text box, type 5, and then click OK.

e. Deselect the range.

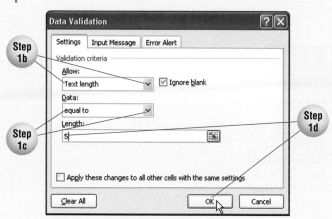

Step 1b

Step 1c

Step 1d

2. Add a new record to the table to test the client identification validation rule by completing the following steps:

a. Right-click row number 27 and then click *Insert* at the shortcut menu.

b. Make A27 the active cell, type **FL-325**, and then press Tab.

c. Type **1010411** in B27 and then press Tab. Since this value is greater than the specified number of characters allowed in the cell, the default error message appears.

d. Click the Retry button.

e. Delete the selected text, type **1010**, and then press Tab. Since this value is less than the specified text length, the default error message appears again. Using a Text Length validation rule ensures that all entries in the range have the same number of characters. This rule is useful to validate customer numbers, employee numbers, inventory numbers, or any other data that requires a consistent number of characters.

f. Click the Cancel button, type **10104**, and then press Tab. Since this entry is five characters in length, Excel moves to the next field.

g. Enter the remaining fields as follows:

Date	10/09/2009
Last_Name	Ferreira
First_Name	Joseph
Attorney_FName	Marty
Attorney_LName	O'Donovan
Area	Divorce
Billable_Hrs	5.75
Rate	85.00

3. Save, print, and then close **ExcelL2_C3_P2.xlsx**.

roject **3** **Group and Subtotal Related Records**

You will convert the billing summary table to a normal range, sort the rows by the attorney names, and then add subtotals to display total fees due, a count of fees, and the average billable hours and fees due for each attorney.

Converting a Table to a Normal Range

A table can be converted to a normal range using the Convert to Range button in the Tools group of the Table Tools Design tab. Convert a table to a range in order to use the Subtotal feature or if you no longer need to treat the table data as a range independent of data in the rest of the worksheet.

Subtotaling Related Data

A range of data with a column that has multiple rows with the same field value can be grouped and subtotals created for each group automatically. For example, a worksheet with multiple records with the same department name in a field can be grouped by the department names and a subtotal of a numeric field calculated for each department. You can choose from a list of functions for the subtotal such as Average or Sum and you can also create multiple subtotal values for each group. Prior to creating subtotals, sort the data by the fields in which you want the records grouped. Also, make sure no blank rows exist within the range to be grouped and subtotaled. Excel displays a summary total when the field value for the specified subtotal column changes content. A grand total is also automatically included. Excel displays the subtotals with buttons along the left side of the worksheet area used to show or hide the details for each group using Excel's Outline feature. Excel can create an outline with up to eight levels. Figure 3.6 illustrates the data you will group and subtotal in Project 3a displayed with the worksheet at level 2 of the outline. In Figure 3.7, the same worksheet is shown with two attorney groups expanded to show the detail records.

Create Subtotals
1. Select range.
2. Click Data tab.
3. Click Subtotals button.
4. Select field to group by in *At each change in* list box.
5. Select desired function in *Use function* list box.
6. Select field(s) to subtotal in *Add subtotal to* list box.
7. Click OK.
8. Deselect range.

Figure 3.6 Worksheet with Subtotals by Attorney Last Name Displaying Level 2 of the Outline

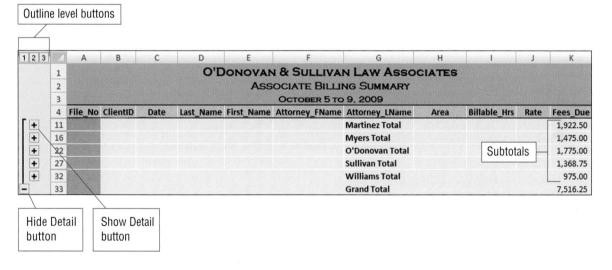

Figure 3.7 Worksheet with Subtotals by Attorney Last Name with Martinez and Sullivan Groups Expanded

1 2 3		A	B	C	D	E	F	G	H	I	J	K
	1					**O'DONOVAN & SULLIVAN LAW ASSOCIATES**						
	2					**ASSOCIATE BILLING SUMMARY**						
	3					**OCTOBER 5 TO 9, 2009**						
	4	**File_No**	**ClientID**	**Date**	**Last_Name**	**First_Name**	**Attorney_FName**	**Attorney_LName**	**Area**	**Billable_Hrs**	**Rate**	**Fees_Due**
	5	EL-632	10225	10/6/2009	Armstrong	Daniel	Rosa	Martinez	Employment	3.25	65.00	211.25
	6	EL-632	10225	10/8/2009	Armstrong	Daniel	Rosa	Martinez	Employment	4.50	65.00	292.50
	7	PL-512	10290	10/8/2009	Tonini	Sam	Rosa	Martinez	Pension	3.75	85.00	318.75
	8	PL-348	10420	10/7/2009	Torrez	Alexander	Rosa	Martinez	Patent	5.00	100.00	500.00
	9	PL-348	10420	10/9/2009	Torrez	Alexander	Rosa	Martinez	Patent	2.25	100.00	225.00
	10	EP-685	10495	10/9/2009	Kinsela	Frank	Rosa	Martinez	Estate	3.75	100.00	375.00
	11							**Martinez Total**				1,922.50
	16							**Myers Total**				1,475.00
	22							**O'Donovan Total**				1,775.00
	23	CL-412	10125	10/5/2009	Schmidt	Hilary	Toni	Sullivan	Corporate	5.25	75.00	393.75
	24	CL-521	10334	10/7/2009	Marsales	Gene	Toni	Sullivan	Corporate	4.25	75.00	318.75
	25	CL-501	10341	10/7/2009	Fletcher	Dana	Toni	Sullivan	Corporate	5.25	75.00	393.75
	26	CL-450	10358	10/9/2009	Poissant	Henri	Toni	Sullivan	Corporate	3.50	75.00	262.50
	27							**Sullivan Total**				1,368.75
	32							**Williams Total**				975.00
	33							**Grand Total**				7,516.25

Project 3a Converting a Table to a Range and Creating Subtotals

1. Open **ExcelL2_C3_P2.xlsx**.
2. Save the workbook with Save As and name it **ExcelL2_C3_P3.xlsx**.
3. Convert the table to a normal range in order to group and subtotal the records by completing the following steps:
   a. Position the active cell anywhere within the table and click the Table Tools Design tab.
   b. Click the *Total Row* check box in the Table Style Options group to remove the total row from the table. The Subtotal feature includes a grand total automatically so the total row is no longer needed.
   c. Click the *Banded Columns* check box in the Table Style Options to remove the banded formatting.
   d. Click the Convert to Range button [Convert to Range] in the Tools group.
   e. Click Yes at the message asking if you want to convert the table to a normal range.

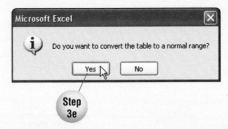

Step 3e

   f. Select columns A–K and adjust the column width to AutoFit.
   g. Deselect the columns.
4. Sort the data by the fields you want to subtotal and group by completing the following steps:
   a. Select A4:K27.
   b. Click the Sort & Filter button in the Editing group in the Home tab and then click *Custom Sort* at the drop-down list.

c. At the Sort dialog box, define three levels to group and sort records as follows:

Column	Sort On	Order
Attorney_LName	Values	A to Z
ClientID	Values	Smallest to Largest
Date	Values	Oldest to Newest

d. Click OK.

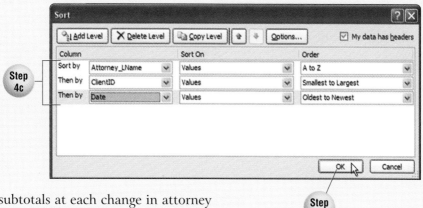

Step 4c

Step 4d

5. Create subtotals at each change in attorney last name by completing the following steps:
   a. With A4:K27 still selected, click the Data tab.
   b. Click the Subtotal button in the Outline group.
   c. At the Subtotal dialog box, click the down-pointing arrow to the right of the *At each change in* list box (current displays *File_No*), scroll down the list, and then click *Attorney_LName*.

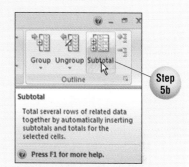

Step 5b

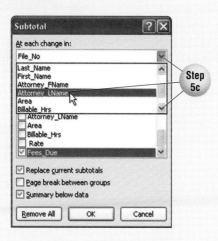

Step 5c

d. With *Use function* set to *Sum* and *Fees_Due* selected in the *Add subtotal to* list box, click OK.
e. Deselect the range.
6. Print the worksheet.

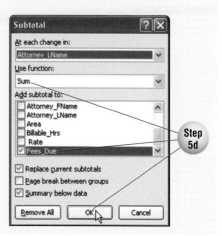

Step 5d

7. Show and hide levels in the outlined worksheet by completing the following steps:

   a. Click the level 1 button located at the top left of the worksheet area below the Name text box. Excel collapses the worksheet to display only the grand total of the *Fees_Due* column.

Step 7a

   b. Click the level 2 button to display the subtotals by attorney last name. Notice a button with a plus symbol displays next to each subtotal in the Outline section at the left side of the worksheet area. The button with the plus symbol is the Show Detail button and the button with the minus symbol is the Hide Detail button. Compare your worksheet with the one shown in Figure 3.6.

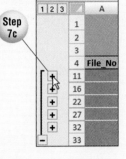

Step 7c

   c. Click the Show Detail button (displays as a plus symbol) next to the row with the Martinez subtotal. The detail rows for the group of records for Martinez are displayed.

   d. Click the Show Detail button next to the row with the Sullivan subtotal.

   e. Compare your worksheet with the one shown in Figure 3.7.

   f. Click the level 3 button to display all detail rows.

8. Save **Excel_L2_C3_P3.xlsx**.

Project 3b   Modifying Subtotals

1. With **ExcelL2_C3_P3.xlsx** open, add a subtotal to count the number of billable records for each attorney for the week by completing the following steps:

   a. Select A4:K33 and click the Subtotal button in the Outline group. The Subtotal dialog box opens with the settings used for the subtotals created in Project 3a.

   b. Click the *Replace current subtotals* check box to clear the check mark. By clearing the check box you are instructing Excel to add another subtotal row to each group.

   c. Click the down-pointing arrow next to the *Use function* list box and then click *Count* at the drop-down list.

   d. With *Fees_Due* still selected in the *Add subtotal to* list box, click OK. Excel adds a new subtotal row to each group with the count of records displayed.

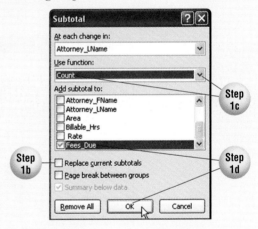

Step 1b

Step 1c

Step 1d

2. Add a subtotal to calculate the average billable hours and average fees due for each attorney by completing the following steps:
   a. With the data range still selected, click the Subtotal button.
   b. Click the down-pointing arrow next to the *Use function* list box and then click *Average* at the drop-down list.
   c. Click the *Billable_Hrs* check box in the *Add subtotal to* list box and then click OK. Excel adds a new subtotal row to each group with the average billable hours and average fees due for each attorney.

Attorney_LName	Area	Billable_Hrs	Rate	Fees_Due
Martinez	Employment	3.25	65.00	211.25
Martinez	Employment	4.50	65.00	292.50
Martinez	Pension	3.75	85.00	318.75
Martinez	Patent	5.00	100.00	500.00
Martinez	Patent	2.25	100.00	225.00
Martinez	Estate	3.75	100.00	375.00
Martinez Average		3.75		320.42
Martinez Count				6
Martinez Total				1,922.50

Average row shown for Martinez group. Average of *Billable_Hrs* and *Fees_Due* columns added to subtotals for all attorneys in Steps 2a–2d.

   d. Deselect the range.
3. Use Save As to save the revised workbook and name it **ExcelL2_C3_P3-Prj3b**.
4. Click the Page Layout tab and scale the height of the worksheet to 1 page.
5. Print the worksheet.
6. Save and then close **ExcelL2_C3_P3-Prj3b.xlsx**.

Grouping and Ungrouping Data

Use the Group and Ungroup buttons when a worksheet is outlined to individually manage collapsing and expanding groups of records at the various levels. For example, in an outlined worksheet with detailed rows displayed, selecting a group of records and clicking the Ungroup button opens the Ungroup dialog box shown in Figure 3.8. Clicking OK with *Rows* selected removes the group feature applied to the selection and the Hide Detail button is removed so the records remain displayed at the outline level. Selecting records that have been ungrouped and clicking the Group button reattaches the group feature to the selection and redisplays the Hide Detail button.

Group Data by Rows
1. Select range to be grouped within outlined worksheet.
2. Click Group button.
3. Click OK.

Figure 3.8 Ungroup Dialog Box

Ungroup Data by Rows
1. Select grouped range within outlined worksheet.
2. Click Ungroup button.
3. Click OK.

Columns can also be grouped and ungrouped. The outline section with the level numbers and Show and Hide Detail buttons displays across the top of the worksheet area. For example, in a worksheet where two columns are used to arrive at a formula, the source columns can be grouped and the details hidden so that only the formula column with the calculated results is displayed in an outlined worksheet.

Project ⓷ᴄ Grouping and Ungrouping Data

1. Open **ExcelL2_C3_P3.xlsx**. Group client data within the Martinez attorney group by completing the following steps:
    a. Select A5:K6. These two rows contain billing information for ClientID 10225.
    b. Click the Group button in the Outline group in the Data tab. (Do not click the down-pointing arrow on the button.)

    Step 1b

    c. At the Group dialog box with *Rows* selected, click OK. Excel adds a fourth outline level to the worksheet and a Hide Detail button is added below the last row of the grouped records in the Outline section.

    Step 1c
    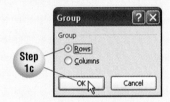

    d. Select A8:K9, click the Group button, and then click OK at the Group dialog box.

    Records grouped at Step 1d.

    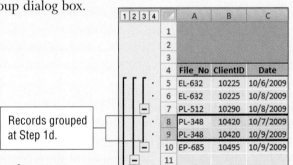

    e. Deselect the range.
2. Experiment with the Hide Detail buttons in the Martinez group by hiding the detail for ClientID 10225 and then hiding the detail for ClientID 10420.
3. Redisplay the detail rows by clicking the Show Detail button for each client.
4. Select A5:K6, click the Ungroup button (do not click the down-pointing arrow on the button), and then click OK at the Ungroup dialog box.
5. Select A8:K9, click the Ungroup button, and then click OK at the Ungroup dialog box.
6. Select A5:K10, click the Ungroup button, and then click OK at the Ungroup dialog box. Notice the Hide Detail button is removed for the entire Martinez group.
7. Deselect the range and then click the level 2 button at the top of the outline section. Notice the Martinez records do not collapse like the others since they are no longer grouped.
8. Close **ExcelL2_C3_P3.xlsx**. Click No when prompted to save changes.

roject **4** **Calculate Statistics Using Database Functions**

You will calculate total and average billable hours by attorney using database functions.

Using Database Functions DSUM and DAVERAGE

Excel includes database functions which can be used to analyze data in a range that meets specified criteria. For example, database functions could be used in the Billing Summary worksheet to produce totals by attorney similar to the Subtotals feature. To use a database function, you create a criteria range outside the range that you want to analyze that specifies the field name and the criteria value that determines the records within the database range to include for the formula calculation. For example, in Figure 3.9 the range K4:K5 is the criteria range for the DSUM function in K8, and K10:K11 is the criteria range for the DSUM function in K14. The structure of a DSUM function is =*DSUM(database,field,criteria)* where *database* is the range containing the data to analyze, *field* is the column that you want to add values from, and *criteria* is the range used to select records.

In the worksheet shown in Figure 3.9, the formula that resides in K8 is =DSUM(A4:I24,H4,K4:K5). The first range in the argument, *A4:I24*, is the range of cells that DSUM is to include in the analysis. The second range in the argument, *H4*, points to the column of values that you want Excel to add. Column H contains billable hours that you want to sum with H4 being the label for the target column. The final range in the argument, *K4:K5*, contains the entries that specify which cells Excel should select to include in the function. The first cell of the criteria range (K4) provides the column label for the column to analyze and the second cell (K5) provides the data that Excel should match in order to include the value in the sum.

QUICK STEPS

Create DSUM Formula
1. Make desired cell active.
2. Click Insert Function button.
3. Change category to *Database*.
4. Select *DSUM*.
5. Click OK.
6. Enter range address or range name in *Database* text box.
7. Enter cell for column heading of column to sum in *Field* text box.
8. Enter range address or range name in *Criteria* text box.
9. Click OK.

Figure 3.9 DSUM Example

	A	B	C	D	E	F	G	H	I	J	K
1		O'DONOVAN & SULLIVAN LAW ASSOCIATES									
2		ASSOCIATE BILLING SUMMARY									
3		OCTOBER 5 TO 9, 2009									
4	File_No	ClientID	Date	Last_Name	First_Name	Attorney	Area	Billable_Hrs	Rate		Area
5	FL-325	10104	10/5/2009	Ferreira	Joseph	Marty O'Donovan	Divorce	6.75	85.00		Corporate
6	EP-652	10106	10/5/2009	Kolcz	Robert	Marty O'Donovan	Wills	3.25	55.00		
7	CL-412	10125	10/5/2009	Schmidt	Hilary	Toni Sullivan	Corporate	5.25	75.00		Corporate Billable_Hrs
8	IN-745	10210	10/6/2009	Boscovic	Victor	Maureen Myers	Insurance	4.25	100.00		23.5
9	EL-632	10225	10/6/2009	Armstrong	Daniel	Rosa Martinez	Employment	3.25	65.00		
10	RE-475	10285	10/6/2009	Cooke	Penny	Kyle Williams	Real Estate	2.75	75.00		Attorney
11	CL-501	10341	10/7/2009	Fletcher	Dana	Toni Sullivan	Corporate	5.25	75.00		Marty O'Donovan
12	CL-521	10334	10/7/2009	Marsales	Gene	Toni Sullivan	Corporate	4.25	75.00		
13	PL-348	10420	10/7/2009	Torrez	Alexander	Rosa Martinez	Patent	5.00	100.00		O'Donovan Billable_Hrs
14	RE-492	10425	10/7/2009	Sauve	Jean	Kyle Williams	Real Estate	3.25	75.00		18.75
15	EL-632	10225	10/8/2009	Armstrong	Daniel	Rosa Martinez	Employment	4.50	65.00		
16	PL-512	10290	10/8/2009	Tonini	Sam	Rosa Martinez	Pension	3.75	85.00		
17	IN-745	10210	10/8/2009	Boscovic	Victor	Maureen Myers	Insurance	4.50	100.00		
18	FL-325	10104	10/8/2009	Ferreira	Joseph	Marty O'Donovan	Wills	3.50	55.00		
19	FL-385	10278	10/8/2009	Moore	Lana	Marty O'Donovan	Separation	5.25	65.00		
20	CL-412	10125	10/5/2009	Schmidt	Hilary	Toni Sullivan	Corporate	5.25	75.00		
21	CL-450	10358	10/9/2009	Poissant	Henri	Toni Sullivan	Corporate	3.50	75.00		
22	IN-801	10346	10/9/2009	Sebastian	Paul	Maureen Myers	Insurance	4.25	100.00		
23	EP-685	10495	10/9/2009	Kinsela	Frank	Rosa Martinez	Estate	3.75	100.00		
24	RE-501	10384	10/9/2009	Eckler	Jade	Kyle Williams	Real Estate	4.50	75.00		

Criteria range

Criteria range

DSUM formula used to total Corporate Billable_Hrs in K8:
=DSUM(A4:I24,H4,K4:K5)

DSUM formula used to total O'Donovan Billable_Hrs in K14:
=DSUM(A4:I24,H4,K10:K11)

The DAVERAGE function uses the same arguments as DSUM and is used to find the arithmetic mean from the specified field. Among the list of database functions that Excel provides are: DAVERAGE, DCOUNT, DCOUNTA, DMAX and DMIN.

A database function can be used on any range of cells set up in a list format with the first row of the range containing labels. Similar to a database table, Excel treats rows as records and columns as fields. Consider assigning a name to the database range for easier entry and readability of the formula.

The criteria range can be placed anywhere within the workbook as long as the first cell in the range contains the column label to be used for selecting records and the cell below the column label specifies the criteria for selecting records. Avoid placing the criteria range immediately below or adjacent to the list in case you want to expand the database in the future. In Project 4, you will place criteria ranges in a separate sheet.

You can use multiple criteria to select records by placing additional text or values below the column label and first criteria cell. For example, in Figure 3.9 the criteria range K4:K5 could be expanded by typing *Patent* in K6. In the DSUM formula, the criteria range would be entered as K4:K6. In this case, Excel would sum the billable hours for those records where *Corporate* or *Patent* is in the Area column.

Project ④ Calculating Statistics Using Database Functions

1. Open **O'Donovan&Sullivan-Billing.xlsx**.
2. Save the workbook with Save As and name it **ExcelL2_C3_P4**.
3. Insert 8 blank rows at the top of the worksheet and then enter the labels shown below.

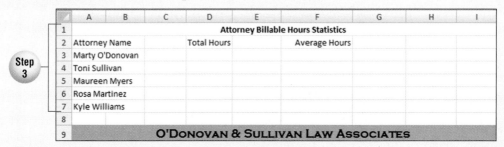

4. Select F12:F13 and copy the cells to the clipboard.
5. Make Sheet2 the active worksheet and paste the cells to A1 in Sheet2. Click the Paste Options button and click *Keep Source Column Widths.*
6. Using copy and paste routines between Sheet1 and Sheet2, create the remaining criteria ranges in the Sheet2 worksheet as shown.
7. Rename Sheet2 to **CriteriaRanges**.
8. Name the following ranges in the CriteriaRanges worksheet:
A1:A2	ODonovan
A4:A5	Sullivan
A7:A8	Myers
A10:A11	Martinez
A13:A14	Williams
9. Make Sheet1 the active worksheet.

10. Select A12:I32 and name the range **Billings**. Deselect the range.
11. Create database functions to sum the billable hours by attorney by completing the following steps:
    a. Make D3 the active cell.
    b. Click the Insert Function button in the Formula bar.
    c. Click the down-pointing arrow next to the *Or select a category* list box and then click *Database* at the drop-down list.
    d. Scroll down the *Select a function* list box, click *DSUM*, and then click OK.
    e. At the Function Arguments dialog box with the insertion point positioned in the *Database* text box, type **Billings** and then press Tab.
    f. Type **h12** in the *Field* text box and then press Tab. The field argument requires only the address of the column label for the column containing the values to be added.
    g. Type **ODonovan** in the *Criteria* text box and then click OK. Excel returns the value 18.75 in the formula cell.

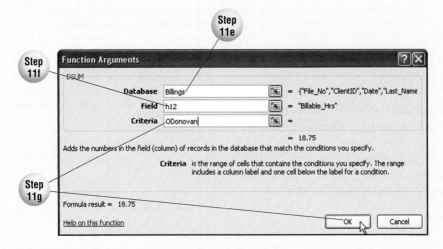

    h. Enter the DSUM functions in D4:D7 by completing steps similar to those in Steps 11a–11g, changing the criteria to the appropriate attorney range name for each cell. When completed the formulas will be as follows:
        D4 =DSUM(Billings,H12,Sullivan)
        D5 =DSUM(Billings,H12,Myers)
        D6 =DSUM(Billings,H12,Martinez)
        D7 =DSUM(Billings,H12,Williams)
12. Select D3:D7 and apply the Comma Style number format.
13. Enter formulas in F3:F7 to average the billable hours for each attorney. Use the database function DAVERAGE. The argument parameters are the same as those used for DSUM. Use the Insert Function button or type the formulas directly into the cells. When completed the formulas will be as follows:
        F3 =DAVERAGE(Billings,H12,ODonovan)
        F4 =DAVERAGE(Billings,H12,Sullivan)
        F5 =DAVERAGE(Billings,H12,Myers)
        F6 =DAVERAGE(Billings,H12,Martinez)
        F7 =DAVERAGE(Billings,H12,Williams)
14. Save, print, and then close **ExcelL2_C3_P4.xlsx**.

Project 5   Calculate Statistics Using a SUBTOTAL Function

You will calculate subtotals in a list using the Math & Trig SUBTOTAL function and then filter the list to view various statistics.

Using the Math & Trig SUBTOTAL Function

HINT

Functions added in a Total row in a table use SUBTOTAL formulas. Consider defining a database or list as a table and then using a Total row to add subtotals.

Math & Trig ▾

In Project 3, you used Excel's Subtotal button in the Outline group of the Data tab to calculate statistics by attorney to view the sum and count of fees due and the average of fees due and billable hours. The Subtotal button is the easier method with which to display subtotals in a database or list. The feature uses the SUBTOTAL function found in the Math & Trig category of the function library. In some cases you may need to edit a SUBTOTAL function created by the Subtotal button, or you may prefer to create your own SUBTOTAL formula and filter a list to view various statistics. The structure of a SUBTOTAL formula is *=SUBTOTAL(function_num,ref1,ref2, . . .)* where *function_num* is the number for the desired function, and *ref1* is the range of cells containing the data you want to subtotal. Multiple ranges can be included in the function by separating each range with a comma. Table 3.2 provides the function numbers with the corresponding function formula for four subtotal functions. Additional functions are available beyond those described in Table 3.2. For example, you can specify MAX or MIN in a SUBTOTAL function using function number 4 or 5. Use Excel's Help feature to view additional function numbers if you want to summarize values in a database or list using a function other than SUM, AVERAGE, COUNT, or COUNTA.

Table 3.2   SUBTOTAL Function Numbers

Function_num to include values in hidden rows in the Subtotal result	Function_num to ignore values in hidden rows in the Subtotal result	Function
1	101	AVERAGE
2	102	COUNT
3	103	COUNTA
9	109	SUM

Assume the list from which you want to generate a subtotal is the range A5:A20. To calculate the average of the values within the range and include any hidden rows in the calculation, you would enter the formula *=SUBTOTAL(1,A5:A20)*. To calculate the average of the values in the range ignoring any hidden rows, you would enter the formula *=SUBTOTAL(101,A5:A20)*. Using the SUBTOTAL function allows you to filter the list or database and view updated results for the filtered records, whereas SUM or AVERAGE functions do not update when the list is filtered.

1. Open **O'Donovan&Sullivan-Billing.xlsx**.
2. Save the workbook with Save As and name it **ExcelL2_C3_P5**.
3. Create a subtotal formula to calculate the sum of the billable hours by completing the following steps:
   a. Make B26 the active cell and then type **Total Billable Hours**.
   b. Make D26 the active cell, type **=subtotal(9,h5:h25)**, and then press Enter.

24	RE-501	10384	10/9/2009	Eckler	Jade
25					
26			Total Billable Hours	=subtotal(9,h5:h24)	

Step 3a

Step 3b

4. Create a subtotal formula to calculate the arithmetic mean of the billable hours by completing the following steps:
   a. Make F26 the active cell and then type **Average Billable Hours**.
   b. Make H26 the active cell, type **=subtotal(1,h5:h25)**, and then press Enter.

24	RE-501	10384	10/9/2009	Eckler	Jade	Kyle Williams	Real Estate	4.50	75.00
25									
26		Total Billable Hours		86.00		Average Billable Hours		4.30	

Step 4a

Step 4b

5. Filter the billing summary data and view updated total and average statistics for the filtered rows by completing the following steps:
   a. Select A4:I24.
   b. If necessary, click the Home tab.
   c. Click the Sort & Filter button in the Editing group and then click *Filter* at the drop-down list.
   d. Deselect the range.
   e. Click the filter arrow button next to *Attorney* in F4.
   f. Click the *(Select All)* check box to clear the check mark from the box, click the *Marty O'Donovan* check box to insert a check mark, and then click OK. Excel filters the list and updates the values in D26 and H26 to display the sum and average of only those rows that are currently displayed.

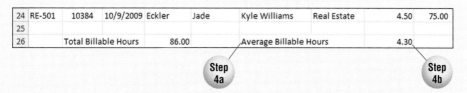

4	File_⏷	ClientI⏷	Date ⏷	Last_Nan⏷	First_Nan⏷	Attorney ⏷	Area ⏷	Billable_H⏷	Rate ⏷
5	FL-325	10104	10/5/2009	Ferreira	Joseph	Marty O'Donovan	Divorce	6.75	85.00
6	EP-652	10106	10/5/2009	Kolcz	Robert	Marty O'Donovan	Wills	3.25	55.00
18	FL-325	10104	10/8/2009	Ferreira	Joseph	Marty O'Donovan	Wills	3.50	55.00
19	FL-385	10278	10/8/2009	Moore	Lana	Marty O'Donovan	Separation	5.25	65.00
25									
26		Total Billable Hours		18.75		Average Billable Hours		4.69	

Subtotals update to reflect the sum and average of only the rows shown in the filtered list in Step 5f.

6. Print the filtered worksheet.
7. Click the filter arrow button next to *Attorney* in F4 and then click *Clear Filter From "Attorney"* at the drop-down list. All rows are redisplayed and the subtotal formulas update to reflect all data.
8. Save, print, and then close **ExcelL2_C2_P5.xlsx**.

CHAPTER summary

- A table in Excel is a range of cells similar in structure to a database in which no blank rows exist and the first row of the range contains column headings.

- Define a range as a table using the Table button in the Tables group of the Insert tab.

- Columns in a table are called fields and rows are called records.

- A table automatically expands to include data typed in a row or column immediately adjacent to a range that has been defined as a table.

- Typing a formula in the first row of a new column causes Excel to define the column as a calculated column and automatically copy the formula to the remaining rows in the table.

- The contextual Table Tools Design tab contains options for formatting tables.

- The Table Styles gallery contains several options with which you can change the visual appearance of a table.

- Banding rows or columns in a table formats every other row or column differently to make reading a large table easier.

- You can add emphasis to the first column or the last column in a table. Excel generally formats the column with a darker fill color and reverse font or bold font and borders depending on the Table Style in effect.

- The row containing field names in a table can be shown or hidden using the *Header Row* option in the Table Style Options group.

- Adding a Total row to a table causes Excel to add the word *Total* in the leftmost column and create a Sum function in the last numeric column in the table. You can add additional functions by clicking in the desired column in the Total row and selecting a function from the pop-up list.

- Excel includes a filter arrow button automatically at the top of each column in a table with which you can filter and sort the table.

- A column containing text that you want to split can be separated into multiple columns using the Text to Columns button in the Data Tools group of the Data tab. The Convert Text to Columns wizard contains three dialog boxes to define how to split the data.

- Using the Remove Duplicates dialog box, you can instruct Excel to compare records within a worksheet and automatically delete rows that are duplicated.

- Data can be validated as it is being entered into a worksheet and invalid data either prevented from being stored or a warning issued to inform that data has been entered that does not conform to the restrictions.

- At the Settings tab in the Data Validation dialog box you define the validation criteria for the cell entry. You can allow data based on values, dates, times, text length, or restrict the entries to values within a drop-down list.

- At the Input Message tab in the Data Validation dialog box you can define a message that pops up when a cell for which data is restricted becomes active.

- At the Error Alert tab in the Data Validation dialog box you define the type of error alert to display and the content of the error message.

- Convert a table to a normal range to use the Subtotal feature or when you no longer need to treat a range of cells independently from the rest of the worksheet.
- Sort a worksheet by the column(s) for which you want to group data for subtotals before opening the Subtotals dialog box.
- The Subtotals button is located in the Outline group of the Data tab.
- Excel adds a subtotal automatically at each change in content for the column you specify as the subtotal field. A grand total is also automatically added to the bottom of the range.
- You can display more than one subtotal row for a group to calculate multiple functions such as Sum and Average.
- A subtotaled range is outlined and detail records can be collapsed or expanded using level number, Hide Detail, and Show Detail buttons.
- Use the Group and Ungroup buttons when a worksheet is outlined to manage the display of individual groups.
- Database functions summarize data within a range based on the contents of a criteria range.
- Create the criteria range for a database function outside the range that will be analyzed.
- The structure of the DSUM function is =DSUM(*database,field,criteria*) where *database* is the list range, *field* is the column heading for the column with the values to sum, and *criteria* is the range containing the field and field value that determines which records are selected to be added to the total.
- The SUBTOTAL function in the Math and Trigonometry function list is used to summarize data in a range.
- The structure of a SUBTOTAL function is =SUBTOTAL(*function_num,ref1*) where *function_num* is the number for AVERAGE, SUM, COUNT, or COUNTA, and *ref1* is the range of cells to subtotal.

COMMANDS review

FEATURE	RIBBON TAB, GROUP	BUTTON	KEYBOARD SHORTCUT
Convert Text to Columns	Data, Data Tools		
Convert to Range	Table Tools Design, Tools	Convert to Range	
Create table	Insert, Tables		Ctrl + T
Data Validation	Data, Data Tools	Data Validation	
Database functions	Formulas, Function Library	*fx*	Shift + F3
Group	Data, Outline		Shift + Alt + Right arrow key
Remove Duplicates	Data, Data Tools OR Table Tools Design, Tools	Remove Duplicates	
Table Styles	Table Tools Design, Table Styles		
Sort & Filter table	Home, Editing		
Subtotals	Data, Outline		
SUBTOTAL function	Formulas, Function Library	Math & Trig	Shift + F3
Total row	Table Tools Design, Table Style Options		Ctrl + Shift + T
Ungroup	Data, Outline		Shift + Alt + Left arrow key

CONCEPTS check

Test Your Knowledge

Completion: In the space provided at the right, indicate the correct term, command, or number.

1. The first row of a table that contains the column headings is called the field names row or this row. _____

2. Typing a formula in the first row of a column in a table causes Excel to define the field as this type of column. _____

3. This is the term that describes the formatting feature in a table in which even rows are formatted differently than odd rows.

_____

4. Change the visual appearance of a table using this gallery in the Table Tools Design tab.

_____

5. Clicking this button causes the Convert Text to Columns wizard to appear.

_____

6. Open this dialog box to instruct Excel to compare the entries in the columns you specify and automatically delete rows that contain repeated data.

_____

7. Open this dialog box to restrict entries in a cell to those that you set up in a drop-down list.

_____

8. This option in the *Allow* list box is used to force data entered into a cell to be a specific number of characters.

_____

9. This is the default error alert style which prevents invalid data from being entered into a cell.

_____

10. The Convert to Range button is found in this tab.

_____

11. Prior to creating subtotals using the Subtotal button in the Outline group of the Data tab, arrange the data in this order.

_____

12. In a worksheet with subtotal rows only displayed, click this button next to a subtotal row in order to view the grouped rows.

_____

13. Click this button in an outlined worksheet to collapse the rows for a group.

_____

14. In a DSUM function, the argument *database* refers to this range.

_____

15. In a DSUM function, the argument *field* refers to this cell.

_____

16. In a DSUM function, the argument *criteria* refers to this range.

_____

17. The SUBTOTAL function formula is located in this function category.

_____

SKILLS check

Demonstrate Your Proficiency

Assessment

1 CREATE AND FORMAT A TABLE

1. Open **Vantage-ClassicVideos.xlsx**.
2. Save the workbook with Save As and name it **ExcelL2_C3_A1**.
3. Format the range A4:K23 as a table using Table Style Medium 9 (second from left in second row in Medium section).
4. Add a calculated column to the table in column L. Type the label **TotalCost** as the column heading and create a formula in the first record that multiplies the number of copies in column G times the cost price in column K.
5. Adjust the three rows above the table to merge and center across columns A through L.
6. Adjust all column widths to AutoFit.
7. Band the columns instead of the rows and emphasize the last column in the table.
8. Add a Total row to the table. Add Average functions to the total row that calculate the average number of copies and the average cost price of a classic video.
9. Format the average value in the *Copies* column of the Total row to zero decimals.
10. The video Blue Hawaii cannot be located and the manager of Vantage Videos would like to remove the record from the table. Delete the row in the table for the record with StockNo CV-1015.
11. Move the clip art images above the table as necessary to improve the layout.
12. Save, print, and then close **ExcelL2_C3_A1.xlsx**.

Assessment

2 USE DATA TOOLS

1. Open **ExcelL2_C3_A1.xlsx**.
2. Save the workbook with Save As and name it **ExcelL2_C3_A2**.
3. Remove the banding on the columns and band the rows.
4. Insert a new blank column to the right of the column containing the director names.
5. Split the director names into two columns. Edit the column headings to **Director_FName** and **Director_LName**, respectively.
6. Use the Remove Duplicates feature to find and remove any duplicate rows using *Title* as the comparison column.
7. Create the following validation rules.
   a. Create a validation rule for the *StockNo* column that ensures all new entries are seven characters in length. Add an input message to the column to advise the user that stock numbers need to be seven characters. You determine the title and message text. Use the default error alert options.
   b. The manager would like to ensure that five copies is the maximum inventory of any individual classic video in the collection. Create a validation rule that restricts entries in the copies column to a number less than six. Add an appropriate input and error message. Use the default Stop error alert.

c. Create a drop-down list for the *Genre* column with the entries provided. Do not enter an input message and use the default error alert settings.

   Action,Comedy,Drama,Family,Horror,Musical,Thriller,War

8. Add the following record to the table to test the data validation rules. Initially enter incorrect values in the *StockNo*, *Genre*, and *Copies* columns to make sure the rule and the messages work correctly.

StockNo	CV-1019
Title	Bonnie and Clyde
Year	1967
Genre	Drama
StockDate	01/15/2009
Director_FName	Arthur
Director_LName	Penn
Copies	2
VHS	No
DVD	Yes
Category	2-day rental
CostPrice	9.12

9. Right-align the StockNo in A22.
10. Save, print, and then close **ExcelL2_C3_A2.xlsx**.

Assessment

3 GROUP AND SUBTOTAL RECORDS

1. Open **ExcelL2_C3_A2.xlsx**.
2. Save the workbook with Save As and name it **ExcelL2_C3_A3.xlsx**.
3. Remove the total row, remove the row banding, and remove the emphasis from the last column in the table.
4. Convert the table to a normal range.
5. Adjust all column widths to AutoFit and then adjust the position of the clip art images above the list to improve the layout.
6. Sort the list first by the genre, then by the director's last name, and then by the title of the video. Use the default sort values and sort order for each level.
7. Add subtotals using the Subtotal button in the Outline group of the Data tab to the *TotalCost* column to calculate the sum and average total costs of videos by genre.
8. Display the worksheet at Level 2 of the outline.
9. Show the details for the Comedy, Drama, and Family genres.
10. Print the worksheet.
11. Save and then close **ExcelL2_C3_A3.xlsx**.

4 SUMMARIZE DATA USING FUNCTIONS

1. Open **Vantage-ClassicVideos.xlsx**.
2. Save the workbook with Save As and name it **ExcelL2_C3_A4.xlsx**.
3. Enter the labels in the cells indicated.
   - B25   Average copies of VHS videos
   - B26   Average copies of DVD videos
4. Create a criteria range in M4:M5 to select a row if the value in the VHS column is Yes. Name the criteria cells **VHS**.
5. Create a criteria range in N4:N5 to select a row if the value in the DVD column is Yes. Name the criteria cells **DVD**.
6. Name the range A4:K23 **Database**.
7. Create DAVERAGE formulas in C25 and C26 to calculate the average copies of VHS and DVD videos, respectively, using the appropriate range names for the database and criteria arguments and G4 as the field argument.
8. Format C25:C26 to display zero decimals.
9. Save, print, and then close **ExcelL2_C3_A4.xlsx**.

CASE study
Apply Your Skills

Part 1

Rajiv Patel, Vice-President of NuTrends Market Research, has sent you a file named **NuTrends-Qtr1MktPlans.xlsx**. The workbook contains client information for the company's first quarter marketing plans for three marketing consultants. Rajiv would like you to improve the reporting in the file by completing the following tasks:

- Set up the data as a table sorted first by the consultant's last name and then by the marketing campaign's start date. Rajiv would prefer that the consultant names be split into two columns.
- Improve the formatting of the dollar values.
- Add a total row to sum the columns containing dollar amounts.
- Add formatting to the titles above the table that are suited to the colors in the table style you selected.
- Make any other formatting changes you think would improve the worksheet's appearance.

Save the revised workbook and name it **ExcelL2_C3_CS_P1**. Print the worksheet in landscape orientation with the width scaled to 1 page.

Part 2

Rajiv would like statistics for each consultant added to the workbook. Specifically, Rajiv would like to see the following information:

- The total marketing plan budget values being managed by each consultant as well as the planned expenditures by month.
- The average marketing plan budget being managed by each consultant as well as the planned expenditures by month.

Rajiv would like a printout that displays only the total and average values for each consultant as well as the grand average and grand total. Save the revised workbook and name it **ExcelL2_C3_CS_P2**. Print and then close the worksheet.

Part 3

Rajiv is preparing for a performance review meeting with Yolanda Robertson. Rajiv has asked that you provide another report from the file named **NuTrends-Qtr1MktPlans.xlsx**. Specifically, Rajiv would like a printout of the worksheet that shows the original data at the top of the worksheet and, a few blank rows below the worksheet, Rajiv would like to see the marketing plan details for Yolanda Robertson's clients that have a campaign starting after January 31, 2009.

You recall seeing the Advanced Filter button in the Sort & Filter group of the Data tab and decide this is likely the feature that will automatically duplicate the records you need below the existing worksheet. Research in Help how to filter a range of cells using Advanced Filter. Make sure you read how to copy rows that meet your filter criteria to another area of the worksheet. Using the information you learned in Help, open **NuTrends-Qtr1MktPlans.xlsx**, insert three new rows above the worksheet and use these rows to create the criteria range. Filter the list as per Rajiv's specifications. Rows that meet the criteria should be copied below the worksheet starting in A21. Add an appropriate title to describe the copied data in A20. Make any formatting changes you think would improve the appearance of the worksheet. Save the revised workbook and name it **ExcelL2_C3_CS_P3**. Print the worksheet in landscape orientation scaled to fit 1 page width and then close the workbook.

Part 4

Rajiv has requested further assistance from you in preparation for the performance review with Yolanda Robertson. Rajiv is looking for information on current salary ranges for a market researcher in the United States. Use the Internet to find the information for Rajiv. If possible, find salary information that is regional to your city or state. Create a workbook that summarizes the results of your research. Include in the workbook the Web site addresses as hyperlinked cells next to the salary range information for the data you have selected. Find a minimum of three resources and a maximum of five. Using the SUBTOTAL function, create a formula below the data that calculates the average salary from the data that you found. Use the AVERAGE function number that ignores hidden rows in the formula. Save the workbook and name it **ExcelL2_C3_CS_P4**. Print the worksheet and then close the workbook.

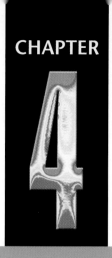

CHAPTER 4

Summarizing and Consolidating Data

PERFORMANCE OBJECTIVES

Upon successful completion of Chapter 4, you will be able to:

- Summarize data by creating formulas with range names that reference other worksheets
- Modify the range assigned to a range name
- Summarize data by creating 3-D formulas
- Create formulas that link to cells in other workbooks
- Edit a link to a source workbook
- Break a link to an external reference
- Use the Consolidate feature to summarize data in multiple worksheets
- Create, edit, and format a PivotTable
- Create and format a PivotChart
- Format the x-, y-, or z-axis in a chart
- Modify or remove chart gridlines
- Add a trendline to a chart to forecast future values
- Modify trendline options

Tutorial 4.1
Consolidating Worksheets and
   Creating PivotTable Reports
Tutorial 4.2
Sorting and Formatting
   PivotTable Reports and
   Creating PivotChart Reports

Various methods for summarizing data include creating formulas that reference cells in other areas of the active worksheet, in other worksheets within the same workbook, or by linking to cells in other workbooks. The Consolidate feature can also be used to summarize data from other worksheets or other workbooks into a master worksheet. Once the data has been summarized, consider presenting or analyzing the data by creating and formatting a PivotTable or a PivotChart. Charts are also reintroduced in this chapter with advanced chart formatting options.

Note: Before beginning computer projects, copy to your storage medium the Excel2007L2C4 subfolder from the Excel2007L2 folder on the CD that accompanies this textbook and then make Excel2007L2C4 the active folder.

Project ① Calculate Park Attendance Totals

You will create and modify range names and calculate total park attendance at three national parks from data stored in separate worksheets and by linking to a cell in another workbook. You will also edit a linked workbook and update the link in the destination file.

Summarizing Data in Multiple Worksheets Using Range Names

QUICK STEPS

Sum Multiple Worksheets Using Range Names
1. Make formula cell active.
2. Type =sum(.
3. Type first range name.
4. Type comma ,.
5. Type second range name.
6. Type comma ,.
7. Continue typing range names separated by commas until finished.
8. Type).
9. Press Enter.

Modify a Range Name or Range Reference
1. Open workbook.
2. Click Formulas tab.
3. Click Name Manager button.
4. Click range name to be modified.
5. Click Edit button.
6. Change name and/or modify range address(es).
7. Click OK.
8. Click Close.

A workbook that has been organized with data in separate worksheets can be summarized by creating formulas that reference cells in other worksheets. When you create a formula that references a cell in the same worksheet you do not need to include the sheet name in the reference. For example, the formula =A3+A4 causes Excel to add the value in A3 in the active worksheet to the value in A4 in the active worksheet. Assume you want Excel to add the value in A3 that resides in Sheet2 to the value in A3 that resides in Sheet 3 in the workbook. To do this you need to include the worksheet name in the formula by typing =Sheet2!A3+Sheet3!A3 into the formula cell. This formula contains worksheet references as well as cell references. A worksheet reference precedes the cell reference and is separated from the cell reference with an exclamation point. Absent a worksheet reference, Excel assumes the active worksheet. A formula that references the same cell in a range that extends over two or more worksheets is often called a **3-D reference**. 3-D formulas can be typed directly in the cell or entered using a point and click approach.

As an alternative, consider using range names to simplify formulas that summarize data in multiple worksheets. A range name includes the worksheet reference by default; therefore typing the range name in the formula automatically references the correct worksheet. For example, assume A3 in Sheet 2 has been named *ProductA* and A3 in Sheet 3 has been named *ProductB*. To add the two values you would type the formula =*ProductA*+*ProductB* in the formula cell. Notice you do not need to remember worksheet references. Another advantage to using range names is that the name can describe the worksheet with the source data. By using range names you also do not have to make each worksheet identical in organizational structure. Remember that cell references in range names are absolute references.

1. Open **ParkAttendance-May.xlsx**.
2. Save the workbook with Save As and name it **ExcelL2_C4_P1**.
3. Click each Sheet tab and review the data. Each park has attendance data entered as a separate worksheet. In the workbook, range names have already been created for two of the three parks. Create the third range name needed for the data in the MesaVerde sheet by completing the following steps:
   a. Click the MesaVerde sheet tab to activate the worksheet.
   b. Select B7:B22.
   c. Hold down the Ctrl key and then select E7:E21.
   d. Click in the Name text box, type **Mesa**, and then press Enter.
4. Check each range name to make sure the cell references are correct before creating the summary formula by completing the following steps:
   a. Click the down-pointing arrow next to the Name text box and then click *Bryce* at the drop-down list. Notice the BryceCanyon sheet is active and the ranges B7:B22 and E7:E21 are selected.
   b. Click the down-pointing arrow next to the Name text box and then click *Grand* at the drop-down list. Notice the GrandCanyon sheet is active and the range B7:B22 is selected. This range is missing the entries for days 17 through 31. You will correct this range in Step 5.
   c. Click the down-pointing arrow next to the Name text box and then click *Mesa* at the drop-down list. The MesaVerde sheet is active and the ranges B7:B22 and E7:E21 are selected.
5. Modify the references in a range name by adding the data in column E of the GrandCanyon worksheet to the range named *Grand* by completing the following steps:
   a. Click in any cell to deselect the *Mesa* range.
   b. Click the Formulas tab.
   c. Click the Name Manager button 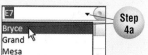 in the Defined Names group.
   d. Click *Grand* in the *Name* list at the Name Manager dialog box.
   e. Click the Edit button.

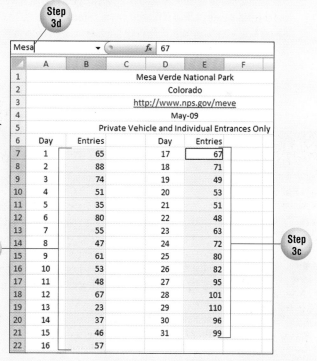

Step 3d

	A	B	C	D	E	F
1				Mesa Verde National Park		
2				Colorado		
3				http://www.nps.gov/meve		
4				May-09		
5				Private Vehicle and Individual Entrances Only		
6	Day	Entries		Day	Entries	
7	1	65		17	67	
8	2	88		18	71	
9	3	74		19	49	
10	4	51		20	53	
11	5	35		21	51	
12	6	80		22	48	
13	7	55		23	63	
14	8	47		24	72	
15	9	61		25	80	
16	10	53		26	82	
17	11	48		27	95	
18	12	67		28	101	
19	13	23		29	110	
20	14	37		30	96	
21	15	46		31	99	
22	16	57				

Step 3b

Step 3c

Step 4a

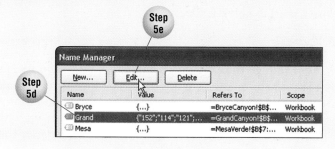

Step 5e

Step 5d

f. At the Edit Name dialog box, click the Collapse Dialog button located at the end of the *Refers to* text box (currently displays *=GrandCanyon!$B$7:$B$22*). The GrandCanyon worksheet is active with the range B7:B22 selected.

g. Hold down the Ctrl key and select E7:E21.

h. Click the Expand Dialog button to restore the Edit Name dialog box. Notice that cell addresses in range names are absolute references.

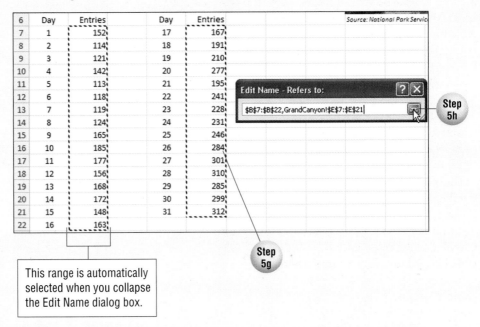

Step 5h

Step 5g

This range is automatically selected when you collapse the Edit Name dialog box.

i. Click OK to close the Edit Name dialog box.

j. Click Close to close the Name Manager dialog box.

k. Click the down-pointing arrow next to the Name text box and then click *Grand* at the drop-down list to make sure the revised range name is referencing B7:B22 and E7:E21 in the GrandCanyon worksheet.

6. Create the formula to add the attendance for May at all three parks by completing the following steps:

a. Click the AttendanceSummary tab to activate the worksheet.

b. If necessary, make F7 the active cell.

c. Type **=sum(bryce,grand,mesa)** and press Enter. Notice that in a Sum formula, multiple range names are separated with commas. Excel returns the result *9620* in F7 of the AttendanceSummary worksheet.

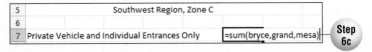

Step 6c

7. Save and then close **ExcelL2_C4_P1.xlsx**.

A disadvantage to using range names applies when several worksheets need to be summarized since you have to create the range name reference in each individual worksheet. If several worksheets need to be summed, a more efficient method is to use a 3-D reference as long as each worksheet is set up with the data in identical cells. In Project 1b, you will calculate the same attendance total for the three parks using a 3-D reference instead of range names.

1. Open **ParkAttendance-May.xlsx**.
2. Save the workbook with Save As and name it **ExcelL2_C4_P1b-3DRef**.
3. Calculate the attendance total for the three parks using a point and click approach to creating a 3-D reference by completing the following steps:
   a. With F7 in the AttendanceSummary worksheet the active cell, type **=sum(**.
   b. Click the BryceCanyon sheet tab.
   c. Hold down the Shift key and click the MesaVerde sheet tab. Using the Shift key while clicking a sheet tab selects all worksheets from the first sheet tab through to the last sheet tab clicked. Notice in the formula bar the formula reads *=sum('BryceCanyon:MesaVerde'!*
   d. With BryceCanyon the active worksheet, select B7:B22, hold down the Ctrl key, and select E7:E21.
   e. Type) and press Enter. Excel returns the value *9620* in F7 in the AttendanceSummary worksheet.
4. Press the Up Arrow key to move the active cell back to F7 and compare your formula with the one shown in Figure 4.1.
5. Save and then close **ExcelL2_C4_P1b-3DRef.xlsx**.

6	Day	Entries	Day	Entries
7	1	44	17	67
8	2	52	18	28
9	3	30	19	44
10	4	28	20	38
11	5	55	21	62
12	6	31	22	78
13	7	20	23	55
14	8	22	24	63
15	9	45	25	71
16	10	18	26	49
17	11	21	27	55
18	12	60	28	67
19	13	18	29	81
20	14	27	30	85
21	15	37	31	90
22	16	41		
23				
24				
25				
26				

SUM(number1, [number2], ...)

AttendanceSummary   BryceCanyon   GrandCanyon   MesaVerde

Step 3d

Figure 4.1 3-D Formula to Sum Two Ranges in Three Adjacent Worksheets

3-D formula created in Project 1b, Step 3 using point-and-click approach.

F7   fx =SUM(BryceCanyon:MesaVerde!B7:B22,BryceCanyon:MesaVerde!E7:E21)

	A	B	C	D	E	F	G	H	I	J	K
1			National Park Service								
2			U.S. Department of the Interior								
3			May-09								
4			Attendance Summary								
5			Southwest Region, Zone C								
6											
7	Private Vehicle and Individual Entrances Only					9620					

Summarizing Data by Linking to Ranges in Other Workbooks

Create Link to External Reference
1. Open source workbook.
2. Open destination workbook.
3. Arrange windows as desired.
4. Make formula cell active in destination workbook.
5. Type =.
6. Click to activate source workbook.
7. Click source cell.
8. Press Enter.

Using a similar method as that used in Project 1a or Project 1b, you can summarize data in one workbook by linking to a cell, range, or range name in another workbook. This method incorporates external references and requires that a workbook name reference be added to a formula. For example, linking to cell A3 in a sheet named ProductA in a workbook named Sales would require that you enter =[Sales.xlsx]ProductA!A3 in the formula cell. Notice the workbook reference is entered first in square brackets. The workbook in which the external reference is added becomes the destination workbook. The workbook containing the data that is linked to the destination workbook is called the source workbook. In Project 1c you will create a link to an external cell containing the attendance total for the tour group entrances for the three parks. The point-and-click approach to creating a linked external reference creates an absolute reference to the source cell. Delete the dollar symbols in the cell reference if you plan to copy the formula and need the source cell to be relative. Note that workbook and worksheet references remain absolute regardless.

Project 1c   Summarizing Data by Linking to Another Workbook

1. Open **ExcelL2_C4_P1.xlsx**.
2. Open **GroupSalesbyPark-May.xlsx**. This workbook contains tour group attendance data for the three national parks. Tour groups are charged a flat rate entrance fee and their attendance values represent bus capacity and not actual counts of patrons on each bus.
3. Click the View tab, click the Arrange All button in the Window group, and then click *Vertical* in the *Arrange* section of the Arrange Windows dialog box.
4. Create a linked external reference in the worksheet you created in Project 1a to the total attendance in the worksheet with the commercial tour vehicle attendance data by completing the following steps:
   a. Click in the **ExcelL2_C4_P1.xlsx** worksheet to make the worksheet active.
   b. Make A9 the active cell, type **Commercial Tour Vehicles Only**, and then press Enter.
   c. Make F9 the active cell.
   d. Type =.
   e. Click the **GroupSalesbyPark-May.xlsx** title bar to activate the worksheet and then click F7. Notice the formula that is being entered into the formula cell contains a workbook reference and a worksheet reference in front of the cell reference.
   f. Press Enter.

g. Press the Up Arrow key to move the active cell back to F9 and then compare your worksheet with the one shown below.

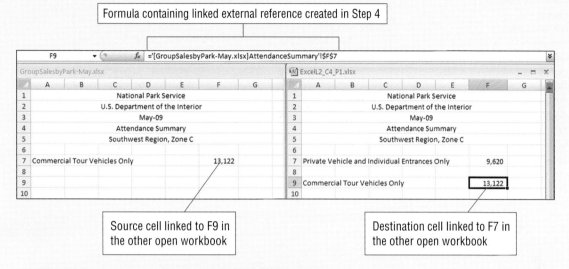

Formula containing linked external reference created in Step 4

Source cell linked to F9 in the other open workbook

Destination cell linked to F7 in the other open workbook

5. Click the Maximize button in the **ExcelL2_C4_P1.xlsx** title bar.
6. Make A11 the active cell, type **Total Attendance**, and then press Enter.
7. Make F11 the active cell and then create a formula to add the values in F7 and F9.
8. Format F7:F11 to the Comma Style number format with no decimals and then deselect the range.
9. Print the AttendanceSummary worksheet in **ExcelL2_C4_P1.xlsx**.
10. Save and then close **ExcelL2_C4_P1.xlsx**.
11. Close **GroupSalesbyPark-May.xlsx**. Click No when prompted to save changes.

Maintaining External References

When you link to an external reference, Excel includes the drive and folder names in the path to the source workbook. If you move the source workbook or change the workbook name, the link will no longer work. By default, when you open a workbook with a linked external reference, automatic updates is disabled and Excel displays an alert message from which you can enable the content. Links can be edited or broken at the Edit Links dialog box shown in Figure 4.2. If more than one link is present in the workbook, begin by clicking the link to be changed in the Source list. Click the Change Source button to open the Change Source dialog box in which you can navigate to the drive and/or folder in which the source workbook was moved or renamed. Click the Break Link button to permanently remove the linked reference and convert the linked cells to their existing values. The Undo feature does not operate to restore a link. If you break a link that you decide you want to restore, you will have to recreate the linked formula.

QUICK STEPS

Edit Link to External Reference
1. Open destination workbook.
2. Click Data tab.
3. Click Edit Links.
4. Click link.
5. Click Change Source.
6. Navigate to drive and/or folder.
7. Double-click source workbook file name.
8. Click Close.
9. Save and close destination workbook.

Figure 4.2 Edit Links Dialog Box

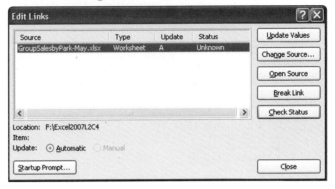

Break Link to External Reference
1. Open destination workbook.
2. Click Data tab.
3. Click Edit Links.
4. Click link.
5. Click Break Link.
6. Click Break Links.
7. Click Close.
8. Save and close destination workbook.

Project 1d Editing Source Data and Updating an External Link

1. Open **GroupSalesbyPark-May.xlsx**.
2. Save the workbook with Save As and name it **ExcelL2_C4_P1-Source**.
3. Edit the attendance data values at each park by completing the following steps:
   a. Click the BryceCanyon tab.
   b. Make B8 the active cell and then change the value from *52* to **312**.
   c. Click the GrandCanyon tab.
   d. Make B20 the active cell and then change the value from *26* to **260**.
   e. Click the MesaVerde tab.
   f. Make E21 the active cell and then change the value from *312* to **468**.
4. Click the AttendanceSummary tab. Note the updated value in F7 is *13,772*. Print the AttendanceSummary worksheet.
5. Save and then close the **ExcelL2_C4_P1-Source.xlsx**.
6. Open **ExcelL2_C4_P1.xlsx**. Notice the security warning that appears in the Message bar above the worksheet area with the message that automatic update of links has been disabled. Instruct Excel to allow automatic updates for this workbook since you are sure the content is from a trusted source by completing the following steps:
   a. Click the Options button in the Message bar located between the ribbon and the worksheet area.

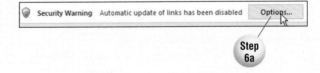

Step 6a

b. At the Microsoft Office Security Options dialog box, click *Enable this content* and then click OK.

7. Edit the link to retrieve the data from the workbook revised in Steps 2–5 by completing the following steps:

a. Click the Data tab.

b. Click the Edit Links button in the Connections group.

c. At the Edit Links dialog box click the Change Source button.

d. At the Change Source: GroupSalesbyPark-May.xlsx dialog box, double-click **ExcelL2_C4_P1-Source.xlsx** in the file list box. Excel returns to the Edit Links dialog box and updates the source workbook file name and path.

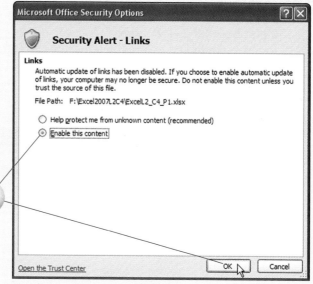

Step 6b

Updated source workbook file name and path edited in Steps 7a–7d

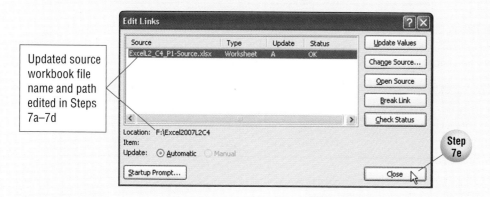

Step 7e

e. Click the Close button.

8. Click F9 in the AttendanceSummary worksheet to view the updated linked formula. Notice the workbook reference in the formula is [ExcelL2_C4_P1-Source.xlsx] and the drive and path are included in the formula.

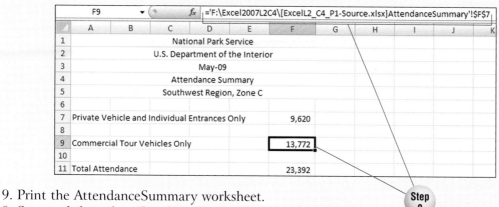

Step 8

9. Print the AttendanceSummary worksheet.

10. Save and then close **ExcelL2_C4_P1.xlsx**.

1. Open **ExcelL2_C4_P1.xlsx**.
2. Remove the linked external reference to attendance values for commercial tour vehicles by completing the following steps:
   a. With Data the active tab, click the Edit Links button in the Connections group.
   b. Click the Break Link button at the Edit Links dialog box.

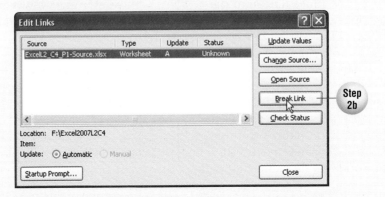

Step 2b

   c. Click the Break Links button at the Microsoft Office Excel message box that says breaking links permanently converts formulas and external references to their existing values and cannot be undone and asks if you are sure you want to break the links.

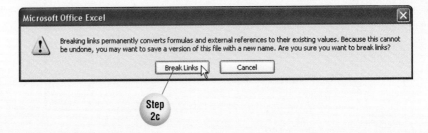

Step 2c

   d. Click the Close button at the Edit Links dialog box with no links displayed.
3. With F9 in the AttendanceSummary worksheet the active cell, look in the Formula bar. Notice the linked formula has been replaced with the latest cell value, *13772*.
4. Save and then close **ExcelL2_C4_P1.xlsx**.
5. Open **ExcelL2_C4_P1.xlsx**. Notice that since the workbook no longer contains a link to an external reference, the security warning message no longer appears in the Message bar.
6. Close **ExcelL2_C4_P1.xlsx**. Click No if prompted to save changes.

roject **2** **Calculate Total Fees Billed by Three Dentists**

You will use the Consolidate feature to summarize the total dental fees billed by treatment category for three dentists.

Summarizing Data Using the Consolidate Feature

The Consolidate feature is another method that can be used to summarize data from multiple worksheets or from another workbook into a master worksheet. Open the Consolidate dialog box shown in Figure 4.3 from the Consolidate button located in the Data Tools group in the Data tab.

By default, the Sum function is active. Change to a different function such as Count or Average using the *Function* drop-down list. In the *Reference* text box, type the range name or use the Collapse Dialog button to navigate to the cells to be consolidated. If the cells are located in another workbook, use the Browse button to navigate to the drive and/or folder and locate the file name. Once the correct reference is inserted in the *Reference* text box, click the Add button. Continue adding references for each unit of data to be summarized. Click *Top row* or *Left column* in the *Use labels in* section to indicate where the labels are located in the source ranges. Click the *Create links to source data* to instruct Excel to update the data automatically when the source ranges change. Make sure enough empty cells are available to the right and below the active cell when you open the Consolidate dialog box since Excel populates the rows and columns based on the size of the source data.

QUICK STEPS

Consolidate Data
1. Make starting cell active.
2. Click Data tab.
3. Click Consolidate button.
4. If necessary, change *Function*.
5. Enter first range in *Reference* text box.
6. Click Add.
7. Enter next range in *Reference* text box.
8. Click Add.
9. Repeat Steps 7–8 until all ranges have been added.
10. Select *Top row* and/or *Left column* check boxes.
11. If necessary, click *Create links to source data*.
12. Click OK.

Figure 4.3 Consolidate Dialog Box

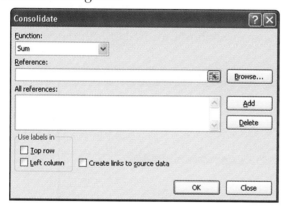

Project ② Consolidating Data

1. Open **NewAgeDental-Qtr1FeeSummary.xlsx**.
2. Save the workbook using Save As and name it **ExcelL2_C4_P2**.
3. The workbook is organized with the first quarter's fees for each of three dentists entered in a separate worksheet. Range names have been defined for each dentist's first quarter earnings. Review the workbook structure by completing the following steps:
   a. Click the down-pointing arrow in the Name text box and then click *Popovich* at the drop-down list. Excel makes the Popovich worksheet active and selects the range A2:F13. Deselect the range.
   b. Display the defined range for the range name *Vanket* and then deselect the range.
   c. Display the defined range for the range name *Jovanovic* and then deselect the range.

4. Use the Consolidate feature to total the fees billed by treatment category for each month by completing the following steps:
   a. Make FeeSummary the active worksheet.
   b. With A5 the active cell, click the Data tab.
   c. Click the Consolidate button in the Data Tools group.
   d. With *Sum* already selected in the *Function* list box at the Consolidate dialog box, and with the insertion point positioned in the *Reference* text box, type **Popovich** and then click the Add button.

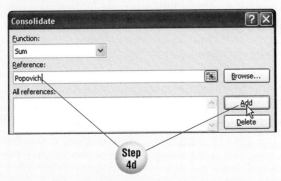

Step 4d

   e. With the text *Popovich* selected in the *Reference* text box, type **Vanket** and then click the Add button.
   f. With the text *Vanket* selected in the *Reference* text box, type **Jovanovic** and then click the Add button.
   g. Click the *Top row* and *Left column* check boxes in the *Use labels in* section to insert a check mark in each box.
   h. Click OK.

Step 4g

Step 4h

5. Deselect the consolidated range in the FeeSummary worksheet.
6. Adjust the width of each column in the FeeSummary worksheet to AutoFit.
7. Move the data in E5:E15 to F5:F15 and then AutoFit the column width.
8. Use Format Painter to apply the formatting options for the column headings and the total row from any of the three dentist worksheets to the FeeSummary worksheet.
9. Print the FeeSummary worksheet.
10. Save and then close **ExcelL2_C4_P2.xlsx**.

Project 3   Analyze Fitness Equipment Sales Data in a PivotTable and PivotChart

You will create and edit a PivotTable and a PivotChart to analyze fitness equipment sales by region and by salesperson.

Creating a PivotTable Report

Create PivotTable
1. Select source range.
2. Click Insert tab.
3. Click PivotTable button.
4. Click OK.
5. Add fields as needed using PivotTable Field List pane.

A PivotTable is an interactive table that organizes and summarizes data based on category labels you designate from row headings and column headings. A numeric column you select is then grouped by the row and column category and the data summarized using a function such as Sum, Average, or Count. PivotTables are useful management tools since you can analyze data in a variety of scenarios by filtering a row or column category and instantly seeing the change in results. The interactivity of a PivotTable allows one to examine a variety of scenarios with just a few mouse clicks.

Before creating a PivotTable, examine the source data and determine the following elements before you begin:

- Which row and column headings will define how to group the data?
- Which numeric field contains the values that should be grouped?
- Which summary function will be applied to the values? For example, do you want to sum, average, or count?
- How do you want the layout of the table to be structured? For example, which label do you want used as a row heading and which do you want to use as a column heading?
- Do you want the ability to filter the report as a whole as well as by columns or rows?
- Do you want the PivotTable to be beside the source data or in a new sheet?
- How many reports do you want to extract from the PivotTable by filtering fields?

HINT

Make sure the source data contains no blank rows or columns and that the data is structured in such a way that repeated data in columns or rows can be grouped.

To begin a PivotTable, select the source range or make sure the active cell is positioned within the list range, click the Insert tab and then click the PivotTable button in the Tables group. At the Create PivotTable dialog box, confirm the source range is correct and select whether to place the PivotTable in the existing worksheet or in a new worksheet. Figure 4.4 presents the initial PivotTable report and PivotTable Field List pane in which you define the report layout. Each column or row heading in the source range becomes a field in the PivotTable Field List.

PivotTable

Figure 4.4 PivotTable Report and PivotTable Field List Pane Used to Define Report Layout

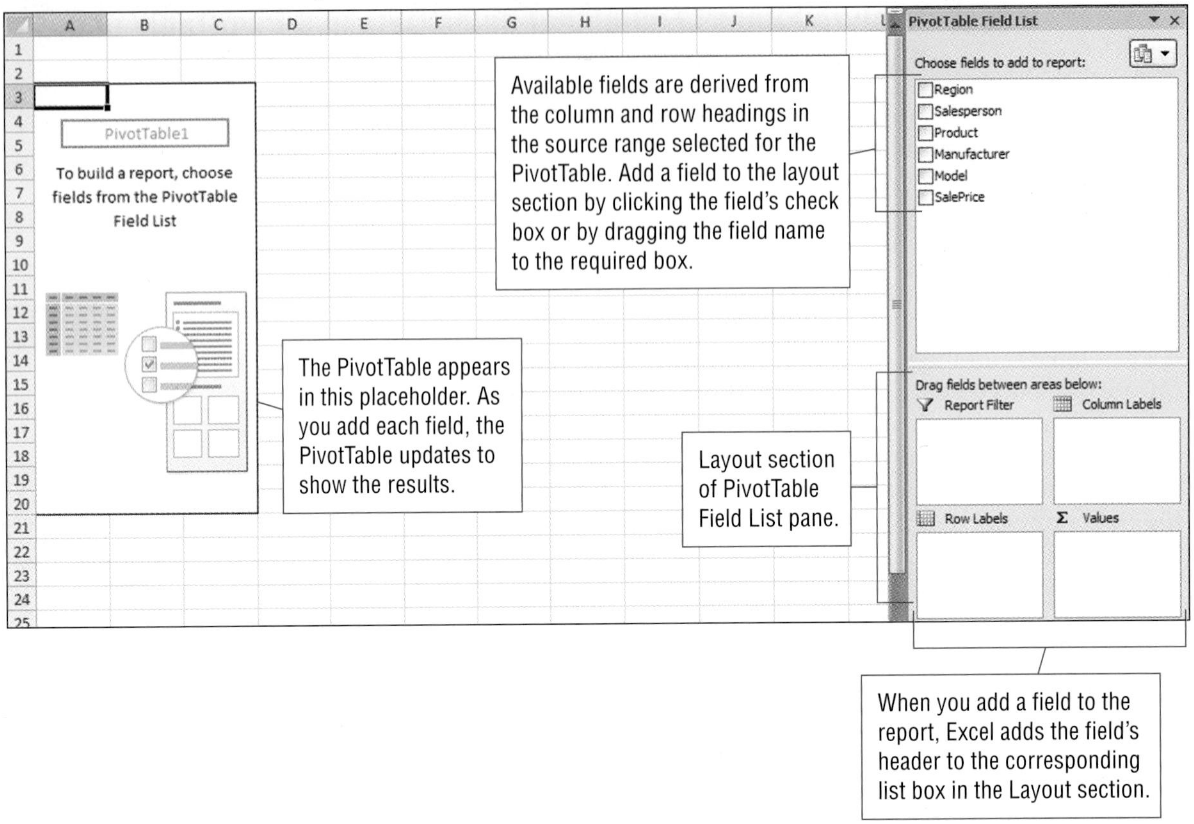

Available fields are derived from the column and row headings in the source range selected for the PivotTable. Add a field to the layout section by clicking the field's check box or by dragging the field name to the required box.

The PivotTable appears in this placeholder. As you add each field, the PivotTable updates to show the results.

Layout section of PivotTable Field List pane.

When you add a field to the report, Excel adds the field's header to the corresponding list box in the Layout section.

Build a PivotTable by selecting fields in the PivotTable Field List pane. Click the check box next to a field to add it to the PivotTable. By default, non-numeric fields are added to the *Row Labels* box and numeric fields are added to the *Values* box in the layout section of the pane. You can move a field to a different box by dragging the field header or by clicking the field header to display a pop-up menu. As you add each field, the PivotTable report updates to show the results. If you do not like the results, uncheck the field's check box to remove it from the report. Figure 4.5 displays the PivotTable you will build in Project 3a.

Figure 4.5 PivotTable for Project 3a

	A	B	C	D	E	F	G	H	I	J
1	Model	(All)	▼							
2										
3	Sum of SalePrice	Column Labels	▼							
4	Row Labels ▼	Adams	Clarke	Fernandez	Kazmarek	Grand Total				
5	Central	5520	4470		8474	18464				
6	East	7682	1199	4090	3540	16511				
7	North	2250	7120	4545	8099	22014				
8	South		4744	6295		11039				
9	West	3974	4838	2944	2574	14330				
10	Grand Total	19426	22371	17874	22687	82358				

PivotTable Field List

Choose fields to add to report:

☑ Region
☑ Salesperson
☐ Product
☐ Manufacturer
☑ Model
☑ SalePrice

Drag fields between areas below:

▼ Report Filter	▥ Column Labels
Model ▼	Salesperson ▼

▥ Row Labels	Σ Values
Region ▼	Sum of SalePr... ▼

☐ Defer Layout Update   [Update]

Sheet1 / JanSales / Sheet2 / Sheet3

Project 3a Creating a PivotTable Report

1. Open **PremiumFitness-JanSales.xlsx**.
2. Save the workbook with Save As and name it **ExcelL2_C4_P3**.
3. Create a PivotTable report to summarize the fitness equipment sales by region and by salesperson as shown in Figure 4.5 by completing the following steps:
   a. A range name has been defined to select the list data. Click the down-pointing arrow in the Name text box and then click *JanSales* at the drop-down list.
   b. Click the Insert tab.
   c. Click the PivotTable button in the Tables group. (Do not click the down-pointing arrow on the button.)
   d. At the Create PivotTable dialog box, with *JanSales!$A$4:$F$47* entered in the *Table/Range* text box and *New Worksheet* selected for *Choose where you want the PivotTable report to be placed*, click OK.

Step 3b

Home   Insert

Step 3c   PivotTable Table Picture

Tables

Step 3d

e. Click the *Region* check box in the PivotTable Field List pane. *Region* is added to the *Row Labels* list box in the layout section of the pane and the report updates to show one row per region with a filter arrow button at the top of the column and a Grand Total row automatically added to the bottom of the table. Since *Region* is a non-numeric field, Excel automatically placed it as a row label.

f. Click the *Salesperson* check box in the PivotTable Field List pane. Excel automatically adds *Salesperson* to the *Row Labels* list box in the layout section. In the next step you will correct the placement of the field to move it to the *Column Labels* list box.

g. Click the *Salesperson* field header in the *Row Labels* list box in the layout section and then click *Move to Column Labels* at the pop-up list. Notice the layout of the report now displays one row per region and one column per salesperson. In the next step you will drag a field from the PivotTable Field List to the desired list box in the layout section.

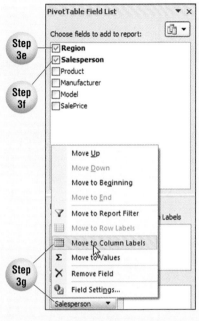

h. Position the mouse pointer over *Model* in the PivotTable Field List, hold down the left mouse button, drag the field to the *Report Filter* list box in the layout section, and then release the mouse. Notice *Model* is added as a filter at the top left of the PivotTable report in A1:B1.

i. Click the *SalePrice* check box in the PivotTable Field List pane. Since the field is a numeric field, Excel adds it automatically to the *Values* list box in the layout section and the report updates to show the Sum function applied to the grouped values in the PivotTable report. Compare your results with the PivotTable shown in Figure 4.5.

4. Save **ExcelL2_C4_P3.xlsx**.

When the active cell is positioned inside a PivotTable, the contextual PivotTable Tools Options tab and PivotTable Tools Design tab become available. Features in the PivotTable Tools Design tab shown in Figure 4.6 are similar to those learned in Chapter 3 for tables.

Figure 4.6 Contextual PivotTable Tools Design Tab

| ☑ Row Headers | ☐ Banded Rows |
| ☑ Column Headers | ☐ Banded Columns |

Subtotals Grand   Report Blank
           Totals▼ Layout▼ Rows▼

Layout   PivotTable Style Options   PivotTable Styles

Project 3D Formatting and Filtering a PivotTable

1. With **ExcelL2_C4_P3.xlsx** open, apply formatting options to the PivotTable to improve the report's appearance by completing the following steps:
   a. With the active cell positioned in the PivotTable report, click the PivotTable Tools Design tab.
   b. Click the More button located at the bottom of the vertical scroll bar in the PivotTable Styles gallery.
   c. Click *Pivot Style Medium 7* at the drop-down gallery (last option in first row of *Medium* section).
   d. Click the *Banded Rows* check box in the PivotTable Style Options group. Excel adds border lines between rows in the PivotTable. Recall from Chapter 3 that banded rows or banded columns add a fill color or border style depending on the style in effect when the option is added.
   e. Select B5:F10, click the Home tab, and then click the Comma Style button in the Number group.
   f. Click the Decrease Decimal button in the Number group twice to remove the zeros to the right of the decimal.
   g. Deselect the range.
   h. Select columns B through F and change the column width to 12.
   i. Right-align the labels in B4:F4.

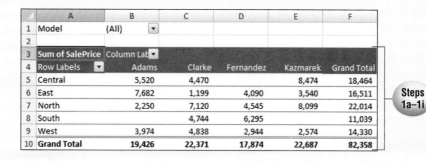

	A	B	C	D	E	F
1	Model	(All)				
2						
3	Sum of SalePrice	Column Lab				
4	Row Labels	Adams	Clarke	Fernandez	Kazmarek	Grand Total
5	Central	5,520	4,470		8,474	18,464
6	East	7,682	1,199	4,090	3,540	16,511
7	North	2,250	7,120	4,545	8,099	22,014
8	South		4,744	6,295		11,039
9	West	3,974	4,838	2,944	2,574	14,330
10	Grand Total	19,426	22,371	17,874	22,687	82,358

Steps
1a–1i

2. Filter the PivotTable report to view sales for a group of model numbers by completing the following steps:

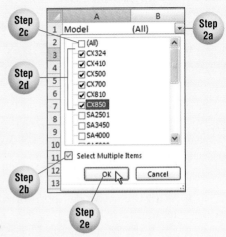

Step 2c **Step 2a** **Step 2d** **Step 2b** **Step 2e**

a. Click the filter arrow button next to *(All)* in B1.
b. Click the *Select Multiple Items* check box to turn on the display of check boxes next to each model number in the drop-down list.
c. Click the *(All)* check box to clear the check marks for all of the model numbers.
d. Click the six check boxes for those model numbers that begin with *CX* to select all of the models from Cybex.
e. Click OK.
f. Print the filtered PivotTable.
g. Click the filter arrow button next to *(Multiple Items)* in B1, click the *(All)* check box to select all model numbers in the drop-down list, and then click OK.
h. Experiment with the Column Labels and Row Labels filter arrow buttons to filter the PivotTable by region or by salesperson.
i. Make sure all filters are cleared and then print the PivotTable.
3. Save **ExcelL2_C4_P3.xlsx**.

 Project 3C **Changing the Values Function in a PivotTable**

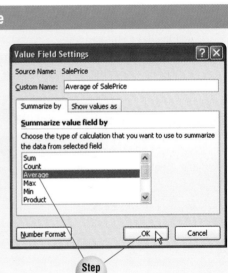

Step 2c **Step 2d**

1. With **ExcelL2_C4_P3.xlsx** open, use Save As and name the workbook **ExcelL2_C4_P3-Avg**.
2. Change the function for the *SalePrice* field from Sum to Average by completing the following steps:
a. Make A3 the active cell in the PivotTable. This cell contains the label *Sum of SalePrice*.
b. Click the PivotTable Tools Options tab.
c. Click the Field Settings button in the Active Field group.
d. At the Value Field Settings dialog box with the Summarize by tab active, click *Average* in the *Summarize value field by* list box and then click OK.
3. Print the revised PivotTable.
4. Save and then close **ExcelL2_C4_P3-Avg.xlsx**.

Creating a PivotChart

A PivotChart visually displays the data from a PivotTable in chart form. As with a PivotTable, you can filter the data to examine various scenarios between categories. Excel displays the PivotChart Filter Pane when a PivotChart is active so that you can filter the data as needed. As you make changes to the PivotChart, the PivotTable that is associated with the PivotChart is also updated. Figure 4.7 displays the PivotChart you will create in Project 3d.

In a worksheet that already contains a PivotTable, position the active cell anywhere within the PivotTable, click the PivotTable Tools Option tab, and then click the PivotChart button in the Tools group to create a chart from the existing summary data. Excel displays the Insert Chart dialog box in which you choose the type of chart to create. Once the PivotChart has been generated, the PivotTable and PivotChart become connected. Changes made to the data by filtering in one object cause the other object to update with the same filter. For example, filtering the chart by an individual salesperson name causes the PivotTable to also filter by the same salesperson name.

If you open a worksheet that does not contain a pre-existing PivotTable and create a PivotChart, Excel displays a blank chart window with the PivotTable Field List pane and a PivotChart Filter Pane. Build the chart using the same techniques you used to build a PivotTable. Before you begin creating a PivotChart from scratch, examine the source data and determine the following elements:

- Which row or column heading contains the labels that you want to display along the x-axis? In other words, how do you want to compare data when viewing the chart—by time period such as months or years, by salesperson names, by department name, or by some other category?
- Which row or column heading contains the labels that you want to display as legend fields? In other words, how many data series (bars in a column chart) do you want to view in the chart—one for each region, product, salesperson, department, or some other category?
- Which numeric field contains the values you want to graph in the chart?

As you build a PivotChart from scratch, Excel will also build a PivotTable in the background that is connected to the PivotChart.

QUICK STEPS

Create PivotChart from PivotTable
1. Make cell active within PivotTable.
2. Click PivotTable Tools Options tab.
3. Click PivotChart button.
4. Select desired chart type.
5. Click OK.

Create PivotChart without Existing PivotTable
1. Make cell active within list range.
2. Click Insert tab.
3. Click down-pointing arrow on PivotTable button.
4. Click *PivotChart*.
5. Click OK.
6. Add fields as needed in PivotTable Field List pane to build chart.

PivotChart

Move Chart

Figure 4.7 PivotChart for Project 3d

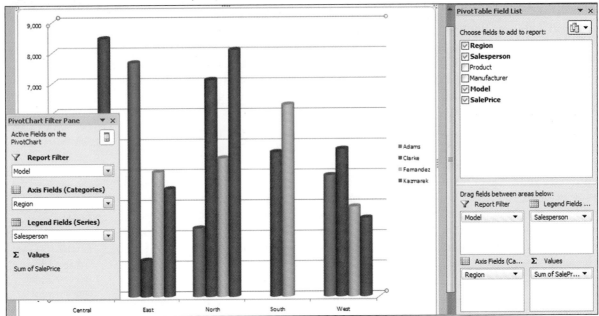

Project 3d **Creating a PivotChart**

1. Open **ExcelL2_C4_P3.xlsx**.
2. Create a PivotChart to visually present the data in the PivotTable by completing the following steps:
   a. If necessary, click any cell within the PivotTable to activate the PivotTable contextual tabs.
   b. Click the PivotTable Tools Options tab.
   c. Click the PivotChart button in the Tools group.
   d. At the Insert Chart dialog box, with *Column* selected in the left pane, click *Clustered Cylinder* (first option in second row in *Column* section) and then click OK.

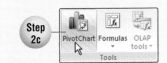

Step 2c

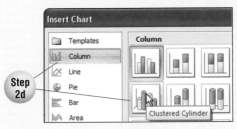

Step 2d

3. Filter the PivotChart to display sales for only one salesperson by completing the following steps:
   a. Click the filter arrow button in the PivotChart Filter Pane for Legend Fields (Series) (currently displays *Salesperson*).
   b. Click the *(Select All)* check box to clear all of the check boxes.
   c. Click the *Kazmarek* check box and then click OK.

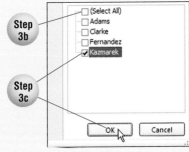

Step 3b

Step 3c

d. If necessary, drag the chart to the right or left of the PivotChart Filter Pane so that you can view all of the chart.
e. Notice the PivotTable behind the chart is also filtered to reflect the chart's display.

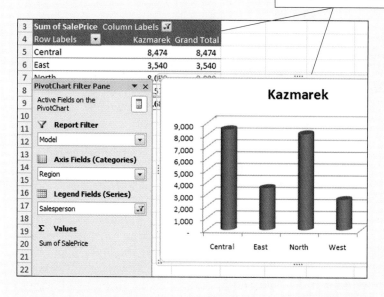

PivotTable is updated to reflect the current filter settings in the PivotChart.

f. Click the filter arrow button in the PivotChart Filter Pane for Legend Fields (Series) and then click *Clear Filter From "Salesperson"*.

4. Move the PivotChart to a separate worksheet by completing the following steps:
   a. Click the Move Chart button in the Location group of the PivotChart Tools Design tab.
   b. At the Move Chart dialog box, click *New sheet*, type **PivotChart** in the *New sheet* text box, and then click OK. Excel moves the PivotChart to a separate worksheet. Compare your PivotChart with the one shown in Figure 4.7.
   c. Close the PivotTable Field List pane in the PivotChart worksheet.
   d. Close the PivotChart Filter Pane.

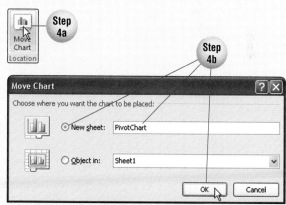

5. Print the PivotChart.
6. Rename the sheet tab for the worksheet containing the PivotTable (Sheet1) to **PivotTable**.
7. Save and then close **ExcelL2_C4_P3.xlsx**.

1. Open **PremiumFitness-JanSales.xlsx**.
2. Save the workbook with Save As and name it **ExcelL2_C4_P3-Chart**.
3. Create a PivotChart to chart the sales by manufacturer by region by completing the following steps:

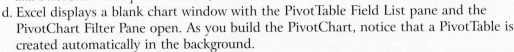

   Step 3a

   a. With the active cell positioned in A5, click the Insert tab.
   b. Click the down-pointing arrow on the PivotTable button in the Tables group and then click *PivotChart* at the drop-down list.
   c. At the Create PivotTable with PivotChart dialog box, with *JanSales!$A$4:$F$47* entered in the *Table/Range* text box and with *New Worksheet* selected in the *Choose where you want the PivotTable and PivotChart to be placed* section, click OK.

   Step 3b

   d. Excel displays a blank chart window with the PivotTable Field List pane and the PivotChart Filter Pane open. As you build the PivotChart, notice that a PivotTable is created automatically in the background.
   e. Click the *Manufacturer* check box in the PivotTable Field List. Excel adds the field to the *Axis Fields (Categories)* list box in the layout section.
   f. Click the *Region* check box in the PivotTable Field List. Excel adds the field below *Manufacturer* in the *Axis Fields (Categories)* list box in the layout section.
   g. Click the *Region* field header in the *Axis Fields (Categories)* list box and then click *Move to Legend Fields (Series)* at the pop-up list. Excel moves the field and updates the chart and the PivotTable.

   Step 3g

   h. Click the *SalePrice* check box in the PivotTable Field List. Excel graphs the sum of the SalePrice values in the PivotChart and updates the PivotTable.
4. Close the PivotTable Field List pane and the PivotChart Filter Pane.
5. Move the PivotChart below the PivotTable aligning the chart at the top of row 9 and centered below the PivotTable.
6. Print the PivotTable and PivotChart worksheet.
7. Rename the sheet containing the PivotTable and PivotChart (Sheet1) to **SummaryData**.
8. Save and then close **ExcelL2_C4_P3-Chart.xlsx**.

Step 5

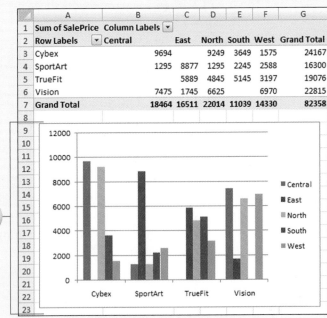

	A	B	C	D	E	F	G
1	Sum of SalePrice	Column Labels					
2	Row Labels	Central	East	North	South	West	Grand Total
3	Cybex	9694		9249	3649	1575	24167
4	SportArt	1295	8877	1295	2245	2588	16300
5	TrueFit		5889	4845	5145	3197	19076
6	Vision	7475	1745	6625		6970	22815
7	Grand Total	18464	16511	22014	11039	14330	82358

 roject **④** **Format the Axes in a Chart and Add a Trendline**

You will create a chart to display sales data by region and then edit the chart axes, gridlines, and add a trendline to predict future values.

Advanced Chart Formatting Techniques

Excel generates a chart based on the content in the source data range and the selected chart type. In many cases, the default options applied to the various chart elements are suited to the purpose for which the chart was created. Chart editing generally involves adding or removing chart elements such as a title or legend, or changing the font, color, or size of category labels or value labels. In some cases, you may wish to control the scale of the value axis or the gridlines or add advanced options such as a trendline to predict future values in a chart.

Formatting Chart Axes

Two-dimensional charts have two axes: a vertical axis called the value axis or the y-axis, and a horizontal axis called the x-axis or category axis. Three-dimensional charts have an additional axis called the z-axis, series axis, or depth axis. Some charts do not have axes such as a pie chart or a doughnut chart. When you select the source range for a chart, Excel places textual entries evenly-spaced along the horizontal axis. Numeric data is plotted on the vertical axis and scaled automatically based on minimum and maximum values within the data range. You can customize the scale if you prefer to control the minimum and maximum value and the tick mark intervals. Right-click the axis that you want to format and then click *Format Axis* at the shortcut menu or activate the Chart Tools Layout tab and click the Axes button in the Axes group to choose from predefined options.

Chart Gridlines

Chart gridlines are horizontal and vertical lines across the plot area of the chart that facilitate reading the chart. Show or hide gridlines using the Gridlines button in the Axes group of the Chart Tools Layout tab. Gridlines are drawn for major and/or minor units. Set the interval between major and minor units when you format the value axis for horizontal gridlines and the category axis for vertical gridlines.

QUICK STEPS

Format Value Axis
1. Right-click value axis.
2. Click *Format Axis*.
3. Change *Minimum, Maximum, Major unit,* and *Minor unit* options as required.
4. Click Close.

Axes

QUICK STEPS

Show or Hide Gridlines
1. Click Chart Tools Layout tab.
2. Click Gridlines button.
3. Point to *Primary Horizontal Gridlines* or *Primary Vertical Gridlines.*
4. Click desired gridline option.

Gridlines

1. Open **PremiumFitness-3YrSales.xlsx**.
2. Save the workbook with Save As and name it **ExcelL2_C4_P4**.
3. Create a column chart to graph the sales by region for 2007 through to 2009 and move the chart to its own worksheet by completing the following steps:
   a. Select A4:D9.
   b. Click the Insert tab.
   c. Click the Column button in the Charts group and then click *3-D Clustered Column* at the drop-down list (first option in *3-D Column* section). Excel creates the chart and drops the chart in the middle of the worksheet area.
   d. With the Chart Tools Design tab active, click the Move Chart button in the Location group.
   e. Click *New sheet* at the Move Chart dialog box and then type **ColumnCht** in the *New sheet* text box.
   f. Click OK.
   g. Print the chart.

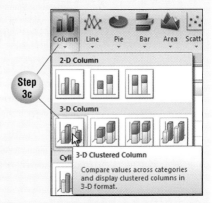

Step 3c

4. Format the value axis in the chart to customize the minimum and maximum value and major gridline interval by completing the following steps:
   a. Point to any of the values displayed in the vertical axis along the left edge of the chart until the ScreenTip displays *Vertical (Value) Axis*, right-click, and then click *Format Axis* at the shortcut menu and Mini toolbar.
   b. At the Format Axis dialog box with *Axis Options* selected in the left pane, click *Fixed* next to *Minimum* in the *Axis Options* section of the right pane, select the current text in the adjacent text box, and then type **100000**.
   c. Click *Fixed* next to *Maximum*, select the current text in the adjacent text box, and then type **1000000**.

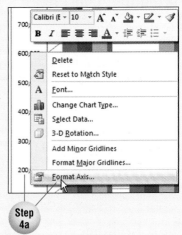

Step 4a

Step 4b

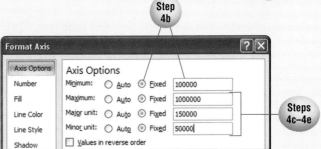

Steps 4c–4e

   d. Click *Fixed* next to *Major unit*, select the current text in the adjacent text box, and then type **150000**.
   e. Click *Fixed* next to *Minor unit*, select the current text in the adjacent text box, and then type **50000**.
   f. Click the Close button. Notice the scale has changed from the original chart and fewer horizontal gridlines display at the revised major unit intervals.

5. Modify the display of the chart gridlines to show and then hide minor gridlines by completing the following steps:
   a. Click the Chart Tools Layout tab.
   b. Click the Gridlines button in the Axes group.
   c. Point to *Primary Horizontal Gridlines* and then click *Minor Gridlines* at the drop-down list. A minor gridline is added to the chart at each 50,000 unit interval on the value axis.
   d. After reviewing the chart you decide to remove the minor gridlines to make the chart appear less cluttered. Click the Gridlines button, point to *Primary Horizontal Gridlines* and then click *Major Gridlines* at the drop-down list.

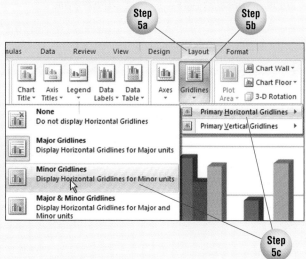

6. Print the revised chart.
7. Save **ExcelL2_C4_P4.xlsx**.

Adding a Trendline to a Chart

A trendline added to a chart illustrates the direction or trend that the data is presenting within the chart. By displaying a trendline one can attempt to predict future values based on the past history displayed in the chart. Excel includes six types of trendlines that are described in Table 4.1. Add a trendline by selecting the series upon which to base the trendline direction, click the Chart Tools Layout tab, click the Trendline button in the Analysis group and then select the type of line you want to add. Right-click a trendline in a chart and select *Format Trendline* to customize the trendline options. Trendlines cannot be added to 3-D or stacked chart subtypes, or to doughnut, pie, radar, or surface charts.

Add Trendline
1. Make chart active.
2. Click data series upon which to base trendline.
3. Click Chart Tools Layout tab.
4. Click Trendline button.
5. Click desired trendline option
OR
1. Click More Trendline Options.
2. Click desired Trend/Regression Type.
3. Click Close.

Trendline

Table 4.1 Trendline Options in Format Trendline Dialog Box

Trend/Regression Type	Description
Exponential	Uses a curved line to display values that are increasing or decreasing at higher rates.
Linear	Use for values that increase or decrease at a steady rate to be displayed in a best-fit straight line.
Logarithmic	Use for values that increase or decrease quickly and then level out. Displays as a best-fit curved line.
Polynomial	Use for values that fluctuate. Displays as a curved line. Enter a value from 2 to 6 in the *Order* text box to specify the number of bends you want in the line.
Power	Use for values that increase at a specific rate. Displays as a curved line.
Moving Average	Uses a curved line to display values with fluctuations smoothed out in order to show a pattern. Requires a number for period that represents a value between 2 and the number of data points minus 1. Period determines the data point averages that become the points in the trendline.

Project 4D · Adding and Modifying a Trendline to a Chart

1. With **ExcelL2_C4_P4.xlsx** open, use Save As and name the chart **ExcelL2_C4_P4-Trendline**.
2. Change the chart to a two-dimensional type by completing the following steps:
   a. Click the Chart Tools Design tab.
   b. Click the Change Chart Type button in the Type group.
   c. Click *Clustered Column* (first option in first row of *Column* section) at the Change Chart Type dialog box and then click OK.
3. Right-click any of the data series bars representing 2007 Sales (blue bars) and then click *Delete* at the shortcut menu. This removes the 2007 data from the chart, leaving only 2008 Sales and 2009 Sales.
   Removing the earliest data will make the chart less cluttered and the trendline easier to analyze.
4. Add a trendline based upon the 2008 Sales data by completing the following steps:
   a. Click any of the data series bars representing 2008 sales data (red bars).
   b. Click the Chart Tools Layout tab.
   c. Click the Trendline button in the Analysis group and then click *More Trendline Options* at the drop-down list.

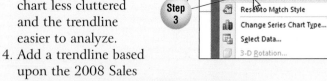

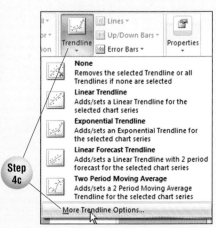

d. At the Format Trendline dialog box, click *Polynomial* in the *Trend/Regression Type* section, select the current text in the *Order* text box, and then type 3.

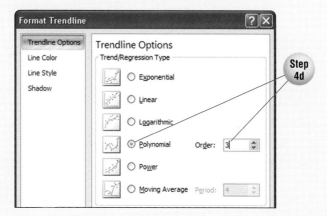

e. Click Close.
5. Add a trendline based upon the 2009 Sales data by completing the following steps:
   a. Click any of the data series bars representing the 2009 sales data (green bars).
   b. Click the Trendline button and then click *Linear Trendline* at the drop-down list. Excel adds a linear trendline to the 2009 Sales series.
6. Format the 2009 Sales trendline to set it apart from the 2008 Sales trendline by completing the following steps:
   a. Right-click the linear trendline for the 2009 Sales.
   b. Click *Format Trendline* at the shortcut menu.
   c. At the Format Trendline dialog box, click *Line Color* in the left pane.
   d. Click *Solid line* in the Line Color section in the right pane.
   e. Click the Color button and then click *Purple* in the *Standard Colors* section of the color palette.

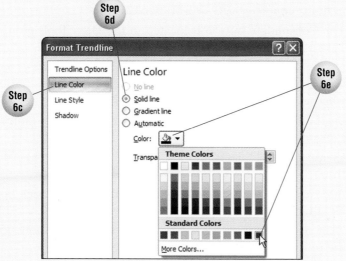

   f. Click Close.
7. Print the chart.
8. Save and then close **ExcelL2_C4_P4-Trendline.xlsx**.

CHAPTER summary

- A formula that references a cell in another worksheet within the same workbook contains a worksheet reference as well as a cell reference separated by an exclamation point.

- Range names can be used to simplify references to cells in another worksheet since the worksheet reference is automatically included in the range name definition.

- A disadvantage to using range names to reference other worksheets exists if there are several worksheets to be summarized since each name has to be defined before you can create the formula.

- A 3-D reference is used to summarize the same cell in a range that extends over two or more worksheets.

- A 3-D reference includes the starting worksheet name and the ending worksheet name separated by a colon similar to the method used to define a range of cells.

- Formulas that reference a cell in another workbook must include a workbook reference in front of the worksheet and cell reference. Workbook references are enclosed in square brackets.

- When you create a formula that links to an external reference, Excel includes the drive and folder name in the path to the source workbook. If you move the location of the source workbook or change the source workbook file name, you have to edit the linked reference.

- Open the Edit Links dialog box to edit or remove a linked external reference.

- The Consolidate feature is another method that can be used to summarize data in multiple worksheets or workbooks.

- The Consolidate button is located in the Data Tools group in the Data tab.

- At the Consolidate dialog box, choose the summary function you want to use for the data that will be aggregated, add the references containing the data you want to summarize, specify the location of the labels to duplicate, and indicate whether to create a link to the source data.

- PivotTables are interactive tables that organize and summarize data based on categories in rows or columns.

- Create a PivotTable using the PivotTable button in the Tables group in the Insert tab.

- Add fields to the PivotTable using the field name check boxes in the PivotTable Field List pane.

- Once created, a PivotTable can be used to view a variety of scenarios by filtering the row, column, or report headings.

- Use buttons in the contextual PivotTable Tools Options and Design tabs to format the PivotTable and/or edit the features used in the table.

- A PivotChart displays the data in a PivotTable in a specified chart type.

- Filter a PivotChart using buttons in the PivotChart Filter Pane.

- Customize a value axis in a chart by specifying a fixed value for the *Minimum*, *Maximum*, *Major unit*, or *Minor unit* intervals at the Axis Options dialog box.

- Primary horizontal or vertical gridlines are spaced at intervals defined in the Axis Options dialog box.
- Show or hide gridlines in a chart using the Gridlines button in the Axes group in the Chart Tools Layout tab.
- Trendlines depict the direction or trend that a data series is expected to follow based on the data plotted in the chart.
- Adding a trendline to a chart allows you to see whether there is a pattern to the data and whether you can forecast future values.
- Excel includes six types of trendlines in the Format Trendline dialog box: *Exponential, Linear, Logarithmic, Polynomial, Power,* and *Moving Average.*
- Consider formatting a trendline to a different color when adding more than one to a chart.

COMMANDS review

FEATURE	RIBBON TAB, GROUP	BUTTON	KEYBOARD SHORTCUT
Axis Options	Chart Tools Layout, Axes OR PivotChart Tools Layout, Axes		
Consolidate	Data, Data Tools	Consolidate	
Edit Links	Data, Connections	Edit Links	
Gridlines	Chart Tools Layout, Axes OR PivotChart Tools Layout, Axes		
Manage range names	Formulas, Defined Names		Ctrl + F3
PivotChart	Insert, Tables OR PivotTable Tools Options, Tools		
PivotTable	Insert, Tables		
Trendline	Chart Tools Layout, Analysis OR PivotChart Tools Layout, Analysis		

CONCEPTS check

Test Your Knowledge

Completion: In the space provided at the right, indicate the correct term, command, or number.

1. This symbol separates a worksheet reference from a cell reference.

   _____

2. This term describes a formula that references the same cell in a range that spans two or more worksheets.

   _____

3. Assume a workbook contains the following defined range names that reference cells in four worksheets: Qtr1, Qtr2, Qtr3, and Qtr4. Provide the Sum formula to add the data in the four ranges.

   _____

4. This would be the formula entry to link to an external reference C12 in a worksheet named Summary in a workbook named QtrlySales.

   _____

5. Open this dialog box to change the source of a linked external reference if you moved the source workbook to another folder.

   _____

6. Click this button to permanently remove a linked external reference and convert the linked cells to their existing values.

   _____

7. This is the default function active when you open the Consolidate dialog box.

   _____

8. Add fields to a PivotTable report by clicking the field check box in this pane.

   _____

9. The PivotTable Styles gallery is accessible from this tab.

   _____

10. Change the summary function for a PivotTable numeric field by clicking this button in the PivotTable Tools Options tab.

    _____

11. A PivotChart visually displays the data from this source.

    _____

12. Buttons to filter a PivotChart are found in this pane.

    _____

13. The horizontal axis in a chart is called the category axis or this.

    _____

14. The vertical axis in a chart is called the value axis or this.

    _____

15. Add this line to a chart to predict future values based on a pattern in the selected data series.

    _____

SKILLS check
Demonstrate Your Proficiency

Assessment

1 SUMMARIZE DATA IN MULTIPLE WORKSHEETS USING RANGE NAMES

1. Open **NewAgeDental-Qtr1FeeSummary.xlsx**.
2. Save the workbook with Save As and name it **ExcelL2_C4_A1**.
3. The workbook contains three worksheets with dental fees earned in January, February, and March for three dentists at the dental clinic. Define a range name in F13 of each worksheet to reference the total fees earned by the dentist for the quarter as follows:
   a. Name F13 in the Popovich worksheet PopovichQ1Total.
   b. Name F13 in the Vanket worksheet VanketQ1Total.
   c. Name F13 in the Jovanovic worksheet JovanovicQ1Total.
4. Make FeeSummary the active worksheet and then type the following label in A6:

   Quarter 1 fees for Popovich, Vanket, and Jovanovic
5. Make F6 the active cell and create the Sum formula to add the total fees earned by each dentist.
6. Format F6 to the Accounting Number Format style and then adjust the column width to AutoFit.
7. Print the FeeSummary worksheet.
8. Save and then close **ExcelL2_C4_A1.xlsx**.

Assessment

2 SUMMARIZE DATA USING LINKED EXTERNAL REFERENCES

1. Open **PremiumFitness-SalesSummary.xlsx**.
2. Save the workbook with Save As and name it **ExcelL2_C4_A2**.
3. Open **PremiumFitness-Qtr1.xlsx**, **PremiumFitness-Qtr2.xlsx**, **PremiumFitness-Qtr3.xlsx**, and **PremiumFitness-Qtr4.xlsx**.
4. Tile all of the open workbooks.
5. Starting in cell B5 in **ExcelL2_C4_A2.xlsx**, create formulas to populate the cells in column B by linking to the appropriate source cell in **PremiumFitness-Qtr1.xlsx**. *Hint: In B5, use a relative reference to the source cell so you can copy and paste the formula in B5 to B6:B9.*
6. Create formulas to link to the appropriate source cells for the second, third, and fourth quarter sales.
7. Close the four quarterly sales workbooks.
8. Maximize **ExcelL2_C4_A2.xlsx**.
9. Print the SalesSummary worksheet.
10. Save and then close **ExcelL2_C4_A2.xlsx**.

Assessment

3 BREAK LINKED REFERENCES

1. Open **ExcelL2_C4_A2.xlsx**.
2. Convert the formulas to their existing values by breaking the links to the external references in the four quarterly sales workbooks.
3. Save, print, and then close **ExcelL2_C4_A2.xlsx**.

Assessment

4 SUMMARIZE DATA USING 3-D REFERENCES

1. Open **ParkAttendance-May.xlsx**.
2. Save the workbook with Save As and name it **ExcelL2_C4_A4.xlsx**.
3. With AttendanceSummary the active worksheet, summarize the data in the three park worksheets using 3-D references as follows:
   a. Delete the label in A7.
   b. Copy A6:A22 from any of the park worksheets and paste to A6:A22 in the AttendanceSummary worksheet.
   c. Copy D6:D21 from any of the park worksheets and paste to D6:D21 in the AttendanceSummary worksheet.
   d. Type the label **Entries** right-aligned in B6 and E6.
   e. Make B7 the active cell and then create a 3-D formula to sum the attendance values in the three park worksheets for Day 1. Copy and paste the formula to the remaining cells in column B to complete the summary to Day 16.
   f. Make E7 the active cell and then create a 3-D formula to sum the attendance values in the three park worksheets for Day 17. Copy and paste the formula to the remaining cells in column E to complete the summary to Day 31.
   g. Type the label **Total Vehicle and Individual Entrances** in A24.
   h. Create a Sum formula in E24 to compute the grand total.
   i. Apply formatting options to the grand total as desired to make the total stand out.
4. Print the AttendanceSummary worksheet.
5. Save and then close **ExcelL2_C4_A4.xlsx**.

Assessment

5 SUMMARIZE DATA IN A PIVOTTABLE AND PIVOTCHART

1. Open **NewAgeDental-09FeeSummary.xlsx**.
2. Save the workbook with Save As and name it **ExcelL2_C4_A5**.
3. Create a PivotTable in a new worksheet as follows:
   a. Display the range named *FeeSummary* and then insert a PivotTable in a new worksheet.
   b. Add the *Service Provided* field as row labels.
   c. Add the *Dentist* field as column labels.
   d. Sum the *FeesBilled* field.
4. Apply Pivot Style Medium 20 to the PivotTable (sixth from left in third row in *Medium* section).

5. Format the values to the Comma Style number format with zero decimals and right-align the dentist names.
6. Name the worksheet **PivotTable** and then print the PivotTable.
7. Create a PivotChart from the PivotTable using the Clustered Column chart type and move the chart to its own sheet named **PivotChart**.
8. Close the PivotTable Field List pane and the PivotChart Filter Pane.
9. Modify the value axis in the PivotChart to fix the minimum value to 1,000, the maximum value to 55,000, and the major unit to 5,000.
10. Select the data series representing Popovich and then add a two-period moving average trendline.
11. Move the legend to the bottom of the chart.
12. Print the PivotChart.
13. Save and then close **ExcelL2_C4_A5.xlsx**.

CASE study

Apply Your Skills

Part 1

Yolanda Robertson of NuTrends Market Research is continuing to work on the franchise expansion plan for the owners of Pizza by Mario. Yolanda has received a new workbook from the owners with profit information for each of the existing franchise locations. Yolanda would like your assistance with summarizing the data. Open the workbook named **PizzabyMario-Sales&Profits.xlsx** and review the structure of the data and check for existing range names. Yolanda would like a report that provides the average gross sales and the average net income by store by state. You determine how to organize the layout of the report. *Hint: You can add more than one numeric field to the **Values** list box*. Remove any unnecessary grand totals that might be included depending on how you structure the report. For example, if you organize the report with the city names in row labels, grand totals which Excel automatically adds for each row at the right end of the table are not needed. Use the Grand Totals button in the Layout group of the PivotTable Tools Design tab to add or remove grand totals. Apply formatting options to improve the report's appearance and make sure the report prints on one page in landscape orientation. Rename the worksheet containing the table **PivotTable**. Save the revised workbook and name it **ExcelL2_C4_CS_P1**.

Part 2

Yolanda would like a chart that summarizes the Net Income data for the state of Michigan only. Revise the PivotTable created in Part 1 and then generate a chart placed in its own sheet named **PivotChart**. You determine an appropriate chart style and elements to include in the chart. Yolanda has asked that a polynomial trend line with the order set to 4 be included in the chart. Yolanda will be using this chart at an upcoming meeting with the franchise owners and wants the chart to be of professional quality. Print the chart. Save the revised workbook and name it **ExcelL2_C4_CS_P2** and then close the workbook.

Part

3

Open **ExcelL2_C4_CS_P1.xlsx**. Use the Help feature to find out how to rename the field titles within a PivotTable. Using the information you learned in Help, rename the field headings for the numeric entries from *Average of Gross_Sales* and *Average of Net_Income* to a title that uses less space. Print the PivotTable. Save the revised workbook using the same name and then close the workbook.

Part

4

Yolanda would like you to do some comparison research of another pizza franchise. Use the Internet to research the sales and net income information of a pizza franchise with which you are familiar. Create a workbook that compares the total annual sales and net income values of the pizza franchise you researched with the Pizza by Mario information in **ExcelL2_C4_CS_P1.xlsx**. Provide the URL of the Web site from which you obtained the competitive data. Create a chart that visually presents the comparison data. Save the workbook and name it **ExcelL2_C4_CS_P4**. Print the comparison data and the chart. Close **ExcelL2_C4_CS_P4.xlsx**.

Advanced Formatting, Formulas, and Data Management

Unit 1

ASSESSING proficiency

In this unit, you have learned to apply advanced formatting options such as conditional formatting and custom number formats; perform advanced sort and filtering techniques; create functions that incorporate conditional logic, look up data, convert text, and calculate financial results; define a table and apply data management features to a table or list range; consolidate and summarize data and present summary information in PivotTables or PivotCharts.

Note: Before beginning assessments, copy to your storage medium the Excel2007L2U1 subfolder from the Excel2007L2 folder on the CD that accompanies this textbook and then make Excel2007L2U1 the active folder.

Assessment 1 Conditionally Format and Filter a Help Desk Worksheet

1. Open **RSR-HelpDeskRpt.xlsx**.
2. Save the workbook using the name **ExcelL2_U1_A1**.
3. Apply conditional formatting to display the *3 Flags* icon set to the values in the *Priority* column. For example, calls with a priority code of 1 should display a red flag, priority 2 calls should display a yellow flag and priority 3 calls should display a green flag.
4. Create a custom format for the values in the *Time Spent* column. The format should display leading zeros, two decimal places, and the text *hrs* at the end of the entry.
5. Create two conditional formatting rules for the values in the *Time Spent* column as follows:
   a. For all entries where the time spent is less than 1 hour, apply bold and a pale green fill color.
   b. For all entries where the time spent is more than 2 hours, apply a bright yellow fill color.
6. Filter the worksheet by the bright yellow fill color applied in the *Time Spent* column.
7. Print the filtered worksheet.
8. Clear the filter and the filter arrow buttons and then print the worksheet.
9. Save and then close **ExcelL2_U1_A1.xlsx**.

Assessment 2 Use Conditional Logic Formulas in a Help Desk Worksheet

1. Open **ExcelL2_U1_A1.xlsx**.
2. Save the workbook using the name **ExcelL2_U1_A2.xlsx**.

3. Create range names for the following ranges. You determine appropriate names.
   a. Name the cells in A4:E6 which will be used in a lookup formula.
   b. Name the entries in the *OperatorID* column.
   c. Name the values in the *Time Spent* column.
   d. Name the cells in the *Status* column.
4. In I4 create a COUNTA formula to count the number of help desk calls in March using column A as the source range.
5. In I5 and I6 create COUNTIF formulas to count the number of active calls (I5) and the number of closed calls (I6). Use range names in the formulas.
6. Create COUNTIF formulas in K3 through K6 to count the calls assigned to OperatorID 1, 2, 3, and 4, respectively. Use range names in the formulas.
7. Create SUMIF formulas in L3 through L6 to calculate the total time spent on calls assigned to OperatorID 1, 2, 3, and 4, respectively. Use range names in the formulas. Format the results to display two decimal places.
8. Create AVERAGEIF formulas in M3 through M6 to find the average time spent on calls assigned to OperatorID 1, 2, 3, and 4, respectively. Use range names in the formulas. Format the results to display two decimal places.
9. Create the HLOOKUP formula with an exact match in F8 to return the last name for the operator assigned to the call. Use the range name for the lookup table in the formula.
10. Create the HLOOKUP formula with an exact match in G8 to return the first name for the operator assigned to the call. Use the range name for the lookup table in the formula.
11. Copy the HLOOKUP formulas in F8:G8 and paste to the remaining rows in the list.
12. Save, print, and then close **ExcelL2_U1_A2.xlsx**.

Assessment 3 Use Table and Data Management Features in a Help Desk Worksheet

1. Open **ExcelL2_U1_A2.xlsx**.
2. Save the workbook using the name **ExcelL2_U1_A3.xlsx**.
3. Format A7:I26 as a table using Table Style Medium 14.
4. Add a calculated column to the table that multiples the time spent times 15.00. Use the column heading *Cost* in J7. Format the results to display Comma Style number format.
5. Add a total row to the table. Display a sum total in columns H and J.
6. Add emphasis to the last column in the table and band the columns instead of the rows.
7. Create a drop-down list for the *OperatorID* column that displays the entries 1, 2, 3, 4.
8. RSR has a policy that help desk operators cannot spend more than three hours on a call. Calls that require more than three hours must be routed to the Help Desk manager and assigned to another group. Create a validation rule in the *Time Spent* column that ensures no value greater than 3 is entered. Create appropriate input and error messages.

9. Add the following two records to the table:

Date	3/29/2009	3/29/2009
TicketNo	12029	12030
Priority	2	2
Type of Call	Email	Password
OperatorID	3	4
TimeSpent	.75	.25
Status	Active	Closed

10. Filter the table to display only those calls with a *Closed* status.
11. Print the filtered list.
12. Filter the worksheet to display only those calls with a *Closed* status where the type of call was *Password*.
13. Print the filtered list.
14. Clear both filters.
15. Save, print, and then close **ExcelL2_U1_A3.xlsx**.

Assessment 4 Add Subtotals and Outline a Help Desk Worksheet

1. Open **ExcelL2_U1_A3.xlsx**.
2. Save the workbook using the name **ExcelL2_U1_A4**.
3. Remove the total row from the table.
4. Convert the table to a normal range.
5. Sort the list first by the operator's last name, then by the operator's first name, then by the call priority, and finally by the type of call, all in ascending order.
6. Add a subtotal to the list at each change in the operator last name to calculate the total cost of calls by operator.
7. Display the outlined worksheet at level 2 and then print the worksheet.
8. Display the outlined worksheet at level 3 and then print the worksheet.
9. Save and then close **ExcelL2_U1_A4.xlsx**.

Assessment 5 Use Financial and Text Functions to Analyze Data for a Project

1. Open **AllClaims-OfficeRelocation.xlsx**.
2. Save the workbook using the name **ExcelL2_U1_A5**.
3. With the LoanRelocation tab active, create formulas to analyze the cost of the loan from NEWFUNDS TRUST and DELTA CAPITAL as follows:
   a. In C9 and E9, calculate the monthly loan payments from each lender.
   b. In C11 and E11, calculate the principal portion of each payment for the first loan payment.
   c. In C13 and E13, calculate the total loan payments that will be made over the life of the loan from each lender.
4. In E19, use the text function *=PROPER* to return the loan company name for the loan that represents the lowest total cost to AllClaims Insurance. **Hint: The argument for the function will reference either C3 or E3**.
5. In E20, use the text function *=LOWER* to return the loan application number for the loan company name you displayed in E19.
6. Print the LoanRelocation worksheet.
7. Make the NPV-Relocation worksheet active.
8. Calculate the net present value of the relocation project in C14.
9. Print the NPV-Relocation worksheet.
10. Save and then close **ExcelL2_U1_A5.xlsx**.

Assessment 6 **Analyze Sales Using a PivotTable and PivotChart**

1. Open **Precision-BulkSales.xlsx**.
2. Save the workbook using the name **ExcelL2_U1_A6**.
3. Select A4:I22 and create a PivotTable in a new worksheet named PivotTable as follows:
   a. Add the *Category* field as the report filter field.
   b. Add the *Distributor* field as the row labels.
   c. Sum the North, South, East, and West sales values.
4. Apply formatting options to the PivotTable to make the data easier to read and interpret.
5. Print the PivotTable.
6. Create a PivotChart in a separate sheet named **PivotChart** that graphs the data from the PivotTable in a Clustered Cylinder chart.
7. Edit the chart fields to display only the sum of the North and the South values.
8. Move the legend to the bottom of the chart.
9. Print the chart.
10. Save and then close **ExcelL2_U1_A6.xlsx**.

Assessment 7 **Link to an External Data Source and Calculate Distributor Payments**

1. Open **Precision-DistributorPymnt.xlsx**.
2. Save the workbook using the name **ExcelL2_U1_A7**.
3. Open **ExcelL2_U1_A6.xlsx**.
4. Save the workbook using the name **ExcelL2_U1_A7-Source**.
5. Make the PivotTable worksheet active and then edit the PivotTable Field List so that *Sum of Total* is the only numeric field displayed in the table.
6. Save **ExcelL2_U1_A7-Source.xlsx**.
7. Arrange the display of the two workbooks vertically.
8. Create linked external references starting in D6 in **ExcelL2_U1_A7.xlsx** to the appropriate source cells in the PivotTable in **ExcelL2_U1_A7-Source.xlsx** so that the distributor payment worksheet displays the total sales for each distributor. *Note: Since you are linking to a PivotTable, Excel automatically generates a GETPIVOTDATA function formula in each linked cell.*
9. Close **ExcelL2_U1_A7-Source.xlsx**.
10. Maximize **ExcelL2_U1_A7.xlsx**.
11. Format D6:D8 to the Accounting number format with zero decimals.
12. Precision Design and Packaging pays each distributor a percentage of sales depending on the total sales achieved. If the distributor generates more than $900 thousand in sales, Precision pays a distributor fee of 4% on the total sales. If the distributor generates more than $600 thousand in sales, Precision pays 2%. For all other sales $600 thousand and less, Precision pays 1%. Calculate the payment owed for the distributors in H6:H8. Perform the calculation using either one of the following two methods—choose the method which you find easier to understand.
    - Create a nested IF statement; OR
    - Create a lookup table in the worksheet that contains the sale ranges and the three percentage values. Next, add a column next to each distributor with a lookup formula to return the correct percentage and then calculate the payment using total sales times the percent value.

13. Format H6:H8 to the Comma Style number format.
14. Add the label TOTALS in B10 and then create formulas in D10 and H10 to calculate the total sales and total payments respectively. Format the totals and adjust column widths as necessary.
15. Print the worksheet. Write the GETPIVOTDATA formula for D6 at the bottom of the printout.
16. Break the link to the external references and convert the formulas to their existing values.
17. Save and then close **ExcelL2_U1_A7.xlsx**.

WRITING activities

The following activities give you the opportunity to practice your writing skills along with demonstrating an understanding of some of the important Excel features you have mastered in this unit. Use appropriate word choices, correct grammar, capitalization, and punctuation when setting up new worksheets. Labels should clearly describe the data that is presented.

Activity 1 Create a Worksheet to Track Video Rental Memberships

Vantage Video Rentals is offering a new membership program for their frequent customers. Customers will pay an annual membership fee which then entitles them to a discount on video rentals based on their membership category. Table U1.1 provides the three membership levels and discounts. The manager of Vantage Video Rentals has asked you to create a worksheet that will be used to provide a master list of customers who are participating in the membership program, the membership level they have paid, and the discount on video rentals they are entitled to receive. The worksheet will need to provide in list format the following information:

• Date annual membership needs to be renewed
• Customer name
• Customer telephone number
• Membership level
• Annual membership fee
• Discount on video rentals

Create a worksheet for the membership list. Use a lookup table to populate the cells containing the membership fee and the discount level. Create a drop-down list for the cell containing the membership level that restricts the data entered to the three membership categories. Use a special number format for the telephone number column so that all telephone numbers include the area code and are displayed in a consistent format. Enter a minimum of five sample records to test the worksheet with your settings. The manager anticipates approximately 35 regular customers will subscribe to the membership program. Format enough rows with the data features to include at least 35 memberships. Save the completed worksheet and name it **ExcelL2_U1_Act01**. Print and then close the worksheet.

Table U1.1 Activity 1

Membership Category	Annual Fee	Discount on Video Rentals
Gold	$35.00	15%
Silver	$25.00	12%
Classic	$15.00	10%

Activity 2 Create a Worksheet to Log Hours Walked in a Company Fitness Contest

The company at which you work is sponsoring a contest this year to encourage employees to participate in a walking fitness program during lunch hours. The company is offering to pay for a spa weekend at an exclusive luxury resort for participating employees in the department that logs the most miles or kilometers walked during the year. You work in Human Resources and are in charge of keeping track of each department's walking records. Create a worksheet that can be used to enter each department's totals by month and summarize the data to show the total distance walked for the entire company at the end of the year as follows:

- Four departments have signed up for the contest: Accounting, Human Resources, Purchasing, and Marketing. Create a separate worksheet for each department.

- Each department will send you a paper copy of their walking log each month. You will use this source document to enter the miles or kilometers walked by day. At the end of each month you want to calculate statistics by department to show the total distance walked, the average distance walked, and the number of days in the month in which employees walked during their lunch hour. When calculating the average and the number of days, include only those days in which employees logged a distance. In other words, exclude from the statistics those days in which employees did not log any distance. *Hint: Consider adding a column that contains Yes or No to record whether or not employees participated in the walking program each day to use as the criteria range.*

- Create a summary worksheet that calculates the total of all miles or kilometers walked for all four departments.

Enter at least five days of sample data in each worksheet to test your settings. Save the completed workbook and name it **ExcelL2_U1_Act02**. Print the entire workbook and then close the workbook.

Optional: Using the Internet or other sources, find information on the health benefits of walking. Prepare a summary of the information and include it in a memo announcing the contest. The memo is to be sent from Human Resources to all departments. Save the memo and name it **ExcelL2_U2_Act02_Memo**. Print the memo and close the file.

INTERNET research

Create a Worksheet to Compare Online Auction Listing Fees

You are assisting a friend who is interested in selling a few items by auction on the Internet. Research a minimum of two Internet auction sites for all selling and payment fees associated with selling online. For example, be sure to find out costs for the following activities involved in an auction sale:

- Listing fees (sometimes called insertion fees)
- Optional features that can be attached to an ad such as reserve bid fees, picture fees, listing upgrades, and so on
- Fees paid when the item is sold based on the sale value
- Fees paid to a third party to accept credit card payments (such as PayPal)

Create a worksheet in which you compare the fees for each auction site you researched. Include for each auction site two sample transactions and calculate the total fees that would be paid.

Sample transaction 1   Item sold at $24.99
Sample transaction 2   Item sold at $49.99

- Add optional features to the listing such as a picture and/or a reserve bid
- Assume in both sample transactions the buyer pays by credit card using a third party service

Based on your analysis, decide which auction site is the better choice from a cost perspective. Apply formatting options to make the worksheet easy to read and decipher your recommendation for the lower cost auction site. Save the completed worksheet and name it **ExcelL2_U1_Act03**. Print and then close the worksheet.

Microsoft®

excel

Unit 2: Managing and Integrating Data and the Excel Environment

➤ Using Data Analysis Features

➤ Protecting and Sharing Workbooks

➤ Automating Repetitive Tasks and Customizing Excel

➤ Importing, Exporting, and Distributing Data

Benchmark Microsoft® Excel 2007 Level 2

Microsoft Certified Application Specialist Skills—Unit 2

Reference No.	Skill	Pages
1	**Creating and Manipulating Data**	
1.3	Modify cell contents and formats	
1.3.1	Cut, copy, and paste data and cell contents	154-156
1.4	Change worksheet views	
1.4.1	Change views within a single window	242-244
2	**Formatting Data and Content**	
2.1	Format worksheets	
2.1.1	Use themes to format worksheets	245-251
2.1.2	Show and hide gridlines and headers	242-244
3	**Creating and Modifying Formulas**	
3.1	Reference data in formulas	
3.1.1	Create formulas that use absolute and relative cell references	171-174
5	**Collaborating and Securing Data**	
5.1	Manage changes to workbooks	
5.1.1	Insert, display, modify, and resolve tracked changes	205-209
5.2	Protect and share workbooks	
5.2.1	Protect workbooks and worksheets	195-204
5.2.2	Enable workbooks to be changed by multiple users	188-195
5.3	Prepare workbooks for distribution	
5.3.1	Remove private and other inappropriate data from workbooks	285-289
5.3.2	Restrict permissions to a workbook	296
5.3.3	Add keywords and other information to workbook properties	186-188
5.3.4	Add digital signatures	292-295
5.3.5	Mark workbooks as final	289-290
5.4	Save workbooks	
5.4.1	Save workbooks for use in a previous version of Excel	290-292
5.4.2	Using the correct format, save a workbook as a template, a Web page, a macro-enabled document, or another appropriate format	222-235, 251-253

Note: The Level 1 and Level 2 texts each address approximately half of the Microsoft Certified Application Specialist skills. Complete coverage of the skills is offered in the combined Level 1 and Level 2 text titled *Benchmark Series Microsoft® Excel 2007: Levels 1 and 2*, which has been approved as certified courseware and which displays the Microsoft Certified Application Specialist logo on the cover.

Using Data Analysis Features

PERFORMANCE OBJECTIVES

Upon successful completion of Chapter 5, you will be able to:

- Switch data arranged in columns to rows and vice versa
- Perform a mathematical operation during a paste routine
- Copy and paste comments
- Populate a cell using Goal Seek
- Save and display various worksheet models using Scenario Manager
- Create a scenario summary report
- Create a one-variable data table to analyze various outcomes
- Create a two-variable data table to analyze various outcomes
- View relationships between cells in formulas
- Identify Excel error codes and troubleshoot a formula using formula auditing tools
- Circle invalid data
- Use the Watch Window to track a value

Tutorial 5.1
What If Analysis and Projecting Values
Tutorial 5.2
Auditing Worksheets

Excel's Paste Special dialog box includes several options for pasting copied data. You can choose to paste attributes of a copied cell or alter the paste routine to perform a more complex operation. A variety of *what-if* analysis tools allow you to manage data to assist with decision-making or management tasks. Formula auditing tools can be used to troubleshoot a formula or view dependencies between cells.

Note: Before beginning computer projects, copy to your storage medium the Excel2007L2C5 subfolder from the Excel2007L2 folder on the CD that accompanies this textbook and then make Excel2007L2C5 the active folder.

Project  Analyze Data from a Request for Proposal

You will manipulate a worksheet containing vendor quotations for an enterprise resource planning information system by copying and pasting using Paste Special options.

Pasting Data Using Paste Special Options

The Paste Special dialog box shown in Figure 5.1 can be used after data has been copied to the Clipboard to paste specific attributes of the source data, perform a mathematical operation in the destination range based on values in the source range, or carry out a more complex paste sequence. For example, you can copy a cell containing a comment and paste only the comment to the destination.

Figure 5.1 Paste Special Dialog Box

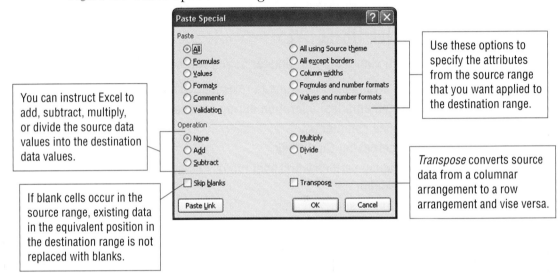

You can instruct Excel to add, subtract, multiply, or divide the source data values into the destination data values.

If blank cells occur in the source range, existing data in the equivalent position in the destination range is not replaced with blanks.

Use these options to specify the attributes from the source range that you want applied to the destination range.

Transpose converts source data from a columnar arrangement to a row arrangement and vise versa.

Transposing Data

QUICK STEPS

Transpose a Range
1. Select source range.
2. Click Copy button.
3. Click starting cell in destination range.
4. Click Paste button arrow.
5. Click *Transpose*.

A worksheet may have data arranged in a way that is not suitable for the analysis you want to perform. For example, examine the worksheet shown in Figure 5.2. This is the worksheet you will be working with in Project 1. Notice the layout of the information shows each company that submitted a proposal arranged in a separate column with the criteria for analysis, such as the cost of the hardware, arranged in rows. While at first glance this layout may seem appropriate, consider how you would analyze this data if you wanted to examine only those vendors that offer a five-year contract. To use the filter feature on this data, you need the contract term in a columnar format. Rearranging the data in this worksheet manually would be a tedious process. The *Transpose* option in the Paste drop-down menu or the Paste Special dialog box will convert columns to rows and rows to columns.

Figure 5.2 Project 1 Worksheet

	A	B	C	D	E	F
1			**Precision Design and Packaging**			
2			**Enterprise Resource Planning Information System**			
3			**Finance Department RFP Analysis**			
4	RFP No. 385-XR-78					
5	Company	Westerveld Inc.	Kampson Ltd.	Jensen Systems	Core Solutions	NuTech Partners
6	Hardware	675,000	588,000	615,000	625,000	596,000
7	Software	212,000	280,000	267,000	250,000	292,000
8	Maintenance	22,500	21,675	20,750	23,450	26,432
9	Service Level	Same day	24 hours	24 hours	Same day	Same day
10	Term	5	4	5	5	4
11	Total Cost	909,500	889,675	902,750	898,450	914,432

Project 1a Converting Data from Rows to Columns

1. Open **Precision-ERPSystem.xlsx**.
2. Save the workbook with Save As and name it **ExcelL2_C5_P1**.
3. Convert the worksheet to arrange the company names in rows and the criteria data in columns by completing the following steps:
   a. Select A5:F11.
   b. Click the Copy button.
   c. Click A13.
   d. Click the Paste button arrow and then click *Transpose* at the drop-down list.

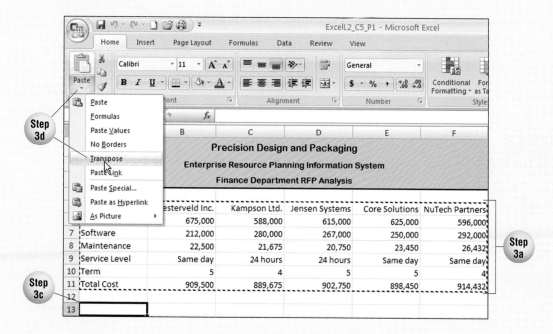

   e. Press the Esc key to remove the moving marquee from the source range and then click in any cell to deselect the range.
4. Delete rows 5–12.
5. Add a thick bottom border to G3 and right-align the labels in row 5.
6. Correct the merge and centering in rows 1–3 to extend the three titles across columns A–G.
7. Select A5:G10, turn on the Filter feature, and then click in any cell to deselect the range.

8. Click the filter arrow button in F5 and then filter the worksheet to display only those vendors offering a 5-year contract.

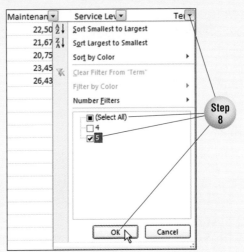

Step 8

9. Click the filter arrow button in E5 and then filter the remaining rows to display only those vendors offering same day service.

Compa ▼	Hardwa ▼	Softwa ▼	Maintenan ▼	Service Lev ▼	Te ▼	Total C ▼
Westerveld Inc.	675,000	212,000	22,500	Same day	5	909,500
Core Solutions	625,000	250,000	23,450	Same day	5	898,450

Step 9

10. Make A6 the active cell and then print the filtered worksheet in landscape orientation.
11. Turn off the Filter feature and then save **ExcelL2_C5_P1.xlsx**.

QUICK STEPS

Performing a Mathematical Operation while Pasting

Perform Mathematical Operation during Paste
1. Select source range values.
2. Click Copy button.
3. Click starting cell in destination range.
4. Click Paste button arrow.
5. Click *Paste Special*.
6. Click desired mathematical operation.
7. Click OK.

A range of cells in a copied source range can be added to, subtracted from, multiplied by, or divided by the cells in the destination range by opening the Paste Special dialog box and selecting the mathematical operation you want to perform. For example, in the worksheet for Project 1, the values entered in the Maintenance row relate to annual maintenance fees charged by each vendor. To compare the total cost of the system from all of the vendors, you want to see the maintenance value for the life cycle of the contract. In Project 1b, you will copy and paste using a multiply operation to avoid having to add a row to the worksheet to perform the calculation for you.

1. With **ExcelL2_C5_P1.xlsx** open, select F6:F10.
2. Click the Copy button.
3. Paste the source range and instruct Excel to multiply the values when pasting by completing the following steps:
   a. Click D6.
   b. Click the Paste button arrow and then click *Paste Special* at the drop-down list.
   c. Click *Multiply* in the *Operation* section of the Paste Special dialog box and then click OK.

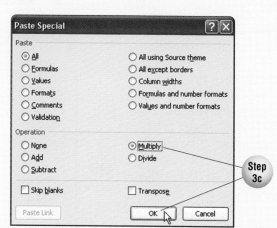

   d. Press the *Esc* key to remove the moving marquee from the source range and then click in any cell to deselect the range.
4. Print the worksheet.
5. Save **ExcelL2_C5_P1.xlsx**.

Pasting Comments

A comment that has been added to a cell can be copied and pasted to one or more cells. After copying the source cell, click the destination cell and then open the Paste Special dialog box. Click *Comments* in the *Paste* section and then click OK.

Selecting Other Paste Special Options

Other options at the Paste Special dialog box include *Formulas* or *Values* to paste the source formulas or displayed values only, *Formats* to paste only formatting options from the source, *Validation* to paste a validation rule, *All using Source theme* to apply the theme from the source, *All except borders* to paste everything except borders from the source, and *Column widths* to adjust the destination cells to the same column width as the source. To paste values or formulas including the number formats from the source click the *Formulas and number formats* or *Values and number formats* option.

QUICK STEPS

Copy and Paste Comments
1. Select source cell containing comment.
2. Click Copy button.
3. Click destination cell(s).
4. Click Paste button arrow.
5. Click *Paste Special*.
6. Click *Comments*.
7. Click OK.

Show All Comments

Launch Dialog Box

1. With **ExcelL2_C5_P1.xlsx** open, make A6 the active cell.
2. Add a comment to the cell by completing the following steps:
   a. Click the Review tab.
   b. Click the New Comment button in the Comments group.
   c. Type **Waiting for reference list from vendor** and then click outside the comment box.

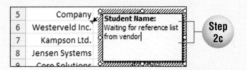

Step 2c

3. Copy and paste the comment to two other vendor names by completing the following steps:
   a. Make A6 the active cell, click the Home tab, and then click the Copy button.
   b. Click A8, hold down the Ctrl key, and then click A10.
   c. Click the Paste button arrow.
   d. Click *Paste Special*.
   e. Click *Comments* in the *Paste* section of the Paste Special dialog box and then click OK.
   f. Press the Esc key to remove the moving marquee from the source cell and then click in any cell to deselect the range.

Step 3e

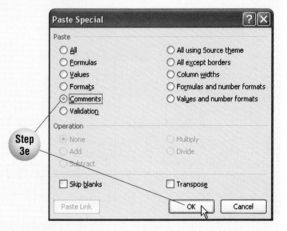

4. Hover the mouse pointer over A8 and view the comment box.
5. Hover the mouse pointer over A10 and view the comment box.

Step 5

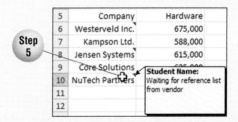

6. Print the worksheet with the comments as displayed by the cells by completing the following steps:
   a. Click the Review tab.
   b. Click the Show All Comments button in the Comments group.
   c. Click the Page Layout tab.
   d. Click the Page Setup: Sheet dialog box launcher in the Sheet Options group.
   e. Click the down-pointing arrow at the right of the *Comments* list box in the *Print* section and then click *As displayed on sheet* at the drop-down list.
   f. Click OK.
   g. Print the worksheet.

Step 6e

7. Click the Review tab and then click the Show All Comments button to turn off the display of the comment boxes.
8. Save and then close **ExcelL2_C5_P1.xlsx**.

roject ② **Calculate a Target Test Score**

Using a grades worksheet for a student, you will determine the score a student needs to earn on a final test in order to achieve a specified final average grade.

Using Goal Seek to Populate a Cell

Excel's Goal Seek feature returns a value based upon a target that you want to achieve in another cell that is dependent on the cell you want Goal Seek to populate. For example, the worksheet shown in Figure 5.3 shows Whitney's grades on the first four tutoring assessments. The value in B11 (average grade) is calculated as the average of the five values in B5:B9. Note that the final test is showing a grade of zero although the test has not yet occurred. Once the final test grade is entered, the value in B11 will update to reflect the average of all five scores. Suppose Whitney wants to achieve a final grade of 76% in her course. Using Goal Seek, you can determine the score she needs to earn on the final test in order to achieve the 76% average.

In Project 2 you will return a value in B9 that the Goal Seek feature will calculate based on the target value you will set in B11. Goal Seek causes Excel to calculate in reverse—you specify the ending value and Excel figures out the input numbers that will achieve the end result you want. Note that the cell in which you want Excel to calculate the target value must be referenced by a formula in the *Set cell* box. Goal Seek is useful for any situation where you know the result you want to achieve but are not sure what value will get you there.

QUICK STEPS

Use Goal Seek to Return a Value
1. Make desired cell active.
2. Click Data tab.
3. Click What-If Analysis button.
4. Click *Goal Seek*.
5. Enter desired cell address in *Set cell* text box.
6. Enter desired target value in *To value* text box.
7. Enter dependent cell address in *By changing cell* text box.
8. Click OK.
9. Click OK or Cancel to accept or reject results.

HINT

The cell in which you want Excel to calculate the target value must be referenced by a formula in the *Set cell* box.

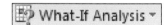

Figure 5.3 Project 2 Worksheet

	A	B	C
1	**Math by Janelle Tutoring Service**		
2	**Student Assessment Report**		
3	**Whitney Orlowicz**		
4	**Assessments**	**100**	**Session**
5	Objective test	64.5	1
6	Performance test	72.0	6
7	Problem-solving test	83.5	10
8	Comprehensive test	78.5	15
9	Final test	0.0	20
10			
11	Average grade	59.7	

Goal Seek can determine the value that needs to be entered for the final test in order to achieve an average grade that you specify in B11.

Project ② Using Goal Seek to Return a Target Value

1. Open **JanelleTutoring-OrlowiczRpt.xlsx**.
2. Save the workbook with Save As and name it **ExcelL2_C5_P2**.
3. Use Goal Seek to find the score Whitney needs to earn on the final test to achieve a 76% average grade by completing the following steps:
   a. Make B11 the active cell.
   b. Click the Data tab.
   c. Click the What-If Analysis button in the Data Tools group and then click *Goal Seek* at the drop-down list.

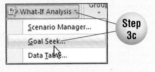
   Step 3c

   Step 3e

   Step 3f

   d. If necessary, drag the Goal Seek dialog box to the right of the worksheet so that you can see all of the values in column B.

   Step 3g

   e. With *B11* already entered in the *Set cell* text box, click in the *To value* text box and then type 76.
   f. Press Tab and then type b9 in the *By changing cell* text box.
   g. Click OK.
   h. Click OK at the Goal Seek Status dialog box that shows Excel found a solution.

   Step 3h

4. Notice that Excel entered the value *81.5* in B9. This is the score Whitney must earn in order to achieve a final average grade of 76%.
5. Print the worksheet.
6. Assume that Whitney wants to achieve a final average grade of 80%. Use Goal Seek to find the value that she will need to earn on the final test to accomplish the new target by completing the following steps:
   a. Click the What-If Analysis button in the Data Tools group and then click *Goal Seek* at the drop-down list.
   b. Click in the *To value* text box, type 80, and then press Tab.
   c. Type **b9** in the *By changing cell* text box and then click OK.
   d. Click OK.
   e. Notice that the value returned in B9 is 101.5. This is the new value Excel has calculated Whitney needs on the final test in order to earn an 80% final average grade.
   f. Click the Cancel button at the Goal Seek Status dialog box to restore the previous values.

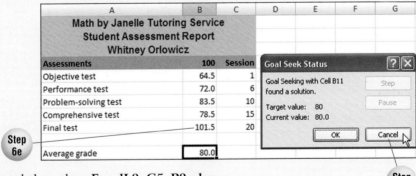

Step 6e

Step 6f

7. Save and then close **ExcelL2_C5_P2.xlsx**.

roject ③ **Forecast a Budget Based on Various Inflation Rates**

You will determine the impact on a department's budget of various inflation rates to determine the funding request to present to management to maintain service.

Creating Assumptions for What-If Analysis Using Scenario Manager

The Scenario Manager allows you to store multiple sets of assumptions about data and then view the impact of those assumptions on your worksheet. You can switch the display between scenarios to test the various inputs on your worksheet model. You can save each scenario using a descriptive name such as *Best Case* or *Worst Case* to indicate the type of data assumptions you have stored. Examine the worksheet shown in Figure 5.4. In this worksheet, the Computing Services department budget for the next year has been calculated based on projected increases for various expense items. Assume that the department manager has more than one estimate for the percentages based on different inflation rates or vendor rate increases for next year. The manager can create and save various scenarios in order to view the impact on total costs for a combination of different forecasts.

QUICK STEPS

Add a Scenario
1. Click Data tab.
2. Click What-If Analysis button.
3. Click *Scenario Manager.*
4. Click Add button.
5. Type name in *Scenario name* text box.
6. Type or select variable cells in *Changing cells* text box.
7. Click OK.
8. Enter values for each changing cell.
9. Click OK.
10. Click Close button.

Figure 5.4 Project 3 Worksheet

	A	B	C	D
1	@ National Wholesale Marketing Inc. @			
2	Computing Services Department			
3		Current budget	Projected increase	New budget
4	Wages and benefits	345,550	3.5%	357,644
5	Computer supplies	148,750	1.5%	150,981
6	Training and development	57,600	10.0%	63,360
7	Other administrative costs	61,243	5.0%	64,305
8				
9	Total costs:	613,143		636,291

Using the Scenario Manager dialog box shown in Figure 5.5 you can create as many models as you want to save in order to test various what-if conditions. For example, two scenarios have been saved in the example shown in Figure 5.5, *Low_Inflation* and *High_Inflation*. When you add a scenario you define which cells will change and then enter the data to be stored under the scenario name.

HINT

Create a range name for each changing cell. This allows you to see a descriptive reference next to the input text box rather than the cell address when adding a scenario.

Figure 5.5 Scenario Manager Dialog Box and Scenario Values Dialog Box

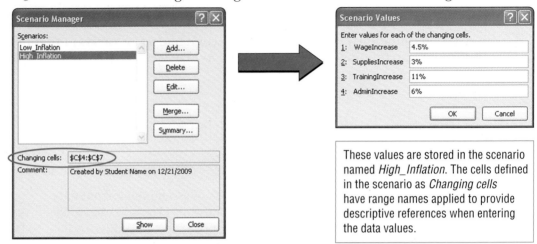

These values are stored in the scenario named *High_Inflation*. The cells defined in the scenario as *Changing cells* have range names applied to provide descriptive references when entering the data values.

Project 3a   Adding Scenarios to a Worksheet Model

1. Open **NationalCSDept-Budget.xlsx**.
2. Save the workbook with Save As and name it **ExcelL2_C5_P3**.
3. View the range names already created in the worksheet by clicking the down-pointing arrow at the right of the Name text box and then clicking *WageIncrease* at the drop-down list. The active cell moves to C4. A range name has been created for each data cell in column C to allow a descriptive label to show when you add scenarios in Steps 4 and 5.
4. Add a scenario with values assuming a low inflation rate for next year by completing the following steps:
   a. Click the Data tab.
   b. Click the What-If Analysis button in the Data Tools group and then click *Scenario Manager* at the drop-down list.
   c. Click the Add button at the Scenario Manager dialog box.
   d. At the Add Scenario dialog box with the insertion point positioned in the *Scenario name* text box, type **Low_Inflation** and then press Tab.
   e. Type **c4:c7** in the *Changing cells* text box and then press Enter or click OK. (As an alternative, you can move the dialog box out of the way and select the cells that will change in the worksheet.)

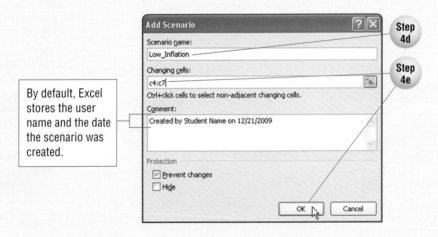

By default, Excel stores the user name and the date the scenario was created.

f. With the insertion point positioned in the first text box labeled *1: WageIncrease*, type 2% and press Tab.

g. Type 1% and press Tab.

h. Type 5% and press Tab.

i. Type 1.5% and then press Enter or click OK.

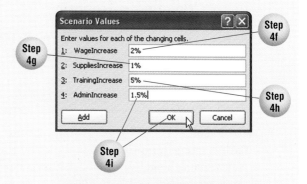

Step 4f

Step 4g

Step 4h

Step 4i

5. Add a second scenario to the worksheet assuming a high inflation rate by completing the following steps:

a. Click the Add button at the Scenario Manager dialog box.

b. Type **High_Inflation** in the *Scenario name* text box and then click OK. Notice the *Changing cells* text box already contains the range C4:C7.

c. At the Scenario Values dialog box, add the following values in the text boxes indicated:

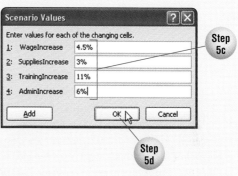

Step 5c

Step 5d

1: WageIncrease	4.5%
2: SuppliesIncrease	3%
3: TrainingIncrease	11%
4: AdminIncrease	6%

d. Click OK.

6. Add a third scenario named *Original_Forecast* that contains the original worksheet's values by completing the following steps:

a. Click the Add button at the Scenario Manager dialog box.

b. Type **Original_Forecast** in the *Scenario name* text box and then click OK.

c. At the Scenario Values dialog box, notice the original values are already entered in each text box. Click OK.

7. Click the Close button to close the Scenario Manager dialog box.

8. Save **ExcelL2_C5_P3.xlsx**.

Applying a Scenario

After you have created the various scenarios you want to save with the worksheet, you can apply the values stored in a scenario to the variable cells to view the effects on your worksheet model. To do this, open the Scenario Manager dialog box, click the name of the scenario that contains the values you want to apply to the worksheet and then click the Show button. Generally, you should create a scenario with the original values in the worksheet since Excel replaces the changing cell's contents when you show a scenario.

Editing a Scenario

Change the values associated with a scenario by opening the Scenario Manager dialog box, clicking the name of the scenario that contains the values you want to change, and then clicking the Edit button. At the Edit Scenario dialog box, change the name associated with the scenario, the cells that will change, or click OK to open the Scenario Values dialog box to edit the individual values associated with each changing cell. Click OK and then Close when finished editing.

QUICK STEPS

Display Scenario
1. Click Data tab.
2. Click What-If Analysis button.
3. Click *Scenario Manager*.
4. Click desired scenario name.
5. Click Show button.
6. Click Close button.

Deleting a Scenario

To delete a scenario, open the Scenario Manager dialog box, click the scenario you want to remove, click the Delete button, and then click the Close button.

Project 3b Applying a Scenario's Values to the Worksheet

1. With **ExcelL2_C5_P3.xlsx** open, apply the scenario containing the values for the low inflation rate assumptions by completing the following steps:
   a. With Data the active tab, click the What-If Analysis button and then click *Scenario Manager* at the drop-down list.
   b. Click *Low_Inflation* in the *Scenarios* list box and then click the Show button. Excel changes the values in the range C4:C7 to the values stored within the scenario. Notice the total cost of the new budget under a low inflation assumption is $625,340.
2. With the Scenario Manager dialog box still open, change the worksheet to display the high inflation rate assumptions by clicking *High_Inflation* in the *Scenarios* list box and then clicking the Show button. Notice the total cost of the new budget under the high inflation assumption is $643,166.

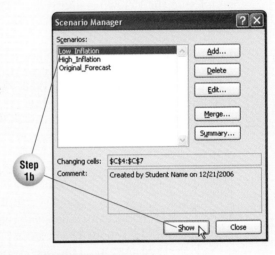

Step 1b

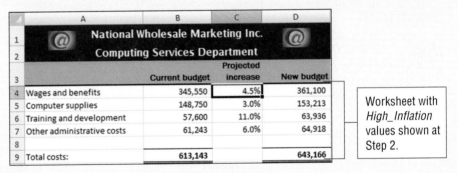

Worksheet with *High_Inflation* values shown at Step 2.

3. Show the worksheet with the *Original_Forecast* scenario's data values.
4. Click the Close button.
5. Save **ExcelL2_C5_P3.xlsx**.

QUICK STEPS

Create Scenario Summary Report
1. Click Data tab.
2. Click What-If Analysis button.
3. Click *Scenario Manager.*
4. Click Summary button.
5. Click OK.

Compiling a Scenario Summary Report

You can create a scenario summary report to compare scenarios side-by-side in a worksheet or a PivotTable. At the Scenario Summary dialog box shown in Figure 5.6 in the *Result cells* text box, enter the formula cell or cells that change by applying the data in the various scenarios. Enter multiple cell addresses in this text box separated by commas.

Figure 5.6 Scenario Summary Dialog Box

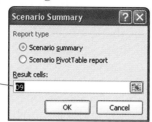

Enter the cell address of the cell containing the total or other formula results that is impacted by the changing cells in each scenario. Enter multiple results cell addresses separated by commas.

Project ③C Generating a Scenario Summary Report

1. With **ExcelL2_C5_P3.xlsx** open, display a scenario summary report by completing the following steps:
   a. With Data the active tab, click the What-If Analysis button and then click *Scenario Manager* at the drop-down list.
   b. Click the Summary button at the Scenario Manager dialog box.
   c. At the Scenario Summary dialog box, with the *Report type* set to *Scenario summary* and the *Result cells* displaying the address D9, click OK.

Step 1c

2. Examine the Scenario Summary sheet added to the workbook. The summary report displays each changing cell with the input values for each scenario. Below the Changing Cells table, Excel displays the Result Cells values given each scenario's input.

Scenario Summary worksheet created at Step 1.

Scenario Summary				
	Current Values:	Low_Inflation	High_Inflation	Original_Forecast
Changing Cells:				
WageIncrease	3.5%	2.0%	4.5%	3.5%
SuppliesIncrease	1.5%	1.0%	3.0%	1.5%
TrainingIncrease	10.0%	5.0%	11.0%	10.0%
AdminIncrease	5.0%	1.5%	6.0%	5.0%
Result Cells:				
$D$9	636,291	625,340	643,166	636,291

Notes: Current Values column represents values of changing cells at time Scenario Summary Report was created. Changing cells for each scenario are highlighted in gray.

3. Print the Scenario Summary worksheet in landscape orientation.
4. Save and then close **ExcelL2_C5_P3.xlsx**.

Project ④ Compare Impact of Various Inputs Related to Cost and Sales Pricing

Using a one-variable and a two-variable data table, you will analyze the impact on the cost per unit and selling price per unit of a manufactured container.

Performing What-If Analysis Using Data Tables

A data table is a range of cells that contains a series of input values. Excel calculates a formula substituting each input value in the data table range and places the result in the cell adjacent to the value. You can create a one-variable and a two-variable data table. A one-variable data table calculates a formula by modifying one input value in the formula. A two-variable data table calculates a formula substituting two input values. Data tables provide a means to analyze various outcomes in a calculation that occur as a result of changing a dependent value without creating multiple formulas.

Creating a One-Variable Data Table

Create One-Variable Data Table
1. Create variable data in column at right of worksheet.
2. Enter formula one row above and one cell right of variable data.
3. Select data range including formula cell.
4. Click Data tab.
5. Click What-If Analysis button.
6. Click *Data Table*.
7. Type cell address for variable data in source formula in *Column input cell* text box.
8. Press Enter or click OK.

Design a one-variable data table with the variable input data values either in a series down a column or across a row. Examine the worksheet shown in Figure 5.7. Assume that management wants to calculate the effects on the cost of each unit when production volumes vary due to spoilage or other inventory variations given a standard set of costs per factory shift. The worksheet displays the total costs for direct materials, direct labor, and overhead.

Figure 5.7 Project 4a One-Variable Data Table

	A	B	C	D	E	F	G	H
1		**Precision Design and Packaging**						
2		**Cost Price Analysis**						
3		**"E" Container Bulk Cargo Box**						
4	Factory costs per shift:				Variable unit production impact on cost			
5	Direct materials	$ 575,000						
6	Direct labor	875,452			425,000			
7	Overhead	145,045			450,000			
8	Total cost	$ 1,595,497			475,000			
9					500,000			
10	Standard production	500,000	units		525,000			
11					550,000			
12	Cost per unit	$ 3.19			575,000			

> In this area of the worksheet, you can calculate the change in cost per unit based on varying the production volume using a data table.

The formula in B8 sums the three cost categories. Based on a standard production volume of 500,000 units, the cost per unit is $3.19, calculated by dividing the total costs by the production volume (B8/B10). In E6:E12, the factory manager has input varying levels of production. The manager would like to see the change in the cost per unit for each level of production volume assuming the costs remain the same. In Project 4a, you will use a data table to show the various costs. This data table will manipulate one input value, production volume; therefore, the table is a one-variable data table.

Project **4a**

1. Open **Precision-EBoxCost.xlsx**.
2. Save the workbook with Save As and name it **ExcelL2_C5_P4-Cost**.
3. Calculate the cost per unit for seven different production levels using a one-variable data table by completing the following steps:
   a. A data table requires that the formula for calculating the various outcomes be placed in the cell in the first row above and one column right of the table values. The data table's values have been entered in E6:E12; therefore, make F5 the active cell.
   b. The formula that calculates the cost per unit is =B8/B10. This formula has already been entered in B12. Link to the source formula by typing =b12 and then pressing Enter.
   c. Select E5:F12.
   d. Click the Data tab.
   e. Click the What-If Analysis button and then click *Data Table* at the drop-down list.

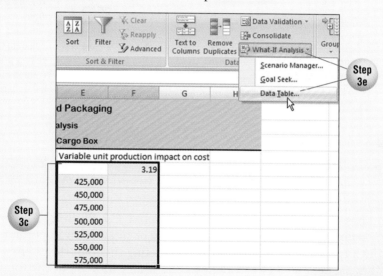

					Variable unit production impact on cost	
$	575,000				=b12	
	875,452		425,000			
	145,045		450,000			
$	1,595,497		475,000			
			500,000			
	500,000	units	525,000			
			550,000			
$	3.19		575,000			

Step 3b

d Packaging
alysis
Cargo Box

Variable unit production impact on cost	
	3.19
425,000	
450,000	
475,000	
500,000	
525,000	
550,000	
575,000	

Step 3c

Step 3e

   f. At the Data Table dialog box, click in the *Column input cell* text box, type **b10**, and then press Enter or click OK. At the Data Table dialog box, Excel needs to know which reference in the source formula is the address for which the variable data is to be inserted. (The production volume is B10 in the source formula.)

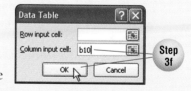

Data Table

Row input cell: [ ]
Column input cell: [b10]

OK   Cancel

Step 3f

   g. Click in any cell to deselect the range.
4. Print the worksheet in landscape orientation.
5. Save and then close **ExcelL2_C5_P4-Cost.xlsx**.

Variable unit production impact on cost	
	3.19
425,000	3.75
450,000	3.55
475,000	3.36
500,000	3.19
525,000	3.04
550,000	2.90
575,000	2.77

Costs calculated by the data table at each production volume. Notice the costs are higher at lower volumes and decrease as production volume increases.

Creating a Two-Variable Data Table

Create Two-Variable Data Table
1. Create variable data at right of worksheet with one input series in a column and another in a row across the top of the table.
2. Enter formula in top left cell of table.
3. Select data table range.
4. Click Data tab.
5. Click What-If Analysis button.
6. Click *Data Table*.
7. Type cell address for variable data in source formula in *Row input cell* text box.
8. Press Tab.
9. Type cell address for variable data in source formula in *Column input cell* text box.
10. Press Enter or click OK.

A data table can substitute two variables in a source formula. To modify two input cells, design the data table with a column along the left containing one set of variable input values and a row along the top of the table containing the second set of variable input values. In a two-variable data table, the source formula is placed at the top left cell in the table. In the worksheet shown in Figure 5.8, the source formula will be inserted in E5, which is the top left cell in the data table.

Figure 5.8 Project 4b Two-Variable Data Table

	A	B	C	D	E	F	G	H
1		Precision Design and Packaging						
2		Selling Price Analysis at Variable Production and Markups						
3		"E" Container Bulk Cargo Box						
4	Factory costs per shift:				Variable unit production impact on sell price			
5	Direct materials	$ 575,000				50%	52%	55%
6	Direct labor	875,452			425,000			
7	Overhead	145,045			450,000			
8	Total cost	$ 1,595,497			475,000			
9					500,000			
10	Standard production	500,000	units		525,000			
11					550,000			
12	Cost per unit	$ 3.19			575,000			
13	Markup	52%						
14	Selling price per unit	$ 4.85						

This data table contains two input variables—production units and markup percentage. The data table will calculate a selling price at each production volume and at each markup percentage.

Project 4b Creating a Two-Variable Data Table

1. Open **Precision-EBoxSellPrice.xlsx**.
2. Save the workbook with Save As and name it **ExcelL2_C5_P4-Sell**.
3. Calculate the selling price per unit for seven different production levels and three different markups using a two-variable data table by completing the following steps:
   a. In a two-variable data table, Excel requires the source formula in the top left cell in the data table; therefore, make E5 the active cell.
   b. Type **=b14** and press Enter. The formula that you want Excel to use to create the data table is in B14. The selling price is calculated by adding to the cost per unit (B12) an amount equal to the cost per unit times the markup percentage (B13).

			Variable unit
$	575,000		=b14
	875,452		425,000
	145,045		450,000
$	1,595,497		475,000
			500,000
	500,000	units	525,000
			550,000
$	3.19		575,000
	52%		
$	4.85		

Step 3b

c. Select E5:H12.

d. Click the Data tab.

e. Click the What-If Analysis button and then click *Data Table* at the drop-down list.

f. At the Data Table dialog box with the insertion point positioned in the *Row input cell* text box, type **b13** and press Tab. Excel needs to know which reference in the source formula is the address relating to the variable data in the first row of the data table. (The markup value is in B13 in the source formula.)

g. Type **b10** in the *Column input cell* text box and then press Enter or click OK. As in Project 4a, Excel needs to know which reference relates to the production volume in the source formula.

h. Click in any cell to deselect the range.

Step 3f

Data Table

Row input cell: b13

Column input cell: b10

OK   Cancel

Step 3g

Variable unit production impact on sell price			
$ 4.85	50%	52%	55%
425,000	5.63	5.71	5.82
450,000	5.32	5.39	5.50
475,000	5.04	5.11	5.21
500,000	4.79	4.85	4.95
525,000	4.56	4.62	4.71
550,000	4.35	4.41	4.50
575,000	4.16	4.22	4.30

Selling prices calculated by the data table at each production volume and at each percentage markup

4. Print the worksheet in landscape orientation.

5. Save and then close **ExcelL2_C5_P4-Sell.xlsx**.

Project 5 Audit a Worksheet to View and Troubleshoot Formulas

You will use buttons in the Formula Auditing group to view relationships between cells that comprise a formula, identify error codes in a worksheet, and troubleshoot errors using error checking tools.

Using Auditing Tools

The Formula Auditing group in the Formulas tab shown in Figure 5.9 contains buttons that are useful for viewing relationships between cells in formulas. Checking a formula for accuracy can be difficult when the formula is part of a complex sequence of operations. Opening a worksheet created by someone else can also present a challenge in understanding the relationships between sets of data. When Excel displays an error message in a cell, viewing the relationships between the dependencies of cells assists with finding the source of the error.

QUICK STEPS

Trace Precedent Cells
1. Open worksheet.
2. Make desired cell active.
3. Click Formulas tab.
4. Click Trace Precedents button.
5. Continue clicking until all relationships are visible.

Trace Dependent Cells
1. Open worksheet.
2. Make desired cell active.
3. Click Formulas tab.
4. Click Trace Dependents button.
5. Continue clicking until all relationships are visible.

Figure 5.9 Formula Auditing Group in Formulas Tab

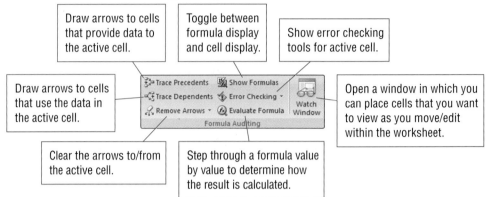

Trace Precedents and Trace Dependents

Precedent cells are cells that provide data to a formula cell. For example, if cell B3 contains the formula =B1+B2, cell B1 and cell B2 are precedent cells. Dependent cells are cells that contain a formula that refers to other cells. In the previous example, cell B3 would be the dependent cell to cells B1 and B2 since B3 relies on the data from cells B1 and B2. Click a cell and click the Trace Precedents button to draw tracer arrows that show direct relationships to cell(s) that provide data to the active cell. Click the button a second time to show indirect relationships to cell(s) that provide data to the active cell at the next level. Continue clicking the button until no further arrows are drawn. Excel will sound a beep when you click the button if no more relationships exist.

Click a cell and click the Trace Dependents button to draw tracer arrows that show direct relationships to other cell(s) in the worksheet that use the active cell's contents. As with the Trace Precedents button, you can click a second time to show the next level of indirect relationships and continue clicking the button until no further tracer arrows are drawn.

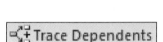

Excel draws blue tracer arrows if no error is detected in the active cell and red tracer arrows if an error condition is detected within the active cell.

Project **5a**   **Viewing Relationships between Cells and Formulas**

1. Open **ExcelL2_C5_P4-Sell.xlsx**.
2. View relationships between cells and formulas by displaying tracer arrows between cells by completing the following steps:
   a. Make B8 the active cell.
   b. Click the Formulas tab.
   c. Click the Trace Precedents button in the Formula Auditing group. Excel draws a blue tracer arrow that shows the cells that provide data to B8.
   d. Click the Remove Arrows button in the Formula Auditing group. The blue tracer arrow leading to B8 is cleared.

> Blue precedent arrow drawn to B8 at Step 2c.

4	Factory costs per shift:		
5	Direct materials	$	575,000
6	Direct labor		875,452
7	Overhead		145,045
8	Total cost	$	1,595,497

Step 2a

---

e. Make B14 the active cell.

f. Click the Trace Precedents button.

g. Click the Trace Precedents button a second time to show the next level of cells that provide data to B14.

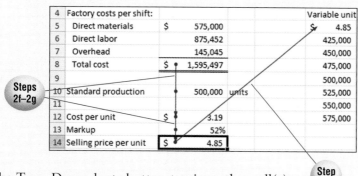

h. Click the Trace Dependents button to view other cell(s) dependent on B14.

3. Click the Remove Arrows button to clear all of the arrows.

4. Click the Show Formulas button to display cell formulas. Click the Show Formulas button again to turn off the display of formulas.

5. Close **ExcelL2_C5_P4-Sell.xlsx**. Click No when prompted to save changes.

Troubleshooting Formulas

Formulas in Excel can contain various types of errors. Some errors are obvious because Excel displays an error message such as #VALUE!. Other errors can occur that do not display error messages but are incorrect because the logic is flawed. For example, you could enter a formula in a cell which Excel does not flag as an error because the syntax is correct; however, the calculation could be incorrect for the data and the situation. Logic errors are difficult to find and require that you check a worksheet by entering proof formulas or by individually checking accuracy. A proof formula is a formula entered outside the main worksheet area that checks key figures within the worksheet. For example, in a payroll worksheet, a proof formula to check the total net pay column could add the total net pay to the totals of all of the deduction columns. The total displayed should be equal to the total gross pay amount in the worksheet.

Excel displays an error message code in a cell which is detected to have an error. Two types of error flags can occur. A green diagonal triangle in the upper left corner of a cell indicates an error condition. Activate the cell with the green triangle and an error checking button displays with which you can access error checking tools. Other cells indicate an error by displaying an entry such as #NAME?. Figure 5.10 displays a portion of the worksheet you will use in Project 5b to troubleshoot errors. Table 5.1 describes the three error codes that are displayed in Figure 5.10.

HINT

Reference errors can also occur—the formula uses correct syntax and logic but refers to the wrong data. These errors are difficult to find and only a thorough review and test of key figures reveal their existence.

QUICK STEPS

Trace Errors
1. Click cell containing error message.
2. Click Formulas tab.
3. Click down-pointing arrow on Error Checking button.
4. Click *Trace Error*.

Figure 5.10 Project 5b Partial Worksheet

	A	B	C	D	E	F	G	H	I	J	K
1		Precision Design and Packaging									
2		Bulk Container 2012 Sales Target by Region (in millions)								Sales Target Assumptions	
3	Model Number	Description	Base	East	West	North	South	Total			
4	PD-1140	Gaylord with lid	2.75	#NAME?	#N/A	2.81	0.05	#NAME?		East	1.50%
5	PD-2185	Premium Gaylord with lid	2 14	#VALUE!	#VALUE!	#VALUE!	#VALUE!	#VALUE!		West	#N/A
6	PD-1150	Gaylord bottom	2.33	#NAME?	#N/A	2.38	0.04	#NAME?		North	2.15%
7	PD-1155	Gaylord lid	1.85	#NAME?	#N/A	1.89	0.03	#NAME?		South	1.75%
8	PD-3695	Telescoping top and bottom	2.45	#NAME?	#N/A	2.50	0.04	#NAME?			
9	PD-3698	Telescoping bottom	2.96	#NAME?	#N/A	3.02	0.05	#NAME?			

Table 5.1 Error Codes in Worksheet Shown in Figure 5.10

Error Code	Description of Error Condition
#N/A	A required value for the formula is not available
#NAME?	This error code indicates the formula contains an unrecognized entry
#VALUE!	A value within the formula is of the wrong type or otherwise invalid

The Error Checking button in the Formula Auditing group can be used to assist with finding the source of an error condition in a cell by displaying the Error Checking dialog box or by drawing a red tracer arrow to locate the source cell that is contributing to the error. The Evaluate Formula button can be used to step through a formula value by value to determine the position within the formula where an error exists.

Project 5b Troubleshooting Formulas

1. Open **Precision-RegSalesTrgt.xlsx**.
2. Save the workbook with Save As and name it **ExcelL2_C5_P5**.
3. Solve the #N/A error by completing the following steps:
   a. Make E4 the active cell.
   b. Point to the Trace Error button that displays next to the cell and read the ScreenTip that displays below the button.
   c. Look in the Formula bar at the formula that has been entered into the cell. Notice that the formula includes a reference to a named cell. You decide to use the tracer arrows to locate the source of the named cell.

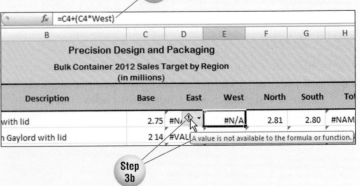

d. Click the down-pointing arrow to the right of the Error Checking button in the Formula Auditing group of the Formulas tab and then click *Trace Error* at the drop-down list. Excel moves the active cell to K5 and draws a red tracer arrow from K5 to E4. Look in the Formula bar and notice that *#N/A* displays as the entry in K5. Also notice the cell name *West* displayed in the Name text box. Since a value does not exist in the cell named *West* which is K5, the dependent cell E4 was not able to calculate its formula.

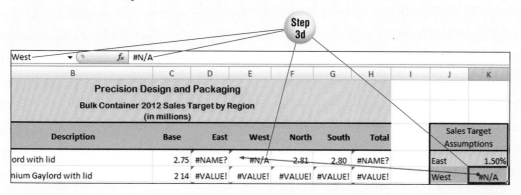

e. With K5 the active cell, type **1.25%** and press Enter. The red tracer arrow changes to blue now that the error is corrected and the #N/A error messages have disappeared.

f. Click the Remove Arrows button to clear the blue tracer arrow.

4. Solve the #NAME? error by completing the following steps:

a. Make D4 the active cell, point to the Trace Error button that appears, and then read the ScreenTip that appears. The message indicates that the formula contains unrecognized text.

b. Look at the entry in the Formula bar: *=C4+(C4*East)*. Notice the formula is the same as the formula you reviewed in Step 3c except that the named range is *East* instead of *West*. The formula appears to be valid.

c. Click the down-pointing arrow to the right of the Name text box and view the range names in the drop-down list. Notice that a range named *East* is not in the list.

d. Click *North* at the Name drop-down list. The active cell moves to K6. You know from this Step and from Step 3d that the named ranges should reference the percentage values within column K.

e. Make K4 the active cell, type **East** in the Name text box, and press Enter. The #NAME? error is resolved.

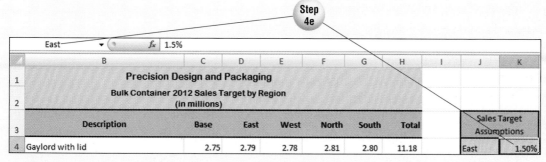

5. Solve the #VALUE! error by completing the following steps:

a. Make D5 the active cell, point to the Trace Error button that appears, and then read the ScreenTip that appears. The message indicates that a value within the formula is of the wrong type.

b. Click the Trace Precedents button in the Formula Auditing group to display tracer arrows showing you the source cells that provide data to D5. Two blue arrows appear indicating two cells provide the source values: K4 and C5.

c. Make K4 the active cell and look at the entry in the Formula bar: *1.5%*. This value is valid.

d. Make C5 the active cell and look at the entry in the Formula bar: *2 14*. Notice there is a space instead of a decimal point between 2 and 1.

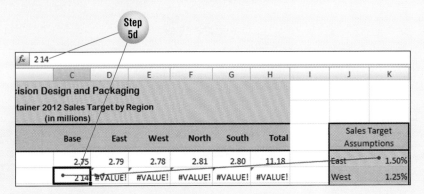

e. Click in the Formula bar and then edit the formula to delete the space between 2 and 1 and type a period to insert a decimal point. Press Enter. The #VALUE! error is resolved.

f. Click the Remove Arrows button to clear the blue tracer arrows.

6. Scroll to the bottom of the worksheet to make sure no other error messages are visible.

7. Save **ExcelL2_C5_P5.xlsx**.

QUICK STEPS

Circle Invalid Data
1. Open worksheet containing validation rules.
2. Click Data tab.
3. Click down-pointing arrow on Data Validation button.
4. Click *Circle Invalid Data*.

Watch a Formula Cell
1. Click Formulas tab.
2. Click Watch Window button.
3. Click Add Watch button.
4. Click desired cell.
5. Click Add button.

Circling Invalid Data

Recall from Chapter 3 that Data Validation is a feature used to restrict entries entered into cells. If data validation rules have been set up after data has been entered, existing values are not tested against the new rules. In this situation, you can use the Circle Invalid Data feature to draw red circles around cells that do not conform to the new rule.

Watching a Formula

In a large worksheet, a dependent cell may not always be visible while you are making changes to other cells that affect a formula. You can open a Watch Window and add a dependent cell to the window so that you can view changes to the cell as you work within the worksheet. You can add multiple cells to the Watch Window providing a single window in which you can keep track of key formulas within a large worksheet.

Consider assigning a name to a cell that you want to track using the Watch Window. At the Watch Window, the cell's name will appear in the *Name* column providing you with a descriptive reference to the entry being watched. You can expand the width of the *Name* column if a range name is not entirely visible.

The Watch Window can be docked to the top, left, bottom, or right edge of the worksheet area by dragging the title bar of the window to the desired edge of the screen. Excel changes the window to a Watch Window task pane.

1. With **ExcelL2_C5_P5.xlsx** open, view the Data Validation rule in effect for column C by completing the following steps:
   a. Make any cell containing a value in column C active.
   b. Click the Data tab.
   c. Click the Data Validation button in the Data Tools group. The Data Validation dialog box opens.
   d. Review the parameters for data entry in the Settings tab. Notice the restriction is that values should be greater than or equal to 1.57.
   e. Click OK.

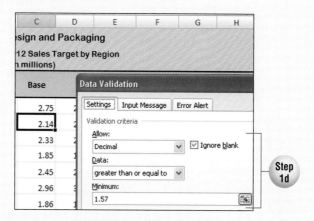

2. Click the down-pointing arrow to the right of the Data Validation button in the Data Tools group and then click *Circle Invalid Data* at the drop-down list. Three cells are circled in the worksheet: C11, C13, and C16.

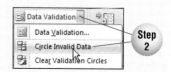

3. Watch the grand total cell update as you correct the invalid data by completing the following steps:
   a. Make H22 the active cell and then click the Formulas tab.
   b. Click the Watch Window button in the Formula Auditing group. A Watch Window opens.
   c. Click the Add Watch button in the Watch Window.
   d. At the Add Watch dialog box, move the dialog box out of the way if necessary to view cell H22. Notice H22 is entered by default as the watch cell. Click the Add button.

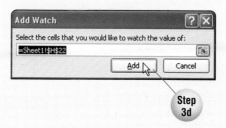

   e. Scroll up the worksheet if necessary until you can view C11. If necessary, drag the Watch Window to an out-of-the-way location in the worksheet.
   f. Make C11 the active cell, type 1.58, and press Enter. Notice the red circle disappears since you have now entered a value that conforms to the validation rule. Look at the value for H22 in the Watch Window. The new value is *153.67*.

g. Make C13 the active cell, type 1.61, and press Enter. Look at the updated value for H22 in the Watch Window.

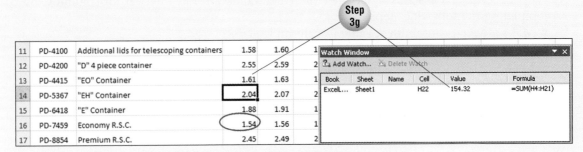

Step 3g

h. Make C16 the active cell, type 1.57, and press Enter.
i. Click the Watch Window button to close the Watch Window.
4. Print the worksheet in landscape orientation with the height and width scaled to fit 1 page.
5. Save and then close **ExcelL2_C5_P5.xlsx**.

Checking a worksheet for accuracy using auditing and error checking tools is an important skill to develop. Worksheets provide critical information to decision-makers who rely on the validity of the data. After completing a worksheet, examine it carefully, looking for data entry mistakes, values that do not appear realistic, or other indications of potential errors that should be checked.

CHAPTER summary

- Open the Paste Special dialog box to paste attributes of the source cell(s), or perform a mathematical operation during the paste.

- Transposing data during a paste routine means that data arranged in columns is converted to a row arrangement and rows are converted to columns.

- Click the Paste button arrow and then click *Paste Special* to access paste special options.

- The Goal Seek feature returns a value in a cell based on a target value you specify for another cell. The two cells must have a dependent relationship for Excel to calculate a value.

- Click the What-If Analysis button in the Data Tools group of the Data tab to locate the Goal Seek, the Scenario Manager, or the Data Table command.

- Scenario Manager allows you to save multiple sets of values for key cells in a worksheet. Switch between scenarios to view the impact of changing the input cells to one of the worksheet's saved data sets.

- A scenario summary report presents the input data for each key cell in a scenario in a tabular format with a results cell below each data set displaying the value if the data set is applied.

- A data table is a range of cells containing a series of input values with a calculated formula result adjacent to each input value.

- A one-variable data table modifies one input value within a formula.

- A two-variable data table modifies two input values within a formula.

- Design a one-variable data table with the input values in a columnar arrangement and the formula cell one row above and one column right of the input values.

- Design a two-variable data table with one set of input values in a columnar arrangement and the other set of input values starting in the first column right and first row above the first set of values. Add the formula cell to the top left cell within the input table.

- Buttons in the Formula Auditing group of the Formulas tab allow you to view relationships between cells and find and resolve errors.

- Use the Trace Precedents button to draw tracer arrows to cells that feed data into the active cell.

- Use the Trace Dependents button to draw tracer arrows to cells that use data from the active cell.

- Click the Trace Precedents or Trace Dependents button a second time to display an indirect set of relationship arrows at the next level.

- Some errors in a worksheet are syntax-related, meaning they are typed incorrectly with respect to punctuation such as a space, colon, comma, missing bracket, or misspelled function name.

- Logic errors occur when the formula is not correct for the data or the situation.

- Reference errors occur when a formula points to the wrong data cell.

- Use proof formulas to test the accuracy of key figures in a worksheet. A proof formula is entered outside the main worksheet area and double-checks data within the worksheet.
- Excel displays two types of error flags in a cell where an error has been detected.
- A green diagonal triangle in the upper left corner of the cell indicates an error is presumed. Click the active cell and use the Trace Error button to access error checking options.
- Error codes within a cell also indicate an error. For example, #NAME? means that the formula contains text that Excel cannot recognize.
- Other error codes include #VALUE?, which means a value within the formula is not valid, and #N/A, which means a value needed by the formula is not available.
- When a worksheet has data validation rules in force, data that was in existence before the rule was created is not tested. Use the Circle Invalid Data feature from the Data Validation button to place red circles around cells that do not test correct with the new rule.
- A Watch Window is a window that remains visible in the worksheet area while you scroll and edit other parts of a large worksheet. Add cells to the Watch Window that you want to keep an eye on while you make changes.
- After completing a worksheet, take time to examine the data carefully for data entry errors or logic errors that could impact the results.

COMMANDS review

FEATURE	RIBBON TAB, GROUP	BUTTON
Circle Invalid Data	Data, Data Tools	Data Validation
Data Table	Data, Data Tools	What-If Analysis
Goal Seek	Data, Data Tools	What-If Analysis
Paste Special	Home, Clipboard	
Remove tracer arrows	Formulas, Formula Auditing	Remove Arrows
Scenario Manager	Data, Data Tools	What-If Analysis
Trace Dependents	Formulas, Formula Auditing	Trace Dependents
Trace Error	Formulas, Formula Auditing	Error Checking
Trace Precedents	Formulas, Formula Auditing	Trace Precedents
Transpose	Home, Clipboard	
Watch Window	Formulas, Formula Auditing	

CONCEPTS check

Test Your Knowledge

Completion: In the space provided at the right, indicate the correct term, command, or number.

1. This option from the Paste drop-down menu will convert columns to rows and rows to columns.

   _____

2. Open this dialog box after copying to paste only the comment text from the source cell to the destination cell.

   _____

3. Use this feature if you know the end result you want to obtain but are not sure what input value you need to achieve the end value.

   _____

4. This feature allows you to store various sets of data for specified cells under a name.

   _____

5. This report compares various saved data sets side-by-side so you can view all of the results in one page.

   _____

6. A one-variable data table requires the formula to be entered at this location within the data table range.

   _____

7. In a two-variable data table, the source formula is entered at this location within the data table range.

   _____

8. The Data Table feature is accessed from this button.

   _____

9. Click this button to draw arrows to cells that feed data into the active cell.

   _____

10. Click this button to draw arrows to cells that use the data in the active cell.

    _____

11. This button in the Formula Auditing group can be used to assist with locating the source cell that is causing an error code.

    _____

12. This error code indicates that a value needed to calculate the formula result is not available.

    _____

13. This type of error occurs when the formula is typed correctly but is not the correct mathematical operation for the data or the situation.

    _____

14. This type of error occurs when you enter a formula using incorrect punctuation such as missing a bracket or a comma.

    _____

15. Use this feature to test existing data in a worksheet that has had a new data validation rule created.

    _____

SKILLS check
Demonstrate Your Proficiency

Assessment

1 CONVERT COLUMNS TO ROWS; ADD SOURCE CELLS TO DESTINATION CELLS; FILTER

1. Open **CutRate-CarRFP.xlsx**.
2. Save the workbook with Save As and name it **ExcelL2_C5_A1**.
3. Copy and paste A4:F11 below the worksheet, converting the data arrangement so that the columns become rows and vice versa.
4. Delete the original source data rows from the worksheet.
5. Adjust the merge and centering of the title rows across the top of the worksheet, adjust column widths as desired, and change any other formatting options you think would improve the appearance of the revised worksheet.
6. Copy the values in the *Shipping* column. Paste the values to the *Total Cost* values using an Add operation so that the Total Cost now includes the shipping fee.
7. Filter the worksheet on the *Total Cost* column using a *Less Than Number Filter* and display only those bids with a total cost less than $850,000.
8. Filter the worksheet again to show only those companies offering a 60-month warranty.
9. Print the filtered worksheet in landscape orientation.
10. Clear all filters.
11. Save, print, and then close **ExcelL2_C5_A1.xlsx**.

Assessment

2 USE GOAL SEEK

1. Open **NationalCSDept-Budget.xlsx**.
2. Save the workbook with Save As and name it **ExcelL2_C5_A2**.
3. Make D9 the active cell and open the Goal Seek dialog box.
4. Find the projected percentage increase for Wages and benefits that will make the total cost of the new budget equal $630,000.
5. Accept the solution Goal Seek calculates.
6. Save, print, and then close **ExcelL2_C5_A2.xlsx**.

Assessment

3 USE SCENARIO MANAGER

1. Open **Precision-CdnTarget.xlsx**.
2. Save the workbook with Save As and name it **ExcelL2_C5_A3**.
3. Create scenarios to save various percentage data sets for the four regions using the following information:
   a. A scenario named *OriginalTarget* that stores the current percentage values in K4:K7.

b. A scenario named *LowSales* with the following rates:

East	1.00%
West	1.50%
Ontario	2.75%
Quebec	2.50%

c. A scenario named *HighSales* with the following rates:

East	3.00%
West	4.50%
Ontario	6.75%
Quebec	5.50%

4. Apply the *LowSales* scenario and then print the worksheet. ***Note: The worksheet is set to print in landscape orientation.***
5. Edit the *HighSales* scenario to change the Ontario value from 6.75% to 6.50%. ***Hint: After selecting the scenario name and clicking the Edit button, click OK at the Edit Scenario dialog box to show the scenario values.***
6. Create a scenario summary report displaying H18 as the result cell.
7. Print the Scenario Summary sheet.
8. Save and then close **ExcelL2_C5_A3.xlsx**.

Assessment

4 CREATE A TWO-VARIABLE DATA TABLE

1. Open **NationalCSDept-HlpDeskCalls.xlsx**.
2. Save the workbook with Save As and name it **ExcelL2_C5_A4**.
3. Create a two-variable data table that will calculate the average cost per call in the data table for each level of total call minutes logged and at each average cost per minute.
4. Format the average costs to display two decimal places.
5. Save, print, and then close **ExcelL2_C5_A4.xlsx**.

Assessment

5 FIND AND CORRECT FORMULA ERRORS

1. Open **NationalCSDept-CapitalBudget.xlsx**.
2. Save the workbook with Save As and name it **ExcelL2_C5_A5**.
3. Make D5 the active cell and use formula auditing tools to solve the #VALUE! error.
4. Make D19 the active cell and draw tracer arrows to find the source cell creating the #N/A error.
5. Print the worksheet.
6. The CS department manager advises the cost of a PIX firewall is $4,475.00. Enter this data in the appropriate cell to correct the #N/A error.
7. Remove the tracer arrows.
8. The worksheet contains a logic error in one of the formulas. Find and correct the error.
9. Save, print, and then close **ExcelL2_C5_A5.xlsx**.

CASE study

Apply Your Skills

Yolanda Robertson is continuing her work on the marketing information package for prospective new franchise owners. She has sent you a workbook named **PizzabyMario-StartupInvt.xlsx**. The workbook contains information on the estimated capital investment required to start up a new franchise along with estimated sales and profits for the first year. The workbook calculates the number of months in which a new franchisee can expect to recoup his or her investment based on estimated sales and profits for the first year. Yolanda wants you to apply what-if analysis to find out how much a franchise has to make in its first year of sales in order to pay back the initial investment in 12 months (instead of 14). Accept the proposed solution and use Save As to name the revised workbook **ExcelL2_C5_CS_P1**. Print the worksheet.

After reviewing the printout from Part 1, Yolanda is concerned that the revised sales figure is not attainable in the first year. Restore the sales for year 1 to the original value of $550,000. Yolanda has created three models for the startup investment worksheet.

Item	Conservative	Optimistic	Aggressive
Projected Sales	$550,000	$590,000	$615,000
Profit Percent	20%	22%	18%

Yolanda would like you to set up the worksheet to save each of these models. Create a report that shows Yolanda the input variables for each model and the impact of each on the number of months to recoup the initial investment. Save the revised workbook as **ExcelL2_C5_CS_P2**. Print the summary report in landscape orientation. Switch to the worksheet and show the model that reduces the number of months to recoup the initial investment to the lowest value. Print the worksheet. Save **ExcelL2_C5_CS_P2**.

Part 3

Yolanda would like you to check each formula in the worksheet to make sure the formulas are accurate before submitting this worksheet to the client. Since you did not create this worksheet, you decide to check if there is a feature in Excel that navigates to formula cells automatically so that you do not miss any calculated cells. Use the Help feature to find out how to select cells that contain formulas. Based on the information you learned in Help, select the cells within the worksheet that contain formulas and then review each formula cell in the Formula bar to ensure the formula is logically correct. ***Hint: When the formula cells are selected as a group, press the Enter key to move to the next formula cell without losing the selection***. When you are finished reviewing the formula cells, type the name of the feature you used in a blank cell below the worksheet. For auditing purposes print a copy of the worksheet with precedent tracer arrows displayed to show the relationships between all of the formula cells. Save the revised workbook and name it **ExcelL2_C5_CS_P3**.

Part 4

When meeting with a prospective franchise owner, Yolanda expects that the money required for the initial capital investment will present a challenge for some people that do not have an excellent credit rating. Assume that the owners of Pizza by Mario would be willing to finance the initial investment. Search the Internet for current lending rates for secured credit lines at the bank at which you have an account. In a new worksheet within the workbook, document the current loan rate that you found and the URL of the bank Web site from which you obtained the rate. Add two percentage points to the lending rate to compensate the owners for the higher risk associated with financing the startup. Create a linked cell in the new worksheet to the Total Estimated Initial Investment in Sheet1. Calculate the monthly loan payment for a term of five years. Add appropriate labels to describe the data and format the worksheet as desired to improve the worksheet appearance. Save the revised workbook and name it **ExcelL2_C5_CS_P4**. Print the loan worksheet.

Project 1 Add Workbook Properties and Share a Workbook

You will add information to a workbook's Document Information Panel in order to provide the author's name and other descriptive information to other readers and then share the workbook with other users for editing purposes.

QUICK STEPS

Add Information to Properties
1. Click Office button.
2. Point to *Prepare*.
3. Click *Properties*.
4. Type data in desired fields.
5. Close Document Information Panel.

Adding Workbook Properties Using the Document Information Panel

Workbook properties include information about the workbook such as the author's name, a title, a subject, a category to which the workbook is related (such as Finance), and general comments about the workbook. This information can be added to the file using the Document Information Panel shown in Figure 6.1.

Other information not shown in the Document Information Panel is added to file properties automatically by Microsoft Excel. For example, workbook statistics such as the date the workbook was created, the date the workbook was last modified, and the name of the last person to save the workbook are also maintained. This information can be viewed by opening the workbook's Properties dialog box shown in Figure 6.2. Workbook properties are sometimes referred to as *metadata*. Metadata is a term used to identify descriptive information about data.

Figure 6.1 Document Information Panel

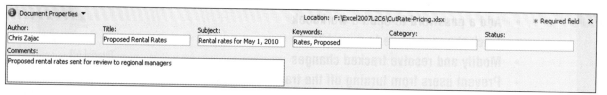

Figure 6.2 Properties Dialog Box with Statistics Tab Selected

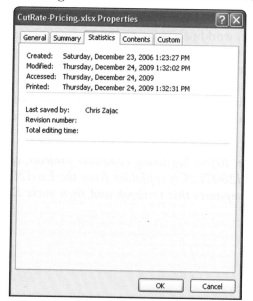

To open the Document Information Panel to add an author's name or other descriptive information about a workbook, click the Office button, point to *Prepare* and then click *Properties* at the drop-down list. By default, Excel inserts in the *Author* text box the name of the computer user (as defined when Microsoft Office is installed) when a new workbook is created. Click the Property Views and Options button in the Document Information Panel and then click *Advanced Properties* at the drop-down list to view workbook statistics in the Properties dialog box. You cannot modify workbook statistics since they are tracked by Microsoft Excel automatically. In Chapter 8, you will learn how to strip metadata including personal information from the file if you do not wish this information to be included when distributing a workbook outside your organization. Personal information can be useful, however, when you are browsing a list. The *Author, Title, Subject, Size,* and *Date Modified* appear in a ScreenTip when the mouse pointer rests on a workbook name in the Open dialog box. This information helps you select the correct file.

Project 1a Adding Information to Workbook Properties and Viewing Workbook Statistics

1. Open **CutRate-Pricing.xlsx**.
2. Save the workbook with Save As and name it **ExcelL2_C6_P1**.
3. Change the author's name associated with the workbook, add a title, add a subject, and enter keywords to associate with the workbook by completing the following steps:
   a. Click the Office button, point to *Prepare*, and then click *Properties*.
   b. Select the current entry in the *Author* text box and press Delete to remove the current author's name.
   c. Type **Chris Zajac** and press Tab.
   d. With the insertion point positioned in the *Title* text box, type **Proposed Rental Rates** and press Tab.
   e. With the insertion point positioned in the *Subject* text box, type **Rental rates for May 1, 2010** and press Tab.
   f. With the insertion point positioned in the *Keywords* text box, type **Rates, Proposed** and press Tab.
   g. Click in the *Comments* text box and then type **Proposed rental rates sent for review to regional managers**.
   h. Compare your Document Information Panel with the one shown in Figure 6.1.
4. Save **ExcelL2_C6_P1.xlsx**.
5. View workbook statistics in the Properties dialog box by completing the following steps:
   a. Click the Property Views and Options button located at the top left corner of the Document Information Panel (just above the *Author* text box).

Step 3a

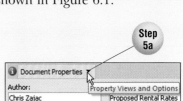

Step 5a

b. Click *Advanced Properties* at the drop-down list.

c. At the ExcelL2_C6_P1.xlsx Properties dialog box with the
   General tab selected, click the Summary tab and review the
   information in the dialog box. Notice the Summary tab
   provides similar text boxes as the Document Information
   Panel.

d. Click the Statistics tab.

e. Review the dates shown for
   Created, Modified, Accessed, and
   Printed. Note the name shown
   next to Last saved by. The name
   displayed is the name entered as
   the user name when Microsoft
   Office was installed on the
   computer you are using.

f. Click OK to close the Properties dialog box.

6. Click the Close button located at the top right corner of the Document Information Panel.

7. Close **ExcelL2_C6_P1.xlsx**.

QUICK
STEPS

Share Workbook
1. Open workbook.
2. Click Review tab.
3. Click Share Workbook button.
4. Click *Allow changes by more than one user at the same time* check box.
5. Click OK to close Share Workbook dialog box.
6. Click OK to continue.

Sharing a Workbook

A workbook may need to be circulated among several people so they can review,
add, delete, or edit data. One method that is available for collaborating with other
users is to share a workbook. A shared workbook is generally saved to a network
folder that is accessible by the other individuals that need the file. Excel tracks
each person's changes and displays a prompt when conflicts to a cell occur if two
people have the file open at the same time and make changes to the same data.

To share a workbook, click the Review tab and then click the Share Workbook
button in the Changes group. At the Share Workbook dialog box with the Editing
tab active shown in Figure 6.3, click the *Allow changes by more than one user at the
same time* check box.

Figure 6.3 Share Workbook Dialog Box with Editing Tab Selected

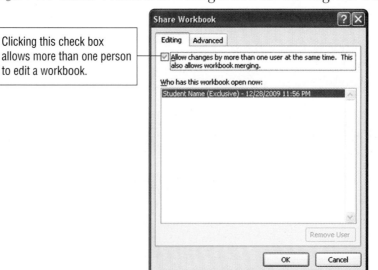

Clicking this check box allows more than one person to edit a workbook.

Click the Advanced tab in the Share Workbook dialog box to define the sharing options shown in Figure 6.4. A shared workbook should be saved to a network folder that is designated as a shared folder accessible by the other users. A network administrator is usually the person who creates a folder on a networked server designated with the read/write access rights for multiple accounts (referred to as a *network share*) and can assist you with navigating to and saving to a network share. All individuals with access to the shared network folder have full access to the shared workbook. One drawback of a shared workbook is that it cannot support all Excel features. If you need to use a feature that is unavailable or make a change to a feature that is not allowed, you will first need to remove shared access. In a later section you will learn how to lock/unlock worksheets and cells for editing if you want to protect the worksheet or sections of the worksheet from change.

QUICK STEPS

View Other Users of Shared Workbook
1. Open shared workbook.
2. Click Review tab.
3. Click Share Workbook button.
4. Review names in *Who has this workbook open now* list box.
5. Click OK.

Figure 6.4 Share Workbook Dialog Box with Advanced Tab Selected

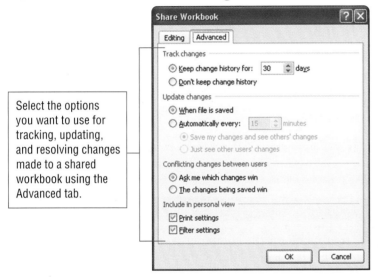

Select the options you want to use for tracking, updating, and resolving changes made to a shared workbook using the Advanced tab.

Project 1b   **Sharing a Workbook**

1. Open **ExcelL2_C6_P1.xlsx**.
2. Save the workbook with Save As and name it **ExcelL2_C6_P1-Shared**.
3. Assume that you are Chris Zajac, regional manager of CutRate Car Rentals. You want feedback on the proposed rental rates from another manager. Share the workbook so that the other manager can make changes directly within the file by completing the following steps:
   a. Click the Review tab.
   b. Click the Share Workbook button in the Changes group.
   c. At the Share Workbook dialog box with the Editing tab selected, click the *Allow changes by more than one user at the same time* check box to insert a check mark.

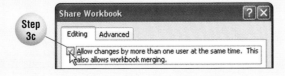

Step 3c

d. Click OK.

e. At the Microsoft Office Excel message box informing you that the workbook will now be saved and asking if you want to continue, click OK.

4. Notice that Excel adds [Shared] in the Title bar next to the workbook file name to indicate the workbook's status.

5. Close **ExcelL2_C6_P1-Shared.xlsx**.

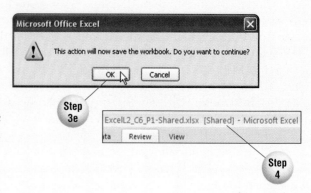

Step 3e

Step 4

Change User Name
1. Click Office button.
2. Click Excel Options button.
3. Select current entry in *User name* text box.
4. Type new user name.
5. Click OK.

Changing the User Name

When a workbook is shared, Excel tracks the name of the user who edits a shared workbook. When Microsoft Office is installed, the user name information is entered by the person completing the installation. You can change the user name associated with the copy of Excel by opening the Excel Options dialog box.

Excel Options

Project 1c Changing the User Name and Editing a Shared Workbook

1. At a blank Excel screen, change the user name for the computer you are using to simulate an environment in which another manager is opening the shared workbook from a network share location by completing the following steps:

a. Click the Office button.

b. Click the Excel Options button located near the bottom right of the drop-down list.

c. At the Excel Options dialog box with *Popular* selected in the left pane, make a note of the existing entry in the *User name* text box in the *Personalize your copy of Microsoft Office* section. **Note: You will be restoring the original user name in Project 1e. If necessary, write the user name down so you do not forget the correct entry.**

d. Select the current entry in the *User name* text box, type **Aaron Rubin** and then click OK.

Step 1d

Personalize your copy of Microsoft Office

User name: Aaron Rubin

Choose the languages you want to use with Microsoft Office: Language Settings...

OK   Cancel

2. Open **ExcelL2_C6_P1-Shared.xlsx**.
3. Assume you are Aaron Rubin and you decide to make a few changes to the proposed rental rates.
   a. Make F5 the active cell and change the entry from *15%* to **12%**.
   b. Make B10 the active cell and change the entry from *85.99* to **92.99**.
   c. Make D10 the active cell and change the entry from *299.99* to **333.99**.
4. Save **ExcelL2_C6_P1-Shared.xlsx**.

Project 1d Viewing Other Users of a Shared Workbook

1. Start a new copy of Excel by clicking the Start button, pointing to *All Programs*, pointing to *Microsoft Office*, and clicking *Microsoft Office Excel 2007*. **Note: You are opening another copy of Excel to simulate an environment in which multiple copies of the shared workbook are open. You will also change the user name to continue the simulation using a different identity.**
2. Open the Excel Options dialog box and change the *User name* in the new copy of Excel to **Chris Zajac**. Refer to Project 1c, Steps 1a–1d if you need assistance with this step.
3. Open **ExcelL2_C6_P1-Shared.xlsx**.
4. Assume you are Chris Zajac and want to see who else is working on a shared workbook. View other users working on a shared workbook by completing the following steps:
   a. Click the Review tab.
   b. Click the Share Workbook button in the Changes group.
   c. At the Share Workbook dialog box with the Editing tab selected, look at the names in the *Who has this workbook open now* list box.

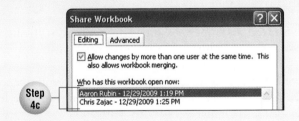

   d. Click OK.
5. Leave both copies of Excel open for the next project.

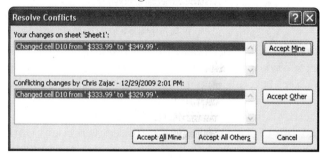

QUICK
STEPS

Resolving Conflict in Shared Workbook
1. Open shared workbook.
2. Make desired edits.
3. Click Save button.
4. Click Accept Mine or Accept Other button at each conflict.
5. Click OK.

Resolving Conflicts in a Shared Workbook

When two users have a copy of a shared workbook open and each makes a change to the same cell, Excel prompts the second user to resolve the conflict by displaying the Resolve Conflicts dialog box shown in Figure 6.5. The cell address, original entry, and revised entry are shown for each user. You can choose to click the Accept Mine button to save your revision or the Accept Other button to remove your change and restore the cell to the entry made by the other user. Click Accept All Mine or Accept All Others to avoid being prompted at each individual cell that has a conflict.

HINT

Open the Share Workbook dialog box and click the Advanced tab to instruct Excel not to display the Resolve Conflicts dialog box by selecting *The changes being saved win* in the *Conflicting changes between users* section.

Figure 6.5 Resolve Conflicts Dialog Box

Project **1e**   **Resolving Conflicts in a Shared Workbook**

1. With **ExcelL2_C6_P1-Shared.xlsx** open, assume that you are still Chris Zajac and that you decide to make a change to a proposed rental rate which will conflict with a change made by Aaron Rubin.
   a. Make sure the copy of Excel that is active is the second copy you opened for Project 1d in which you viewed the users with the shared workbook open using the identity Chris Zajac.
   b. Make D10 the active cell and change *333.99* to **329.99**.
   c. Save **ExcelL2_C6_P1-Shared.xlsx**.
2. Switch to the other copy of Excel using the Taskbar. Assume that Aaron Rubin has decided to change the weekly luxury rate again. Edit the worksheet and resolve the conflict by completing the following steps:
   a. Make D10 the active cell and change the entry to **349.99**.
   b. Click the Save button. Since this change conflicts with the change made by Chris Zajac in Step 1b, Excel prompts the second user with the Resolve Conflicts dialog box.
   c. Click the Accept Other button to restore the cell to the value entered by Chris Zajac.

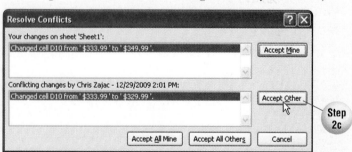

Step 2c

d. At the Microsoft Office Excel message box informing you that the workbook has been updated with changes saved by other users, click OK.

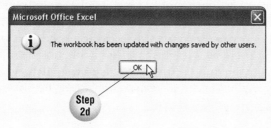

Step 2d

3. Notice that a cell in which a conflict was resolved is displayed with a colored border. Hover the mouse over the colored border in D10 to view the pop-up box with the name, date, and time the cell change was saved as well as the original and revised data entries.
4. Exit the active copy of Excel.
5. With the other copy of Excel active, close **ExcelL2_C6_P1-Shared.xlsx**.
6. Change the user name back to the name you recorded in Project 1c, Step 1c.

Removing Shared Workbook Access

Before changing the status of a shared workbook to an exclusive workbook, consider printing the change history in order to have a record of the workbook's editing actions made by all users who worked on the file. To do this, click the Review tab, click the Track Changes button, and then click *Highlight Changes* at the drop-down list. At the Highlight Changes dialog box shown in Figure 6.6, change *When* to *All*, clear the *Who* and *Where* check boxes, click the *List changes on a new sheet* check box and then click OK. By default, Excel displays a colored border in changed cells. When you hover the mouse pointer over a cell with a colored border, Excel displays in a pop-up box the cell's change history. Clear the *Highlight changes on screen* check box if you prefer not to highlight changed cells in the worksheet.

QUICK STEPS

Print History Sheet
1. Open shared workbook.
2. Click Review tab.
3. Click Track Changes button.
4. Click *Highlight Changes*.
5. Change *When* to *All*.
6. If necessary, clear *Who* check box.
7. If necessary, clear *Where* check box.
8. If desired, clear *Highlight changes on screen* check box.
9. Click *List changes on a new sheet* check box.
10. Click OK.
11. Print History sheet.

Figure 6.6 Highlight Changes Dialog Box

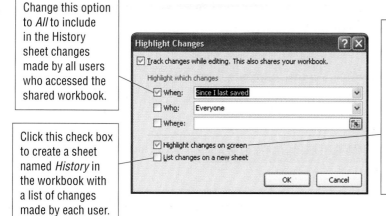

Change this option to *All* to include in the History sheet changes made by all users who accessed the shared workbook.

Click this check box to create a sheet named *History* in the workbook with a list of changes made by each user.

By default, this option is selected, which causes a colored border to display in changed cells. Hovering the mouse pointer over a highlighted cell causes a pop-up box to display with the change history.

HINT

Before changing a shared workbook's status to exclusive, make sure no one else is currently editing the workbook since once you remove shared access users with the file open will not be able to save their changes.

Stop Sharing Workbook
1. Open shared workbook.
2. Click Review tab.
3. Click Share Workbook button.
4. Clear *Allow changes by more than one user at the same time* check box.
5. Click OK.
6. Click Yes.
7. Close workbook.

To prevent multiple users from accessing a workbook that was defined as a shared workbook, open the shared workbook, click the Review tab, and then click the Share Workbook button. At the Share Workbook dialog box with the Editing tab selected, clear the check box for *Allow changes by more than one user at the same time*. When you click OK, Excel displays a message box informing you that changing the workbook to exclusive status will erase all of the change history in the workbook and prevent users who might have the workbook open from saving their changes. Consider copying and pasting the cells in the History sheet to a new workbook and saving the history as a separate file since the History sheet is removed when the shared workbook is saved.

Project 1f   Printing the History Sheet and Removing Shared Access to a Workbook

1. Open **ExcelL2_C6_P1-Shared.xlsx**.
2. Create a new sheet named *History* and print the record of changes made to the shared workbook by completing the following steps:
   a. If necessary, click the Review tab.
   b. Click the Track Changes button in the Changes group and then click *Highlight Changes* at the drop-down list.
   c. At the Highlight Changes dialog box, click the down-pointing arrow at the right of the *When* list box and then click *All* at the drop-down list.
   d. If necessary, clear the *Who* check box if a check mark is displayed in the box.
   e. If necessary, clear the *Where* check box if a check mark is displayed in the box.
   f. Clear the *Highlight changes on screen* check box to clear the check mark.
   g. Click the *List changes on a new sheet* check box to insert a check mark and then click OK.
   h. Print the History sheet.
3. Stop sharing the workbook by completing the following steps:
   a. Click the Share Workbook button.
   b. Click the *Allow changes by more than one user at the same time* check box to clear the check mark.

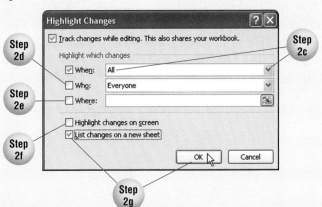

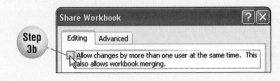

c. Click OK.

d. At the Microsoft Office Excel message box informing you that the workbook will be removed from shared use, click Yes to make the workbook exclusive.

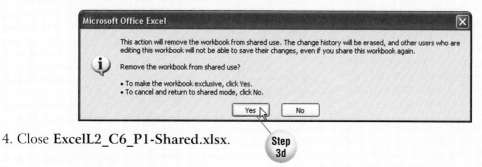

4. Close **ExcelL2_C6_P1-Shared.xlsx**.

Step 3d

roject ② **Lock and Unlock a Workbook, a Worksheet, and Ranges**

Project ② **Lock and Unlock a Workbook, a Worksheet, and Ranges**

You will protect worksheets, unlock ranges, grant permissions to ranges that can be edited, prevent changes to the structure of a workbook, and add a password to open a workbook.

Protecting Worksheets

Protecting a worksheet prevents another user from editing cells that you do not want accidentally deleted, modified, or otherwise changed. By default, when a worksheet is protected, each cell in the sheet is locked. This means no one can insert, delete, or modify the content. In most cases, some cells within the worksheet contain data that you want to allow another user to be able to change; therefore, in a collaborative environment, protecting the worksheet generally involves two actions:

1. Clear the lock attribute on those cells that will be allowed to be edited.
2. Protect the worksheet.

To unlock the cells that will be allowed to be modified, select the cells, click the Home tab, and then click the Format button in the Cells group. Click *Lock Cell* in the *Protection* section at the drop-down list to turn off the lock attribute. Next, turn on worksheet protection by clicking the Review tab and then clicking the Protect Sheet button in the Changes group. At the Protect Sheet dialog box shown in Figure 6.7, select the actions you want to allow and then click OK. You can also choose to assign a password to unprotect the sheet. Be cautious if you add a password to remove protection since you will not be able to unprotect the worksheet if you forget the password.

QUICK STEPS

Protect Worksheet
1. Open workbook.
2. Activate desired sheet.
3. Click Review tab.
4. Click Protect Sheet button.
5. Type password to unprotect sheet.
6. Choose allowable actions.
7. Click OK.
8. Retype password.
9. Click OK.

Unlock Cells
1. Open workbook.
2. Select cell(s).
3. Click Home tab.
4. Click Format button.
5. Click *Lock Cell*.
6. Deselect cell(s).

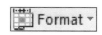

Protect Sheet

Figure 6.7 Protect Sheet Dialog Box

You can choose to add a password that will need to be entered in order to unprotect the worksheet.

Select the actions that users of the protected worksheet can do in this list box.

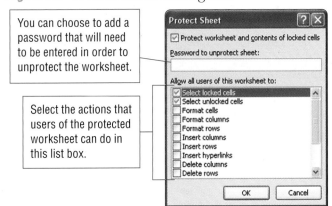

Project 2a Protecting an Entire Worksheet

1. Open **CutRate-FinalRates.xlsx**.
2. Save the workbook with Save As and name it **ExcelL2_C6_P2**.
3. Protect the entire FinalRates worksheet by completing the following steps:
   a. Make sure FinalRates is the active sheet.
   b. Click the Review tab.
   c. Click the Protect Sheet button in the Changes group.
   d. At the Protect Sheet dialog box with the insertion point positioned in the *Password to unprotect sheet* text box, type **f4R$c** and then click OK.
   e. At the Confirm Password dialog box with the insertion point positioned in the *Reenter password to proceed* text box, type **f4R$c** and then press Enter or click OK.
   f. Make any cell active in the FinalRates sheet and attempt to delete the data or type new data. Since the entire worksheet is now protected, all cells are locked and Excel displays a message that the cell is read-only. Click OK at the Microsoft Office Excel message indicating that you need to unprotect the sheet to modify the protected cell.

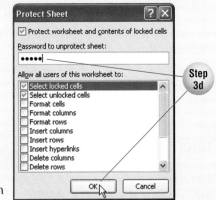

Step 3d

Step 3e

Step 3f

4. Notice the Protect Sheet button changes to the Unprotect Sheet button when a worksheet has been protected.
5. Save **ExcelL2_C6_P2.xlsx**.

1. With **ExcelL2_C6_P2.xlsx** open, make TargetRevenue the active sheet.
2. Unlock the weekday target rental data cells that you want to allow to be edited by completing the following steps:
   a. Select C5:C10.
   b. Click the Home tab.
   c. Click the Format button in the Cells group.
   d. At the Format drop-down list, look at the icon next to *Lock Cell* in the *Protection* section. The highlighted icon indicates the lock attribute is turned on.

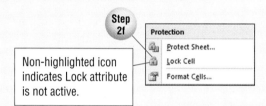

   Step 2d

   Highlighted icon indicates Lock attribute is active.

   e. Click *Lock Cell* at the Format drop-down list to turn the lock attribute off for the selected range.
   f. Click any cell within the range C5:C10 and click the Format button in the Cells group. Look at the icon next to *Lock Cell* in the drop-down list. The icon is no longer highlighted, indicating the cell is unlocked.

   Step 2f

   Non-highlighted icon indicates Lock attribute is not active.

   g. Click within the worksheet area outside the drop-down list to close the menu.
3. Unlock the remaining target rental ranges to allow the cells to be edited by completing the following steps:
   a. Select F5:F10, hold down the Ctrl key, and select I5:I10 and L5:L10.
   b. Click the Format button in the Cells group and then click *Lock Cell* at the drop-down list.
   c. Click any cell to deselect the ranges.
4. Protect the TargetRevenue worksheet by completing the following steps:
   a. Click the Review tab.
   b. Click the Protect Sheet button.
   c. Type **f4R$c** in the *Password to unprotect sheet* text box.
   d. Click OK.
   e. Type **f4R$c** in the *Reenter password to proceed* text box and press Enter or click OK.
5. Save **ExcelL2_C6_P2.xlsx**.
6. Test the worksheet protection applied to the TargetRevenue sheet by completing the following steps:
   a. Make B8 the active cell and press the Delete key.
   b. Click OK at the Microsoft Office Excel message box indicating the protected cell is read-only.
   c. Make C8 the active cell and press the Delete key. Since C8 is unlocked, the contents of C8 are deleted and dependent cells are updated.
   d. Click the Undo button on the Quick Access toolbar to restore the contents of C8.
7. Save and then close **ExcelL2_C6_P2.xlsx**.

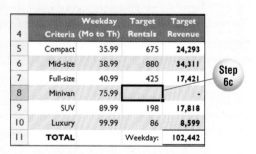

	Criteria (Mo to Th)	Weekday Rentals	Target Rentals	Target Revenue
4				
5	Compact	35.99	675	24,293
6	Mid-size	38.99	880	34,311
7	Full-size	40.99	425	17,421
8	Minivan	75.99		-
9	SUV	89.99	198	17,818
10	Luxury	99.99	86	8,599
11	**TOTAL**		Weekday:	102,442

Step 6c

Unprotecting a Worksheet

When a worksheet has protection turned on, the Protect Sheet button in the Changes group of the Review tab changes to the Unprotect Sheet button. To remove worksheet protection, click the Unprotect Sheet button. If a password was entered when the worksheet was protected, the Unprotect Sheet dialog box shown in Figure 6.8 appears. Type the password and press Enter or click OK.

Figure 6.8 Unprotect Sheet Dialog Box

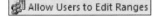

Assigning Permissions to Specific Users to Edit Ranges

In a workgroup environment where the computer system you are using is part of a Windows domain (a group of connected resources such as computers and printers defined by a name), you can grant permissions to specific individuals (who are also connected to the domain) to make changes to an identified range within the worksheet. Individuals specified in the Permissions dialog box can edit the range without a password while other users who open the workbook are prompted for a password if they try to change the identified range.

Select the range for which you want to assign individual permissions, click the Review tab, and then click the Allow Users to Edit Ranges button in the Changes group. At the Allow Users to Edit Ranges dialog box (see Figure 6.11), click the New button to define a new range. This opens the New Range dialog box shown in Figure 6.9. If you want to use this feature, set up the permissions for users before protecting the worksheet since this feature becomes unavailable when worksheet protection is turned on.

Figure 6.9 New Range Dialog Box

Type title to identify range for which permissions are being created.

Range that was selected before opening dialog box is automatically entered. If neccessary, use the Collapse Dialog button and select the range in the worksheet area.

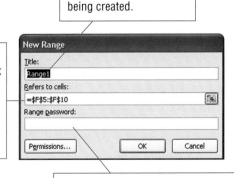

Type password to edit range for those users not on the same domain that you want to give access to. You will need to give each user the password to edit the range.

Type a title to identify the restricted range in the *Title* text box. The range that you selected before opening the dialog box will automatically appear in the *Refers to cells* text box. Type a password to unlock the range for people not connected to the same domain that you want to grant access to and then click OK. You will need to confirm the password a second time. At the Allow Users to Edit Ranges dialog box (see Figure 6.11), the new range is added to the list. Click the Permissions button to opens the Permissions for [Range Name] dialog box, where [Range Name] is the title assigned to the range, in which you assign access rights to the individual persons connected to the domain.

Figure 6.10 Permissions for [Range Name] Dialog Box

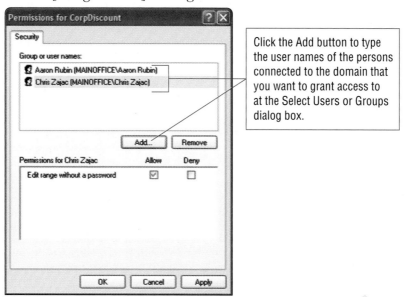

Click the Add button to type the user names of the persons connected to the domain that you want to grant access to at the Select Users or Groups dialog box.

Click the Add button at the Permissions dialog box shown in Figure 6.10 and then type the user names of the individuals separated by semicolons in the Select Users or Groups dialog box. For example *Aaron Rubin; Chris Zajac*. Click OK until you are returned to the Allow Users to Edit Ranges dialog box shown in Figure 6.11 that you started from. Click the Protect Sheet button and then follow the steps you learned to protect the worksheet. When finished, save the workbook.

Figure 6.11 Allow Users to Edit Ranges Dialog Box

Ranges that have been defined appear here.

Click Permissions to add names of persons connected to the domain that can edit the range without the password.

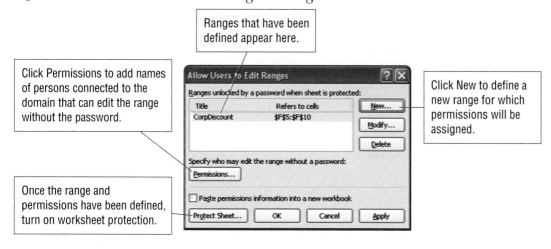

Click New to define a new range for which permissions will be assigned.

Once the range and permissions have been defined, turn on worksheet protection.

Note: Check with your instructor before completing this project. At Step 4c, you will need the names of two user names on the same domain. If necessary, complete this project skipping Step 4 if you cannot add user names to the Permissions dialog box.

1. Open **CutRate-Pricing.xlsx**.
2. Save the workbook with Save As and name it **ExcelL2_C6_P2-Permissions**.
3. Assume that you want to grant permissions to specific users to edit the corporate discount rates. Define the range of cells containing the corporate discount rates as a new range that can be edited by specific users only by completing the following steps:
   a. Select F5:F10.
   b. If necessary, click the Review tab.
   c. Click the Allow Users to Edit Ranges button in the Changes group.
   d. At the Allow Users to Edit Ranges dialog box, click the New button.
   e. With *Range1* selected in the *Title* text box, type **CorpDiscount**.
   f. Click in the *Range password* text box, type **cR$nx**, and then press Enter or click OK.

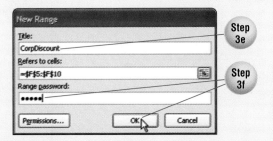

g. At the Confirm Password dialog box, type **cR$nx** in the *Reenter password to proceed* text box and then press Enter or click OK.
4. *Note: Skip this step if you do not have the names of two users on the same domain.*
   Add the individual users for which permissions to edit the *CorpDiscount* range will be granted by completing the following steps:
   a. At the Allow Users to Edit Ranges dialog box, with *CorpDiscount* selected in the ranges list box, click the Permissions button.
   b. Click the Add button at the Permissions for CorpDiscount dialog box.
   c. With the insertion point positioned in the *Enter the object names to select* text box at the Select Users or Groups dialog box, type the two user names provided by your instructor separated by a semicolon and one space; for example, **Aaron Rubin; Chris Zajac**.
      Note: Do not use your own user name for the domain.
   d. Click OK.

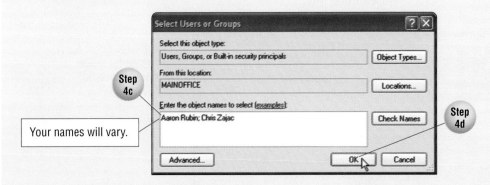

e. Click OK at the Permissions for CorpDiscount dialog box.

5. Protect the worksheet by completing the following steps:

a. At the Allow Users to Edit Ranges dialog box, click the Protect Sheet button.

b. At the Protect Sheet dialog box, with the insertion point positioned in the *Password to unprotect sheet* text box, type f4R$c and press Enter or click OK.

c. Type f4R$c and press Enter or click OK at the Confirm Password dialog box.

6. Deselect the range, save, and then close **ExcelL2_C6_P2-Permissions.xlsx**.

7. Test the range protection by completing the following steps:

a. Open **ExcelL2_C6_P2-Permissions.xlsx**.

b. Make F5 the active cell.

c. Press the Delete key.

d. Since you are not in the list of users that were granted permissions to the range, you are prompted for the password at the Unlock Range dialog box. With the insertion point positioned in the *Enter the password to change this cell* text box, type cR$nx and press Enter or click OK.

e. The cell entry is deleted. Type 10% and press Enter.

8. Save and then close **ExcelL2_C6_P2-Permissions.xlsx**.

Step 5a

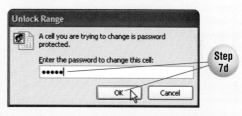

Step 7d

Protecting the Structure of a Workbook

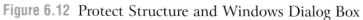

The Protect Workbook button in the Changes group of the Review tab can be used to prevent changes to the structure of a workbook such as inserting a new sheet, deleting a sheet, or unhiding a hidden worksheet. At the Protect Structure and Windows dialog box shown in Figure 6.12 you can also turn on protection for the workbook's windows. Clicking the *Windows* check box prevents a user of the workbook from resizing or changing the position of the windows in the workbook.

As with protecting worksheets, an optional password can be entered that will be required to unprotect the workbook in the future.

QUICK STEPS

Protect Workbook Structure
1. Open workbook.
2. Click Review tab.
3. Click Protect Workbook button.
4. Type optional password if desired.
5. Click OK.
6. Retype optional password if entered at Step 4.
7. Click OK.

Protect Workbook

Figure 6.12 Protect Structure and Windows Dialog Box

1. Open **ExcelL2_C6_P2.xlsx**.
2. Protect the workbook structure by completing the following steps:
   a. If necessary, click the Review tab.
   b. Click the Protect Workbook button in the Changes group.
   c. At the Protect Structure and Windows dialog box with the insertion point positioned in the *Password (optional)* text box, type **w4R!c** and press Enter or click OK.
   d. At the Confirm Password dialog box with the insertion point positioned in the *Reenter password to proceed* text box, type **w4R!c** and press Enter or click OK.
3. Test the workbook protection by attempting to insert a new worksheet by completing the following steps:
   a. Right-click the TargetRevenue sheet tab.
   b. Look at the shortcut menu. Notice that all of the options related to managing worksheets are dimmed, meaning the options are unavailable.
   c. Click within the worksheet area outside the pop-up list to close the menu.
4. Save and then close **ExcelL2_C6_P2.xlsx**.

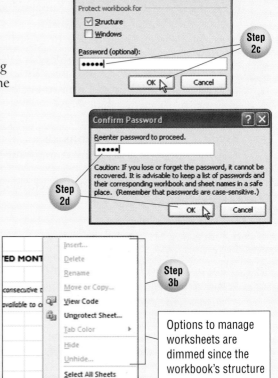

Step 2c

Step 2d

Step 3b

Step 3a

Options to manage worksheets are dimmed since the workbook's structure is protected.

Unprotecting a Workbook

When the structure of a workbook has been protected, the Protect Workbook button in the Changes group of the Review tab changes to the Unprotect Workbook button. To remove workbook protection, click the Unprotect Workbook button. If a password was entered when the workbook was protected, the Unprotect Workbook dialog box shown in Figure 6.13 appears. Type the password and press Enter or click OK.

Figure 6.13 Unprotect Workbook Dialog Box

Adding a Password to a Workbook

QUICK STEPS

You can prevent unauthorized access to Excel data by requiring a password to open the workbook and/or a password to modify the data in the workbook. Passwords to open the workbook are encrypted while passwords to modify the workbook are not encrypted. To add a password to a workbook, open the Save As dialog box and click the Tools button located near the bottom left corner of the dialog box. Click General Options at the Tools menu to open the General Options dialog box shown in Figure 6.14.

Type a password in the *Password to open* text box and/or a password in the *Password to modify* text box. If you plan to use both password options, create a different password for each option. Click the *Read-only recommended* check box if you want the ability to prompt users who open the file to open the workbook as read-only. This prompt can help prevent accidental changes; however, the prompt is a recommendation only and does not prevent the user from opening the workbook normally. After clicking OK you will need to confirm each password.

When you create passwords, a guideline to follow is to include a combination of four character elements: uppercase letters, lowercase letters, symbols, and numbers. Passwords constructed according to this model are considered secure and more difficult to crack. Note also that if you or another user forget your password, you will be unable to open the workbook. If necessary, write down the password and store the written copy in a safe location.

Add Workbook Password
1. Open workbook.
2. Click Office button.
3. Click *Save As*.
4. Click Tools button.
5. Click *General Options*.
6. Type password.
7. Press Enter or click OK.
8. Type password.
9. Press Enter or click OK.
10. Click Save.
11. Click Yes to replace existing file.

Figure 6.14 General Options Dialog Box

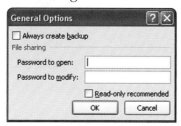

Project 2e **Adding a Password to Open a Workbook**

1. Open **ExcelL2_C6_P2.xlsx**.
2. Add a password to open the workbook by completing the following steps:
   a. Click the Office button.
   b. Click *Save As* at the drop-down list.
   c. At the Save As dialog box, click the Tools button located near the bottom left corner of the dialog box.
   d. Click *General Options* at the pop-up menu.

e. Type **p4E#c** at the General Options dialog box with the insertion point positioned in the *Password to open* text box.

f. Press Enter or click OK.

g. Type **p4E#c** at the Confirm Password dialog box with the insertion point positioned in the *Reenter password to proceed* text box and then press Enter or click OK.

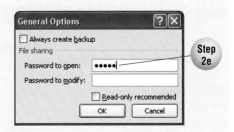

Step
2e

Step
2g

h. Click the Save button to save the workbook using the same name.

i. Click Yes to replace the existing file.

3. Close **ExcelL2_C6_P2.xlsx**.

4. Test the password security on the workbook by completing the following steps:

a. Open **ExcelL2_C6_P2.xlsx**.

b. At the Password dialog box with the insertion point positioned in the *Password* text box, type a password that is incorrect for the file and press Enter.

c. At the Microsoft Office Excel message box indicating that the password you supplied is not correct, click OK.

d. Open **ExcelL2_C6_P2.xlsx**.

e. Type **p4E#c** in the *Password* text box and then press Enter or click OK.

Step
4e

5. Close **ExcelL2_C6_P2.xlsx**.

Removing a Workbook Password

To remove a password from a workbook, open the workbook using your password to open or modify the workbook. Open the Save As dialog box and, using the Tools menu, open the General Options dialog box. Select and delete the password in the *Password to open* and/or *Password to modify* text boxes and click OK. Save the file using the same name by clicking Yes to replace the existing file.

roject ③ **Track and Resolve Changes Made to a Workbook**

You will begin tracking changes made to a workbook, view changes made by two users, and accept and reject changes.

Tracking Changes to a Workbook

As you learned in Project 1, by default Excel tracks changes made to the workbook by each user when you share a workbook. As you saw with the History sheet in Project 1f, you can display and print a record of the changes. If a workbook is not shared, you can turn on the Track Changes feature and Excel will automatically share the workbook. To do this, click the Track Changes button in the Changes group of the Review tab and click *Highlight Changes* at the drop-down list. At the Highlight Changes dialog box, click the *Track changes while editing* check box and click OK.

As the owner of a shared workbook you might need to view the worksheet with all cells highlighted that have had changes made to the data. Figure 6.15 displays the worksheet you will edit in Project 3 with all changes highlighted. As you hover the mouse pointer over a highlighted cell, a pop-up box displays the name of the person who changed the cell along with the date, time, original entry, and revised entry.

Track Changes
1. Open workbook.
2. Click Review tab.
3. Click Track Changes button.
4. Click *Highlight Changes.*
5. Click *Track changes while editing* check box.
6. Click OK twice.

Highlight Changes
1. Open tracked workbook.
2. Click Review tab.
3. Click Track Changes button.
4. Click *Highlight Changes.*
5. Change *When* to *Not yet reviewed.*
6. Make sure *Who* is *Everyone.*
7. Click OK.

Track Changes ▾

Figure 6.15 Project 3 Worksheet with Changes Highlighted

	A	B	C	D	E	F	G	H	I	J	K	L	M
1						CutRate Car Rentals							
2						Estimated Monthly Revenue							
3						West Region							
4	Effective Date: 1-May-10												
5	Criteria	Weekday (Mo to Th)	Target Rentals	Target Revenue	Weekend	Target Rentals	Target Revenue	Weekly (*Min 5 days)	Target Rentals	Target Revenue	Monthly (*Min 21 days)	Target Rentals	Target Revenue
6	Compact	35.99	375	Sam Forwell, 12/30/2009 9:42 AM: Changed cell C6 from ' $362.00 ' to ' $375.00 '.			,958	175.99	52	9,151	675.99	10	6,760
7	Mid-size	38.99	285				,480	185.99	25	4,650	692.99	10	6,930
8	Full-size	40.99	175				,949	215.99	30	6,480	775.99	8	6,208
9	Minivan	75.99	155	11,778	130.99	68	8,907	251.99	28	7,056	866.99	8	6,936
10	SUV	89.99	135	12,149	139.99	42	5,880	249.99	28	7,000	885.99	10	8,860
11	Luxury	99.99	55	5,499	155.99	30	4,680	329.99	10	3,300	999.99	5	5,000
12	TOTAL		Weekday:	61,208		Weekend:	46,854		Weekly:	37,636		Monthly:	40,693

Changed cells in a shared workbook can be displayed with a colored border to identify which cells were revised. Each person's changes are identified with a different color.

Accepting and Rejecting Tracked Changes

Accept and Reject Changes
1. Open tracked workbook.
2. Click Review tab.
3. Click Track Changes button.
4. Click *Accept/Reject Changes*.
5. Make sure *When* is *Not yet reviewed*.
6. Make sure *Who* is *Everyone*.
7. Click OK.
8. Click Accept or Reject button at each change.

As well as displaying the worksheet with the changes highlighted, you can elect to navigate to each change and accept or reject the revision. To do this, click the Track Changes button in the Changes group of the Review tab and then click *Accept/Reject Changes* at the drop-down list. At the Select Changes to Accept or Reject dialog box shown in Figure 6.16, define which changes you want to review and then click OK.

Excel navigates to the first cell changed and displays the Accept or Reject Changes dialog box shown in Figure 6.17. Review the information in the dialog box and click either the Accept or Reject button. If you reject a change, the cell is restored to its original value. As you respond to each changed cell, the colored border is removed since the cell has been reviewed. The dialog box includes an Accept All button and a Reject All button to do a global review if desired. Be cautious with accepting and rejecting changes since Undo is not available after you review the cells.

Figure 6.16 Select Changes to Accept or Reject Dialog Box

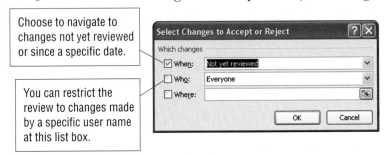

Choose to navigate to changes not yet reviewed or since a specific date.

You can restrict the review to changes made by a specific user name at this list box.

Figure 6.17 Accept or Reject Changes Dialog Box

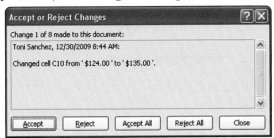

Project 3a Tracking Changes Made to a Workbook

1. Open **CutRate-WestRegion.xlsx**.
2. Save the workbook with Save As and name it **ExcelL2_C6_P3**.
3. Begin tracking changes made to the workbook by completing the following steps:
   a. If necessary, click the Review tab.
   b. Click the Track Changes button in the Changes group.
   c. Click *Highlight Changes* at the drop-down list.
   d. At the Highlight Changes dialog box, click the *Track changes while editing* check box. Notice that turning on the Track Changes feature automatically shares the workbook.

   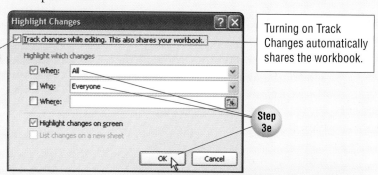

   Turning on Track Changes automatically shares the workbook.

   e. With *When* set to *All* and *Who* set to *Everyone* by default, click OK.
   f. At the Microsoft Office Excel message box indicating that this action will now save the workbook, click OK to continue.

   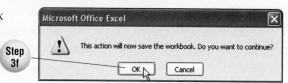

4. Close **ExcelL2_C6_P3.xlsx**.

Project 3b Editing a Tracked Workbook

1. Assume that you are Toni Sanchez, the SUV rental manager for the west region at CutRate Car Rentals. You have been asked to edit the target rental values for SUVs. At a blank Excel window, change the user name to **Toni Sanchez**. If necessary, refer to Project 1c, Step 1 if you need assistance with changing the user name. *Note: Make sure you make a note of the original user name, which you will restore in Project 3c.*
2. Open **ExcelL2_C6_P3.xlsx**.
3. Edit the SUV target data as follows:

C10 from	*124*	to	135
F10 from	*22*	to	42
I10 from	*22*	to	28
L10 from	*8*	to	10

4. Save and then close **ExcelL2_C6_P3.xlsx**.
5. Assume that you are Sam Forwell, the compact rental manager for the west region at CutRate Car Rentals. You have been asked to edit the target rental values for compact cars. At a blank Excel window, change the user name to **Sam Forwell**.
6. Open **ExcelL2_C6_P3.xlsx**.
7. Edit the compact target data as follows:

C6 from	*362*	to	375
F6 from	*165*	to	160
I6 from	*33*	to	52
L6 from	*15*	to	10

8. Save and then close **ExcelL2_C6_P3.xlsx**.

1. Assume that you are the west region operations manager. You decide to review the changes made by Toni Sanchez and Sam Forwell. At a blank Excel window, change the user name back to the original user name for the computer that you are using.
2. Open **ExcelL2_C6_P3.xlsx**.
3. Highlight cells with changes made by all users that have not yet been reviewed by completing the following steps:
   a. Click the Track Changes button in the Changes group of the Review tab.
   b. Click *Highlight Changes* at the drop-down list.
   c. At the Highlight Changes dialog box, click the down-pointing arrow at the right of the *When* list box and then click *Not yet reviewed* at the drop-down list.
   d. With *Who* set to *Everyone* by default, click OK.

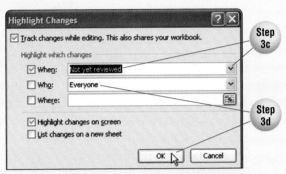

4. Accept and reject changes as you navigate the worksheet by completing the following steps:
   a. Press Ctrl + Home to move the active cell to A1.
   b. Click the Track Changes button and then click *Accept/Reject Changes* at the drop-down list.
   c. At the Select Changes to Accept or Reject dialog box, with *When* set to *Not yet reviewed*, and *Who* set to *Everyone* by default, click OK.

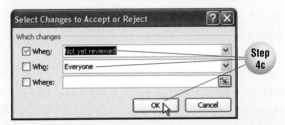

   d. Excel moves the active cell to C10 where the first change was made and displays the Accept or Reject Changes dialog box. Click the Accept button to leave C10 at 135.
   e. Excel moves the active cell to F10. Click the Reject button to restore F10 to the original value of 22. *Note: If necessary, drag the Accept or Reject dialog box out of the way to see the cell being reviewed in the worksheet area.*

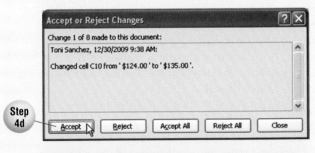

   f. Respond to the remaining changes as follows:

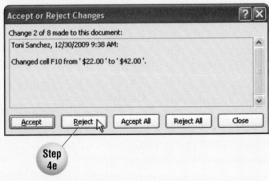

      Accept   I10
      Accept   L10
      Reject   C6
      Accept   F6
      Reject   I6
      Accept   L6
5. Print the worksheet scaled to fit one page in width and one page in height.
6. Save and then close **ExcelL2_C6_P3.xlsx**.

Stopping the Tracking of Changes in a Workbook

When you no longer need to track the changes made to a workbook, click the Track Changes button and click *Highlight Changes* at the drop-down list. At the Highlight Changes dialog box, clear the *Track changes while editing* check box and click OK. Excel displays the warning message that the workbook will no longer be shared and the change history will be erased. Click Yes to complete the action.

If you have not reviewed all changes made to the workbook, consider printing a copy of the History sheet before turning off the track changes feature. Refer to Project 1f, Step 2 for assistance with printing a history sheet.

roject ④ **Protect a Shared Workbook**

You will share a workbook and prevent the shared users from turning off the Track Changes feature or removing the shared workbook status.

Protecting and Sharing a Workbook

You can prevent the Track Changes feature from being removed by any of the users in a shared workbook using the Protect and Share feature. At the same time you can add an optional password that prevents unauthorized users from removing the protected sharing feature unless he or she has the correct password.

Click the Protect and Share Workbook button in the Changes group of the Review tab to restrict the Track Changes feature. At the Protect Shared Workbook dialog box shown in Figure 6.18 click the *Sharing with track changes* check box. Add a password to remove protected sharing of the workbook if desired and then click OK. If a password was entered, you will need to type the password again to confirm the first entry.

Figure 6.18 Protect Shared Workbook Dialog Box

1. Open **CutRate-WestRegion.xlsx**.
2. Save the workbook with Save As and name it **ExcelL2_C6_P4**.
3. Prevent users from stopping the Track Changes feature and add a password to remove the protected sharing of the workbook by completing the following steps:
   a. If necessary, click the Review tab.
   b. Click the Protect and Share Workbook button in the Changes group.
   c. At the Protect Shared Workbook dialog box, click the *Sharing with track changes* check box.
   d. Click in the *Password (optional)* text box and type p4E#c.
   e. Click OK.
   f. Type p4E#c in the *Reenter password to proceed* text box at the Confirm Password dialog box and press Enter or click OK.
   g. Click OK at the message that the workbook will be saved.

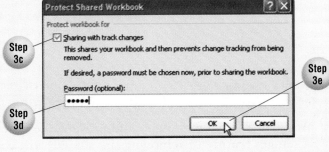

4. Close **ExcelL2_C6_P4.xlsx**.
5. Test the security features of the Protect and Share Workbook feature by completing the following steps:
   a. Open **ExcelL2_C6_P4.xlsx**.
   b. Click the Track Changes button and then click *Highlight Changes* at the drop-down list.
   c. Look at the *Track changes while editing* check box. Notice the option is not available.

   > The Track Changes feature cannot be turned off.

   d. Click OK.
   e. Click OK at the message that no changes were found with the specified properties.
   f. Click the Unprotect Shared Workbook button in the Changes group of the Review tab.
   g. At the Unprotect Sharing dialog box with the insertion point positioned in the *Password* text box, type unprotect and press Enter or click OK.
   h. Click OK at the message box indicating that the password supplied is not correct.

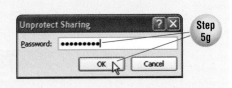

6. Close **ExcelL2_C6_P4.xlsx**.

Excel provides several methods to share and collaborate with other users of data in Excel. The method that you choose depends on factors such as the availability of a network share folder, the need to protect ranges or otherwise restrict access to sensitive data, and the resources available by the users who will receive the data. In Chapter 8 you will explore other features that are important to consider when you will be distributing a workbook which restrict access, certify a workbook's content, and remove personal information.

CHAPTER summary

- Workbook properties include descriptive information about the workbook such as the author's name, title, subject, keywords, or comments.
- Workbook properties are sometimes referred to as *metadata*.
- Open the Document Information Panel to add information to a workbook's properties.
- Open the Properties dialog box to view more detailed statistics about the workbook.
- Sharing a workbook generally involves turning on the sharing feature and saving the workbook to a folder on a networked server that is accessible to the other users who need the file.
- Use the Share Workbook button in the Changes group of the Review tab to turn on the sharing feature.
- When Microsoft Office is installed, a user name is defined for the computer upon which the software has been copied. Excel automatically inserts this name in the *Author* workbook property as a new workbook is created.
- You can change the user name at the Excel Options dialog box.
- View other users who have a shared workbook open at the Share Workbook dialog box.
- When a workbook is shared, Excel automatically tracks the changes made by each person who accesses the file.
- If two users have a shared workbook open at the same time and each person makes a change to the same cell, a Resolve Conflicts dialog box appears when the second user saves the workbook.
- At the Resolve Conflicts dialog box, the second user can choose to accept the change made by him or her or restore the cell to the entry made by the last person to save the file.
- Print a History sheet that provides a detailed record of all changes made to a shared workbook before removing shared access to the workbook.
- When a shared workbook is changed to an exclusive workbook, all change history is removed from the file.
- An entire worksheet can be protected to prevent another person from accidentally inserting, deleting, or changing data that you do not want modified.
- Protect a worksheet using the Protect Sheet button in the Changes group of the Review tab.
- You can add a password that is required to unprotect a worksheet.
- Each cell in a worksheet has a lock attribute which activates when the worksheet is protected.
- To allow individual cells in a protected worksheet to be editable, select the cell(s) and turn off the lock attribute before protecting the worksheet.
- In a workgroup environment, you can grant permission to specific users in the same domain to edit ranges in a worksheet. These users will be able to edit the range without knowing a password. Other users not on the same domain can edit the range by typing the password.

- Assign permissions to users in the same domain using the Allow Users to Edit Ranges button in the Changes group of the Review tab.
- Define a new range first before assigning permissions.
- After the range is defined and the permissions added, protect the worksheet.
- The Protect Workbook button in the Changes group of the Review tab is used to protect a workbook from a user inserting, deleting, renaming, or otherwise managing worksheets in the workbook.
- You can prevent unauthorized access to an Excel workbook by adding a password to open and/or modify the workbook.
- Passwords to open the workbook are encrypted while a password to modify the workbook is not.
- Add a workbook password at the Save As dialog box by clicking the Tools button and then *General Options*.
- Turn on or off the Track Changes feature or display changes in a shared workbook by opening the Highlight Changes dialog box.
- The Accept/Reject Changes feature is used to navigate to each changed cell in a worksheet and accept or reject the revision.
- Prevent the Track Changes feature from being turned off using the Protect and Share Workbook button in the Changes group of the Review tab. An optional password can also be set up that is required to remove protected sharing of the workbook.

COMMANDS review

FEATURE	RIBBON TAB, GROUP	BUTTON	OFFICE BUTTON DROP-DOWN LIST
Accept/Reject Changes	Review, Changes	Track Changes ▾	
Add password to a workbook			Save As
Allow users to edit ranges	Review, Changes	Allow Users to Edit Ranges	
Change user name		Excel Options	Excel Options
Document Information Panel			Prepare, Properties
Highlight Changes	Review, Changes	Track Changes ▾	
Protect and Share Workbook	Review, Changes	Protect and Share Workbook	
Protect Workbook	Review, Changes		
Protect Worksheet	Review, Changes		
Share Workbook	Review, Changes		
Track Changes	Review, Changes	Track Changes ▾	
Unlock cells	Home, Cells	Format ▾	

CONCEPTS check

Test Your Knowledge

Completion: In the space provided at the right, indicate the correct term, command, or number.

1. Open this panel to add descriptive information about a workbook such as a title or subject heading.

   _____

2. Open this dialog box to turn on the feature that allows changes by more than one user at the same time.

   _____

3. Change the user name for the computer that you are using by opening this dialog box.

   _____

4. When two users have the same workbook open at the same time and each makes a change to the same cell, this dialog box appears when the second person saves the workbook.

   _____

5. Open this dialog box to create a History sheet that includes a record of all changes made to a shared workbook.

   _____

6. Add a password that is required to unprotect a worksheet at this dialog box.

   _____

7. Select a cell that you want to allow changes to and then click this button and menu option to unlock the cell before protecting the worksheet.

   _____

8. Click this button if you want to add permissions to specific users on the same domain to edit ranges in a protected worksheet.

   _____

9. Prevent users from inserting or deleting worksheets in a workbook by opening this dialog box.

   _____

10. The General Options dialog box can be opened from this button at the Save As dialog box.

    _____

11. Turn this feature on and Excel automatically changes the workbook to a shared workbook if it is not already shared.

    _____

12. Excel applies this formatting to cells in a shared workbook that have been modified in order to make the revised cells stand out.

    _____

13. Turn on this feature to navigate to each changed cell in a shared workbook and decide whether to leave the change or restore the cell back to its previous value.

    _____

14. This feature is not available to restore cells to their previous values after you have finished reviewing tracked changes. _____

15. Open this dialog box to share a workbook and prevent users from turning off the feature that automatically records changes. _____

SKILLS check
Demonstrate Your Proficiency

Assessment

1 ENTER AND DISPLAY WORKBOOK PROPERTIES

1. Open **NationalCSDept-Off07Licenses.xlsx**.
2. Save the workbook with Save As and name it **ExcelL2_C6_A1**.
3. Open the Document Information Panel and enter the following data:

Author	Student Name (substitute your name for *Student Name*.)
Title	Chargeback for MSO 2007 Licenses
Subject	Journal entry by department for software licenses
Keywords	Office 2007, License, Costs
Category	Journal entry supporting document
Status	Posted
Comments	Audit worksheet for Office 2007 site license with internal chargebacks

4. Press the PrintScreen key to copy the screen image to the Clipboard.
5. Close the Document Information Panel.
6. Save and close **ExcelL2_C6_A1.xlsx**.
7. Open a blank Microsoft Word document and paste the screen image to the document.
8. Save the Microsoft Word document and name it **ExcelL2_C6_A1**.
9. Print **ExcelL2_C6_A1.docx** and then exit Word.

Assessment

2   SHARE A WORKBOOK; EDIT A SHARED WORKBOOK; PRINT A HISTORY SHEET

1. Open **Precision-MfgTargets.xlsx**.
2. Save the workbook with Save As and name it **ExcelL2_C6_A2**.
3. Share the workbook.
4. Change the user name to **Lorne Moir** and then edit the following cells:

C11	from	*4,352*	to	5520
C18	from	*15,241*	to	15960

5. Save the workbook.
6. Change the user name to **Gerri Gonzales** and then edit the following cells:

F4	from	*3,845*	to	5126
F9	from	*7,745*	to	9320

7. Save the workbook.
8. Create a History sheet with a record of the changes made to the data by all users.
9. Print the History sheet.
10. Save and then close **ExcelL2_C6_A2.xlsx**.
11. Change the user name back to the original user name for the computer you are using.

Assessment

3   REMOVE SHARED ACCESS

1. Open **ExcelL2_C6_A2.xlsx**.
2. Save the workbook with Save As and name it **ExcelL2_C6_A3**.
3. Remove the shared access to the workbook.
4. Close **ExcelL2_C6_A3.xlsx**.

Assessment

4   PROTECT AN ENTIRE WORKSHEET; ADD A PASSWORD TO A WORKBOOK

1. Open **ExcelL2_C6_A1.xlsx**.
2. Save the workbook with Save As and name it **ExcelL2_C6_A4**.
3. Protect the entire worksheet using the password L$07j to unprotect.
4. Add the password J07$e to open the workbook.
5. Close **ExcelL2_C6_A4.xlsx**.
6. Open **ExcelL2_C6_A4.xlsx** and test the password to open the workbook.
7. Unprotect the worksheet to test the password to unprotect.
8. Close **ExcelL2_C6_A4.xlsx** without saving changes.

5   UNLOCK CELLS AND PROTECT A WORKSHEET; PROTECT WORKBOOK STRUCTURE

1. Open **Precision-MfgTargets.xlsx**.
2. Save the workbook with Save As and name it **ExcelL2_C6_A5**.
3. Select the range C4:F21 and unlock the cells.
4. Deselect the range and then protect the worksheet using the password **Mt12#** to unprotect.
5. Rename Sheet1 to **2012MfgTargets**.
6. Delete Sheet2 and Sheet3.
7. Protect the workbook structure to prevent users from inserting, deleting, or renaming sheets using the password **Mt12!shts** to unprotect.
8. Save and then close **ExcelL2_C6_A5.xlsx**.

6   PROTECT AND SHARE A WORKBOOK; ACCEPT/REJECT CHANGES

1. Open **ExcelL2_C6_A5.xlsx**.
2. Save the workbook with Save As and name it **ExcelL2_C6_A6**.
3. Protect and share the workbook to prevent users from removing the Track Changes feature using the password **Mt12!shre** to remove protected sharing.
4. Change the user name to **Grant Antone** and then edit the following cells:

D4	from	*3,251*	to	3650
D17	from	*5,748*	to	6080

5. Save, change the user name to **Jean Kocsis**, and then edit the following cells:

E6	from	*6,145*	to	5840
E11	from	*2,214*	to	4175

6. Save and then change the user name back to the original user name for the computer you are using.
7. Highlight all changes made by everyone in the worksheet.
8. Accept and Reject changes as follows:

Accept	D4
Reject	D17
Reject	E6
Accept	E11

9. Create and print a History sheet of the changes made to the worksheet with the printout scaled to fit one page.
10. Print the 2012MfgTargets worksheet.
11. Save and then close **ExcelL2_C6_A6.xlsx**.

CASE study
Apply Your Skills

Part 1

Yolanda Robertson of NuTrends Market Research is working with Nicola Carlucci of Pizza by Mario on a workbook with projected franchise startups for 2012. The workbook is currently in draft format in a file named **PizzabyMario-TargetFranchises.xlsx**. Open the workbook and use Save As to name the workbook **ExcelL2_C6_CS_P1**. Add an appropriate title and subject to the workbook's properties and include comment text to explain that the draft workbook was created in consultation with Nicola Carlucci. Yolanda has asked for your assistance with protecting the workbook to prevent accidental data modifications or erasure when the workbook is shared with others. Yolanda and Nicola have agreed that the city, state, and store numbers should remain fixed. When sharing the workbook, the month a new store is planned to open and the names of prospective franchisees could change. Share the workbook making sure that no one who uses the shared workbook can turn off the Track Changes feature. Yolanda and Nicola have agreed on the following passwords:

- Password to unprotect the worksheet is **U12@s**.
- Password to open the workbook is **SbM@12**.
- Password to remove sharing of the workbook is **Ushr12@s**.

Part 2

Use Save As to name the workbook **ExcelL2_C6_CS_P2**. Yolanda has reviewed her research files and meeting notes and has the following changes to make to the data. Make sure the user name is correct so that the following changes are associated with Yolanda:

Store 124	Franchisee is Jae-Dong Han
Store 135	Franchisee is Leslie Posno

Save the workbook. Nicola is in charge of logistics planning and has two changes to make to the months that stores are scheduled to open. Make sure the user name is correct so that the following changes are associated with Nicola:

Store 125	Open in February
Store 141	Open in December

Save the workbook and then display the worksheet with all of the changes made by Yolanda and Nicola highlighted. Create a History sheet. Print the worksheet with the cells highlighted and also print the History sheet scaled to fit one page. Restore the worksheet to exclusive use. Close **ExcelL2_C6_CS_P2.xlsx**. Change the user name back to the original user name for the computer you are using.

Yolanda will be sending the shared workbook from Part 1 to Leonard Scriver, a colleague at the Michigan office of NuTrends Market Research. Yolanda wants Leonard to review the data and add his recommendations; however, Yolanda would prefer that Leonard save his copy using a different name so that the original shared version is not disrupted. Open **ExcelL2_C6_CS_P1.xlsx**. Use Save As to name the workbook **PizzabyMario-TargetFranchises-LScriver**. Based on Leonard's experience with franchise startups, he has the following recommendations. Make sure the user name is correct so that the following changes are associated with Leonard:

Store 136   Open in April
Store 138   Open in August
Store 140   Open in September
Store 141   Change the franchisee to Corporate-owned

Save the revised workbook and then change the user name back to the original user name for the computer that you are using. Close **PizzabyMario-TargetFranchises-LScriver.xlsx**. Research in Help how to use the Compare and Merge Workbooks command to merge copies of a shared workbook. Open **ExcelL2_C6_CS_P1.xlsx**. Use Save As to name the workbook **ExcelL2_C6_CS_P3**. Using the information you learned in Help, merge the changes made by Leonard in **PizzabyMario-TargetFranchises-LScriver.xlsx** into **ExcelL2_C6_CS_P3.xlsx**. Save, print, and then close **ExcelL2_C6_CS_P3.xlsx**. Remove the Compare and Merge Workbooks button from the Quick Access Toolbar.

Mario Carlucci has commented that the password to open the workbook is not intuitive for him and he has had trouble remembering the password. He wants to change the workbook password to something more user-friendly such as *Target12*. Yolanda and Nicola chose the passwords they have used in the workbook carefully based on their understanding of strong passwords that are more difficult to crack by unauthorized users. Yolanda has asked you to assist with a training package for Mario that will educate him on strong passwords. Research on the Internet the guidelines for creating strong passwords. Based on what you have learned from your research create a document in Microsoft Word that highlights the components of a strong password. Include a table of dos and don'ts for creating strong passwords in a user-friendly easy-to-understand format for Mario. Finally, create a minimum of three examples that show a weak password improved by a stronger password. Include a suggestion for how to use the phrasing technique to create strong passwords so that they are easier to remember. Save the document and name it **ExcelL2_C6_CS_P4**. Print and then close **ExcelL2_C6_CS_P4.docx**.

Automating Repetitive Tasks and Customizing Excel

PERFORMANCE OBJECTIVES

Upon successful completion of Chapter 7, you will be able to:

- Record and run a macro
- Save a workbook containing macros as a macro-enabled workbook
- Create a macro that is run using a shortcut key combination
- Change the macro security settings
- Edit and delete a macro
- Save a macro to the Personal Macro Workbook for use in all workbooks
- Create and delete a custom fill series
- Pin and unpin a frequently used file to the Recent Documents list
- Add and remove buttons for frequently used commands to the Quick Access toolbar
- Hide the ribbon to increase space in the work area
- Customize the work area to hide gridlines and column and row headers
- Create a custom workbook theme
- Create and use a template

excel Chapter 7

Tutorial 7.1
Creating Macros and
    Customizing Toolbars
Tutorial 7.2
Using Templates and
    Workspaces

Automating and customizing the Excel environment can increase your efficiency and allow you to change the environment to accommodate your preferences. Create a macro when you find yourself repeating the same task frequently to save time and ensure consistency. Customize the Excel environment by adding a button for a frequently used command to the Quick Access toolbar to provide single-click access to the feature. Other ways to customize can involve tasks such as pinning frequently used files to the Recent Documents list or creating a custom fill series, template, or theme. In this chapter you will explore ways to make Excel more adaptable to your work requirements.

Note: Before beginning computer projects, copy to your storage medium the Excel2007L2C7 subfolder from the Excel2007L2 folder on the CD that accompanies this textbook and then make Excel2007L2C7 the active folder.

Project ① Create Macros

You will create, edit, run, and delete macros to automate tasks including assigning a macro to a shortcut key and storing a macro in the Personal Macro Workbook.

QUICK STEPS

Record Macro
1. Click View tab.
2. Click down-pointing arrow on Macros button.
3. Click *Record Macro*.
4. Type macro name.
5. Click in *Description* text box.
6. Type description text.
7. Click OK.
8. Perform desired actions.
9. Click Stop Recording button.

Creating a Macro

A macro is a series of instructions stored in sequence that can be recalled and carried out whenever the need arises. Macros are generally created when a task that is never varied is repeated frequently. Saving the instructions in the macro not only saves time but ensures that the steps are consistently reapplied which can avoid errors in data entry, formatting, or other worksheet options.

To create a macro, you begin by turning on the macro recorder. A macro is identified by assigning a unique name to the steps that will be saved. Macro names must begin with a letter and can be a combination of letters, numbers, and underscore characters. A macro name cannot include spaces—use the underscore character if you want to separate words in a macro name. At the Record Macro dialog box shown in Figure 7.1, you also choose the location in which to save the macro. By default, Excel saves the macro within the current workbook meaning that once the workbook is closed, the macro is not available to other workbooks. In a later section you will learn how to save macros to the Personal Macro Workbook, which makes the macros available to all new workbooks.

Figure 7.1 Record Macro Dialog Box

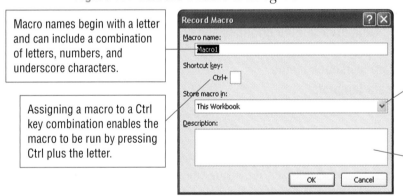

Macro names begin with a letter and can include a combination of letters, numbers, and underscore characters.

Assigning a macro to a Ctrl key combination enables the macro to be run by pressing Ctrl plus the letter.

Store a macro in the current workbook or in the personal macro workbook.

Including a description of the macro's purpose, the name of the person who created the macro, and the date recorded is useful for others who might need to run or edit the macro.

Macros can be assigned to a Ctrl shortcut key combination, which allows the macro to be run more quickly by pressing Ctrl plus the chosen lowercase or uppercase letter. Entering a description of the macro's purpose provides information to other users who might use or edit the macro. In a macro workbook that will be shared, also consider entering the creator's name and date into the description box for reference purposes. Before you begin recording, determine if the active cell location at the time the macro is run will be a factor. During recording, you can position the active cell using a shortcut key or Go To command. Do not be concerned if you make a typing mistake or have to cancel a dialog box while recording—correct your mistakes as you go since only the end result is saved. Click OK when you are finished identifying the macro and the recorder begins saving the text and/or steps that you perform. Once you have completed the tasks you want saved, click the Stop Recording button in the Status bar to end recording.

HINT

While creating the macro, mouse clicks to select tabs within the ribbon are not saved.

Stop Recording Macro

Saving Workbooks Containing Macros

If a workbook contains a macro, save it using the new macro-enabled file format in Excel 2007. The default XML-based file format (.xlsx) cannot store VBA macro code (VBA stands for Visual Basic for Applications). When a macro is created in Excel, the commands are written and saved in Microsoft Visual Basic. The macro recorder that you use in Project 1a converts your actions to Visual Basic statements for you behind the scenes. You can view and edit the Visual Basic code, or you can create macros from scratch by using the Visual Basic Editor in Microsoft Visual Basic. In Project 1e you will look at the Visual Basic statements created when the Acctg_Documentation macro was recorded and edit an instruction.

To save a workbook as a macro-enabled workbook, do one of the following actions:

- *New workbook.* Click the Save button on the Quick Access toolbar. Type the file name and change *Save as type* to *Excel Macro-Enabled Workbook (*.xlsm).* Click the Save button.

- *Existing workbook.* Click Office button, point to *Save As*, and then click *Excel Macro-Enabled Workbook.* Type the file name and then click the Save button.

QUICK STEPS

Save Macro-Enabled Workbook
1. Click Office button.
2. Click *Save As.*
3. Type file name.
4. Click *Save as type* list arrow.
5. Click *Excel Macro-Enabled Workbook (*.xlsm).*
6. Click Save.

Project 1a **Creating a Macro and Saving a Workbook as a Macro-Enabled Workbook**

1. Assume that you work in the Accounting department at a large company. The company has a documentation standard for all Excel workbooks that requires each worksheet to show the department name, the author's name, the date the workbook was created and a revision history. You decide to create a macro that will insert row labels for this data to standardize the documentation.
2. At a new blank workbook, create the documentation macro by completing the following steps:
   a. Make C4 the active cell and then click the View tab. You are making a cell other than A1 the active cell because within the macro you want to move the active cell to the top left cell in the worksheet.
   b. Click the down-pointing arrow on the Macros button in the Macros group.
   c. Click *Record Macro* at the drop-down list.

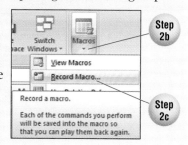

Step 2b

Step 2c

d. At the Record Macro dialog box with the insertion point positioned in the *Macro name* text box, type **Acctg_Documentation**.

e. Click in the *Description* text box and then type **Accounting department documentation macro. Created by [Student Name] on [Date].** where your name is substituted for [Student Name] and the current date is substituted for [Date].

f. Click OK. The macro recorder is now turned on as indicated by the Stop Recording button in the Status bar (displays as a blue square next to *Ready*).

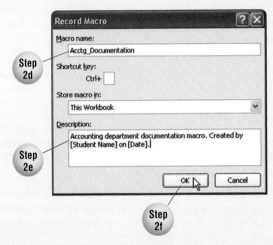

g. Press Ctrl + Home to move the active cell to A1. Including this command in the macro ensures that the documentation will always begin at A1 in all workbooks.

h. Type **Accounting department** and press Enter.

i. With the active cell in A2, type **Author** and press Enter.

j. With the active cell in A3, type **Date created** and press Enter.

k. With the active cell in A4, type **Revision history** and then press Enter three times to leave two blank rows before the worksheet will begin.

l. Click the Stop Recording button located near the left side of the Status bar next to *Ready*.

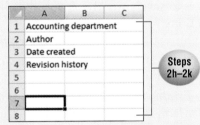

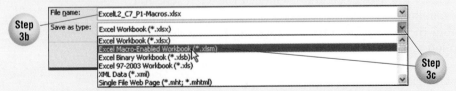

3. Save the workbook as a macro-enabled workbook by completing the following steps:

a. Click the Save button on the Quick Access toolbar.

b. Type **ExcelL2_C7_P1-Macros** in the *File name* text box.

c. Click the down-pointing arrow next to the *Save as type* text box and then click *Excel Macro-Enabled Workbook (*.xlsm)* at the drop-down list.

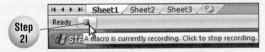

d. Click the Save button.

Running a Macro

QUICK
STEPS

Run Macro
1. Click View tab.
2. Click Macros button.
3. Double-click macro name.

Running a macro is also sometimes referred to as playing a macro. Since a macro is a series of recorded tasks, running the macro involves instructing Excel to *play back* the recorded tasks. To do this, view a list of macros by clicking the Macros button in the Macros group of the View tab. This opens the Macro dialog box shown in Figure 7.2. Click the macro name you want to run and then click the Run button, or double-click the macro in the *Macro name* list box.

Figure 7.2 Macro Dialog Box

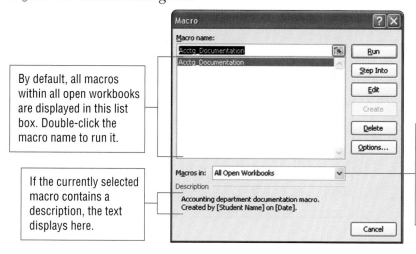

By default, all macros within all open workbooks are displayed in this list box. Double-click the macro name to run it.

If the currently selected macro contains a description, the text displays here.

Change the list of macros you want to view using this list arrow. You can view macros contained in all open workbooks, the current workbook only, or select a specific open workbook name.

Project 1b   Running a Macro

1. With **ExcelL2_C7_P1-Macros.xlsm** open, run the Acctg_Documentation macro to test that the macro works correctly by completing the following steps:
   a. Select A1:A4 and press the Delete key to erase the cell contents.
   b. You want to test the Ctrl + Home command in the macro by making sure A1 is not active when the macro begins. Click any cell within the worksheet area other than A1 to deselect the range.
   c. Click the Macros button in the Macros group of the View tab. Do not click the down-pointing arrow on the button.
   d. At the Macro dialog box with *Acctg_Documentation* already selected in the *Macro name* list box, click the Run button.

Step 1c

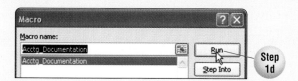

Step 1d

2. Save and then close **ExcelL2_C7_P1-Macros.xlsm**.

Assigning a Macro to a Shortcut Key

Assign Macro to Shortcut Key
1. Click View tab.
2. Click down-pointing arrow on Macros button.
3. Click *Record Macro*.
4. Type macro name.
5. Click in *Shortcut key* text box.
6. Type desired letter.
7. Click in *Description* text box.
8. Type description text.
9. Click OK.
10. Perform desired actions.
11. Click Stop Recording button.

Launch Dialog Box

Record New Macro

When you record a macro you have the option of assigning the macro to a Ctrl key combination. A macro that is assigned to a shortcut key can be run without displaying the Macro dialog box. You can choose any lowercase letter or uppercase letter for the macro. Excel distinguishes the case of the letter you choose when you type the letter at the *Shortcut key* text box at the Record Macro dialog box. For example, if you type an uppercase P, Excel defines the shortcut key as *Ctrl + Shift + P* as shown in Figure 7.3.

Figure 7.3 Record Macro Dialog Box with Shortcut Key Assigned

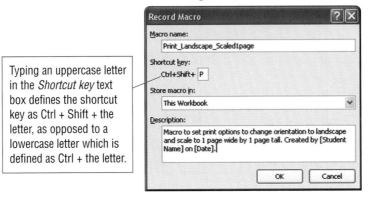

Typing an uppercase letter in the *Shortcut key* text box defines the shortcut key as Ctrl + Shift + the letter, as opposed to a lowercase letter which is defined as Ctrl + the letter.

If an Excel feature is assigned to the key combination that you choose, your macro will override Excel's shortcut. For example, pressing Ctrl + p in Excel causes the Print dialog box to appear. If you create a macro and assign the macro to Ctrl + p, your macro's instructions are invoked instead of the Print dialog box. You can view a list of Excel-assigned keyboard shortcuts in Help by typing **keyboard shortcuts** in the Search text box of the Excel Help window. Select *Excel shortcut and function keys* in the Results list.

Project 1C **Creating and Running a Macro Using a Shortcut Key**

1. Open **ExcelL2_C7_P1-Macros.xlsm**.
2. The default security setting for any workbook that is opened containing a macro is *Disable all macros with notification*. This causes a security warning to appear in the message bar (between the ribbon and the work area) notifying you that macros have been disabled. Enable the macros in the workbook by completing the following steps:
   a. Click the Options button in the message bar.

Step 2a

b. At the Microsoft Office Security Options dialog box, click *Enable this content* and then click OK.

Step
2b

3. Create a macro assigned to a keyboard shortcut that changes print options for a worksheet by completing the following steps:
   a. Once a macro has been recorded and stopped in an Excel session, the Stop Recording button in the Status bar changes to the Record New Macro button. Click the Record New Macro button located at the left side of the Status bar next to *Ready*. If you exited Excel before starting this project, start a new macro by clicking the View tab, clicking the down-pointing arrow on the Macros button, and then clicking *Record Macro*.
   b. Type Print_Landscape_Scaled1page in the *Macro name* text box.
   c. Click in the *Shortcut key* text box, hold down the Shift key, and press the letter p.
   d. Click in the *Description* text box and then type Macro to set print options to change orientation to landscape and scale to 1 page wide by 1 page tall. Created by [Student Name] on [Date]. Substitute your name for [Student Name] and the current date for [Date].
   e. Click OK.

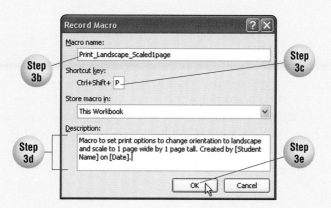

Step
3b

Step
3c

Step
3d

Step
3e

   f. Click the Page Layout tab.
   g. Click the Page Setup Dialog Box launcher located at the bottom right of the Page Setup group.

h. At the Page Setup dialog box with the Page tab selected, click *Landscape* in the *Orientation* section.

i. Click *Fit to* in the *Scaling* section to scale the printout to 1 page wide by 1 page tall.

j. Click OK.

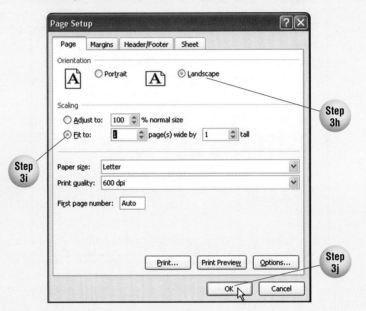

k. Click the Stop Recording button.

4. Click the New button on the Quick Access toolbar, or press Ctrl + N to start a new blank workbook.

5. Press Ctrl + Shift + p to run the Print_Landscape_Scaled1page macro.

6. Type your name in A1, press Enter, and then press Ctrl + F2 to display the worksheet in Print Preview. Notice the page orientation is landscape. Click the Page Setup button in the Print group of the Print Preview tab. Notice the orientation and scaling options set by the macro. Click OK to close the Page Setup dialog box and then click the Close Print Preview button.

7. Close the new workbook without saving changes.

8. Save **ExcelL2_C7_P1-Macros.xlsm**.

Changing Macro Security Settings

QUICK STEPS

Change Macro Security Setting
1. Click Office button.
2. Click Excel Options.
3. Click *Trust Center* in left pane.
4. Click Trust Center Settings button.
5. Click *Macro Settings* in left pane.
6. Click desired setting.
7. Click OK twice.

In Excel 2007, the Trust Center initially controls workbooks containing macros. Before a workbook can have the macros enabled, the Trust Center checks for a valid and current digital signature signed by an entity that is stored in the Trusted Publishers list. The Trusted Publishers list is maintained by you on the computer you are using. A trusted publisher is added to the list when you enable content from an authenticated source and click the option to *Trust all content from this publisher*. Depending on the active macro security setting, if the Trust Center cannot match the digital signature information with an entity in the Trusted Publishers list or the macro does not contain a digital signature, the security warning displays in the message bar. Changing the macro security setting in Excel does not affect the macro security setting in other Microsoft programs such as Word or PowerPoint.

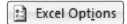

Although most macros you work with will only contain a series of stored keystrokes or mouse clicks such as those you created in Project 1a and Project 1c, in recent years Excel workbooks have become the target for distributing malware. For this reason, the recommended setting of *Disable all macros with notification* should be used to ensure you do not unknowingly allow macros to run that will infect your computer with a virus. In Project 1c, you enabled the macro because you knew the content was from a trusted source (yourself). Table 7.1 describes the four options for macro security. In some cases, you may decide to change the default macro security setting by opening the Trust Center dialog box. You will explore the Trust Center in Project 1d.

HINT

Macros are often circulated within workbooks sent by e-mail. If you receive a workbook as an e-mail attachment, always scan the workbook for viruses using up-to-date virus definitions before opening.

Table 7.1 Macro Security Settings for Workbooks Not Opened from a Trusted Location

Macro Setting	Description
Disable all macros without notification	All macros are disabled; security alerts will not appear.
Disable all macros with notification	All macros are disabled; security alert appears with the option to enable content if you trust the source of the file. This is the default setting.
Disable all macros except digitally signed macros	A macro that does not contain a digital signature is disabled; security alerts do not appear.
	If the macro is digitally signed by a publisher in your Trusted Publishers list, the macro is allowed to run.
	If the macro is digitally signed by a publisher not in your Trusted Publishers list, you receive a security alert.
Enable all macros (not recommended, potentially dangerous code can run)	All macros are allowed; security alerts do not appear.

Project ⑩ Viewing Macro Security Settings

1. With **ExcelL2_C7_P1-Macros.xlsm** open, explore the current settings in the Trust Center by completing the following steps:
   a. Click the Office button.
   b. Click the Excel Options button located near the bottom right of the drop-down list.
   c. Click *Trust Center* in the left pane of the Excel Options dialog box.
   d. Click the Trust Center Settings button in the *Microsoft Office Excel Trust Center* section.

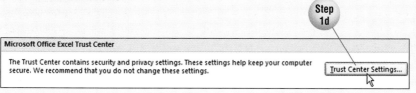

e. At the Trust Center dialog box, click *Macro Settings* in the left pane.

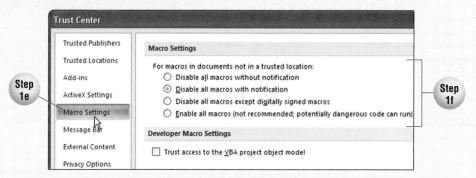

f. Review the options under the section titled *For macros in documents not in a trusted location*. Note which option is active on the computer you are using. The default option is *Disable all macros with notification*. **Note: The security setting on the computer you are using may be different than the default option. Do not change the security setting without the permission of your instructor.**

g. Click *Trusted Publishers* in the left pane. If any publishers have been added to the list on the computer you are using, the names of the entities will be shown in the list box. If the list box is empty, no trusted publishers have been added.

h. Click *Trusted Locations* in the left pane. Review the path and description of folders added to the trusted locations list. By default, Excel adds folders created upon installation of Microsoft Office Excel that contain files provided by Microsoft to the list. Additional folders may also appear that have been added by a system administrator or network administrator.

i. Click OK to close the Trust Center dialog box.

2. Click OK to close the Excel Options dialog box.

QUICK STEPS

Edit Macro
1. Open workbook containing macro.
2. Click View tab.
3. Click Macros button.
4. Click desired macro name.
5. Click Edit button.
6. Make desired changes in Visual Basic code window.
7. Click Save button.
8. Click File.
9. Click *Close and Return to Microsoft Excel.*

Editing a Macro

The actions that you performed while recording the macro are stored in Visual Basic program code. Each macro is saved as a separate module within a VBAProject for the workbook. A module can be described as a receptacle for the instructions. Each macro is contained within a separate module within the workbook. Figure 7.4 displays the Visual Basic macro code for the macro created in Project 1a.

Edit a macro if you need to make a change that is easy to decipher within the Visual Basic statements. If you need to make several changes to a macro or do not feel comfortable with the Visual Basic code window, you can re-record the macro. Excel prompts you to replace an existing macro if you record a new macro with the same name as an existing macro.

Figure 7.4 Microsoft Visual Basic Code Window for Project 1a Acctg_Documentation Macro

Text that appears in green and preceded with an apostrophe is a comment. Comments are explanatory text that are ignored when the macro is run.

The macro's actions are in this section. Each action is a separate line.

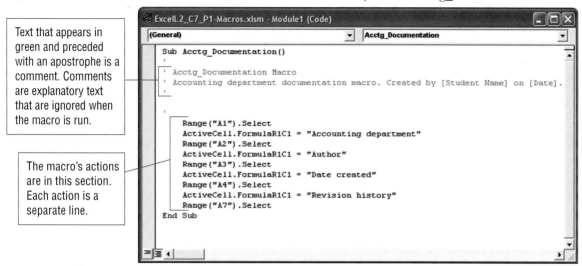

```
ExcelL2_C7_P1-Macros.xlsm - Module1 (Code)

(General)                                    Acctg_Documentation

    Sub Acctg_Documentation()
    '
    ' Acctg_Documentation Macro
    ' Accounting department documentation macro. Created by [Student Name] on [Date].
    '

    '
        Range("A1").Select
        ActiveCell.FormulaR1C1 = "Accounting department"
        Range("A2").Select
        ActiveCell.FormulaR1C1 = "Author"
        Range("A3").Select
        ActiveCell.FormulaR1C1 = "Date created"
        Range("A4").Select
        ActiveCell.FormulaR1C1 = "Revision history"
        Range("A7").Select
    End Sub
```

Project **1e** Editing a Macro

1. With **ExcelL2_C7_P1-Macros.xlsm** open, edit the Acctg_Documentation macro to leave only one blank row after the last entry by completing the following steps:
   a. If necessary, click the View tab.
   b. Click the Macros button in the Macros group.
   c. At the Macro dialog box with *Acctg_Documentation* already selected in the *Macro name* list box, click the Edit button. A Microsoft Visual Basic window opens with the program code displayed for ExcelL2_C7_P1-Macros.xlsm Module 1 (Code).

Step 1c

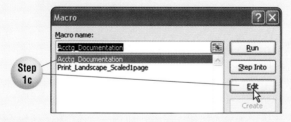

```
Macro                                          ? X

Macro name:
Acctg_Documentation                                    Run

Acctg_Documentation
Print_Landscape_Scaled1page                            Step Into

                                                       Edit

                                                       Create
```

   d. Read the statements between the blue *Sub* and *End Sub* statements. *Sub* indicates the beginning of a procedure and *End Sub* indicates the end of the procedure. A procedure is a set of Visual Basic statements that perform actions. The name of the procedure is placed after the opening *Sub* statement and is the macro name. The lines beginning with a single apostrophe (') are comments. Comments are used in programming to insert explanatory text that describes the logic or purpose of a statement. Statements that begin with the apostrophe character are ignored when the macro is run. The commands that are executed when the macro is run are the indented lines of text below the comment lines.
   e. Position the insertion point at the beginning of the last statement before *End Sub* that reads *Range("A7").Select* and click the left mouse button. This is the last action in the macro that makes A7 the active cell. Notice the entry two lines above reads *Range("A4").Select*. To edit the macro and leave only one blank row you need to change the address from *A7* to *A6*.

f. Use the Right Arrow key to move the insertion point, delete 7, and type 6 so that the edited line reads *Range("A6").Select*.

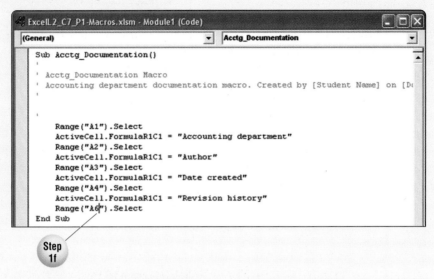

Step
1f

g. Click the Save button on the toolbar.
2. Click File and then click *Close and Return to Microsoft Excel*.

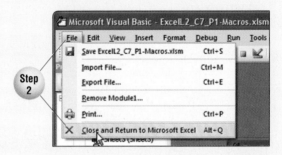

Step
2

3. Test the edited macro to make sure only one blank row is left before the active cell by completing the following steps:
   a. Select A1:A4 and press the Delete key.
   b. Make any cell other than A1 the active cell.
   c. Click the Macros button in the Macros group of the View tab. Do not click the down-pointing arrow on the button.
   d. At the Macro dialog box, double-click *Acctg_Documentation* in the *Macro name* list box.
4. Save and close **ExcelL2_C7_P1-Macros.xlsm**.

Saving a Macro to the Personal Macro Workbook

By default, macros are stored within the workbook that is active when the macro is recorded. When you close the workbook, the macros within the file are no longer available. If you create macros that you want to use in other workbooks, one solution is to leave the workbook containing the macros open since the Macro dialog box, by default, displays macros in the *Macro name* list box from all open workbooks. Another solution is to store macros that you want to make available for other workbooks in the Personal Macro Workbook file. To do this, change *Store macro in* to *Personal Macro Workbook* at the Record Macro dialog box.

The Personal Macro Workbook is created by Excel automatically the first time you record a new macro to it and is named Personal.xlsb. The file extension .xlsb is a Microsoft Office Excel binary worksheet. Once created, the workbook is opened each time you start Excel; however, you do not see the workbook because Excel hides the file. If necessary, you can unhide the workbook to edit, rename, or delete a macro saved in it.

If you want to copy a Personal Macro Workbook to another computer you will need to locate the file on the hard drive. The workbook PERSONAL.XLSB is saved in the path [d:]\Documents and Settings*user name*\Application Data\Microsoft\Excel\XLSTART. You will need to display hidden files to locate the workbook since Application Data is a hidden folder.

QUICK STEPS

Save Macro in Personal Macro Workbook
1. Click View tab.
2. Click down-pointing arrow on Macros button.
3. Click *Record Macro*.
4. Type macro name.
5. Click down-pointing arrow to right of *Store macro in*.
6. Click *Personal Macro Workbook*.
7. Click in *Description* text box.
8. Type description text.
9. Click OK.
10. Perform desired actions.
11. Click Stop Recording button.

Project ⑪ Creating a Macro in the Personal Macro Workbook

1. Press Ctrl + N to start a new blank workbook.
2. Create a macro that inserts your name in a footer and store the macro in the Personal Macro Workbook file by completing the following steps:
   a. Click the Record New Macro button at the left side of the Status bar.
   b. Type **Footer_Name** in the *Macro name* text box.
   c. Click the down-pointing arrow next to the *Store macro in* list box and then click *Personal Macro Workbook* at the drop-down list.
   d. Click in the *Description* text box and then type **Name centered in footer macro. Created by [Student Name] on [Date].** Substitute your name for [Student Name] and the current date for [Date].
   e. Click OK.
   f. Click the Page Layout view button in the Workbook Views group of the View tab.
   g. Scroll to the bottom of the page, click over the text *Click to add footer*, type your name at the bottom center of the page, and then click in the worksheet area to close the footer.

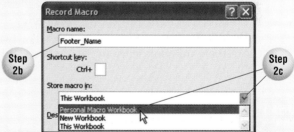

Step 2b   Step 2c

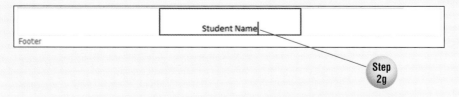

Footer   Student Name

Step 2g

h. Click the Normal button in the Workbook Views group of the View tab.

i. Press Ctrl + Home to move the active cell to A1.

j. Click the Stop Recording button.

3. Test the macro to make sure the macro works in a new workbook in a new Excel session by completing the following steps:

a. Close the workbook without saving changes. You will save the macro workbook in the next step.

b. Exit Excel. At the Microsoft Office Excel message box asking if you want to save the changes made to the Personal Macro Workbook, click Yes.

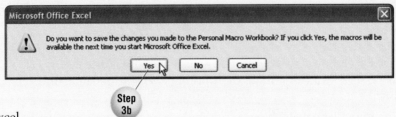

Step 3b

c. Start Excel.

d. Click the View tab and then click the Macros button.

e. Notice the macro named *Footer_Name* preceded with *PERSONAL.XLSB!* in the *Macro Name* list box.

f. Click the Run button.

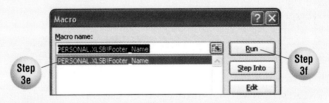

Step 3e

Step 3f

g. Type your name in A1, press Enter, and then press Ctrl + F2 to view the worksheet in Print Preview.

h. Look at the footer in the Print Preview window and then click the Close Print Preview button.

4. Close the workbook without saving the changes.

Deleting a Macro

Delete Macro
1. Open Macro dialog box.
2. Click macro name.
3. Click Delete button.
4. Click Yes.

If you no longer need a macro, the macro can be deleted at the Macro dialog box. Open the Macro dialog box, select the macro name in the *Macro name* list box and then click the Delete button.

Hide

Unhide

1. At a blank Excel window, unhide the Personal Macro Workbook by completing the following steps:
   a. If necessary, click the View tab.
   b. Click the Unhide button in the Window group.
   c. With *PERSONAL.XLSB* selected in the *Unhide workbook* list box at the Unhide dialog box, click OK.

2. Delete the Footer_Name macro by completing the following steps:
   a. Click the Macros button.
   b. With *Footer_Name* selected in the *Macro name* list box, click the Delete button.

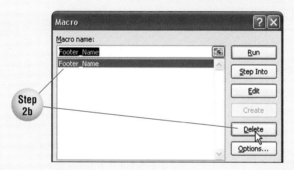

   c. At the Microsoft Office Excel message box asking if you want to delete the macro named Footer_Name, click Yes.
3. Click the Hide button in the Window group.
4. Exit Excel. Click Yes when prompted to save changes made to PERSONAL.XLSB.

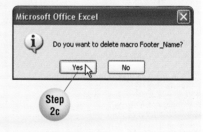

Project 2 Add a Custom List and Pin a Workbook to the Recent Documents List

You will add a custom list to Excel to enable you to populate cells using the fill handle and make a file that is used frequently more easily accessible by attaching the workbook name to the Recent Documents list.

Creating a Custom Fill Series

Create Custom List by Importing
1. Type list entries in worksheet.
2. Select list range.
3. Click Office button.
4. Click Excel Options button.
5. Click Edit Custom Lists button.
6. Click Import button.
7. Click OK twice.

HINT

You may also create a custom list to define an unusual sort order by which to sort a list. For example, if you have a list of items that you want to sort by an order other than alphanumeric ascending or descending, create a custom list with the items in the correct order. To perform a sort by the custom list, open the Sort dialog box, change *Order* to *Custom List* and then select the custom list.

The fill handle is used often to facilitate data entry by dragging the handle to populate cells from a list or by copying a formula. For example, a popular method of setting up a worksheet with the months of the year is to type **January** in a cell and then drag the fill handle to fill the remaining adjacent cells with *February*, *March*, *April*, and so on. Excel recognizes several series based on the source cell(s) selected before dragging the fill handle.

You can also create your own custom lists that can be used to fill a series using the Custom Lists dialog box shown in Figure 7.5. Open the dialog box using the Edit Custom Lists button in the Excel Options dialog box with the *Popular* category selected. A long list can be created by first typing the entries within the worksheet and using the Import button to identify the range to add to the *List entries* list box. Another method is to type the entries directly into the *List entries* list box pressing Enter after each item and then click the Add button. Once the list is added you can populate the cells in a worksheet by typing the first entry in the list and then using the fill handle to fill the remaining cells.

Figure 7.5 Custom Lists Dialog Box

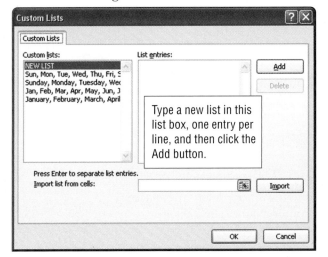

Type a new list in this list box, one entry per line, and then click the Add button.

Excel Options

Project 2a   **Creating a Custom List Series by Importing**

1. Start Excel and then open **NationalAcctgDept-JE-HelpDesk.xlsx**.
2. Save the workbook with Save As and name it **ExcelL2_C7_P2**.
3. Assume that the list of departments in column A represents entries that you need to fill frequently in other worksheets. Create a custom list to allow you to fill the series using the fill handle by completing the following steps:
   a. Select A7:A17.
   b. Click the Office button.
   c. Click the Excel Options button.

d. With *Popular* selected in the left pane, click the Edit Custom Lists button in the *Top options for working with Excel* section.

e. At the Custom Lists dialog box with *$A$7:$A$17* entered in the *Import list from cells* text box, click the Import button.

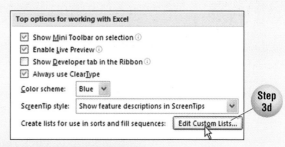

Step 3d

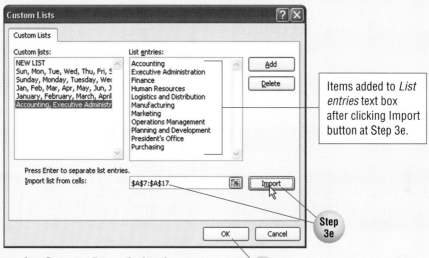

Items added to *List entries* text box after clicking Import button at Step 3e.

Step 3e

f. Click OK to close the Custom Lists dialog box.

g. Click OK to close the Excel Options dialog box.

h. Click any cell to deselect the range.

Step 3f

4. Test the custom list in a new worksheet by completing the following steps:

a. Click the Sheet2 tab to activate a new worksheet.

b. With A1 the active cell, type **Accounting** and press Enter.

c. Press the Up Arrow key to move the active cell back to A1 and then drag the fill handle down to A11.

d. Click any cell to deselect the range.

e. Make Sheet1 the active sheet.

Steps 4b–4c

5. Save and then close **ExcelL2_C7_P2.xlsx**.

	A	B	C
1	Accounting		
2	Executive	Administration	
3	Finance		
4	Human Resources		
5	Logistics and Distribution		
6	Manufacturing		
7	Marketing		
8	Operations Management		
9	Planning and Development		
10	Presidents Office		
11	Purchasing		
12			

Deleting a Custom List

To remove a custom list that is no longer needed, open the Custom Lists dialog box, select the list to be removed in the *Custom lists* list box and then click the Delete button. At the Microsoft Office Excel message box informing you that the list will be permanently deleted, click OK.

QUICK STEPS

Delete Custom List
1. Click Office button.
2. Click Excel Options button.
3. Click Edit Custom Lists button.
4. Click desired list in *Custom lists* list box.
5. Click Delete button.
6. Click OK three times.

1. Press Ctrl + N to start a new blank workbook.
2. Delete the custom list created in Project 2a by completing the following steps:
   a. Click the Office button.
   b. Click the Excel Options button.
   c. With *Popular* selected in the left pane, click the Edit Custom Lists button in the *Top options for working with Excel* section.
   d. At the Custom Lists dialog box, click *Accounting, Executive Administration* in the *Custom lists* list box.
   e. Click the Delete button.

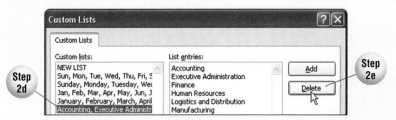

f. Click OK at the Microsoft Office Excel message box informing you the list will be permanently deleted.
g. Click OK to close the Custom Lists dialog box.
3. Click OK to close the Excel Options dialog box.

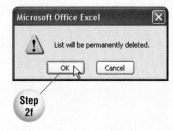

Pinning Workbooks to the Recent Documents List

Pin Workbook to Recent Documents List
1. Make sure workbook has been opened recently.
2. Click Office button.
3. Click pin icon next to workbook name.

Unpin Workbook from Recent Documents List
1. Click Office button.
2. Click green pin icon next to workbook name.

Unpinned Workbook

Pinned Workbook

When you click the Office button, the left pane displays file management options and the right pane displays the *Recent Documents* list. By default, Excel shows 17 most recently opened workbook file names in the list. To open a workbook you used recently, click the workbook name in the *Recent Documents* list. A workbook that you want to make readily accessible can be permanently added to the *Recent Documents* list. To do this, make sure you have recently opened the workbook, click the Office button, and then click the pin icon next to the workbook name. A workbook that is permanently pinned to the list displays with a green push pin icon. Clicking the green push pin icon unpins a workbook from the list.

To change the number of workbooks shown in the Recent Documents list, open the Excel Options dialog box and click *Advanced* in the left pane. Change the number in *Show this number of Recent Documents* text box in the *Display* section to the desired number of workbooks.

1. With a blank worksheet displayed, pin two workbooks to the *Recent Documents* list by completing the following steps:
   a. Click the Office button.
   b. Click the pin icon to the right of ExcelL2_C7_P2.xlsx in the *Recent Documents* list.

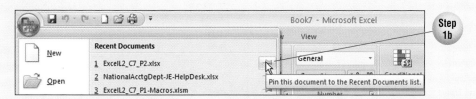

   c. Click the pin icon to the right of **Excel_L2_C7_P1-Macros.xlsm**.
   d. Click in the worksheet area outside the drop-down list to close the menu.
2. Click the Office button and then click **ExcelL2_C7_P2.xlsx** in the *Recent Documents* list to open the workbook.
3. Close **ExcelL2_C7_P2.xlsx**.
4. Unpin the two workbooks by completing the following steps:
   a. Click the Office button.
   b. Click the green push pin icon to the right of **ExcelL2_C7_P2.xlsx**.
   c. Click the green push pin icon to the right of **ExcelL2_C7_P1-Macros.xlsm**.
   d. Click in the worksheet area outside the drop-down list to close the menu.

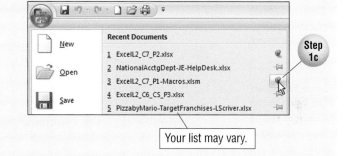

Your list may vary.

Project ③ Customize the Excel Work Environment

You will customize the Excel environment by adding buttons to the Quick Access toolbar to make features more accessible, minimize the ribbon to create more space in the work area, and change display options.

Customizing the Quick Access Toolbar

As you work with Excel you may find that some features that you use frequently you would prefer to access from the Quick Access toolbar to save time and mouse clicks. Click the Customize Quick Access Toolbar button located at the right end of the toolbar to open the Customize Quick Access Toolbar drop-down list shown in Figure 7.6.

Customize Quick Access Toolbar

A few less popular features are only available by adding a button to the Quick Access toolbar. If a feature you are trying to locate is not available in any tab of the ribbon, search for the feature in the *All Commands* list.

Figure 7.6 Customize Quick Access Toolbar Drop-down List

Add Button to Quick Access Toolbar
1. Click Customize Quick Access Toolbar button.
2. Click desired button.
OR
1. Click Customize Quick Access Toolbar button.
2. Click *More Commands*.
3. Click down-pointing arrow at right of *Choose commands from*.
4. Click desired category.
5. Double-click desired command in commands list box.
6. Click OK.

Remove Button from Quick Access Toolbar
1. Click Customize Quick Access Toolbar button.
2. Click desired button.
OR
1. Click Customize Quick Access Toolbar button.
2. Click *More Commands*.
3. Click desired command in right list box.
4. Click Remove button.
5. Click OK.

Click *More Commands* to open the Excel Options dialog box with *Customize* selected. Scroll through command lists grouped by categories to locate the feature you want to add to the toolbar.

Click *More Commands* at the drop-down list to open the Excel Options dialog box with *Customize* selected in the left pane. Change the list of commands shown in the left list box by clicking the down-pointing arrow to the right of *Choose commands from* and then clicking the desired category. Scroll the list box to locate the command and then double-click the command name to add it to the Quick Access toolbar.

Figure 7.7 Excel Options Dialog Box with *Customize* Selected

Begin by selecting the category from which to choose commands.

Next, double-click the command you wish to add from this list box.

Change the order in which the buttons are arranged on the toolbar or remove buttons using this list box.

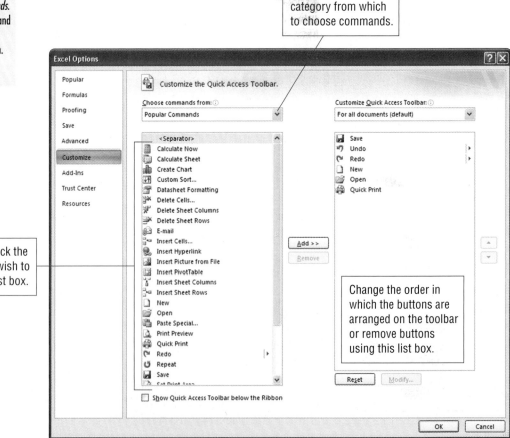

1. With a blank workbook open, add the Print Preview and Sort commands to the Quick Access toolbar by completing the following steps:

   a. Click the Customize Quick Access Toolbar button located at the right end of the Quick Access toolbar.

   b. Click *Print Preview* at the drop-down list. Print Preview is added to the end of the Quick Access toolbar. ***Note: Go to Step 1d if Print Preview is already present on your Quick Access toolbar***.

   c. Click the Customize Quick Access Toolbar button.

   d. Click *More Commands* at the drop-down list.

   e. At the Excel Options dialog box with *Customize* selected in the left pane, click the down-pointing arrow next to *Choose commands from* and then click *All Commands*.

   f. Scroll down the All Commands list box and then double-click the *Sort* option that displays the ScreenTip *Data Tab | Sort & Filter | Sort....(SortDialog)*.

   g. Click OK. The Sort button is added to the end of the Quick Access toolbar.

2. Type your name in A1, press Enter, and then click the Print Preview button on the Quick Access toolbar to display the worksheet in Print Preview.

3. Click the Close Print Preview button.

4. Click the Sort button on the Quick Access toolbar to open the Sort dialog box.

5. Click the Cancel button at the Sort dialog box.

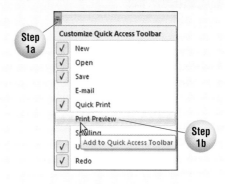

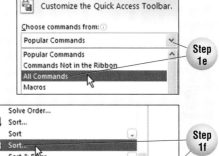

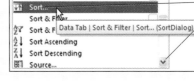

1. With a blank workbook open, remove the Print Preview and Sort buttons from the Quick Access toolbar by completing the following steps:

   a. Click the Customize Quick Access Toolbar button.

   b. Click *Print Preview* at the drop-down list. ***Note: Check with your instructor if Print Preview was already present on the Quick Access toolbar before Project 3a. Your school may want the customized Quick Access toolbar to remain unchanged; go to Step 1d in this case***.

   c. Click the Customize Quick Access Toolbar button.

   d. Click *More Commands* at the drop-down list.

   e. At the Excel Options dialog box with *Customize* selected in the left pane, click *Sort* in the right list box and then click the Remove button.

   f. Click OK.

2. Close the workbook without saving changes.

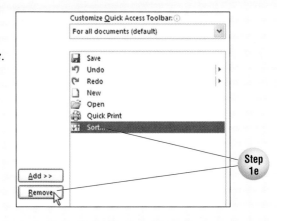

QUICK STEPS

Minimize Ribbon
Double-click any tab.
OR
1. Click the Customize Quick Access Toolbar button.
2. Click *Minimize the Ribbon*.

Customize Display Options
1. Click Office button.
2. Click Excel Options button.
3. Click *Advanced* in left pane.
4. Change display options as required.
5. Click OK.

Changing Display Options to Customize the Work Area

The Excel Options dialog box contains many options for customizing the environment when the default options do not suit your needs. As shown in Figure 7.8, Excel groups options that affect the display of Excel by those that are global display settings, those that affect the entire workbook, and those that affect the active worksheet. Changes to workbook and/or worksheet display options are saved with the workbook.

Minimizing the Ribbon

When you are working with a large worksheet, you may find it easier to work with the ribbon minimized to provide more space within the work area. Figure 7.9 shows the worksheet you will use in Project 3c to customize the display options and minimize the ribbon. With the ribbon minimized, clicking a tab temporarily redisplays the ribbon to allow you to select a feature. As soon as you select the feature, the ribbon returns to the minimized state. Use any of the following methods to toggle on or off the ribbon:

- Double-click a tab
- Click the Customize Quick Access Toolbar button and then click *Minimize the Ribbon*
- Press Ctrl + F1

Figure 7.8 Excel Options Dialog Box with Display Options Shown

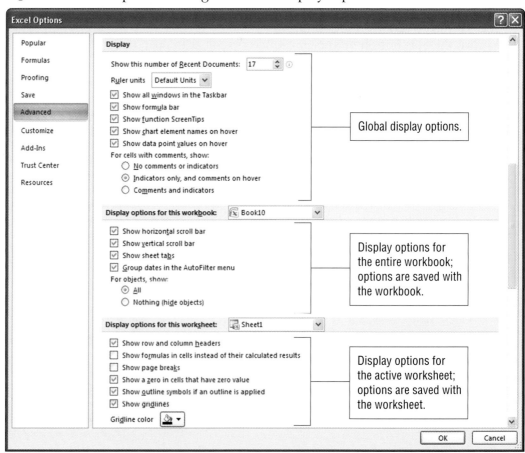

Figure 7.9 Project 3c Worksheet with Customized Display Options and Minimized Ribbon

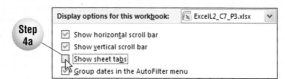

		ExcelL2_C7_P3.xlsx - Microsoft Excel				
Home	Insert	Page Layout	Formulas	Data	Review	View

Double-click a tab to show or hide the ribbon.

Noranda Sportsplex
Winter Swimming Schedule

Day	Start time	End time	Pool	Activity
MORNINGS				
Monday, Wednesday	6:30	7:50	All	Adult swim
Tuesday, Thursday, Friday	6:30	7:50	All	Moms & tots swim
Monday, Wednesday	8:00	8:45	Blue, Green	Beginner aquafit
Tuesday, Thursday, Friday	8:00	8:45	Blue, Green	Adult swim
Monday, Wednesday	8:00	8:45	Red	Deep water aquafit
Tuesday, Thursday, Friday	8:00	8:45	Red	Deep water aquafit
Monday, Wednesday	9:00	9:45	Blue, Green	Intermediate aquafit
Tuesday, Thursday, Friday	9:00	9:45	Blue, Green	Leisure swim
Monday, Wednesday	9:00	9:45	Red	Senior aquafit
Tuesday, Thursday, Friday	9:00	9:45	Red	Beginner aquafit
Monday, Wednesday	10:00	11:45	All	Leisure swim
Tuesday, Thursday, Friday	10:00	11:45	Blue, Green	Senior aquafit
Tuesday, Thursday, Friday	10:00	11:45	Red	Deep water aquafit
Saturday, Sunday	9:00	11:45	All	Swimming lessons
AFTERNOONS				
Monday, Wednesday	1:00	1:45	Blue	Moms & tots swim
Tuesday, Thursday, Friday	1:00	1:45	Blue	Adult swim
Monday, Wednesday	1:00	1:45	Red, Green	Beginner aquafit
Tuesday, Thursday, Friday	1:00	1:45	Red, Green	Intermediate aquafit
Monday, Wednesday	2:00	3:45	All	Leisure swim
Tuesday, Thursday, Friday	2:00	3:45	Blue, Green	Private bookings
Tuesday, Thursday, Friday	2:00	3:45	Red	Diving club
Monday, Wednesday	2:00	3:45	Blue, Green	Intermediate aquafit
Tuesday, Thursday, Friday	2:00	3:45	Blue, Green	Beginner aquafit
Monday, Wednesday	4:00	4:45	Red	Adult lane swim

Ready | 100%

Project 3c Customizing Display Options and Minimizing the Ribbon

1. Open **NorandaSportsplex-WinterSwimSch.xlsx**.
2. Save the workbook with Save As and name it **ExcelL2_C7_P3**.
3. Turn off the display of the formula bar since no formulas exist in the workbook by completing the following steps:
   a. Click the Office button.
   b. Click the Excel Options button.
   c. Click *Advanced* in the left pane.
   d. Scroll down the Excel Options dialog box to the *Display* section and then click the *Show formula bar* check box to clear the check mark.

   Step 3d

   Display
   Show this number of Recent Documents: 17
   Ruler units Default Units
   ☑ Show all windows in the Taskbar
   ☐ Show formula bar
   ☑ Show function ScreenTips
   ☑ Show chart element names on hover

4. Turn off the display of the sheet tabs since only one sheet exists in the workbook by completing the following step:
   a. Scroll down the Excel Options dialog box to the *Display options for this workbook* section and then click the *Show sheet tabs* check box to clear the check mark.

   Step 4a

   Display options for this workbook: ExcelL2_C7_P3.xlsx
   ☑ Show horizontal scroll bar
   ☑ Show vertical scroll bar
   ☐ Show sheet tabs
   ☑ Group dates in the AutoFilter menu

5. Turn off the display of row and column headers and gridlines by completing the following steps:
   a. Scroll down the Excel Options dialog box to the *Display options for this worksheet* section and then click the *Show row and column headers* check box to clear the check mark.
   b. Click the *Show gridlines* check box to clear the check mark.

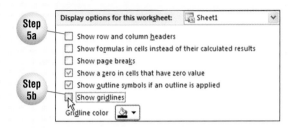

   c. Click OK.
6. Double-click the Home tab to minimize the ribbon.
7. Compare your screen with the one shown in Figure 7.9.
8. Save and then close **ExcelL2_C7_P3.xlsx**.

Project 3d **Restoring Default Display Options**

1. Press Ctrl + N to start a new blank workbook.
2. Notice the display options that were changed in Project 3c that affect the workbook and the worksheet are restored to the default options. The formula bar remains hidden since this option is a global display option. The ribbon remains minimized since the display of the ribbon is a toggle on/off option.
3. Open **ExcelL2_C7_P3.xlsx**.
4. Notice the sheet tabs, the row and column headers, and the gridlines remain hidden since these display option settings are saved with the workbook.
5. Close **ExcelL2_C7_P3.xlsx**.
6. Double-click the Home tab to redisplay the ribbon.
7. Redisplay the Formula bar by completing the following steps:
   a. Open the Excel Options dialog box.
   b. Click *Advanced* in the left pane.
   c. Scroll down the Excel Options dialog box to the *Display* section, click the *Show formula bar* check box to insert a check mark and then click OK.
8. Close the workbook.

Project 4 **Create a Custom Theme**

You will modify an existing theme's colors and fonts and save the changes as custom theme colors and custom theme fonts. Next, you will apply the custom colors and custom fonts, choose a theme effect, and then save the combination as a custom theme.

Creating a Custom Theme by Modifying Existing Theme Elements

QUICK STEPS

Create Custom Theme Colors
1. Click Page Layout tab.
2. Click Theme Colors button.
3. Click *Create New Theme Colors.*
4. Change color options as desired.
5. Select text in *Name* text box.
6. Type desired name.
7. Click Save button.

A theme is a set of predefined theme colors, theme fonts, and theme effects. Microsoft provides the same set of built-in themes in Word, Excel, and PowerPoint. A new workbook defaults to the *Office* theme. You can change to any of the other built-in themes or a custom theme that you have created. Within a theme, you can also change any of the three theme elements to your preferences for colors, fonts, or effects.

A custom theme is created by modifying and saving an existing theme's colors, fonts, or effects and then saving the combination in a new theme. A theme you create will display in the Themes drop-down gallery in a section labeled *Custom*.

Modifying Theme Colors

To modify theme colors, click the Page Layout tab, click the Theme Colors button, and then click *Create New Theme Colors* at the drop-down gallery. This displays the Create New Theme Colors dialog box shown in Figure 7.10. Theme colors contain four text and background colors, six accent colors, and two hyperlink colors. Change a color by clicking the color button at the right side of the color option and then clicking the desired color at the color palette.

After you have made all desired changes to colors, click in the *Name* text box, type a name for the custom color theme, and then click the Save button. This saves the custom theme colors and also applies the color changes to the current workbook.

If you make changes to colors at the Create New Theme Colors dialog box and then decide you do not want to keep the color changes, click the Reset button located in the lower left corner of the dialog box.

HINT
By applying the same theme across Word, Excel, and PowerPoint, you can "brand" your business communications with a professionally-designed, consistent look.

Figure 7.10 Create New Theme Colors Dialog Box

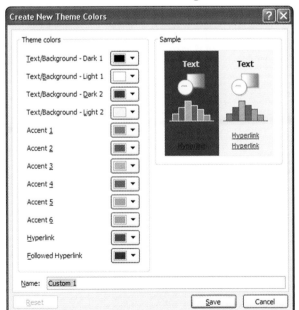

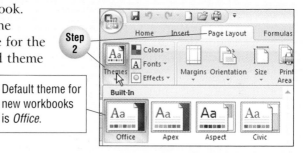

1. Press Ctrl + N to start a new blank workbook.
2. Click the Page Layout tab and then click the Themes button to check the current theme for the workbook. Notice that *Office* is the selected theme at the drop-down gallery.

   Step 2

   Default theme for new workbooks is *Office*.

3. Click in the worksheet area to close the drop-down gallery.
4. Modify the theme colors for the *Office* theme by completing the following steps:

   a. Click the Theme Colors button in the Themes group and then click *Create New Theme Colors* at the drop-down gallery.

   b. At the Create New Theme Colors dialog box, click the color button that displays at the right of *Text/Background - Light 1* and then click the *Aqua, Accent 5, Lighter 80%* color square at the color palette (fourth from right in second row of *Theme Colors* section).

   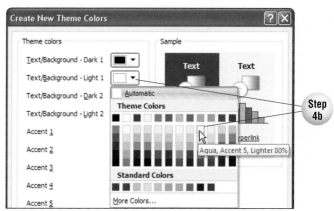

   Step 4b

   c. Click the color button at the right of *Accent 1* and then click the *Yellow* color square at the color palette (fourth from left in *Standard Colors* section).

   d. Click the color button at the right of *Hyperlink* and then click the *Dark Red* color square at the color palette (first from left in *Standard Colors* section).

   Step 4c

   Step 4d

   e. Click the color button at the right of *Followed Hyperlink* and then click the *Light Green* color square at the color palette (fifth from left in *Standard Colors* section).

   Step 4e

   Steps 5a–5b

   Step 5c

   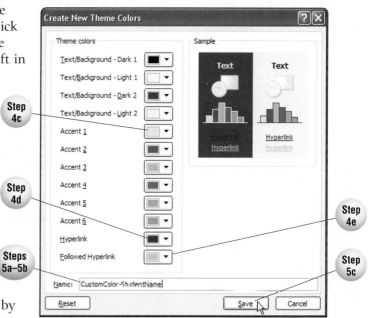

5. Save the custom theme colors by completing the following steps:

   a. Select the current text in the *Name* text box.

   b. Type **CustomColor-StudentName**, substituting your name for *StudentName*.

   c. Click the Save button.

6. Look in the ribbon at the buttons in the Themes group. Notice the colors have changed on the face of the buttons to denote the custom color choices.
7. Close the workbook. Click No when prompted to save changes.

Modifying Theme Fonts

To modify theme fonts, click the Page Layout tab, click the Theme Fonts button, and then click *Create New Theme Fonts* at the drop-down gallery to open the Create New Theme Fonts dialog box shown in Figure 7.11. Make the desired changes to the *Heading font* and *Body font* options, type a name for the custom fonts in the *Name* text box, and then click the Save button. Excel applies the new fonts to the current workbook and adds the custom font to the top of the Theme Fonts drop-down gallery.

QUICK STEPS

Create Custom Theme Fonts
1. Click Page Layout tab.
2. Click Theme Fonts button.
3. Click *Create New Theme Fonts*.
4. Change fonts as desired.
5. Select text in *Name* text box.
6. Type desired name.
7. Click Save button.

Figure 7.11 Create New Theme Fonts Dialog Box

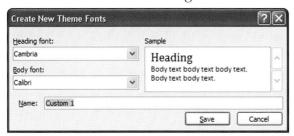

Project 4b Modifying and Saving Custom Theme Fonts

1. Press Ctrl + N to start a new blank workbook.
2. If necessary, click the Page Layout tab.
3. Modify the theme fonts and then save the custom theme fonts by completing the following steps:
   a. Click the Theme Fonts button in the Themes group and then click *Create New Theme Fonts* at the drop-down gallery.
   b. At the Create New Theme Fonts dialog box, click the down-pointing arrow at the right of the *Heading font* list box, scroll up the list, and then click *Arial*.
   c. Click the down-pointing arrow at the right of the *Body font* list box, scroll down the list, and then click *Century Gothic*.
   d. Select the current text in the *Name* text box.
   e. Type **CustomFont-StudentName**, substituting your name for *StudentName*.
   f. Click the Save button.

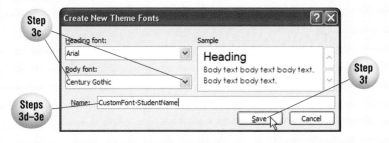

4. Close the workbook. Click No when prompted to save changes.

Applying Custom Theme Colors and Fonts

After saving custom theme colors or fonts, you can apply the selections to a workbook by clicking the Theme Colors or Theme Fonts button in the Themes group in the Page Layout tab and then clicking the name of the saved theme colors or fonts at the drop-down gallery. Custom themes appear at the top of the drop-down gallery in a section titled *Custom*.

Applying Theme Effects

**Save Custom
Workbook Theme**
1. Click Page layout tab.
2. Apply desired custom theme colors.
3. Apply desired custom theme fonts.
4. Apply desired theme effects.
5. Click Themes button.
6. Click *Save Current Theme*.
7. Type desired name.
8. Click Save.

The options in the Theme Effects drop-down gallery apply sets of lines and fill effects to drawn shapes, SmartArt, charts, or other graphic objects in the workbook. You cannot create your own theme effects but you can apply a theme effect and then save the formatting as a component within your own custom theme.

Saving a Workbook Theme

After you have customized theme colors and fonts and applied a theme effect to a workbook you can save the combination as a custom workbook theme. To do this, click the Themes button in the Themes group in the Page Layout tab and then click *Save Current Theme* at the drop-down gallery to open the Save Current Theme dialog box. Type a name for the custom workbook theme in the *File name* text box and then click the Save button.

Project **4C**   **Applying Custom Theme Colors, Custom Theme Fonts, and Theme Effects and Saving a Custom Workbook Theme**

1. Open **NationalAcctgDept-JE-TSR.xlsx**.
2. Save the workbook with Save As and name it **ExcelL2_C7_P4**.
3. Apply the custom theme colors and custom theme fonts from Project 4a and 4b by completing the following steps:
   a. If necessary, click the Page Layout tab.

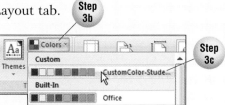

   b. Click the Theme Colors button in the Themes group.
   c. Click *CustomColor-StudentName* where your name is substituted for *StudentName* located in the *Custom* section at the top of the drop-down gallery.
   d. Click the Theme Fonts button.
   e. Click *CustomFont-StudentName* where your name is substituted for *StudentName* located in the *Custom* section at the top of the drop-down gallery.

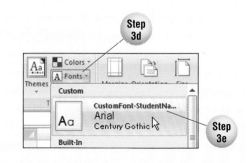

4. Apply a theme effect by clicking the Theme Effects button and then clicking *Concourse* at the drop-down gallery.
5. Make A3 the active cell, click the Home tab, and then change the Fill Color to *Dark Blue, Text 2* (fourth from left in first row of *Theme Colors* section) at the drop-down color palette.
6. If necessary, select the WordArt object in A3 and move it until it is centered within columns A–H.
7. Save the custom theme colors, theme fonts, and Concourse theme effect as a custom workbook theme by completing the following steps:
   a. Click the Page Layout tab.
   b. Click the Themes button.
   c. Click *Save Current Theme* at the bottom of the drop-down gallery.
   d. At the Save Current Theme dialog box, type **CustomTheme-StudentName** substituting your name for StudentName in the *File name* text box and then click the Save button. ***Note: Check with your instructor before saving in case you should save the custom theme to the Excel2007L2C7 folder on your storage medium.***

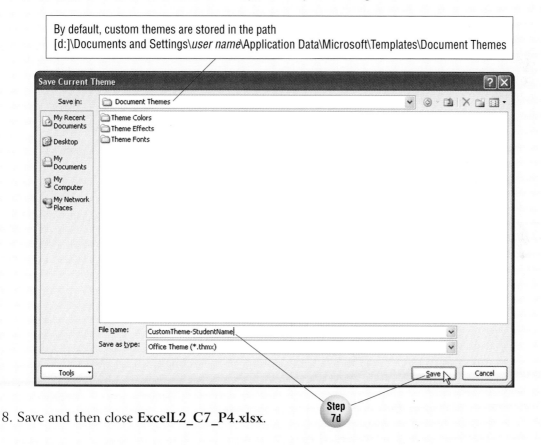

By default, custom themes are stored in the path
[d:]\Documents and Settings*user name*\Application Data\Microsoft\Templates\Document Themes

Step 7d

8. Save and then close **ExcelL2_C7_P4.xlsx**.

Deleting Custom Themes

**Delete Custom Theme
Colors or Custom
Theme Fonts**
1. Click Page Layout tab.
2. Click Theme Colors or
   Theme Fonts button.
3. Right-click custom
   name.
4. Click *Delete*.
5. Click Yes.

**Delete Custom
Workbook Theme**
1. Click Page Layout tab.
2. Click Themes button.
3. Click *Save Current
   Theme*.
4. Click theme name.
5. Press Delete key.
6. Click Yes.
7. Close Save Current
   Theme dialog box.

To delete custom theme colors, click the Theme Colors button, right-click the theme you want to delete, and then click *Delete* at the shortcut menu. At the message asking if you want to delete the theme colors, click Yes. To delete custom theme fonts, click the Theme Fonts button, right-click the theme you want to delete, and then click *Delete* at the shortcut menu. At the message asking if you want to delete the theme fonts, click Yes.

Delete a custom workbook theme (includes custom colors, fonts, and effects) at the Save Current Theme dialog box by clicking the Themes button and then clicking *Save Current Theme* at the drop-down gallery. Click the custom theme name in the file list and then click the Delete button on the dialog box toolbar, or press the Delete key. At the message asking if you are sure you want to send the theme to the Recycle Bin, click Yes.

Project ④⓪ Deleting Custom Themes

1. Press Ctrl + N to start a new blank workbook.
2. If necessary, click the Page Layout tab.
3. Click the Theme Colors button, right-click *CustomColor-StudentName* where your name is substituted for *StudentName*, and then click *Delete* at the shortcut menu.

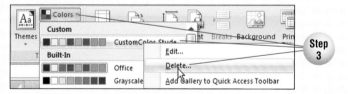

4. At the Microsoft Office Excel message box asking if you want to delete these theme colors, click Yes.
5. Click the Theme Fonts button, right-click *CustomFont-StudentName* where your name is substituted for *StudentName*, click *Delete* at the shortcut menu, and then click Yes at the message box asking if you want to delete these theme fonts.
6. Delete the custom workbook theme by completing the following steps:
   a. Click the Themes button.
   b. Click *Save Current Theme* at the bottom of the drop-down gallery.

c. At the Save Current Theme dialog box, click *CustomTheme-StudentName.thmx* where your name is substituted for *StudentName* in the file list box. If necessary, navigate to the Excel2007L2C7 folder on your storage medium if you saved the custom theme to this location in Project 4c, Step 7d.

d. Press the Delete key.

e. At the Confirm File Delete dialog box, click Yes.

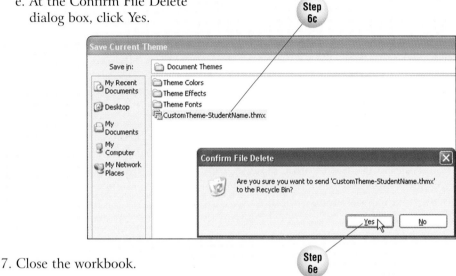

Step 6c

Step 6e

7. Close the workbook.

P roject ⑤ **Save a Workbook as a Template**

You will modify an existing workbook and save the revised version as a template.

Saving a Workbook as a Template

Templates are workbooks with standard text, formulas, and formatting. Cells are created and formatted for all of the entries that do not change. Cells are also created for variable information which has formatting applied but which are left empty since these cells will be filled in when the template is used to generate a worksheet. Examples of worksheets that would be suited to a template include an invoice, a purchase order, a time card, or an expense form. These templates would be reused often to fill in information that is different for each individual invoice, purchase order, time card, or expense.

Several templates have already been created and are available to you either installed on the computer or by download from Microsoft Office Online. New templates are made available through Microsoft Office Online frequently. Before creating a custom template, search the Microsoft Office Online Web site to see if a template already exists that is suited to your purpose.

QUICK STEPS

Save Workbook as Template
1. Open workbook.
2. Make desired changes.
3. Click Office button.
4. Click *Save As*.
5. Change *Save as type* to *Excel Template (*.xltx)*.
6. Type desired file name.
7. Click Save button.

HINT

If macros exist in the template workbook, change the *Save as type* to *Excel Macro-Enabled Template (*.xltm)*.

If no template exists that meets your needs, you can create your own custom template. To do this, create a workbook that contains all of the standard data, formulas, and formatting applied. Leave cells empty for any information that is variable; however, format these cells as required. When you are ready to save the workbook as a template, use the Save As dialog box and change *Save as type* to *Excel Template (*.xltx)*.

Consider protecting the worksheet by locking all cells except those that will hold variable data before saving the workbook as a template.

Project 5a — Saving a Workbook as a Template

1. Open **ExcelL2_C7_P3.xlsx**.
2. Assume that you work at the Noranda Sportsplex and have to publish swimming schedules often. The sportsplex manager never changes the days or times the pool operates; however, the activities and assigned pools will often change. You decide to modify this workbook and then save it as a template to be reused whenever the schedule changes.
3. Make the following changes to the workbook:
   a. Clear all of the contents in the *Pool* column within the Mornings, Afternoons, and Evenings sections.
   b. Clear all of the contents in the *Activity* column within the Mornings, Afternoons, and Evenings sections.
   c. Delete *Winter* in *Winter Swimming Schedule* so that the subtitle reads *Swimming Schedule*.
   d. Insert a new row below *Swimming Schedule* and merge and center the cells in the new row to match the subtitle. This will be used later to enter the timeframe for the new schedule.

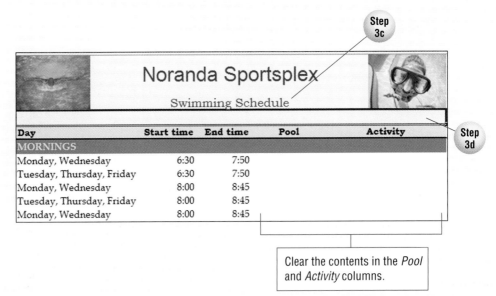

Step 3c

Step 3d

Clear the contents in the *Pool* and *Activity* columns.

   e. Select and turn off the lock attribute for those cells that will hold variable information. For example, A3 will vary as well as the ranges within the pool and activity columns for each of the timeframes.
   f. Protect the worksheet. Do not assign a password to unprotect.
4. Save the revised workbook as a template by completing the following steps:
   a. Click the Office button.
   b. Click *Save As*.

c. Click the down-pointing arrow next to *Save as type*, scroll down the list box, and then click *Excel Template (*.xltx)*.

d. Select the current text in the *File name* text box and then type **SwimSchTemplate-StudentName**, substituting your name for *StudentName*.

Step 4d

Step 4e

Step 4c

| File name: | SwimSchTemplate-StudentName |
| Save as type: | Excel Template (*.xltx) |

Save

e. Click the Save button.

5. Close **SwimSchTemplate-StudentName.xltx**.

Using a Custom Template

To use a template that you created yourself, click the Office button and then click *New* at the drop-down list. At the New Workbook dialog box, click *My templates…* in the *Templates* section of the left pane. This opens the New dialog box shown in Figure 7.12. Double-click the desired template.

QUICK STEPS

Use Custom Template
1. Click Office button.
2. Click *New*.
3. Click *My templates…*.
4. Double-click desired template.

Figure 7.12 New Dialog Box

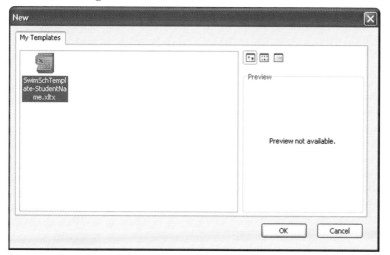

Project **5b** **Using a Custom Template**

1. At a blank Excel screen, open the template created in Project 5a by completing the following steps:
   a. Click the Office button.
   b. Click *New*.
   c. At the New Workbook dialog box, click *My templates…* in the *Templates* section of the left pane.

Step 1c

d. At the New dialog box, double-click *SwimSchTemplate-StudentName.xltx* where your name is substituted for *StudentName*.

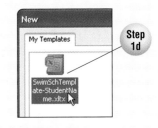

2. Look at the workbook name in the title bar. Notice that Excel has added *1* to the end of the name.
3. Make A3 the active cell and then type **Winter 2010**.
4. Enter data for the first two rows in the MORNINGS section by making up a pool name and activity for each row.
5. Click the Save button on the Quick Access toolbar.
6. Excel opens the Save As dialog box and automatically changes the *Save as type* option to *Excel Workbook (*.xlsx)*. Type **ExcelL2_C7_P5** in the *File name* text box, navigate to the Excel2007L2 folder on your storage medium, and then click the Save button.
7. Close **ExcelL2_C7_P5.xlsx**.

QUICK STEPS

Delete Custom Template
1. Click Office button.
2. Click *New*.
3. Click *My templates....*
4. Right-click desired template name.
5. Click *Delete*.
6. Click Yes.
7. Close New dialog box.
8. Close New Workbook dialog box.

Deleting a Custom Template

To delete a custom template, click the Office button and then click *New* at the drop-down list. At the New Workbook dialog box, click *My templates...* in the *Templates* section of the left pane. At the New dialog box, click the template you want to delete and then press the Delete key. At the Confirm File Delete dialog box, click Yes.

Project 5c **Deleting a Custom Template**

1. At a blank Excel screen, delete the template created in Project 5a by completing the following steps:
   a. Click the Office button.
   b. Click *New*.
   c. At the New Workbook dialog box, click *My templates...* in the *Templates* section of the left pane.
   d. At the New dialog box, right-click *SwimSchTemplate-StudentName.xltx* where your name is substituted for *StudentName*.
   e. Click *Delete* at the shortcut menu.
   f. At the Confirm File Delete dialog box, click Yes.
2. Close the New dialog box.
3. Close the New Workbook dialog box.

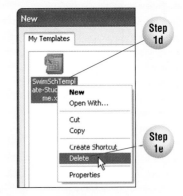

CHAPTER summary

- A macro is a set of stored instructions.
- Create a macro for a task that you repeat frequently in which the steps do not vary.
- Start creating a new macro by clicking the View tab, the down-pointing arrow on the Macros button in the Macros group, and then *Record Macro*.
- At the Record Macro dialog box, assign a name to the macro, an optional shortcut key, and a description.
- The macro recorder is turned on after you click OK to close the Record Macro dialog box. All commands and keystrokes are recorded until you click the Stop Recording button.
- Workbooks that contain macros are saved in the *Excel Macro-Enabled Workbook (*.xlsm)* file format.
- Run a macro by opening the Macro dialog box and double-clicking the macro name.
- A macro assigned to a shortcut key is run by pressing Ctrl + the assigned letter.
- Excel differentiates the case of the letter typed in the *Shortcut key* text box at the Record Macro dialog box. An uppercase letter is assigned the shortcut key Ctrl + Shift + the assigned letter.
- If you assign a shortcut key to a macro that is the same as a shortcut key assigned to an Excel feature, the macro overrides the Excel shortcut.
- Check the macro security settings at the Trust Center dialog box, which is accessed from the Excel Options dialog box.
- By default, Excel sets the security level to *Disable all macros with notification*. This means that when you open a workbook containing macros, the macros are disabled and a security warning appears in the message bar. You have the option of enabling the macros if the workbook is from a trustworthy source.
- Other macro security settings you can change to are: *Disable all macros without notification, Disable all macros except digitally signed macros,* and *Enable all macros (not recommended, potentially dangerous code can run)*.
- A macro's instructions are recorded in Visual Basic program code. To edit a macro, open the Macro dialog box, click the macro name to be edited, and then click the Edit button. A Microsoft Visual Basic window opens with a code window in which you edit the macro's program code.
- After editing the macro, save the changes and then click File and Close and Return to Microsoft Excel.
- If you are not comfortable with editing a macro in Visual Basic, you can record a new macro to correct the steps using the same name to replace the existing macro.
- Macros are stored in the workbook in which they are created. When you open the Macro dialog box, all macros from all open workbooks are made accessible; therefore, to use a macro stored in another workbook you will need to open the other workbook first.
- Another option to make macros accessible to other workbooks is to store the macro in the Personal Macro Workbook. To do this, change *Store macro in* to *Personal Macro Workbook* at the Record Macro dialog box.

- The Personal Macro Workbook is created the first time you store a macro within it. Once the workbook exists, Excel automatically opens the workbook whenever you start Excel, making the macros available to all new workbooks.
- By default, Excel hides the Personal Macro Workbook file. You can unhide the workbook if you need to edit or delete a macro stored within PERSONAL.XLSB.
- Delete a macro at the Macro dialog box.
- Open the Excel Options dialog box and click the Edit Custom Lists button in the *Popular* section to create or delete a custom fill series.
- The entries for a custom fill series can be typed at the Custom Lists dialog box or imported from a range in the active worksheet.
- Pin a workbook that you want to make permanently available in the *Recent Documents* list at the Office drop-down list.
- A pinned workbook displays with a green push pin icon. Clicking the green push pin icon unpins the workbook from the list.
- Add or delete a button to the Quick Access toolbar using the Customize Quick Access Toolbar button. Click *More Commands* from the drop-down list to open the Excel Options dialog box with *Customize* selected to locate a feature you want to add in the commands list box.
- Display options in Excel are grouped by global display options, options that affect the current workbook, and options that affect the current worksheet.
- Customized workbook and worksheet display options are saved with the file.
- Minimize the ribbon to open more space in the work area when working with a large worksheet. The minimized ribbon displays only the tabs. Clicking a tab temporarily redisplays the ribbon to allow you to select a feature.
- A theme is a set of predefined theme colors, theme fonts, and theme effects.
- Theme colors can be customized by modifying an existing theme's colors and saving the revision at the Create New Theme Colors dialog box.
- Theme fonts can be customized by modifying an existing theme's fonts and saving the revision at the Create New Theme Fonts dialog box.
- A theme's effects cannot be customized but you can select the effect option you want to store with a custom workbook theme.
- To customize a workbook theme, apply the combination of theme colors, theme fonts, and theme effects options to a workbook, click the Themes button, click *Save Current Theme*, and then enter a name in which to store the theme options at the Save Current Theme dialog box.
- Custom theme colors or custom theme fonts can be deleted by right-clicking the custom name at the drop-down gallery and clicking *Delete* at the shortcut menu.
- A custom workbook theme is deleted by opening the Save Current Theme dialog box and deleting the theme name in the file list.
- Templates are workbooks with standard text, formatting, and formulas.
- A custom template is created from an existing workbook by saving the workbook as an *Excel template (*.xltx)* at the *Save as type* drop-down list at the Save As dialog box.
- To use a custom template, open the New Workbook dialog box and click *My templates...* to open the New dialog box in which you double-click the custom template name.
- Delete a custom template at the New dialog box by deleting the template name in the file list.

COMMANDS review

FEATURE	RIBBON TAB, GROUP	BUTTON	OFFICE BUTTON DROP-DOWN LIST	KEYBOARD SHORTCUT
Custom fill series		Edit Custom Lists...	Excel Options	
Customize Quick Access toolbar			Excel Options	
Delete macro	View, Macros			Alt + F8
Display options		Excel Options	Excel Options	
Edit macro	View, Macros			Alt + F8
Macro security settings		Excel Options	Excel Options	
Minimize ribbon	Double-click any tab			Ctrl + F1
Record macro	View, Macros	OR		
Run macro	View, Macros			Alt + F8
Save as a macro-enabled workbook			Save As	F12
Theme colors	Page Layout, Themes	Colors ▾		
Theme effects	Page Layout, Themes	Effects ▾		
Theme fonts	Page Layout, Themes	A Fonts ▾		
Themes	Page Layout, Themes	Aa		
Use custom template			New	

CONCEPTS check
Test Your Knowledge

Completion: In the space provided at the right, indicate the correct term, command, or number.

1. Macro names must begin with a letter and can contain a combination of letters, numbers, and this other character.

_____

2. Click this button to indicate you have finished the tasks or keystrokes you want saved in the macro.

_____

3. A workbook containing a macro is saved in this file format.

_____

4. A macro can be assigned to a shortcut key that is a combination of a lowercase or uppercase letter and this other key.

_____

5. This is the default macro security setting in the Trust Center dialog box.

_____

6. Macro instructions are stored in this program code.

_____

7. Save a macro to this workbook to make the macro available for all new workbooks whenever Excel is started.

_____

8. Click this button in the Excel Options dialog box to create a custom fill series.

_____

9. A workbook that you use frequently can be permanently added to the Recent Documents list by clicking this icon next to the workbook name.

_____

10. Click this option at the Customize Quick Access Toolbar drop-down list to locate a feature to add to the toolbar from a commands list box.

_____

11. Display options are shown in the Excel Options dialog box with this option selected in the left pane.

_____

12. Do this mouse action on any tab name to minimize the ribbon.

_____

13. Click this option at the Themes drop-down gallery to save the current combination of theme colors, theme fonts, and theme effects as a custom workbook theme.

_____

14. Change *Save as type* to this option at the Save As dialog box to save the current workbook as a standard workbook that can be opened from the New dialog box.

_____

15. Click this option in the New Workbook dialog box to view a list of custom templates.

_____

SKILLS check
Demonstrate Your Proficiency

1 CREATE MACROS

1. At a new blank workbook, create the following macros storing both of them within the Personal Macro Workbook:
   a. Create a macro named **Landscape** that changes the page orientation to landscape, sets custom margins at top = 1 inch; bottom, left and right = 0.5 inch; and centers the worksheet horizontally. Assign the macro to the shortcut key Ctrl + Shift + L. Enter an appropriate description that includes your name and the date the macro was created.
   b. Create a macro named **Technic** that applies the theme named *Technic* and turns off the display of gridlines in the active worksheet. Assign the macro to the shortcut key Ctrl + t. Enter an appropriate description that includes your name and the date the macro was created.
2. Close the current workbook without saving changes.
3. Exit Excel. Click Yes when prompted to save changes to the Personal Macro Workbook.

2 RUN MACROS

1. Start Excel and open **NationalAcctgDept-JE-HelpDesk.xlsx**.
2. Save the workbook with Save As and name it **ExcelL2_C7_A2.xlsx**.
3. Press Ctrl + t to run the Technic macro.
4. Press Ctrl + Shift + L to run the Landscape macro.
5. Save, print, and then close **ExcelL2_C7_A2.xlsx**.

3 CREATE MACROS; SAVE AS A MACRO-ENABLED WORKBOOK

1. Open **ExcelL2_C7_A2.xlsx**.
2. Save the workbook with Save As and name it **ExcelL2_C7_A3**.
3. Create the following two macros and store both of them within the current workbook:
   a. Create a macro named **FormulaBarOff** that turns off the display of the formula bar and protects the worksheet. Do not enter a password to unprotect the sheet. Assign the macro to the shortcut key Ctrl + Shift + F. Enter an appropriate description that includes your name and the date the macro was created.

b. Create a macro named **FormulaBarOn** that turns on the display of the formula bar and unprotects the worksheet. Assign the macro to the shortcut key Ctrl + Shift + U. Enter an appropriate description that includes your name and the date the macro was created.

4. Test each macro to make sure the shortcut key runs the correct commands.
5. Save **ExcelL2_C7_A3** as a macro-enabled workbook.
6. Close **ExcelL2_C7_A3.xlsm**.

4 PRINT MACROS; UNHIDE THE PERSONAL MACRO WORKBOOK AND DELETE MACROS

1. Open **ExcelL2_C7_A3.xlsm** enabling the content.
2. Open the Macro dialog box and edit the FormulaBarOff macro.
3. At the Microsoft Visual Basic window with the insertion point blinking in the code window, click File on the Menu bar and then click *Print*. At the Print - VBAProject dialog box, click OK. ***Note: The FormulaBarOn macro code will also print since both macros are stored within the VBA Project.***
4. Click File on the Menu bar and then click *Close and Return to Microsoft Excel*.
5. Close **ExcelL2_C7_A3.xlsm** without saving.
6. Unhide the Personal Macro Workbook file PERSONAL.XLSB.
7. Open the Macro dialog box and edit the Landscape macro.
8. At the Microsoft Visual Basic window with the insertion point blinking in the code window, click File on the Menu bar and then click *Print*. At the Print - VBAProject dialog box, click OK. ***Note: The Technic macro code will also print since both macros are stored within the VBA Project.***
9. Click File on the Menu bar and then click *Close and Return to Microsoft Excel*.
10. Delete the Landscape and the Technic macros.
11. Hide the PERSONAL.XLSB workbook.
12. Exit Excel. Click Yes when prompted to save changes to the Personal Macro Workbook.
13. Start Excel and make sure the Formula bar is visible. If necessary, open the Excel Options dialog box and turn on the display of the formula bar.

5 CREATE A CUSTOM LIST; SORT BY A CUSTOM LIST

1. Open **O'Donovan&Sullivan-Jan29Billing.xlsx**.
2. Save the workbook with Save As and name it **ExcelL2_C7_A5**.
3. Create a custom list that stores the law firm's attorney names in the following order:
   Toni Sullivan
   Marty O'Donovan
   Kyle Williams
   Rosa Martinez
   Maureen Myers

4. The names in the custom list are the order by which the managing partners would like the billing summary sorted. Select A4:I23 and open the Sort dialog box.
5. Sort by the *Attorney* column using the order in the custom list created in Step 3.
6. Save, print, and close **ExcelL2_C7_A5.xlsx**.
7. Start a new blank workbook.
8. Open the Custom List dialog box and delete the custom list created in Step 3.
9. Close the workbook without saving.

Assessment

6 CUSTOMIZE THE EXCEL ENVIRONMENT

1. Open **O'Donovan&Sullivan-Jan29Billing.xlsx**.
2. Save the workbook with Save As and name it **ExcelL2_C7_A6**.
3. Make the following changes to the Display options:
   a. Turn off the horizontal scroll bar.
   b. Turn off sheet tabs.
   c. Turn off row and column headers.
   d. Turn off gridlines.
4. Change the current theme to *Median*.
5. Freeze the first four rows in the worksheet.
6. Save, print, and then close **ExcelL2_C7_A6.xlsx**.

Assessment

7 CREATE AND USE A TEMPLATE

1. Open **ExcelL2_C7_A6.xlsx** and turn on the display of row and column headers.
2. Make the following changes to the workbook:
   a. Select and delete all of the data below the column headings in row 4.
   b. Delete the text in A3.
   c. Edit the subtitle in A2 to *Associate Weekly Billing Summary*.
3. Save the revised workbook as a template named **BillingSummary-StudentName** with your name substituted for *StudentName*.
4. Close **BillingSummary-StudentName.xltx**.
5. Start a new workbook based on the **BillingSummary-StudentName.xltx** template.
6. Type the dates for Monday to Friday of the current week in A3 in the format *January 12 to 16, 2009*.
7. Enter the following two billings using Monday's date of the current week. Enter dates in the format mm/dd/yyyy. For example, *01/12/2009*.

| IN-774 | 10665 | [Monday's date] | Rankin | Jan | Maureen Myers | Insurance | 4.50 | 100.00 |
| EP-895 | 10996 | [Monday's date] | Knox | Velma | Rosa Martinez | Estate | 3.50 | 100.00 |

8. Save the worksheet as an Excel workbook named **ExcelL2_C7_A7**.
9. Print and then close **ExcelL2_C7_A7.xlsx**.

10. Display the New dialog box and right-click the template **BillingSummary-StudentName.xltx**. Select *Copy* at the shortcut menu. Open a My Computer window and navigate to the Excel2007L2C7 folder on your storage medium and then paste the template. Close the My Computer window.
11. Display the New dialog box and then delete the custom template named **BillingSummary-StudentName.xltx**.

CASE study
Apply Your Skills

Part 1

Yolanda Robertson of NuTrends Market Research would like you to help her become more efficient by creating macros for the frequently performed tasks in the list below. In order to share the macros with colleagues in the office you decide to save all of the macros in a macro-enabled workbook named **ExcelL2_C7_CS_P1-Macros**. Delete Sheet2 and Sheet3 from the workbook. Rename Sheet1 to **MacroDocumentation**. Document the macros in the workbook by typing the macro names, the shortcut keys you assigned to each macro, and descriptions of the actions each macro performs. This documentation will assist your colleagues by informing them about the macros in the file. For example, in column A type the name of the macro, in column B type the macro's shortcut key, and in column C enter a description of the actions the macro performs.

Create a separate macro for each of the following tasks. At the Record Macro dialog box, type your name and the current date in the *Description* text box for each macro.

- Apply the theme named *Equity* and show all comments.
- Set the active column's width to 20.
- Apply conditional formatting to highlight the top 10 in a selected list. Accept the default formatting options.
- Apply the Accounting format with zero decimals.
- Create a footer that prints your name centered at the bottom of the worksheet.

Print the MacroDocumentation worksheet. Open the Macro dialog box and edit the first macro. At the Microsoft Visual Basic window, print the macros in the VBAProject. Close the Visual Basic window to return to the worksheet. Save **ExcelL2_C7_CS_P1-Macros.xlsm**.

Part 2

Yolanda has received the file named **PizzabyMario-TargetFranchRev.xlsx** from Nicola Carlucci. She wants you to format the workbook using the macros created in Part 1. Open the workbook and use Save As to name it **ExcelL2_C7_CS_P2**. Run each macro created in Part 1 using the following information:

- Set all of the column widths to 20 except column C.
- Run the number formatting and the conditional formatting with the values in column E selected.
- Run the theme and footer macros.

Print the worksheet making sure the comments print as displayed. Save and then close **ExcelL2_C7_CS_P2.xlsx**. Close **ExcelL2_C7_CS_P1-Macros.xlsm**.

Part 3

Yolanda Robertson from NuTrends Market Research and Nicola Carlucci from Pizza by Mario will be exchanging several workbooks during their project that may contain macros. Yolanda and Nicola want to each set up a folder on their computer and define the folder as a trusted location. Each of them will save the files they exchange to the trusted location folder so that the Trust Center does not block the macros. Yolanda has asked for your help to instruct her on how to create a trusted location. Research in Help how to add a new location to the *Trusted Locations* list. Add the Excel2007L2C7 folder on your storage medium to the list. Open **ExcelL2_C7_CS_P1.xlsm** stored in the Excel2007L2C7 folder to test whether you can now open the workbook without the security warning requiring that you enable the content. Run one of the macros to make sure they have been enabled.

Compose a memo to Yolanda using Microsoft Word that provides the steps on how to add a folder to the *Trusted Locations* list. Save the Word memo and name it **ExcelL2_C7_CS_P3**. Print and then close **ExcelL2_C7_CS_P3.docx** and exit Word. Remove the Excel2007L2C7 folder from the Trusted Locations list.

Part 4

Yolanda would like to customize the Quick Access toolbar but finds the process cumbersome using the Excel Options dialog box to locate commands. Use Excel Help to learn how to add a button to the Quick Access toolbar directly from the ribbon. Test the information you learned by adding two buttons to the Quick Access toolbar using the ribbon. For example, add the Orientation button from the Page Layout tab and the New Comment button from the Review tab. Compose a memo to Yolanda that describes the steps to add a button to the Quick Access toolbar directly from the ribbon. With Excel active, use Print Screen to capture the screen showing the two buttons you added to the toolbar. Paste the screen at the bottom of the memo. Save the Word memo and name it **ExcelL2_C7_C3_P4**. Print and then close **ExcelL2_C7_CS_C4.docx** and exit Word. Remove the two buttons you added to the Quick Access toolbar.

Importing, Exporting, and Distributing Data

PERFORMANCE OBJECTIVES

Upon successful completion of Chapter 8, you will be able to:

- Import data from an Access table
- Import data from a Web site
- Import data from a CSV text file
- Append data from an Excel worksheet to an Access table
- Embed and link data in an Excel worksheet to a Word document
- Copy and paste data in an Excel worksheet to a PowerPoint presentation
- Export data as a comma delimited text file
- Scan and remove private or confidential information from a workbook
- Mark a workbook as final
- Check a workbook for incompatible features with earlier versions of Excel
- Add a digital signature to a workbook
- Describe how digital rights management restricts access to specific users to view, edit, or print a workbook

excel Chapter 8

Tutorial 8.1
Importing Data into Excel
Tutorial 8.2
Exporting Data from Excel

Exchanging data contained in one program with another by importing or exporting eliminates duplication of effort and reduces the likelihood of data errors or missed entries that would arise if the data was retyped. One of the advantages of working with a suite of programs such as Word, Excel, Access, and PowerPoint is the ability to easily integrate data from one program to another. In this chapter you will learn how to bring data into an Excel worksheet from sources external to Excel and how to export data in a worksheet for use with other programs. During an import or export routine, the program containing the original data is called the *source*, and the program to which the data source is being copied, embedded, or linked, is called the *destination*. You will also learn to use features that allow you to restrict access to information and certify content in a workbook that will be distributed to other readers.

Note: Before beginning computer projects, copy to your storage medium the Excel2007L2C8 subfolder from the Excel2007L2 folder on the CD that accompanies this textbook and then make Excel2007L2C8 the active folder.

Project 1 Import Data from External Sources to Excel

You will import U.S. Census Bureau data related to a market research project from an Access database, from the U.S. Census Bureau's Web site, and from a text file previously downloaded from the Census Bureau.

QUICK STEPS

Import Access Table
1. Make active cell at which to begin import.
2. Click Data tab.
3. Click From Access button.
4. Navigate to drive and/or folder.
5. Double-click source database file name.
6. If necessary, click desired table name and OK.
7. Select desired view format.
8. Click OK.

Importing Data into Excel

The Get External Data group in the Data tab contains buttons used to import data from external sources into an Excel worksheet. Make the cell active at which you want the import to begin and click the button representing the source application, or click the Other Sources button to select the source from a drop-down list. A connection can be established to an external data source to avoid having to repeat the import process each time you need to analyze the data in Excel. Once a connection has been created, you can repeat the import in another worksheet by simply clicking the connection file in the Existing Connections dialog box.

Importing Data from Access

Exchanging data between Access and Excel is a seamless process since data in an Access datasheet is structured in the same row and column format as an Excel worksheet. You can import the Access data as an Excel table, a PivotTable Report, or as a PivotChart and a PivotTable report. The imported data can be placed in a cell you identify in the active worksheet or in a new worksheet. To import an Access table, click the Data tab and then click the From Access button in the Get External Data group. At the Select Data Source dialog box, navigate to the drive and/or folder in which the source database resides and then double-click the Access database file name in the file list. If the source database contains more than one table, the Select Table dialog box opens in which you choose the table containing the data you want to import. If the source database contains only one table you are not prompted to select a table name. Once the table is identified, the Import Data dialog box shown in Figure 8.1 appears. Choose how you want to view the data and the location to begin the import and click OK.

HINT
Only one table can be imported at a time. To import all of the tables in the source database, repeat the Import process for each table.

From Access

Figure 8.1 Import Data Dialog Box

Choose the format in which you want the Access table imported in this section.

Choose where to place the imported data in this section.

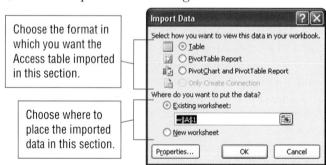

1. Open **NuTrendsMktRsrch-CensusData.xlsx**.
2. Save the workbook with Save As and name it **ExcelL2_C8_P1**.
3. Import four years of U.S. state population estimates compiled by the U.S. Census Bureau that are stored in an Access database by completing the following steps:
   a. With PopulationEstimates the active worksheet, make A5 the active cell.
   b. Click the Data tab.
   c. Click the From Access button in the Get External Data group.
   d. At the Select Data Source dialog box, navigate to the Excel2007L2C8 folder on your storage medium and then double-click *NuTrendsMktRsrch-CensusData.accdb*.

   e. Since the source database contains more than one table, the Select Table dialog box appears. Click *PopulationByState* in the *Name* column and then click OK.

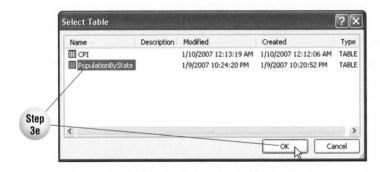

   f. At the Import Data dialog box with *Table* selected in the *Select how you want to view this data in your workbook* section and *=$A$5* in the *Existing worksheet* text box in the *Where do you want to put the data?* section, click OK.

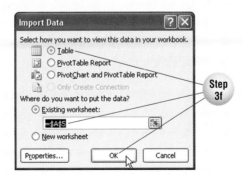

4. Scroll down the imported table data. Notice the data is formatted as a table with filter arrow buttons.

5. Make the following changes to the worksheet:
   a. The clip art image at the top of the worksheet became skewed when the columns were automatically widened upon import. Display the sizing handles on the image and decrease the width to the approximate width shown.
   b. Remove the filter arrow buttons.
   c. Change the table style to Table Style Medium 1 (first from left in *Medium* section) at the Format as Table drop-down gallery.
   d. Format all of the values to display a comma in the thousands and zero decimals.

	A	B	C	D	E	F
1			NuTrends Market Research			
2			U.S. Population Estimates by State			
3						
4	Source: U.S. Census Bureau					
5	ID	State	Pop_July1_06	Pop_July1_05	Pop_July1_04	Pop_Jul1_03
6	1	Alabama	4,599,030	4,548,327	4,517,442	4,495,089
7	2	Alaska	670,053	663,253	656,834	647,747
8	3	Arizona	6,166,318	5,953,007	5,745,674	5,582,252
9	4	Arkansas	2,810,872	2,775,708	2,746,823	2,723,645
10	5	California	36,457,549	36,154,147	35,841,254	35,466,365

Steps
5a–5d

6. Print the PopulationEstimates worksheet scaled to fit 1 page in width and height.
7. Save **ExcelL2_C8_P1.xlsx**.

Importing Data from a Web Site

Import Data from Web Page
1. Make active cell at which to begin import.
2. Click Data tab.
3. Click From Web button.
4. Navigate to desired Web page.
5. Click arrows next to tables to import.
6. Click Import button.
7. Click OK.

Tables in a Web site can be downloaded directly from the Web source using the New Web Query dialog box shown in Figure 8.2. Make active the cell at which you want to begin the import, click the Data tab, and then click the From Web button in the Get External Data group. Use the Address bar and Web navigation buttons to go to the page containing the data you want to use in Excel. At the desired page, Excel displays black right-pointing arrows inside yellow boxes next to elements on the page that contain importable tables. Point to an arrow and a blue border surrounds the data Excel will capture if you click the arrow. Click the arrow for those tables you want to bring into your Excel worksheet and then click the Import button. In Project 1b, you will import multiple sections of data about Florida from the U.S. Census Bureau QuickFacts Web page.

Figure 8.2 New Web Query Dialog Box

Navigate to the desired Web site as you would in a browser window.

Point to an arrow in a yellow box to display a blue border around a table on the Web page. Click the arrow to select the table and then click the Import button to copy the data into the active cell.

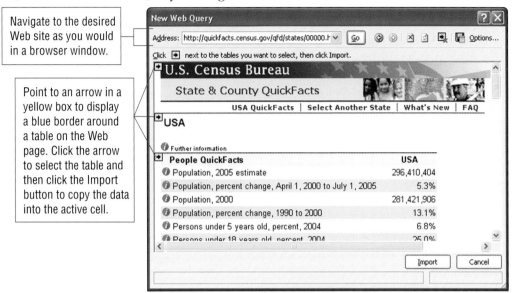

Project 1b | **Importing a Table from a Web Page**

1. With **ExcelL2_C8_P1.xlsx** open, make FloridaGeographicData the active worksheet.
2. Import statistics related to Florida from the U.S. Census Bureau QuickFacts Web page by completing the following steps:
   a. Make A6 the active cell.
   b. Click the From Web button in the Get External Data group of the Data tab.
   c. At the New Web Query dialog box, select the current entry in the *Address* text box, type http://www.census.gov and press Enter.
   d. Click the Data Tools link located near the top left of the Web page.
   e. At the Data Access Tools page, scroll down the page if necessary and then click the QuickFacts link in the Interactive Internet Tools section.
   f. At the State & County QuickFacts page, resize the New Web Query dialog box until you can see the entire map of the USA.

g. Click on the state of Florida in the map.

h. At the Florida QuickFacts page, notice the black right-pointing arrows inside yellow boxes along the left edge of the page. Point to one of the arrows to see the blue border that surrounds a section of data; the border indicates the data that will be imported into Excel if you click the arrow.

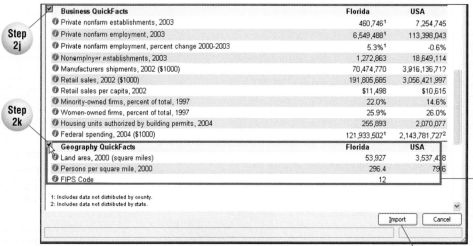

Step 2g

i. Scroll down the page to the section titled *Business QuickFacts*.

j. Click the black right-pointing arrow inside the yellow box next to *Business QuickFacts* to select the table. The arrow changes to a check mark inside a green box when the table is selected for import.

k. Click the arrow next to *Geography QuickFacts* to select the table.

l. Click the Import button.

Step 2j

Step 2k

Business QuickFacts	Florida	USA
Private nonfarm establishments, 2003	460,746[1]	7,254,745
Private nonfarm employment, 2003	6,549,488[1]	113,398,043
Private nonfarm employment, percent change 2000-2003	5.3%[1]	-0.6%
Nonemployer establishments, 2003	1,272,863	18,649,114
Manufacturers shipments, 2002 ($1000)	70,474,770	3,916,136,712
Retail sales, 2002 ($1000)	191,805,685	3,056,421,997
Retail sales per capita, 2002	$11,498	$10,615
Minority-owned firms, percent of total, 1997	22.0%	14.6%
Women-owned firms, percent of total, 1997	25.9%	26.0%
Housing units authorized by building permits, 2004	255,893	2,070,077
Federal spending, 2004 ($1000)	121,933,502[1]	2,143,781,727[2]
Geography QuickFacts	**Florida**	**USA**
Land area, 2000 (square miles)	53,927	3,537,438
Persons per square mile, 2000	296.4	79.6
FIPS Code	12	

1: Includes data not distributed by county.
2: Includes data not distributed by state.

[Import] [Cancel]

A blue border displays around the data that will be imported to Excel if the table is selected.

m. At the Import Data dialog box with *=$A$6* in the *Existing worksheet* text box in the *Where do you want to put the data?* section, click OK. Excel imports the data from the Web page into the Excel worksheet starting in A6.

Step 2l

Step 2m

3. Make the following changes to the worksheet:

a. Move the clip art image to approximately center it horizontally and vertically within the range C1:D5.

b. Select the cells in Column A that contain imported text, click the Home tab, and then click the Wrap Text button in the Alignment group.

c. Decrease the width of column A to 35.00 (250 pixels).

d. AutoFit the height of A6:A22.

e. Align the text in C6:D6 at the center.

f. Change the page orientation to landscape and scale to fit one page width by one page height.

4. Print the FloridaGeographicData worksheet.

5. Save **ExcelL2_C8_P1.xlsx**.

Importing Data from a Text File

A text file is often used to exchange data between dissimilar programs since the file format is recognized by nearly all applications. Text files contain no formatting and consist of letters, numbers, punctuation symbols, and a few control characters only. Two commonly used text file formats separate fields with either a tab character (delimited file format) or a comma (comma separated file format). The text file you will use in Project 1c is shown in a Notepad window in Figure 8.3. If necessary, you can view and edit a text file in Notepad prior to importing.

QUICK STEPS

Import Data from Comma Separated Text File

1. Make active cell at which to begin import.
2. Click Data tab.
3. Click From Text button.
4. Double-click .csv file name.
5. Click Next.
6. Click *Comma* check box.
7. Click Next.
8. Click Finish.
9. Click OK.

From Text

Figure 8.3 Project 1c Text File Contents

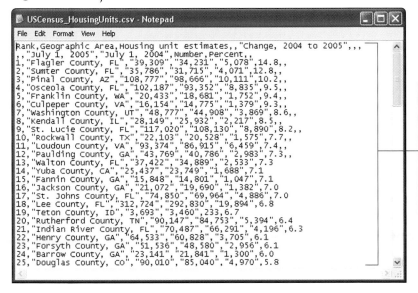

Text files contain no formatting codes. A comma separated file (.csv) contains a comma separating each field. During the import, Excel starts a new column at each comma. Notice also that quotes surround text data. Excel strips the quotes from the data upon importing.

To import a text file into Excel, use the From Text button in the Get External Data group of the Data tab and then select the source file at the Import Text File dialog box. Excel displays in the file list any file in the active folder that ends with a text file extension *.prn, .txt,* or *.csv.* Once the source file is selected, Excel begins the Text Import Wizard, which guides you through the import process through three dialog boxes.

HINT

Most programs can export data in a text file. If you need to use data from a program that is not compatible with Excel, check the source program's export options for a text file format.

1. With **ExcelL2_C8_P1.xlsx** open, make HousingUnitData the active worksheet.
2. Import statistics related to the top-growing U.S. counties based on changes in housing units downloaded from the U. S. Census Bureau Web site in a text file by completing the following steps:
   a. Make A7 the active cell.
   b. Click the Data tab.
   c. Click the From Text button in the Get External Data group.
   d. At the Import Text File dialog box, double-click the file named **USCensus_HousingUnits.csv** in the file list.
   e. At the Text Import Wizard - Step 1 of 3 dialog box, with *Delimited* selected in the *Original data type* section, click Next. Notice the preview window in the lower half of the dialog box displays a sample of the data in the source text file. Delimited files use commas or tabs as separators, while fixed-width files use spaces.

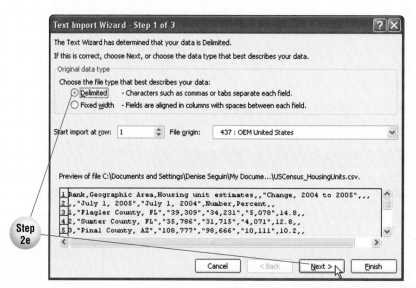

Step 2e

   f. At the Text Import Wizard - Step 2 of 3 dialog box, click the *Comma* check box in the *Delimiters* section to insert a check mark and then click Next. Notice after you select the comma as the delimiter character, the data in the *Data preview* section updates to show the imported data arranged in Excel columns.

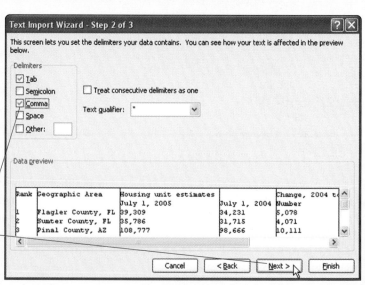

Step 2f

g. Click Finish at the Text Import Wizard - Step 3 of 3 dialog box to import all of the columns using the default *General* format. Formatting can be applied after the data has been imported into the worksheet.

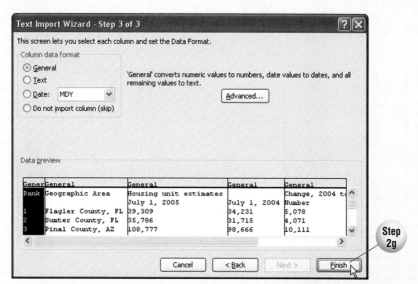

h. At the Import Data dialog box with *=$A$7* in the *Existing worksheet* text box in the *Where do you want to put the data?* section, click OK.

3. Scroll down the worksheet and view the imported data. The text file contained the top 100 counties in the United States ranked by change in housing units from 2004 to 2005. The number of housing units and the percent change are included.

4. Make the following changes to the data:
   a. Select C7:D7, click the Home tab, and then click the Merge & Center button in the Alignment group.
   b. Merge and center E7:F7.
   c. Align the text in E8 at the right.
   d. Change the width of columns C, D, and E to 14.00 (103 pixels).

5. Print the HousingUnitData worksheet.
6. Save and then close **ExcelL2_C8_P1.xlsx**.

Project ② Export Data in Excel

You will copy and paste data related to car inventory from an Excel worksheet to integrate with an Access database, a Word report, and a PowerPoint presentation. You will also save a worksheet as a comma separated text file for use in a non-Microsoft program.

Exporting Data from Excel

Excel data can be exported for use in other programs by copying the cells to the clipboard and pasting into the destination document or by saving the worksheet as a separate file in another file format. To use Excel data in Word, PowerPoint, or Access, use the copy and paste routine since the programs within the Microsoft Office Suite are designed for integration. To export the Excel data for use in other programs, open the Save As dialog box and change the *Save as type* option to the desired file format. If the file format for the destination program that you want to use does not appear in the *Save as type* list, you can try copying and pasting the data or go to the Microsoft Office Online Web site and search for a file format converter that you can download and install.

Append Excel Data to Access Table
1. Open Excel workbook.
2. Select cells.
3. Click Copy button.
4. Start Access.
5. Open database.
6. Open table in Datasheet view.
7. Click Paste button arrow.
8. Click *Paste Append*.
9. Click Yes.
10. Deselect pasted range.

Copying and Pasting Worksheet Data to an Access Table

Data in an Excel worksheet can be copied and pasted to an Access table datasheet, query, or form using the clipboard. To paste data into a table datasheet, make sure that the column structure in the two programs match. If the Access datasheet already contains records, you can choose to replace the existing records or append the Excel data to the end of the table. If you want to export Excel data to an Access database that does not have an existing table in which to receive the data, perform an import routine from Access. Start Access, click the External Data tab, and then click the Import Excel spreadsheet button.

Project 2a   **Copying and Pasting Excel Data to an Access Datasheet**

1. Open **CutRate-Inventory.xlsx**.
2. Copy and paste the rows in the NewInventory worksheet to the bottom of an Access table by completing the following steps:
   a. Make sure NewInventory is the active worksheet.
   b. Select A2:G30 and click the Copy button in the Clipboard group in the Home tab.
   c. Start Microsoft Office Access 2007.
   d. At the Getting Started with Microsoft Office Access screen, click the Office button and then click *Open* at the drop-down list.
   e. At the Open dialog box, navigate to the Excel2007L2C8 folder on your storage medium and then double-click the database named ***CutRate-CarInventory.accdb***.
   f. Double-click the object named *CarPurchaseInventory : Table* in the Navigation pane at the left side of the Access window. This opens the CarPurchaseInventory table in Datasheet view. Notice the structure of the columns in the datasheet is the same as the source worksheet in Excel.

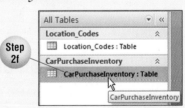

Step 2f

g. With the table open in Datasheet view, click the down-pointing arrow on the Paste button in the Clipboard group and then click *Paste Append* at the drop-down list.

h. At the Microsoft Office Access message box informing you that you are about to paste 29 records and asking if you are sure, click Yes.

Step 2g

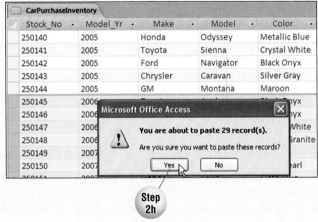

Step 2h

i. Click any cell within the datasheet to deselect the pasted records.

3. Print the datasheet in Access in landscape orientation by completing the following steps:

   a. Click the Office button, point to *Print*, and then click *Print Preview*.

   b. Click the Landscape button in the Page Layout group in the Print Preview tab.

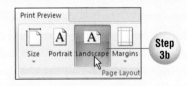

Step 3b

   c. Click the Print button in the Print group and then click OK at the Print dialog box.

   d. Click the Close Print Preview button in the Close Preview group.

4. Click the Close button located at the top right of the datasheet to close the CarPurchaseInventory datasheet.

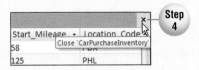

Step 4

5. Click the Office button and then click the Exit Access button located at the bottom right of the drop-down list.

6. Click any cell to deselect the range in the NewInventory worksheet and press the Esc key to remove the moving marquee.

Copying and Pasting Worksheet Data to a Word Document

Embed Excel Data in Word Document
1. Open Excel workbook.
2. Select cells.
3. Click Copy button.
4. Start Word.
5. Open document.
6. Position insertion point at desired location.
7. Click Paste button arrow.
8. Click *Paste Special.*
9. Click *Microsoft Office Excel Worksheet Object.*
10. Click OK.
11. Save and close Word document.
12. Deselect range.

Link Excel Data in Word Document
1. Open Excel workbook.
2. Select cells.
3. Click Copy button.
4. Start Word.
5. Open document.
6. Position insertion point at desired location.
7. Click Paste button arrow.
8. Click *Paste Special.*
9. Click *Microsoft Office Excel Worksheet Object.*
10. Click *Paste link.*
11. Click OK.
12. Save and close Word document.
13. Deselect range.

Using a process similar to the one in Project 2a, you can copy and paste Excel data, copy and embed Excel data as an object, or copy and link Excel data as an object in a Word document. Use the copy and paste method if the data being brought into Word is not likely to be updated or require editing once the source cells are pasted in the Word document. Copy and embed the data if you want to have the ability to edit the data once it is inserted in Word using Excel's editing tools and features. Copy and link the data if the information being pasted into Word is likely to be changed in the future and you want the document in Word updated if the data in the source file changes.

Embedding Excel Data into Word

To embed copied Excel data into a Word document, open the desired Word document, move the insertion point to the location at which you want to insert the copied Excel data, and then open the Paste Special dialog box. At the Paste Special dialog box, click *Microsoft Office Excel Worksheet Object* in the *As* list box and then click OK.

To edit an embedded Excel object in Word, double-click over the embedded cells to open the cells for editing in a worksheet. Word's ribbon is temporarily replaced with Excel's ribbon. Click outside the embedded object to restore Word's ribbon and close the worksheet object in Word.

Linking Excel Data into Word

Linking Excel data to a Word document means that the source data exists only in Excel. Word places a shortcut to the source data file name and range in the Word document. When you open a Word document containing a link, Word prompts you to update the links. Since the data resides in the Excel workbook only, be careful not to move or rename the original workbook from which you copied the cells or the link will no longer work.

To paste copied Excel data as a link in a Word document, open the desired Word document, move the insertion point to the location at which you want to link the cells, open the Paste Special dialog box, click *Microsoft Office Excel Worksheet Object* in the *As* list box, click *Paste link*, and then click OK.

Project 2b Embedding Excel Data in a Word Document

1. With **CutRate-Inventory.xlsx** open, copy and embed the data in the CarCosts worksheet to a Word document by completing the following steps:
   a. Make CarCosts the active worksheet.
   b. Select A4:F9.
   c. Click the Copy button in the Clipboard group.

d. Start Microsoft Office Word 2007.
e. Open **CutRate-CarReport.docx**.
f. Save the document with Save As and name it
   ExcelL2_C8_P2.
g. Press Ctrl + End to move the insertion point to the
   end of the document.
h. Click the down-pointing arrow on the Paste button
   and then click *Paste Special* at the drop-down list.
i. At the Paste Special dialog box, click *Microsoft Office
   Excel Worksheet Object* in the *As* list box and then click OK.

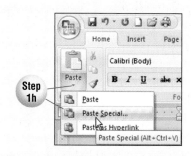

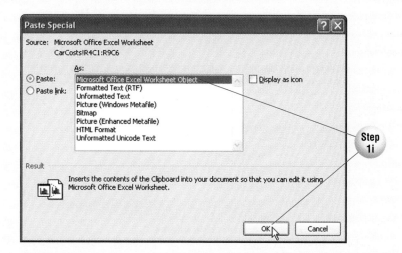

2. Save **ExcelL2_C8_P2.docx**.
3. When you use Paste Special, the copied cells are embedded as an object in the Word
   document. Edit the embedded object using Excel's editing tools by completing the following
   steps:
   a. Double-click over any cell in the embedded worksheet object. The object is surrounded
      with a border and Excel's column and row headers appear with the cells. Word's ribbon
      is temporarily replaced with Excel's ribbon.
   b. Select B5:F9 and then click the Accounting Number Format button in the Number group.

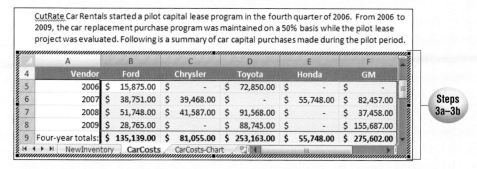

   c. Click in the document outside the embedded object to close the object and restore
      Word's ribbon.
4. Save, print, and then close **ExcelL2_C8_P2.docx**.
5. Click the Office button and then click the Exit Word button.
6. Click any cell to deselect the range in the CarCosts worksheet.

1. With **CutRate-Inventory.xlsx** open, copy and link the data in the CarCosts worksheet to a Word document by completing the following steps:
   a. With CarCosts the active worksheet, select A4:F9 and click the Copy button.
   b. Start Microsoft Office Word 2007.
   c. Open **CutRate-CarReport.docx**.
   d. Save the document with Save As and name it **ExcelL2_C8_P2-Linked**.
   e. Press Ctrl + End to move the insertion point to the end of the document.
   f. Click the down-pointing arrow on the Paste button and then click *Paste Special* at the drop-down list.
   g. At the Paste Special dialog box, click *Microsoft Office Excel Worksheet Object* in the *As* list box and then click *Paste link*.
   h. Click OK.

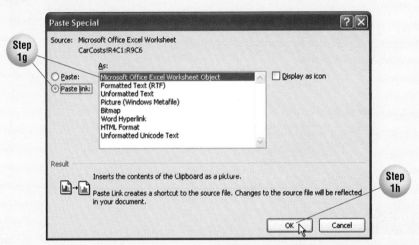

2. Save and then close **ExcelL2_C8_P2-Linked.docx**. When data is linked, the data exists only in the source program. In the destination document, Word inserted a shortcut to the source range. Edit the source range and view the update to the Word document by completing the following steps:
   a. Click the button on the Taskbar representing the Excel file named **CutRate-Inventory.xlsx**.
   b. With CarCosts the active worksheet, press the ESC key to remove the moving marquee from the source range and then make E5 the active cell.
   c. Type **85000** and press Enter.
   d. Click the button on the Taskbar representing Word.
   e. Open **ExcelL2_C8_P2-Linked.docx**.
   f. At the Microsoft Office Word message box asking if you want to update the document with data from the linked files, click Yes.

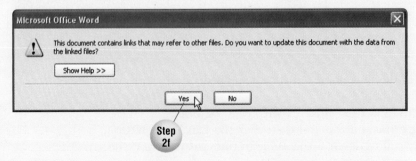

3. Notice the data inserted in the Excel worksheet is also shown in the linked Word document.
4. Save and then print **ExcelL2_C8_P2-Linked.docx**.
5. Exit Word.
6. With CarCosts the active worksheet in **CutRate-Inventory.xlsx**, delete the contents of E5.

Breaking a Link to an Excel Object

If you linked Excel data to a Word document and later decide you no longer need to maintain the link, you can break the connection between the source and destination files so that you are not prompted to update the object each time you open the document. Breaking the link means that the data in the Word document will no longer be connected to the data in the Excel workbook. If you make a change to the original source in Excel, the Word document will not reflect the updated information. To break a link, open the document, right-click over the linked object, point to *Linked Worksheet Object* and click *Links* at the shortcut menu. This opens the Links dialog box. If more than one linked object exists in the document, click the source object for the link you want to break and then click the Break Link button. Click Yes to confirm you want to break the link at the message box that appears.

Project **2d** | **Breaking a Link**

1. Start Word and open **ExcelL2_C8_P2-Linked.docx**.
2. At the message asking if you want to update links, click Yes.
3. Break the link between the Excel workbook and the linked object by completing the following steps:
   a. Right-click over the linked Excel worksheet object.
   b. Point to *Linked Worksheet Object* and then click *Links* at the shortcut menu.
   c. At the Links dialog box, with the linked object file name selected in the Source file list box, click the Break Link button.

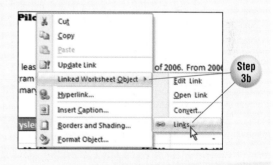

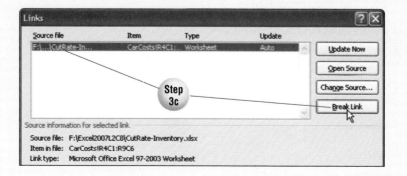

d. At the Microsoft Office Word dialog box asking if you are sure you want to break the selected link, click Yes.

4. Save **ExcelL2_C8_P2-Linked.docx** and then exit Word.

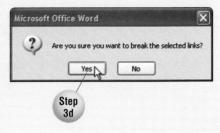

Step 3d

Copying and Pasting Worksheet Data to a PowerPoint Presentation

As with Word, you can copy and paste, copy and embed, or copy and link Excel data to slides in a PowerPoint presentation. Although you can create tables and charts in a PowerPoint slide, some people prefer to use Excel for these tasks and then copy and paste the data to PowerPoint. Presentations often incorporate charts to visually depict numerical data in a graph format that is easy to understand. In the Office 2007 suite, the charting system is fully integrated within Word, Excel, and PowerPoint. A chart inserted in a Word document or PowerPoint presentation is created as an embedded object with the source data used to generate the chart stored in an Excel worksheet; the Excel worksheet with the source data becomes part of the document or presentation file.

Since the chart feature is fully integrated within Word, Excel, and PowerPoint, you can edit a chart in a PowerPoint presentation using the same techniques you learned to edit a chart in Excel. Clicking a chart on a PowerPoint slide causes the contextual Chart Tools Design, Chart Tools Layout, and Chart Tools Format tabs to become active with the same groups and buttons available in Excel.

Project 2e | **Embedding Excel Data in a PowerPoint Presentation**

1. With **CutRate-Inventory.xlsx** open, copy and embed the chart in the CarCosts-Chart worksheet to a slide in a PowerPoint presentation by completing the following steps:
   a. Make CarCosts-Chart the active worksheet.
   b. Click in a blank area around the chart to select the chart object.
   c. Click the Home tab and then click the Copy button.
   d. Start Microsoft Office PowerPoint 2007.
   e. Open **CutRate-CarReport.pptx**.
   f. Save the presentation with Save As and name it **ExcelL2_C8_P2**.

g. Click slide 3 in the Slides pane.

h. Click the Paste button in the Clipboard group. Since all charts are embedded by default, you do not need to use Paste Special.

2. Resize the chart to the approximate height and width shown and position the chart in the center of the slide horizontally.

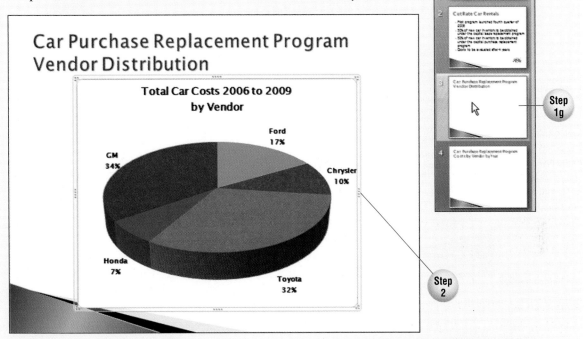

3. Copy and embed the table used to generate the chart in the CarCosts worksheet to the next slide in the PowerPoint presentation by completing the following steps:

a. Click slide 4 in the Slides pane.

b. Click the button on the Taskbar representing the Excel workbook **CutRate-Inventory.xlsx**.

c. Make CarCosts the active worksheet, select A1:F9 and click the Copy button.

d. Click the button on the taskbar representing the PowerPoint presentation **ExcelL2_C8_P2.pptx**.

e. Click the down-pointing arrow on the Paste button and then click *Paste Special* at the drop-down list.

f. With *Microsoft Office Excel Worksheet Object* selected in the *As* list box, click OK.

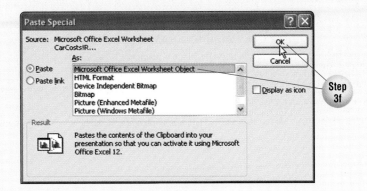

4. Resize and position the embedded table to the approximate height, width, and position shown.

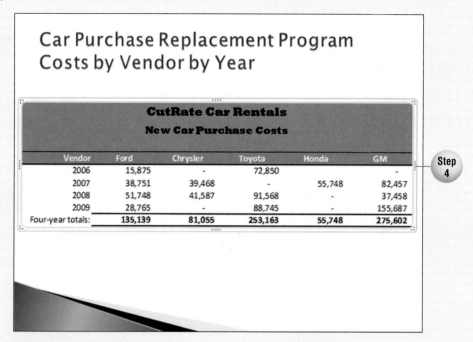

Car Purchase Replacement Program
Costs by Vendor by Year

Vendor	Ford	Chrysler	Toyota	Honda	GM
CutRate Car Rentals					
New Car Purchase Costs					
2006	15,875	-	72,850		-
2007	38,751	39,468	-	55,748	82,457
2008	51,748	41,587	91,568	-	37,458
2009	28,765	-	88,745	-	155,687
Four-year totals:	**135,139**	**81,055**	**253,163**	**55,748**	**275,602**

Step 4

5. Click the Office button and then click *Print*. Change *Print what* to *Handouts*. Make sure *Slides per page* is *6*, and then click OK.
6. Save and close **ExcelL2_C8_P2.pptx** and then exit PowerPoint.
7. Press the ESC key to remove the moving marquee and then click any cell to deselect the range in the CarCosts worksheet.

Step 5

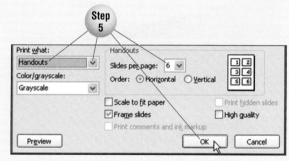

QUICK STEPS

Export Worksheet as Text File
1. Open workbook.
2. Make desired sheet active.
3. Click Office button.
4. Click *Save As*.
5. Type file name.
6. Change *Save as type* to desired text file format.
7. Click Save button.
8. Click OK.
9. Click Yes.

Exporting Excel Data as a Text File

If you need to exchange Excel data with a person who is not able to import a Microsoft Excel worksheet or cannot copy and paste using the clipboard, you can save the data as a text file. Excel provides several text file options including file formats suitable for computers that use the Macintosh operating system as shown in Table 8.1. To save a worksheet as a text file, open the Save As dialog box and change *Save as type* to the desired option. Type a file name for the text file and then click the Save button. Click OK at the message box that informs you that only the active worksheet is saved and then click Yes at the next message box to confirm you want to save the data as a text file.

Table 8.1 Supported Text File Formats for Exporting

Text File Format Option	File Extension
Text (tab delimited)	.txt
Unicode text	.txt
CSV (Comma delimited)	.csv
Formatted text (Space delimited)	.prn
Text (Macintosh)	.txt
Text (MS-DOS)	.txt
CSV (Macintosh)	.csv
CSV (MS-DOS)	.csv

HINT

Why so many text file formats? Although all systems support text files, differences occur across platforms. For example, a Macintosh computer denotes the end of a line in a text file with a carriage return character, Unix uses a linefeed character, and DOS inserts both a linefeed and a carriage return character code at the end of each line.

Project ② Exporting a Worksheet as a Text File

1. With **CutRate-Inventory.xlsx** open, export the NewInventory worksheet data as a text file by completing the following steps:
   a. Make NewInventory the active worksheet.
   b. Click the Office button and then click *Save As*.
   c. Type ExcelL2_C8_P2 in the *File name* text box.
   d. Click the down-pointing arrow to the right of the *Save as type* list box, scroll down the list, and then click *CSV (Comma delimited) (*.csv)* at the drop-down list.
   e. Click the Save button.

Step 1d

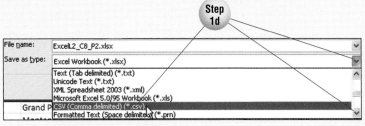

   f. Click OK to save only the active sheet at the Microsoft Office Excel message box that informs you the selected file type does not support workbooks that contain multiple worksheets.

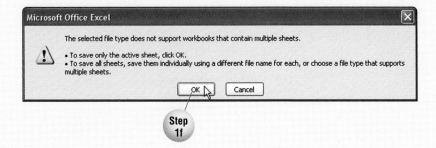

Step 1f

g. Click Yes to save the workbook in this format at the next message box that informs you Excel_L2_C8.csv may contain features that are not compatible with CSV (Comma delimited).

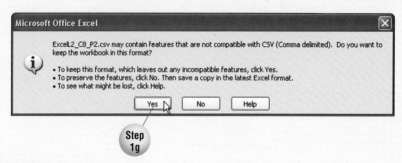

Step
1g

2. Close **ExcelL2_C8_P2.csv**. Click No when prompted to save changes.
3. Open Notepad and view the text file created in Step 1 by completing the following steps:
   a. Click the Start button, point to *All Programs*, point to *Accessories*, and then click *Notepad*.
   b. Click File on the Notepad Menu bar and then click *Open*.
   c. Navigate to the Excel2007L2C8 folder on your storage medium.
   d. Click the down-pointing arrow next to *Files of type* and then click *All Files* at the drop-down list.
   e. Double-click **ExcelL2_C8_P2.csv**.
   f. Scroll down to view all of the data in the text file. Notice that a comma has been inserted between each column's data.

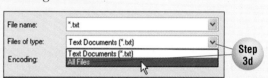

Step
3d

A comma is inserted at each column change in a csv text file.

Step
3f

4. Click File on the Notepad Menu bar and then click *Print*. Click the Print button at the Print dialog box.
5. Exit Notepad.

Project ③ Prepare a Workbook for Distribution

You will remove confidential information from a workbook, mark the workbook as final, and attach a digital signature.

Preparing a Workbook for Distribution

In today's workplace, you often work as part of a team both within and outside your organization. Excel workbooks are frequently exchanged between workers via e-mail message attachments; by saving to a shared network folder, a document management server, or a company Web site; or by other means of electronic distribution. Prior to making a workbook available for others to open, view, and edit, Excel provides several features on the Prepare menu from the Office drop-down list that allow you to protect and/or maintain confidentiality.

Removing Information from a Workbook before Distributing

Prior to distributing a workbook electronically to others, you should consider using the Document Inspector feature to scan the workbook for personal or other hidden information that you would not want others to be able to view. Recall from Chapter 6 that a workbook's properties, sometimes referred to as *metadata*, include information that is tracked automatically by Excel such as the names of the individuals that accessed and edited a workbook. If a workbook will be sent electronically by e-mail or made available on a document management server or other Web site, consider the implications of recipients of that workbook being able to look at some of this hidden information. Ask yourself if this information should remain confidential and if so, remove sensitive data and/or metadata before distributing the file. To do this, click the Office button, point to *Prepare*, and then click *Inspect Document*. This opens the Document Inspector dialog box shown in Figure 8.4. By default, all check boxes are selected. Clear the check boxes for those items that you do not need or want to scan and remove and then click OK.

Note also that before removing sensitive data, you can save a copy of the original file that retains all content using password protection or other security measures to limit access. Another helpful use of the Document Inspector is as a tool to reveal the presence of headers, footers, hidden items, or other invisible items in a workbook for which you are not the original author.

QUICK STEPS

Use Document Inspector to Remove Private Information
1. Open workbook.
2. Click Office button.
3. Point to *Prepare*.
4. Click *Inspect Document*.
5. Clear check boxes for those items you do not want to scan and remove.
6. Click Inspect button.
7. Click Remove All button in those sections with items you want removed.
8. Click Close button.

Figure 8.4 Document Inspector Dialog Box

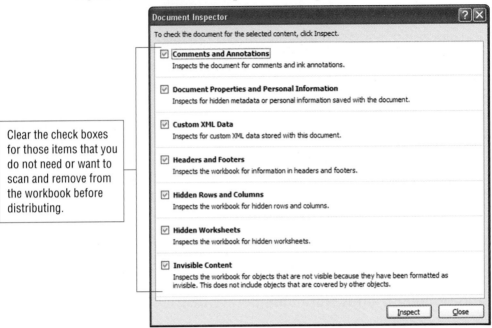

Clear the check boxes for those items that you do not need or want to scan and remove from the workbook before distributing.

The Document Inspector scans the workbook for the existence of any of the checked items. When completed, a dialog box similar to the one shown in Figure 8.5 appears. Excel displays a check mark in the sections for which no items were found and a red exclamation mark in the sections in which items were detected within the workbook. Click the Remove All button in the section that contains content you decide you want to remove. Click OK when finished and then distribute the workbook as needed.

Figure 8.5 Document Inspector Dialog Box with Inspection Results Shown

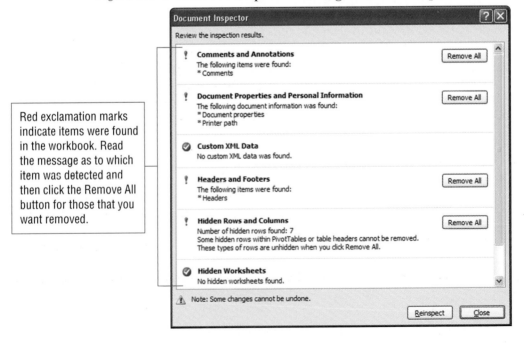

Red exclamation marks indicate items were found in the workbook. Read the message as to which item was detected and then click the Remove All button for those that you want removed.

1. Open **CutRate-PilotPrjRpt.xlsx**.
2. Save the workbook with Save As and name it **ExcelL2_C8_P3**.
3. Examine the workbook for private and other confidential information by completing the following steps:
   a. Click the Office button, point to *Prepare,* and then click *Properties*.
   b. Read the information in the property fields in the Document Information Panel.
   c. Click the Property Views and Options button and then click *Advanced Properties* at the drop-down list.

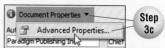

Step 3c

   d. Click the Custom tab in the ExcelL2_C8_P3.xlsx Properties dialog box.
   e. Position the mouse pointer on the right column boundary for the *Value* column in the *Properties* list box until the pointer changes to a vertical bar with a left- and right-pointing arrow and then drag the column width right until you can read all of the text within the column.
   f. Notice that the extra information added to the workbook properties contains names and other data that you might not want widely circulated.

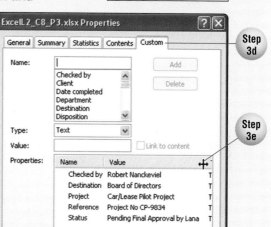

Step 3d

Step 3e

   g. Click OK.
   h. Close the Document Information Panel.
   i. Click the Review tab and then click the Show All Comments button in the Comments group.
   j. Read the two comments displayed in the worksheet area.

Step 3j

4. Scan the workbook for other confidential information using the Document Inspector by completing the following steps:
   a. Click the Office button, point to *Prepare,* and then click *Inspect Document*.
   b. At the Microsoft Office Excel message box indicating the file contains changes that have not been saved, click Yes to save the file now.
   c. At the Document Inspector dialog box with all check boxes selected, click the Inspect button to check for all items.
   d. Scroll down the Document Inspector dialog box and review the messages in each section that display with a red exclamation mark.

e. Click the Remove All button in the *Document Properties and Personal Information* section. Excel deletes the metadata and the section now displays with a check mark indicating the information has been removed.

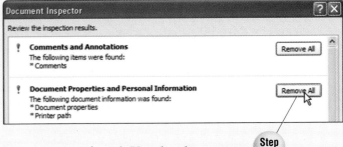

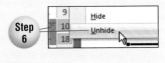

Step 4e

f. Notice the inspection results indicate a header and seven hidden rows were found. You decide to review these items before removing them. Click the Close button to close the Document Inspector dialog box.

5. Display the worksheet in Page Layout View and view the header.

6. Look at the row numbers in the worksheet area. Notice that after row 10, the next row number is 18. Select row numbers 10 and 18, right-click the selected rows, and then click *Unhide* at the shortcut menu to display rows 11–17.

Step 6

7. Change to Normal view and click any cell to deselect the range. Review the information that was in the hidden rows. Notice an additional comment is now displayed.

8. You decide the rows that were initially hidden should remain displayed but want to remove the header and the comments from reviewers of the workbook. Use the Document Inspector to remove these items by completing the following steps:

a. Click the Office button, point to *Prepare*, click *Inspect Document*, and then click Yes to save the changes to the workbook.

b. Clear the check boxes for all items except *Comments and Annotations* and *Headers and Footers*.

c. Click the Inspect button.

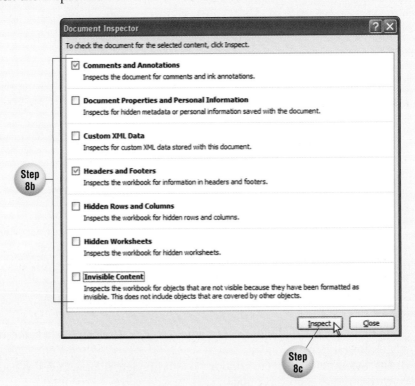

d. Click the Remove All button in the *Comments and Annotations* section.

e. Click the Remove All button in the *Headers and Footers* section.

f. Click the Close button.

9. Notice the comments have been deleted from the worksheet. Switch to Page Layout view and check for the header text. Notice the header has been deleted. Switch back to Normal view.

10. Click the Show All Comments button in the Comments group of the Review tab to turn the feature off.

11. Save, print, and then close **ExcelL2_C8_P3.xlsx**.

Marking a Workbook as Final before Distributing

A workbook that will be distributed to others can be marked as final which means the workbook is prevented from having additions, deletions, or modifications made to cells. The workbook is changed to read-only and the status property is set to *Final*. In addition to protecting the workbook, marking a workbook as final also serves to indicate to the recipient(s) of the workbook that you consider the content complete. To mark a workbook as final, click the Office button, point to *Prepare*, and then click *Mark as Final*. Note that marking a workbook as final should not be considered as secure as using password-protected, locked ranges. The workbook's read-only and final status property can be removed by simply clicking the Office button, pointing to *Prepare*, and then clicking *Mark as Final*.

As an alternative to *Mark as Final*, consider distributing a workbook published as a PDF document. Microsoft has made available for download an add-in that allows you to save in PDF or XPS format. Click the Office button, point to *Save As*, and then click *Find add-ins for other file formats*. This opens an Excel Help window where you will find a link to Microsoft's Web site with the PDF download.

Project **3b** **Marking a Workbook as Final**

1. Open **ExcelL2_C8_P3.xlsx**.

2. Save the workbook with Save As and name it **ExcelL2_C8_P3-Final**.

3. Mark the workbook as final to prevent changes and set the Status property to *Final* by completing the following steps:

a. Click the Office button, point to *Prepare*, and then click *Mark as Final*.

b. Click OK at the message box that says the workbook will be marked as final and then saved.

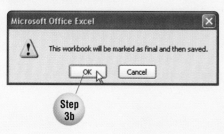

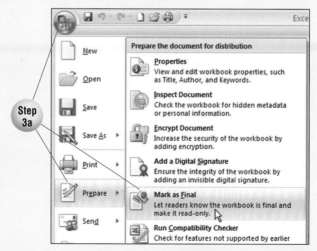

c. Click OK at the second message box that says the workbook has been marked as final to indicate that editing is complete and that this is the final version of the document. ***Note: If this message box does not appear, it has been turned off by a previous user who clicked the*** Don't show this message again *check box.*

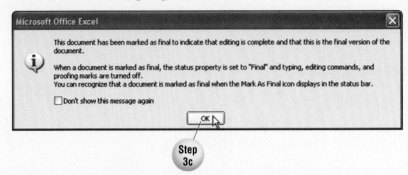

Step
3c

4. Notice the visual indicators that the workbook is final by the addition of *[Read Only]* next to the file name in the Title bar and the *Marked as Final* icon in the Status bar next to *Ready*.
5. Open the Document Information Panel. Notice the *Status* property reads *Final*.
6. Close the Document Information Panel.
7. Make any cell active and attempt to insert or delete text in the cell. Since the workbook is now read-only, you cannot open the cell for editing or delete the contents.
8. Look at the ribbon and notice most of the buttons are dimmed for features that would be used to edit the workbook.
9. Close **ExcelL2_C8_P3-Final.xlsx**.

QUICK
STEPS

Check Workbook for Compatibility
1. Open workbook.
2. Click Office button.
3. Point to *Prepare*.
4. Click *Run Compatibility Checker*.
5. Read information in Summary report.
6. If desired, click *Copy to New Sheet* OR click Close.

Using the Compatibility Checker

If you have a workbook that will be exchanged with other users that do not have Excel 2007, you can save the workbook in the Excel 97-2003 file format. When you save the file in the earlier version's file format, Excel automatically does a compatibility check and prompts you with information about loss of functionality or fidelity. If you prefer, you can run the compatibility checker before you save the workbook so that you know in advance areas of the worksheet that may need changes prior to saving.

In the Compatibility Checker Summary report, if an issue displays a Fix hyperlink, click Fix to resolve the problem. If you want more information about a loss of functionality or fidelity, click the Help hyperlink next to the issue.

1. Open **CutRate-BuyLeaseAnalysis.xlsx**.
2. Run the Compatibility Checker to check the workbook in advance of saving in an earlier Excel file format by completing the following steps:
   a. Click the Office button.
   b. Point to *Prepare*.
   c. Click *Run Compatibility Checker*.

   d. At the Microsoft Office Excel - Compatibility Checker dialog box, read the information in the *Summary* box in the *Significant loss of functionality* section.
   e. Scroll down and read the information displayed in the *Minor loss of fidelity* section.
   f. Scroll back up to the top of the dialog box.
   g. Click the Copy to New Sheet button.

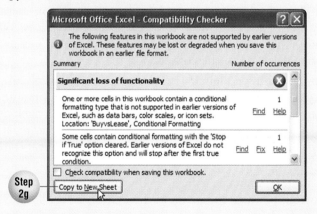

3. At the Compatibility Report sheet, read the information in the box with the hyperlink 'BuyvsLease'!D13:D16 and then click the hyperlink. The BuyvsLease sheet becomes active with the cells selected that have conditional formatting applied that is not supported in the earlier version of Excel.

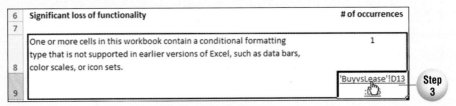

4. Make the Compatibility Report sheet active and then print the worksheet.
5. Use Save As to save the revised workbook and name it **ExcelL2_C8_P3-CompChk**.
6. Make BuyvsLease the active worksheet and deselect the range.
7. Click the Office button, point to *Save As*, and then click *Excel97-2003 Workbook*. Click the Save button at the Save As dialog box to accept *ExcelL2_C8_P3-CompChk.xls* as the *File name* and with *Save as type* changed to *Excel 97-2003 Workbook (*.xls)*. Click the Continue button at the Compatibility Checker dialog box.
8. Close **ExcelL2_C8_P3-CompChk.xls**.

Signing a Workbook with a Digital Signature

You can digitally sign a workbook to authenticate the workbook as originating from you when sending the workbook electronically to another person, or to indicate acceptance or agreement with content within the workbook. Think of a digital signature as an electronic stamp that certifies your identity and "return address." For example, a workbook that contains pricing for a contract could be digitally signed by you to authenticate your acceptance of the prices. When you add a digital signature to a workbook, the workbook becomes read-only and is protected from having changes made to the content.

Before attaching a digital signature, you must first obtain a digital certificate, which is essentially a file from a commercial certification authority (CA) which establishes and verifies your identity. A third party CA, such as VeriSign, charges a fee for dispensing a certificate and requires that the certificate be renewed periodically or the certificate expires and becomes unusable. Some organizations and government agencies can create their own digital certificates.

If you have a digital certificate and want to sign the active workbook, click the Office button, point to *Prepare*, and then click *Add a Digital Signature*. Click OK at the Microsoft Office Excel message box that displays with information about the integrity of digital signatures. This causes the Sign dialog box to open, in which you type the purpose for signing the workbook and then click the Sign button. Click OK at the Signature Confirmation dialog box that informs you the signature was successfully saved with the workbook. The Signatures pane opens at the right side of the worksheet area with a list of all of the valid signatures added to the workbook.

Creating Your Own Digital ID

If you do not have a digital ID from a third-party CA, Microsoft has provided the ability to create your own, which is saved on the computer used to create the digital signature. To create a digital signature, click the Office button, point to *Prepare*, and then click *Add a Digital Signature.* At the Microsoft Office Excel message box that displays information about the integrity of a digital signature, click OK. Excel checks the computer for a valid digital signature file and, if none exists, displays the Get a Digital ID dialog box shown in Figure 8.6. Click *Create your own digital ID* and then click OK. This opens the Create a Digital ID dialog box shown in Figure 8.7. Add your name, e-mail address, organization, and location information and then click Create.

HINT
Creating your own digital ID does not allow recipients of a workbook you signed to authenticate your identity. Your digital ID can only be verified on the computer on which you created the signature. IDs purchased from third parties provide the additional key that others use to verify authenticity.

Figure 8.6 Get a Digital ID Dialog Box

Click here to create your own digital ID on the computer you are using. This ID cannot be used to verify your signature in a workbook that is opened on any computer other than the one you are currently using.

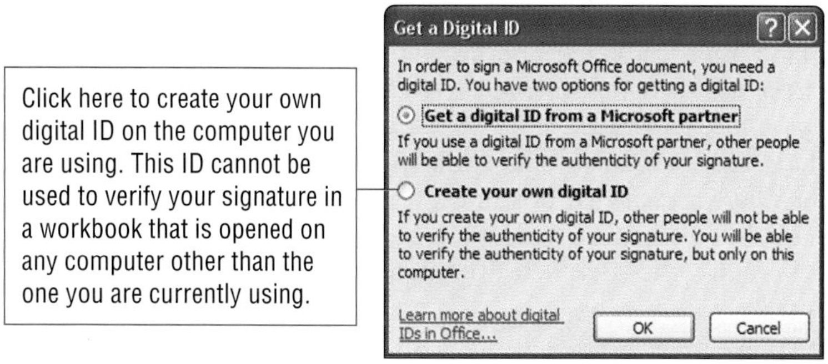

Figure 8.7 Create a Digital ID Dialog Box

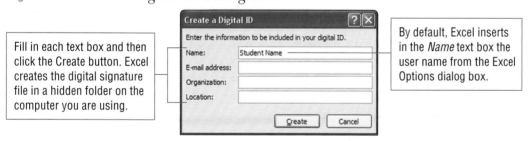

Fill in each text box and then click the Create button. Excel creates the digital signature file in a hidden folder on the computer you are using.

By default, Excel inserts in the *Name* text box the user name from the Excel Options dialog box.

Note: Check with your instructor before completing this project. If you are working in a school computer lab, you may not be able to create the digital ID.

1. Open **ExcelL2_C8_P3.xlsx**.
2. Save the workbook with Save As and name it **ExcelL2_C8_P3-Signed**.
3. Create a digital ID and sign the workbook by completing the following steps:
   a. Click the Office button, point to *Prepare*, and then click *Add a Digital Signature*.
   b. At the Microsoft Office Excel message box displaying information about digital signatures, click OK.
   c. At the Get a Digital ID dialog box, click *Create your own digital ID* and then click OK.

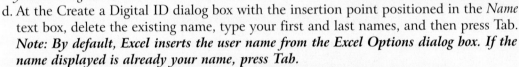

Step 3c

   d. At the Create a Digital ID dialog box with the insertion point positioned in the *Name* text box, delete the existing name, type your first and last names, and then press Tab. *Note: By default, Excel inserts the user name from the Excel Options dialog box. If the name displayed is already your name, press Tab.*
   e. Type your e-mail address in the *E-mail address* text box and then press Tab.
   f. Type your school's name in the *Organization* text box and then press Tab.
   g. Type the city in which your school is located in the *Location* text box.
   h. Click the Create button. Excel creates the digital ID file and then opens the Sign dialog box.

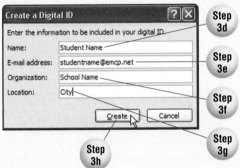

Step 3d

Step 3e

Step 3f

Step 3h

Step 3g

   i. At the Sign dialog box, type Certifying the buy values are correct in the *Purpose for signing this document* text box.
   j. Click the Sign button.

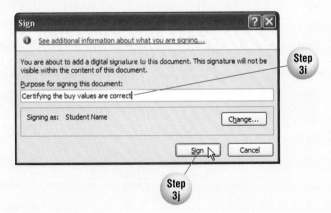

Step 3i

Step 3j

k. At the Signature Confirmation dialog box informing you that your signature has been successfully saved with the document, click OK. The Signatures pane opens at the right side of the worksheet area.

4. Notice the visual indicators that the workbook has been protected with a digital signature by the addition of *[Read Only]* next to the file name in the Title bar and the Signatures button in the Status bar next to Ready.

5. Look at the ribbon and notice most of the buttons are dimmed for features that would be used to edit the workbook.

6. View the digital signature details by pointing to your name in the Signatures task pane, clicking the down-pointing arrow that appears, and then clicking *Signature Details* at the drop-down list.

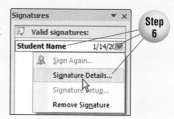

Step 6

7. Read the information in the Signature Details dialog box and then click the Close button.

8. Click the Close button located at the top right corner of the Signatures task pane.

9. Close **ExcelL2_C8_P3-Signed.xlsx**.

Once the digital ID has been created, the next time you want to add a digital signature and are using the same computer, when you click the Office button, *Prepare*, and then *Add a Digital Signature*, you are taken directly to the Sign dialog box where you type the purpose for signing.

Removing a Digital Signature

You can remove a digital signature that has been attached to a workbook. When you remove the signature, the workbook becomes available for formatting and editing. Remove the digital signature at the Signatures task pane. Open the Signatures task pane by clicking the Signatures button that displays at the left end of the Status bar next to Ready. At the task pane, point to the signature you want to remove, click the down-pointing arrow that appears, and then click *Remove Signature* at the drop-down list. Click Yes at the Remove Signature dialog box that asks if you are sure you want to permanently remove the signature and informing you that the action cannot be undone.

Viewing Digital Signatures in a Workbook Received from Someone Else

If you receive a workbook that has been digitally signed by someone else, you are notified in the message bar when you open the file that the document contains signatures. Click the View Signatures button in the Message bar to open the Signatures task pane and view the certificates added to the workbook. If the message bar has been turned off on the computer you are using, you can click the Signatures button that displays at the left end of the Status bar next to *Ready* to open the Signatures task pane.

Create Digital ID and Sign Workbook
1. Open workbook.
2. Click Office button.
3. Point to *Prepare*.
4. Click *Add a Digital Signature.*
5. Click OK.
6. Click *Create your own digital ID.*
7. Click OK.
8. Enter name, press Tab.
9. Enter e-mail address, press Tab.
10. Enter organization name, press Tab.
11. Enter location.
12. Click Create button.
13. Type purpose for signing workbook.
14. Click Sign button.
15. Click OK.

Signatures

Restricting Permissions to a Workbook

In Microsoft Office 2007, Information Rights Management (IRM) is used to restrict permissions to a workbook. Permissions is the term given to the viewing and editing rights that you assign to an individual. You can grant one person the ability to read but not change the workbook and another person the ability to read and edit but not print the workbook. By restricting the workbook you can prevent confidential data from being changed, printed, or copied. You can also add an expiration date on a workbook so that after the specified date, the workbook no longer is available.

To be able to use the Restrict Permission feature, you must have previously installed the Windows Rights Management Software (RMS). The computer that you are using requires the RMS client. You also need the ability to connect to a Windows 2003 or later server running RMS. The server is used to distribute licenses to individuals who want to access a restricted workbook. For example, if you grant permission to a person to edit a workbook, the first time the individual opens the restricted workbook, he or she connects to the server for authentication and downloads a license.

If you have the RMS client software and access to a licensing server, you can restrict permissions to the active workbook by clicking the Office button, pointing to *Prepare*, pointing to *Restrict Permission*, and then clicking *Do Not Distribute*. This opens the Permission dialog box. Click the *Restrict permission to this document* check box and then assign the access rights you want to grant to individual users. Users are identified by e-mail address. The following permission levels are available:

- *Read*. Individual can read the workbook but cannot edit, print, or copy.
- *Change*. Individual can read, edit, and save changes but cannot print.
- *Full Control*. Individual can read, edit, save changes, and print; essentially any task that the author can do is also available to a person granted full control permission.

If you receive a workbook that is restricted, a *Do Not Distribute* message appears in the message bar when the workbook is opened.

Deciding the best method to protect information when distributing workbooks to others both within and outside the organization depends on the nature of the data and the purpose for distributing the workbook. Keep in mind that e-mail is not secure and the possibility exists that a private e-mail with a workbook attachment can be intercepted. Consider also that e-mail is easily forwarded and that you cannot control an e-mail message once it leaves your inbox. Safeguarding against unexpected disclosure of information is a good strategy. Employ the prevention techniques learned in this section and use password and protection strategies learned in Chapter 6 to circumvent unintended changes to data or more serious breeches of security or privacy.

CHAPTER summary

- The Get External Data group in the Data tab contains buttons to use for importing data into an Excel worksheet from Access, from the Web, or from a text file.

- Data in an Access table can be imported into Excel as an Excel table, a PivotTable Report, or a PivotChart and a PivotTable report.

- Only one Access table can be imported at a time.

- Tables in a Web site can be imported to Excel using the New Web Query dialog box.

- Text files are often used to exchange data between dissimilar programs since the file format is recognized by nearly all applications.

- Text files generally separate data between fields with either a tab character or a comma.

- The Text Import Wizard guides you through the process of importing a text file through three dialog boxes where you define the source file as delimited and select the delimiter character.

- Data in an Excel worksheet can be copied and pasted or copied and appended to an existing Access table.

- To append records to the Access table, open the datasheet in Access, click the Paste button arrow, and then click *Paste Append* at the drop-down list.

- Worksheet data can be embedded or linked to a Word document. Embedding inserts a copy of the source data in the Word document and allows the object to be edited using Excel's tools within the Word environment, whereas linking the object inserts a shortcut to the Excel workbook from which the source data is retrieved.

- To embed cells copied to the clipboard into the current Word document, click the Paste button arrow and then click *Paste Special*. Click *Microsoft Office Excel Worksheet Object* and click OK.

- To link cells copied to the clipboard into the current Word document, open the Paste Special dialog box, click *Microsoft Office Excel Worksheet Object,* click *Paste link*, and click OK.

- Breaking a link involves removing the connection between the source and destination programs so that the object is no longer updated in the destination document when the source data changes.

- You can embed and link objects to slides in a PowerPoint presentation using the same techniques as you would to embed or link cells to a Word document.

- In Office 2007, the charting tools are fully integrated. A chart copied and pasted from Excel to a PowerPoint presentation or Word document is embedded by default.

- Open the Save As dialog box and change *Save as type* to a text file format to save a copy of the active worksheet in a text file.

- Excel includes several text file formats to accommodate differences that occur across operating system platforms that configure text files using various end of line character codes.

- The Document Inspector feature allows you to search for personal or hidden information and remove it before distributing a file.
- Click the Office button, point to *Prepare*, and then click *Inspect Document* to open the Document Inspector dialog box.
- Once the workbook has been inspected, Excel displays a red exclamation mark in each section in which Excel detected the presence of the requested item. Clicking the Remove All button deletes the items from the workbook.
- Mark a Workbook as Final to change the workbook to a read-only file with the status property set to *Final*.
- Run the Compatibility Checker feature before saving a workbook in an earlier version of Excel to determine if a loss of functionality or fidelity will occur.
- The results of the compatibility check can be copied to a new worksheet for easy referencing and documentation purposes.
- Adding a digital signature to a workbook changes the workbook to read-only.
- If you do not have a digital signature from a third-party certification authority (CA), you can create a digital ID in Excel which is valid only on the computer in use.
- Click the Office button, point to *Prepare*, and then click *Add a Digital Signature* to add a third-party signature, or create and then add your own digital ID.
- Open the Signatures task pane by clicking the Signatures button in the Status bar to remove a signature or view signature details.
- Information Rights Management (IRM) is used to restrict permissions to a workbook to only those individuals for whom you grant read, change, or full control access. A workbook can also have an expiration date attached using the Permission dialog box.
- To use IRM, you need to install the Windows Rights Management Software (RMS) client application on the computer you are using and have access to a Windows server that authenticates and distributes licenses to open and change documents to the users that have been granted permissions.

COMMANDS review

FEATURE	RIBBON TAB, GROUP	BUTTON	OFFICE BUTTON DROP-DOWN LIST	KEYBOARD SHORTCUT
Add digital signature			Prepare, Add a Digital Signature	
Compatibility checker			Prepare, Run Compatibility Checker	
Copy	Home, Clipboard			Ctrl + C
Document inspector			Prepare, Inspect Document	
Import from Access table	Data, Get External Data	From Access		
Import from text file	Data, Get External Data	From Text		
Import from Web page	Data, Get External Data	From Web		
Mark workbook as final			Prepare, Mark as Final	
Paste Special	Home, Clipboard			
Restrict permission (require RMS software installed)			Prepare, Restrict Permission, Do Not Distribute	
Save As			Save As	F12

CONCEPTS check

Test Your Knowledge

Completion: In the space provided at the right, indicate the correct term, command, or number.

1. This group in the Data tab contains buttons for importing data into Access from external sources.

   _____

2. If the source database used to import data contains more than one table, this dialog box appears after you select the data source to allow you to choose the desired table.

   _____

3. To import tables from a Web page, open this dialog box to browse to the Web site and click arrows next to tables on the page that you want to import.

   _____

4. These are the two commonly used delimiter characters in delimited text file formats.

   _____

5. To add to the bottom of the active Access datasheet, cells that have been copied to the clipboard, click this option at the Paste button drop-down list.

   _____

6. Choosing *Microsoft Office Excel Worksheet Object* at the Paste Special dialog box in a Word document and then clicking OK inserts the copied cells as this type of object.

   _____

7. If the Excel data you are pasting into a Word document is likely to be updated in the future and you want the Word document to reflect the updated values, paste the data as this type of object.

   _____

8. A chart copied from Excel and pasted to a slide in a PowerPoint presentation is pasted as this type of object by default.

   _____

9. Export the active worksheet as a text file by opening this dialog box.

   _____

10. This feature scans the open workbook for personal and hidden information and provides you with the opportunity to remove the items.

   _____

11. A workbook that has been marked as final is changed to this type of workbook to prevent additions, deletions, and modifications to cells.

   _____

12. Use this feature to check the current workbook for formatting or features used that are not available with earlier versions of Excel and which could cause loss of functionality if saved in the earlier file format.

   _____

13. Before you can add a digital signature to a workbook, you must first obtain this from a third-party certification authority to allow authentication beyond the computer you are using. _____

14. Once a digital signature has been added to a workbook, open this task pane to view the signature details. _____

15. This dialog box allows you to restrict access to a workbook to individual users provided you have the Windows Rights Management software installed on the computer you are using and have access to an Information Rights Management server that dispenses licenses. _____

SKILLS check
Demonstrate Your Proficiency

Assessment

1 IMPORT DATA FROM ACCESS AND A TEXT FILE

1. Open **Dollarwise-ResearchServices.xlsx**.
2. Save the workbook with Save As and name it **ExcelL2_C8_A1**.
3. Make A6 of the CPIData worksheet the active cell and import the table named CPI from the Access database named **NuTrendsMktRsrch-CensusData.accdb**.
4. Make the following changes to the worksheet:
   a. If necessary, move and/or adjust the size of the clip art images in row 1.
   b. Apply Table Style Medium 15 to the imported cells.
   c. Format the values in all columns *except* column A to one decimal place.
   d. Remove the filter arrow buttons and then center the column headings.
   e. If necessary, adjust column widths to accommodate the data.
5. Print the CPIData worksheet.
6. Make UIRate-MI the active worksheet.
7. With A6 the active cell, import the comma delimited text file named **USDeptofLabor-MichiganUIRATE.csv**.
8. Make the following changes to the data:
   a. Change the width of column B to 8.00 (61 pixels).
   b. Change the width of columns D–F to 15.00 (110 pixels).
   c. Change the width of column G to 9.00 (68 pixels).
   d. Move and/or resize the clip art image in G1.
   e. Format the values in columns D–F to Comma Style with no decimals.
   f. Format the values in column G to display one decimal place.
   g. Right-align and bold the column headings.
   h. Center the months in column C.
9. Print the UIRate-MI worksheet.
10. Save and then close **ExcelL2_C8_A1.xlsx**.

Assessment

2 LINK DATA TO A WORD DOCUMENT

1. Open **MacadamRealty-SeptSales.xlsx**.
2. Save the workbook with Save As and name it **ExcelL2_C8_A2**.
3. With SalesByDate the active worksheet, link A3:G25 to the end of the Word document named **MacadamRealty-SeptRpt.docx**.
4. Use Save As to name the revised Word document **ExcelL2_C8_A2.docx**.
5. Switch to Excel and then press the Esc key to remove the moving marquee and deselect the range.
6. Change the value in E4 to 525000.
7. Change the value in F4 to 3.00%.
8. Save **ExcelL2_C8_P2.xlsx**.
9. Switch to Word, right-click the linked object, and then click *Update Link* at the shortcut menu.
10. Print the Word document.
11. Break the link in the Word document.
12. Save **ExcelL2_C8_P2.docx** and then exit Word.
13. Save and then close **ExcelL2_C8_A2.xlsx**.

Assessment

3 EMBED DATA IN A POWERPOINT PRESENTATION

1. Open **MacadamRealty-SeptSales.xlsx**.
2. Save the workbook with Save As and name it **ExcelL2_C8_A3**.
3. Make SalesByAgent the active worksheet.
4. Display the worksheet at outline level 2 so that only the sales agent names and commissions display.
5. Create a column chart in a separate sheet to graph the sales commissions earned by each sales agent. You determine an appropriate chart style, title, and other chart elements.
6. Start PowerPoint and open **MacadamRealty-SeptRpt.pptx**.
7. Save the presentation with Save As and name it **ExcelL2_C8_A3**.
8. Embed the chart created in Step 5 on Slide 3 of the presentation.
9. Print the presentation as Handouts with three slides per page.
10. Save **ExcelL2_C8_A3.pptx** and then exit PowerPoint.
11. Save and then close **ExcelL2_C8_A3.xlsx**.

Assessment

4 EXPORT DATA AS A TEXT FILE

1. Open **MacadamRealty-SeptSales.xlsx**.
2. With SalesByDate the active worksheet, save the worksheet as a CSV (Comma delimited) (*.csv) text file named **ExcelL2_C8_A4**.
3. Close **ExcelL2_C8_A4.csv**. Click No when prompted to save changes.
4. Start Notepad and open **ExcelL2_C8_A4.csv**.

5. Delete the first two rows at the beginning of the file that contain the title text from the top of the worksheet. The first words in the file should begin at the first column heading, *Sale Date*.
6. Delete the bottom three rows in the file that contain the total commission value and the ending commas.
7. Print the document.
8. Save **ExcelL2_C8_A4.csv** and then exit Notepad.

Assessment

5 PREPARE A WORKBOOK FOR DISTRIBUTION

1. Open **MacadamRealty-2010Sales.xlsx**.
2. Save the workbook with Save As and name it **ExcelL2_C8_A5**.
3. Open the Document Information Panel and read the information in the *Author, Title,* and *Subject* properties. Open the Properties dialog box and read the information in the Statistics and Custom tabs. Close the Properties dialog box and close the Document Information Panel.
4. Display the Open dialog box, click once to select **ExcelL2_C8_A5.xlsx** in the file list, and then change the View to display the Properties pane.
5. Use PrintScreen to copy the screen image to the clipboard. Open a Microsoft Word document, paste the image from the clipboard, and then print the document. Exit Word without saving. Close the Open dialog box in Excel.
6. Turn on the display of all comments and then read the comments that appear.
7. Change to Page Layout view and check for a header or footer in the workbook.
8. Use the Document Inspector feature to check the workbook for private and hidden information. Leave all options selected at the Document Inspector dialog box.
9. Remove all items that display with a red exclamation mark and then close the dialog box.
10. Turn off the Show All Comments feature and switch to Normal view.
11. Run the Compatibility Feature to check for loss of functionality or fidelity in the workbook if saved in an earlier Excel version. Save the Summary report to a new sheet and then print the Compatibility Report sheet.
12. Mark the workbook as final.
13. Print another copy of the properties pane for **ExcelL2_C8_A5.xlsx** in the Open dialog box by completing steps similar to those in Steps 4–5. Change the view at the Open dialog box back to the *List* before closing the dialog box.
14. Close **ExcelL2_C8_A5.xlsx**.

Assessment

6 ADD A DIGITAL SIGNATURE

Note: Complete this assessment only if you were able to create the digital ID in Project 3d.

1. Open **MacadamRealty-2010Sales.xlsx**.
2. Save the workbook with Save As and name it **ExcelL2_C8_A6**.
3. Sign the document using your digital ID. Type **Final sales report approved** as the purpose for signing the workbook.
4. Display the Signature Details dialog box.
5. Use PrintScreen to capture an image of the screen with the dialog box open. Paste the image to a Word document. Print the Word document and then exit Word without saving.
6. Close the Signature Details dialog box and then close the Signatures task pane.
7. Close **ExcelL2_C8_A6.xlsx**.

CASE study
Apply Your Skills

Part 1

Yolanda Robertson of NuTrends Market Research would like new research data from the U.S. Census Bureau for her Pizza by Mario franchise expansion project. The franchise expansion is planned for the states of Illinois, Indiana, Kentucky, Missouri, and Minnesota. Start a new workbook and set up five worksheets named using the state names. In each sheet, using the New Web Query feature, display the Web page http://quickfacts.census.gov/qfd/, and import the People Quickfacts table for the state. Once the data is imported, delete column A, which is the definitions information. Save the workbook and name it **ExcelL2_C8_CS_P1**. Print all five worksheets.

Part 2

To prepare for an upcoming meeting with Mario and Nicola Carlucci of Pizza by Mario, Yolanda would like you to copy selected information from each state to a Word report. Open **PizzabyMario-ExpansionResearch.docx**. Save the document using Save As and name it **ExcelL2_C8_CS_P2**. From the Excel workbook you created in Part 1, copy and paste to the Word document the following data for each state (do not include the data in the *USA* column). Do not embed or link since the data will not be changed or updated.

> Households
> Persons per household
> Median household income
> Per capita money income

If the data you imported does not contain these headings, locate and copy information closely related to number of households and income for the state.

At the bottom of the document, create a reference for the data from the U.S. Census Bureau. Check with your instructor for the preferred format for the reference. Save, print, and then close **ExcelL2_C8_CS_P2.docx**.

Yolanda has noticed that when she opens the workbook you created in Part 1, a message appears in the message bar that says *Data connections have been disabled*. Yolanda has asked what this message means and what she should do at the Options dialog box. Research in Help how to manage connections to external data using the Workbook Connections dialog box. Since the data that was imported does not need to be refreshed in the future, you decide to remove the connections. Open **ExcelL2_C8_CS_P1.xlsx** and enable the data connection content at the Microsoft Office Security Options dialog box. Open the Workbook Connections dialog box and, using the information you learned in Help, remove all of the connections. Save the revised workbook as **ExcelL2_C8_CS_P3**. Close **Excel_L2_C8_CS_P3.xlsx**.

Compose a memo to Yolanda using Microsoft Word that provides a brief explanation of why the security warning message about data connections appeared in the message bar when she opened the workbook in Part 1. Base the memo on the information you learned in Help, making sure that you compose the explanation using your own words. Explain that you have created a new copy of the workbook with the connections removed. Save the Word memo and name it **ExcelL2_C8_CS_P3**. Print and then close **ExcelL2_C8_CS_P3.docx** and then exit Word.

Yolanda wants to know how to obtain a digital signature from a reputable certificate authority so that she can digitally sign macros, workbooks, and e-mails that she exchanges with Nicola Carlucci from Pizza by Mario. Research in Help and on the Internet third party certificate authority companies that provide digital IDs that will be recognized in Microsoft Office. Include in your research the purchase costs and renewal fees if any fees are quoted on the sites you browse. Using Microsoft Word, compose a memo to Yolanda that briefly explains the results of your research. Include in the memo the URL of at least two certificate authorities you visited in case Yolanda wants to check the sites on her own. Save the memo and name it **ExcelL2_C8_CS_P4**. Print and then close **ExcelL2_C8_CS_P4.docx** and exit Word.

Managing and Integrating Data and the Excel Environment

ASSESSING proficiency

In this unit, you have learned to use features in Excel that facilitate performing what-if analysis, identifying relationships between worksheet formulas, collaborating with others by sharing and protecting workbooks, and automating repetitive tasks using macros. You also learned how to customize the Excel environment to suit your preferences and integrate Excel data by importing from and exporting to external resources. Finally, you learned how to prepare a workbook for distribution to others by removing items that are private or confidential, by marking the workbook as final, by checking for incompatible features with earlier versions of Excel, and by adding a digital signature.

Excel Unit 2

Note: Before beginning assessments, copy to your storage medium the Excel2007L2U2 subfolder from the Excel2007L2 folder on the CD that accompanies this textbook and then make Excel2007L2U2 the active folder.

Assessment 1 Use Goal Seek and Scenario Manager to Calculate Investment Proposals

1. Open **DollarWise-InvtPlan.xlsx**.
2. Save the workbook with Save As and name it **ExcelL2_U2_A1**.
3. Use Goal Seek to find the payment amount the client must make each month in order to increase the projected value of the plan to $65,000 at the end of the term. Accept the solution Goal Seek calculates.
4. Assign the range name **AvgReturn** to F8.
5. Create three scenarios for changing F8 as follows:

Scenario name	Interest rate
Moderate	5.5%
Conservative	4.0%
Aggressive	12.5%

6. Apply the *Aggressive* scenario and then print the worksheet.
7. Edit the *Moderate* scenario's interest rate to 8.0% and then apply the scenario.
8. Create and then print a Scenario Summary report.
9. Save and then close **ExcelL2_U2_A1**.

Assessment 2 Calculate Investment Outcomes for a Portfolio Using a Two-Variable Data Table

1. Open **DollarWise-RsrchInvtTable.xlsx**.
2. Save the workbook with Save As and name it **ExcelL2_U2_A2**.

3. Create a two-variable data table that calculates the projected value of the investment plan for each monthly contribution payment and at each interest rate in the range B11:H20.
4. Apply the Comma Style format to the projected values in the table and adjust column widths if necessary.
5. Make F8 the active cell and display precedent arrows.
6. Make B11 the active cell and display precedent arrows.
7. Print the worksheet.
8. Remove the arrows.
9. Save and then close **ExcelL2_U2_A2.xlsx**.

Assessment 3 Solve an Error and Check for Accuracy in Investment Commission Formulas

1. Open **DollarWise-ModeratePortfolio.xlsx**.
2. Save the workbook with Save As and name it **ExcelL2_U2_A3**.
3. Solve the #VALUE! error in F19. Use formula auditing tools to help find the source cell containing the invalid entry.
4. Check the logic accuracy of the formula in F19 by creating proof formulas below the worksheet as follows:
   a. In row 21, calculate the amount from the customer's deposit that would be deposited into each of the six funds based on the percentages in column C. For example, in C21 create a formula to multiply the customer's deposit in C19 times the percentage recommended for investment in the DW Bond fund in C5. Create a similar formula for the remaining funds in D21:H21.
   b. In row 22, multiply the amount deposited to each fund by the fund's commission rate. For example, in C22, create a formula to multiply the value in C21 times the commission rate paid by the DW Bond fund in C17. Create a similar formula for the remaining funds in D22:H22.
   c. In row 23, calculate the total of the commissions for the six funds.
   d. Add appropriate labels next to the values created in rows 21 to 23.
5. Save, print, and then close **ExcelL2_U2_A3.xlsx**.

Assessment 4 Document and Share a Workbook and Manage Changes in an Investment Portfolio Worksheet

1. Open **ExcelL2_U2_A3.xlsx**.
2. Save the workbook with Save As and name it **ExcelL2_U2_A4**.
3. Enter the following data into the workbook properties:
Author	Logan Whitmore
Title	Senior Research Consultant
Subject	Moderate Fund Allocation
Comments	Provides moderate portfolio fund allocation and advisor commission calculator
4. Capture a screen image of the worksheet with the Document Information Panel open. Open Microsoft Word, paste the image to a blank document, print the document, and then exit Word without saving.
5. Close the Document Information Panel.
6. Share the workbook.
7. Change the user name to **Carey Winters** and then edit the following cells:
C7	from	*10%*	to	15%
C8	from	*15%*	to	10%

8. Save **ExcelL2_U2_A4.xlsx**.
9. Change the user name to **Jodi VanKemenade** and then edit the following cells:

E17	from	*2.15%*	to	2.32%
F17	from	*2.35%*	to	2.19%

10. Format F19 to Accounting Number Format.
11. Save **ExcelL2_U2_A4.xlsx**.
12. Create and then print a History sheet.
13. Change the user name back to the original name on the computer you are using.
14. Accept and reject changes made to the ModeratePortfolio worksheet as follows:

Reject	C7
Reject	C8
Accept	E17
Reject	F17

15. Save, print, and then close **ExcelL2_U2_A4.xlsx**.

Assessment 5 Protect a Confidential Investment Portfolio Workbook

1. Open **ExcelL2_U2_A4.xlsx**.
2. Save the workbook with Save As and name it **ExcelL2_U2_A5.xlsx**.
3. Hide rows 21 to 23.
4. Remove the shared access to the workbook.
5. Protect the worksheet allowing editing to C19 only. Assign the password **dW$m28** to unprotect the worksheet.
6. Add the password **Mod%82** to open the workbook.
7. Close **ExcelL2_U2_A5.xlsx**.
8. Test the security features added to the workbook by opening **ExcelL2_U2_A5.xlsx** using the password created in Step 6. Try to change one of the values in the range C5:C10.
9. Make C19 the active cell and then change the value to *10000*.
10. Save, print, and then close **ExcelL2_U2_A5.xlsx**.

Assessment 6 Automate and Customize an Investment Portfolio Workbook

1. Open **ExcelL2_U2_A5.xlsx**.
2. Open the Save As dialog box, remove the password to open the workbook, and name the workbook **ExcelL2_U2_A6**.
3. Unprotect the worksheet.
4. Create two macros to be stored in the active workbook as follows:
   a. A macro named **CustomDisplay** that applies the theme named *Solstice,* and turns off the display of gridlines and row and column headers in the current worksheet. Assign the macro to the shortcut key Ctrl + Shift + T. Enter an appropriate description that includes your name and the date the macro was created.
   b. A macro named **CustomHeader** that prints the text **Private and Confidential** at the left margin and the current date at the right margin. Assign the macro to the shortcut key Ctrl + Shift + H. Enter an appropriate description that includes your name and the date the macro was created.

5. Test the macros by opening **ExcelL2_U2_A1.xlsx**. Make InvestmentPlanProposal the active worksheet and then run the two macros created in Step 4. View the worksheet in Print Preview. Close Print Preview and then close **ExcelL2_U2_A1.xlsx** without saving the changes.
6. Print **ExcelL2_U2_A6.xlsx**.
7. Print the Visual Basic program code for the two macros and then close the Microsoft Visual Basic window and return to Excel.
8. Save **ExcelL2_U2_A6.xlsx** as a macro-enabled workbook.
9. Close **ExcelL2_U2_A6.xlsm**.

Assessment 7 **Create and Use an Investment Planner Template**

1. Open **ExcelL2_U2_A2.xlsx**.
2. Make the following changes to the worksheet:
   a. Change the label in B3 to Investment Planner.
   b. Change the font color of B11 to white. This will make the cell appear to be empty. You want to disguise the entry in this cell because you think displaying the value at the top left of the data table will confuse Dollar Wise customers.
   c. Clear the contents of F5:F7.
   d. Protect the worksheet allowing editing to F5:F7 only. Assign the password p$l@N to unprotect the worksheet.
3. Save the revised workbook as a template named **DollarWise-InvPlan-StudentName** with your name substituted for *StudentName*.
4. Close **DollarWise-InvPlan-StudentName.xltx**.
5. Start a new workbook based on the **DollarWise-InvPlan-StudentName.xltx** template.
6. Enter the following information in the appropriate cells:
   a. *Monthly contribution*   -475
   b. *Number of years to invest*   5
   c. *Forecasted annual interest rate* 7.75%
7. Save the workbook as an Excel workbook named **ExcelL2_U2_A7**.
8. Print and then close **ExcelL2_U2_A7.xlsx**.
9. Display the New dialog box. Copy the template created in this assessment to the Excel2007L2U2 folder on your storage medium.
10. Delete the custom template created in this assessment from the hard disk drive on the computer you are using.

Assessment 8 **Export a Chart and Prepare an Investment Portfolio Worksheet for Distribution**

1. Open **ExcelL2_U2_A6.xlsm** and enable the content at the Microsoft Office Security Options dialog box.
2. Start Microsoft Office PowerPoint 2007 and then open **DollarWise-PortfolioProfiles.pptx**.
3. Save the presentation with Save As and name it **ExcelL2_U2_A8**.
4. Copy the pie chart from the Excel worksheet to Slide 7 in the PowerPoint presentation.
5. Resize the chart on the slide and edit the chart to display data labels to make the chart consistent with the other charts in the presentation.
6. Print the PowerPoint presentation as *Handouts* with nine slides per page.
7. Save **ExcelL2_U2_A8.pptx** and then exit PowerPoint.
8. Deselect the chart in the Excel worksheet.

9. Run the compatibility checker, saving the compatibility report to a new worksheet.

10. Print the Compatibility Report worksheet and then make ModeratePortfolio the active worksheet.

11. Inspect the document, leaving all items checked at the Document Inspector dialog box.

12. Remove all items that display with a red exclamation mark and then close the dialog box.

13. Use Save As to change the file type to *Excel workbook (*.xlsx)* and name it **ExcelL2_U2_A8**. Click Yes when prompted that the file cannot be saved with the VBA Project. Click OK at the privacy warning message box.

14. Mark the workbook as final.

15. Capture a screen image of the worksheet with the Document Information Panel open. Open Microsoft Word, paste the image to a blank document, print the document, and then exit Word without saving.

16. Close the Document Information Panel.

17. Close **ExcelL2_U2_A8.xlsx**.

WRITING activities

The Writing, Internet Research, and Job Study activities give you the opportunity to practice your writing skills while demonstrating an understanding of some of the important Excel features you have mastered in this unit. Use appropriate word choices and correct grammar, capitalization, and punctuation when setting up new worksheets. Labels should clearly describe the data that is presented.

Create a Computer Maintenance Template

The Computing Services department of National Wholesale Marketing Inc. wants to create a computer maintenance template for Help Desk employees to complete electronically and save to a document management server. This system will make it easy for a technician to check the status of any employee's computer from any location within the company. The Help Desk department performs the following computer maintenance tasks at each computer twice per year.

- Delete temporary Internet files
- Delete old .zip files
- Delete temporary document files that begin with a tilde (~)
- Update hardware drivers
- Update emergency boot disk
- Check all power connections
- Reconfirm all serial numbers and asset records
- Have employee change password
- Check that automatic updates for O/S is active
- Check that automatic updates for virus protection is active
- Confirm that automatic backups are being done

- Confirm that employee is archiving data
  - E-mails
  - Documents
- Clean the computer
  - Blow dust and debris from keyboard, printer, and system unit
  - Screen
  - All drives
- Any follow-up work required?

In a new workbook, create a template that can be used to complete the maintenance form electronically. The template should include information that identifies the workstation by asset ID number, the department in which the computer is located, the name of the employee using the computer, the name of the technician that performs the maintenance, and the date the maintenance is performed. In addition, include a column next to each task with a drop-down list with the options: *Completed*, *Not Completed*, *Not Required*. Next to this column include a column in which the technician can type notes. At the bottom of the template include a text box with the following message text:

> Save using the file naming standard CM_StationID##_yourinitials where ## is the asset ID. Example CM_StationID56_JW

Protect the worksheet leaving the cells unlocked that the technician will fill in as he or she completes a maintenance visit. Do not include a password for unprotecting the sheet. Save the template and name it **NationalCMForm-StudentName** with your name substituted for *StudentName*. Start a new workbook based on the custom template. Fill out a form as if you were a technician working on your own computer to test your form's organization and layout. Save the completed form as an Excel workbook named **ExcelL2_U2_Act01**. Print the form scaled to fit one page in height and width. Copy the **NationalCMForm-StudentName.xltx** template file to your storage medium and then delete the template from the computer you are using.

Apply What-If Analysis to a Planned Move

Following graduation, you plan to move out of the state/province for a few years to gain experience living on your own. Create a new workbook to use as you plan this move to develop a budget for expenses in the first year. Research typical rents for apartments in the city in which you want to find your first job. Estimate other living costs in the city including transit, food, entertainment, clothes, telephone, cable/satellite, cell phone, Internet, and so on. Calculate total living costs for an entire year. Next, research annual starting salaries for your chosen field of study in the same area. Estimate the take home pay at approximately 70% of the annual salary you decide to use. Using the take home pay, calculate if you will have a deficit or a surplus after paying all expenses.

Use Goal Seek to find the take home pay you need to earn in order to have a savings of $2,000 at the end of the year. Create three scenarios in the worksheet as follows:

- A scenario named *Original_Values* which includes the current estimates for take home pay, rent, transit, clothes, and entertainment. Include any other expenses you want to vary.

- A scenario named *Lowest_Values* in which you adjust each value down to the lowest amount you think is reasonable.

- A scenario named *Highest_Values* in which you adjust each value up to the highest amount you think is reasonable.

Apply each scenario and watch the impact on the deficit or surplus amount. Display the worksheet in the *Original_Values* scenario. Create a scenario summary report. Print the worksheet scaled to fit one page in width and height and print the scenario summary report. Save the workbook as **ExcelL2_U2_Act02**. Close **ExcelL2_U2_Act02.xlsx**.

Research and Compare Smartphones

You work for an independent marketing consultant who travels frequently in North America and Europe for work. The consultant, Lindsay Somers, would like to purchase a smartphone. Lindsay will use the smartphone while traveling for conference calling, e-mail, Web browsing, text messaging, and making modifications to PowerPoint presentations, Word documents, or Excel worksheets. Research the latest product offerings for smartphones on the Internet. Select three phones from three different manufacturers that you think will suit Lindsay's requirements and provide the best value. Prepare a worksheet that compares the three smartphones, organizing the worksheet so that the main features are shown along the left side of the page by category and each phone's specifications for those features are set in columns. At the bottom of each column, provide the hyperlink to the phone's specifications on the Web. Based on your perception of the best value, select one of the phones as your recommendation and note within the worksheet the phone you think Lindsay should select. Provide a brief explanation of why you selected the phone in a comment box attached to the price cell. Save the worksheet and name it **ExcelL2_U2_Act03**. Print the worksheet in landscape orientation with the page width and height scaled to 1-page. Close **ExcelL2_U2_Act03.xlsx**.

Prepare a Wages Budget and Link the Budget to a Word Document

You work at a small, independent, long-term care facility named Gardenview Place Long-Term Care. As assistant to the business manager, you are helping with the preparation of next year's hourly wages budget. Create a worksheet to estimate next year's hourly wages expense using the following information about hourly paid workers and the average wage costs in Table U2.1:

- The facility runs three 8-hour shifts, 7 days per week, 52 weeks per year.
  - ○ 6 a.m. to 2 p.m.
  - ○ 2 p.m. to 10 p.m.
  - ○ 10 p.m. to 6 a.m.

- Each shift requires two registered nurses, four licensed practical nurses, and two health-care aid workers.

- At each shift, one of the registered nurses is designated as the charge nurse and is paid a premium of 15% of his or her regular hourly rate.
- The 6 a.m.-to-2 p.m. and 2 p.m.-to-10 p.m. shifts require one custodian; the 10 p.m.-to-6 a.m. shift requires two custodians.
- Each shift pays for the services of an on-call physician and an on-call pharmacist.
- Add 14% to each shift's wage costs to cover the estimated costs of benefits such as vacation pay, holiday pay, and medical care coverage plans for all workers *except* the on-call physician and on-call pharmacist, who do not receive these benefits.

Table U2.1 Average Hourly Wage Rates

Wage category	Average wage rate
Registered nurse	27.85
Licensed practical nurse	19.55
Health-care aid worker	13.77
Custodian	9.25
On-call physician	35.00
On-call pharmacist	22.00

Make use of colors, themes, or table features to make the budget calculations easy to read. Save the workbook and name it **ExcelL2_U2_JS**. Create a chart in a separate sheet to show the total hourly wages budget by worker category. You determine the chart type and chart options to present the information. Print the worksheet scaled to fit one page in width and height.

Start Word and open the document named **Gardenview-OpBudget.xlsx**. Edit the year on the title page to the current year. Edit the name and date at the bottom of the title page to your name and the current date. Link the chart created in the Excel worksheet to the end of the Word document. Save the revised document as **ExcelL2_U2_JS**. Print and then close **ExcelL2_U2_JS.docx**. Deselect the chart and close **ExcelL2_U2_JS.xlsx**.

Excel 2007 Feature	Ribbon Tab, Group	Button, Option	Keyboard Shortcut
Accept/Reject Changes	Review, Changes	Track Changes	
Accounting Number Format	Home, Number	$	
Align Text Left	Home, Alignment		
Align Text Right	Home, Alignment		
Axis Options	Chart Tools Layout, Axes OR PivotChart Tools Layout, Axes		
Background Picture	Page Layout, Page Setup		
Bold	Home, Font	B	Ctrl + B
Borders	Home, Font		
Bottom Align	Home, Alignment		
Cell Styles	Home, Styles		
Center	Home, Alignment		
Change Chart Type	Chart Tools Design, Type		
Circle Invalid Data	Data, Data Tools	Data Validation	
Clear cell or cell contents	Home, Editing		
Clip Art	Insert, Illustrations		
Clipboard task pane	Home, Clipboard		
Close workbook		, Close	Ctrl + F4
Conditional formatting	Home, Styles		
Consolidate	Data, Data Tools	Consolidate	
Convert Text to Columns	Data, Data Tools		
Copy	Home, Clipboard		Ctrl + C
Create table	Insert, Tables		Ctrl + T
Custom AutoFilter	Home, Editing	, Filter	Ctrl + Shift + L
Custom number format	Home, Number		Ctrl + 1
Customize Quick Access toolbar		OR , Excel Options	
Cut	Home, Clipboard		Ctrl + X
Data Table	Data, Data Tools	What-If Analysis	
Data Validation	Data, Data Tools	Data Validation	
Database functions	Formulas, Function Library	fx	Shift + F3
Decrease Decimal	Home, Number		
Decrease Indent	Home, Alignment		Ctrl + Alt + Shift + Tab
Default chart in separate sheet			F11
Default chart in worksheet			Alt + F1
Delete cells, rows, columns	Home, Cells	Delete	
Delete comment	Review, Comments		
Delete macro	View, Macros		Alt + F8
Display all comments	Review, Comments	Show All Comments	
Display formulas			Ctrl + `
Document inspector		, Prepare, Inspect Document	
Edit Links	Data, Connections	Edit Links	
Edit macro	View, Macros		Alt + F8
Exit Excel		OR , Exit Excel	
Fill Color	Home, Font		
Financial functions	Formulas, Function Library	Financial	
Find	Home, Editing	, Find	Ctrl + F
Font	Home, Font	Calibri	
Font Color	Home, Font	A	
Font Size	Home, Font	11	
Format	Home, Cells	Format	
Format as Table	Home, Styles		
Format Painter	Home, Clipboard		
Fraction number format	Home, Number	General	Ctrl + 1
Freeze window panes	View, Window	Freeze Panes, Freeze Panes	
Function	Formulas, Function Library	fx	Shift + F3
Go To	Home, Editing	, Go To	Ctrl + G
Goal Seek	Data, Data Tools	What-If Analysis	
Group	Data, Outline		Shift + Alt + Right arrow key
Header and footer	Insert, Text		
Help			F1
Hide worksheet	Home, Cells	Format, Hide & Unhide, Hide Sheet	
Hyperlink	Insert, Links		Ctrl + K
Import data	Data, Get External Data	From Access, From Text, From Web	
Increase Decimal	Home, Number		
Increase Indent	Home, Alignment		Ctrl + Alt + Tab
Insert cells, rows, columns	Home, Cells	Insert	
Insert comment	Review, Comments		Shift + F2
Insert page break	Page Layout, Page Setup	, Insert Page Break	
Insert worksheet			Shift + F11
Italic	Home, Font	I	Ctrl + I
Logical functions	Formulas, Function Library	Logical	
Lookup & Reference functions	Formulas, Function Library	Lookup & Reference	

Excel 2007 Feature	Ribbon Tab, Group	Button, Option	Keyboard Shortcut
Manage range names	Formulas, Defined Names		Ctrl + F3
Margins	Page Layout, Page Setup		
Mark workbook as final		, Prepare, Mark as Final	
Math & Trigonometry functions	Formulas, Function Library	Math & Trig ▾	
Merge & Center	Home, Alignment		
Merge Styles	Home, Styles	, Merge Styles	
Middle Align	Home, Alignment		
Move Chart	Chart Tools Design, Location		
New Workbook		, New	
Number Format	Home, Number	General ▾	
Open workbook		, Open	Ctrl + O
Text Orientation	Home, Alignment		
Page Orientation	Page Layout, Page Setup		
Page Break Preview	View, Workbook Views		
Page Layout View	View, Workbook Views		
Paste	Home, Clipboard		Ctrl + V
Paste Special	Home, Clipboard	, Paste Special	
Percent Style	Home, Number	%	Ctrl + Shift + %
Picture	Insert, Illustrations OR Chart Tools Layout		
PivotChart	Insert, Tables OR PivotTable Tools Options, Tools		
PivotTable	Insert, Tables		
Print Area	Page Layout, Page Setup		
Print Preview		, Print, Print Preview	Ctrl + F2
Print workbook		, Print, Quick Print	
Print worksheet titles	Page Layout, Page Setup		
Protect and Share Workbook	Review, Changes	Protect and Share Workbook	
Protect Workbook	Review, Changes		
Protect Worksheet	Review, Changes		
Record macro	View, Macros	OR	
Remove Duplicates	Data, Data Tools OR Table Tools Design, Tools	Remove Duplicates	
Remove page break	Page Layout, Page Setup	, Remove Page Break	
Repeat			F4 OR Ctrl + Y
Replace	Home, Editing	Replace	Ctrl + H
Run macro	View, Macros		Alt + F8
Save As		, Save As	F12
Save in PDF format		, Save As, PDF or XPS	
Save workbook		, Save	Ctrl + S
Scale	Page Layout, Page Setup		
Scenario Manager	Data, Data Tools	What-If Analysis ▾	
Scientific number format	Home, Number	General ▾	Ctrl + 1
Shapes	Insert, Illustrations OR Chart Tools Layout, Insert		
Share Workbook	Review, Changes		
Shrink to Fit	Home, Alignment		
SmartArt	Insert, Illustrations		
Sort and filter data	Home, Editing		
Special number format	Home, Number		Ctrl + 1
Spelling	Review, Proofing		F7
Split window into pane	View, Window	Split	
Statistical functions	Formulas, Function Library	More Functions ▾	
SUBTOTAL function	Formulas, Function Library	Math & Trig ▾	Shift + F3
Subtotals	Data, Outline		
SUM function	Home, Editing OR Formulas, Function Library	Σ AutoSum ▾	Alt + =
Symbol	Insert, Text	Ω	
Table Styles	Table Tools Design, Table Styles		
Text box	Insert, Text		
Text functions	Formulas, Function Library	Text ▾	
Theme colors, effects, fonts	Page Layout, Themes	Colors ▾ , Effects ▾ , Fonts ▾	
Themes	Page Layout, Themes		
Top Align	Home, Alignment		
Total row	Table Tools Design, Table Style Options		Ctrl + Shift + T
Trace Dependents	Formulas, Formula Auditing	Trace Dependents	
Trace Error	Formulas, Formula Auditing	Error Checking ▾	
Trace Precedents	Formulas, Formula Auditing	Trace Precedents	
Track Changes	Review, Changes	Track Changes ▾	
Underline	Home, Font	U ▾	Ctrl + U
Unfreeze window panes	View, Window	Freeze Panes ▾ , Unfreeze Panes	
Ungroup	Data, Outline		Shift + Alt + Left arrow key
Unhide worksheet	Home, Cells	Format ▾ , Hide & Unhide, Unhide Sheet	
Unlock cells	Home, Cells	Format ▾	
WordArt	Insert, Text	WordArt ▾	
Wrap Text	Home, Alignment		